THE MYSTERIES
OF CHRISTIANITY

THE MYSTERIES
OF CHRISTIANITY

By
MATTHIAS JOSEPH SCHEEBEN

TRANSLATED BY CYRIL VOLLERT, S.J.

A Herder & Herder Book
The Crossroad Publishing Company
New York

Imprimi potest: Joseph P. Zuercher, S.J., Praep. Prov. Missour.
Nihil obstat: Fr. Innocentius Swoboda, O.F.M., Censor Librorum.
Imprimatur: ✠ Georgius J. Donnelly, Adminisrator, Sede vacante.
Sti. Ludovici, die 25 Martii, 1946.

The Crossroad Publishing Company
www.CrossroadPublishing.com

Printed in the United States of America

ISBN-13: 978-0-8245-2430-2
ISBN-10: 0-8245-2430-6

Translator's Preface

This book is a translation of *Die Mysterien des Christentums*, by Matthias Joseph Scheeben. The translation was made from the 1941 edition, published by Herder & Co., G.m.b.H., of Freiburg im Breisgau, and edited by Joseph Höfer. Certain historical circumstances, which impart an extraordinary value to this edition and make previous editions obsolete, deserve to be recounted.

Toward the end of 1887 Scheeben's friend and publisher, Benjamin Herder, requested him to prepare a second edition of the book, which had appeared originally in 1865. The great theologian immediately set to work, and in June of the following year wrote that he could send Herder the greatest part of the new edition, so that printing could begin at once; he would prefer, however, to wait until the whole was finished. This was Scheeben's last letter to the publisher. A month later an untimely death put an end to his fruitful apostolate of the pen.

Scheeben had prepared for the projected new edition by extensively annotating two personal copies of the original edition. L. Küpper, the editor of the second edition, which appeared in 1898, knew of one of these, but made slight and uncritical use of it, preferring to inject his own views into Scheeben's book, without indicating in the text the changes he had introduced. Subsequently Scheeben's annotated copy was forgotten. When A. Rademacher worked on the third edition, published in 1912, apparently he was unaware of its existence. He further modified Scheeben's text by adding changes of his own to Küpper's edition.

Of the two copies of the first edition annotated by Scheeben, one had been carefully and copiously worked through. The other contains only rough drafts of new sentences and paragraphs, marginal notes, and underlinings. Höfer made full and scholarly use of both

TRANSLATOR'S PREFACE

of them, and thus has succeeded in editing a text that is substantially the same as that which Scheeben would have issued had he lived a few months longer.

Since Scheeben's labor on the new edition is the last scientific work of his that we possess, *The Mysteries of Christianity* as published in the 1941 edition gives us a comprehensive view of the whole of his theology in its most mature form.

Scheeben had not been able to carry through his work of revision quite to the end. However, the first seven parts (as they appear in the present translation) had been so thoroughly gone over in detail that they certainly constitute the "greatest part" which the author had regarded as finished.

Part X, which deals with "The Science of the Mysteries of Christianity, or Theology," very likely represents Scheeben's definitive doctrine on the subject. If he had wished to indicate any modifications of his views, he would have had ample opportunity to do so in the first chapter, which treats of the mystery of Christianity in general. Thus we may confidently assert that, with the exception of Parts VIII and IX, the whole book underwent Scheeben's final revision.

If we compare the 1941 edition with the first edition, we shall find scarcely a page free from stylistic alterations. More important, there are numerous, and often extensive, doctrinal changes and additions to the text. A few omissions also occur. These concern mostly polemical matters or references to the author's *Natur und Gnade* and *Die Herrlichkeiten der göttlichen Gnade,* from which youthful works *The Mysteries of Christianity* in the present edition is much more widely separated than in its original form. Scheeben's additions and changes have all been incorporated by Höfer in the text without further indication, as conforming to the author's plan for his own second edition.

The Mysteries of Christianity is a work unique in the literature of theology. Its scope differs greatly from that of the ordinary theological manual. It aims to present a unified view of the whole vast panorama of revealed truth in terms of the nine key mysteries of Christianity, and to relate them to modern life. That the author has succeeded in his task is borne out by the general agreement of theologians with the verdict pronounced by A. M. Weiss, O.P., who called *The Mysteries of Christianity* "the most original, the most profound, and the most brilliant work which recent theology has produced."

The book is not intended for the exclusive use of professional theologians. Scheeben himself envisaged a larger circle of readers. In his preface to the first edition he wrote: "I cherish the deep conviction that speculative theology is of supreme importance for the truest and highest formation of mind and heart, and that under the guidance of the great doctors of the Church secure roads must be built, reaching to the very summits of divine truth, roads that can be traveled without excessive hardship not only by a few privileged spirits, but by anyone who combines courage and energy with a sufficiently sound education. . . . I have endeavored to keep the presentation as simple and clear as possible, and hope that even those readers who have not had the advantage of philosophical training can follow me without too great effort."

Among the heartening signs of the times are intimations that theology is moving from the classrooms of universities and seminaries to a wider public of the faithful. Lectures on the theology and philosophy of St. Thomas, a growing determination to read the *Summa theologica* itself, courses in Sacred Scripture for lay adults, articles in theological journals on dogma for the laity, requests of college students for instruction in dogmatic theology, projected courses of theology for our teaching sisterhoods, demands for a clarification of the theological foundations of the liturgy, are but a few of the indications of the trend. For all such groups, as well as for students in theological faculties and seminaries, who may desire to complement the analytical method pursued in formal classes by a reading of the greatest synthesis of theology written in modern times, the arduous task of translating Scheeben's masterpiece was undertaken. Perhaps no book in the entire history of theological writing so effectively brings dogma to life, or so impressively shows the connection between theology and Christian living.

The Mysteries of Christianity is not a book for those who are in quest of an elementary catechism. Scheeben rises to the very summit of metaphysical speculation. In every one of the nine mysteries he brings out phases and consequences of revealed truths that will strike the attention of even the specialist in theology. In some points of doctrine he seems almost to have reached the uttermost boundaries beyond which the human intellect cannot advance. But the reader who is willing to scale the heights with Scheeben will find, after some tribulation, that he is able to breathe quite comfortably in the rarefied atmosphere to which the brilliant theologian has led him.

Perhaps the greatest difficulty encountered in reading Scheeben, as in translating his works, is his vocabulary. This difficulty arises from the loftiness of the objects he treats, and the profundity with which he discusses them. The light of his intellect penetrated so deeply into the mysteries that it could no longer hold the sharpness of its focus. Since the mysteries of faith are of their very nature obscure, the language in which they are expressed must also, at times, be obscure.

The present translation retains all of Scheeben's own footnotes. In the manner of great writers, his method of referring to sources is frequently vague; wherever I thought the reader might wish a more exact citation or a fuller context, I have ascertained patristic passages in Migne's *Patrologia latina* (*PL*) and *Patrologia graeca* (*PG*), as also in the *Corpus scriptorum ecclesiasticorum latinorum* (*CSEL*). These citations I have inserted without any further indication that they are my own additions.

On the other hand, many of the footnotes with which Dr. Höfer has enriched the German edition are omitted. These refer mainly to contemporary theological literature in German or French; scholars who could profit by them would read Scheeben's book in the original. However, some of Höfer's notes have been utilized, mostly in a modified and adapted form; in a few cases I have supplied footnotes of my own. To avoid cumbersome apparatus, all footnotes which are not Scheeben's are indicated by the device [Tr.]. Needless to say, in employing this designation I have no intention of diverting Dr. Höfer's scholarship to my own credit.

Quotations from Sacred Scripture are from the Douay Version, with the exception of Ephesians 5:32, which I have rendered from the Greek. All other translations, whether from the Fathers or from later theologians, are my own.

Cyril Vollert, S. J.

St. Mary's College
St. Marys, Kansas

Contents

                                       PAGE

TRANSLATOR'S PREFACE iii

INTRODUCTION

CHAPTER

   I. THE MYSTERY OF CHRISTIANITY IN GENERAL 3

PART ONE

THE MYSTERY OF THE MOST HOLY TRINITY

  II. THE OBSCURITY OF THE MYSTERY 25

 III. THE INTELLIGIBLE ASPECT OF THE MYSTERY 49

 IV. THE PRODUCTION OF THE SECOND AND THIRD PERSONS 87

  V. FUSION OF LIGHT AND DARKNESS IN THE MYSTERY . 118

 VI. THE SIGNIFICANCE OF THE MYSTERY OF THE TRINITY . 124

VII. THE MISSIONS OF THE DIVINE PERSONS 149

    APPENDIX I 181

    APPENDIX II 190

PART TWO

THE MYSTERY OF GOD IN THE ORIGINAL CREATION

VIII. CREATION AND ORIGINAL JUSTICE 201

 IX. ORIGINAL JUSTICE IN THE HUMAN RACE AND THE WORLD 229

PART THREE

THE MYSTERY OF SIN

  X. SIN IN GENERAL 243

 XI. ORIGINAL SIN 273

CONTENTS

PART FOUR

THE MYSTERY OF THE GOD-MAN AND HIS ECONOMY

CHAPTER   PAGE

XII. THE GOD-MAN 313

XIII. OUR KNOWLEDGE OF THE GOD-MAN 335

XIV. THE GOD-MAN IN HIS RELATIONS WITH THE TRINITY, THE HUMAN RACE, AND THE WORLD   357

XV. MYSTICAL POSITION AND SIGNIFICANCE OF THE GOD-MAN AS MEDIATOR BETWEEN THE TRINITARIAN GOD AND THE WORLD   405

XVI. ACTIVITY OF THE GOD-MAN IN THE EXECUTION OF HIS DIVINE PLAN 431

PART FIVE

THE MYSTERY OF THE EUCHARIST

XVII. THE REAL PRESENCE AND TRANSUBSTANTIATION . . . 469

XVIII. SIGNIFICANCE OF THE EUCHARIST 512

PART SIX

THE MYSTERY OF THE CHURCH AND THE SACRAMENTS

XIX. THE MYSTERY OF THE CHURCH 539

XX. THE SACRAMENTS OF THE CHURCH 558

XXI. CHRISTIAN MATRIMONY 593

PART SEVEN

THE MYSTERY OF CHRISTIAN JUSTIFICATION

XXII. NATURE OF CHRISTIAN JUSTIFICATION 613

XXIII. THE PROCESS OF JUSTIFICATION 631

PART EIGHT

THE MYSTERY OF GLORIFICATION AND THE LAST THINGS

XXIV. GLORIFICATION AND THE BEATIFIC VISION 651

XXV. TRANSFIGURATION OF THE BODY 666

CONTENTS

PART NINE

THE MYSTERY OF PREDESTINATION

CHAPTER

PAGE

XXVI. NATURE OF PREDESTINATION 697

XXVII. THE TRUE MYSTERY OF PREDESTINATION 712

PART TEN

THE SCIENCE OF THE MYSTERIES OF CHRISTIANITY, OR THEOLOGY

XXVIII. THEOLOGY AS SCIENCE 733

XXIX. FAITH AND REASON 762

INDEX 797

Christian Mysteries

By the Spirit He speaketh mysteries.
I Cor. 14:2

CHAPTER I

The Mystery of Christianity in General

▀▀

1. Interest of the Subject

CHRISTIANITY entered the world as a religion replete with mysteries. It was proclaimed as the mystery of Christ,[1] as the "mystery of the kingdom of God." [2] Its ideas and doctrines were unknown, unprecedented; and they were to remain inscrutable and unfathomable.

The mysterious character of Christianity, which was sufficiently intelligible in its simplest fundamentals, was foolishness to the Gentiles and a stumbling block to the Jews; and since Christianity in the course of time never relinquished and could never relinquish this character of mystery without belying its nature, it remained ever a foolishness, a stumbling block to all those who, like the Gentiles, looked upon it with unconsecrated eyes or, like the Jews, encountered it with uncircumcised hearts. With bitter scorn they would ever scoff at its mysterious nature as obscurantism, superstition, fanaticism, and absurdity.

After the mystery of Christianity had, in spite of all this, succeeded in making its way and became firmly entrenched in the belief of the nations, it found other and less malevolent adversaries. Many souls were too noble to disdain the lofty and beneficent force of Christianity, or too respectful of the faith of their childhood and the heritage of their fathers to turn from it in arrogance, but still not humble enough to surrender themselves to it with childlike trust. They sought to snatch the veil from the sanctuary of Christianity, to cleave the mystery so as to liberate the kernel of truth from the dark prison of its shell and bring it to light.

[1] Rom. 16:25-27; Col. 1:25-27.
[2] Mark 4:11; Luke 8:10.

Even friends and zealous defenders of Christianity could not always suppress a certain dread when they stood in the obscurity of its mysteries. To buttress belief in Christian truth and to defend it, they desired to resolve it into a rational science,[3] to demonstrate articles of faith by arguments drawn from reason, and so to reshape them that nothing would remain of the obscure, the incomprehensible, the impenetrable. They did not realize that by such a procedure they were betraying Christianity into the hands of her enemies and wresting the fairest jewel from her crown.

The greater, the more sublime, and the more divine Christianity is, the more inexhaustible, inscrutable, unfathomable, and mysterious its subject matter must be. If its teaching is worthy of the only-begotten Son of God, if the Son of God had to descend from the bosom of His Father to initiate us into this teaching, could we expect anything else than the revelation of the deepest mysteries locked up in God's heart? Could we expect anything else than disclosures concerning a higher, invisible world, about divine and heavenly things, which "eye hath not seen, nor ear heard," and which could not enter into the heart of any man?[4] And if God has sent us His own Spirit to teach us all truth, the Spirit of His truth, who dwells in God and there searches the deep things of God,[5] should this Spirit reveal nothing new, great, and wondrous, should He teach us no sublime secrets?

Far from repudiating Christianity or regarding it with suspicious eyes because of its mysteries, we ought to recognize its divine grandeur in these very mysteries. So essential to Christianity are its mysteries that in its character of truth revealed by the Son of God and the Holy Spirit it would stand convicted of intrinsic contradiction if it brought forward no mysteries. Its Author would carry with Him a poor recommendation for His divinity if He taught us only such truths as in the last analysis we could have learned from a mere man, or could have perceived and adequately grasped by our own unaided powers.

I would go even further: the truths of Christianity would not stir us as they do, nor would they draw us or hearten us, and they would

[3] Such was the endeavor of G. Hermes (d. 1831; censured 1835, Denz., 1618–21). [Tr.]
[4] Cf. I Cor. 2:9.
[5] Cf. John 16:13 and I Cor. 2:10 f.

not be embraced by us with such love and joy, if they contained no mysteries. What makes many a man recoil from the Christian mysteries as from sinister specters is neither the voice of nature nor the inner impulse of the heart nor the yearning for light and truth, but the arrogance of a wanton and overweening pride. When the heart thirsts after truth, when the knowledge of the truth is its purest delight and highest joy, the sublime, the exalted, the extraordinary, the incomprehensible all exercise an especial attraction. A truth that is easily discovered and quickly grasped can neither enchant nor hold. To enchant and hold us it must surprise us by its novelty, it must overpower us with its magnificence; its wealth and profundity must exhibit ever new splendors, ever deeper abysses to the exploring eye. We find but slight stimulation and pleasure in studies whose subject matter is soon exhausted and so leaves nothing further for our wonderment. But how powerfully sciences enthrall us when every glance into them suggests new marvels to divine, and every facet of the object imprisons new and greater splendors!

The greatest charm in knowledge is astonishment, surprise, wonderment. The less we previously knew of a thing, especially the less we dared hope to learn about it by ourselves and the more we marvel at its existence, the more fortunate we regard ourselves when at length we come to know it. The more exalted an object is, the more its beauty and greatness impress us and the more it compels our admiration, the more even the slightest glance that we dare fix on it captivates us. In a word, the charm of truth is proportionate to its abstruseness and mystery. Must not Christianity, too, be especially valuable and dear to us because of the mysteries it involves? And indeed is it not all the more precious the greater are the mysteries which it harbors within itself? Does not Christianity impress us so powerfully just because it is one vast mystery, because it is the greatest of mysteries, the mystery of God?

Fundamentally, of course, it is not exactly the obscurity engulfing an object that makes the mystery so highly prized and attractive for us. Our souls, born of Light and destined for Light, flee darkness and long for light; darkness as such has no enticement for them. Why does the dawn exercise so enchanting an influence over us, why does it charm us more than the full light of day? Not because the light is mixed with darkness, but rather because it disperses the darkness that surrounded us, and brings in its train the light we have yearned for so long and so earnestly, and because our anxious hearts are cheered by the ever-growing glories of the sun.

What captivates us is the emergence of a light that had been hidden from us. Mysteries must in themselves be lucid, glorious truths. The darkness can be only on our side, so far as our eyes are turned away from the mysteries, or at any rate are not keen enough to confront them and see through them. There must be truths that baffle our scrutiny not because of their intrinsic darkness and confusion, but because of their excessive brilliance, sublimity, and beauty, which not even the sturdiest human eye can encounter without going blind.

When truths which had been entirely inaccessible to us become manifest, when God by His grace makes it possible for us, if only from afar, to cast a timid glance into their depths, a wondrous light dawns in us and the rosy morning glow of a heavenly world breaks over us; and although the darkness that surrounded us and still surrounds us strikes our consciousness only when we have such an experience, a single ray of the higher light that shines upon us is powerful enough to fill us with unutterable rapture.

The fascination of mystery is so strong that almost all religious and social organizations that exercise or have exercised an inspiring and lasting influence on mankind have wrapped themselves up in the obscurity of mystery, and have even gloried in the mysteries which they were aware of, although they disdained Christianity because of its mysteries. Their mysteries, products of human invention, are of course mere caricatures of the divine mysteries. Either they are plain mystifications with which to dupe the uninitiate, or they are in part genuine, in part spurious truths which lose the noble character of mystery by the very fact that they are proposed to the initiate as evident. The Christian, on the other hand, is really initiated into the mysteries of God. He rightly regards this initiation as an illumination replete with wonder and grace; but for this very reason he is filled with the deepest reverence for the sublimity of his mysteries. He acknowledges the grace of God with holy gratitude, but without despising the uninitiated. He earnestly desires that they too may participate in this same tremendous grace; and if in former ages Christians kept their mysteries hidden from unbelievers, it was only because of their solicitude that what was sacred should not be profaned and defiled in the eyes and hands of the unclean.

But when the Christian humbly receives the revelation of God's mysteries as a great grace, he is entitled to a holy pride. With holy pride he can and ought to glory in the exalted mysteries that he possesses by the grace of God; he can and should regard himself as the object of an extraordinary illumination, as an initiate into the great mysteries, which are hidden from the mighty and wise of this world. Today especially, when a superficial enlightenment with its deceptive glimmer is intent on supplanting the mysteries of our faith, the Christian must be conscious of his sublime illumination and proud of the dawn of a higher, fairer, supernatural world that has risen over him in the faith. How can we call forth and strengthen this lofty consciousness, this holy pride? Not by denying the darkness which still shrouds the mysteries from the eyes of the initiate, but by pointing out that even the feeble ray gleaming forth from the darkness is strong enough at least to herald the incredible magnificence of the mysteries. Such demonstration is what we have desired to furnish in the present work, and thus we hope to make a contribution to the advancement of Christian knowledge and Christian life.

In order at the very outset to disclose the plan that we are following in this book, and the principles that guide us, we must first of all, by a careful analysis, come to an understanding about the notion of mystery.

2. THE NOTION OF MYSTERY IN GENERAL AND OF CHRISTIAN MYSTERY IN PARTICULAR

What do we mean by mystery in general? We mean all that is secret, hidden from us; consequently everything that is not seen or known by us, and that cannot be either seen or known by us.

But if this is the case, does it not follow that as soon as a thing comes to our actual knowledge, as soon as it becomes manifest to us, it ceases to be a mystery? To be sure, so far as it becomes really known by us and becomes really manifest to us, it can no longer remain hidden from us, can no longer be a secret, and hence can no longer be a mystery. But cannot a thing which is manifest to us still present obscurity in some respects, and thus remain hidden from us? In fact, is it not usually the case that we know things only according to some aspect, or in general have only a superficial acquaintance with them, without comprehending them from all angles or penetrating into their innermost nature? Indeed, is it not usually true that even what we know of a thing remains obscure and perplexing for the very reason that we cannot reach down into its innermost depths and hence cannot conceive and explain it in terms of its ultimate essence? And in particular, when we have to sketch a composite picture of a thing's nature from the various properties which it displays, is not this picture ordinarily as dark and enigmatic as a silhouette, because we lack an intimate and thorough understanding of the relationships among its various properties?

Nearly all the objects of our knowledge, even the simplest, the most natural, and the most familiar, continue to remain mysteries for us in some respect. The light that falls upon them cannot dispel all darkness from them. Everything remains to some extent inconceivable to us, because our concepts and representations do not embrace all the knowable details of an object; likewise, everything is unfathomable, because the more deeply our gaze penetrates into an object the weaker and less certain it becomes. Further, an essential characteristic of the knowledge we have of a thing is an awareness of the imperfection, deficiency, and obscurity of that knowledge; we do not deceive ourselves that the little we perceive is all that can be perceived. If we were thus to deceive ourselves, we should be regarding darkness itself as light, and we should betray the fact that the light does not shine for us even where its rays actually fall. All true philosophers have quite rightly considered the consciousness of lack of knowledge as an essential factor of true knowledge. Conscious lack of knowledge was for them a "learned ignorance" and enabled them to mark off light from shadow, and thus to bring out in sharper prominence the clear lines of their system of philosophy.[6]

But the basic reason why our cognition does not perfectly and thoroughly illuminate its objects is the feebleness and limitation of the inner light from which it proceeds. Only God's cognition excludes all mysteries, because it springs from an infinite Light which with infinite power penetrates and illuminates the innermost depths

[6] The views of St. Thomas Aquinas on the limits of the human reason are clearly set forth in the Proemium to Book IV of the *Summa contra Gentiles*. Among the Scholastics the outstanding proponent of *docta ignorantia* was Nicholas of Cusa. [Tr.]

of everything that exists. But the created intellect, no matter how pure and perfect it may be, will never with its finite power comprehend and conceive everything that is; its eye is impeded by its very nature from reaching into the deepest foundations of things, and so it cannot perfectly fathom all objects. Much less can the human intellect do so, because it is not a pure spirit but is shackled to matter. Angels have an immediate perception at least of themselves. But man, whether we consider him in himself or with regard to objects outside of himself, has an immediate perception only of the phenomena, the external appearances, the accidents proper to things, from which he may grope toward some knowledge of essences. His reason makes it possible for him, even demands of him, that he pass beyond the phenomenon so that he may perceive not only the phenomenon itself, but also the essence which externalizes and expresses itself in the phenomenon, and thereby to some extent explain and understand the phenomena themselves. His intelligence not only perceives the signs and manifestations that strike the eye, but from them reasons to the cause without which they cannot exist and endure. He reads beneath the surface into the essence which the external appearances disclose to him, and into the cause which confronts him in its effects and which lies concealed behind the effects. But since no essence is entirely revealed in its phenomena, and no cause in its effect, the ray of light with which we penetrate the shell cannot expose the kernel. Knowledge of an essence gained from its phenomena will never equal knowledge gained from immediate intuition, and therefore even the understanding of the phenomena will never be perfect. The former as well as the latter will always remain obscure and full of of mystery.

If by mystery we mean nothing more than an object which is not entirely conceivable and fathomable in its innermost essence, we need not seek very far to find mysteries. Such mysteries are found not only above us, but all around us, in us, under us. The real essence of all things is concealed from our eyes. The physicist will never fully plumb the laws of forces in the physico-chemical world and perfectly comprehend their effects; and the same is true of the physiologist with regard to the laws of organic nature, of the psychologist with regard to the soul, of the metaphysician with regard to the ultimate basis of all being.

Christianity is not alone in exhibiting mysteries in the above-mentioned sense. If its truths are inconceivable and unfathomable, so in greater part are the truths of reason. This by itself does not imply anything against Christianity, nor does it imply much in its favor. As will be shown, however, the truths that are specifically proper to Christianity are inconceivable and unfathomable in an exclusively special sense. To appreciate this fact, we must go on to consider another aspect of the notion of mystery.

When a person understands a truth, it is no longer a mystery for him but is clear to him, to the extent that he understands it. But do we not ordinarily say that he who understands a truth which he had not previously been aware of and did not suspect, or which others are not yet aware of, knows a secret or mystery? That is so; still, the truth is no longer a mystery for him. Well then, what if he were of himself utterly incapable of discovering the truth which he now knows, and which even now, after it has become manifest to him, is known only because another to whom he lends credence has communicated it to him, and which, finally, even now he does not grasp by the light of his own intellect but only by faith? In this case the truth, in spite of such revelation, still remains hidden, because it does not lie open to our scrutiny and is not perceived in itself. If, in addition, the truth which has been revealed by another has absolutely no similiarity, or but very slight similarity, with anything which we ourselves have ever seen or experienced, then naturally we are much less capable of forming a clear idea of it than we are of other things which do not extend beyond our experience. Thus in a double respect it will be obscure in its own way even after it has been revealed, and accordingly will be and will remain a mystery in a quite special sense.

Mysteries of this sort are, to some extent, found even in the natural order. Let us suppose, for instance, that a traveler from a foreign country, to which we cannot go, gives us an account of a plant whose color, blossom, and fragrance have practically no similarity with any we have seen; or that someone should discourse on light and its effects to a man born blind. In such cases, of course, the mystery is not absolute, and does not obtain for all men, since it is not at all obscure for some, or even for a large number. But let us take a truth to which no men, no creatures at all can attain by the natural means of cognition at their disposal, which they can perceive only by a supernatural illumination, which can be grasped only by belief in God's word, and which is remote from everything that the creature naturally knows, as remote as heaven is from earth. Then we have a mystery in its absolute form as a truth whose existence the creature cannot ascertain without belief in God's word, and whose subject matter he cannot represent and conceive directly, but only indirectly by comparison with dissimilar things.

Mystery in its absolute form, as we have just described it, is Christian mystery, that is, mystery which divine revelation in the person of the incarnate Word proposes to the world for belief.

In accordance with our description, two elements are essential to a mystery: first, that the existence of the proposed truth is attainable by no natural means of cognition, that it lies beyond the range of the created intellect; secondly, that its content is capable of apprehension only by analogous concepts. If either one of these two elements is lacking, a truth cannot be called a mystery of Christianity in the strict sense, even if it has actually been proposed by Christian revelation. Owing to the absence of the first element, the doctrine of the existence of God and His essential attributes, for example, is not a mystery in this sense. For, although we apprehend all this only by analogous concepts, so that our notion must always remain obscure, reason can know that the objects apprehended really exist.[7] Conversely, we are aware of many of God's works only through divine revelation (for example, the establishment of the Church as a juridical society pertaining to divine right, prescinding

---

[7] The importance of this element was emphasized by the Provincial Council of Cologne in 1860: "What we say of mysteries is to be accepted not only in the sense in which we rightly assert that we do not understand the intimate nature even of well-known things, but also in the sense that we cannot with certitude demonstrate even the existence of the truths which are called the mysteries of religion, or, in other words, that we cannot perceive why they must be. Reason indeed demonstrates God's existence and infinity, although it perceives far less of the manner of His infinity than it does of the nature of created things. But reason alone, by its own powers and cognitive principles, not only cannot demonstrate or understand how there are three persons in one essence, but it cannot demonstrate or perceive that there are three really distinct, divine persons in one essence, even after the fact has been revealed" (*Collectio Lacensis*, V, 279 f.).

Still more decisive is the Vatican Council (Sessio III, De fide et ratione, can. 1 [Denz., 1816]): "If anyone should maintain that no true and properly so-called mysteries are contained in divine revelation, but that all the dogmas of faith can be understood and demonstrated by the cultured intellect from natural principles: let him be anathema." [Tr.]

from its interior, supernatural character), the abstract notion of which, however, presents no special difficulty, because such things are similar to objects of our natural perception. Hence they are not mysteries in the narrower sense.

Mystery is generally defined as a truth concerning which we know that it is, but not how it is; that is, according to the usual explanation, we know that the subject and the predicate are really connected, but we are unable to determine and perceive the manner of the association.

This definition, if rightly explained, agrees in essentials with ours as given above. But it requires a detailed clarification, which is explicitly contained in our definition, and is not sufficiently expressed in the customary explanation.[8]

[8] The definition appears to intimate that the obscurity of the mystery lies only in the *How*, not in the *That*. The *That* of the truth, namely, its objective existence, the reality of the nexus between subject and predicate, can frequently be known by the mind, even when the mode of the connection remains impenetrable. In this case the truth would not be simply hidden from our natural vision, and hence would not be simply a mystery. The definition must therefore be further clarified so as to suppose that the *That* in the mystery is rendered accessible to us only through a positive revelation. As for the mode of the nexus between subject and predicate, the term is ordinarily understood to apply both to the objective reason for the nexus, and to the manner of the nexus. Thus, it seems, we can perfectly grasp subject and predicate without at the same time understanding the reason and the manner of the connection. But as a rule this is impossible. The obscurity of the mode of connection lies in the obscurity of our concept, of our notion both of the subject and of the predicate; and this in turn, with regard to the mysteries of Christianity, is rooted in the fact that our concepts are not direct, are not gained from an intuition of the object, but are indirect, analogous, and transferred from very dissimilar objects. Therefore the specific kind of obscurity in the subject matter of the Christian mysteries is not indicated in that explanation, and in general the obscurity is not sufficiently declared. By the mode of the objective reality we must rather understand not merely the mode of the connection between subject and predicate, but also the manner of conceiving the entire content of the mystery. If, however, the obscurity of the mode of the nexus is referred to the fact that we cannot perceive the compatibility of subject and predicate, and that both involve an apparent contradiction for our understanding, only a quite subordinate and secondary element in the obscurity is stressed. This element does not universally occur, or in most cases can almost entirely be mastered by our own investigation. We could better account for this obscurity by saying that its nature is such that we cannot positively perceive the possibility of the nexus between subject and predicate. For this is universally the case when we have only analogous, and therefore obscure, concepts of both subject and predicate. The mode of the nexus which we spoke of above is

Hence we shall do well to adhere to our definition, which is in no need of all these explanations and supplementary qualifications. In simpler form we can phrase it thus: Christian mystery is a truth communicated to us by Christian revelation, a truth to which we cannot attain by our unaided reason, and which, even after we have attained to it by faith, we cannot adequately represent with our rational concepts.

3. THE PLACE OF MYSTERIES IN THE SYSTEM OF CHRISTIAN REVELATION

That Christianity contains mysteries of this kind is beyond question. It is likewise clear that not all its truths, but only those to which our definition applies, in contrast to the rest to which it does not apply, deserve to be called mysteries in the full and proper sense of the term. Accordingly we are entitled to detach the mysteries from the rest of the truths, and to consider them under a special category.

I am well aware that difficulties are raised in some quarters against such a division, partly out of zeal for the mysteries, partly in the interests of reason, according as it is argued that the truths of Christianity are all either equally remote from the reason, or are equally proximate to it.

Obviously there can be no question of a like remoteness or proximity in every respect. Who would undertake to maintain that all truths are equally hard or equally easy to learn? Even if such an undertaking should occur to anyone, we have no need to waste words in arguing with him. Those whom we have in mind do not take

precisely the manner in which the nexus is to be thought of as possible, from the standpoint of the reason for it and of the mutual relationship of the terms.

Moreover, the obscurity of the mode of the nexus, as it is commonly understood in the definition we are criticizing, could give occasion to error, as would be the case with mysteries, should we have no knowledge whatever of the mode, the reason, and the manner of the nexus between subject and predicate. On the contrary, in the same relationship in which we understand subject and predicate more or less clearly, we also grasp the reason and the manner of the nexus. Later in the present work we shall have more than one opportunity to demonstrate this truth. In many cases revelation itself instructs us not only about the existence of the nexus, but also about the reason for it, although as a rule less concerning the intrinsic than the extrinsic reason, particularly the ultimate reason, that is, the motive whereby the realization of the nexus is effected.

such a stand. The only contention, with reference to the boundaries set up by our definition, is either that all the truths of Christianity lie without the horizon of the reason, or that all lie within it.

The first of these two contentions is found in the article "Mysterien" of the first edition of the *Freiburger Kirchen-Lexikon*,[9] which in other respects is very stimulating, and is especially good in its criticism of the usual definition of mystery. The article insists that the whole of Christianity is a single great mystery, because it can be known as a whole only through divine revelation; and although its incomprehensibility does not equally pertain to all parts of the whole, it cannot by itself alone yield any definite norm for singling out individual parts of the whole, particularly since there is no special basis for such selection.

Unlike the superficial, inconsistent view of mysteries which occupied the author of the article mentioned above, and which received a sharp criticism from him, this theory is in part quite correct. It is true, and we ourselves have pointed it out above, that inconceivability alone, taken in general, can furnish no definite norm for the distinction; only later, after the necessity of revelation for the knowledge of the existence of the mystery has become apparent, does it prove decisive. Likewise it is perfectly true that Christianity, or rather the content of Christianity taken as a whole, and particularly its specific content, is a mystery in the sense that it can be known only through divine revelation. Lastly it is true that even if the only non-mysterious elements were subordinate truths regarded individually in themselves, we could not rightly consider the primary truths as the sole mysterious section of the whole, since such subordinate truths, which have no meaning apart from the whole, merge with the whole and hence participate in its mysterious character.

But here our ways part. Without doubt Christianity comprises many truths knowable by reason. To such belongs all that concerns the nature of man, man's utter dependence on God, and the existence of this personal God Himself (apart from the precision of His

---

[9] This edition (1847–60) was later withdrawn from circulation, owing to the condemnation of Günther, whose disciples had to some extent collaborated on the work. The article in question is found in Vol. VII, pp. 428–37. The author is Scheeben's severe critic, W. Mattes. The second edition (1882 ff.), which reflects Scheeben's influence, does not contain the entry "Mysterien." [Tr.]

personality in the Trinity). These truths constitute a definite system in themselves; and they are related to the truths that lie beyond the reach of the reason not as secondary truths to primary truths, but as the body to the soul which is above it but at the same time dwells in it, or as the foundation to the edifice constructed thereon, or as the vestibule to the interior of the temple, or as two juxtaposed but subordinate parts of the same whole.

The mysterious part, as the superior, is at once the soul and the proper essence of the whole, gives its name to the whole, and renders the latter specifically distinct from any other whole. So when I say that Christianity as a whole is mysterious, and is a single vast mystery, I do not mean that everything in Christianity is a mystery, but only that the higher and nobler part of it, that part which renders it specifically distinct from every other system of religious truths, even from true and uncontaminated natural religion, is mysterious and a mystery throughout; in the same way as we should say that man, although visible in body, is invisible in his essential form, his soul. And as I should say that the body itself is invisible so far as it belongs to the whole, that is, in its conjunction and union with the soul, so I might say of Christianity likewise, that its naturally known truths are themselves mysterious when considered in their conjunction and relation with the mysterious part. But in this case they are not taken by themselves alone; only their conjunction with the mysterious is designated as a mystery, and the mysterious character of this relationship can be perceived in the very fact that we single out and study the mysterious character of the one part in opposition to the non-mysterious character of the other.

That the relationship of rational truths to mysterious truths is such as we have just described, will be found to be one of the first fruits of our work, which will definitely show that Christianity is essentially a tremendous mystery at every point. That the learned author of the above-mentioned article does not share this view, is owing to the fact, if we understand him aright, that objectively and subjectively he establishes too close a connection between genuinely mysterious truths and the truths which we have designated as rational truths, that he excessively confuses both, and hence notably defrauds reason in its own domain. Thus, for example, he maintains that without a knowledge of the Trinity in God we can have no true notion of God at all, and consequently that any teaching about God is true only in terms of a mystery that comes to our knowledge through revelation. We can admit neither of these propositions, the first if only for the reason that the second would thereupon follow. In the second proposition we discern a decided encroachment on reason in its own realm, and in the first a confusion between a false notion and a one-sided, inadequate notion. I shall later have more to say about this.

Zeal for the mysterious character of the whole of Christianity dictated this protest against the elimination of mysteries from the sum total of Christian truths. At the other extreme is the error, still frequently proclaimed, that all the truths of Christianity lie as close to the reason as any part of them.[10]

No one, to be sure, would deny that to attain to some of the truths of Christianity reason stands in greater need of revelation than in the case of other truths. The view is even put forward that reason by itself could not have discovered them, that they were hidden from reason prior to revelation. But, this view adds, subsequently to revelation, and guided by revelation, reason can direct its gaze toward such truths and by concentrated contemplation can actually perceive them. And in fact there can be no controversy that Christianity makes known in this sense many a truth which had been hidden from us before. But such truths must lie within the range of our natural vision. Hence they are not absolute mysteries, because reason, though not without external assistance, can attain to them by its own inner light, and because, consequent upon revelation, they stand out clearly within the horizon of reason. There is no essential difference between them and the truths discovered by us prior to revelation; they are rational truths just as much as are these latter. Revelation of such truths would not open up the prospect of an entirely new and unknown domain, but would merely guide the reason and assist it in the mastery of its own province.

No, we may not have so mean an estimate of the riches and grandeur of divine revelation. We must certainly be grateful that revelation has pointed out the right path leading to the reason's richest development; but we should prove ungrateful were we to

---

[10] Endeavors to rationalize Christian truth, so prevalent in the schools of Hermes and Günther, are today no longer operative in Catholic theology. [Tr.]

be thankful only for this, were we, enamored of the fancied greatness of our reason, to restrict the inestimable wealth of Christ to
so narrow a compass. Incomparably greater is the call upon our
gratitude for the communication of truths lying entirely beyond
the sphere of investigation possible for our natural reason, truths to
which reason itself, in spite of the greatest endeavor and the most
competent guidance, can never attain. Our gratitude to revelation
for such truths must be all the greater inasmuch as they lie absolutely beyond the reach of reason, and inasmuch as these suprarational truths are more sublime, more precious, more valuable than
purely rational truths, so that even the slightest knowledge of them
calls for the greatest esteem and appreciation on our part.

In fact, it is precisely the objective sublimity and grandeur of
certain truths of Christianity that place them above the horizon
of our reason. Whatever the finite reason, precisely because it is
finite, cannot reach and grasp, must of necessity lie beyond all that
it can reach and grasp. Suprarationality is a consequence, and hence
the best sign, of the greatness and sublimity of a truth. It coincides
with the supernaturality in which the objective sublimity of a thing
is expressed. Deny the suprarationality of a part of Christian truth,
and you destroy its supernatural grandeur and sublimity, its intrinsic excellence and wealth. Vice versa, if you deny the supernaturalness of these truths, they cease automatically to transcend reason,
and so the absolute necessity and the highest value of revelation itself vanish.

4. Guiding Principles and Method of Our Discussion of Mysteries

Thus far we have seen that we may classify the mysteries of
Christianity as a special category of the truths which it teaches; and
we have also fixed upon the reason why such a classification and a
special consideration of them are useful and profitable, if not necessary.

Our purpose in isolating the mysteries from the other truths of
Christianity is to understand and present them in their supernatural
grandeur and sublimity, so as to bring together in one comprehensive
view all that Christianity possesses beyond anything that the human
mind and heart can discover or contrive in the realm of beauty and

greatness, and thus to unveil its proper, intrinsic nature in all its wealth. This we undertake in the hope of being able to show that precisely those doctrines which appear to the proud mind as horrible wraiths, as senseless, impossible enigmas, infinitely surpass in beauty and clarity all that reason in its loftiest flights can achieve. And we hope further that, considered precisely as mysteries, whether singly or in their mutual relationships, they will stand forth in as clear a light as possible here on earth.

We trust that we shall be able to bring together the mysteries of Christianity into an independent, well-ordered system in which they will appear to be a great, mystic cosmos erected, out of the depths of the divinity, upon the world of nature which is visible to the bodily eye, and upon the world of spirit which is visible only to the mind. Lastly, we believe that for the scientific understanding of Christianity, for theology, nothing is more important and rich in blessings, and today in particular nothing is more seasonable, than this specialized and systematic treatment of the doctrine of mysteries.

There is in our day a pronounced tendency toward the strict separation of the various branches of knowledge. The supposition is that each science will come to full and distinct self-consciousness if it is studied in its opposition to other sciences. But how can theology build up a science of its own, and especially how can it detach itself objectively from philosophy, unless it becomes conscious of its own proper domain in which alone it is at home, and into which philosophy cannot follow? And where is its most proper domain situated if not in its doctrine of mysteries?

Such clear self-consciousness is necessary for theology if it is to be quite at home in its own sphere and is to be brought to a genuinely scientific form.

The treatment of those doctrines of Christianity which are really mysteries in the sense explained cannot be fruitful and successful unless we clearly determine and keep before our eyes the position of the reason and its natural objects with respect to these suprarational and supernatural objects. If this is not done, there is a proximate danger of confusing the higher objects with the lower, of drawing the higher down within the orbit of the reason, and of treating them in the same manner as the lower. The result is that these higher objects are viewed obliquely and in a false light by the contemplating eye. Instead of appearing in their extraordinary greatness and harmony, they become disarranged and distorted, if not actually deformed. Thus, instead of gaining in clarity they become darker, even though to a diseased or unfocused eye they seem distinct and beautiful.

Mysteries become luminous and appear in their true nature, their entire grandeur and beauty, only when we definitely recognize that they are mysteries, and clearly perceive how high they stand above our own orbit, how completely they are distinct from all objects within our natural ken. And when, supported by the all-powerful word of divine revelation, we soar upon the wings of faith over the chasm dividing us from them and mount up to them, they temper themselves to our eyes in the light of faith which is supernatural, as they themselves are; then they display themselves to us in their true form, in their heavenly, divine nature. The moment we perceive the depth of the darkness with which heaven veils its mysteries from our minds, they will shine over us in the light of faith like brilliant stars mutually illuminating, supporting, and emphasizing one another; like stars that form themselves into a marvelous system and that can be known in their full power and magnificence only in this system. Lastly, the more we bring ourselves to a realization of the supernaturality in the suprarationality, and of the suprarationality in the supernaturality of these mysteries, the less will the darkness of the incomprehensibility enveloping them trouble and bewilder us. Yet we can never forget that this incomprehensibility is part of their sublimity. Any confusion or apparent contradiction involved in this incomprehensibility will tend to vanish the more we recall the sublimity of these objects and guard against mixing them up with the objects of our natural perception or measuring them with the norm of the latter, and the more careful we are, under the guidance of faith, to refer the natural to them only as an analogy.

Guided by such reflections, we desired to make the attempt to present the higher Christian truths, so far as they are intelligible, in their supernatural magnificence and consummate harmony. To accomplish this task, we must specify the mysterious character of these truths. We believe that, as correct perspective is indispensable to astronomy and the graphic arts, an accurate determination of the mysterious character of the higher Christian truths is indispensable to an understanding and presentation of the mysteries themselves. For thousands of years astronomy had judged the magnitude and relations of the heavenly bodies according to their superficial appearance, and came to a correct appreciation of these matters only when man had learned to determine the distance of the stars from our eye and terrestrial objects by means of the parallax. Similarly theology will understand its exalted objects with greater accuracy and clarity the more exactly we learn to determine their distance from our natural intellect and from the latter's near-by natural objects. Sculpture and painting could achieve their perfection only after man had learned to apply the right perspective to pictorial presentation. In like manner theology will be able to display faithful and lifelike pictures to its disciples only when it succeeds in drawing its designs according to all the laws of correct perspective.

In all departments of experimental science and the graphic arts perspective has in our day come into its full importance. We have studied its laws with zeal and success, and have applied it universally with happy results. In the field of theology the great doctors of the Church, and especially the princes of medieval Scholasticism, investigated and applied its laws with nice judgment, at a time when those laws were scarcely known and but slightly esteemed in the sphere of physical observation and technical works. Far from neglecting them, theology must devote its attention to them more than ever at the present time, when it is apparently being summoned to a new and noble resurgence, so that the sacred sciences may keep pace with the secular sciences, and Christian learning with the renewal of Christian life and the revival of sacred art.

Rationalism, which believes that it alone possesses the philosopher's stone and pretends to be the sole representative of science even in the domain of faith, is the only tendency that will object to the fundamental postulate of theological science. It is not so long ago that a Catholic philosopher in the name of science raised a protest against the withdrawal of the mysteries from the natural purview of the reason, as though theological science would be rendered radically impossible unless confined to the domain of reason. Concerning the validity and necessity of such segregation, the head of the Church has instructed him; concerning the havoc wrought upon science not by the withdrawal, but by the denial of mysteries, science itself will instruct him.[11]

[11] Scheeben is thinking of J. Frohschammer (1821–93), whose views were censured in 1862 (Denz., 1666–76). [Tr.]

The following studies on the mysteries of Christianity are worked out in line with the procedure explained above. We have selected nine of the mysteries as being the most important; all the others are reducible to these nine. We have taken pains to indicate and determine the supernatural, mysterious character of each of them, so as to pave the way for as clear and lucid an exposition of its subject matter as is possible, in view of the obscurity which shrouds it and of our own feeble powers. The light derived from the consideration of each separate mystery spreads automatically far and wide over the inner relationship and the wonderful harmony pervading them all, and thus the individual pictures take their places in an orderly gallery, which comprises everything magnificent and sublime that theology possesses far in excess of all the other sciences, including even philosophy.

PART ONE

The Mystery of the Most Holy Trinity

No one knoweth the Son but the Father;
neither doth anyone know the Father but
the Son, and he to whom it shall please the
Son to reveal Him.

Matt. 11:27

CHAPTER II

The Obscurity of the Mystery

▪▪▪

5. Proof of its Indemonstrability

WE begin with the mystery which more than any other is buried in the depths of the Godhead. The Blessed Trinity is the mystery of mysteries, before which even the seraphim veil their countenances, singing with astonished wonder their thrice-repeated "Holy." [1]

Our first task will be to demonstrate and explain the mysterious character of this doctrine; only by doing so can we succeed in placing it in its proper light and in bringing out its tremendous fullness and far-reaching significance. The more we realize the remoteness of our reason from this exalted object, the more surely will faith present it to our spiritual vision under the right aspect and in its true form.

The thought that the Trinity of persons existing in the one divine nature may be demonstrated by rational arguments has often occurred among Christian philosophers in the past, and today perhaps more than ever a number of apologists seem attracted by the same ambition. The tendency appeared in its crassest form in Raymond Lully, the renowned scientific dilettante; the happiest and most reasonable attempts along the same lines seem [2] to be those made by St. Anselm and Richard of St. Victor, the forerunners and to some extent the standard-bearers of Scholasticism. In recent times the

[1] Cf. Isa. 6:3. Because of the triple "Holy" the text is interpreted in a Trinitarian sense by many Fathers and Scholastics. Such an exegesis does not conform to the literal meaning of the words, but is a theological adaptation in the light of New Testament revelation. [Tr.]

[2] We make this qualification because we believe that their treatment admits of an interpretation incompatible with the claim of a purely rational demonstration.

school of Günther has gloried in its claim of having transformed
this as well as all the other mysteries of Christianity into an evident,
easily understood rational truth.

A simple glance at the dogma as it is proposed to us by the Church
is all that is needed to perceive that not the Trinity, but the
indemonstrability of the Trinity, admits of strict theological and
philosophical proof. This is the firm, unanimous view of practically
all theologians from St. Thomas down to the most recent times,[3]
a view which a Provincial Council has not long ago expressly
sanctioned, and the denial of which, even in its most qualified form,
has lately been censured by the Holy See.[4]

What does the Church teach about the Blessed Trinity? That in
God there is one essence, one nature, in three hypostases or persons.
Each of the persons possesses the entire nature in its entire perfection,
with its entire omnipotence, wisdom, and goodness. Like the nature
itself, the divine activity having its term outside of God is common
to all three persons, for it is exercised only by the power of the common nature. Father, Son, and Holy Ghost are a single principle of
all things: *unum universorum principium.*[5]

From this it follows that only the unity of the divine nature, but
by no means the distinction between the divine persons, can be deduced from God's external activity. Does a study of God's works
enable us to deduce anything more than the power by which they
are produced, the omnipotence which calls them into being, the wisdom which is reflected in them, the goodness which endows them
with life, moves them, and beatifies them? In a word, to account
for creation can we require anything more than the existence of

[3] Cf. St. Thomas Aquinas, *De veritate*, q. 10, a. 13; *In Boetium de Trinitate*,
q. 1, a. 4; on Scotus, see below, note 11; Suarez, *De Trinitate*, I, cc. 11, 12;
Ruiz de Montoya, *De Trinitate*, Disp. 41 ff., which in general is the best
treatise on this entire question; my *Dogmatik*, Bk. II, section 6.

[4] Cf. the Provincial Council of Cologne (1860), *Decreta*, Part. I, tit. 2, c. 9
(*Col. Lac.*, V, 285). Among the Rosminian propositions, condemned December 14, 1887, cf. no. 25: "Once the mystery of the Blessed Trinity has
been revealed, its existence can be demonstrated by purely speculative
arguments which, though negative and indirect, are such as to recall the
truth of the Trinity to the philosophical sphere, so that this proposition
becomes scientific, like any other. For if this truth were denied, the purely
rational theosophic doctrine would remain not only incomplete, but would
bristle with all sorts of absurdities and thus would be demolished" (Denz.,
1915). See also no. 26 (Denz., 1916).

[5] Conc. Lat., IV, c. 1 de fide (Denz., 428).

an infinitely perfect, transcendent, and supramundane Being? Of course this power can be no mere form but must be a substance; and this Being must be self-subsistent, essentially distinct from the universe, and self-sufficient. The mind knows no abstract divinity, but the concrete, definite, actual God, since only the concrete, actual God can be Creator of the world. But the mind by no means perceives that this is one God in three persons. We can show that the divine nature subsists in itself, and not in a subject really distinct from the nature; but we cannot show how it subsists in itself, whether it subsists in one or several subjects, whether it belongs to one or several subjects. From the fact that the divine nature is seen to be externally operative and generous, we know that it is supremely self-sufficient and personal; but the conclusion by no means follows that it is productive within its own nature, and that it can and must communicate itself.

The Apostle says that the invisible attributes of God are clearly perceived by a consideration of created things.[6] But what are these invisible attributes of God? We are to understand thereby His eternal power and providence, all which appears in the works of God, and by which the works are produced. The divinity is invisible in itself, and is visible only in its works. But precisely because the divinity remains invisible in itself, because we know it only in broken rays through its works and not as it is in itself in the pure fullness of its light, whereas the persons pertain to the divinity as it is in itself, they remain absolutely invisible. Thus God is visible and accessible in the nimbus which He has cast about Himself in His works; nevertheless, according to the Apostle, as He is in Himself He inhabits "light inaccessible, whom no man hath seen nor can see." [7] Therefore St. John rightly says: "No man hath seen God at any time; the only-begotten Son who is in the bosom of the Father, He hath declared Him"; [8] and still more clearly God's Son Himself: "No one knoweth the Son but the Father; neither doth anyone [naturally] know the Father but the Son, and he to whom it shall please the Son to reveal Him." [9] Hence only the divine persons themselves, who dwell in the inaccessible light of the Godhead, can know them-

[6] Rom. 1:20.
[7] Cf. I Tim. 6:16.
[8] John 1:18.
[9] Matt. 11:27.

selves in their distinction from one another and also in their mutual relations. Only the Father and the Son and the Holy Ghost, who proceeds from both, the Spirit who dwells in God and "searcheth all things, yea, the deep things of God," [10] only they know one another in themselves. Not alone the human intellect, but all created intellects, know these persons solely through their gracious condescension and revelation, not by intuition or inquiry, but exclusively by way of instruction, from God's positive communication.

The mind perceives that of itself it cannot arrive at a knowledge of the Trinity; and revelation for its part declares that it alone can disclose this mystery. The natural reason, the reason of the creature, knows only the nature of God. And this it knows only according to its external manifestation as the supreme cause of created nature, without being able to penetrate into the inner depths of the Godhead. Filled with astonishment and bowed down in adoration, the reason, like the seraphim, must veil its countenance, or rather remain standing before the impenetrable veil covering the countenance of God, until God in His grace vouchsafes with His own hand to raise this veil, until He Himself lays open His inner nature and shows us the incomprehensible mysteries of His bosom and His heart, at present in the disturbing obscurity of faith, but one day in the glorious clarity of vision.

This mystery is so great and sublime that reason, without previous revelation, could not even surmise it. In the entire created universe there is nothing that could bring one to the thought of a Trinity of persons in God. Nowhere do we find a nature in three persons; and not only do we not find it, but such a phenomenon among creatures is quite unthinkable. Only in the infinite perfection of the divine nature is it possible that the one nature suffices and constitutes three persons. But by natural means we cannot positively perceive or prove even this possibility. Once we have been convinced by inerrant faith of the existence of the Trinity, we must presume that its possibility involves no contradiction; and with the full effort of reason enlightened by faith we can decisively point out the inconclusive character of the arguments advanced to show a contradiction in the object of our faith. But without revelation, or prescinding from it, we have nothing that could vouch for the possibility.

The objection could be raised that also in the case of the attributes

[10] Cf. I Cor. 2:10.

of the divine nature, e.g., omnipresence, eternity, or liberty, we cannot positively grasp and demonstrate their possibility and the absence of contradiction. Yet we are able not merely to surmise them with our natural reason, but we can know them definitely and certainly. But first of all the incomprehensibility of these objects is not so profound as that of the Trinity; we can almost always find apt analogies in the created world that will illustrate both the intelligibility and the obscurity that are in them. Then again—and this is the principal point—our intellects are aware of reasons that compel us to admit the reality of these objects and hence also their possibility. God must be omnipresent, eternal, and free, for otherwise He could not be the creative cause of the universe. But are we cognizant of any evidence thus compelling us to acknowledge the existence of the Trinity? Certainly not; this is precisely what we indicated above as inadmissible. At this juncture we desire to explain the matter further, as we proceed to take up the reasons alleged in support of this contention.

6. Negative Proof of the Indemonstrability of the Mystery. Criticism of Attempts to Establish the Truth of the Trinity by Means of the Unaided Reason

The Trinity of persons is objectively necessary in God; it is actually as necessary as is the divine nature, which in fact can subsist only in three persons. Consequently there must be a necessary, objective reason for the Trinity. But the question here is not whether there is objectively such a reason, but whether it is also subjectively and naturally knowable as such to us.[11] The latter is what we deny, and what we demand proof for.

We omit a host of arguments which in these latter times have been put forward as wonders of science, but which, since they proceed from philosophical principles that are fundamentally false and completely distort the dogma, cannot be admitted to this inquiry. We confine ourselves to those which are specious enough to appeal even

[11] Scotus states decisively that Richard of St. Victor adduces *rationes necessariae* for the Trinity, but not *evidenter necessariae*, because the principles from which he argues are not evident. Cf. *III Sent.*, d.24, q.un., no. 20; *I Sent.*, d.42, q.un., no. 4; *Reportata*, prol., no. 18.

to the sound judgment of a sincere believer. The discussion of them must cast some light upon the nature of the dogma, as well as upon its knowability.

As their starting point, all such arguments must take the nature of God as it is known to us from its works. There is no other medium for arriving at the natural knowledge of God. Whoever does not concede this, cannot as a matter of course be permitted to give evidence, because he would not produce evidence in accord with an established principle, and as the nature of the evidence requires. But once this truth is supposed, we shall see that any adversary, in adducing his proofs, so long as he proceeds logically, will either wander around in a circle and represent the Trinity as a mere factor in the unfolding or revealing processes of nature, thus contradicting the dogma, or, if he chooses to remain faithful to the dogma, will emerge from this circle with a bound and thus break the thread of the proof, by furtively or unintentionally introducing an article of faith.[12]

1. The first alleged proof runs as follows: God, as the supreme cause of the world, must possess, along with all the other perfections we find in creatures, especially life in the highest and truest sense. He must be a living God, He must be Life itself. Life, however, is movement proceeding from an interior principle; life is activity in the noblest and most perfect sense. But in what would movement in God consist if not in the process, the procession of the persons; what would God's activity be without the production of the persons? Some of our adversaries add that life is inconceivable without a certain real multiplicity of factors, without mutual relationship and reciprocal action. Therefore God would appear as a dead Monad, as a rigid, motionless unity, if we did not think of Him in the Trinity of persons.

Who would deny that the production of the persons in God is bound up with His infinite vitality, and that the vitality of God manifests itself in its entire profundity and fullness in such production? Who would deny that we should have but an exceedingly

---

[12] We can say of all such arguments what Kuhn (*Chr. Lehre von der Trinität*, p. 504) pointedly remarked on a similar occasion, that they involve a false notion and a distortion of the dogma, just as concupiscence involves sin; that is, if carried to their logical conclusion they lead to error as inevitably as concupiscence in the same supposition leads to sin. We see this in the Trinitarian doctrine of Abelard, of Lessing (in his *Erziehung des Menschengeschlechts*), and, to some extent, also of Günther.

imperfect idea of God's vitality if we did not know of the Trinity of persons? Generation is indeed the supreme vital act even in the world of creatures. But why? Because it is a communication of life, a propagation of existing life. The act that communicates life presupposes in the generating individual a life that does not consist in the generative activity itself, but is rather the basis of this activity. Thus in God, too, we must acknowledge a life that does not consist formally in the production of new persons, but that is rather the basis for such production; a life that the Father possesses and communicates to the Son, a life that also the Holy Ghost shares, even though He produces no further person. This is the life of the divine nature, and like the nature is common to all three persons. We can and must think of the divine nature itself as living, prescinding from the communication of the nature from one person to another. It is only this life of the nature as such that we can infer from the concept of God as the supreme cause of created things. The interior communicability, productivity, and fecundity are an attribute of this life which is not revealed in its external activity and manifestation, but remains hidden in its own depths. Hence it cannot be inferred from any external manifestation of it; as far as the natural reason is concerned, it is and remains an absolute mystery.

The falsity of the statement that we can think of the life of God only in terms of the Trinity of the persons is evident from the fact that in the Old Testament God constantly manifests Himself and gives witness of Himself as one living God, and that He was acknowledged and understood as such by the Jews, without any distinct revelation of the Trinity, or at any rate without the Trinity being conceived and understood by the great masses. This observation affects also all those who maintain that no one can have a correct and true idea of the real God unless aware of His triple personality. The Jews had a true idea of God, but knew nothing of the three persons. To be sure, such an idea is inadequate and incomplete, but it is not on that account false. It is so correct that it could be employed in preparation for the revelation of the fuller and clearer concept of God in the Christian dispensation. The concept becomes incorrect only when its further clarification and completion are excluded, that is, when a communication of the divine life to different persons is positively repudiated. That is what the Jews did later, when confronted by the fullness of the Christian revelation, and with them the Arians. It was only in opposition to them that the Church had to condemn their idea of a sterile and uncommunicative divine unity, and to stigmatize it as a heresy against the fecundity of the divine life as known by revelation.

How, then, can we account for the life of the divine nature if it does not consist in the production and mutual activity of the divine persons? How shall we be able to retain the notion of life as immanent movement? When we describe life as movement, we must be careful to distinguish the figure from the reality, the accidental from the essential. Life is an activity of the living being, an activity proceeding from within and remaining within that being. Since all visible activity becomes known through the movement it produces, and since a real transition from potency to act takes place in every created activity, or better, this activity is conceivable only in terms of such a transition, we generally describe every activity as a movement, and vital activity as an immanent movement. But in God no transition from potency to act is thinkable; nevertheless, or rather for this very reason, He possesses the purest and most perfect activity; He is His own activity. Therefore He must possess the purest and most perfect life, and must be Life itself, although no real movement can be predicated of His life. His immanent activity, His life, being the life of a pure spirit, consists in knowing and willing. We conceive of this knowing and willing as proceeding from Him after the analogy of the corresponding activity in creatures; in reality both acts are identical with His essence. But just as His activity does not cease to be true activity because of this identity, so it does not cease to be true life; in fact, only thus will it be perfectly immanent, and hence life in the highest sense of the word.

2. A protest may be lodged at this point: an activity is inconceivable unless a product issues from it; consequently in God, too, we must admit a product of the activity of His knowledge and will, the Word as product of the former, the Holy Ghost as product of the latter.

This is the node of the entire difficulty, and it merits our full attention. First of all, we must remark that if every activity in God postulates a product that is distinct from and that issues from the active subject, then also the Son and the Holy Ghost must utter a Word distinct from themselves, since both have the activity of knowledge; and the Holy Ghost must breathe forth another

Spirit distinct from Himself since He, too, has the activity of volition. Thus the argument, taken as it stands, would prove not merely
a Trinity but a Quinternity. Indeed, carried to its logical conclusion,
it would prove an infinite number of persons in God. Some error
must lurk in it. Where is the error?

Among created spirits, in the activities of knowing and willing
the actual knowing and willing are also the act in which the activity
terminates. This act is a real product of the knowing and willing
spirit and of the corresponding faculties of intellect and will, and as
such is really distinct from the spirit and from the faculties. The
act of knowing and willing is not imposed on the spirit from without,
but is produced from within by the spirit's own power, and therefore
is called an action, in contradistinction to passion. In everyday life
we indifferently employ the terms "action" or "act" (*actio, actus*)
of knowing and willing; more accurately, however, action signifies
the placing of the deed or act.

Doubtless in God, too, knowing and willing are deeds or acts,
which are not imposed on Him, but are in Him through Himself.
But these acts are not in Him because He puts them forth from Himself, because He actuates a potency in producing the acts, as is the
case with us. In God there is no transition from potency to act;
potency and act coincide in Him. His knowledge and volition are
one and the same as His essence, and therefore they are in Him and
through Him inasmuch as He is essentially His own knowledge and
volition. Is God to be less active just because He need not first produce the act, but already has it in Himself in so eminent a way?

If this exposition is too subtle, we can make a simpler reply to the
question, "How is God active from eternity, what does He do?"
He beholds Himself and He loves Himself. But according to our concepts, vision and love are actions, whether or not anything is really
produced by the vision and love.

Thus we can form a notion of God as infinitely active in His knowing and willing, that is, in the knowledge and love of Himself, without including any real production and procession in such a notion.
Yet it is true that the divine faculty of cognition and the divine will
do bring forth real products. But with respect to these products we
have to consider not the divine intellectual act as such, but the Word
in which God expresses Himself; not the divine love, but the Breath
in which He reveals Himself and pours Himself forth. Hence it

would have to be proved that the divine intellect must of necessity express itself in a Word which is distinct from the Speaker, and that the divine love must of necessity issue in a Breath which is distinct from the Breather. This is the cardinal point on which the whole problem turns, but a point to which not enough heed has been paid. This is the way we must formulate the question if we are seeking the ultimate answer. But we have only to inspect it frankly to perceive that it is insoluble for the unaided mind of a creature. From God's external manifestations and products we perceive the infinite wisdom which is stamped upon them, and the eternal love which streams forth in them. But we cannot learn anything from them about the inner manifestations and products of God. We do not learn from them that God in His inner Being expresses His knowledge in an image like to Himself, and that He pours forth His love in a personal Breath.

It is striking how this point was overlooked even by St. Anselm, who more than any other sought not merely to explain the Trinity in God in this way, but to advance cogent reasons in proof. In his case, especially if we compare him with St. Thomas, we can clearly detect the error commonly made in this matter. With incomparable precision and acumen he unfolds in the first chapters of his *Monologium* the process of the natural knowledge of God derived from creatures. He shows that we must conceive God as the simplest and most perfect of substances, which is endowed with knowledge and love, or rather is its own knowledge and love. He does not contend that the *Verbum* is formally the divine wisdom; for then the Father would possess wisdom through the Son—which the saint expressly denies. But he advances not a syllable of proof that, in thinking of the divine wisdom and knowledge, we must think of a Word proceeding from it, a Word distinct from the original possessor of the wisdom and knowledge as its product. Here, accordingly, he makes a leap, by taking over from faith the idea of a real production of the intellectual Word.[13] St. Thomas, in his *Summa*, was keenly aware of this error and carefully avoided it. He develops with

---

[13] We shall see later how St. Anselm's procedure, which recurs when he deals with other truths of faith, admits of a justifiable interpretation. For the time being we may content ourselves with the remark that it is to be taken in a sense resembling the doctrine of Richard of St. Victor and St. Bonaventure, to which we shall come presently.

purely philosophical arguments all that concerns God's nature, as well as God's knowledge and love. But as soon as he passes to the Trinity he expressly takes over the idea of the processions and productions from supernatural revelation,[14] and then proceeds to unfold the entire doctrine of the Trinity by pursuing his argumentation along the same lines as St. Anselm.

Like St. Anselm's procedure are the more recent attempts to construct the doctrine of the Trinity from the divine self-consciousness. Ultimately, in fact, the procedures are identical, and differ only in expression. The argument runs as follows. Since God is conscious of Himself and thinks of Himself and knows Himself, He confronts Himself with His thought. This thought must be personal, because everything that is in God is God Himself. Likewise, and for the same reason, the love with which God embraces Himself and His knowledge must be personal. Thus we have three personalities, or persons, in God. Although the argument is proposed in other forms, too, this may do for all; in any case, none of the other forms is better or more happily phrased.

Thus, for example, if one should prefer to say that God appears as both subject and object in His self-consciousness, and that both must be persons in God, with the result that we have two persons, the argument is patently absurd in the extreme. For self-consciousness consists precisely in the fact that one and the same person makes himself the object of his knowledge; in self-consciousness a person confronts himself not with another but with himself.

So let us go back to the form originally proposed. God's knowledge of Himself and His love for Himself must be personal; but why, and in what way? Because the thought is a person other than the thinker and the object represented, and the love is a person other than the lover and the beloved? This would have to be proved, and the argument brought forward proves exactly the opposite. The thought and the love must be personal in God, it is urged, because they cannot be accidents of the divine substance, but must be this substance itself. Well and good; but then they are really identical with the knowing and loving person, and are personal only in and on account of the personality of this person. There is nothing to show

[14] "In reply I state that in relation to God Holy Scripture employs terms which signify procession" etc. (*Summa*, Ia, q. 27, a. 1).

that they constitute other persons, distinct from this person.[15]

Nevertheless the divine self-consciousness is not unconnected with the Trinity of persons. The Father in knowing Himself confronts Himself with the Son, as the expression of this self-knowledge and the image of its object; and inasmuch as the Father and the Son love each other reciprocally, this love seeks its bond and its expression in the Holy Ghost. But this productivity in the process of the divine self-consciousness can be inferred neither from the nature of self-consciousness in general, nor from the nature of the divine self-consciousness in particular, so far as our reason can know it.

7. Continuation of the Criticism

The arguments thus far attempted all begin with the divine nature as we know it from creatures. They all necessarily come to grief for the reason that nothing can be inferred from a consideration of the divine nature except what belongs to its constitution or

[15] With special reference to Günther's arguments the Provincial Council of Cologne declares: "The holy Fathers and Doctors of the Church, while endeavoring to illustrate this most august mystery of the Trinity for the instruction of the faithful, unanimously proclaim that it is ineffable and incomprehensible. And rightly so. For since the invisible things of God are clearly seen, being understood by the things that are made (Rom. 1:20), we should have to attain to the Trinity of persons by a consideration of created things. But this is impossible, since the act by which God created the world is common to the three persons, and therefore manifests the unity of the divine essence, but not the Trinity of the divine persons (*Summa*, Ia, q.45, a.7). True, since the holy Fathers gather from the Scriptures that the processions of the persons in God take place through acts of the intellect and will, it may be said that man, endowed as he is with intellect and will, is not only, like other things, a vestige, but in a certain sense an image of the Trinity, for there is in him a mental word that is conceived and a love that proceeds (*ibid.*). This similarity can serve in some degree to illustrate the Trinity, but by no means to demonstrate or understand the Trinity, for it is highly imperfect (St. Augustine, *De Trinitate*, XV, c.11, no. 20); and either we cannot straightway transfer to the divine intellect what we apprehend in our own intellect, or if it seems that such transference may be made, we do not understand how it is to be made; and even if something in God corresponds to the triple operation of our mind, we are not at all justified in concluding with certitude that this something is the Trinity. Therefore let teachers as well as the faithful beware lest the threat be fulfilled in them: 'He that is a searcher of majesty, shall be overwhelmed by glory' (Prov. 25: 27); and let them be convinced that it suffices for them to hold with unshakable faith what has been revealed with infallible truth" (*Col. Lac.*, V, 285).

unfolding. The persons, however, do not constitute the nature, but possess it; and the production of the persons is no unfolding of the divine nature, which in any case is not capable of any real evolution, but is a communication of the complete, perfect, simple nature to distinct subjects. Other arguments, which seek directly to demonstrate the necessity of such a communication of the nature, are much more in accord with the dogmatic idea of the Trinity, although they, too, come not a hairbreadth closer to a real proof than do the preceding attempts.[16]

1. Thus, according to one line of reasoning, the ability of creatures to communicate their natures is a great perfection. This perfection cannot be lacking in God since, as the cause of creatures, He possesses all their perfections in richest abundance and in purest form. An appeal is made even to the testimony of God Himself, who has said: "Shall not I that make others to bring forth children, Myself bring forth?"[17] All this would be true enough if we could show with our natural reason that the infinity and simplicity of God actually admit of a communication of His nature. Among creatures the communication of nature does not take place without multiplying the nature. The divine nature cannot be multiplied. But whether a communication without multiplication is admissible in God and involves no imperfection, we do not know from reason, and so we cannot maintain that it actually takes place. And as for the words "Shall not I that make others to bring forth children, Myself bring forth?" we need not necessarily refer them to generation within God. The context rather indicates that God claims for Himself a similar, nay a greater, productivity with regard to created beings than that which He has given to others. But even supposing that the words refer to God's fecundity within the divinity, as was argued by some of the Fathers in their defense of the Trinity, then, as uttered by God or considered from the standpoint of His revelation, they serve for the justification, but not for a proof, of the reality of eternal generation. For if God has bestowed so great a fecundity on creatures, we may not deprive God Himself of an interior fecundity, until we have demonstrated the incommunicability of the

[16] The following arguments are taken substantially from Richard of St. Victor (*De Trinitate*, lib. III) and Raymond of Sabunde (*Theologia naturalis*, tit. 47–51).

[17] Isa. 66:9.

divine nature; especially in the face of revelation, persistency in such denial would be blasphemy.

2. To this argument is related that proposed by Richard of St. Victor and others, who hold that we would conceive of God as impotent or at least as lacking infinite power, if we did not attribute to Him the power of communicating His nature. God would be impotent, because He could not do all that is conceivable; He would be lacking in infinite power, because from the standpoint of the external term of His activity He could not effect an infinite product. Unless, therefore, He brought forth such a product within Himself, He would be able to effect no infinite product at all.

Reason, to be sure, can know that God, who is Being itself and the source of all being, must be able to actuate all that is conceivable. But does the reason of itself know with equal certitude that the communication of the divine nature is something conceivable, that it involves no contradiction? And is it true that the power of God would not appear to be infinite unless it put forth an infinite product? Whence does the unaided reason know that God's power must be infinite in this sense? Reason knows the power of God only from its external works, and has no more than the right to term it infinite in so far as it operates as no finite cause can, that is, by creation, and thus operates in a sphere that knows no limits other than those of possibility and conceivability. In order to extend the infinity of God's power to an infinite product, the reason must know that such a product is not a chimera.

If reason could really prove that God must have the power to communicate His nature, nothing further would be required to demonstrate that such communication actually and necessarily takes place. For, since everything that concerns the inner nature of God is necessary, that power would necessarily have to bring forth its product; otherwise something contingent would occur in God. But since reason cannot demonstrate such power, all the arguments which postulate the actuation of it have no foundation.

3. As power makes a production possible, it is goodness in its various forms that impels or inclines to the realization of the possible.

The goodness which is meant here is self-communicating goodness. "Goodness is self-diffusive," according to a profound, time-honored theological maxim. The good tends, as far as possible, to pour itself out and communicate itself. Since God is infinitely and necessarily good, since He is goodness itself, He must necessarily communicate Himself in the highest and most perfect manner. But the most perfect manner of communication is the communication of the divine substance and nature to other hypostases. Thus speaks St. Bonaventure,[18] and also Richard of St. Victor. However, they are not really arguing from the standpoint of reason, but are merely explaining the content of faith so far as it is intelligible.[19]

A further distance must be traversed before one, setting out from this general idea of communication, arrives at the clear notion of communication to two definite persons; but this gap may perhaps be closed by introducing other factors, if only the principle remains firm. What are we to say of the principle? Shall we deny that God is infinitely good? Perish the thought! Shall we deny that reason can know God as infinitely good? No, not that either. But we do deny that reason knows the goodness of God as the source and form of the substantial communication of His essence. The reason perceives that God is infinitely good in the sense that He includes in Himself all conceivable perfections, that He embraces these perfections with infinite love, and in consequence of this love is inclined to communicate and manifest them. But reason can extend this inclination only to such manners of communication as it knows are possible. Since reason cannot know that substantial communication of the divine nature is possible, it dare not decide that the infinite goodness of God consists in this particular communication, just as it is not justified in

---

[18] *Itinerarium mentis ad Deum*, c.6.

[19] The procedure of these two kindred souls is attributable to their point of view, which is contemplative rather than analytic. Their ecstatic spirits take flight to the heights which faith points out to them; and when they look about them with their natural reason, everything seems as near and obvious to them as objects that reason actually perceives by itself. The arguments they adduce for the Trinity really prove, that is, they are objectively sound; and in the supposition of their truth the conclusion follows with evident necessity, at least to some extent. But when their glance travels back along the path of reason, they assert that the basis for the Trinity is a "truth that transcends reason" (Richard, *Benjamin minor*, lib. IV, cc.2, 3); and in one passage St. Bonaventure says expressly: "The Trinity of persons is not knowable by a creature who ascends by way of reason from the creature to God" (*I Sent.*, d.3, a.1, q.4). According to Richard (*loc. cit.*), the mind can attain to objects that surpass reason only when it is joined to faith: "In the investigation, discussion, and assertion of these objects, the human reason accomplishes absolutely nothing unless it is joined to faith."

concluding that God's omnipotence consists in such communication. The reason may indeed term God infinitely good, because it knows in general that He possesses all conceivable good and is the inexhaustible source of all good outside Himself. Further, since reason does not behold God's goodness as it is in itself, it may and even must suppose and assume that unknown and incalculable treasures of goodness and love lie locked up within it; but it must forgo investigation of them the more it is convinced of the infinity of the divine goodness.

The proof turns out no better if, instead of considering God's goodness as communicative, self-surrendering love, we consider it as possessive love, the love of enjoyment; or, in other words, if we fasten our attention on God's infinite beatitude. Richard of St. Victor is of the opinion that the infinite beatitude of God could not be conceived by us unless God had associates in His happiness; the finest constituent of every joy would be lacking, namely, the consciousness of loving others and of being loved by them, and of being able to share one's joy with them. Therefore he postulates in God a loving person, another who is the worthy object of the love of the first, and a third who is to be the co-beloved (*condilectus*) in this union of three.

I do not wish to say that this argument proves nothing; it contains a profound truth, which I shall presently explain at greater length. But at least from the standpoint of natural reason it proves nothing. Reason of course perceives that God as the absolute Being must be absolutely self-sufficient and happy. But even though God must be self-sufficient, even though He must be happy in the possession and enjoyment of the infinite good which is the divine essence, will reason find it necessary to assign Him associates in this possession? Creatures seek their fellows because they are not self-sufficient but must be supplemented by others and have a share in the fortunes of others. Hence it is precisely because of the absolute self-sufficiency of God that we must incline to the conclusion that He does not stand in need of any associates. And, in fact, God does not need another person to complement His happiness; each of the divine persons is infinitely happy by reason of the fullness of the divine nature which He possesses and which is equal in all the persons. Not the limitation of any of the persons, but the superabundance of His riches demands the participation of other persons in possession and enjoyment; each of the persons enjoys the entire fullness of His riches only in and with the other persons for the very reason that the wealth of one person is manifest in the joint possession and enjoyment of the others. It would really, therefore, have to be proved that the wealth of God, in the enjoyment of which He finds His infinite happiness, admits and requires coproprietors; otherwise the infinite happiness of the persons is vindicated at the expense of the infinity of each of them, since the happiness of each would have to be supplemented by the other persons. Such a proof would be reducible to the argument that the infinite perfection of God demands plurality of persons, a position which, after all that has been said, cannot be sustained.

Nevertheless I have remarked that the argument under consideration, as also that which immediately precedes, proves something. It proves, after faith has instructed us about the existence of the Trinity, that the loveliest feature of the divine beatitude, the tenderest work of the divine goodness and love, the most sublime proof of the divine power, are and remain eternally hidden and impenetrable to the mind which is dependent on its own illumination. These arguments show that, if the communication of the divine nature is possible, then the divine power and perfection, the divine goodness and love, shine forth in that communication with a magnificence and splendor which we could call an infinity raised to the second power, and which merits our greater wonderment the less reason can push on from its exterior, inadequate, negative concept of the infinity of the divine nature to this interior, adequate, full concept of the triune God.

In his terse fashion St. Thomas has this to remark about such arguments: the observations contained in them prove true in God and confirm belief in the Trinity, if faith itself is made their root and foundation; that is, if we accept the possibility and existence of the Trinity, and then by means of such observations show how emphatically in this revealed truth the greatness and infinity of the divine power, goodness, and beatitude are brought out. But they could not demonstrate the root itself, because all these reasons suppose that the Trinity in God is known as admissible and possible; but this is known only because revelation proposes it to us as true.[20]

[20] Cf. *Summa*, Ia, q.32, a.1 ad 2: "Reason may be said to have a twofold function: first, to establish a principle by sufficient proof. . . . Secondly,

And in fact all such observations are nothing but blossoms which an attentive study of the dogma proposed by faith coaxes forth as from a root, in order to unfold its entire beauty and glory before our eyes. They are only a development of the idea furnished by the dogma, and serve only to place us on terms of intimate familiarity with the dogma's content. But they cannot convince us of the reality of its content if this has not been proposed and accepted as true. They cannot do so any more than the blossoms can bear the root from which they are sprung. Still, since we generally appraise the quality and value of a root from its flowers, so in this case an unbeliever, on whom the dogma has not yet taken hold, can be induced by the sight of its magnificent blossoms to allow the dogma to strike root in his soul through faith, and thus to make the treasure really his own after admiring its beauty. If a person refuses to take faith as the root, and insists on deducing the Trinity on the purely rational plane, he must take the natural idea of God as root. Then, however, he may regard the power, perfection, goodness, and beatitude of God as blossoms of this root, that is, so far as they are factors and attributes of the creative nature of God, but not so far as they are factors of a process by which that nature itself is communicated.

The proof that we adduced at the beginning for the indemonstrability of the divine Trinity has received striking confirmation

---

it is called upon not to establish a principle by sufficient proof, but to show the congruity of certain effects with a principle previously established. . . . However, reason thus employed does not furnish adequate proof, because possibly some other theory might explain the phenomena. Reason can be employed in the first way to demonstrate that God is one, and the like. But in the investigation of the Trinity reason functions in the second way; for, once the Holy Trinity has been revealed, the arguments proposed by the reason show the congruity of this truth, but cannot adequately demonstrate the Trinity. This is evident from a consideration of the arguments alleged. For God's infinite goodness is manifested in creation, because production from nothing requires infinite power. If God communicates Himself by His infinite goodness, it is not necessary that an infinite effect proceed from God, but merely that the created object participate in the divine goodness according to its own capacity. Further, the statement that the joyful possession of a good requires the partnership of others, is true only when perfect goodness is not found in one person, in which case such goodness must be supplemented by the good of some associate in order to render the complete goodness of happiness possible. Finally, the similarity between intellectual procession in God and in us is not sufficient to prove anything about God, because the intellect is not found univocally in God and in us. Therefore Augustine says that by faith we arrive at knowledge, but not conversely."

from our review of the various attempts at rational demonstration, which were to have demolished our theory. For, to arrive at a conclusion, all such attempts must become irrational on account of their unsound inferences, or must become suprarational by having recourse to truths of faith. Indeed, we may add, the reasons favoring our proposition are such that they hold good not only for us human beings, but in general for every created intellect, even for the angels. For the angels, too, know God in a natural way only from His works, although they know these, and therefore also God, incomparably better than we men do; but we have just shown that the divine Trinity cannot be known from the works of God. Theologians are still arguing whether the Trinity can be known from certain of God's supernatural works; but these, in turn, are not discernible to the natural vision of the created intellect. We must hold as a universal truth that the Trinity cannot be perceived or inferred from any created object, but can be seen only in itself in the immediate intuition of God, which is absolutely supernatural for every created intellect. All the greater, therefore, is the obligation laid on us human beings to thank God for His grace since He has so generously and lovingly revealed to us this inscrutable mystery, to which even the angels cannot draw near.

8. The Supernaturalness of the Mystery as the Reason for Its Inconceivability

As was remarked in the introductory chapter, the general reason for the obscurity of mysteries is their excessive sublimity, or their supernaturalness. Only what is natural is the proper object of natural, rational cognition; the supernatural is for that very reason suprarational.

Where in the Trinity shall we place the supernaturality which is the ground of its suprarationality? The problem is not without difficulty. Do we say that the Trinity is supernatural with reference to the nature of God? But the divine nature is the summit—nothing rises above it; moreover, the three divine persons are really identical with this nature. Do we say that the Trinity is supernatural with reference to created nature? But is not the divine nature, too, supernatural for the latter, without thereby being an absolute mystery, since it is knowable to the natural reason of creatures?

We call the Trinity supernatural in both respects, with reference to the divine nature as well as to created nature. We must go on to explain the sense in which we mean this statement, and the right we have to make it.

1. We consider the matter first from the standpoint of created nature; generally, and also appropriately, the supernatural is held to be that which is above created nature.

The divine nature itself is infinitely above created nature; as it is in itself it cannot be known from created nature, any more than the Trinity can thus be known. But through His nature and its activity God stands in a certain relation and union with His creatures as their Creator, Preserver, and Ruler; created nature simply cannot be conceived and explained apart from its relation to the divine nature, which therefore is the foundation stone and the keystone, as well as the center, of the natural order of created natures. On the other hand, God has no connection with created natures by reason of the Trinitarian relations and Trinitarian activity; because the persons operate externally not in their personal, individual character, but through the nature common to them. Their hypostatic relations and activities occur among themselves and constitute a closed order, which rises above all connection with the created, natural order of things. God enters into the natural order of things by virtue of His nature, although as an exempt and dominating member; as triune, however, He remains entirely outside and above the natural order.[21]

In this sense we call the divine nature a natural truth, and the Trinity a supernatural truth. The former is a natural truth, because it is knowable in a natural manner and, indeed, is knowable to the extent that it enters into relation with created nature as such. The latter is a supernatural truth, because it it knowable only in a supernatural manner; and the reason why it is knowable only in this manner is the fact that it transcends every relationship with created nature. But the divine nature as it is in itself, in its oneness with the Trinity,

[21] Scheeben's terminology is not quite accurate in this sentence, owing to his concern to emphasize the difference between the natural and the supernatural order and the absolute superiority of the latter. God does not enter into the natural order as a "member." Rather, with His entire Being and power He is present in every single member and in the totality of creation by His production, conservation, and government of the universe, as the First Cause and Last End of all. Concerning the special presence of the Trinity in the supernatural order of life, cf. section 30. [Tr.]

in its essence and subsistence, is a supernatural truth, and therefore is known only in the supernatural intuition of God.

2. Can we likewise say that the Trinity is supernatural with respect to the divine nature? Evidently, as has been remarked above, it cannot be supernatural in the sense that it contains a special, higher reality that surpasses the reality of the divine nature. This would contradict the simplicity of God and the infinity of His nature, which must be one supreme reality identical with the persons, *una summa res.* But on account of its infinite riches and our own finite intellectual powers, which do not permit us to exhaust it with a single glance, we must study this one, supreme reality from different sides. From the standpoint of our reason we must split up the one perfection of the divine nature into various perfections, that we may render its riches intelligible; just as we must break up the pure sunbeam by means of a prism into varicolored rays so as to arrive at an accurate knowledge of its make-up. Especially when we contemplate this one supreme reality both in the light of reason and in the light of revelation, it necessarily becomes known to us under different aspects; and so it can happen, and indeed inevitably must happen, that the one divine perfection when viewed in the light of revelation appears to us under an incomparably more splendid and sublime aspect than when viewed in the light of reason. Therefore when we state that the Trinity of persons is supernatural with regard to the divine nature, and hence something higher than the divine nature, this cannot mean that the Trinity is a special, higher reality; it can only mean that in the Trinity God appears according to a higher aspect, in a higher perfection, than He appears when considered only according to His nature. Consequently the concept of God that is gained in a supernatural manner does not have as its object a different, higher reality than the natural concept, but represents the same object according to a higher aspect.

And in fact the natural concept of God exhibits to us only the divine nature, without its communicability and fecundity. It shows us God in the power and goodness required to produce all things that are outside Himself; it exhibits Him only as the infinite cause of the finite. But the concept gained from revelation shows us God the Father as the principle of the equally infinite Son, and together with the Son as the principle of the equally infinite Spirit. The natural concept represents God only so far as He communicates a finite nature to creatures; the supernatural concept represents Him so far as He communicates His own infinite nature to the Son and the Holy Ghost. Since the products of the Trinitarian activity infinitely transcend the products of the activity of the divine nature which terminates outside of God, that is, created natures, God as the principle of the former activity necessarily appears infinitely more perfect than He does as the principle of the latter activity. Therefore the concept of the Trinity discloses to us a perfection which is not contained in the purely rational concept of the divine nature, but immensely surpasses it. The object of the supernatural concept, namely, the Trinitarian process, is much more exalted than the object of the natural concept, namely, the divine nature, with respect to which, accordingly, it is supernatural; and precisely because it is supernatural, it cannot be inferred from our idea of the divine nature. Consequently it is likewise suprarational, whereas the divine nature itself, not indeed in its identity with the Trinity, but in its relation with created nature, is a rational truth that is knowable in a natural manner.

3. According to the explanation set forth in the introductory chapter, the suprarationality of mysteries implies, besides the inaccessibility of the reality, also the incomprehensibility, the inconceivability of the object. Both follow immediately from the supernaturalness of the mystery. As the knowability of the existence of the Trinity differs essentially from the knowability of the divine nature as such, so likewise the inconceivability of its object must be essentially different.

The divine nature also is inconceivable, for any knowledge of it gained from its works is most imperfect and superficial. Nevertheless the divine nature and its attributes are revealed in its works, and the principle of causality furnishes us with a means that enables us to construct a representation, a concept of it from its reflection in its works. In other words, the concepts that we derive from created natures in order to form some representation of the divine nature, must be purified and elevated. But this purification and elevation are effected by an illumination native to the reason with the aid of the principle of causality, by which God is apprehended as the exemplar, unrealized it is true, of created natures, and by which His invisible perfections are in some sense perceived in His works.

But for acquiring an idea of the Trinity our natural concepts are far more inadequate still, since this object is far higher beyond our reach than is the divine nature as such. Hence our concepts are in much greater need of purification and elevation; moreover, our guiding light, the principle of causality, fails us here, since the Trinity is not reflected in creation, for the reason that as such it is not the cause of creation. In default of this inner light, we can acquire some notion of this sublime object only if we recast and clarify our natural concepts in accord with the norm of divine revelation received in faith; and hence it is inevitable that our representations and ideas of the Trinity will be obscure to a far higher degree than our ideas of the divine nature and its attributes.

In brief, both the Trinity and the divine nature are inconceivable to us inasmuch as we cannot represent the content of either to ourselves by concepts acquired from an intuition of them (*per conceptus proprios*) but only by concepts that we transfer to them from other objects. But in the case of the divine nature we perceive the inner nexus between the domain whence we derive our concepts and the domain to which we transfer them; we look from one domain into the other. In the case of the Trinity this clearly perceived nexus is lacking, and moreover the domains are separated by a much greater distance, even in their points of similarity. Consequently the analogy is more obscure and more feeble than in the prior case, and our concepts are less adequate and distinct, even though with the aid of revelation we accurately determine their analogous value.

This inconceivability of the Trinity further implies that our ability to perceive the inner unity and relation between the several factors presented by our concepts is very imperfect, so much so that at times these factors appear mutually incompatible and contradictory. Suprarationality involves an apparent irrationality.

Even in the case of the divine nature we do not perceive how the individual perfections and actions which we discern in it can be united in one absolutely simple perfection and action. But we do perceive clearly that the absolute and infinite divine perfection must embrace them all in one simple reality. In the Trinity, on the contrary, this very absoluteness and infinity in conjunction with the simplicity constitute a seeming contradiction between the Trinity of the persons and the unity of the essence. The absoluteness and infinity of the persons seem to conflict with the production of one person by another, for according to our notions every such production involves dependence and subordination. And even if we are finally successful in our attempts to realize that the plenitude of infinite perfection, as existing in one simple reality, is conceivable in one subject, it is incomparably more difficult to conceive that this perfection is identical with three mutually distinct subjects which, each in His own proper way, are to possess it. For in the former case the distinctions that we conceive in one and the same divine subject need not imply a real distinction in God; but the distinction between essence and person must establish such a distinction among the persons, and accordingly, as it seems, must itself be a real distinction, even though all the others are not.

Thus the light of our rational concept of the divine nature seems to rule out the conceivability of the Trinity, and to obscure and disorganize its content. The inconceivability of the Trinity is, therefore, specifically different from, and higher than, the inconceivability of the divine nature, although we do not mean to say that its obscurity can in no way be illuminated, or that its apparent confusion can in no way be resolved. Simply because a thing is not absolutely conceivable, we cannot conclude that it is absolutely inconceivable.

The inability to associate the various notes of an object, plus the inability to comprehend its harmony and unity, accounts for the inconceivability of its content. It is evident that the doctrine of the Trinity is eminently inconceivable in both respects, and hence that its content is as obscure as its existence is undiscoverable.

And so we come to the conclusion: owing to its absolutely supernatural sublimity, the Trinity of divine persons is a truth hidden from the natural cognition of every creature. Without belief in God's revelation it cannot be known at all; and even for believers it is incomprehensible in an exceptionally high degree, indeed, in the highest degree. Therefore it is a mystery in the truest, highest, most beautiful sense of the word.

CHAPTER III

The Intelligible Aspect of the Mystery

9. Transition from Darkness to Light

IT is high time that we introduce some light into the darkness which we have endeavored at such length and in so great detail to bring to the consciousness of our intellect. We have earnestly sought to restrain reason from its rash attempts to pierce the darkness of the night by sending up its own rockets. Certainly we did not do this out of any love for darkness, or because we did not eagerly desire to see it illuminated. We wished to show that the night which shrouds our mystery is too thick to be dispelled by any earthly torch, and that we must accordingly long for a heavenly light that would transform the night, if not into clear day, at least into a serene, cheering, hopeful dawn. We were afraid that the earthly torch would not display the object of our quest in its true form, but would disclose some monstrous phantom in its stead. In fact, all rational proofs for the Trinity are either no proofs at all or, if they prove anything, they prove something other than the real Trinity. At best they blind us in such a way that we mistake the knowledge of faith for rational knowledge, and that we think we behold in the light of our earthly torch the vital truth which in reality is brought near to us only in the light of the dawn from heaven. Our purpose was to banish all deception, all delusion, all ambiguity, and confine the range of natural light to its own sharply defined boundaries; thus the supernatural light of faith would be free to develop its entire power. Only when we accurately fix the point beyond which reason can no longer advance and from which the wings of faith alone can carry it farther, can the mystery of the Trinity be scientifically unfolded and light be shed over it. But once this is done, the light becomes so brilliant that many of **those**

49

philosophers who grope about for a rational demonstration of the Trinity are not even aware that it is shining.

Reason by itself can advance to the divine nature, but no farther. Here its course is arrested. It can pass from that point to the Trinity of persons only by a leap, a leap that falls short of the mark; for either the reasoning process harbors a fallacy or the conclusion contains an error. It can reach the higher sphere only if faith supports it at one stage of its progress, in one principle (*fide subnixa*, as Richard of St. Victor says). Arrived at the divine nature, reason is impeded by intrinsic necessity from farther advance. Knowledge of the Trinity cannot be the fruit of the intellect, unless it be an aborted monster. Solely when it is joined to faith, when it bases further development upon a principle taken over from faith as a fecundating seed (*fidei admixta*, says Richard of St. Victor again), can reason bring knowledge of the Trinity to maturity, in the measure possible here on earth, as a faithful and comely image of the heavenly exemplar.

I assert: one single principle taken from the revealed doctrine of the Trinity is sufficient for reason to construct and develop the dogma in its entire rich content. The dogma is so symmetrical, and with all its rich detail so simple a tapestry, that starting with any thread at random we can trace the whole pattern from one end to another. Just as I can deduce all the attributes of the divine nature from any one of them, I can start with any Trinitarian proposition that I receive from faith and develop all the others by proceeding either backward analytically or forward synthetically.[1]

---

[1] The principle thus enunciated by Scheeben closely coordinates revealed truth with natural reason. Its application makes possible the construction of a speculative theology, the discovery of new points of view for the contemplation of revealed truth, and a composite view of the truths of faith whose intimate relations were not previously perceived. However, such cooperation of reason with a principle of faith does not result in the certitude of faith, although the conclusion thus arrived at has great theological certitude, on account of the union of natural reasoning with faith. A very pronounced difference is to be noted between theology, which is the reasoned investigation of truth presented by faith, and faith itself, which objectively is the substance of this truth, and subjectively is a divine, infused virtue. Therefore no conclusion drawn from a revealed truth and a naturally known proposition can be raised to the status of an article of faith; nor can such a conclusion be properly defined as a revealed dogma, although the Church can declare that it is infallibly true. On the other hand, a conclusion derived from two propositions that are recognized as certainly revealed truths can

For example, let us take the dogma in its most concise formulation: "There are three persons in God." If there are three persons in God, it is straightway evident that they are consubstantial; for all three must possess the one divine nature, which cannot be multiplied. Therefore they are one God; and since there can be no composition in God, they are in reality also the Godhead. Hence they are not distinct in nature and substance, nor are they distinct from the nature and substance itself. Accordingly they can be distinct only in the different manner in which they possess and are this substance itself. But a different mode of possessing the same nature is impossible if each of the persons possesses the nature originally of and from Himself; for thus all three would possess it in the same way.² Therefore only one person can originally possess the nature of Himself; the two others must receive it from Him, and the Third Person, indeed, must receive it in a manner different from that of the Second; which would not be the case if He received the nature from the First Person alone, as does the Second; and so the Third Person receives it from both the First and the Second Person. Therefore the persons are not absolute,³ but relative persons; that is, the characteristic of the personality of each consists in the fact that each possesses the nature only in relation to the others, and consequently in common with them. This is evident in the case of the two persons who are produced, since they have the nature from the First Person, and accordingly are what they are only in relation to Him. But the same is no less clear with regard to the First Person, too; for He possesses the nature only so far as He possesses it in a characteristic manner, as a special person, to give it to the other two persons. Briefly, the three persons cannot really be three divine persons, cannot possess the nature as their common good, unless they stand in essential relationship to one another, in a relationship which is the reason both for community of possession and for distinction in possession. This in turn takes us

---

be pronounced an article of faith. Scheeben here appears as the intellectual heir of an abstract, speculative tradition which had all but disappeared in his day; at the same time he was guided more by the data of revelation than by any systematizing principle of reason. [Tr.]

² On the validity of this conclusion, cf. Suarez, *De Trinitatis mysterio*, I, c.4; Ruiz, *De Trinitate*, disp. I.

³ We shall see later to what extent the divine persons are also to be termed absolute.

back to the origin of one person from the others, and of the Second and Third from the First. With this thread the entire doctrine of the Trinity can be spun out step by step. But we do not wish to anticipate.

In like manner, we can draw upon the dogma for the fact that there are two real distinctions in God, and then, with the aid of what reason teaches us concerning the simplicity of God, prove that these distinctions are personal and relative. There can be distinctions only between the persons; otherwise there would be real distinctions in one and the same person, who would then necessarily appear as composite—which contradicts God's simplicity. Really distinct persons, on the contrary, would not enter into composition with one another; they constitute a plurality, not a whole constructed of different parts. Likewise the distinctions must be relative, that is, they must be distinctions among relative things, which are distinct only in and through their relationship to one another; otherwise the distinction would be such as to destroy the unity in God, and this again contradicts God's simplicity, which admits of opposition but not division.

A more natural process still would be to start with the truth that in God there are four real relations, or two real mutual relations. For the real relations are the objective reason both for the real distinction among the persons and for their unity. A relation distinguishes its subjects from one another at the same instant that it brings them into relationship, and hence into union with one another. It necessitates distinctions, and these distinctions cannot be situated in the divine nature as such or in one of the divine persons without destruction of simplicity. Therefore it necessitates several persons, and the four relations in God necessitate three persons, because not more and not fewer are needed to constitute the four relations. But because the relations of the distinct persons are necessary and essential and because the persons are opposed only with reference to one another, they can be no other than relations of the persons as persons in their personal characteristic, that is, in the proper way in which each possesses the common nature. Consequently the relations must concern the characteristic manner of possessing the nature; and this is essentially relative only so far as it either essentially depends on the communication of the nature to another person, as with the Second and Third Persons, or is essentially ordained to the communication of the proper, original possession, as with the First Person.

In all these deductions, which could be further developed and extended to the entire doctrine of the Trinity, no other leap need be made, because the transition to the higher sphere in which the reason moves about freely was effected right at the beginning. Nowhere in this sequence need a link be forced in arbitrarily, once the reason has received the first link from faith, and strung all the rest to it as on a golden chain. No longer does reason weave the empty air, once revelation has supplied it with the warp for its tapestry, to which it need merely furnish the woof.

For all that, the point of the dogma from which the demonstration is begun is not a matter of indifference. While I can start at any point and trace the entire pattern up or down, there can be only one point from which to survey the whole in correct alignment. This is the point from which the objective unfolding of the dogma proceeds, and from which accordingly I can follow it as it were in its genesis; and again, as we shall see, this is the point at which the simplest and most natural transition is made from the divine nature to the Trinity of persons, from knowledge of God by reason to knowledge of God by faith, from natural to supernatural knowledge.

No doubt it has been noticed that in the developments already undertaken we have had to follow, for the most part, an analytic, retrogressive method; we have been compelled to work our way from the Trinity of persons, from the distinctions and relations in God, to the processions, productions, and communications that take place in God. The processions in God and the corresponding productions lead to the relations, and through the relations to the personal distinctions. For the relations between the producing and the produced persons arise from the productions and processions. But these relations must be personal relations, relations between persons; because in God nothing can be produced in the same person or in the nature, as otherwise that person would be composed of a producer and a product, and the divine nature is itself neither produced nor can it in any way whatever be completed by a product. Therefore the object of the production can be nothing else than this, that another person is put in possession of the same nature. Hence the production is essentially a communication of the nature to another person, who thereby enters into the most intimate relation with the producing person. Consequently, too, the distinctions which the relations involve are personal distinctions, and comprise a multiplicity of persons in the same nature.

Accordingly the productions and processions make the genesis of the Trinity clear to us, as indeed the terms themselves imply. They disclose the Trinity to us in its very origin. They constitute the ray of light in which the unity of the divine essence is displayed as the Trinity of divine persons; in which we see the latter enter into union with the former, or more accurately, issue from it. Reason shows us God in the unity of His nature, but does not show us the fecundity of God in the real productions that take place within His own nature. Then faith comes along and teaches us that God can be and is productive and fruitful not merely in His external works, but also in His innermost being, and so points out the way that enables us to develop the doctrine of the Trinity from its source. Thus by means of the doctrine of the productions our knowledge of God is caught up and forwarded at the very point at which reason has left off. In this teaching not only do we behold the Trinity as a ripe fruit upon the divine tree; we behold it at the instant it springs forth as a tender shoot, and with clear vision we can follow its course step by step from the first bud to its full flowering in all the splendor of its glory.[4]

No one has understood this better, no one has applied it with greater success, than St. Thomas in his *Summa*. This is why his treatise on the Trinity is the clearest, the soundest, and the most perfect that has ever been written. As has already been remarked, he expressly designates the first proposition with which he begins this treatise as an article of faith, whereas up to this point—with the sole exception of the doctrine of predestination, which involves the supernatural destiny of creatures—he has regarded and treated everything that was to be said about the divine nature and its activ-

---

[4] Thus we prefer to present what in recent times has been called the "construction" of the Trinity. This is nothing but a dialectical process of development by which, for our better understanding, we split up into its component elements the content of the dogma that is so infinitely beyond our comprehension in its objective simplicity. From these elements we can then construct a composite representation of the dogma, without of course carrying the dissection and the gradual genesis of our ideas over to the object itself. Obviously such a construction can rest only upon a foundation supplied to us by divine revelation.

ity as truths of reason. This article of faith is no other than that of the two processions and productions. From the processions and productions he then goes on to derive the relations, from the relations the persons in their plurality and their real distinctions, and he concludes this construction of the Trinity with a retrospective glance at our knowledge of it. After he has thus built up the dogma he turns to a contemplation of the finished structure, first to a consideration of the individual persons with their different names and properties, then to a comparison of the persons with the unity of the essence as well as with the relations, the personal properties, and the productions, and finally to a comparison of the persons among themselves. All that he says in the second section about the several parts of the structure and their relationships has its foundation in the construction of the first section, and this construction in turn is nothing but a development of the root-principle with which he began.[5]

We have no desire to follow him throughout this process. Not every point of his development is equally clear and manifest, nor equally interesting and attractive. We have found it preferable to render the dogma as intelligible as possible in its most vital and interesting features, and to dwell on whatever can promote the intimacy of the believing soul with the highest object of our faith and provide rich material for arousing love and encouraging meditation of this mystery, or whatever appears of importance for the understanding of the other mysteries and of the whole of Christianity. However, it is by no means necessary to depart from the Angelic Doctor's scientific method and principles. On the contrary, nothing is more advantageous for our purpose than a rigorous adherence to such procedure.

We shall take pains to enrich St. Thomas' train of ideas by the addition of other elements, and where necessary to point his thought more sharply and develop it further, or, as the case may require, to modify it. We do not wish to give the impression that we are averse to progress in this field. In particular we shall endeavor to utilize

[5] The expression "construction" of the Trinity, employed by German idealism and related schools, strikes us as out of place. The union of vigorous speculation and firm faith in Scheeben excludes its presumptuous connotation. Present-day theology does not consciously engage in "constructing" the Trinity. It studies the mystery in connection with the person of the Godman, Christ. Its attitude and the starting point of its thought are primarily determined by the reality of Christ and His economy of salvation. [Tr.]

not only the further developments of later Scholasticism, but also the masterly contributions of the predecessors of St. Thomas, notably those of St. Augustine (*De Trinitate libri 15*), St. Anselm (*Monologium*), and Richard of St. Victor (*De Trinitate libri 6*). Richard of St. Victor, to be sure, is not equally felicitous in all departments, and in particular he has taken less adequate account of the inner relationship of the divine productions to the divine knowledge and love. But he is so fertile in highly original and profound thoughts and develops so sharp and adroit a dialectic, that the mine of information he has bequeathed us is far richer than most of the philosophical ventures of later times in this same province.

10. The Root-principle of the Trinity: the Productions in the Divine Knowledge and Love

The divine nature is completely alive; consequently the productions which take place in it must be productions of the vitality of this nature, as their very names, generation and spiration, indicate. They must occur through the vital acts of this nature; and since in God these vital acts are spiritual, and hence reducible to knowledge and love, the productions must take place through acts of knowledge and love. In God such acts are infinite and substantial, and therefore must issue in an infinite and substantial product.

That the productions in God take place through the activities of the nature, and indeed the activities of knowledge and love, is evidently ascertainable in the mere supposition that there are productions in God; and as a rule theologians derive their more detailed descriptions of the productions from the fact that they cannot be conceived in God in any other way, and that there are no other interior activities in God than those of the intellect and will. Although this demonstration may not be clear to everyone, such determinate account of the divine productions can and must be accepted as somehow proposed in divine revelation. The truth is so distinctly revealed and so unanimously and decisively accepted by the Fathers and theologians, that it cannot be regarded merely as an ingenious hypothesis or a freely discussed theological opinion, but must prevail as the only admissible and hence perfectly certain and authentic description of the divine productions. Though it is not explicitly of faith, it cannot be denied without great temerity.

We do not here intend to demonstrate this proposition from the standpoint of positive theology. With his usual masterly skill Kleutgen has in recent times presented this proof in his *Theologie der Vorzeit*. Whoever wishes still further information on the matter need only have recourse to the most available of those theologians of antiquity who are not exclusively speculative.[6] Besides, the very use we shall make of this doctrine, and the light it casts upon the entire content of revelation and the Church's teaching, will suffice as a guaranty of its truth.

But, that this idea may be a safe guide and become a source of abundant light, we must examine it and determine its implications as accurately as possible; and here again we must insist on fixing the precise point where reason and faith meet, where the former leaves off and the latter takes up.

Reason furnishes us with the idea not only of the divine nature, but also of its substantial vitality. It teaches us that the divine substance is at once purest being and purest activity, and that this activity of God consists in the most perfect knowledge and love of Himself. However, reason does not inform us that this knowledge and love in God produce something, but only that knowledge and love are the substance of the knower and lover as well as of the object known and loved. Therefore reason cannot state whether the knowledge and love constitute a new person, but only that they are perfections of that person to whom they belong.

Faith now enters in and reveals that the activity of the divine life is productive. It tells us that God not only knows and loves Himself, but that He gives expression to His knowledge and that His love issues in a product; that He utters the knowledge which He has of Himself in an interior Word, and imprints or radiates it in an image of Himself; that He breathes forth the love which He bears for Himself and His Word in an interior sigh of love, seals it with a kiss, formulates it in a pledge. Knowledge and love in God are not produced, any more than is the nature to which they belong and which they constitute in its actual vitality. Hence they do not formally establish any opposition, any relation, any distinction in God, nor, consequently, any distinct persons. Accordingly we

[6] Cf. Kleutgen, *Theologie der Vorzeit*, I (2nd ed., Münster, 1867), 265–313; Suarez, *De Trinitatis mysterio*, I, c.5; Ruiz, *De Trinitate*, disp. II; my *Dogmatik*, I, sect. 116.

cannot say, if we are to speak quite accurately, that the divine knowledge and love are formally a real production or procession, a bringing forth or a going forth. This much only is clear: through the knowledge and love of the First Person in the Godhead, the original possessor of the divine nature and its life-activity, the expression, or utterance and manifestation, the revelation of this knowledge and this love, is really produced, as something really distinct from the producing person, something that stands in real relationship to Him.

The distinction we are here making is somewhat subtle, but can be made sufficiently clear in its main features to any thinking intellect. That its full precision is not ordinarily grasped is simply owing to the fact that, whereas it is observable in our own intellectual life, it is not quite as obvious in us as in God.

Knowledge and love can be expressed in a twofold manner, exteriorly and interiorly. External expression is better known and more intelligible to us, as regards both ourselves and God, and we must start with it in order to explain internal expression.

As regards ourselves, however, external expression is again twofold: there is an expression that is vital, but more intangible; and there is another that is not in itself vital, but is more concrete. We give expression to our knowledge by the word in which we represent our thought, and by the image in which we depict it.[7] We give ex-

---

[7] As in the things themselves, there is a curious linguistic relationship between word and image. For "word" has, like "verbum," ῥῆμα (from the root 'ΡΕ'Ω), λόγος (from λέγω), and דָּבָר , the basic meaning of gathering and putting together, and thus suggests a formed image. And herein is perceived the striking difference between conveying thought by a word and by a sigh or an exclamation of joy. This is clearer in Latin. *Suspirium* (sigh) is the sounded *aspiratio* (impulse toward a thing), which is called forth in vehement emotion. Relative to our subject, St. Francis de Sales in his Pentecost sermon calls the product of divine love "un soupir, une respiration, un souffle d'amour." When the Apostle says that the Holy Spirit pleads in us, God's children, with unutterable groanings [Rom. 8:26], he indicates that the Holy Spirit Himself is a "gemitus inenarrabilis," which streams forth from the heart of the Father and the Son. We might better call Him, with one of the Fathers of the Church, "iubilus Patris et Filii," as in His relation to the Father and the Son He is the expression not of languishing love, but of love overflowing with rapture. The swelling and outpouring of the heart, though not always voiced in a sigh, is always in some way perceptible, and is the most natural and direct indication both of emotion in general, and especially of love, the source and mistress of the emotions. Particularly significant is the Hebrew word יוֹבֵל , "clang, peal" (from יָבַל , to bubble up, pour forth), since in this connotation the sound of jubilation appears as the effect of the

pression to love through the sigh or aspiration in which it streams forth, and by means of the pledge or gift in which we embody it, and by which we desire to unite ourselves with the object of our love.

God gives external expression to His knowledge and love in a similar manner. All things that God has called into existence are an expression of His knowledge, an impress of His thoughts, and as such they are words He has uttered, in which He has manifested Himself, and images which He has fashioned according to His ideas. And everything among creatures that partakes of life and happiness is an expression and outpouring of the divine love, a breath that flows forth from it, a pledge and a gift by which that love clasps the creature to itself.

On the analogy of this external expression of knowledge and love, let us turn to the consideration of an internal expression of knowledge and love, as it takes place in ourselves—and according to revelation we must speak of God in like manner. Let us consider an expression that does not pass beyond the knowing and loving soul, that is not directed to other subjects.

We conceive knowledge as the production of a representation of a thing, and of a judgment concerning it. Just as the artist reproduces his ideas by means of the visible picture, and as we express our judgment by means of the external word, so we ordinarily regard our idea itself as an image of the object known, and our inner judgment as a word of our soul. More accurately, the actual idea is the expressed species (*species expressa*) of the image impressed on our soul by the object (*species impressa*), and the actual judgment is the expression of an observed relationship perceived by the soul and habitually residing therein. The cognition which comes to expression in the interior image and word is not the actual but the habitual cognition (the *memoria*); it is true in the strictest sense of the word that the actual idea and the actual judgment are produced from this habitual knowledge and by it. But if I consider cognition as the act by which the soul is rendered actually knowing, then that image or word is no longer the expression of the cognition, but is the

---

welling up and overflowing of the heart through the breath. Partially related to this word is הֶבֶל, *exhalavit, spiravit*, from which הֶבֶל , *halitus, vapor,* ἀτμίς, a notion which Sacred Scripture expressly applies to the eternal wisdom issuing from the mouth of God (Wisd. 7:25-27).

cognition itself. Hence it is produced only so far as the cognition itself, the act of knowing, is a product of the soul. Briefly, the word or image is a real product, a real expression of the soul which passes from habitual to actual cognition, but is not a product or an expression of the actual cognition or of the cognitive act, with which it is identical.[8]

The process must be entirely different in God. In His cognition He too gives forth a real expression, a really produced image and word; but this image and word must be thought of otherwise than in the created soul. God's completed, actual cognition cannot be the object of a real production—for then God would not be essentially knowing, would not be pure Act—and hence word and image, so far as they constitute actual cognition, cannot be really produced, as with us. We can make no real, actual distinction between God's being as the object of His cognition, and the representation of it in the cognitive act. Subject and object, idea and reality, coincide in God in one undivided existence. In our soul the intellectual word or image is a product of the soul, as is the cognition itself by which the soul is actuated; but God is purest actuality without any potentiality. Therefore the reason which demands in us a real distinction, a real relation between the knower and his intellectual word and image, is entirely lacking in Him. God cannot produce His word and image in order to know Himself; He produces it because He knows Himself,[9] out of the overflowing fullness and actuality of His knowledge, which does not remain sterile but is infinitely fruitful. This infinite fecundity impels it to give adequate expression of itself in a word and image remaining within God.

Again: the creature produces its cognitive act in its intellectual

[8] Nevertheless, even in actual cognition the perception of a truth or the apprehension of it, and the assertion or pronouncement in favor of its objective truth, and the substantiation and awareness of a perfect understanding of it in the judgment, can be distinguished at least as principle and consequence, if not as cause and effect.

[9] We shall discuss later the sense in which the First Person knows Himself only through His *Verbum,* or rather in His relation to the *Verbum,* and to what extent He could not know Himself for what He really is without the production of the *Verbum.* Cf. the Council of Cologne, 1860 (*Col. Lac.,* V, 286): "It cannot be said that only by generating the Son does the Father acquire that knowledge or cognition of Himself which, if God is to be true God, cannot be lacking in Him, in whom 'to be is to know, and essence is wisdom' " (St. Augustine, *De Trinitate,* XV, c.7, no. 12).

conception; it produces because it is not pure and real actuality by its very essence. God, however, is pure and perfect actuality by His essence. Consequently, the mind judges, that mode of production by which knowledge itself becomes the object of the production does not occur in God. But faith informs us that another and higher production takes place, one that is rooted not in imperfection, but in the immense, inexhaustible riches of God.

Strictly speaking, we can say no more than that the expression of God's cognition, as its word and image, is produced and that it is produced by the cognition itself. Moreover, because the word is uttered in God, His knowledge is expressed in that word; and because the image is formed in God, His knowledge and its object are impressed in the image. But we cannot invert the order of these causal clauses; for to utter a thought does not mean to produce the thought, but the expression of it, and to copy or impress an image does not mean to produce the image itself, but a reproduction of it.

When we consider love, we find that the process is similar. The act of love in the human soul proceeds from the will as a product of the soul. We consider this act either as an activity by which the soul itself is actuated and becomes loving *actu*, or as the product of this activity, as an impulse which the soul produces in itself as a result of its tendency toward the beloved object, as a bond by which the soul attaches itself to the object, and the object to itself. And since love manifests itself outwardly by a sigh flowing forth from the heart, by which it moves toward the beloved object, or by the gift which is given and received as a pledge of love, we cannot better characterize the interior product, the inner expression or rather the outpouring of the loving soul and its activity, than by calling it a sigh of love and a love-token or a giving of self.

But, as has been stated, we can discern this inner sigh of love, this inner pledge of love, from the act of love itself only with the greatest difficulty and by reflecting on the matter. For the act of love itself is this impulse and pledge, as the outpouring of the habitual affection and union with the beloved object. We cannot speak of the production of such a sigh or pledge unless the act of love itself is produced in us.[10]

---

[10] In actual love, however, as analogously in actual cognition, we can distinguish at least mentally the complacency toward the beloved good which represents the impression aroused by the good, from a delight and awareness

If we wish to think that in God, too, a real process and a real production take place in and through love, naturally we can do so only on the analogy of what goes on in us. But we must remember that this is only according to analogy, that is, that it is verified in God in an incomparably higher, and, in part, reverse sense. The act of love in God does not proceed from the *habitus* or potency, and so is not a true product. God is His love, in the purest and fullest actuality. But, as faith teaches us, precisely because God's love is not an elicited act, because it is an eternal and aboundingly rich act, it is no less fruitful than the divine cognition. Therefore in His love God puts forth an immense sigh, an aspiration of love and an infinite pledge of love. God pours forth His love in this aspiration; not the love, however, but the aspiration is produced. And God expresses His love in this pledge; not the love, however, but the pledge of love proceeds from the Lover as something distinct from Him.

Therefore, according to revelation, there are productions in the divine knowledge and love, which manifest their infinite fecundity in the productions. The light of God's knowledge shines forth in the reflection of an infinite likeness, and the fire of the divine love flares up in an infinite flame. *Reflection, word,* and *image* are the designations for the expression of the divine cognition; *flame, aspiration,* and *self-donation* or *pledge* are the quite parallel designations for the outpouring of the divine love.

Holy Scripture employs these and similar terms to describe the products of the inner divine productions. Thus the product of the first production is known as the "pure emanation of the glory of the almighty God," "the brightness of eternal light, and the unspotted mirror of God's majesty, and the image of His goodness," [11] the *Logos,* the "Word" of God,[12] the character or "figure of His substance." [13] Since the second production is generally represented in Sacred Scripture in its extension to the outer world, we observe that the names assigned to it appear only in this connection, although we may easily reason back to the inner product in its absolute

---

resulting from that complacency on account of an interior, loving aspiration and caress, which represents an outpouring and pledging of love for the good.

[11] Wisd. 7:25 f.

[12] John 1:1, and elsewhere frequently. On the meaning of the term *Logos,* cf. Petavius, *De Trinitate,* VI, cc. 1-3.

[13] Heb. 1:2.

essence. Later we shall have occasion to discuss this matter more fully.[14]

Of course in these explanations we are not yet considering the two products in God as persons. We wish first to make clear how and why there must be persons, and indeed, distinct persons. As, however, the dogma teaches that the second production issues not from the First Person alone, but likewise from the product of the first production as from a second person, we may and ought to take this fact into consideration in determining the mode in which the divine love is fruitful. This we do by looking upon the love of two persons for each other as fruitful love, as a source of being.

God's utterance, the expression of His knowledge, supposes no other person than the speaker who is impelled to manifest His knowledge of Himself and to glorify its object by reproducing it; or, if there be needed a person to whom He speaks, this, as will be shown, is none other than the Word He utters and in which He formulates the expression of His knowledge. The case with love is somewhat different.

If God did not bring forth another person through His cognition, He could be and would have to be thought of as having an infinite love for Himself, that is, an infinite complacency in His own infinite goodness. As was stated in the first edition at this point, in this case it does not at all appear impossible to conceive of this complacency as being fruitful in a manner similar to the intuition of the divine perfection, but without understanding this specifically as

[14] Among the Scholastics the designations which we have listed for the product of divine love, and which seem quite obvious to us, are not yet sufficiently taken into consideration. They, too, usually assign for the second production names that are parallel to the terms *verbum* and *imago;* thus *amor* corresponds to *verbum*, and *donum* to *imago*. But *amor* in itself simply means love, not the product of love. The Scholastics themselves are aware of this, for they call the outpouring of love *amor notionalis* (that is, the notion which represents a distinctive property of one of the divine persons), while they call the divine love as such *amor essentialis*. However *amor* in comparison with *caritas* can naturally be employed according to the original meaning of the words as a specific term to serve as a variant for the latter, or to indicate the welling up and overflow of love. They explain the term *donum* as applied to God only according to the relation into which the product of the divine love for creatures can enter. But in this connection the relationship of the product to its producing principles ought to be expressed, for upon them the special relationship to creatures is based. We shall speak of this later at a more suitable opportunity.

complacency in the good of another person and as affection for Him. This complacency is fruitful in an infinite delight that manifests itself as a glorification of the beloved good and as joy over its possession. And it is fruitful in an exhalation which envelops the beloved good like a precious odor of incense ascending from its fire, glorifies it, and makes known to the Lover the entire sweetness of His possession. And if a second person were necessary, such a one is present in the person who, as we shall see, is brought forth by the outpouring of love. In fact, the Greek Fathers in their account of the product of the divine love prescind altogether from mutual love. They regard it simply as the odor and breath of the divine sanctity, hence as an outpouring of the holy love of God for His absolutely perfect essence.

Nevertheless, love appears more adequately and perfectly to be the fecund principle of an outpouring of love for the beloved if a lover and a beloved confront each other as two distinct subjects, if one is attracted to the other, and both pour out their love for each other. The conception of a pledging of love points to such a love even more, for love strives to unite and bind together two distinct subjects that love each other, or at least to crown and seal an already existing union and bond in a common effusion. If the fecundity of the divine love is to be perfectly understood, it must be represented in this fashion, that is, it must be regarded as the reciprocal love of two distinct persons.

This point of view is not greatly emphasized in the deductions of St. Thomas, especially in the *Summa contra Gentiles*. St. Bonaventure, on the contrary, explicitly stresses the point that the love by which the second production in God takes place is a mutual love.[15] Long before this the Eleventh Council of Toledo had stated in its famous Creed: "The Holy Ghost proceeds from both the Father and the Son, because He is the charity or sanctity of both."[16] St. Augustine, who was the first among the Latin Fathers to go into a deeper explanation of the person of the Holy Ghost, outdoes himself in the tenderest and sublimest expressions and images, in order to bring out the thought previously uttered by his teacher, St. Ambrose. Let the Holy Ghost, he says, be the substantial love of the Father and the Son, who are both consubstantial; if appropriate, let

[15] *I Sent.*, d. 10, q. 3.
[16] Cf. Denz., 277. [Tr.]

Him be called "friendship"; but more suitably He may be called "caritas." "What is love," he asks, "but a certain life that unites two beings or seeks to unite them, the lover and the one who is loved? What does the friend love in his friend, if not the friend? And so there are these three, the lover, the beloved, and the love." And therefore he repeatedly calls the product of the second process in God "communion, embrace, kiss, bond, unity; by these the two are joined together, and preserve their unity of spirit in the bond of peace." [17]

In like manner St. Bernard calls the Holy Spirit "the most sweet kiss of Father and Son," because He is "both the mutual knowledge and the love of Father and Son," and therefore is "the tranquil peace of Father and Son, their bond of union, their singular love." [18] As these words of St. Bernard show, the clearest and most comprehensive of all these terms which express the manifestation and sealing of the mutual love between Father and Son, and also the most common among the Fathers, is that of the *osculum*, or kiss, which among human beings is the most perfect attestation of love and at the same time is most closely connected with the notion of the exhalation of love. The kiss is the caress of love in the most exquisite sense.[19]

11. Further Discussion of the Products of the Eternal Productions; Their Immanence and Substantiality

Let us again take up the thread of our discourse.

In order to regard the Word and the Spirit as real products, we must distinguish the Word of God's knowledge from the knowledge, and the sigh of love from the love itself. But we may not dissociate

---

[17] *Tract. 105 in Io.; De Trin.*, VI, c.5; VII, c.3; VIII, c.10.

[18] *In Cant. Cant.*, VIII, 1-2. See the selections from the Fathers cited in my *Dogmatik*, Bk. II, no. 942.

[19] Scheeben ends this paragraph with a philological observation. He remarks that the German term *Liebkosung* ("caress") is derived from *Kusz* ("kiss"), although the sequence is inverted in Latin (*suavium* from *suavis, suavitas*), and in Greek (*philema* from *philos, philia*). These two languages, he thinks, form words signifying "kiss" according to its spiritual significance, from the sweetness and friendliness of the love which is expressed in it.

The peoples of eastern Asia do not express love by kissing. In fact, they detest kissing as practiced by Europeans and Americans. This alone is sufficient to show that the kiss cannot, without qualification, be regarded as "the most perfect attestation of love." [Tr.]

the Word from the knowledge, or the sigh from the love. If the divine productions which we are here speaking of are interior, immanent productions, the expression of knowledge cannot be completely detached from the knowledge, nor the aspiration of love from the love. The Word is Word only because the knowledge is formulated in it, is contained in it; and the breath of love is breath of love only because the love is breathed forth in it, lives and manifests itself in it.

To be sure, we do not really embody our knowledge, but only a sign of it, in external words; and we do not give forth love itself, but only an effect and symbol of it, in external, audible sighs. Similarly God's knowledge as manifested by externally uttered words, that is, in the images of creatures which express the divine thoughts, is merely like the idea of the artist as represented in his work of art. Again, God's love as conveyed by externally manifested sighs, that is, in the life and happiness of creatures, resembles merely some energy that is perceived in an effect distinct from the energy itself.

But such is not the case with the Word and sigh of God which are produced interiorly. God must place in this Word the very knowledge which He expresses in it, just as it is; He must pour forth into this sigh the love which He breathes out in it, just as it is. And since, as is always the case with God, no real composition is conceivable between the expression and the knowledge reflected in it, between the sigh and the love surging in it, the Word must really be the knowledge itself, and the sigh must really be the love itself. The Word and the sigh as such are produced, whereas the knowledge and the love as such are not produced.

A further consideration follows.

An expression of knowledge is at the same time an expression of the object known. With us, however, knowledge does not in reality contain its object, whether our knowledge extends to things outside of us or is confined to our soul itself. Therefore the interior product of our cognitive faculty is a mere word by which the object is signified, rather than a true image in which the object is imbedded. God's knowledge, on the contrary, is really identical with the object known, with the divine nature and essence: its object is truly and literally, not merely ideally, present in the cognition. Consequently the expression of the cognition must be a real counterpart of the object known, namely, the divine Being. It cannot simply be a word, but must also be a real image, in which the essence of the speaker is not only signified, but is actually presented. But the essence of the First Person in God can be thus really present solely for the reason that God's essence is contained in the real image just as His knowledge is formulated in the Word. It follows that the reproduction or counterpart in God really comprises in itself the essence of the First Person, and further that it is really identical with this essence, without ceasing to be distinct from the First Person; but it is identical with the divine essence quite otherwise than the First Person is. The counterpart is identical with the essence because and so far as the essence is incorporated in it; but the original Person is identical with the essence so far as He originally possesses it, and indeed possesses it in such a way that He can express it in a word and imprint it in an image.

An analogous observation is in order with regard to production as it takes place in divine love. Love among creatures does not really contain in itself the good that pleases it in the beloved or the good that it would present to the beloved, any more than the cognition of creatures really contains its object or is identical with it. We say, indeed, that lovers would like to give themselves, their very being, to each other in their love. But this mutual giving is a donation only according to affection, it is a mere affection without a real union, just as the representation of an object in us is no more than a thought. We can give real expression to a thought by projecting outside of ourselves a real though lifeless picture of the object known. In the same way lovers can, as signs of their love, give real pledges of the union by which they desire to belong to each other. But their essence is no more really present in the pledges which they give to each other than their love is really present in their sighs.

In God, however, the love of the first two persons is really identical with the goodness of the essence which they love in each other and which they both possess. Hence in consummating their mutual love and making it fruitful in an inner product, they can and must, together with and in their love, pour forth and incorporate in this product, as in a real pledge, their mutual or rather their common good, their common essence. As the expression of God's knowledge is a real expression of His essence, and is both a true word and a real image, so the outpouring of His love is an outpouring of the goodness of the divine essence, while at the same time it is an aspiration and a real pledge. As product of the loving persons, this pledge is really distinct from them. Nevertheless it is identical with their essence, but in a way different from the way the producing persons are identical with their essence. This pledge is identical with their essence only because it takes and receives the essence from the first two persons. Accordingly it is at once identical with these two persons and distinct from them, but in a different respect: it is identical with them in what they are and possess, distinct from them in the manner of being and possessing.

At this point we reach the climax of our development, where we can and must show how and why the divine processions are personal processions, how and why the products of the divine cognition and love can and must be called true persons in their own right, as in fact they are.[20]

St. Thomas proposes his course of reasoning and exposition as follows. From the divine productions there arise in God relations between the producer and the produced. These relations in God cannot be conceived as inhering in the substance, as accruing to it, as really distinct from it; this would contradict the divine simplicity. Therefore they must be really identical with the divine substance; and since the divine substance is in the highest sense subsistent, the relations (namely, the oppositions called forth by the relations) must likewise be subsistent. But because the relations are distinct from one another like paternity and filiation, seeing that they are opposed to one another, they must, so far as they cannot exist in one another, engender oppositions and distinctions in the subsistence. Hence beside the First Person, who proceeds from no anterior person, there are in God two other modes of subsistence, corresponding to the two productions; consequently there are two other subjects to whom these proper modes of subsistence belong. But that which in a substance or nature subsists in an individual manner as opposed to another, we call hypostasis or suppositum; and if the substance or

----

Note that our discussion of the products of divine knowledge and love, in three successive steps as proposed in sections 10–13, corresponds exactly to the three clauses of the first verse of St. John's Gospel. "In the beginning was the Word" (section 10: expression of cognition); "and the Word was with God" (section 11: immanence, or the substantial existence of the Word within God); "and the Word was God" (sections 12–13: divine personality of the Word).

nature is rational, we call it a person. Accordingly there are in God distinct hypostases and supposita, distinct persons, and indeed three.

Without wishing to impair the genuine depth and consistency of these deductions, we believe that another road will lead more easily to the same objective, and that the personal character of the inner products of God can be developed more clearly and understandably in another way.

12. Analysis of the Concepts of Hypostasis and Person

First of all, what do we mean by a person?

This concept, as applied in the sphere of revelation, will never be adequately apprehended unless the more general concept of hypostasis has previously been clearly determined. This point has often been entirely disregarded in the German theology of the nineteenth century. It was thought that the notion of personality was set forth in its full splendor only in recent times, as the finest fruit of the scientific movement; and some thinkers were so inspired by the "new" idea that they practically exempted themselves from a calm analysis of it. Personality is the most conspicuous perfection of the spirit as opposed to blind nature; it is the aggregate of the spirit's self-consciousness, and of the liberty which rests thereon: such is the leading idea which runs through all disquisitions on the concept. But when we come to theology, where we must admit and account for three persons in one divine nature, and the two natures of Christ in one person, we must conceive of personality not in opposition to what we are accustomed to call nature in the concrete, that is, to the visible, material world, but above all in opposition to spiritual, rational nature; and, further, not in opposition to a foreign, external being which we call nature, but also in opposition to the proper, inner essence of the person himself. This latter opposition is verified in the person in common with the hypostasis. Indeed, it is formally emphasized in the concept of hypostasis. Moreover, hypostasis is the original term, first employed by the Church for indicating distinction in God and unity in Christ: a further reason for not underrating its importance.

1. To the Greek word *hypostasis*, which is used both concretely to signify a thing and abstractly to signify a mode of being, the Latin *subsistentia* corresponds well enough for the abstract use, and *sup-*

positum or even *subsistens* for the concrete. German usage has sanctioned no single, definite word for it; the language retains the Latin and Greek expressions, which for that matter have long been canonized, although composite terms can render them very pregnantly.[21]

In its original meaning, "hypostasis" denotes that which, although existing and reposing in itself, is capable of bearing and containing something else. The notion of existing and reposing in itself, is indicated by the Latin *subsistere;* and the notion of bearing and containing, by the Latin *suppositum.* Hence everything that must in any way be regarded as existing in another, reposing in another, intrinsically belonging to another, is not a hypostasis in the absolute sense. Thus the accidents, actions, and properties that are in a thing and belong to it, are not hypostases. Even substances are not always hypostases in the full sense. Thus a part of the human body, for example, the head, although itself a bearer of properties and accidents, is not a real hypostasis, for it in turn exists in a whole, in the body, or rather in the man himself; it belongs to this whole and has its origin in the whole. Indeed, not even the entire human nature, the entire essence of a man, taken abstractly, is a hypostasis, because it has existence only in individual men, and because it belongs to them, is borne by them and possessed by them. "Hypostasis" is rather the individual, real bearer and proprietor of the nature, the subject to which the nature with all its parts, properties, and activities belongs and is attributed.

According to the usual definition, "hypostasis" is an individual substance. Rightly understood, this definition is in perfect agreement with the one given. But we must render the Latin *individuum* not by "indivisible" (from *dividere aliquid*), but by "incommunicable." The substance which originates in a superior whole belongs to it (as a member); and the substance which dwells in several distinct subjects is communicated to it (as a generic substance); accordingly neither of these is individual in the strict sense of the word. A substance is truly and fully a *substantia individua* only when it is taken as identical with the ultimate subject to which it pertains. Where communicability ceases, possession or proprietorship begins; as soon

[21] English, too, retains the Latin terms, for which no convenient Anglo-Saxon equivalents are available. Even "hypostasis," unchanged from the Greek, is an English word in good standing. [Tr.]

as I assert that the substance no longer belongs to a subject,[22] I affirm that it belongs to itself, that it reposes in itself and subsists.

Hypostases are found at all levels of existence or being, wherever there is a nature, essence, or substance. Every nature and essence must exist and rest somewhere, must be in a subject, must have a support. Even sensible and material substances, from minerals up to animals, are true hypostases, inasmuch as they are self-contained and have an independent existence. But we find persons and personality only in spiritual substances.

2. The person is a special, eminently perfect kind of hypostasis. A person differs from other hypostases in this respect: the nature of which the person is the hypostasis, bearer, and possessor, is exclusively a spiritual nature.[23]

The spiritual nature or essence itself, with all its properties, with its consciousness and its liberty, is not necessarily a person by the mere fact of its spirituality, for these attributes do not even constitute it a hypostasis. On the other hand, the hypostasis of this nature is personal or a person only in the supposition that this nature is spiritual. Both conditions are equally necessary to verify the notion of a person, namely, that the bearer and proprietor of the nature be subsistent, and that this nature itself be spiritual.

The second condition modifies the first. For the very reason that the person is bearer of a spiritual nature, he must possess this nature in a much more perfect manner than other hypostases possess their natures, and hence must be independent in a far higher sense than these.

The tree or the brute possesses its parts and the faculties through which it operates, but has no real right over them, no conscious

---

[22] "Subject" here as elsewhere is equivalent to *suppositum* in Scheeben's terminology. Scheeben's exposition leaves open the question disputed among Thomists, Scotists, and Molinists, whether the "belonging-to-itself" is a real perfection added to the singular substance, and in what it consists metaphysically. [Tr.]

[23] That is, it is a real substance, not composed of matter and form, but unextended and independent of matter. Scheeben develops the concept of person from a theological point of view, on the model of God, whose spiritual nature and independent subsistence are the supreme and absolute exemplar of human personality, which can be no more than an analogous imitation of it. Anton Günther, whose position Scheeben opposes, held with John Locke that the one factor constituting person was self-consciousness (*Persona est substantia sui conscia*). [Tr.]

enjoyment of them, no free dominion over them. The person, on the contrary, has a true, inviolable right over his parts and faculties. Thanks to his spiritual nature, the person is a *hypostasis cum dignitate,* a noble, honorable proprietor of all that he has and is. Thanks further to the rationality of his nature, he is endowed with consciousness of his essence and of the goods he possesses, as well as of the very fact of his proprietorship; only by reason of such consciousness does proprietorship become full proprietorship, an enjoyment of proprietorship and possessions. Even more: from the rationality of the nature arises, along with self-consciousness, the ability to direct all activities more or less independently to self-appointed ends, and to apply all faculties, all the means at one's command, to the attainment of these ends. Thus self-determination and the free use of property issue in enjoyment, *usus* results in *fructus.* Such free usage alone is true dominion, and hence is alone the sign of full possession.

However, to the essence of personality pertains not actual self-consciousness, not the actual use of liberty, but only that aptitude for such acts which is necessarily implied in spiritual nature. What is essential is the dignity, the worth of the person, owing to which he is deserving of respect in his possession and his being, as proprietor of a rational nature, even though he is not yet able to enjoy or exercise his proprietorship, or at any rate cannot fully enforce it externally. The former is the case with children who have not yet attained to the use of reason; the latter is the case with minors.

Since persons, owing to their rational nature, possess their nature more perfectly than other hypostases do, they are subsistent in a far higher sense than the latter. Other hypostases, for example, in the plant and animal kingdoms, have no complete perseverance in being. They are corruptible and transitory by nature; the individual perishes to give way to a successor; they exist more for the sake of the species than for themselves. But personal hypostases have an imperishable existence, at least so far as their nature is spiritual; for a spiritual nature is indestructible. They exist not merely to represent their species, but to have for themselves the eternal possession and enjoyment of the advantages which pertain to the species; they are ends in themselves. And since they are ends in themselves, whereas other hypostases are not, the latter with all that they are and have can be subordinated to persons and become their property; they can and should serve the enjoyment of persons and be subjected to their dominion. But persons, because of their dignity, can never be treated as mere things; for they are not only autonomous but *sui iuris*. And therefore persons cannot be employed as mere means to some end foreign to themselves.

Nevertheless created persons are not their own ultimate ends. Because they are created, they depend upon a higher personality as upon their first cause and last end, and hence they by no means have unrestricted, absolute possession, enjoyment, and use of self. Only God is absolutely self-possessive, self-dependent, self-governing. He alone has personality in the absolute sense of the word.

But if the Absolute is of necessity only one, does it not follow that there is only one absolute personality, only one absolute person, and hence only one divine person? As there is and can be only one divine nature, so there can be only one divine personality, if by this is meant the dignity, the power, and the liberty whereby the person is elevated above other hypostases, and a divine person above all outside of God. But if we recall that a person is properly the bearer and proprietor, the hypostasis of rational nature, we can by no means deduce from the unity of the divine nature that there is only one divine person, or even that there is only one personality in God, since by personality we understand that whereby different bearers of the same rational nature are constituted as such and are rendered distinct from one another.

If now we go on to prove that the internal divine productions issue in bearers and proprietors of the divine nature, we shall have demonstrated, as we set out to do, that they are productions resulting in persons; and thus we shall have some account of the Trinity of persons in the one divine nature.

13. The Divine Productions as Personal Productions, and Their Products as Hypostases and Persons

The demonstration will not be difficult after the explanation that has been given. As has been remarked, God's productivity within the divinity must issue in some product really distinct from the producing subject; otherwise there would be no real production. This product, however, cannot be regarded as something contributing to the perfection, actuation, completion of the producing subject, as is the case with processes that take place in our souls; otherwise the producing subject would not be pure and perfect actuality. Hence nothing remains but that the producing subject, operating out of the fullness of His actuality, communicates His own perfection to another subject, and places another subject in the copossession of His own perfection. But God can communicate interiorly only His entire nature and essence, since everything in Him is really nature and essence. In communicating this nature and essence, He places another subject in the possession of it. And since this subject has no existence apart from such communication—for He receives the divine nature and essence only by communication, and without nature and essence no subject is conceivable—the subject is produced by the very fact that He is placed in possession of the divine nature and essence. Therefore by production in God we must mean that the producing person produces a copossessor, a receiver, bearer, and proprietor of His nature and essence. But the proprietor and bearer of a nature is a suppositum, a hypostasis; and the proprietor and bearer of a rational nature is a person. Consequently the products of the divine productions are true persons, and indeed persons who are really distinct from the producing person since they possess the same nature in different manners.

Let us apply this in detail.

Prior to every other consideration, we must unquestionably assume in God an original bearer and possessor of the divine nature, an unproduced person. This person originally has the divine cognition, the knowledge of Himself and of His essence. Therefore He must be the principle of the Word in which this knowledge is expressed, and of the image in which its object is imprinted.[24] In producing the Word as an expression of His cognition and essence distinct from Himself, He formulates in the Word and communicates to Him His own knowledge and essence. The Word therefore receives from

[24] The Greek Fathers Athanasius, Basil, Gregory of Nazianzus, Gregory of Nyssa, and others call the Father the "source" of the Trinity, and assign "innascibility" as His distinguishing characteristic. Gregory of Nyssa uses the simile of "three torches": the Father gives His light to the Second Person, and through Him to the Third Person. St. Augustine, the Latin Fathers, Thomas Aquinas and most of the latter's disciples place more stress on the oneness in essence and the circumincession of the divine persons. Richard of St. Victor and Bonaventure follow the Greeks in their Trinitarian doctrine. Scheeben, too, derives his view of the Trinity as a fellowship in divine life from the Greek Fathers. [Tr.]

the First Person the latter's knowledge and essence, and with it the entire divine nature. Thus the Word appears as the recipient, and consequently as the possessor and proprietor, of the divine nature. But since He is proprietor only by reason of this communication, He is as such distinct from the original proprietor; He is a real proprietor of the nature, distinct from the original proprietor. As real proprietor of a nature the Word is therefore a true suppositum; as proprietor of a rational nature He is a true person; and as proprietor of the divine nature He is a divine person.

Thus we perceive that the interior Word of God is a personal Word, a Word which is not merely a medium for the disclosure and communication of thought, as our words are, but is at the same time the recipient of the thought and of its real content, and even becomes the bearer of the thought. The First Person in God expresses Himself in His Word and communicates Himself in such wise that the Word receives the communication itself and possesses that which is communicated. The First Person not only speaks through His Word, but also speaks to it as to another subject. Further, this Word is not merely a personification, but is the personal representative of the wisdom of the First Person. He is the latter's representative because He is the adequate expression of Him; and He is the personal representative because He not only manifests this wisdom, but really possessses it, because He possesses it as truly and perfectly as does He to whom it originally belongs, and finally because He is the actual bearer and proprietor of it just as the First Person is.

The case of the second production in God, spiration, is similar. The sigh which proceeds from the mutual love of the First Person and His personal Word is necessarily something other than these two persons, who pour forth their love and the real content of their love into Him, and flood Him with the goodness of their essence. And since the two do not perfect themselves by this production of a third but rather transfer their perfection to Him, they produce this third as a recipient of their substantial love and goodness, they make Him a proprietor and bearer of their love and goodness, and thereby of the entire divine nature. The love with which Father and Son embrace each other in the communion of their goodness and lovableness, of their nature and essence, aims in its infinite fruitfulness at transferring this same nature and essence to a third subject, a third hypostasis; and the bliss which these two enjoy in the possession of the same nature can achieve a real expression in no other way than by taking a third person into this communion, by sharing with a third the entire and indivisible good which they possess, without losing it.

The sigh of the divine love is therefore a personal sigh, a person, and a person distinct from them who breathe Him forth in their love; and the pledge of the divine love, the bond which crowns the love of the first two persons, is a personal pledge and bond, a new person who takes His place with them and stands in their midst. This sigh is not only a manifestation of the love of two hearts for each other, which wish their life, their ardor, to flow over to each other. It is a sigh in which two divine persons, out of the absolute oneness and fullness of their common heart,[25] prove their love with utter efficacy, in that they transmit this oneness to a third person. And the pledge cannot be a mere bond between two lovers who desire to unite themselves to each other, but is a bond which must be the adequate expression of their absolute oneness, and which therefore must enter into the same relationship, the same unity in which they stand to each other. Lastly, the first two persons cannot surrender themselves to each other more thoroughly than they already possess each other by reason of their mutual relationship to each other. Consequently if their love is to be manifested in a gift, that which is given must be given to a third. This Third Person must therefore receive all that the other two had in their possession to give to each other; He must receive their own nature and possess it in a manner proper to Himself; He must be a personal gift, a person to whom the divine nature is given, and who seals and crowns the mutual surrender of the other two persons by what He receives.[26]

[25] Hence the spiration of the Holy Ghost would more appropriately be called *unicors* than *concors*.

[26] Here we may call attention to the beautiful theory so ingeniously propounded by Richard of St. Victor, even though it leaves much to be desired in precision of expression. Richard holds that when only two persons love each other, perfect communion in love is impossible; for since each loves the other, they love different objects. Hence a third person is required; the affections of the other two are fused into one by the fire of their love for this third person, for then their love has the same object (*De Trinitate*, III, c. 19). Thus the Father willed a Second Person, equal to Himself in dignity (*condignum*), to whom He might communicate the wealth of His infinite greatness; and He willed a Third Person, the object of the love of the first two

Accordingly, as the expression of the divine knowledge is a personal expression of the knowledge, so the outpouring of the divine love is a personal outpouring of this love. And as the Word is the subsisting personal representative of the divine wisdom, so the outpouring of the love is no mere poetic personification, but is a real person, a proprietor of this love, which He not only manifests, but possesses in as true a sense as the other two persons do. He represents this love in a superlative way, manifests it in Himself, and brings it to expression in Himself for the sole reason that He receives and possesses it in His own proper manner and is, moreover, the pledge of this love; for this reason alone He is in a distinctive sense called the personal love (not personified love, but love manifested in a person).

We should do well to abandon figurative language and say that the Third Person in God is the person of love, that is, the person corresponding to the fruitfulness of divine love. For properly the love itself is not personal, that is, a person, since it is common to all the divine persons; only the outpouring of it is a person, and when I employ the word "love" instead of "outpouring of love," I am using a figure of speech. In the same way there is a great difference whether I say that the Second Person is the personal Word or the personal wisdom of God. The Word is truly a person in the proper sense, really distinct from the speaker and from the sigh of love. But the wisdom is not; the wisdom is common to all the persons, and is something proper, distinct, subsistent, only when I employ it figuratively as the expression of wisdom, as the *verbum sapientiae*.

Does it still appear necessary to explain why knowledge and love in creatures are not activities that constitute persons? That they do not do so, every rational being knows, and requires no proof. But the contrast between these activities and the divine activities enables us to obviate the many misunderstandings that usually creep in at this point. This contrast will also serve to throw new light on the character of divine personality.

In a human soul the acts of cognition and love are accidents of the substance and the person. The intelligible word and the volitional love-impulse are at bottom really the same as the completed acts of

---

(*condilectum*), so that upon Him might be lavished the delights of divine love: "for supreme happiness consists in perfect communion of love" (*ibid.*, VI, c.6; cf. St. Bonaventure, *1 Sent.*, d. 10, a. 1, q. 2).

cognition and love, and hence are themselves accidents of the human substance and person. To be persons, they would first of all have to be substantial. But they are not, and so they can serve only to perfect the person to whom they pertain. They actuate the consciousness and enjoyment of the person, and carry him to the full realization and development of his own personality. Therefore the created person needs the interior productions for the perfection of himself, whereas in God the First Person possesses the actual knowledge and love of Himself in His very substance, and by production merely manifests the fullness of His riches in order to give origin to other, equal persons. The created person conveys not a substantial, but an accidental wisdom and love in his word and sigh; neither his word nor his sigh is a substance. The divine person, on the contrary, formulates a substantial wisdom in His Word, a substantial love in His sigh; accordingly both are consubstantial to Him. Since they proceed from Him, they are products distinct from Him, and hence persons.

By his external word the created person can manifest himself only to other persons, already existing; by his internal word he can manifest himself only to himself, but not to the word as to another person. But the First divine Person by His external word calls into existence with creative omnipotence the beings and persons to whom He wills to manifest Himself; and with still greater power He calls forth in His internal Word another person, not so as to become known to Himself by this Word, but to manifest and communicate Himself to this Word. It is true that the First Person, as opposed to the other divine persons, as a distinct person, as Father, knows Himself only in and through the others, or better, in His relation to them. But the inference by no means follows that the personality of the Father is completed by His Word and His sigh; for to be at once the complement of a person and a subsistent person is a contradiction. This alone follows, that the person of the Father stands in essential relationship to the person of the Son and the Holy Ghost; accordingly He can know Himself in His own subsistence and totality only in this relationship.

Further, as man gives to another person no more than an impersonal pledge of his love in the signs of love that he manifests, so the interior expression of love which he bears for himself serves only to make him pleased with himself. But God by the aspiration of love which He directs outside Himself brings into being not only the goods which He communicates to His creatures, but also the recipients of these goods. Similarly, in breathing forth the pledge of their love, the Father and the Word place Him in the co-enjoyment of their love and beatitude; He does not cause the happiness of their communion in Him. Briefly, the created spirit expresses his internal word within himself in order to become manifest to himself, and puts forth his impulse of love for himself in order to rejoice in himself. God expresses His Word in order to manifest the fullness of His self-knowledge to the Word Himself; God breathes forth His love in order to communicate to this sigh His own superabundant goodness.

Therefore the products of the internal divine productions must be true hypostases and persons distinct from each other. Accordingly the productions themselves must, like their products, be called hypostatic, personal productions.

They are hypostatic productions, in the first place, because they issue in hypostases. More than this, they are purely hypostatic, because they bring forth absolutely nothing except hypostases. For the nature which the produced hypostasis receives is not produced, but communicated. Lastly, these productions are shown to be hypostatic because the divine hypostases as such are distinct from one another only by reason of these productions and with respect to them.

The productions are completely hypostatic, and they are also completely personal; and first of all, because they are completely hypostatic: a person is nothing but a hypostasis with a rational nature. But they are personal in a way that is quite special; for the producing principle, which constitutes the persons, is also manifested as a person in them. For the First Person brings forth the Second only by the act of self-consciousness and self-knowledge, which is characteristic of a person above and beyond all other hypostases; and the First together with the Second Person produces the Third only by the act of love, which likewise is predicable of persons alone. By virtue of their origin, therefore, the persons in God are distinct from one another not only hypostatically but also personally. The second hypostasis is distinct from the first only for the reason that the second proceeds from the self-consciousness of the first, and consequently is known as distinct from Him in this self-consciousness; likewise the third hypostasis is distinct from the first two only for the reason that He proceeds from their love for each other, and consequently is willed as distinct from them in this love.

But we wished to make these rather subtle remarks only in passing, in order to counteract certain erroneous notions and expressions of recent theologians and philosophers.[27]

More important and also more comprehensible is the further determination of the notion of divine persons, and the establishing of those concepts and terms by which we have to apprehend and designate concretely and clearly the individuals as true persons, and their respective origins as personal origins.

As we endeavor in the following pages to ascertain these concepts and terms, or rather to explain them as imparted to us in revelation through the Church, we shall have many another opportunity to determine more accurately and to develop further the doctrine already proposed.

14. Notion and Definition of the Divine Hypostases and Persons

In general we define "person" as the bearer and possessor of a rational nature. This definition is valid also for the divine persons; but we have to add that they are possessors of the divine nature. Yet even this does not indicate the characteristic way the divine persons possess their nature and are distinct from one another, in contrast to the way non-divine persons possess their nature. Since an infinite difference obtains in this matter, the concept of a divine person would remain extremely vague unless we could succeed in delineating it more sharply. The very difference involves the consequence that the notion of hypostasis and person which we abstract from creatures is applicable to the divine hypostases and persons only in an analogous sense, hence with qualifications. Accordingly the concept must be reduced to its analogous value by the determination of that difference, for only thus can it be transferred to God.

Created persons of the same nature, for example, several men, are distinct from one another as persons by the fact that different individuals possess the same nature; the nature is not numerically one

[27] Scheeben has in mind the terminology of Anton Günther and his school. [Tr.]

in them, but multiplied. Hence they can be distinct from one another and subsistent even if none of them originates from another or, for that matter, even if they stand in no relationship to one another. Indeed, all relationships which they have to one another, even that of father and son, suppose their difference and subsistence, and hence establish not an essential, but only an accidental difference.

But the case is the opposite in God. All the divine persons possess one and the same individual, indivisible, and simple nature. The bearers of this nature must even be really identical with it, otherwise they would not be simple, but composite. Therefore, if the bearers of this nature are to be distinct from one another, they must possess the one nature and be identical with it in different manners. And in fact, as we have seen, the First Person possesses this nature of Himself, the Second possesses it from the First, and the Third from the First and Second. Accordingly the internal distinction and also the inner being of these persons are constituted by the relations in which they stand to one another as possessors of the same nature. This is obvious in the case of the produced persons: they are proprietors, and subsistent proprietors, of the divine nature because and so far as they are recipients of it. But the First Person, too, is relative to the others in His possession, because He owes His possession of the nature to the communication of it just as much as they do. And the First Person is for His part essentially bound up with this communication, because He possesses the nature only to communicate it. And thus the divine persons are perceived to be such only in and through the relations in which they stand to one another. Therefore in our definition we must take these relations into account, and say that the divine persons are relative proprietors of the divine nature, that is, as just explained, they are proprietors of the nature in and through their relationship to other proprietors of the same nature.[28]

Under another aspect, however, these same divine persons are absolute persons, that is, free, untrammeled by any real dependence

[28] This teaching, the elements of which are discernible in the Greek Fathers, was developed by St. Augustine, Boethius, and others, and received its classical expression in St. Anselm's formula: "In divinis omnia sunt unum, ubi non obviat relationis oppositio" (*De processione Spiritus Sancti*, c.II). This proposition was taken over by the Council of Florence (bull *Cantate Domino*, 1441; Denz., 703) as a certain theological doctrine, common to both the Greeks and the Latins. [Tr.]

or restriction. All created persons are relative in this respect; they are essentially dependent on a higher power which has freely called them into existence; and for this reason they are limited, are not absolutely autonomous, are not their own absolute ends, and lack the dignity of person in the fullest, most comprehensive sense. The divine persons are relative only among themselves. They are not dependent on any higher being outside themselves, since they all have the same supreme and independent nature. They are not even dependent on one another, because the person who gives origin to another is related as essentially to the latter as the latter is to the former, and mutual relations in the same order are equalized. Still less are they limited; for each of the divine persons possesses the entire divine nature, and in it the highest dignity, the greatest riches that can come to a person. That each possesses this nature in common with the others, implies no limitation; for the copossession partitions neither the ownership nor the property. We might even say that the latter is doubled and tripled in each person, since each in His own way possesses the others as His inseparable product or His inseparable origin; and moreover, being united in the essence with which they are really identified, the persons are also united in oneness among themselves.

We readily perceive that the absoluteness of the divine persons comes in the first instance from the absolute nature which they possess and are. Yet they remain essentially relative among themselves. Indeed, if they did not, they could not all be absolute; for they would have to be distinguished from one another by something else than the sole mode of possession. One would not only have to possess in a different way, but would have to possess, and therefore be, something else than the others; and so not all would possess the same absolute nature.

Thus the relativity of the divine persons not only does not destroy their absoluteness, but definitively secures it. These persons are relative in the difference of their hypostatic characters, absolute in the dignity which marks the hypostases as persons. In both respects they are essentially different from all created hypostases and persons. And thus we can transfer and apply the concept of hypostasis and person to God only in an analogous sense.

In the created order the individual, that is, the singular substance that does not pertain to a higher whole, is by that very fact a hypostasis; and if the substance is endowed with reason, it is a person. But the divine substance is not a hypostasis by the mere fact that it is singular, not generic, pertaining to no higher whole, and independent. According to the teaching of faith it does not appear in the last instance as individual, incommunicable, and uncommunicated by reason of its singularity and independence. We must go further and conceive of several subjects, not standing over it or embracing it, but really identical with it, subjects in which it is and to which it is communicated. In the last instance, the divine substance appears as individual, and hence as hypostasis, only in these subjects, and as identical with each of them.

Hence the formal concept of hypostasis in God does not coincide with the concept of singularity and totality of substance and nature, and hence the plurality of hypostases in God requires no multiplication of the nature, but only a distinction, based upon communication, in the possession of the same indivisible nature.

The similarity between divine and created hypostases lies in this, that in God there are really distinct possessors of the same nature; the dissimilarity between divine and created hypostases lies in this, that in God distinct possession is based not on a multiplication of the object possessed, but on the communication of the same object. The analogous concept of the divine hypostases is formed with the aid of this positive and this negative factor.

That the dignity of the divine hypostases, whereby they are persons, can likewise be conceived by us only through analogous concepts, is sufficiently clear. We can more readily understand this truth when we realize that this dignity is nothing else than the perfection of the divine nature, which indeed is reflected in the corresponding dignity and perfection of creatures, but at the same time remains infinitely superior to them.

15. The Concrete Concept and Name of the Several Persons and Their Productions; Necessity and Possibility of a Deeper Understanding of Ecclesiastical Terms

If the divine persons are essentially relative, we can assign to them no names capable of designating them in their personal characteristic unless such names express their relationship. This is the reason why the First Person is called Father, that is, Father of the Son; and the Second is called Son, Son of the Father. With the Third Person this relationship is not so readily perceived, since the term "Spirit" is used also absolutely. But strictly understood, it must be taken relatively so as to designate the Third Person, since in using the term "Spirit" we mean the Spirit, that is the sigh or breath, of the Father and the Son.

We must explain these names in detail because they are the most commonly used in the language of Sacred Scripture and the Church; but also—and this is why their usage is favored—because without further qualification they stress and indicate in the most concrete fashion the personal character of the three oppositions in God.

We have already learned several names for the Second and Third Persons, names that are proper to them. The Second Person really, and He only, is the Word and image of the First. But there are also impersonal, entirely non-subsistent words and images; hence in expressions of this kind the personality of their object is not brought out, and must be indicated by apposition. The same is the case with the names sigh, pledge, and bond, which we attribute to the Third Person. But for the First Person we had as yet no name at all; at best we were able to call Him "Speaker," seeing that He is principle of the Word. His personality is indeed expressed, or rather supposed, in this name; but it does not explicitly bring out His relation to another person proceeding from Him, since the product appears only as Word. But if the relative name is really to characterize one of the divine persons in His entire, concrete subsistence, it must designate Him in His personal relationship, that is, as personal principle of a person, or, as the case may be, as personal product of another person.

Our purpose is attained in the case of the first two persons if the First is called Father, and the Second is called Son. For a father is always a hypostasis and a personal hypostasis, and is also the principle of another personal hypostasis; and a son likewise is always a hypostasis and a personal hypostasis, and a product of another personal hypostasis.

This reciprocal designation of the first two persons can be based only on the fact that the Second proceeds from the First by way of generation—for only a generative principle is father, and only a generated product is son. And if this is to be a characteristic, proper designation of these two persons, if these names are to be proper names, only the reciprocal relation of these two persons, to the exclusion of the relation of the Third Person to them, can be based on generation.

If we wish to understand and explain why and how the first two persons, and they alone, are designated by the proper names of Father and Son, we must endeavor to understand and explain why and how the production of the Second Person from the First, and indeed exclusively in contrast to the other divine production, is called generation. There are really two questions, whether and how the first production can and must be called generation, and whether and how this term and the concept underlying it is proper to it alone, and not to the second production also. These questions, however, need not be treated separately. For if the first production pre-empts the term on account of its own special character, the second production is thereby deprived of it; and even supposing that the term is suitable for the second production also, it would then cease to point out the characteristic feature of the first.

Weighty reasons seem to deter us from this inquiry. The words of the Prophet are recalled: "Who shall declare His generation?" [29] Formidable hosts of the holy Fathers are marshaled, who hold it boundless temerity to seek to understand the generation of God and to fathom the difference between this generation and the production of the Holy Ghost. They insist that we must embrace such truths on faith, and not trouble ourselves with futile endeavors to penetrate with our natural reason what is reserved to the faithful in heaven.

But let us banish fear. All this concerns primarily those who think and speak of the inner mysteries of God in the light of reason alone, or merely under the impetus of faith, but not under the guidance of faith itself. We approach an understanding of these matters from faith and its data. It concerns further all those who, like the Eunomians against whom the Fathers especially inveigh, seek to fathom and exhaust the mystery completely. But our intention is to understand only the meaning of the expression with which revelation designates the origin of the Second Person, without pretending fully to explore its content. We desire merely to investigate why and to what extent revelation has applied to God the term and concept

[29] Isa. 53:8.

derived from the material world. But since we do not perfectly understand the inner nature even of animal generation, we shall by no means claim to comprehend from a feeble imitation the ideal which is imperceptible to our very intellect.

If our faith is to be an enlightened faith, rich in substance, we must strive to grasp as clearly as possible the meaning and inter-relations of revealed truths. We may not content ourselves with clinging to empty formulas and giving up their import as inde-terminable. Certain utterances of the Fathers, it is true, give the impression that this is what they contend. But the reason for this was that during their era systematic investigation had not yet sufficiently illuminated the inner organism of the Trinity, and in fact had not sufficiently clarified even the full, profound sense of the term. Yet they had to maintain against heretics that the names of the Son and the Holy Ghost were not interchangeable.

Since that ancient time theological science has advanced by tremendous strides. Through scientific investigation and super-natural contemplation, in which the saints made our dogma their object, the doctrine of the Trinity has been set forth in clearer, more distinct outline; and so we may well venture to take up our question without meriting the reproach of temerity. This we may undertake with greater confidence since we have already explained and accounted for the real distinction between the Second and Third Persons, and have now only to assign the fundamental reason for their names.

CHAPTER IV

The Production of the Second and Third Persons

▄▄▄

16. THE PRODUCTION OF THE SECOND PERSON IN GOD AS GENERATION, AND ITS PRODUCT AS THE SON

THE term "generation" is of course employed, in the first place, to indicate that the production of the Second Person in God is wholly different from creation, the act by which non-divine beings come into existence. Creation is a free act of the divine will, whereby God calls into being things which of themselves were nothing, and communicates to them an existence which is essentially different from His own. But God brings forth His interior Word by communicating to Him His own being, His own substance. The Word proceeds from the Father's innermost substance, which passes over to the Word and places Him in full possession of the very nature that is proper to the Father. Such transference of substance is likewise the most striking feature that differentiates generation in creatures from every other mode of production: something passes over from the substance of the producing principle to the product, and the product itself is similar in its substance to the producing principle. As a rule both these conditions are verified together in creatures; the second is everywhere and always found associated with the first, although the reverse is not true. Thus, for example, in the case of parasites that grow on trees, something from the substance of the tree enters materially into the product; but the specific nature of the tree does not. In God, however, the two conditions are so essentially interrelated that they can scarcely be distinguished from each other. The divine substance is absolutely simple; hence not merely a part of it passes over to the progeny, as is the case with even the most perfect animal generation, but the entire substance. This substance is utterly perfect and living; therefore it is transmitted not as matter which is to be informed and animated, but as absolute perfection and pure life, with which the produced subject is to be endowed. Accordingly, since the entire substance with its entire perfection is communicated to the product, the first two conditions of generation are verified in the production of the Second Person in the most perfect sense possible.

But these two conditions are verified likewise in the production of the Third Person in God. He, too, is not created; He, too, proceeds from the substance of the First, and this substance with its entire perfection is communicated to Him. He, too, springs from the interior of the Father, and is just as perfect a likeness of the Father as is the Second Person. Moreover, if this point is considered essential, He proceeds from the Father with the same necessity.

The reason why the Second Person alone is generated and is called Son, whereas the Third is not, can be accounted for only by the fact that they receive and possess the divine nature and essence in different ways, and that only the Second Person's mode of origin conforms to what we call generation in the created order.

According to the dogma, the most decisive difference between the production of the Second Person and the production of the Third Person is the fact that the former proceeds from one person, and the latter proceeds from two persons. But this alone provides no basis for applying the term generation to the former production rather than to the latter.

If we are to proffer some explanation, we must go more deeply into the matter and uncover the ultimate reason why the Second Person proceeds from one person, whereas the Third Person proceeds from two persons. The Second Person proceeds from the First alone, because He is the expression, the Word, the image of the knowledge which the First Person has of Himself and His essence; the Third Person proceeds from two persons because He is the sigh and the outpouring of the love of the first two persons for each other. The First Person's productivity through His cognition, and in conjunction with the Second Person through His love, must be the ultimate reason not only for the distinction of the persons, but also for all the individual distinctions and further determinations of the persons as well as of their origins. No matter how deeply we may probe

PRODUCTION OF SECOND AND THIRD PERSONS

in our endeavor to establish the conditions which verify the concept of generation, it remains true that the Second Person alone is generated and is alone Son, because He alone is the Word of the First Person; and that the Third Person is not generated and is not Son, because He is not the Word of the First Person.

Thus far nearly all theologians since the time of St. Thomas are in agreement, although they are not all successful in explaining clearly why the concept of generation conforms to the intellectual production and to it alone. Let us try briefly and simply to present here the result of the best investigations into this problem.

Our knowledge of generation is derived in the first instance from the material world, that is, from living beings, whether plants, animals, or men. We distinguish generation as the highest species of formation. We apply the term formation in general to all production, all bringing-forth, interior or exterior, whether it is accomplished by nature or by art and the exercise of free will, so far as all production makes known to us, or bears witness to, the power or art of the acting subject. But we reserve the term generation for the highest kind of production, whereby the generating being gives evidence of itself in the most perfect manner, expresses itself. Generation takes place when a living being—for only such is capable of generation—gives origin from its own substance to another living being that is like to the generating being, and bears the latter's essence and nature in itself; the generating being fashions from its own substance an image like to itself, manifests itself exteriorly with its entire nature and perfection, expresses itself exteriorly, and thereby gives witness of itself in the most perfect manner. Thus quite appropriately we define generation as the origin or production of a living being from the substance of another living being *unto* similarity of nature.[1] We do not say merely *in* similarity of nature; for the similarity is not only a necessary element in generation, but is formally the end to which it tends; the self-witness of the generator by means of the generated offspring is achieved only by effecting this similarity. Accordingly the assimilation of the offspring to the generator is always the supreme and principal factor in generation.[2]

[1] "Productio (passiva processio) viventis de vivente coniuncto in similitudinem naturae." By *coniunctio* is meant a connection in the substance which in whole or in part passes from the parent to the offspring.

[2] Here we forbear to translate two brief paragraphs in which Scheeben seeks to establish some sort of etymological connection between the terms

Like nature, which gives witness of itself and expresses itself in its offspring, the mind generates the word in which it expresses its ideas, its knowledge. This is indicated at any rate in Latin, in which the intelligible word, the mental representation of a thing, is called a *conceptus* or *conceptio*. This is true especially of the representation or the mental word in which the intellect knows itself. For in this case the mind forms an image of itself in itself and from itself; it imprints itself in this image. Not only can the cause and exemplar of the image be recognized in the image, which is the case even in animal generation; rather it must recognize itself in the image, which is the cognition itself. Consequently the mind mirrors itself, attests and expresses itself in its image in an incomparably higher manner than nature can mirror and express itself in its products. Further, we have here not a dead image, but a living image, as the cognition itself is something alive; an image which participates in the spiritual nature of its generator, since it, too, is spiritual; lastly, an image that proceeds from the innermost depths of the spirit, since it is brought forth from the spirit's innermost vital faculty as a likeness of its substance.

In many respects, therefore, this intellectual generation in its ideal form is not only equal to but superior to animal generation. Espe-

---

signifying to generate and to bear witness, with a resulting play on words that cannot be imitated in English. The reader who understands German may be interested in Scheeben's exposition, which follows.

Es ist zwar keineswegs ausgemacht, dass das erzeugende Zeugen und das bezeugende Zeugen ursprünglich und etymologisch zusammenhängen. Vielmehr hat wohl die Grundform von ersterem (Wurzel tuh, duco) die Bedeutung von ziehen, die des letzteren (W. dih, in dico, δείκνυμαι) die Bedeutung von zeigen. Wie aber die Begriffe "hervorziehen" oder "erzeugen" (genau = producere) und "bezeigen" oder "bezeugen" tatsächlich in derselben Lautbildung "zeugen" zusammengeflossen sind: so fügen sich auch die beiden Begriffe harmonisch zusammen, um die vollkommenste Art des Erzeugens zu charakterisieren, und deuten zugleich an, wie dieselbe auf geistigem Gebiet zu denken ist.

Die Verwandtschaft der beiden Begriffe weist nämlich bei näherer Betrachtung eine merkwürdige Wechselbeziehung der geistigen Welt mit der sinnlichen auf. Man bezeugt eigentlich nur Gedanken, wie man auch nur Gedanken ausspricht. Und in der Tat legt auch das zeugende Wesen in der sinnlichen Welt nicht so sehr Zeugnis ab von seiner konkreten, individuellen Natur, als von der göttlichen Idee der Natur im allgemeinen, welche sich in jedem Individuum dieser Natur offenbart und bezeugt und sich von dem zeugenden zu dem gezeugten Individuum fortbezeugt. Gleichwohl sagen wir nicht, dass die göttliche Idee die Individuen zeuge, da sie anderer Natur ist als diese and sie deshalb auch nicht aus ihrem Schosse hervorbringt.

cially the attestation of the generator is formally more perfect because it makes the generator known and also contains in itself the very knowledge. But, as regards the reality and subsistence of the generated likeness, it remains far behind material generation; for its product is not a substantial product to which the substantial nature of the generator can be transmitted, and hence is not a new, subsistent being. So it is hard to decide in which of the two the notion of generation is more truly and perfectly verified. In both cases, in both material and spiritual nature, there is an expression, an attestation, of nature in its likeness, and hence the most proper and characteristic manifestation of nature. But in the one case generation can result only in a real likeness, in the other only in a mental likeness. Should we not then find the very ideal of generation, the most perfect generation of all, if we could point to a production whose product would be at once the intelligible and the real likeness, and so in an eminent sense a spoken and speaking image of the generator?

In God, in whom all that is found scattered in creatures is one, faith reveals to us the production of the Word from the substance of the Father. This Word is an intelligible image of its principle, because it proceeds from the latter's cognition and manifests it. It is likewise a real, substantial, personal image, because the cognition and also the object of the cognition, the essence of the First Person, which is really one with the cognition, are expressed and impressed in this Word. The Second Person in the Godhead is produced because the First Person wills to utter and attest Himself, to express and manifest His nature. The Second Person receives the Father's nature in order to exhibit and manifest it in Himself. What then is to prevent us from saying that He is truly generated, nay, that His generation is the perfect ideal of all generation, and that, in accord with the words of Holy Scripture, all fatherhood in heaven and on earth is so called after the generating fatherhood of His principle? [3] Although we transfer the notion of generation to God from creatures, since we form it from creatures, we perceive that the object of this concept in its purest, most perfect, and ideal sense is found originally in God alone, and therefore the corresponding production of creatures merits the name of generation only in a secondary and partial sense. [4]

[3] "I bow my knees to the Father of our Lord Jesus Christ, of whom all paternity in heaven and earth is named" (Eph. 3:14 f.).
[4] St. Thomas, in *Summa contra Gentiles*, IV, c.11, proceeds much as we

But does the name and concept of generation apply only to the Second Person? Does it not apply also to the production of the Third Person? No, it does not belong to the Third Person, because we have just shown from the characteristic nature of the first production that it can and must be called generation. The first production is generation because it is the utterance of a word and the impression of an image; if this characteristic does not pertain to the second production, it is obviously not generation. In point of fact, the second production in God takes place not through cognition but through love. Hence it produces not a word, but an aspiration of love; not

---

have done; he develops the nature of the Son's production and all that Sacred Scripture says of it from the idea of the *Verbum*. Then he goes on to explain the scriptural expressions by which the various phases of generation, which is absolutely simple in God, are illustrated by the successive moments of generation in creatures. The entire chapter merits quotation here, but to save space we shall give only the concluding section.

"We must note that what is generated is said to be conceived, so long as it remains in the parent. God's Word is begotten of God in such wise that He does not depart from the Father but remains in Him. Therefore God's Word may rightly be said to be conceived of God. This is the reason why the Wisdom of God affirms: 'The depths were not as yet, and I was already conceived' (Prov. 8:24).

"There is, however, this difference between the conception of God's Word and the material conception which we observe in creatures: at the moment of conception and all during the period of gestation the offspring has not yet attained the ultimate perfection that will enable it to subsist by itself apart from its parent. Hence in the corporal generation of an animal the conception must be distinct from its birth, when, having been brought forth from the womb, it is locally separated from its parent. But the Word of God, even though remaining in God the speaker, is perfect, subsistent, and distinct from God the speaker; no local separation is required, for the sole distinction is that of relationship. Accordingly in the generation of God's Word conception and birth are identical; and so, after stating, 'I was already conceived,' Wisdom continues: 'Before the hills I was brought forth' (verse 25).

"Further, since conception and birth in corporal things are accompanied by movement, some succession must take place in them; for the term of conception is the existence of the conceived being in the conceiving being, and the term of birth is the separate existence of the offspring apart from the parent. Hence in corporal nature the being that is in process of conception does not yet exist, and while parturition is taking place the offspring that is being brought forth is not distinct from the parent. But the conception and birth of an intelligible word is free from motion and succession; hence it exists at the instant of conception, and has a separate existence at the instant of parturition; just as an object is illuminated the very instant light shines upon it, since there is no succession in the diffusion of light. And what is thus observed in our intelligible word is eminently applicable to God's Word, not only because His conception and birth are in the intelan image of a person reflecting upon Himself, but a pledge that binds together two loving persons, the original and the image. Therefore it does not attest what the producing person is, or the nature which the latter possesses; if it attests anything, it is the love and unity in which the two persons, who as original and image possess the same nature, conform.

Of course the divine nature is communicated in the second production just as well as in the first. But it is not communicated *per modum naturae*, as some theologians aptly remark; it is not communicated in the way in which nature as nature is communicated. Nature as nature operates only in attesting what it is in itself, in expressing, irradiating the likeness in which it manifests itself. Spiritual nature

---

lectual order, but because both are coincident with eternity, in which priority and succession are impossible. Thus after Wisdom had stated, 'Before the hills I was brought forth,' the text continues, in order to preclude any notion that He did not exist while He was being brought forth: 'When He prepared the heavens, I was present' (verse 27); for, whereas in the carnal generation of animals the offspring is first conceived, then brought forth, and finally stands in the presence of the parent, associating with the latter as a distinct being, all these phases must be undertood as simultaneous in divine generation; for the Word of God is simultaneously conceived, brought forth, and present.

"Again, what is brought forth issues from the womb. For a similar reason the generation of God's Word, which is called birth to indicate His perfect distinction from His Father, is called birth from the womb, according to Psalm 109:3: 'From the womb before the day star I begot Thee.' However, the distinction of the Word from the speaker does not prevent the Word from existing in the speaker. Hence, just as the Word is said to be begotten or brought forth from the womb, to indicate His distinct existence, so to show that this distinction does not exclude the Word from existence in the speaker, revelation assures us that He 'is in the bosom of the Father' (John 1:18).

"Finally, we must advert to the fact that the carnal generation of animals is effected by an active and a passive principle. The father has an active, the mother a passive part. Hence for the procreation of offspring the father has one function, the mother a different one: the father confers nature and species on the progeny, whereas the mother, as passive and receptive principle, conceives and gives birth. Procession is predicated of the Word inasmuch as God understands Himself; but the divine intelligence involves no passive element, but is wholly active, so to speak, since the divine intellect is not in potency but exclusively in act. Therefore in the generation of God's Word there is no maternal function, but only a paternal function. Hence the various functions which pertain to the father and the mother in carnal generation, are all attributed by Scripture to the Father in His generation of the Word: the Father is said to give life to the Son (cf. John 5:26), to conceive Him, and to bring Him forth."

operates as nature only in its cognition by which it reflects and expresses itself in itself; and we, too, when we describe the nature of spiritual beings, call them intellectual, not volitional beings. Thus the divine nature acts precisely as nature only in the utterance of its personal Word.

The Third Person, on the other hand, receives the divine nature with just as great natural necessity as the Second does, and in this sense receives it naturally, but not *per modum naturae*, not in the manner and way of nature as such, but in the manner and way of the will, of love, of donation. The nature is not communicated to Him in order to be represented in Him. Rather, the first two persons, the begetter and the begotten, in virtue of their mutual love take their nature in order to deposit it in the Third Person as the pledge of their love, and thereby to crown their union with each other. Thus, to be sure, they produce this person *in* the similarity of their nature, not however *into* the similarity, but rather into the fellowship of their nature, that is, into the copossession of their nature, which is given to the Third Person through love. In generation, too, a communication of nature takes place. But in generation the communication is a secondary factor or a consequence of the directly intended manifestation of the nature in a witness. On the other hand, a manifestation of the nature takes place also in the production of the Holy Ghost; but it is only a secondary factor or a consequence of the directly intended communication of the nature to a Third Person.[5]

We can say briefly and to the point: the Holy Ghost is not generated, because He proceeds from the heart of the Father and the Son, but not from the bosom of the Father. For the infinite fullness of love in God is what the heart is in sentient beings, while His cognition is the fount of light from which He irradiates His very likeness. We cannot be induced to regard the fruitfulness of God's love as generation any more than we can associate the heart with human generation as its principle. We shall later take up the question whether we can discover in creatures a production from the heart which would correspond to the production of the Third Person in God.

[5] For other insufficient or inconclusive reasons which several Fathers and theologians suggest to explain why the second divine procession is not generation, cf. Petavius, *De Trinitate*, VII, c.13.

Accordingly the Second Person in God is truly generated, in the fullest and highest sense of the word; and this generation is peculiar to Him, belongs to Him alone, not only in opposition to creatures, but also in opposition to the Third Person. And so without further qualification we are able to apply to Him a name which adequately expresses and clearly illustrates His procession as that of a true, independent suppositum. This fact supplies us at the same time with substantive terms which designate His being as well as that of His principle. The product of true generation we call son, especially when the nature communicated to the product is rational and thereby confers the dignity of personality. The term "Son" designates the first product in God as a suppositum, and likewise as a personal suppositum, as a person. And since the First Person is perceived to be subsistent only when He appears as the generative principle of the Son, the name Father is just as fitting and significant for Him as the name Son is for the Second Person.

17. The Third Person as Spirit, Breath of the Father and the Son, and His Production as Spiration

Shall we be able to find for the production of the Third Person in God a term which indicates His hypostatic and personal character as decisively and characteristically as the other production is characterized by the term generation?

No; we have no expression for the second production which is perfectly parallel to the term generation, that is, which with equal clarity manifests the product as hypostatic and personal. The reason for this is easy to perceive. We nowhere observe among creatures, from which we should have to derive such an expression, a naturally effected production of a similar, living suppositum except by way of generation; or at least—if the thought should occur that there is an essential distinction between certain modes of reproduction in plants and lower animals and real generation—we observe no such production as would resemble the second production in God according to its specific character.[6]

[6] Our own opinion is that one instance can be found in human nature of a production of one person from another, effected by supernatural intervention, which is remarkably analogous to the production of the Third Person in God. Actually, however, revelation has not derived the hypostatic name of the Third Person from this production. Moreover, the novelty and delicate

In our efforts to find a personal, concrete designation for the Third Person, we must apparently get along as best we may. There is the further difficulty that those designations which revelation and the Church usually apply to the Third Person as roughly corresponding to the terms Son and generation, seem on account of their apparent indefiniteness and generality to suggest only a very vague portrayal of His Person, and seem to be assigned to Him arbitrarily. The name "Spirit" or "Holy Spirit" can quite rightly be attributed to the two other divine Persons also, since they possess an eminently spiritual and holy nature. The term "procession" indicates in general any origin whatever, personal as well as impersonal, procession by way of generation no less than procession by way of volition. Hence it has no advantage over the other two terms "aspiration" and "donation" which we previously declared unsatisfactory; on the whole it gives us no definite idea, to say nothing of a clear and vivid idea, of the origin of the Third Person in the Godhead. In spite of all this we hope to be able to show that these expressions, notwithstanding their seeming indefiniteness, and indeed partly on this very account, possess such elasticity and pregnancy that all the notions which we have thus far gained concerning the Third Person and His procession may be concentrated in them. And we hope to show that these notions supply a sketch of those expressions which, though less sharply outlined, is all the richer in coloring and vividness.

Before all else we must observe that the word "spirit" in established usage means a subsistent being, a person, and that the word "procession" can indicate the origin of a person at least as appropriately as it can the origin of any other object. Accordingly, as far as concreteness of terminology is concerned, we are better able to deal with these expressions than with the terms sigh and pledge, spiration and donation. But how can they be employed as characteristic, specific names of the Third Person and His procession?

As has been remarked, God the Father is a spirit and God the Son is a spirit, that is, immaterial and intellectual being. All three persons

---

nature of the matter deter us from attaching too great weight to this analogy. Accordingly we are for the present omitting this notion of ours, and offer it to the judicious reader in an appendix at the close of Part I, without claiming too much for what is after all only a personal view.

are spirits in this sense, because they are God; for "God is a spirit" [7] and the most pure spirit. The Third Person Himself could not be a spirit if the persons from whom He proceeds were not spirit. He is but Spirit of Spirit. "The Holy Spirit is from both as Spirit from Spirit: for God is Spirit," says St. Epiphanius.[8] Thus far considered, the term does not denote any characteristic of the Third Person, nor does it in any way touch upon His relative position to the Father and the Son.

The first step toward specification we find in St. Augustine, who follows St. Ambrose in this matter. As St. Augustine points out, since the term is appropriate for the first two persons, it suits the Third Person in a special way because He is the common bond of the two.[9] This point becomes clearer if we proceed further and take into consideration the fact that the Third Person is the expression and seal of the spiritual unity which the Father and the Son have in each other as one spirit, and that the absolute spirituality of the other persons is most distinctly expressed in Him and culminates in Him as in its summit.

But even so the term does not indicate with sufficient clarity the proper, relative character of the Third Person; nor will it be of any aid to us in our quest so long as it signifies no more to us than an immaterial being.

The word "spirit," as applied to God and generally to immaterial beings, is a transferred term. If we use the term, as we have just done, to designate God simply as an immaterial substance, it is transferred from sensible, aeriform substances, so far as these are distinguished from crassly material substances by their lightness, elasticity, and invisibility; these qualities supply us with some image of the nature and character of immaterial substances. As applied to the Third Person, especially when He is called not simply Spirit but "Spirit of the Father and the Son," it has another origin. This origin, however, is connected with the previous derivation; in this case it is transferred not from aeriform substances, but from those

[7] John 4:24.

[8] *Haereses*, 30, c.4, no. 7. (*Haeres.*, 74, c.7, PG, XLII, 488.)

[9] "Ut ex nomine, quod utrique convenit, utriusque communio significetur, vocatur donum amborum Spiritus Sanctus" (*De Trinitate*, V, c.11 fin.); "quia communis est ambobus, id vocatur ipse proprie, quod ambo communiter" (*ibid.*, XV, c.19 fin.).

which stream forth from the interior of living beings as sigh and breath.[10] This derivation is more obvious in the Greek πνεῦμα and the Latin *spiritus* than in German [or in English]. The German word *Geist* [spirit] is only the more elegant and flexible term for *Odem* [breath], which is not used so much in the transferred sense.

Thus understood, the name "Spirit" doubtlessly expresses the relation of the Third Person to the others. "Spiritus alicuius aspirantis est, ergo ad Patrem Filiumque refertur," says St. Fulgentius.[11] However, thus taken it appears to be merely a concrete diction for the name "Sigh of love" (*aspiratio*), which, as we have previously noted, corresponds to the Third Person as the name "Verbum" does to the Second Person. Nevertheless, a more accurate investigation will show that its force and meaning are far richer than this, and that it is not much inferior to the name "Son" for the Second Person.

As the name "Son" gathers up and includes all that is implied in the terms "word" and "image," so the name "Spirit" comprises what is contained in the terms "aspiration," "pledge," and "gift." As a word is in itself a witness, but appears as truly generated and as a person only when it is at the same time a real image of its generator, so aspiration is a sigh of the heart. But the sigh of the heart will signify to us the procession of a person in God, as generation does,

---

[10] That the term "spirit" as applied to the Third Person is really derived from man's breath is evident from the constant usage of the corresponding words πνεῦμα and *spiritus* in Scripture and the Fathers. The Fathers find that this is the case especially in the Savior's action of breathing upon the apostles: our Lord intended to symbolize not only the external procession, but also the internal procession of the Third Person from the Son and the Father. "Christ breathed Him [the Holy Spirit] into His disciples by a bodily action," says St. Cyril of Alexandria, "thereby showing that, as the breath issues corporally from the mouth of man, so the Spirit, who proceeds from Him, issues from the divine substance in a manner befitting the deity" (*In Ioannem*, IX, 810; *PG*, LXXIV, 257). In another passage he asserts even more categorically that the Son of God emphatically represented the nature of the Holy Spirit proceeding from Him in His divinity by the exhalation of His human breath (*De Trinitate dialogi*, IV, 532; *PG*, LXXV, 908). And so he could remark, relative to the Holy Spirit's name: "Give the name Holy Spirit to that divine person who issues forth substantially from God the Father through the Son, and who in the symbol of breath exhaled from the mouth makes known to us His own proper mode of subsistence" (*ibid.*, II, 423; *PG*, LXXV, 724).

[11] *De Trinitate*, c.6.

only when we perceive in it a real outpouring of the divine substance and life.

When we wish to express the intimacy of union between two persons, we say that they are of one spirit, or even that they are one spirit. We mean by this that by their love and affection they live for each other and in each other. For spirit here means life itself, which in the animal kingdom is manifested especially by means of the breath. This unity of life and spirit rests on the fact that the lover does everything for the beloved as for himself, and all that the beloved suffers and feels he regards as if he suffered and felt it himself. It rests also on the fact that the lover transforms himself, as far as his affection goes, into the beloved; this is what is called the ecstasy of love. But this affectual ecstasy of love, this affectual oneness of life that is characteristic of lovers, tends by natural inclination to become a real union.[12] Lovers seek in all reality to pour out their mutual life into each other, and to fuse their lives into a single life. The most perfect and adequate expression of this striving must be sought, in the created order, where union in love has its most natural and real basis and is manifested in the purest and tenderest manner. The child on the bosom of its mother, who has carried it under her heart, from whom it received its life, and from whose breast it still continues to draw that same life—wherein does it give more lively expression to its intimate love than in the kisses which it presses on her mouth; and what does the mother's heart long for more than once again to breathe her life into the fruit of her womb through her kiss?

In this act the desired unity of life is brought about in the most perfect and real manner possible through the overflowing of the breath of life and the flame of love burning in it from one heart to the other, from one soul to the other.[18] In the meeting and fusing of their life-breath their hearts and souls meet and fuse into one life,

[12] Says St. Augustine (*De Trin.*, VIII, c.10): "Amor est iunctura quaedam, duo aliqua copulans vel copulare appetens." "Quod dicit copulans," comments St. Thomas (*Summa*, Ia IIae, q.28, a.1), "refertur ad unionem affectus, sine qua non est amor; quod vero dicit, copulare intendens, pertinet ad unionem realem."

[18] "Ii qui se osculantur, non sunt labiorum praelibatione contenti, sed spiritum suum sibi videntur infundere" (St. Ambrose, *De Isaac et anima*, c.3; cf. St. Francis de Sales, *The Love of God*, Bk. I, especially chap. 9).

one spirit. The simple sigh by which lovers give expression to their
love even while separated from each other, becomes a full, living
surrender; and the surrender by which they can belong to each other
even at a distance, becomes a mutual, living fusion when they
meet.

When we thus consider the sigh as the breath of life whereby
the oneness in life which love strives for is achieved and expressed
in a kiss, its import must appear far richer and more striking than
when we see in it only an aspiration of love. Regarded in this way
it will furnish us with a much more concrete and vigorous analogue
for the Third Person in the Godhead.

Obviously we may and ought to regard it in its significance as an
analogue of the Third Person. The holy Fathers are fond of referring to Him by the charming terms "kiss of the Father and the
Son; most sweet but secret kiss," as St. Bernard says so tenderly.[14]
If anywhere there is not only oneness of love but also oneness of
life between two persons, if anywhere two lovers are of one spirit
and are one spirit, surely the Father and the Son are such in their
one divine nature. Here, in fact, there are not two lives which melt
into one; there is only one life and one heart. Therefore the "kiss"
cannot be merely a vehicle, a medium to procure unity of life; it
must be its expression. Hence the Father and the Son do not pour
their breath of life into each other by their "kiss," but from the
interior of their common heart they pour it out into a third person,
in whom the oneness of their love and life is manifested.

As the Third Person receives His essence only through the outpouring of the breath of life, He is nothing but this breath itself.
As such He is obviously more than a mere aspiration of love, and
more than a mere pledge. He is both together in most vital unity,
just as the Son as Son is both Word and image of the Father. He is
an aspiration to which is really given all that the lovers bear in their
heart, and a pledge and bond which is derived from the innermost
heart of the lovers, and which, along with the aspiration of love,
flows forth from that heart in living flood. Further, since the breath
of life proceeding from the Father and the Son clearly involves an
outpouring, a communication of their own life, the Third Person
straightway appears as bearer of the life which is poured forth
into Him, as recipient and proprietor of the life, and hence in most

[14] *Sermones in cantica*, VIII, 2.

concrete fashion as an independent hypostasis and person, just as the Son, who is at once Word and image, is perceived to be generated, and therefore a subsistent, living being. Accordingly the name "Breath or Spirit of the Father and the Son" is at once the richest, the most vivid, and the most concrete that we can find or even may desire for the Third Person in God. The terms "Breath" and "Spirit" are, strictly understood, identical; in fact, Greek and Latin have only the one word. In general we prefer the name "Spirit," because the oneness of life in God, which is exhibited in the Third Person, is wholly spiritual and immaterial, and because in any case the word "spirit" is in common use to designate the possessor of spiritual life, although for that very reason its relative significance, which must be retained, is not emphasized so much.

The objection may be raised that the term "spirit," in its strict acceptance as breath of life, does not, like the name "son," suggest a hypostasis, a proprietor of nature and life, since with men it is only a sign and vehicle of life and the unity of life, but is not this life and does not possess it. In point of fact a man's breath of life is not in itself, like his son, a hypostatic image of the corresponding divine hypostasis. But that does not prevent it, when transferred to God, from designating the corresponding divine hypostasis almost as strikingly and concretely as the name Son designates the other person. Among men, too, the breath appears in some respect as bearer of life. To be sure, this is only in so far as it is a vehicle of life. Hence it does not possess life in itself and for itself, but only in order to convey life from the person from whom it proceeds to the other person with whom unity of life is to be established. But as soon as the figure is transferred to God, we see that the breath cannot be bearer of life as a mere vehicle; it is the outpouring of an existing, infinitely intimate unity of life between the Father and the Son, which requires no real intermediary, and does not even admit one. The life-stream in God is not transmitted from the Father to the Son, or vice versa, through their breath, but passes from the unity of the Father and the Son over to their breath, in order to terminate therein. Evidently, therefore, God's breath is a bearer of the divine life as its recipient and proprietor, and is seen to be such without further consideration as soon as it is regarded as the breath of God or of divine persons.

This will become clearer presently: we have still to discuss the most concrete of all the designations for the procession of the Holy Spirit.

As the term "generation" corresponds to the name "Son," so the term "spiration," *spiratio*, ἐκπνευσις, corresponds to the name "Spirit," understood as the proper name of the last proceeding person, to designate His procession. The Third Person is Spirit in a special sense, because He is breathed forth, spirated, because He is the *spiramen* and *flamen* of the Father and the Son. But we must understand this breathing (*spirare*) in a richer, fuller sense than before. Previously we regarded the breathing only as aspiration, as simple manifestation of the affection of love, and in this sense we declared it insufficient to symbolize and express the production of a new, living being. But now we regard it in its complete and full sense, in the entire meaning which breathing has in animal life. When inhaled, the breath is the propelling force; when exhaled, it is the outpouring of the animal life that surges and swells within the animal. Thus it is a striking representation of the overflow, the communication of life. Understood thus in its most pregnant sense, the term "spiration" suggests the procession of the Third Person as a true communication of life, and consequently as a personal procession. We perceive that the Third Person proceeds not from the bosom, but from the heart, of the other two persons; their entire life is conveyed in their love and from their love over to the Third Person.

Although among created beings exhalation never brings forth a new being as generation does, and although in this respect it is not as definite a figure as generation, it furnishes us with a more graphic image, owing to the richness and vividness of its connotation. Moreover, since it is a most convincing manifestation and natural sign of life, we can easily conceive that the infinitely powerful outbreathing of the divine life produces a living being as well as generation does. In breathing, we fancy we perceive how one life wakens another, how the flame of life flashes from one being to another, penetrates it, and ignites it. And does not Sacred Scripture itself in a number of passages employ the same figure to illustrate the animation of lifeless matter and thereby the production of a living being? [15]

[15] The animation of the first man at his creation is thus represented: "The Lord God formed man of the slime of the earth, and breathed into his face the breath of life, and man became a living soul" (Gen. 2:7). This notion is more graphically developed in Ezech. 37:4-10: "Ye dry bones," God bids

Accordingly we believe we can maintain without misgivings that the term spiration, taken in its full implication, should be placed on a par with the term generation, as far as concreteness and clarity are concerned. We need no longer say that we have only the general, indefinite term *processio* for the procession of the Holy Spirit; we have a quite definite, specific, characteristic expression that is deeply significant.

Even the general term, procession, in its special application to the Holy Spirit, is not so vague and indefinite as is commonly supposed. It has a pregnant sense that is unique, and stresses the most significant point in the term spiration.

The word *procedere* ("to proceed") means primarily a movement from one place to another. Although every production, including generation, involves a procession and movement, inasmuch as it is a drawing forth of the product from its principle, the analogy of movement applies to the spiration of the Holy Ghost in a special way. He is movement in His very being, as it were, just as love is. The irradiation of the Father's cognition in the Word and the imprinting of His nature in the Son rather connote the repose of terminated activity, as is proper to their relationship of Father and Son. But in the production of the Holy Ghost they commune with each other, move and live in each other; there is an eternal surrendering and accepting in the most literal sense, an infinitely powerful living breath which emanates from one to the other and from both, the mighty pulsation of an infinite heart which surges with the supreme ardor of affection, the blazing flame of an infinite fire of love. There is, in brief, the intensity, the activity, the effusion and the torrent of love in which Father and Son fuse and pour forth their nature into the Holy Ghost. This is why the Holy Ghost is symbolized in the roaring wind that shook the house of the apostles on Pentecost, and in the darting, flaming tongues that hovered over the heads of the apostles.[16] This is why the Savior compares Him

---

the Prophet say, "hear the word of the Lord. Thus saith the Lord God to these bones: Behold, I will send spirit into you, and you shall live." And when the Prophet gave the Lord's command, "Come, spirit, from the four winds and blow upon these slain, and let them live again," it came forthwith: "the spirit came into them [i.e. the bones, which God had clothed with sinews, flesh, and skin] and they lived; and they stood up upon their feet, an exceeding great army."

[16] Acts 2:2 f.

to a brimming stream of living water.[17] "What is the meaning of the expression: He proceeds?" asks St. Chrysostom. "To avoid the term generation, so as not to call the Holy Spirit Son, Scripture says: The Holy Spirit 'who proceedeth from the Father.' [18] Scripture represents Him as proceeding like water that gushes forth from a fountain, as is said of Paradise: 'a river went out of the place of pleasure': [19] He proceeds, He issues forth. The Father is called the fountain of living water by the prophet Jeremias: 'They have forsaken Me, the fountain of living water.' [20] . . . But what is it that proceeds? The Holy Spirit. How? Like water from a fountain." [21] In proof of this last statement St. Chrysostom adduces the Savior's words: "He that believeth in Me, as the Scripture saith: Out of his belly shall flow rivers of living water." Whereupon the Evangelist adds: "Now this He said of the Spirit which they should receive who believed in Him." [22]

Therefore when we say that the Holy Ghost proceeds from the Father and the Son, we mean not only that He has His origin from them, but that this origin takes place in the manner of an out-gushing movement, which is accomplished in the effusion of love and the donation of life from the Father and the Son to the Holy Ghost.[23]

[17] John 7:38 f.
[18] John 15:26.
[19] Gen. 2:10.
[20] Jer. 2:13.
[21] Hom. *De Sancto Spiritu* ("Heri a nobis"); *PG*, LII, 814 f.
[22] John 7:38 f.
[23] No one, so far as we know, has discussed the import of *procedere*, as predicated of the Third Person in distinction to the origin of the Second Person, so thoroughly and exhaustively as St. Albert the Great, *Summa tract.*, VII, q. 31, membr. 4. Indeed, he is practically the only author who professedly sets out to treat the question fully. For this reason, notwithstanding some heaviness of style, we are here setting down the main points of his doctrine.
"It is characteristic of a spirit, whether corporeal or incorporeal, always to proceed. Wherefore, even according to philosophers, an incorporeal spirit, when it proceeds from an intellect that acts through the will, conveys to its effects the forms of the active intelligence; for example, the spirit of an artificer which proceeds from his mind conveys, while it proceeds, the forms of art to the artificer's hands, to his axe and hatchet, and to the stones and beams he is working with. This is the bearing of the statement in Wisdom 1:7: 'The Spirit of the Lord hath filled the whole world, and that which containeth all things'; and in Job 26:13 we read: 'His Spirit hath adorned the heavens'; and Psalm 32:6: 'By the word of the Lord the heavens were established; and all the power of them by the Spirit of His mouth.' Similarly it is characteristic of love, whether spiritual or carnal, always to proceed

The pregnant sense of streaming forth which we may and must assign to the Latin *procedere*, since it is parallel to *spirari*, is implied more clearly and definitely in the Greek term which corresponds to *procedere* in the Creed. For ἐκπορεύεσθαι is etymologically the equivalent of "to set out from." Hence it is never used by the Greek Fathers for the procession of the Son, which they designate rather as προϊέιν, that is, "to step forth from." With the Greeks only this προϊέιν, as regards etymology and general meaning, is parallel to *procedere*, whereas ἐκπορεύεσθαι is a specific term for the procession of the Holy Spirit, and in Latin would be rendered more or less by *emitti* or *emanare*.

Of course the emphasis placed on the infinite movement discerned in the Holy Spirit and His procession is not incompatible with the eternal repose reigning therein. The profoundest peace rules in God, and the most untroubled happiness. For all its energy, that movement is not violent or restless, because it is a tranquil motion of love which

---

and flow and never to remain still. For this reason Chrysostom says that when the Holy Spirit has entered into the heart of a man, He flows more copiously than any fountain and does not stand still, but progresses. And John 7:38 f.: 'He that believeth in Me, as the Scripture saith: Out of his belly shall flow rivers of living water.' And the Evangelist adds: 'Now this He said of the Spirit.'

"And so Dionysius says that divine love causes ecstasy, that is, transports: for it transports the lover into the beloved and does not allow him to remain in himself. Hence even grammarians say that the verb *amo* [I love] is a word indicating impetuous transition. Therefore, since the Holy Spirit is a Spirit and is spirated love, it is proper for Him simply to proceed; while it is not proper for one who is generated to proceed, but to exist in the nature received.

"Hence the solution of the first objection is obvious: Procession signifies diffusion and, as it were, movement to another place, which is not implied in generation, and so generation is not simply procession, but a certain kind of procession. On the other hand, spiration, although it is a specific procession like generation, is nevertheless simply procession: for the proper act of a spirit and of love is to proceed. We willingly concede that procession from one or from two does not affect the notion of procession. As for the alleged similarity to generation, which is a transit from a male to a female, the example proves nothing and is very much out of place in a question where all is purity, . . . and surely it seems rash to think or believe that the spirating power of the Son is related to the spirating power of the Father like the female and male faculties in generation. Hence the objection proves nothing.

"Let us turn to our question: Is procession predicated equivocally or univocally? If the term is unqualified, it indicates local motion and voluntary motion. Wherefore even animals, when moved by appetite, are said, in *De*

is not in feverish quest of its object and its end, but eternally possesses and enjoys both; and because the movement is at the same
time a most intimate and close embrace, an embrace in which is
found the imperturbable peace (*pax imperturbabilis*) of St. Bernard.[24]

18. CONTINUATION. FURTHER EXPLANATION OF THE HOLY SPIRIT'S NAMES

St. Augustine uses a striking phrase for the specific characteriza-
tion of the Holy Spirit's procession: "Exiit non quomodo natus, sed
quomodo datus." [25] We have little inclination to contest the correctness of this statement, especially as we have made its underlying
thought the basis of our entire deduction. However, we do think,
as is clear from all that has been said thus far, that it does not supply
an exhaustive, adequate account of our object. Its value would be
depreciated still more if we interpreted the *datus* as *dandus creaturis*,

---

anima, III, to move with a processive motion. To proceed simply by such
motion befits the Holy Spirit, because love and spirit proceed voluntarily,
and, so to speak, processively. Thus understood, procession is not attributed
to the Son except in a qualified sense. But if procession is taken in a sense
similar to the process of an effect from a cause, as Dionysius says in the *Liber
de divinis nominibus*, chap. 4, namely, that things which are multiple in their
processes are one in their principle, then the term procession is employed in
an extended sense, and befits both the generation of the Son and the spiration
of the Holy Spirit; and so there is no reason why it should not befit the Son
in one sense and the Holy Spirit in another, and why the sense in which it
is said of a son in created nature, in which priority and posteriority are possible, should not prevail over the sense in which it is said of the Holy Spirit;
for procession by generation looks toward being, whereas procession by love
in created nature looks only toward well-being. But all this is meaningless in
God, in whom nothing is principal or secondary: just as the Son has His being
from the Father by generation, so the Holy Spirit has His being from the
Father and the Son by spiration. Therefore procession thus understood
equally befits the Son and the Holy Spirit, but in different manners."
Since Albert the Great wrote his *Summa* toward the end of his life, and
hence at least part of it after the year 1274, in which the question of the
Holy Spirit's procession was taken up with the Greeks at the Council of
Lyons [cf. Denz., 461, 463], we may well assume that Albert derived his
more profound notion of procession from these deliberations. Thus the
much-contested supposition that Albert personally took part in that Council
would receive confirmation.—Albert's presence at Lyons is now generally
regarded as demonstrated. [Tr.]
[24] Cf. *Sermo* 23, 16; "Deus tranquillus tranquillat omnia." [Tr.]
[25] *De Trinitate*, V, c.14.

meaning that the Holy Spirit does not proceed as *natus* because His origin is such that He can be given to creatures, and actually is given to them in time. In this case the interior nature of the procession would not be illustrated; its interior character would be merely suggested in a relation to the external world based on that interior character. Only when we pursue and exploit this suggestion, and discover the reason why the Holy Spirit is termed *dabilis* or *dandus* will it yield us a satisfactory explanation.

This reason is that the Holy Spirit has the character of gift also in His eternal relationship to the Father and the Son; He can be regarded in a special sense as the gift of God to the creature, that is, as the supreme gift and the fountainhead of all other gifts, only because He is the outpouring of the mutual love of the Father and the Son. The temporal giving of the Holy Spirit to creatures must be regarded in a sense as the prolongation of the eternal giving from which He Himself proceeds; we could not speak of an outpouring of the Holy Spirit upon creatures were He not essentially an outpouring of the divine love and the divine life. The Father and the Son surrender their nature to the Holy Spirit out of love, and give Him to each other and possess Him in common as the pledge of their love. Therefore, even prescinding from His relation to the outside world, we can and must say that the Holy Spirit "exit non quomodo natus, sed quomodo datus." Of course, if we understand gift in the sense of "a present" (*donum*), and consider the present as a freely offered gift in the ordinary sense, as a gift which the giver can offer or not as he pleases, then the Holy Spirit can be called gift only with reference to creatures.

In the last analysis a gift is essentially an outpouring of love, whether that love is necessary or not. In every act of love and in its every effect, even in necessary love, there is found a certain kind of freedom. This may not always be the freedom of dominion over the act, such as is found in freedom of choice, but at any rate it is the freedom of spontaneity: the lover loves because the object of his love is pleasing to him, and it is this pleasure that impels him to act. In this sense the Scotists say that the spiration of the Holy Spirit, unlike generation, is free, although necessary. Generation, they contend, takes place with natural, physical necessity,[26] which manifests

[26] In material natures natural necessity is involuntary, but in spiritual natures, above all in the divine nature, it is illuminated by the intellect, be-

itself without the intervention of love's complacency and is only accompanied by it; but spiration ensues from the complacency of love and the will, and the necessity of its operation is merely concomitant. Fortified by this subtle distinction, which is worthy of the "Doctor Subtilis" but which is seldom thoroughly understood and hence must be judged cautiously,[27] Scotus takes his stand against St. Thomas, according to whom the Holy Spirit proceeds from the Father and the Son *necessitate naturali*. Bluntly as Scotus here opposes St. Thomas, and vigorously as he is assailed by Thomists and the majority of theologians, in reality both Scotus and St. Thomas appear to say much the same thing. For Scotus does not deny that the necessity with which the Holy Spirit proceeds is rooted in the divine nature; and St. Thomas agrees that the Holy Spirit is produced not by way of nature that unfolds itself involuntarily, without the intervention of the will, but only by love which takes account of no other law than the carrying out of its own impulse and good pleasure.[28]

---

cause these natures are themselves intellectual. Material nature acts unconsciously, following the direction of a higher agent which moves it and which determines the end of its activity. In the generation of the Son, God acts by the light that constitutes His nature; therefore the light does not previously illuminate His operation, so as to hold before Him the advantage and expediency of His act and thereby determine Him to act. It is not the impetus of love, but the need of His nature as such, that seeks expression and determines the necessity of this act.

[27] This view readily inclines to curtailment of the notion of the will's freedom of choice. In fact, the Jansenists appeal to the teaching of Scotus to bolster up their determinist theory. Scotus himself is convinced that he not only refrains from curtailing freedom of choice, but that his view alone can explain it in a manner consistent with the nature of the will. The freedom of choice enjoyed by the will (*libertas arbitrii in arbitrando secundum deliberationem oppositorum*) is, he thinks, no more than an element derived from the liberty found in all acts of the will, which consists in acting out of love for an objective under the guidance of the intellect. *Liberum* is for him equivalent to *voluntarium*. Cf. J. de Rada, *Controversiae inter S. Thomam et Scotum*, I, controv. 13; P. Dechamps, *De haeresi Janseniana*, III, c.22.

[28] Cf. Scotus, *Quaestiones quodlibetales*, q.16, especially the "Additio editoris" at no. 10. Ruiz (*De Trinitate*, disp. 92, sect. 3, nos. 19 f.) calls the spiration of the Holy Spirit an *operatio naturalis*, but expressly declares that this is not *naturalis* in the full sense, as is the generation of the Son. The latter is generated independently of the *voluntas generandi*. Spiration, however, is an "actus spontaneus, libenter, delectabiliter et quasi eligibiliter volitus, procedens a principio se ipsum movente in bonum praesupposita illius cognitione perfectissima."

Like Scotus, his illustrious predecessors in the Franciscan School, Alexander of Hales and St. Bonaventure,[29] had contrasted the *modus procedendi per voluntatem* with *ex natura*, and had further delineated the former as the *modus procedendi per liberalitatem*, through liberality, hence in the form of an open-handed distribution. And in fact we can scarcely describe the sharing impulse which is so characteristic of love, even of necessary love, or its joy in giving, by any other term than liberality. Although the expression readily lends itself to misunderstanding, it contains such a profound kernel of truth that we cannot lightly dismiss it. But if we substitute "loving surrender" or *largitio* for open-handed distribution, and the "sharing impulse" or *largitas* of love for liberality, we have in its pure form the view upheld by St. Francis' disciples, who like their master were quite at home with the mysteries of love; a view which, although more sharply stressed by them, was at bottom the common property of the Catholic schools. The expression would be still more accurate if it connoted that the Holy Spirit proceeds as *donatio*, δωρεά, donation; for on the one hand this indicates more clearly that He is essentially the fruit of a donation and bears the donating love in Himself, and on the other that He is the principle of all love bestowed on creatures.

This view enables us to see quite easily how the Holy Spirit can be understood as and be called *donum* in His eternal relation to the Father and the Son; consequently the statement, "procedit ut datus," as was said above, illustrates this relationship most aptly. Owing to His hypostatic character, the Holy Spirit is the first and the supreme gift, and at the same time the source and end of all other gifts, especially of supernatural gifts, which God confers on His creatures out of love that is absolutely free and gratuitous. The first and highest gift that God bestows on His creatures is the love He showers on them, and hence also the infinite pledge in which this love is embodied. And in this first outpouring of Himself, in which He surges forth with His entire infinite greatness, the torrent of the overflowing divine love rolls forth outside of God in order to flood creatures with the wealth of its gifts. This takes place particularly, as we shall see later, in the bestowal of grace, by which the creature is raised to a participation in God's own life, to a supernatural union with Him, and to the enjoyment of the same delights of beatitude

[29] *In I Sent.*, dist. 10, a. 1, q. 1 et sqq.

which the divine persons possess and enjoy in the Holy Spirit. It is especially in this communication of grace that the Holy Spirit Himself appears as the supreme gift and grace which God confers on His children. In this sense of personal divine love that gives to creatures all good and His entire self in closest union, the Holy Spirit in person is divine grace, *gratia* in the most elevated and perfect meaning of the word, and as such is called *gratia increata*.

But even this loving relationship of the Holy Spirit to creatures, which the term *donum* expresses, is brought out with far greater force and vividness in the all-embracing, significant name "Spirit." As spirit, as breath of God, we behold Him flowing forth from God's heart over creatures, and entwining a living bond about both. We see Him with all the warmth of His affection penetrating the creature, refreshing him, and filling him with ineffable rapture. We behold Him communicating the ardor of His love to creatures; and from the light of the Son from whom He proceeds we see Him transferring to creatures glowing sparks of divine knowledge, and fanning them to brilliant flame. We perceive Him flooding the creature with His own vital energy, freeing him from death and corruption, and filling him with immortal life. We recognize Him finally, in St. Bernard's words, as the *osculum suavissimum* in which God seals the bond of love with the creatures He has favored with His grace.

And so this name is as ineffably sweet and lovable as it is true and expressive; better, it is so sweet and lovable because it is so true and expressive. For, in connoting so strikingly the purest flower of divine love, it gives expression to what is sweetest and most lovable in God; and it does this in so vivid a manner that a more forceful expression is inconceivable. In which of the Third Person's names is He perceived more clearly as the "bliss, the happiness, the beatitude in the Trinity, the delight of the begetter and the begotten," in St. Augustine's words,[30] and therefore the source of all delight for us, than

---

[30] "Ille igitur ineffabilis quidam complexus Patris et Imaginis [Filii] non est sine perfruitione, sine caritate, sine gaudio. Illa ergo dilectio, delectatio, felicitas, sive beatitudo, si tamen aliqua humana voce digne dicitur, usus ab illo [Hilario] appellatus est breviter, et est in Trinitate Spiritus Sanctus, non genitus, sed genitoris genitique suavitas, ingenti largitate atque ubertate perfundens omnes creaturas pro captu earum, ut ordinem suum teneant et locis suis adquiescant" (*De Trin.*, VI, c. 10). Elsewhere (*Contra Maximinum Arian.*, II, c. 16, no. 3) he understands the "oil of gladness" of which Scripture speaks

in the figure of the breath of love and life? This breath, with grateful warmth and refreshing coolness, gently touches and pervades the entire being of Him from whom He proceeds and the being of him to whom He is wafted. And is it not from this name of the Third Person that we best understand why in relation to us He is called the Paraclete, the Comforter, He who with His soft breath cools the fever of our hurts, who like a strong gale raises up the soul bowed down; He in whom the loving paternal heart of God beats against ours and coaxes our timid soul to His fatherly embrace?

But what makes the divine breath of the Father and the Son exquisitely fragrant with heavenly sweetness, what imparts the character of a perfume [31] costly beyond measure, a perfume rising from the fire of the divine love, is the exalted dignity and nobility of those persons who, burning with ardent love, breathe forth the Spirit from their heart; it is further the infinite perfection and purity of the love-fire that consumes these persons; in a word, it is the sanctity of the loving persons and of their love.

Although the Father and the Son are holy—otherwise they could not bring forth anything holy—or rather because they are holy, the Spirit whom they breathe forth is holy in a unique sense. He is the flower and the perfume of the holiness of the Father and the Son, as He is the flower and the apex of their spirituality. Therefore

---

(Ps. 44:8) as meaning the Holy Spirit. St. Ambrose previously had the same idea, which he supports with many scriptural texts (*De Spiritu Sancto*, c. 7 f.).

[31] The Fathers, who after the example of Scripture call the Holy Spirit the oil or ointment flowing from the Father and the Son, thereby signalizing the effluence of the divine love as pleasing, gentle, delightful, are also fond of calling Him the fragrance of the Father and the Son, particularly of the latter. Thus, for example, St. Athanasius remarks: "This unguent is the breath of the Son; he who has the Spirit may say: 'We are the good odor of Christ'" (*Ep. ad Serapionem*, III, 3; PG, XXVI, 628). Again, the substance of the Father and the Son is likened to a perfume from which the fragrance of the Holy Spirit ascends. "The fragrance of perfumes," says St. Cyril of Alexandria, "which is carried to our nostrils, proceeds from the aromatic substances whose strength it has received. . . . In some such fashion, or even to a greater extent, you should think of God and the Holy Spirit. For He is, as it were, the living, all-pervading fragrance of God, and transmits what is divine from God to creatures, upon whom He confers a participation in the supreme substance which is God. For if the fragrance of perfume imparts its strength to clothing, and in a certain sense transforms receptacles which contained it into itself, should not the Holy Spirit, who proceeds from God, make those in whom He dwells partakers of the divine nature?" (*In Ioannem*, XI, c. 2; PG, LXXIV, 452 f.)

holiness is rightly predicated, in an eminent sense, of the Holy Spirit, as the Person representing the holiness of the others in Himself; and so He is called simply the Holiness of God or the Holiness of the Father and the Son, not as though the Father and the Son were holy only because of Him, but because their holiness is manifested in Him.

Consequently when we explicitly characterize the Third Person in His relation to the other persons, as the Spirit of the Father or of the Son or of both together, we do not ordinarily add the adjective "Holy." We do not say: "the Holy Spirit of the Father and the Son," because the Spirit proceeding from the divine persons cannot be other than holy, and holiness in this connection is necessarily understood. For the Third Person, as the outpouring of God's most exalted spirituality, as its culmination and flower, is essentially holy, since holiness in the last analysis coincides with perfect spirtuality conceived in all its purity. But if we use the name "Spirit" without expressly emphasizing His relationship to the spirating persons, we invariably call Him "Holy Spirit," to signify that we are not think- ing of the spirit of some creature, which can be imperfect, but of the Spirit of the purest, most exalted, immutable goodness and love, who can be no other than the Spirit of God.

There is another reason, closely connected with the foregoing, why holiness is not merely predicated of the Third Person in God, but is especially stressed as a characteristic note. As we have seen repeatedly, the Third Person, who is the common breath of love and life of the two other persons, is also the pledge of their love as well as the bond and seal of their absolute physical and moral unity. What confers upon a pledge of love, as also upon a bond and seal of unity, the value which enables them to fulfill their essential func- tion? In the case of a pledge is it not the costliness of the gift, in the case of a bond its firmness, in the case of a seal its unquestioned genuineness? If the love and the unity are divine, must not the infinite costliness of the pledge, the absolute sacredness and inviola- bility of the bond, the absolute authenticity and genuineness of the seal, be expressed and emphasized? But all these sublime attributes are expressed in simplest and noblest fashion by the single word, holiness. Sanctity signifies all that is sublime and estimable, and hence precious, in a good; "sacred" is the term we apply to the firm- est, most inviolable unions and obligations; sacred, too, is the un- swerving loyalty with which they are maintained and kept. Holy means for us, lastly, what is pure and immaculate, what cannot be defiled or adulterated, and especially the love that cannot be desecrated by any gross or even refined self-seeking; while of course love that is contaminated by foul sensual lust is entirely out of the question.

In thus applying the name "Holy Spirit" to the Spirit of the Father and the Son, we behold Him, as it were, in the guise of an infinitely precious diamond of unshatterable compactness and the most limpid purity, crystallized out of the breath of their love and life, a diamond in which in an inexpressibly sublime manner the Father and the Son pledge their love, and secure, seal, and crown their bond of union. In a word, we stress the sanctity of the Spirit as we similarly stress the Son's equality with the Father, which is what manifests Him as the true and perfect Son of the Father; and as we stress the oneness of the Father Himself, by virtue of which He is the original principle of the other persons and the absolutely simple center from which they both proceed in ordered succession like two rays.

The Fathers appear at times to deduce the holiness predicated of the Holy Spirit from the consideration that He communicates holiness to creatures. "The power of sanctification," says St. Cyril of Alexandria, "which naturally proceeds from the Father and confers perfection on the imperfect, we call the Holy Spirit." [32] But the power to sanctify pertains to the Holy Spirit because He is holiness itself, and the holiness that He communicates is only an imitation of His own holiness. For this reason St. Cyril had stated a little previously: "The Spirit is called holy, because He is essentially holy, not by extrinsic accretion. For He is the natural, living, and subsistent activity of God, which perfects creatures in sanctifying them by the communication of Himself." [33]

Later we shall come back to this relationship of the Holy Spirit to the sanctification of creatures, as in any case we must further discuss the relations to creatures endowed with grace that spring from His hypostatic character, and the names corresponding to these relations.

If, as we hope, we have succeeded in our endeavor to bring out the full import of the names which the Church applies to the divine

[32] *Thesaurus, Assertio* 34, p. 352; PG, LXXV, 598.
[33] *Ibid.*, p. 351; PG, LXXV, 595.

persons, we have the best proof for the correctness of the standpoint from which we launched this discussion. "Ecclesiastical specula- tion," as Dieringer pointedly remarks, "must start from the con- viction that ecclesiastical terminology (which is likewise that of revelation itself) is for all its analogy the most correct we can have in such matters, and that the reality signified by the terms we must employ is in objective truth vastly more perfect than the expressions can indicate." [34] On the other hand, our exposition affords some intimation of the wealth and profundity of thought contained in these expressions. For although they are only analogous, their anal- ogy is so suggestive, so cogent, and so striking, that an understanding of them conveys to us a clear and most resplendent notion of the sublime mystery. Truly we must marvel at the infinite wisdom of those persons who willed to reveal themselves to us through the medium of such terms.

19. TRIUNITY IN THE TRINITY

Presupposing the unity and simplicity of the divine essence, and arguing from the revealed doctrine of the interior productions, we have up to the present endeavored to give a logical and progressive account of the most important features of the Trinity. We advanced from the simplest and least definite to the most concrete conception. We believe that we have shown how, from the standpoint of faith, the mysterious doctrine of the divine Trinity in the persons of the Father, the Son, and the Holy Spirit may be scientifically established, developed, and explained; or, if the term be preferred, constructed.[35]

It remains for us to point out that the greatest unity obtains in the divine Trinity which, although a plurality in the most real sense of the word, is thoroughly permeated and pervaded by the highest unity. Our development of the doctrine of the Trinity has brought to light the principles that establish this unity; we need only glance back at these.

Unity rules throughout; the divine nature and substance is one in all three persons, and these in turn are one with the essence, from which they are not really distinct, just as they are not distinct from

[34] *Lehrbuch der katholischen Dogmatik*, 4th ed., p. 192.
[35] This "construction" turned out to be less a logical systematization than a theological interpretation of revealed truth. [Tr.]

one another in essence. They are one supreme Being, *una summa res*. The communication of the essence from one person to the others involves no separation or partition of the essence. On the contrary, the essence can be transmitted to one of the other persons only if this person enters into relationship with the First Person and is united to Him in oneness of essence.

Furthermore, the first principle is one, the original possessor of the divine nature is one; and the distinction among the persons proceeds from this one principle. The distinction issues from the unity, and is in turn stabilized by this same unity. For the Second and Third Persons are distinct from the First Person only because they have their origin from Him and stand in relation to Him by virtue of this origin.

But this is an interior origin, arising from the interior of the producing person and remaining within Him. The Son does not depart from the bosom of the Father at His generation; He remains dwelling therein; He is distinct from the Father, but is not separated from the Father. The Holy Spirit likewise does not retire from the heart of the Father and the Son at His origin; He remains inseparably united to them, as the flame to the fire from which it flares up, as the flower to the plant from which it stems. The order of origins in God not only points to an undivided first principle, but suffers no separation from it to arise. It establishes only a distinction among the persons.

Even this distinction is purely relative, that is, it consists only in the relationship of the persons to one another, specifically of the Second and the Third to the First. It is this relationship which distinguishes one person from the others to whom He is related, but at the same time unites them with one another, both in reality and in our concept; for the relative as such can neither exist nor be conceived apart from the term to which it is related. The Father cannot be God and possess the divine nature without the Son, nor can the Father and the Son without the Holy Spirit. Each possesses the nature in Himself and for Himself, but only in so far as He possesses it also from another or for another: from another, from whom He receives it; for another, to whom He gives it. Thus distinction in possession not only does not exclude common possession, but essentially requires it.

This union and community among the persons appear in higher

relief when we reflect that not only are any two of the persons immediately related and united to each other, but that each of the
three persons is in His own way a center and focus to which the
other two are related and in which they are united to each other.
The Father unites the other two persons with and in Himself as
their common root and source; for He is the common principle of
both: He alone is the principle of the Son, and together with the
Son is the principle of the Holy Spirit, not only mediately, not
merely through the Son, but also immediately. Contrariwise the
Holy Spirit unites the Father and the Son with and in Himself, not
as their principle, but as their common and immediate product; and
more accurately, as the product of their mutual love, in which they
manifest their unity and show themselves to be one Spirit. He is
the crown, the seal of unity in the Trinity, as the Father is its root
and source. Lastly, the Son is neither principle nor product of two
other persons; He is the product of the Father and principle of the
Holy Spirit. As such He occupies a central position, and is thus a
link which joins the other persons in Himself to form a golden chain.
His procession from the Father is the essential prerequisite, as it
were the point of intersection, for the procession of the Holy Spirit,
so much so that the latter's relationship to the Father cannot even
be conceived without the Son. The union of the Holy Spirit with
the Father, like His distinction from the Father, is conceivable only
in the Son and through the Son.

Nowhere in the divine Trinity do we perceive a division, a partition, a separation, or even a distinction which does not imply the
principle of union and unity. Everything in the Trinity is unity,
union, and harmony in the highest and most beautiful sense of the
word. The Trinity does not destroy the unity and simplicity of
God; rather this unity and simplicity manifest themselves in their
full force and grandeur only through the Triunity, through the
absolute accord and harmony with which they pervade and permeate the Trinity in God. This unity appears as a consummate, living
unity, as rich in movement as in repose, in communicativeness as in
self-sufficiency, in plurality as in simplicity, in joint activity as in
autonomy.

Such is the great marvel, the supernatural mystery, which faith
proposes for our contemplation, the mystery which our reason cannot approach without faith, which reason cannot perceive as it is

in itself even though enlightened by faith, to say nothing of exhausting and fathoming its depths, and which, finally, reason discerns and comes to know as an immeasurable ocean of light, as an infinitely profuse system of the most dazzling and sublime truths. It is a mystery which must attract our reason because of its very eminence; for even the slightest glance that reason is enabled to cast into its depths is a source of inexpressible delight.

CHAPTER V

Fusion of Light and Darkness in the Mystery

▪▪

20. LIMITATIONS OF OUR UNDERSTANDING OF THE MYSTERY

OUR intention in proposing a systematic construction, or rather reconstruction, of the mystery, has been to impart a profound, clear, and well-rounded concept of the Trinity. Have we not to fear that our zeal has been excessive and that, contrary to our own theory, we have done away with its mysterious obscurity?

Not at all. Our purpose has not been to establish the reality of its content with the unaided reason. We have accepted the mystery from divine revelation; it is from faith that we have taken over and used, as the basis of further deductions, the reality of an idea: the idea of the internal divine productions which are at the root of the entire dogma. We have erected our structure upon this one foundation, and in the last instance our whole conviction of the reality of the various factors of the mystery rests upon this foundation.

As concerns the obscurity, the incomprehensibility of the content of the mystery, it remains the same after revelation as it was before revelation. The truth contained in the mystery is disclosed to us only in feeble twilight; the darkness prevails over the light.

The concepts by which we grasp and represent the content of the mystery to our minds are only analogous, derived from finite things, even material things, which are not able adequately to exhibit the wealth of their object in its utter simplicity, for the very reason that there are so many of them. The notions of production, of the products of knowledge and love, of hypostasis and person, of generation and spiration: all are drawn from created things. Even if we were able to determine the limitations of their applicability to God, a predominantly negative quality marks the determinations we make according to the norm of revelation and our natural idea of God. The object represented by these determinations is never as distinctly perceptible to our vision as it is in the living reality.

Nevertheless these analogous concepts, recognized in their analogous value, suffice for the realization that they are necessarily stipulated, postulated, and determined; so that, if one of them is true, the rest also must possess objective verity. Our grasp of the interrelationship of the concepts is so sure that we should find an evident contradiction within them if even a single one of them were inapplicable to the object. Thus, for example, if we were to admit productions in God but should not be willing to admit that these productions are personal productions and that their products are true persons, we should be involved in an evident contradiction. Likewise if we should fail to put the products on a par with their producing principle as regards simultaneity and perfection, or should posit a real distinction between the persons and the essence, an intrinsic contradiction would be apparent.

On the other hand our analogous concepts, when exact and definite, enable us decisively to reject as not evident those seeming contradictions which lurk in the dogma, as far as the purely rational understanding is concerned. These apparent contradictions are principally three: (1) the real distinction among the persons, despite the fact that they are one with the essence, and through the essence with one another; (2) the co-eternity of the persons, despite the fact that some of them owe their origin to others; (3) the equality of dignity and perfection among the persons, despite the fact that some of them are related to others as their principle.[1] These alleged contradictions stand only so long as the concepts that meet in them are not

---

[1] Kuhn (*Die christliche Lehre von der göttlichen Dreieinigkeit*, pp. 502 ff.) contends that these three points "remain inconceivable, i.e., impenetrable for us," but that the absence of an evident contradiction, of a real absurdity, can be shown. They may perhaps be reduced to two: namely, the relation of person to essence, and the relation of person to productive activity, since the co-eternity of the product with the producing principle can be sufficiently illustrated by examples drawn from the created world. Thus light and its reflection are simultaneous[!], even though the latter is ever dependent on the former. If the light shone from eternity, its reflection would also be eternal and would eternally depend on it. In some such way the Son of God is the reflection of the eternal, spiritual light shining in the Father.

sharply circumscribed in their analogous applicability. We can admit no real distinction between essence and person in God, but we can admit a virtual distinction, on the strength of which we can assert that the one *summa res* which we call God is at once person and essence. This is true, however, in different senses according to these two respects: as person the one supreme reality is perceived to be relative, as essence it is not relative, and so as person it is really distinct from the term of its relation.[2] The produced persons could

---

[2] "Virtual distinction" is the correct expression for the distinctions we make with reference to one and the same divine subject. The real distinction among the persons, the several subjects as such, does not formally compromise the divine simplicity. This simplicity formally excludes only such real distinctions as are found in the same subject; for it is only distinct elements existing in the same subject that combine to form a whole. The distinction which we make between person and essence in order to distinguish the persons from one another notwithstanding the unity of their essence, cannot be a real distinction in the sense that person and essence would be two different, complementary realities. On the other hand, a purely subjective distinction, a mere *distinctio rationis*, will not suffice, because the real distinction among the persons must be accounted for. In some way or other the distinction must have an objective basis (in the language of the Schools, it must be a *distinctio rationis cum fundamento in re*). This objective basis cannot be the presence of two different realities (person and essence) in the same object, but has to be the fact that one and the same reality (the one *summa res simplex omnino* which we call God) manifests itself as equivalent in the infinite wealth of its simplicity to the various realities which we apprehend in our concepts, so that notwithstanding its simplicity, or better because of it, it must be represented under the form of different "values" (called *rationes* by St. Thomas, *valores* by St. Augustine in *De Trinitate*, XV, c.7). In line with these different values that are discernible in the object and that come to light upon a more accurate and adequate contemplation (hence the distinction κατ' ἐπίνοιαν of the Greek Fathers), the reality itself is objectively verified under different formalities, so that what I can affirm of it in one connection I must deny in another. Thus intellect and will are two different values found in the one simple, divine nature; the first of them, and it alone, is verified in the divine cognition, whereas the second, and it alone, is verified in the divine volition. Although both are one absolutely simple reality, I cannot say that this one reality fulfills according to the first value the function that it actually fulfills only so far as it comprises within itself the second. Similarly, in the *summa res* which we call God, person and nature are different values; both are contained undivided in this one reality, but each according to its own full import. Person and essence are really found in God, a possessing subject and a nature which the subject possesses. Although the *summa res* is both possessing subject and object of possession in the most absolute simplicity, without any composition, no contradiction is involved in the fact that it has a different value as possessing from the value it has as object of possession. In the first respect it can communicate the essence and

not be equally eternal with the producing person if they were produced by a transient act, rather than by an act which consists in the
eternal constituting of some of them by the others; it is in the latter
manner that we can and must conceive divine production. For this
reason, in the language of the Church, we do not call the producing
person *causa* (cause) but *principium* (principle); the former term
connotes more an act proceeding from a fully constituted essence,
whereas the latter indicates in general a constituting power inherent
in an essence. Again, the produced persons could not be equal to
the producing person in dignity and perfection, if production implied a simple dependence on Him, if the First Person could exist
without them, while they could not exist without Him. But they can
well be equal to the producing person if the latter has an essential
ordination to the production and possesses His own subsistence only
in His productivity of them, and if, further, the common essence
must by its very nature exist in one as much as in another of the
persons, and indeed in each of them in relation to the others.

Thus we apprehend in the Trinity the necessary interconnection
of the various concepts applied to it, and at the same time we perceive
that no evident contradiction is discernible in them.

But the perception of the interrelationship among the several concepts is not a perception of the absolute unity of the object in itself,
which such concepts exhibit only in broken rays. And the perception
of the absence of contradiction among the concepts reaches only to
a certain point, and then comes to an abrupt halt. It is only a negative
perception, a realization of the lack of evidence in the alleged contradictions, not a positive insight which would enable us, without the
assurance which faith imparts, simply to assert the absence of contradiction. It rests more upon a sharp delimitation of the concepts by

---

hence multiply the possession, whereas in the second respect it can only be
communicated without being multiplied.

Since we can conceive the various values of the *summa res* only according
to the individual ideas of the perfections to which they correspond in creatures, we must intellectually assemble the different concepts into one composite representation in order to form some notion of the wealth of the
object. But we may not transfer this composition to the object itself. For
the object is but one simple reality which manifests its wealth to us in
multiple broken rays. It sends these rays out from itself in different directions
as from an indivisible point, and therefore enables the spectator, no matter
from what angle he contemplates the object, to trace back the rays to the
point which is their source.

negative determinations than upon a positive, exhaustive survey of their object. The analogously determined concepts by which we solve the contradictions continue to remain most obscure in themselves, and afford us no real view of their object, to say nothing of a penetrating insight. For instance, to remain within the compass of the above-mentioned difficulties, what is the meaning of the statement that a producing person is a definite person only because He produces, and that His productivity consists not in a transient act but in the eternal relation of one person to the others? Again, how can a merely virtual distinction between person and nature issue in the real distinction among the persons within their unity of nature? Our perception of all this is at best very dim; and the reason is that creation nowhere furnishes an example of the relationship of a person to his nature and his productive activity in the same way that this is found in God.

For all that, the very fact that in God everything is otherwise than in creatures, suffices for the realization that no real contradiction can lie at the basis of the apparent contradiction discernible in our defective concepts.[8] In other words: the more clearly we realize that the mystery is inconceivable despite the most perfect analogous presentation, and the more we appreciate its mysterious character, the less we shall be tempted to admit any incompatibility among its individual factors, to concoct a maze of contradictions from its incomprehensible sublimity, or to see in its dazzling brilliance only a desolate blackness.

"He that is a searcher of majesty," says Holy Scripture, "shall be overwhelmed by glory." [4] This is doubly true of our mystery, which comprises the entire greatness of God's majesty. He who seeks to probe into it with his unaided reason, spurning God's gracious condescension in His revelation, and ventures to measure its content by the norm of his natural ideas, will be so blinded by the splendor of the mystery that he will see nothing in it and, instead of the true majesty of God, he will adore an idol set up by himself. But whoever draws near under the guidance of faith, in the humble consciousness that with his reason he can neither reach nor measure the mystery of

[8] Cf. Kuhn, *Die christliche Lehre von der göttlichen Dreieinigkeit,* especially section 35: "Die Denkbarkeit der göttlichen Trinität," one of the best and most profound discussions of this problem.

[4] Prov. 25:27.

the majesty of God Three-in-One and One-in-Three, he, too, will be blinded, but in such wise that the glory of divine majesty will at least dimly enter his eye and with heavenly rapture enthrall his heart. The Psalmist urges and encourages us thus to approach God when he says: "Come ye to Him and be enlightened: and your faces shall not be confounded." [5]

We shall learn to appreciate more adequately the advantage for mind and heart which even a slight knowledge of this mystery affords us, when we examine the subjective and objective significance possessed by the mystery in the organism of Christian revelation. Our intention is to make this particular significance of the mystery of the Trinity and of its knowledge the object of a special inquiry. As a rule theologians devote little or no attention to this phase of the question; and when they do come to treat of it, they seldom attain to a clear appreciation of the undertaking. The task is indeed a difficult one, and we must here more than ever beg the reader's forbearance if we do not conduct him to the goal easily, quickly, and over a well-paved road.

[5] Ps. 33:6.

CHAPTER VI

The Significance of the Mystery of the Trinity

▪▪▪

21. PHILOSOPHICAL SIGNIFICANCE OF THE MYSTERY

AT the present time a good deal is being said about the philosophical significance of the dogma of the divine Trinity. The idea is current in some circles that, if the doctrine has no philosophical import, science need not concern itself greatly about it; it would then be a transcendental dogma that would have to be regarded simply as the object of unscientific faith. Under the persuasion that honor is paid to the dogma if a philosophical significance is attributed to it, an attempt is made to discover such a significance. Some go so far as to assign supreme philosophical significance to it, and maintain that there can be no sound, true philosophy at all unless it is based on this doctrine or reverts to it.

These contentions appear specious; as a matter of fact vast confusion reigns in them.

If anyone were to ask me whether the Trinity has a philosophical significance, I should reply "yes" or "no" according as the question is understood.

Philosophy can be understood in a narrower or a wider sense. In general it means love of wisdom and wisdom itself, and therefore also the divine, supernatural knowledge and science which faith imparts to us. In the stricter sense it means human wisdom, a purely rational knowledge and science.

If "philosophy" is understood in the latter sense, as generally it would be, the question is to be answered with an unqualified negative and a carefully qualified, restricted affirmative.

A philosophical significance can be simply assigned only to those truths that are themselves philosophical, that is, truths that are knowable through the organ of philosophy or that at any rate appear absolutely necessary for the explanation and establishment of the object of philosophy. Can the Trinity be drawn into this category? By no means. If it is a mysterious, supernatural truth in the sense we have indicated above, it cannot be a rational truth nor can it be unconditionally necessary for the explanation and establishment of rational truths. As far as philosophy is concerned, the Trinity is truly transcendental. It lies immeasurably beyond the realm and sphere of philosophy, and no real honor is rendered to its sublimity by drawing it down from its elevated position and enclosing it within the philosophical sphere.

The fear is expressed that unless we assume the Trinity we shall fall into pantheism, or at least shall not be able to demolish pantheism from every angle. But why this fear? To refute and exclude pantheism, is it not enough to demonstrate the existence of the one independent, infinite, personal God? Can we have no concept of the one true God without the concept of the Trinity? But, it is argued, will not God's activity necessarily appear to be an evolution of God in the universe if we cannot show that this activity is productive within the interior of the Godhead? This is not true either. We conceive of God as infinitely active in the knowledge and love of Himself; we conceive that on this account God is sufficient to Himself for His own beatitude, and therefore stands in no need of activity that passes beyond Himself. If this is not enough to guard a person from all inroads of pantheistic thought, neither will the interior productions in God avail any better for his instruction. Have we not seen how in Günther's system a transition is effected from the inner productions in the Godhead to the outer, and how an attempt is made to represent the latter as the necessary development and complement of the former? Even if this is not formally pantheism, in the last analysis it leads to pantheism, just as every doctrine does which represents the universe as the necessary complement of the Infinite.

Shall we, then, deny outright that the doctrine of the Trinity has a great significance for philosophy, particularly for the refutation of pantheism? We deny only that it is necessary for philosophy in its own sphere in order to explain the origin of the world and its relation to God. We concede that it is highly useful to philosophy in this connection. For, in fact, the more clearly we grasp the manner of God's subsistence and personality, the more decisively we can distinguish Him from the universe in His own personality; and if we know that God unfolds an infinite productivity in His own interior, we acquire a more perfect notion of His freedom with regard to His external activity. But even this utility does not accrue to philosophy from the doctrine of the Trinity as from a truth pertaining to its own order, since the doctrine always remains transcendental to it, and is made known to the philosophizing spirit not by reason but by faith. Accordingly when philosophy seeks to derive profit from the doctrine of the Trinity, it draws upon a source that is not its own, and so those who would entirely block off philosophy from faith have no right at all to speak of a philosophical significance of the doctrine of the Trinity.

This much will ever remain certain: reason and natural man cannot and need not know this transcendental truth. Natural man can and need be aware only of his natural relation to God. He must honor God as his supreme Creator and Lord, he must subject himself to God with deepest reverence, must adore and serve Him. The knowledge of God's unity and infinity suffices for this purpose. Natural man has neither the obligation nor the right to know more.

Therefore if God reveals this mystery, He has in view higher ends than the development and perfection of natural man. This revelation is supernatural in every respect, as is the mystery itself; hence it is necessarily connected with a supernatural elevation of man and has a supernatural significance for him. Essentially a theological truth that can be known only through faith, its real significance is to be sought in its relation to the higher theological knowledge itself and to the circle of higher, suprarational truths encompassed by that knowledge. This significance is not philosophical, but is purely theological.

22. Theological Significance of the Mystery of the Trinity

Let us first of all see the significance which the revelation and the corresponding knowledge of the Trinity can have and in fact does have in itself, prescinding from the relations in which the object of this knowledge stands to other connected objects. In other words, why has God revealed this truth which is transcendental with regard to our reason, for what purpose has He proposed it to us for belief? We shall see that these reasons and ends are supernatural and, as lying beyond the calculations of our intellects, are likewise transcendental truths.

We are sometimes told that God has revealed this incomprehensible mystery to humble our reason by the very incomprehensibility of the mystery, and to give us an opportunity for practicing an obedience that honors Him greatly, the blind, unconditional obedience of faith. That is true. But this humiliation does not exclude exaltation, this devoted renunciation of our own judgment does not exclude the wealth of God's grace; far from it. Rather, as we know, self-abasement before God is the way to the highest elevation, and devoted self-abandonment to God brings us the richest gain. The abasement on our part and loving condescension on God's part, devotedness on our part and wealth of grace on God's part, keep pace together and imply one another. The more we realize and acknowledge that of ourselves we have neither the power nor the right to know the divine Trinity without faith and that we must conceive it in accord with faith, the more honorable and ennobling it is for us that we are permitted to come to a knowledge of this sublime mystery at least through faith. The more we must forgo our own judgment in accepting the mystery on faith, the more we shall be rewarded by our reception of the power to make our own the judgment and knowledge which God alone possessed prior to revelation and which was accessible to no creature.

The revelation of the Trinity is an act of tenderest love and most loving generosity, by which God is pleased to honor and gladden creatures in a supernatural manner, and to glorify Himself in a supernatural manner.

1. The statement uttered by the Son of God Himself is true here, if anywhere: "I will not now call you servants. . . . But I have called you friends, because all things whatsoever I have heard of My Father I have made known to you." [1] It is not seemly for the servant to enter into the inner apartment of his master's family; and so it pertains to the creature as he is in himself only to honor God as his Lord; he may not venture to cast a glance into the mysteries of His bosom and His heart. If he is admitted to these mysteries, he thereby enters into a certain friendship with God; for only to friends does

[1] John 15:15.

anyone reveal his most intimate secrets.[2] He ascends far beyond his native lowliness and, initiated into the secrets of his Lord, feels himself summoned to all the other privileges as well as to the duties of a true friend.

2. The revelation of this mystery in its character of extraordinary proof of the divine love for us, calls for a boundless gratitude and return of love; but the mystery itself must be much more effective in enkindling in us a supernatural, childlike love of God. The natural creature knows God rather as the absolute Being on whom every other being depends; and the Old Testament reveals God as He who is, without whom nothing is, and who therefore is enthroned above us as the absolute Lord of all beings. As such, of course, God deserves our love, too, because He makes His goodness known also by giving existence to other beings. But the wealth of the divine goodness comes into prominence only in the divine Trinity. Here God appears to us in an eternal, necessary, absolute surrender and communication of His entire essence; here we perceive that He is good not only because He possesses infinite goods, but that He is good, infinitely good, in the complete communication of His goods.[3] Does He not appear immeasurably more lovable now than before? Must not our love for Him become incomparably more ardent and tender, when we see how the Father gives His entire essence to the Son, and then remains united with His Son in so stupendous a love that a third person proceeds from that love, a person in whom they embrace

[2] "This is a characteristic of friendship, that a man reveal his secrets to a friend. For, since friendship unites affections and, so to speak, makes one heart out of two, we may say that a person does not release from his own heart the secret that he reveals to his friend. Hence our Lord says to His disciples: 'I will not now call you servants. . . . But I have called you friends, because all things whatsoever I have heard of My Father, I have made known to you.' " St. Thomas, *Summa contra Gentiles*, IV, c.21.

[3] This is also St. Bonaventure's point of view in his description of the condition of natural man and of man raised to the supernatural order by the Spirit of God through Christ; cf. his *Itinerarium mentis ad Deum*, cc.5 f. As source of created being, God must possess pure being; but He reveals Himself as inexhaustible, *superabundant* being in the communication of His infinity. Alexander of Hales (*Summa*, II, q.90, m.1, a.1) goes so far in one passage as to say that the divine Trinity is the specific object of supernatural love of God in contradistinction to natural love of God, seeing that it is also the specific object of the supernatural knowledge possessed by faith. As more accurately delineated, this agrees with what we have stated in our volume *Natur und Gnade* concerning the formal and specific object of supernatural love.

each other? No wonder that with Christianity, which first ushered a clear knowledge of the Trinity into the world, a new source of divine love, such as had never been known before, burst forth in the world, that in place of the reverential awe in presence of the Supreme Being which had ruled in the Old Testament, the law of servitude, an enchanting and joyous wonderment at the divine goodness made its appearance. Undoubtedly the consideration that God the Father had given His only-begotten Son to the world out of love for it contributed to this. But this mission of the Son to men, this supernatural love of God for His creatures, had so powerful an effect upon minds and hearts primarily because that mission was a revelation and continuation of the Trinitarian productions, and made men acquainted with the eternal relations existing among Father, Son, and Holy Spirit. But this is a subject to which we shall return later.

3. Thus our initiation into the mystery of the Trinity engenders above all a supernatural, elevated, and tender love for God, a love of friendship. At the same time it gives us a pledge that as friends of God we are further called to the immediate intuition of His essence as it is in itself, to the vision of God face to face. Indeed, is it not true that even the knowledge of the Trinity which is imparted to us by faith enables us to know God not merely as He appears to the outer world, but as He is in Himself, as He subsists in Himself? Once the veil that conceals God's inner being from the sight of His creatures is parted, once the creature rising upon the wings of faith draws so near to God that he comes to know the hidden names and relations of the divine persons, he feels within himself a longing, and with the longing a confidence, that some day the parted veil will drop entirely, that the persons who now show themselves dimly from afar will reveal themselves to us face to face.

The supernatural beatitude which the creature enjoys in the vision of God is thus inaugurated and anticipated by the revelation of the Trinity. Belief in the Trinity is a foretaste of the beatific vision of God; it builds a bridge to heaven for our souls, it lifts them up to God while they tarry still on earth; it introduces them into the joy of their Lord. If the supreme delight of God's own beatitude is the fellowship and mutual relationship of the persons, our very faith in the Trinity enables us in some slight way to savor the innermost sweetness and loveliness of God.

Thus the revelation of the Trinity is more than a supernatural mark of distinction conferred upon the creature, rich in grace though that revelation be; it leads him to a supernatural union with God, here below through a love, in the next world through a fruition, which surpass the utmost love and enjoyment known to nature.

4. Obviously this revelation is likewise full of glory for God Himself. In all God's external works utility comes to the creature, glory to God. Utility to the creature and glory to God go hand in hand. The utility to the creature is greater the more God communicates Himself to him; but the more God communicates Himself, the more He manifests and therefore glorifies Himself. The higher He elevates the creature, the higher He thereby elevates Himself, not by any augmentation, but by the unfolding of His greatness.

If God is glorified by manifesting His power, wisdom, and goodness in created nature, in the visible and invisible worlds with their countless grades, orders, and species of being, how greatly does He not glorify Himself when He reveals the infinite fruitfulness of His bosom, the overflowing fullness of His heart, when He grants us to know the testimony which the Son, His equal in nature, gives of the majesty of the Father, and which the Holy Spirit, equal to them both, gives of the majesty of the Father and the Son! Creatures, too, bear witness of God's glory: "The heavens show forth the glory of God, and the firmament declareth the work of His hands." [4] But the testimony of creatures is only a dull, fading echo of the testimony which the Father receives from His own Word; the shimmering shapes of creatures are only a dark shadow compared with the Son, who as Light of Light is an unsullied mirror of His Father's beauty and a faithful image of His being. And the exultant love song of creatures is scarcely audible alongside that inexpressible sigh of love which the Father and the Son breathe forth in the Holy Spirit. All the tides of life and happiness which surge in the hearts and veins of creatures are dwindling brooklets compared with that inexhaustible torrent of life which floods the Father and the Son in the Holy Spirit. When God reveals the Trinity of persons, and presents these divine persons as witnesses of their own majesty, He glorifies Himself before our eyes quite otherwise than when He merely deputes creatures to give testimony of that majesty to us. The latter is a natural, the former a super-

[4] Ps. 18:2.

natural, glorification; the latter is finite, the former is infinite. They are essentially distinct, separated by the breadth of heaven, and we must be vividly conscious of this difference and never overlook it; for only the difference and contrast between the natural and finite on one side and the supernatural and infinite on the other, will enable us to apprehend and appreciate the entire grandeur and sublimity of the latter.

Such reflections are sufficient to show that the revelation and knowledge of the divine Trinity have a very great and lofty meaning for us, in spite of the fact, or rather because of the fact, that it is a supernatural and suprarational truth, a truth that is transcendental for nature and reason. By revealing this truth which extends so far beyond nature and reason, God raises us above our nature and our reason, and by His grace permits us to mount to the very pinnacle of His mysteries. The mystery is transcendental for purely human, natural science and philosophy. Therefore it becomes the object of a superhuman science and philosophy, namely, theology, in which man does not search for truth, but God communicates His own knowledge.[5] As the divine nature regarded in its unity is the highest object, the crowning point of philosophy, so the divine Trinity is the highest and at the same time the most characteristic object, the center, and the very heart of theology.

23. THE OBJECTIVE REVELATION OF THE TRINITY NOT FORMALLY EFFECTED BY AN ACTIVITY PROPER TO THE INDIVIDUAL PERSONS

We must consider the significance of the Trinity and Triunity of the persons in God from another aspect. Thus far we have been regarding the Trinity only as it is a truth in itself. But it is related to other truths and dogmas, too, and its significance emerges more impressively and comprehensively when viewed in this relationship. The Trinity is the starting point and goal of a whole order of truths that can be proposed and understood only with reference to it. It is the source of an entire scientific system which receives its form and perfection from the inner system of the Trinity, and in which

[5] Scheeben here uses the word "theology" in the broad sense found in some of the Fathers, for whom God's own assertions concerning the mystery of His being, of His decrees, and of His activity constitute theology. [Tr.]

the Trinity is revealed in a sort of objective reflection of itself. Thus the Trinity presents itself anew to our cognition, and imparts to us a knowledge not only of itself but also of its objective manifestations, which then lead to a fuller and more graphic knowledge of itself. This will show us once again that the Trinity is a supernatural truth, a real mystery the significance of which lies in the fact that it is the source and focus of other mysteries in which it is revealed.

To arrive at a thorough realization of this we must examine the way the Trinity appears to the outside world and can make contact with things external to it.

In the first place it is clear, as we pointed out previously, that the Trinity of persons, or the divine persons in their mutual relations and distinctions, do not manifest themselves to the outer world formally by their operations and activity. This could be the case only if each of the persons were externally to manifest an operation exclusively His own, as a result of which each would enter into a special relation with His own effect or the substance upon which He works, and consequently would in this effect manifest Himself alone, in distinction to the other persons.[6] But the Church teaches the contrary; even a superficial study of the dogma enables us to discover the reason for this teaching.

The divine persons are distinct only in their mutual relationships, and these relationships, so far as an activity is connected with them, are actuated only among themselves. God the Father can operate with an action that is exclusively proper to Himself as Father, only in generating the Son; and Father and Son can operate with an action that is exclusively their own, only in spirating the Holy Spirit. As the spirating activity must be ascribed to the Son not in distinction

---

[6] Those philosophers who would like to assign some place to the Trinity in their philosophical systems are fond of regarding the divine persons as the *three divine powers* by which the created world is sustained in being. They intend thereby to arrive at an ideal conception of the dogma, in contrast to the purely notional conception which is that of the simple faithful. They insist on shaping the reality according to an ideal they set up for themselves, and refuse to conform their ideal to the reality. These gentlemen have no notion of the true ideal conception; their distortion of the dogma even bars the way thereto. The persons are, if one will, the representatives of the divine powers, in so far as there can be powers at all, different powers, in the supreme actuality and simplicity which is God; but they are not the powers themselves. Otherwise a real distinction between the persons would be impossible, since a real distinction between the powers as such is impossible.

to the Father, but in union with Him, so a fortiori every other activity must be ascribed to all three persons not according to their distinction, but according to their unity. As, therefore, according to the teaching of the Church, the Father and the Son are one principle of the Holy Spirit, so all three persons are one principle of all external works. On account of this unity in operation, which is based on unity of nature, one person does not have a greater function in any of the works than the other persons; they all act equally through one wisdom, one will, one power.

This is true of all the external works of God not only in the natural order, but also in the supernatural order, as, for example, the works of grace and the Incarnation. All theologians are in accord that the Incarnation, although it terminates in the Son alone, is effected by the common activity of all three persons.[7] With regard to grace, they likewise teach that the whole Trinity is the cause of grace in us, although its bestowal is usually attributed to the Holy Spirit.

How, then, does it happen that Sacred Scripture and ecclesiastical language repeatedly assign a special operation to the individual persons, as, for instance, creation to the Father, redemption to the Son, sanctification to the Holy Spirit?

First of all we must note that redemption in the strict sense, redemption through satisfaction and merit, is exclusively proper to the Son of God. As such, however, it is not a purely divine activity, but an activity of the God-man, which can pertain exclusively to the Son because He alone is man. But usage is not so constant with regard to purely divine operations as to prevent a work generally attributed to one person from being occasionally attributed to the others. The activity which is assigned to the individual persons really belongs to them. To this extent such *appropriatio* (appropriation), as the theologians term it, includes the *proprietas* (property); but this *proprietas* is not an exclusive property from which the other persons are shut out. Therefore when a certain activity is regularly assigned to one of the persons, the appropriateness which it has for Him is merely emphasized, and this for a twofold reason: first, to bring the individual persons close to our understanding in their true

---

[7] "We must believe that the entire Trinity effected the Incarnation of the Son of God, since the operations of the Trinity are indivisible." Symbolum fidei. Conc. Toletanum XI, a.675; Denz., 284.

distinction; secondly, to signalize the activities proceeding from God in a more splendid and striking manner.

For each of the divine attributes and operations, although they are all common to the three persons, has a special connection and relationship with the proper character of the individual persons, and accordingly find in them their personal expression, their special representatives. Thus we saw earlier that the Son as the Word, the expression of the Father's wisdom, is its personal representative, and likewise that the Holy Spirit as the effluence of love is the representative of love. In a similar way the Father, as the original principle in the Godhead, as the first proprietor of the divine being, by the intellectual expression of which He generates the Son, is the representative of the divine power. Is it, then, a matter to excite surprise if the manifestation of divine power, like that of divine wisdom and love, is generally ascribed to one person as the representative of the attribute in question?[8]

Above all, will not the persons themselves, in appearing as representatives of a certain attribute and authors of certain activities, be more strikingly and clearly apprehended as distinct? For us, who do not behold the persons in themselves, who for that matter are accustomed to judge of all things in terms of their activities, this distinction and apportionment of activities is almost a necessity, if we are to distinguish the persons from one another and are to awaken in ourselves a living interest in each of them. The fact that the Second Person has in the Incarnation displayed an activity which in a true sense is exclusively His own, increases this necessity. If a special activity were not likewise ascribed to the Father and to the Holy Spirit, these two persons would, as far as our view is concerned, retire quite to the background. This is the principal reason why the Creed apportions God's external activity among the three divine persons according to its various aspects, so that each may appear operative and so that the personal character of each may shine forth in His activity.

On the other hand, God's activity also shines in a more splendid light if its varying kinds and aspects are appropriated to definite

[8] On the principle and classification of the appropriations, see St. Bonaventure, *Breviloquium*, I, c.6; St. Thomas, *Summa*, Ia, q.39, a.7, 8. In Appendix II to Part I we shall quote at length from the doctrine of St. Thomas on the Holy Spirit's appropriations, which occur the most frequently and in the most varied manner in Sacred Scripture.

persons. Every external activity of God bears the impress and is the manifestation of a divine perfection. When we contemplate the divine perfections in their personal representative, they are more concrete, clearer, and more imposing than when we regard them in themselves. In the same way the impress or manifestation of those perfections strikes our attention more forcefully and vividly when we reflect that it proceeds from the representative of the perfections. If I say: "God the Father, the source of the divine being, has created the world and has given existence to the world," do I not utter the truth in a far more sublime and striking manner than if I merely say: "God has created the world"? Is not this statement: "The eternal Word has given us wisdom, the image of the Father has formed us, the reflection of the infinite Light has enlightened us," quite different from the assertion: "God has given us wisdom, has formed and enlightened us"? Do we not acquire a more vivid notion of the truth when we are told: "The Spirit of God moved over the waters, the Spirit of God animates everything that lives, the Holy Spirit sanctifies and purifies the creature, the Spirit of divine love drops the dew of grace down upon us," than when it is affirmed: "God moved over the waters, God gave us life, sanctification, and grace"?

For the same reasons the language of Scripture and the Church frequently attributes one and the same activity to the several persons according to different respects. This is usually stated in the form: "The Father acts through the Son in the Holy Spirit." Here the various divine attributes which function in every divine action are assigned to their representatives. Our intention might be to say: "God manifests His power through His wisdom in His love." But does not our thought gain tremendously in meaning and vividness if we word it thus: "The Father, as representative of the divine power, acts through His Word, the expression of His wisdom, and in the Holy Spirit, the outpouring of His love"? The proper and the deepest significance of this phraseology is that it serves to indicate how the one common divine activity is truly predicated of the several persons. For, as the nature is transmitted from the Father through the Son to the Holy Spirit, the activity effected by the nature is transmitted from the Father through the Son to the Holy Spirit; and this order, according to which the divine activity pertains to the several persons and is communicated to them without impairment of its joint character, cannot be more plainly and concisely described than by saying that the Father acts through the Son in the Holy Spirit. This does not at all imply that the several persons act externally in different manners. Rather the explanation given to the phrase brings home the truth that all three persons have the same activity and the same mode of acting externally, but that they come into possession of it in different ways.

Consequently, although the appropriation of the divine activities and modes of external action to the several persons is based on solid grounds and has an important bearing on our knowledge, the truth remains, as we insisted above, that the divine persons are not manifested externally according to their inner distinctions and relations by their activity; nor do they acquire any real significance for the outer world by reason of such activity.

24. The Objective Revelation of the Trinity Effected in the Supernatural Works of the Incarnation and of Grace

Is there a further significance for the outer world that we can ascribe to the Trinity of divine persons? There is a great significance in the fact that by their common activity and mode of action the divine persons externally prolong and continue, or imitate and reproduce, their internal relations, and thereby call into being an order of things which is an objective unfolding and revelation of the inner heart of this mystery, and which can be thoroughly understood and perfectly grasped only in the light of the mystery.

This revelation of the Trinity is an objective, as opposed to a merely logical and subjective, revelation, such as is vouchsafed through faith; but it is closely bound up with the latter. Further, this manifestation proceeds from the actual Trinity of divine persons, not merely from its shadow, the appropriated attributes, and therefore provides the ultimate basis for the justification and meaning of the appropriations.

As the Trinity itself is a supernatural and mysterious truth, the order of things in which it manifests itself externally must also be supernatural and mysterious. This order of things must present itself as a specific object of supernaturally revealed faith. Together with the Trinity it must constitute a system of mysteries which, hidden and impenetrable as far as pure reason is concerned, are in themselves clear light and mutually illuminate and clarify one another. Let us endeavor with the eyes of our faith to catch up at least a few rays of this light.

We wish first to show that in fact supernaturally mysterious divine works alone are joined to the Trinity and are intimately connected with it in the manner indicated. This we shall demonstrate by a simple induction.

We have purposely spoken of two distinct ways in which the Trinitarian relations are made known externally: by prolongation and continuance, and by imitation and reproduction. The first takes place if a divine person goes forth from God in His own personal character, and in His going forth preserves or, so to speak, bears with Him into the outer world the same relationship to the other persons which He had in the interior of the Godhead. This occurred—and it can occur in no other way—when one of the divine persons hypostatically united Himself with a created nature and entered the created world by means of this union.

The second is the case if God places a creature, a being existing outside of Himself, in a relationship with Himself similar to that in which the divine persons stand to one another, or so endows the creature that the processes which take place in him become a faithful image of the Trinitarian processes in God. We will show later that in such imitation a certain prolongation of the eternal productions and a certain entrance of their products into the creature must be conceived.

Both these kinds of revelation and manifestation are, if not in equally high degree, at any rate with equal right, absolutely supernatural with respect to the creature and hence absolutely mysterious.

This is quite evident in the first case: no created nature is hypostatically united with a divine person by virtue of its inherent principles, nor can it have any claim whatever to such a union.

In the second instance this is not so obvious. We could readily conclude that the relationship in which the creature, especially the rational creature, originally stands to God, is of itself an image of the relationship in which the divine persons stand to one another. Or we might conclude that the natural processes which take place in the rational creature's self-consciousness and knowledge of God are a reflection of the Trinitarian processes in God. In this case the objective revelation of the Trinity would no longer be mysterious and supernatural, and the Trinity itself would, at least from this point of view, lose its supernatural character and its supernatural significance.

This conception is not without a certain speciousness, and this speciousness rests upon a certain truth. However, this truth is only half understood and is not clearly grasped.

The procession of the creature from God is doubtless somewhat similar to the procession of the Son from the Father; but the dissimilarity surpasses the similarity. The creature does not proceed from the substance of God, but is drawn from nothing by the power of God. In no sense does it receive the nature of God, but a different nature, which is extraneous to God. Both observations are true likewise of rational creatures. Although, in contrast to irrational beings, they are called images of God and are so, their nature is essentially unlike the divine nature; their origin from God can be compared to the generation of the Son from the Father and can be called generation from God only in a highly metaphorical sense. Properly, eternal generation from God has a counterpart in the creature only if God raises the creature above his own nature to a participation in the divine nature, confers His own proper sanctity and glory upon him, and floods him with His own divine life. But such generation and the relation to God based on it are patently supernatural and mysterious to the highest degree; they take place only when the creature is drawn up to the bosom of God and is placed at the side of His only-begotten Son by a purely gratuitous adoption.

Although the relation of the Son of God to the Father is truly revealed in its own proper character in such an imitation, that revelation itself is not only imperceptible to reason, but is incomprehensible. It is, therefore, a revelation sharing in the mysterious character of its prototype, a revelation not granted to reason but reserved to supernatural faith, which the Spirit of God draws into the very depths of the divinity.

Similar is the case with the image of the Trinitarian process that might be conjectured to find its reflection in the interior processes of the rational creature. The Fathers and the theologians discern a certain reflection of the Trinitarian process in the activity which the rational creature directs to himself. For in knowing himself the creature expresses an intelligible word which represents himself, and in the self-knowledge obtained in this word he loves himself, much as God in the Trinitarian process expresses the Word which is an image of Himself, and through the Word breathes forth His love in the Holy Spirit. But we have already seen how inadequate this analogy is. To have a true reflection of the Trinitarian process in God, this natural psychological process would have to revolve around God as its center and object. This process takes place to some extent even in natural knowledge and love of God: in the light in which God appears to it, the soul conceives an intelligible word expressive of God, and in the love which results from this knowledge it seeks to unite itself with God, and God with itself. But since this light is merely natural, since it is confined to created nature and is not the light of God Himself, and since God appears to the soul only in His works and not in His essence, the generative power communicated to the soul is not divine and is not like that of the eternal Father. Moreover, its word is not an immediate, adequate expression of the divine essence. Consequently it is not a proper image of the eternal Word. Lastly, its sigh of love is not filled and pervaded with the real excellence and sweetness of the divine goodness in the way the latter pulsates and lives in the Holy Spirit. In short, this image lacks precisely the divine vitality and power of its exemplar.

If, therefore, the divine ideal is to be reflected in the soul with its full divine resplendence, the soul must be made like its exemplar in a supernatural manner; the soul, raised above its own nature, must participate in the divine nature and be thus enabled to reproduce in itself the processes proper to the divine nature. For if the soul truly participates in the divine nature, if God has shed His own light over it, then He appears to it in His essence, which is inaccessible to any other kind of light. Thus illuminated, the soul conceives a word of like rank with the eternal Word, a word in which the divine essence and its eternal Word are mirrored. Then also the soul embraces with its love the God present in it in His essence, its love is thoroughly permeated and scented with its divine object, and the flame in which it flares up and the sigh which it pours forth are the living, faithful expression of the eternal outpouring of love in God which we have come to know as the Holy Spirit.

Thus the reflection of the Trinitarian process in the creature is essentially supernatural and hence truly mysterious. For the principle and the activities by which and in which it is effected are withdrawn from the purview of the natural intellect; they can be known only in the light that is proper to them. Only in their own proper light do they reveal the ideal of which they are the reflection. The same divine light that enables us to reproduce the Trinitarian processes and to know them in ourselves, likewise permits us to perceive the divine ideal. For along with the immediate vision of the divine essence which it inaugurates, it necessarily reveals also the persons in whom that essence subsists.

And thus we have shown that the imitation of the Trinity in the rational creature, so far as it involves not merely analogous relations and processes but such as manifest the oneness in nature and the divinity of the eternal persons, or, in other words, so far as it exhibits the Trinity as Triunity and indeed as divine Triunity, can be nothing but a supernatural mystery, just as is the Trinity itself.

An exhaustive induction also shows that those works of God to which the Trinity is vitally related, can be nothing short of supernatural and mysterious.

Further, we have achieved some knowledge of the nature of these relationships. One of these relationships in particular is that by which the Trinitarian relations are objectively revealed by the external works in question, and the creatures in which those works are effected are designed for the objective glorification of the mystery of the Trinity. As a result, the Trinity is related to the mystical order of things established by those works much as the root is related to the plant that manifests its intrinsic vitality and nature.

As this order of things is an objective revelation of the Trinitarian root, so this root is the real foundation upon which that order is based and from which it develops. More than this: since this root is truly alive and drives its ramifications deep into that order, it is closely interlaced with the latter. These two functions of the root entail the necessary consequence that whatever grows forth from it is an objective revelation of the root itself.

Our next task will be to expound these two characteristics of the Trinity with reference to the simple order of grace as it is in itself; the explanation of their relationship to the order established by the Incarnation at this point would necessitate a discussion of the entire mystery of the Incarnation, which can better be postponed to a later chapter.

25. THE TRINITY, ROOT OF THE ORDER OF GRACE

If the internal divine relations and processes are externally imitated and reproduced by the communication of the divine nature to rational creatures, in the manner described, the Trinity is clearly the basis for the possibility, as well as the exemplar and goal, of the supernatural order of grace as we actually find it among creatures. The very essence of the Trinity consists in the substantial communication of the divine nature from the Father to the other two divine persons. Hence the true meaning of the Trinity for creatures raised to the supernatural order must be apprehended in the fact that on its basis, according to its model, and for its glorification, a participation in the divine nature is gratuitously communicated to them. Consequently the Trinity is the root from which arises the order of things called forth by this communication.

This significance of the Trinity has particular force for us if we, too, are called to a participation in the divine nature. In this case our vocation and our attitude toward God require that we gain some information about the basis, the exemplar, and the purpose of our elevation and of our relation to Him. Indeed, it is quite impossible to acquire a suitable knowledge of our vocation and position unless we go back to their basis and ideal, unless we evaluate and conceive them in accordance with this ideal. Thus the dogma of the Trinity, which objectively is the root of the order of grace, is subjectively the source of the light that illuminates that order and enables us to understand it.

Let us explain this in detail.

Our natural relationship to God as our Creator and Lord is accounted for simply by the infinity of the divine nature and our dependence on it. We discover the basis for the possibility, the exemplar, and the motive of our existence in the sole fact that God is being itself, that He is infinite being. God can give existence to finite beings because He is being itself; in the contemplation of His perfection He finds the exemplar and ideal of their essence; and in His love for this perfection He possesses the motive for its multiplication and glorification in finite imitations.

1. But the case is otherwise with the grace of divine filiation, with the gratuitous communication of the divine nature to creatures. God's power to communicate His nature externally and to beget

children of grace is conceived by us not on the ground of His creative power, but as correlative to the infinite generative power by which He communicates His nature substantially and begets a Son equal to Himself. Not God's creative power, but His generative power enables us to apprehend that the generation of adoptive children is possible.

2. The very notion of adoptive filiation presupposes natural sonship. We could not properly regard ourselves as adoptive children of God unless natural sonship were present to our minds as the ideal to which we are to be conformed through adoption by God in grace; and God Himself can have the idea of creating adoptive children from no other exemplar than from His own Son. In fact, faith teaches us that He begets us according to the image of His only-begotten Son, and has predestined us to be made conformable to Him.

3. The natural filiation of the Son of God, which is the exemplar, is at the same time God's motive for making us His adoptive children. Only because God has a Son in whom He takes infinite pleasure and whom He loves with an infinite love, can He have reason to multiply outside of Himself the image which He bears in His bosom, and thereby to glorify the more His infinite generative power, as well as His Son Himself, who is reborn in every one of His brethren. He can embrace His creatures with fatherly love in His only-begotten Son alone; only the love which He bears for His Son can become so fruitful for creatures that it raises them up to His bosom and forms them to His supernatural likeness.

The doctrine of the generation of the Son of God from the Father provides us with the key to the understanding of our elevation to the status of children of God. Nothing is truer than this; and we need feel no misgiving in maintaining that God has revealed the inner life of the Trinity for the very purpose of enlightening us concerning our supernatural relationship to Him. He makes Himself known to us not only as God but as Father, that we may realize how and why He can be and wills to be our Father also. And if He demands of our faith the avowal that He is the Father of His only-begotten Son, He thereby wills us openly to profess and acknowledge that He is our Father, too; if He demands that we believe in His Son, He wills that we acknowledge ourselves to be His children.

But how then, the question will arise, is our adoption as God's children rooted in the procession of the Holy Spirit?

Our adoption is rooted in this procession for the very reason that it is rooted in the procession of the Son from the Father and in the Son's relationship to the Father. For this relationship essentially includes the procession of the Holy Spirit in whom the Father and the Son seal their unity, and is adequately knowable only in connection with this procession. Since the entire Trinity forms one single, indivisible organism, the significance which we ascribe to any one phase of it must be attributed to the whole, and consequently at least indirectly to the other phases.

But besides this, the relationship of the second procession in God to the grace of divine filiation is direct, to some extent even more direct than is the relationship of the first procession. For the communication of the divine nature to creatures proceeds from God not by way of natural necessity, but by way of love, of gift, of liberality. From the standpoint of the manner in which it is effected, therefore, it has its exemplar and its basis of possibility more in the procession of the Holy Spirit from the Father and the Son than in the procession of the Son.

That is, we perceive in the Son a communication of the divine nature by way of natural necessity through real generation, whereas we as adoptive children participate in that nature not by generation but through sheer love and grace. We find the basis for this kind of communication only in that internal divine process which communicates the divine nature by way of pure, though also necessary, love and liberality. The Holy Spirit, as the first, all-perfect, and innermost fruit of the self-communicating divine love, is the seed and root of all other fruits which God puts forth by way of His love. In the procession of the Holy Spirit we perceive, according to an aspect different from the generation of the Son, the basis for the possibility of a further communication of the divine nature through gracious love; and this is the perfect exemplar for the external outpouring of love in finite brooklets, and at the same time the motive for still further revealing to creatures, beyond the inner life of the Godhead, that love of the Father for the Son which has already shown itself to be so fruitful and beatifying in the Holy Spirit.

Thus the communication of the divine nature to creatures, thus the order of grace, has its root equally in both of the internal divine processions. There are not, however, two roots independent of each other; there is but one two-branched root in which that order has its principle and from which it grows. For just as these two processes constitute but a single organic whole, and just as one is involved in the other and complemented by it, so they involve and complement each other when there is question of an external communication of the divine nature. Each in its own way, but in mutual relationship, is the basis for the external communication: the procession of the Son is above all the exemplar which determines the nature and the conceivability of the relationship into which we are to enter with God as co-brothers of the Son, whereas the procession of the Holy Spirit is chiefly the motive and standard which determines the way that relationship is realized.

If we were to overlook the procession of the Holy Spirit and attend to that of the Son alone, we might conclude that the divine love, which must be as fruitful as the divine knowledge, would have to pour itself forth outside of the Godhead, and thus its liberty would be impaired. This liberty, and with it the freely given, overflowing grace by which God descends to His creatures, can be grasped only in the realization that the divine love brings forth a product into which it pours itself entirely. On the other hand, without the procession of the Son that of the Holy Spirit is not conceivable at all, because the very concept of the procession of the Holy Spirit essentially supposes the procession of the Son. Further, in the loving communication of the divine nature to creatures, the relationship which exists between the Holy Spirit and the spirating persons must not be reproduced or represented as existing between creatures and God; otherwise creatures would have to be called spirits, not children of God, and they would have to be not only united to God, but would have to be the bond of such a union. No, only the relation between the Father and the Son, the fruit of which is the Holy Spirit and which is so pleasing to God because of this fruit, is to be communicated to creatures and reproduced in them as a result of the pleasure which God takes in it.

To express the full truth we must say: as the first procession terminates in the second, it is the basis and root of the creature's imitation of it in conjunction with the second procession. The second procession, which closes the internal processions and communications, is, so to speak, the conductor for the external transmission of the first procession to the creature. The communication of the divine nature from the Father to the Son by generation can find its way to the creature only in the further communication of the same divine nature to the Holy Spirit by love. And thus the Holy Spirit, who is the product of the union between Father and Son, brings about the union between God and the creature which imitates that relationship.

Is it not, then, true that the knowledge of the Third Person's procession is as necessary for the full understanding of our supernatural relations to God as is the knowledge of the generation of the Son, and consequently that a knowledge of the Trinity in general is most closely bound up with our own supernatural state? Is it not true that as soon as grace raises us above our nature and makes us share in the divine nature, this dogma, which in itself is transcendental for every creature, enters into the most intimate relations with us and ceases to be transcendental for us once we are established upon these heights? Further, is it not clear that in the supernatural order of grace the divine Trinity stands forth externally as such, beyond the absolute unity which is all that is known to the purely natural reason, and appears closely interlaced with the order of grace which imitates it and is attached to it? Is it not obvious why the revelation of the New Testament, in contradistinction to that of the Old, in transmitting to us the clear notion and the rich meaning of divine filiation, is more concerned to stress the several divine persons in their special relations than the one God, and for that purpose to attribute to the individual persons individual, definite relations and operations in regard to us?

For it is the great significance which the properties of the several divine persons acquire for us by our adoption as children of God, that imparts a high value and an especially profound meaning to the appropriations of divine attributes and operations.

We saw earlier that these appropriations are applied to God in order to throw clearer light both on the person to whom is ascribed an attribute or an operation as its representative, and on these attributes and operations themselves, which receive a special luster from their personal representatives. Where are we more clearly enjoined to stress and signalize the individual divine persons in every possible way than here, where we stand in so vital a relationship to them? And where must the attributes, operations, and relations of God to the creature be more emphasized by referring them to the individual persons than in the sphere of grace, where they are so closely connected with the hypostatic character of the persons? Indeed, the appropriations are frequently so prominent in such cases that they can scarcely be distinguished from the properties. We can show this by examples.

By grace we become children of God, not only of the Father, but of all the divine persons, since all communicate their nature to us. But as this relationship of ours to God is modeled on the ideal of the relationship between Father and Son, Scripture generally designates us as children of the Father and brothers of the Son. Likewise it is not the Holy Spirit alone who animates us by grace and dwells in us, so to speak, as the soul of our soul. Nevertheless Sacred Scripture does not as a rule call us temples of the Father or of the Son, because the breathing forth of the divine life is indicated most clearly in the person who in actual fact is the personal breath of the divine life. Hence the Father appears especially as the person who begets us as His children (and truly He does so, although not without the other persons), and the Holy Spirit as the person who, breathed forth by the Father and the Son, breathes into us the life of the Father and the Son. But the Son appears neither as begetter nor as vivifier, but as the person who is born again in us, begins to be and live anew in us; He is born again of the Father, from whom He has His eternal being and who once more impresses His image, this time upon us, and through the Holy Spirit, who proceeds from Him as divine person but on that very account transmits the life received from the Son to the latter's counterpart, the soul in grace. Strictly speaking, we could say that the Father and the Holy Spirit also begin to be and live in us, but not that they are reborn in us, because they do not receive their own being and life by generation.

26. Ramifications of the Trinity in the Order of Grace by Prolongation of the Trinitarian Productions and Entrance of Their Products into the Outer World, or by the Missions of the Divine Persons

In pursuance of this doctrine we have to consider the divine Trinity so far as it is the root of a supernatural order in the creatures which pertain to the order of grace, so far as the order of grace proceeds from the Trinity and is constructed upon it as its foundation, and consequently so far as the imitation of the internal Trinitarian relations and productions is an objective revelation of the Trinity.

But if the Trinity is a truly living root it must not only cause that order to spring forth from itself and support it; it must itself live in that order, plunge its branches into it, and penetrate it from all sides. Only thus will it be seen to be intertwined with its products for the formation of an organic, living whole, as in the realm of botany the root is joined to the plant which springs from it to form one organism with it.

The Trinity of divine persons proves to be the root of the order of grace in this sense, too. It thrusts the branches of its interior organism into the organism which is modeled upon it; that is, it exhibits itself in the order of grace as a prolongation of the eternal productions and processions, and really introduces their eternal products into the creature that is endowed with grace. As has to some extent been indicated, we find many expressions in Holy Scripture and the Fathers which certainly imply more than a mere imitation of the eternal productions and products in the creature. They speak of a real sojourn of the Son of God in us, whereby He is reborn in us, and especially of an interior light He confers upon us, in which He manifests the Father to us. But above all we are confronted throughout the entire New Testament with the idea of an outpouring of the Holy Spirit into creatures, whereby He dwells in creatures and unites them with the divine persons from whom He proceeds.

Viewed thus, the relation of the Trinity to the outer world is clearly perceived to be much closer and more intimate, and its significance for that world far greater and richer in consequences.[9] We cannot better develop this aspect of the truth than by undertaking a more detailed study of the missions of the divine persons, which have so prominent a function in the sacred writings of the New Law. In the view of all theologians these missions must be regarded as a temporal prolongation of the eternal processions, and as the introduction of their products into the creature. At the same time theologians teach that these missions, understood in a strict and proper sense, take place (prescinding from the Incarnation) only in

[9] See the chapters from St. Thomas' *Summa contra Gentiles* quoted in Appendix II to Part I. [Tr.]

and with sanctifying grace.[10] The statements of Holy Scripture and the Fathers provide the surest clue to our present idea, and are the best guaranty for its meaning and truth.

As a rule little is said of this matter, and so we must push our investigations somewhat further. The difficulty of the subject once again impels us to bespeak the reader's patience and forbearance. But we trust that St. Augustine's declaration, "nothing is more laboriously sought, nothing more advantageously discovered," which he uttered with reference to the inner nature of the Trinity, will be verified of its external unfolding also, and with regard to the second clause just as much as to the first, or even more so.

[10] St. Thomas, *Summa*, Ia, q.43, a.3. For commentaries on this passage, see Suarez and Ruiz.

CHAPTER VII

The Missions of the Divine Persons

...

27. GENERAL PRELIMINARY NOTIONS ON THE MISSIONS; DISTINCTION BETWEEN REAL AND SYMBOLIC MISSIONS

A MISSION can be predicated only of those divine persons who proceed from another person; for he who is sent must be deputed by another. And, in fact, Sacred Scripture restricts such sending to the Son and the Holy Spirit. Of the Father it states only that He sends the Son and the Holy Spirit, and of the Holy Spirit only that He is sent; of the Son it states both that He is sent by the Father and that He sends the Holy Spirit.

But as regards both divine persons this process has two characteristics which essentially differentiate it from the process which takes place in creatures when there is question of a mission. In the latter case the person who is sent is under the authority and sovereignty of the person who sends him, and in devoting himself to the purpose of his mission and fulfilling the charge entrusted to him, he withdraws from the person who has sent him and from whom he comes. Matters are quite otherwise in God. The Son and the Holy Spirit are not under the Father's authority, but are equal to Him in power and authority. They proceed from the Father only in the sense that they have their origin from Him as their author. Nevertheless a divine mission is no less perfect in concept than among creatures. For, as in general the Son and the Holy Spirit are what they are and have their being from the Father, they must in every respect be from the Father and through the Father, by proceeding from Him. Thus the divine person who is sent, no matter where He begins to be or to act, can never separate Himself from the person who sends Him, since both are absolutely one in their being, their substance, and their activity. Wherever the person who is sent

149

begins to be or to act, the sending person, owing to the circumincession of the divine persons, is also there with Him or rather in Him,
even though not in the same way that He is there.

Hence, as concerns the movement that must be conceived in the
external going or coming of the person who is sent, the following
must be borne in mind. By virtue of their infinity and omnipresence,
all the divine persons together are from eternity substantially present
everywhere where they can ever be. Therefore they cannot in their
substance begin to be anywhere in time where they were not before;
a local motion is out of the question with them. Only in the variation
of the manner in which these persons and their substance become
present to other beings, come to the latter, and enter into relationship
with them, can any change take place and any movement of the
persons be conceived. Actually this eternal substantial presence
in all other beings is either implicitly understood (for example, in
the case of the dove over the Jordan, which in itself was only an
image of the Holy Spirit, as a statue is the image of a king, but in
which the Holy Spirit really dwelt substantially), or is expressly
postulated, as in the case of all effects ascribed to one of the divine
persons; since the power of God is identical with His substance, He
must be present in His substance wherever He acts.

As has just been stated, the divine persons are one in substance
and are from eternity substantially present everywhere, so that
they cannot be present anywhere without their substance. Let us
now consider more in detail how the Son and the Holy Spirit, as
proceeding from the Father, can in a new way become present to
the creature in time, and in this sense begin to exist outside of God.
Considering the matter thus, we are led to think of the activity
which They begin to develop upon and in the creature. In fact,
Holy Scripture ordinarily represents God's activity in the creature
as a coming of God to the creature, as a visitation to the creature on
the part of God, and depicts this visitation itself as a brief passing-by
or a lengthy sojourn according as the operation is transient or prolonged. More than this: Scripture very frequently mentions that the
persons are sent for the express purpose of exercising an activity in
the creature. Thus, for example, God sends His Word to melt the
ice, and then wafts His Spirit over the waters to make them flow.
Thus the wise man implores God to send him the sharer of His

throne (His personal Wisdom) to enlighten him. Thus the Church prays in scriptural words: "Send forth Thy Spirit, and they shall be created." Thus the Savior Himself says that He will send the Holy Spirit to console us and lead us to all truth.[1]

But if we look merely to the activity for which and in which a divine person is to be sent, the mission itself can be understood only in a sense that is partly inadequate, partly even figurative. For in the full and proper sense I can say that one person is sent by another only if he comes from the latter in such a way that he alone by himself enters and exists in a particular place, or at any rate that he does so in a particular manner in the place where that other is present also. But every external operation is absolutely common to all the divine persons; all three possess efficient power indivisibly in the same perfection. Hence by reason of the activity no divine person can step into the outer world exclusively by Himself. This is so true that even the mission of the Son in the Incarnation, so far as the assumption of the human nature is regarded not in its term but in its origin, as the effecting of the union of the human nature with the Logos, must be considered and is considered by all the Fathers and theologians as an action and proceeding that is not peculiar to the Logos but is common to Him along with the other persons.

In accord with the doctrine previously laid down, an external operation can be ascribed to one person in particular only by appropriation; and the mission itself is only appropriative, hence figurative, because the fundamental condition of the mission, the distinction and procession of the person sent from the sending person, is not verified. At best this can mean only that the sending person would begin to act somewhere along with the person who proceeds from Him hypostatically, that the sending person would act in the place in question and would enter thither along with the person sent, that the sending person would take the latter to that place with Him. In such a case the mission is no more than inadequate; it involves procession, to be sure, but at the same time reveals the common nature of the external undertaking rather than any special characteristic in it.

Hence, if we look only to the activity of a divine person, we cannot in the full and proper sense perceive any mission of the in-

[1] Ps. 147:18; Wisd. 9:4; Ps. 103:30; John 14:16; 15:26.

dividual persons according to their hypostatic characteristic. But it is no less impossible to perceive such a mission without divine activity; for any coming of God or of a divine person to a creature can be apprehended as taking place only in terms of some operation proceeding from God. This activity, by which God is brought to a creature, is in itself common to all the persons; for that reason it is proper in its totality to each of the persons, and therefore can be attributed to each person as well as to all together. Consequently if a special presentation or coming of one of the proceeding persons really takes place, I can ascribe the activity by which this is brought about to the producing person as well as to the proceeding person. In the first case we say that the producing person confers the proceeding person upon the creature, that He gives Him to the creature; in the second, that the proceeding person gives Himself to the creature to whom He makes Himself present, that He comes to him from the producing person. And since both cases are true together, if we make the further supposition that the proceeding person is both given to the creature and betakes Himself to him, then we have the full concept of the sending activity. For the idea of a mission is fulfilled neither by a mere donation of a thing which does not move itself, nor by a mere coming which does not imply the correlative notion of another as cause of the coming. Only the donation with which is associated an independent setting forth of the one given, is called sending or mission in the active sense, and only that coming of a being which includes the donation, the authorship of another being, is designated as mission in the passive sense, or as the execution of the mission.

We must go on to examine the most important point of all. In what does the term, the result of the mission's activity, that is, of the activity which carries out the mission, properly consist? As has been stated, this product is the introduction of the person concerned into the creature and His existence in the creature, an existence that is proper to the person sent, and is not common to Him along with the sending person.

That this special existence cannot formally be a mere presence according to power and operation, has been shown already,[2] and the assumption of a presence that is no more than this would implicate us in a vicious circle. How, then, can a divine person be

[2] Cf. section 24.

established in the creature in a special way and exist in the creature by Himself alone?

This can be done if a divine person exhibits His hypostatic character in some symbol (as the Holy Spirit did in the dove appearing at the baptism in the Jordan), that is, by presenting Himself in His own activity and that of the divine person from whom He Himself proceeds. But if a created person should wish to represent the Holy Spirit to himself or others under a dove's image made by himself or already at hand, we should not say, and in accordance with the preceding doctrine we could not say, that the Holy Spirit is sent; for He can be sent only by those persons with whom He dwells and to whom He belongs. In the supposition we have just made, He would rather be sought by persons who do not have Him with them and who desire to visualize Him.

This kind of mission is indeed hypostatically peculiar to the person sent, for each of the persons has something proper to Himself which can be grasped in a special concept and hence represented in a special image. But it is merely symbolic, since the divine person is visualized by the creature only in a material symbol representing Him, even though that person, as, for example, the Holy Spirit in the dove, also dwells substantially in the symbol by reason of His omnipresence.

As a rule we call this symbolic mission simply a visible mission, because the symbol, to be a symbol for us, must be something visible; or else we call it an external mission, in contrast to the mission that terminates in the interior of our soul. However, the very real mission of the Son of God in the Incarnation is also visible in the fullest sense, and is likewise external. Hence these terms do not especially and exclusively characterize the first kind of mission which we have been discussing.

Obviously this type of mission is imperfect by its very nature, since a merely symbolic representation cannot properly be called an existence of the represented object in the image. The object represented is in the image only for him who sees the image and associates it with its original. Therefore this sort of mission does not possess its end in itself; it serves only to accompany and illustrate in a visible manner the other kinds of mission which are complete in themselves. Thus on the occasion of the baptism in the Jordan the dove was meant to illustrate the union of the Son of God (who had been sent in His human nature) with the heavenly Father in the Holy Spirit; [3] and the symbolic mission of the Holy Spirit on Pentecost Day, under the image of the rushing wind and the fiery tongues, was meant to emphasize His interior mission into the hearts of the apostles. The latter two kinds of mission—in the Incarnation and in grace—can consequently be called real, actual missions in contradistinction to the symbolic mission, although even of them it may be said that the second has a certain analogy with the symbolic mission. For it effects not so much a real union of the person sent with the created nature, as a manifestation of the former in the latter. But this manifestation is so direct and real that it results in a very close union of the divine person with the creature.

28. The Real Mission of the Divine Persons in Sanctifying Grace. First Kind of Mission by Impression and Expression of the Persons Sent

Let us turn to our proper object, the real mission of the divine persons to the souls of rational creatures by grace.

In accordance with the explanation given above, a true existence, a true presence of one of the divine persons in the creature is conceivable only in the case of an effect produced by Him and the other divine persons in common. On the nature of this effect depends whether we can say that one of the divine persons as such, that is, in His divine and hypostatic character, is introduced into the creature or, in other words, whether He comes as proceeding from another person. Not every effect is suited for this. Although even in God's natural effects some reflection of the eternal processions can be perceived and can be regarded as an outflowing of the wisdom and goodness of God originally active in the generation of the Son and

[3] The dove is the loveliest and most striking symbol of the Holy Spirit. Its form and color put us in mind of the grace and purity of the Holy Spirit, its rapid but unagitated flight represents His lively yet controlled motion, its low murmur is like the expression of love which we have come to associate with the Holy Spirit. Following the baptism in the Jordan, the dove hovered between the Father and His incarnate Son, descending from the former to the latter. Thus in eternity, in virtue of His relation to the Father and the Son, the Holy Spirit hovers above and between them; He shelters them, as it were, under His wings, and brings them together in Himself in blissful embrace, crowning and perfecting their love.

the spiration of the Holy Spirit, in such cases the persons are not communicated to the creature, nor formed in him and poured out into him in their specifically divine character. A closer approximation to a real mission would occur in the so-called *gratiae gratis datae* (namely, those graces that are given to a person mainly for the spiritual benefit of others rather than for his own sanctification); for on occasions when such graces are conferred, Sacred Scripture more frequently speaks of a communication and indwelling of the Holy Spirit, although not in the full and strict sense of the word. Again, we cannot speak of the mission of the Holy Spirit in this sense at the communication of actual graces which prepare the way for sanctifying grace. Unmistakably we have in this case a presence of the divine persons only *secundum virtutem*, according to power and operation, and hence only *secundum appropriationem*, by appropriation.

Only where the power and activity of the divine persons are manifested in a particularly sublime manner, in an effect by which the specific divine excellence of a person is communicated to the creature, and in the communication of which the procession of this person is reproduced in the creature according to His specifically divine character; where consequently this person appears as a seal which, stamped upon the creature, impresses in him the divine and hypostatic character of the person—can we say in the full and proper sense of the word that the person Himself, and not merely some gift derived from Him, is lodged in the creature, is given to the creature, manifests Himself and is present in the creature. Then we can truly say that the divine person enters into the creature, not by some indeterminate effusion of His power, but by an outpouring that remains in its original character and, so to speak, in the same channel —an outpouring of the flood in which that person's eternal procession is accomplished. Then, in a word, the divine person Himself is sent into the creature.

All this takes place in sanctifying grace, and in it alone. This was explained and demonstrated previously, when the image of the Trinity and of the Trinitarian productions was under discussion. For by its assimilation to the divine productions and its union with them, the imitation of those productions effects a continuous formation and establishment of them in the creature.

In the outpouring of supernatural, filial, divine love, of *caritas* into our hearts, the interior outpouring of the love between the Father and the Son that is consummated in the Holy Spirit is continued because it is reproduced. So we can say not only that the love is given to us and is poured out upon us, but that the Holy Spirit Himself is given to us and poured out upon us in this love. We should do even better to say that the habit and act of charity, poured forth by the Holy Spirit, come into our heart by the very fact that He Himself, the torrent of divine love, is given and drawn to our soul.[4]

Similarly in the conferring of supernatural divine light and the reflection of the divine nature upon our soul, in the impress of the supernatural likeness of God, the eternal splendor of the Father is irradiated over us, and His consubstantial image, the Son of God, is imprinted in our soul and is reborn in us by an imitation and extension of the eternal production. Thus God's Son Himself in His divine and hypostatic character is lodged in the creature as the seal of the creature's likeness to God. By the impress of this seal the creature is made conformable to the Son Himself, and by fellowship with the Son he receives the dignity and glory of the children of God.[5]

[4] "The charity of God is poured forth in our hearts by the Holy Ghost, who is given to us" (Rom. 5:5). "In this [that is, in charity] we know that we abide in Him, and He in us: because He hath given us of His Spirit" (I John 4:13). This doctrine is borne out by all those texts which indicate that the Holy Spirit lives in us, or that we live in Him, as though He Himself were the breath of life sustaining us. Thus Rom. 8:9: "But you are not in the flesh, but in the Spirit, if so be that the Spirit of God dwell in you. Now if any man have not the Spirit of Christ [the Spirit of love] he is none of His." Ibid., v.14 f.: "Whosoever are led by the Spirit of God, they are the sons of God. For you have not received the spirit of bondage again in fear, but you have received the Spirit of adoption of sons [in filial love] whereby we cry: Abba (Father)." I Cor. 2:12: "We have received not the spirit of this world, but the Spirit that is of God."

[5] "My little children, of whom I am in labor again, until Christ be formed in you" (Gal. 4:19). "Christ is formed in us in an ineffable manner, not as a creature in creatures, but as uncreated God in a created nature, transforming that nature to His own image by the Spirit, and transferring the creature, that is, ourselves, to a dignity higher than that of a creature" (St. Cyril of Alexandria, De Trinitate dialogi, IV, p.530; PG, LXXV, 905); cf. St. Ambrose, De fide, V, c.7. "That Christ may dwell by faith in your hearts" (Eph. 3:17). But the Son of God as Verbum naturally dwells in us by the light of faith only if faith is animated by love. For, as St. Thomas says (Summa, Ia, q.43, a.5 ad 2), "The Son is the Word, not of any sort, but a Word that

The application to the creature of the divine love-flame flaring up in the Holy Spirit by the enkindling of a similar flame, and the reflection upon the creature of the divine glory shining in the Son by the irradiation of a similar splendor: these two images give us a striking illustration of the two divine missions as prolongations of the eternal processions and their entrance into the creature. These images become still more striking if we combine them with the image of the stamp of the seal imprinted by God upon the soul in the spiritual kiss wherein He so pours forth the light of His countenance and the sigh of His heart that the soul is illuminated and transfigured by His light, and inflamed and animated by His breath.

In the case of the Holy Spirit especially the outer procession as a prolongation of the inner is most fittingly expressed by saying that the Father and the Son breathe Him into the creature. This is the exalted sense in which the Fathers expound the words of Genesis: "And the Lord God . . . breathed into his face the breath of life." [6]

The statement just made would suffice in itself to enable us to perceive a true mission of the divine persons (Son and Holy Spirit) in the communication of grace. In this communication the Son and the Holy Spirit, as distinct from the Father and from each other, are present in the creature by virtue of a definite image impressed by each of them, an image which is so vivid and perfect that it infinitely surpasses a mere symbol. They are both so closely connected with this image that they dwell in it, not only as regards our way of conceiving the matter, because of the relation of similarity, but really, with their substance and personality. This is so for the general reason that as God they are everywhere present, and also because, even if they were not already present everywhere in substance for that general reason, they have to be present in so perfect an impress and effluence of their most intrinsic, personal perfections and origins, just as the seal must be present in its counterpart. Indeed, unlike the material seal after an impression has once been made, they cannot even be thought of as removed from immediate contact with the impression, for the latter, which has existence only from them, also has existence only in them.

---

breathes forth love. Whence Augustine says in *De Trinitate*, IX [c. 10]: 'The Word of which we are speaking is knowledge with love.' "

   [6] Gen. 2:7; cf. I Cor. 15:45.

However, if we wish to conform to scriptural teaching and the views of the holy Fathers and theologians, and if we are to present the whole truth, we must stress a further aspect in the communication of sanctifying grace, an aspect that will show us still another kind of interior mission of the divine persons. This latter kind of mission is so essentially bound up with the former and so closely interwoven with it that, in the expressions used by Sacred Scripture and the Fathers, it can often be distinguished from the former only with difficulty or not at all. In fact, the two form a single indivisible, organic whole. But to understand this organic whole in its entire grandeur and beauty, we must keep the single members clearly in view, not disengaging them from their union but rather proceeding in our investigation on the basis of this union.

29. Second Kind of Real Mission: *Habitum et Habens*

The process by which the divine persons and their processions are formed in rational creatures is not a dead process but a living one, living with a spiritual life. It consists in the habit and the acts of supernatural knowledge and love. As a result of the mission explained above, the divine persons become present to the rational creature as object of a living, intimate possession and enjoyment; and this is the second kind of mission. This mission is the one ordinarily most emphasized in scholastic theology, and is the one principally meant in Scripture when it says that the Holy Spirit is given especially as the *arrha* [7] of our inheritance. For "to give" means primarily to deliver something to another for his possession; but a thing is given over to another's possession only for his use or for his delight. The divine persons cannot be given to us for use, therefore for delight; and delight in this instance can be realized only through knowledge and love.[8] But how does this mission take place in such a way that

[7] Cf. Eph. 1:13 f. *Arrha* is a Semitic word borrowed from the legal language of antiquity. It is best translated by "earnest," or "earnest money," and signifies originally the money or other object of value which is paid by a buyer to a seller to bind a bargain and to guarantee the subsequent payment of the full purchase price. [Tr.]

[8] Cf. St. Bonaventure, *I Sent.*, d. 14, a. 2, q. 1: "What has been given is owned or possessed. What is owned or possessed is at the disposal of the owner or possessor. What is at the disposal of the owner or possessor may be either enjoyed or used. Perfect possession is the ownership of an object that can be both used and enjoyed. In the absolute sense, however, only God is the

it involves the necessary conception of a real, substantial, and hypostatic entrance of the Son and the Holy Spirit into our souls?

When God graciously adopts us as His children and truly unites us to Himself in a most intimate manner by the grace of sonship which, as participation in the divine nature is a very real entity, He gives us Himself, His own essence, as the object of our delight. For the divine vital faculties which are contained in the grace of sonship can be satisfied with no other object. They must have the same object to embrace which the life of God Himself possesses and around which it revolves. But this object must be brought into contact with those faculties in a way similar to that by which it is immediately, substantially present to the inner life of God Himself. Hence it is not enough that the divine essence, which is to be the object of our delight, be merely exhibited to those faculties from afar. It must itself be truly present in them, so much so that if it were not already present everywhere, it would have to be substantially lodged in the creature for this very reason and purpose.

As regards the perfect enjoyment of the divine essence in the next life, in the beatific vision, the teaching of theologians is explicit. This vision can be accounted for only by an utterly interior presence of God's substance in the soul. But even the imperfect enjoyment possible in this life requires the real presence of the object to be enjoyed, for it differs from perfect beatitude only in degree, not in kind. The Apostle indicates this truth clearly when he speaks not only of a *pignus* (pledge) but of an *arrha* (earnest) of our future possession. For an *arrha* is already a part of the promised reward; and so, while the *arrha* must in this case be a less perfect and intimate presence, it must nevertheless be a true, actual presence, and, in comparison with every other kind of presence outside of grace, it must be an altogether interior and singular presence of the divine substance in the soul.

In consequence of this presence of the divine essence in the soul and the real union of the soul with God which is effected by grace

object of our enjoyment or beatitude." To the objection that apparently only created grace is given when the divine persons are said to be bestowed on us, St. Thomas answers (*Summa*, Ia, q.43, a.3 ad 1): "By the gift of sanctifying grace the rational creature is perfected so that he can freely use not only the created grace, but can also enjoy the divine person Himself. And therefore, although the invisible mission takes place according to the gift of sanctifying grace, the divine person Himself is given."

and upon which that presence is based, we enjoy God not as an object that lies outside of us and does not belong to us, but as an object that is really and truly in us and is our own. We truly grasp Him with our knowledge and embrace Him with our love.

Hence this sojourn of God in our soul is beyond doubt real and substantial. But is it also hypostatic? Are the individual persons, that is, those who proceed, present in the soul and given to the soul in their hypostatic character, each in His own personal way? This precisely is the question, as has been pointed out again and again; otherwise the most important note of a true mission is lacking, namely, that special coming of the persons sent which formally depends on, and is bound up with, their eternal procession. How can we assign to the Son and the Holy Spirit a special presence involving their eternal procession, their hypostatic character?

When we receive grace, God becomes the object of our possession and enjoyment in His entire essence. Evidently, then, all three persons come to us and give themselves to us, inasmuch as they are one with the essence, and in the essence with each other. Yet the individual persons, too, as distinct from one another and especially so far as one proceeds from another, can give themselves to us for our possession and enjoyment. The proceeding person is presented to us for possession and enjoyment by the producing person, and by that very fact also presents His Author to us for our possession and enjoyment.

This is the way, then, in which the Holy Spirit comes to our soul and becomes present in it formally in His own person, as the outpouring and pledge of the love of the Father and the Son, and hence also as the outpouring and pledge of the fatherly love with which the Father loves us, His adoptive children. He comes to us as the flower of the sweetness and loveliness of God; in a word, as the *osculum* or kiss of the Father and Son which we receive in the innermost recess of our soul. And when we for our own part know and love the Holy Spirit thus dwelling within us in His own character, and rejoice at our possession of Him, we return God's kiss and taste His ineffable sweetness.[9] In the Holy Spirit and through Him we

[9] St. Ambrose (*De Isaac et anima*, c.3; PL, XIV, 506), says: "The soul adheres to God the Word by a kiss, by which the Spirit of Him who kisses is transferred to the soul. They who kiss are not satisfied with a mere brushing of the lips, but seem to pour their very spirits into each other. . . . The

embrace the Son and the Father, who had sent Him to us as the pledge of their love and happiness; with Him and through Him our thoughts and our love are raised to the enjoyment of those persons from whom He proceeds.

In the previous kind of mission we had come to know the Holy Spirit as the *donum Dei*, the gift of God, which in the Savior's words is given to us as a fountain of living water, springing up unto life everlasting; [10] for such pre-eminently is the Holy Spirit, who is the full outpouring of the inner divine life and who communicates His life to us. But in the mission we are now considering He is a gift so far as He is bestowed on us as the special object of our supernatural life. In the former mission He is a gift in the sense that He is the channel of the supernatural grace and love whereby we become partakers of the divine nature and adopted children of God. Here He is a gift so far as God not only bestows His fatherly love on us and makes fruitful in us that same love with which He loves His only-begotten Son, but also incorporates that love in us in the pledge in which it culminates. In both cases, but especially in the latter, the Holy Spirit is the *donum hypostaticum;* this is the way theologians regard Him, as we have seen, when they signalize the name *donum* (or rather *donabilitas,* "giveableness") as a *proprium,* or property, of the Holy Spirit.

In referring to the Holy Spirit as *donum hypostaticum* we frequently mean no more than that a gift distinct from Himself is bestowed on us through Him, who is the ideal and motive of the giving. That is, as we stated above, we suppose that the Holy Spirit must be thought of as the prototype of the communication of divine love poured out upon us (the *caritas creata*) and as the motive for the communication of supernatural grace which contains the *caritas creata.*[11] In the first case, as has been shown, the donation of the prototype involves a real, essential, and hypostatic indwelling in its

---

soul craves a kiss: God the Word pours Himself wholly into that soul." Cf. St. Bernard (*In Cantica,* serm. VIII, no. 2; *PL,* CLXXXIII, 811): "To kiss . . . means here nothing else than to infuse the Holy Spirit."

[10] John 4:10; cf. 4:14.

[11] We treated of the latter in section 24. Many theologians seem to restrict the Holy Spirit's attribute of *donum* to the fact that He is the *ratio dandi,* the reason why God confers the gifts on us. Actually He is such only with reference to the supernatural gifts. But no mission at all is involved therein, to say nothing of a real, substantial, and hypostatic mission.

imitation. In the second case this is not so evident. For, when I
bestow a gift on anyone out of love, I also include my love for him
in the gift. But I do not actually give him my love in the sense in
which I present the gift to him. It is otherwise with the fatherly love
that God showers on us. We possess this love not only in the general sense in which we say that everyone who is loved possesses the
love of another. We possess it in its substantial nature and its hypostatic outpouring; it is substantially in us. We possess the love as
such, as a love that bestows on us and conveys to us not only other
gifts but this love itself as a special gift. The same love with which
the eternal Father loves His Son is in us as it is in the Son, in its inner
essence and with its inner effusion; it is our own property and rests
upon us: "that the love wherewith Thou hast loved Me," says the
Son to the Father, "*may be in them.*" [12] This is the sense in which the
Prince of the Apostles teaches that the Spirit of God rests upon us;
that is, the Spirit of God rests upon us inasmuch as the paternal love
of God, of which He is the outpouring, dwells in us.[18]

Thus the Holy Spirit in Himself, and not merely in His gifts,
although supposing and including them—for He can be united with
us and we can possess and enjoy Him only through them—is in fullest
truth an uncreated and hypostatic gift. Thus this attribute is a true
property peculiar to Him, as He is distinct from the other persons
by reason of it, although His fitness to be sent has its roots in the fact
that He is the pledge and gift in the eternal love between the Father
and the Son.

In this attribute likewise He is truly and in a special sense the
Paraclete. In this character God's Son promised Him, and the
Church reveres Him so lovingly. All that God has given us He gives

---

[12] John 17:26.

[18] "If you be reproached for the name of Christ, you shall be blessed; for
that which is of the honor, glory, and power of God, and that which is His
Spirit, resteth upon you" (I Pet. 4:14). Cf. Luis de la Puente, *Expositio moralis
et mystica in Canticum Canticorum,* 75. This work abounds in profound and
ardent theological ideas, and is incontestably one of the best books ever
written on the Canticle of Canticles and the sublime mysteries of mystical
theology. Although it is, unfortunately, much less known than the same author's famous series of meditations, in our opinion it far surpasses the latter
work in content and in beauty of style. This book has all the fervor and depth,
joined to the clearest, soundest, and most extensive theological knowledge,
that characterize the golden age of Spanish theology, which coincides with
the golden age of general literature in Spain.

for our consolation, so that we may rejoice, take courage, and find solace in our misery. What heartens us more than the consciousness that we are loved by God with fatherly love in the Holy Spirit, what comforts us more than the possession of those gifts in which this fatherly love is imparted to us? This love is imparted to us, first, as it pours out upon us the Holy Spirit as the source of our childlike love for the Father; secondly, and still more as it gives us the very Spirit of the Father for our own. Consequently the Holy Spirit in person is as truly and properly Paraclete in virtue of His origin as, owing to that same origin, He is the pledge of love between the Father and the Son and the *donum hypostaticum.*

The Son also becomes present in our soul in His own person, as the reflection and exact image of the glory of the Father from whom He proceeds. By virtue of His procession He is the perfect, adequate counterpart of His Father; as such He is offered and presented to the soul in grace in the innermost recess of its being for its possession and enjoyment, that in Him and through Him we may know and enjoy the glory of the Father. Our possession of the Father and His glory need not be restricted to our possession of Him through the Son. But the Father as Father and the glory which He has as Father come nearer to us in the Son and through the Son. And therefore theologians say that it is not only by appropriation but also with perfect propriety that we know God in a most excellent way *in Verbo,* in the expression of the Father's own cognition, just as we lovingly embrace Him in the outpouring of His own love, the Holy Spirit. This truth finds exalted expression in the words of the Apostle: "God, who commanded the light to shine out of darkness, hath shined in our hearts, to give the light of the knowledge of the glory of God, in the face of Christ Jesus." [14]

Naturally this sending of the divine persons into our souls will be perfect only when our fruition of them is perfect, that is, when the divine persons immediately show themselves to us in all truth, just as they are, in their real presence. For then we shall experience the Holy Spirit in His entire sweetness, then truly, face to face, we shall behold the eternal Word and in Him the Father.

[14] Cf. II Cor. 4:6. The Apostle is here speaking primarily of the Son as He comes to us in the Incarnation. But the glory of God really shines in our hearts through the Son of man only so far as we know and possess Him by faith as the Son of God, and therefore in Him also the Father.

Here upon earth the divine persons are present to us only in the obscurity of faith. Although present in us in a real way, the Holy Spirit shows Himself to us only by faith, as the pledge of the divine love for us dwelling in us, so that our love for God is enkindled by His mysterious nearness, and our love regales itself and rejoices in the possession of Him. Furthermore, only by faith do we know the Son who is present in us as the image of the Father. Although the knowledge of faith is definite and certain, and although we may say with the Apostle that Christ dwells in our hearts by faith, in comparison with true vision this sort of knowledge can scarcely be called a possession and fruition of its object. So we find but few indications in Scripture that the Son is sent to us here on earth in the manner in which we are at present regarding the missions. But the mission of the Holy Spirit is pointed out frequently and decisively. For, even though the pledge of love will be perfectly possessed and enjoyed only when we come to know Him perfectly, perfect knowledge is not so essential in His case. Love can embrace its object and rejoice in the possession of it even when it does not behold that object, even when all it knows is that the object is there. And so even here below our love can embrace the pledge of God's love for us that is lodged in our hearts, and can rejoice in Him. Indeed, our present possession and enjoyment of this pledge of divine love is the guaranty of our eventual full possession and fruition of the Holy Spirit, and with Him of the Son and the Father, whom the divine love, plighted in the Spirit, will give us in eternity. And the Holy Spirit Himself, now clasped by us in loving embrace, is according to the Apostle the earnest of Himself and the other two persons, inasmuch as they are to be ours entirely in eternity.[15] In this sense the Apostle calls the Holy Spirit who is bestowed on us the "Spirit of promise, who is the pledge [i.e., according to the Greek, "earnest"] of our inheritance." [16]

---

[15] St. Augustine (*Serm. 13 de verbis Apostoli; Serm.* 156, c.15; *PL,* XXXVIII, 858) says of the Holy Spirit: "What is the thing itself, if the pledge is so great? We should call it an earnest rather than a pledge. For when a pledge is given, it is taken back when the thing itself is given. But an earnest is a portion of the thing which is promised, so that when the thing promised is given, what was wanting to the earnest is made up, but the earnest itself does not change hands again."

[16] Eph. 1:13 f.

30. SPECIAL CHARACTERISTICS OF THE SECOND KIND OF MISSION
   AS CONCERNS THE HOLY SPIRIT. ITS RELATION TO THE
         SANCTIFICATION AND ADOPTION OF THE
            CREATURE AND TO THE LATTER'S
               UNION WITH GOD

With regard particularly to the Holy Spirit, who is sent to us here below in a quite unparalleled manner, Sacred Scripture and the holy Fathers speak of still another kind of presence in our hearts, which at first sight seems incompatible with the presence explained above, but is at bottom essentially connected with it. According to Sacred Scripture the Holy Spirit is sent to us as to a temple which belongs to Him and is consecrated to Him.[17] Consequently He not only belongs to us, but He Himself possesses us as His property. Is this kind of mission, too, a real, substantial, and hypostatic mission?

Undoubtedly this presence of the Holy Spirit is real and substantial, for by grace we are really in Him, just as He is really united to us by a real bond. The relationship of possession is essentially reciprocal. If by grace the Holy Spirit dwells in us with His divine substance as the object of our possession, He likewise dwells in us as the proprietor of our soul and our whole being. Evidently, at least in some respect, this possession of our soul is common to the Holy Spirit and the other two persons. For we are the temples of God as such, not of the Holy Spirit alone. That this possession is appropriated, attributed to the Holy Spirit, involves no difficulty, but is rather most natural. For if He is the embrace of the Father and the Son, if both not only surrender themselves to each other but clasp each other in Him, what is more natural than that the Father and the Son should be represented as receiving the surrender of the creature and as taking the creature into their possession in the Holy Spirit, just as they give themselves to the creature in Him?

However, Sacred Scripture and especially the Fathers, when they speak of the temple of the Holy Spirit, repeatedly employ such striking expressions that in this connection, if anywhere, we are led

---

[17] "Know you not that you are the temple of God, and that the Spirit of God dwelleth in you?" (I Cor. 3:16.) "Or know you not that your members are the temple of the Holy Ghost, who is in you, whom you have from God; and you are not your own?" (I Cor. 6:19.)

to think of a possession of the creature that is truly hypostatic and proper to the Holy Spirit. And, in fact, we are of the opinion that this may readily be conceived. Although the divine substance and activity are common to all the persons, the possession of the substance is peculiar to each person. As each distinct person possesses the divine nature in a special way, He can possess a created nature in His own personal way, and to this extent exclusively. We know that this is the case with the Son in the Incarnation. If the Son alone takes physical possession of a created nature, why should not the Holy Spirit be able to take possession of a created being in a way proper to His own person, by means of a less perfect and purely moral possession (by a ἕνωσις σχετική in contradistinction to φυσικὴ καὶ ὑποστατική, i.e., εἰς ὑπόστασιν μίαν [union according to relationship, in contradistinction to a physical and hypostatic union, i.e., according to hypostasis alone])? In this supposition the other divine persons would not directly possess that being in this particular relationship, but only in the Holy Spirit, as is the case with the Son and His humanity.

In His hypostatic character and by virtue of the same the Holy Spirit is truly the pledge in which and by which we possess and embrace the other persons. No less truly He must, likewise in His hypostatic character, be able to be their depositary in whom and by whom they possess us. Furthermore, as proceeding from the other persons, He must be able to dwell in us as in His own temple, that belongs to Him in a special manner, although, because of the oneness of the divine substance and because of His personal relation to the other persons, He cannot take possession of this temple without them. Rather He takes possession for them. Again, as the Holy Spirit is in a special sense the object of our possessive and joyous love, He can also, in His person, be the special object of the *cultus* of our grateful love. We can and should give and consecrate ourselves to Him as His special property, for the other persons give themselves to us in Him. Thus we would belong to the Father and the Son in Him and through Him.[18] Indeed, in view of the fact that the Holy Spirit is given to us by the Father as the pledge of His paternal love, we can and ought to offer Him as the only worthy pledge of our return of love to the Father and the Son. Just as we

[18] Hence the ancient doxology: "Glory be to the Father through the Son in the Holy Spirit."

can worthily thank God for having given us His Son in the Incarnation only by presenting to Him this very Son as a thankoffering, so we can return the love by which God has given us the Holy Spirit only by giving back to Him this very Spirit as the pledge of our love.

Hence it is clear that the two seemingly opposed aspects of the concepts of donation and possession are, in fact, related to each other. Both alike are expressed in the noble words of the hymn in which the Holy Spirit is called the sweet guest of our soul.[19] He takes possession of our soul as guest, but as a sweet guest, who desires to possess us only through our love. He offers Himself to our love for our sweet enjoyment and blissful embrace. As guest, moreover, He is seen to be not only a hypostatic gift, but also a personal gift.

If we examine this kind of mission more closely, we shall discern many other mysteries in this one mystery. Especially we shall understand the full, profound sense of many passages of Sacred Scripture and the Fathers, to which otherwise only a vague or superficial sense is attached. We shall perceive that by dwelling in our soul as a guest the Holy Spirit is in a most exalted and marvelous manner not only the efficient and exemplary cause, but in a certain sense also the formal cause of our supernatural sanctity, of our dignity as sons of God, and of our union with the divine persons. This is the contention of a number of the most distinguished theologians, on the basis of a more profound study of the Fathers.

1. Let us begin with sanctity. When many of the Fathers implicitly, and many learned theologians, such as Petavius, Lessius, and Thomassinus, explicitly maintain that the Holy Spirit is in a certain sense the formal cause of holiness in creatures, they do not thereby exclude holiness as a state inhering in us. Nor do they assert that the Holy Spirit is identical with this state; rather they teach the contrary. Sanctity as a real state of our soul is the supernatural purity and goodness by which the soul becomes an image of the sanctity of the divine nature. The Holy Spirit is regarded as the efficient and exemplary cause for the infusion of sanctity into our souls partly by appropriation, partly by proper attribution. At the same time this state is a disposition for the reception of the Holy Spirit as our most holy guest. On this account the soul is called holy in the sense in which we call a church holy when it is made ready for the celebra-

[19] "Dulcis hospes animae," in the hymn *Veni Creator*.

tion and reception of the Blessed Sacrament by sacred adornment and the bishop's consecration. As the church thus already holy is again sanctified by the reservation of the Blessed Sacrament, so the soul, already holy by the adornment of grace, is again sanctified by the indwelling of the Holy Spirit, by the Holy Spirit Himself with whom it is united, to whom it belongs, and who has given Himself to it. Thus, too, theologians state that the humanity of Christ is formally holy not only by the state of holiness inhering in it, but also by the uncreated holiness of the Logos to whom it belongs. Although in our case the aforesaid indwelling of the Holy Spirit is in reality conferred along with sanctifying grace, it is distinct from sanctifying grace. So we may and must here distinguish the sanctity of consecration as a special excellence from the sanctity of habitual grace. The distinction between the former and the latter resembles that according to which we call the Father and the Son holy in one sense because of their inherent sanctity which they give to the Holy Spirit, and in another sense because of the Holy Spirit Himself, whom they possess as the sanctity proceeding from them. As the Holy Spirit proceeds from the sanctity of the Father and the Son, but for that very reason remains their own, so He enters into the sanctity presented to us by His indwelling, and also becomes ours, not as an inhering quality, but as an indwelling person.

As has been indicated, this sanctity of consecration is effected by the sojourn of the Holy Spirit in our soul as possession and treasure, and likewise as guest and proprietor. For the vessel containing a holy and precious treasure is no less holy than the house in which a holy and noble guest sojourns in order to take possession of it.

2. The Holy Spirit sanctifies us by dwelling in us hypostatically as gift and possessor. He likewise makes us adoptive children of God. This He does as a channel that pours forth supernatural grace and charity into our hearts, and so in a sense He continues His divine life in our souls. The Apostle says: "Whosoever are led by the Spirit of God, they are the sons of God." [20] Usually we understand the sonship of God only in the sense that man becomes conformable to God in a supernatural manner by virtue of the state and disposition of his soul, and so bears in himself a likeness of the divine nature and the divine life.

No one can rightly deny that the grace and charity inhering in

[20] Rom. 8:14.

the soul suffice to make man an adoptive son of God. But we must go further and say that grace and charity constitute the dignity of the sons of God inasmuch as they render the soul conformable to God, but also because they make God's own Spirit the property and innermost possession of the soul.[21] Indeed the proprietorship and indwelling of the Holy Spirit impart to this dignity its highest splendor and value. For we are made like the natural Son of God not only because we are conformable to Him, but most of all because we personally possess within ourselves the very same Spirit that He possesses; and our union with the heavenly Father is so glorious because of the fact that He has incorporated His own Spirit in us. This is why the Apostle calls the Holy Spirit the "Spirit of adoption of sons, whereby we cry: Abba (Father)"; [22] i.e., the Spirit by whom our adoption is effected, and by whom the relation of sonship evoked by this adoption is constituted or, better, sealed. For in another passage the same Apostle says: "Because you are sons [and ought to be perfect sons] God hath sent [in order to crown and seal this dignity and this relationship] the Spirit of His Son into your hearts, crying: Abba, Father." [23] The indwelling of the Holy Spirit seals the relation of adoptive sonship in us much as His procession from the Father and the Son crowns and completes the relation of the natural sonship. For this reason the Apostle calls the inhabitation itself a sealing by the Holy Spirit: "You were signed with the Holy Spirit of promise, who is the pledge of our inheritance." [24]

If the Holy Spirit Himself in person, as the pledge of the fatherly love bestowed upon us and of the inheritance to be hoped for, thus seals us and our relationship to the Father by His possession of us and His indwelling in us, we perceive the full sense of the words,

---

[21] In the following pages Scheeben presents his definitive view concerning the controverted question of the personal inhabitation of the Holy Spirit. [Tr.]

[22] Rom. 8:15.

[23] Gal. 4:6.

[24] Eph. 1:13 f. By the seal of the Holy Spirit we can also understand its impress on our soul, namely, charity and grace, of which we spoke previously; or in a very special sense this impress is the sacramental character which stamps and marks us as Christ's members called to grace. But here the Apostle apparently regards the Holy Spirit Himself in His union with the grace-endowed soul as a seal, for he does not say that we are sealed by the Holy Spirit or through the Holy Spirit, but with Him; and moreover his assertion is based on the fact that the Holy Spirit in person is the pledge (*arrha*) of our inheritance.

"whereby we cry," and "who cries in us: Abba, Father." We address God with the cry, "Father," and the Holy Spirit cries out the same word in us by the fact that filial and trustful love of God is poured forth into us by Him. But this love in turn cries out the name of Father so strongly and trustingly because it possesses and embraces the highest pledge of the Father's love in the Holy Spirit. And most of all the Holy Spirit Himself cries out in us inasmuch as He brings us near to the Father and infuses the tenderest trust in Him into us by His personal possession of us.[25] Lastly, so far as He makes us worthy of the great tenderness of the eternal Father by His indwelling, He in person is the inexpressible sigh begging for us the love and benefits of the Father. To this sigh we add our own inexpressible sighs and prayers by which we long for the full revelation of the glory of the children of God.[26] For God "shall quicken also your mortal bodies," says the Apostle, "because of His Spirit that dwelleth in you"; [27] that is, God will awaken our bodies to glorious, immortal life, and thereby will reveal the full glory of the children of God.

3. Of course the Holy Spirit is the seal of our sonship in God not only because God belongs to us as our Father, but also because we belong to Him as His children, as similarly in God Himself not only the Father belongs to the Son, but also the Son belongs to the Father in the Holy Spirit. Thus, as in the Trinity the Holy Spirit is the bond and seal of the absolute unity of the Father and the Son by His procession from them both, so by His indwelling in us He is the bond and seal of that unity which we are to have with God as His adoptive children. The Son of God Himself had prayed to the Father for this when He said: "I pray . . . that they all may be one, as Thou, Father, in Me, and I in Thee; that they also may be one in Us." And that this may come to pass, that we may be one as He and the Father are one, and may "be made perfect in one," He adds that He has given us the glory which He had received from the Father, and explains the organism of unity by the fact that He is in us and the Father in Him.[28] But if we are one in the

---

[25] Eph. 2:18: "We have access both [Jews and Gentiles] in one Spirit to the Father."

[26] Rom. 8:26: "The Spirit Himself asketh for us with unspeakable groanings."

[27] Rom. 8:11.

[28] John 17:20–23.

Father and the Son, then we are one in the very bond of this unity, the Holy Spirit; and if the Son is truly in us, then He is in His own Spirit, who unites us both to Him and to the Father.

But just as the soul as child of God is sealed and is united to God the Father through the Holy Spirit, and as the Holy Spirit is the *osculum*, or kiss, of the Father whereby the Father takes the soul to Himself as His child and unites it to Himself, so He is likewise the *osculum* of the Son, by which the soul becomes the latter's bride. As bride of the Son the soul in grace prays to Him in the Canticle (1:1): "Let Him kiss me with the kiss of His mouth," so that by His spiritual kiss it may become one with Him in one Spirit.[29] The soul becomes one with the Son as one Spirit in the Holy Spirit, whom He breathes forth into the soul and with whom the soul merges through the breath of love aroused by Him: like a flame which, after it has been enkindled from another flame, meets and fuses with the latter and unites with it to form a single flame. The real indwelling of the Spirit of the bridegroom in His bride is to the spiritual marriage of the Son of God with the soul what corporal union is in corporal marriage, a union to which bride and bridegroom aspire in their reciprocal love. Hence it can be regarded as the consummation and sealing of the affectional union between the Son of God and the soul.[30]

Thus the soul, joined by the Holy Spirit to the Son as sister and bride, and to the Father as child, is taken up by the same Holy

[29] "Know you not that he who is joined to a harlot is made one body? . . . But he who is joined to the Lord is one Spirit" (I Cor. 6:16 f.).

[30] St. Bernard especially, in his characteristically tender and contemplative fashion, speaks of God's kiss in the Holy Spirit and its relations to the soul in grace. Thus in the frequently quoted Serm. VIII *in Cantica*, no. 9 (*PL*, CLXXXIII, 814), he says: "Blessed kiss, by which God is not only recognized, but the Father is loved, He who is not fully known unless He is perfectly loved. How describe that soul of yours which has sometimes heard in the secret depths of its consciousness the Spirit of the Son crying, 'Abba, Father'? Let the soul which perceives that it has the same Spirit possessed by the Son be convinced that it is loved with fatherly affection. Have confidence, O soul, have confidence and do not hold back. In the Spirit of the Son recognize yourself as the child of the Father, as the spouse or sister of the Son. You will find such a soul called by both names. The proof is at hand; I shall not have to belabor it. The voice of the Spouse calls to the soul: 'I am come into My garden, O My sister, My spouse' (Cant. 5:1). The soul is a sister, as child of the same Father; spouse, because in the same Spirit. For if carnal marriage joins two in one flesh, shall not spiritual union much more join two in one Spirit? Whoever cleaves to the Lord is one Spirit."

Spirit into the intimate communion, into the fellowship and company of both, into the wonderful fellowship of the Father and the Son, which St. John depicts as the purpose of the Incarnation.[31] The Holy Spirit is the bond uniting the Father with the Son in His procession from both, and is likewise the bond uniting the Father and the Son with the creature by His coming to lodge in the latter. This is in the highest sense the communication or society (κοινωνία) of the Holy Spirit of which the Apostle speaks,[32] that is, it is not only a fellowship with the Holy Spirit Himself, but a fellowship of the creature with the divine persons through Him and based on His procession from them and His entrance into the creature, a fellowship in which the Holy Spirit unites every individual, and also all sanctified creatures as a body, to the divine persons, and therefore also among themselves, threading and joining all together into a great, golden chain. The spiritual unity which the Apostle exhorts us to preserve [33] consists not only in the union of affection, not only in the concord of the love poured into our hearts by the Holy Spirit. We are to guard the unity of love among us because a spiritual "bond of peace," the Holy Spirit Himself, embraces us all, because there is one Spirit for all who come together in one body,[34] and because the union perfected in the Holy Spirit demands on our part a unity of disposition of all of us with the divine persons, similar to that which the Father and the Son exemplify in the spiration of the Holy Spirit.[35]

[31] "That . . . our fellowship may be with the Father and with His Son, Jesus Christ" (I John 1:3).

[32] "The grace of our Lord Jesus Christ, and the charity of God, and the communication of the Holy Ghost be with you all" (II Cor. 13:13). "If there be . . . any comfort of charity, if any society of the Spirit . . ." (Phil. 2:1).

[33] Eph. 4:3: "Careful to keep the unity of the Spirit in the bond of peace."

[34] Eph. 4:4: "One body and one Spirit."

[35] On the office of the Holy Spirit in our union with God we wish to quote several little known but beautiful passages from the Fathers, which can serve to elucidate and confirm our position. The author of the *Libellus de vita solitaria ad fratres de monte Dei* [probably William of Saint-Thierry; the work is contained in *PL*, CLXXXIV, 307–64; the passage quoted by Scheeben is found in col. 349] says: "This unity [the union of God with man] is called spirit not only because the Holy Spirit brings it about or joins man's spirit in it, but because it is the Holy Spirit Himself, because God is charity. For through Him who is the love of the Father and the Son, and their unity and sweetness and good and kiss and embrace and whatever can be common to both in that supreme unity of truth and truth of unity, man in his way is united to God as the Son is united to the Father in substantial unity, or as the

31. Organic Connection of the Two Kinds of Mission as Factors of a Single Total Mission. Explanation of Remaining Details

1. The doctrine thus described makes clear the distinction between the two kinds of interior mission. Manifestly the second kind, taken in itself, verifies the notion of mission more perfectly than the first. In the first kind of mission the eternal processions are, in fact, merely imitated and are continued only so far as a different sort of procession, an analogous procession of an effect coming from God to creatures, is connected with the divine processions, although the connection is close. In the second mission, on the contrary, the terminus of the eternal procession, the proceeding person as such, is placed in relationship with the creature in order to dwell in the creature and to present Himself to the creature precisely as that which He is by His eternal procession.

Father to the Son. This takes place when the beatified consciousness finds itself, as it were, in the midst of the embrace and kiss of the Father and the Son." St. Augustine had spoken in a similar vein (*Serm. 11 de verbis Domini; Serm.* 71; *PL*, XXXVIII, 454): "Here is indicated the authorship of the Father, the nativity of the Son, the unity of the Father and the Son in the Holy Spirit, and the equality of all three. That, therefore, which the Father and the Son have in common, they wished us to have in common, both among ourselves and with them, and they wished to gather us into one by that gift which they have in common, that is, by the Holy Spirit, God and the gift of God. In Him we are reconciled to the Trinity in which we have our beatitude." Not so closely connected with the doctrine we are here emphasizing, but most beautiful and instructive, is the following passage from St. Fulgentius (*Ad Monimum*, II, c.11; *PL*, LXV, 190 f.): "We pray that the same grace by which the Church became the body of Christ may enable all the members to persevere in corporal unity, joined by the abiding bond of charity. Fittingly we pray that this blessing may be granted us by the gift of that Spirit who is the one Spirit of the Father and the Son; for the holy and natural unity, equality, and charity of the Trinity, which alone is the one true God, sanctify those whom it adopts by the bond of mutual love. In that one substance of the Trinity there is unity in origin, equality in off-spring, and fellowship of unity and equality in love. That unity admits no cleavage, that equality suffers no diversity, that charity never palls. No discord can arise there, for the equality which is loved and is one, the unity which is equal and is loved, and the love that is equal and one, persevere necessarily and immutably. For the love of the Father and the Son is shown to be one by the fellowship, if we may speak thus, of the Holy Spirit. The blessed Apostle commends this fellowship in the following words: 'The grace of our Lord Jesus Christ, and the charity of God, and the communication [fellowship] of the Holy Ghost be with you all' (II Cor. 13:13); and in

In actual truth, however, these two kinds of mission are distinguishable only in concept. We have already stated that they constitute an inseparable, living organism, which must be regarded as the single, integral mission which they combine to form. How is this to be explained?

The explanation is contained in the preceding doctrine. The Holy Spirit, who is the outpouring both of the paternal love of the Father and of the filial love of the Son, can be conceived by us as the pledge of God's fatherly love for us only if we realize that our supernatural filial love for God is poured forth into us as an overflow of the same love from which the Holy Spirit proceeds. Similarly, the love of the Holy Spirit is poured into our hearts only that we may thereby embrace the pledge of God's love proffered by Him in the Holy Spirit. Indeed, in a certain respect this supernatural love is enkindled and inflamed by the Holy Spirit as its object; for the motive of the love is also the fuel and stimulus for it, and the Holy Spirit is such pre-eminently, for He is the living expression, the breathing forth of the divine love for us. Thus at bottom we have only a single stream, a single process in which the Holy Spirit is poured forth into us and is sent into us as prototype, as object, and as stimulus of our love. This triple signification may well be the true interpretation of the Apostle's ineffably profound and suggestive words: "The charity of God [that is, love for God, or also God's own love] is poured forth in our hearts by the Holy Ghost, who is given to us" (Rom. 5:5).[36]

---

another place: If there be 'any comfort of charity, if any society of the Spirit' (Phil. 2:1); wherefore it is written that 'the charity of God is poured forth in our hearts by the Holy Ghost, who is given to us' (Rom. 5:5). Truly the Holy Spirit, the one Spirit of the Father and the Son, accomplishes in those upon whom He has conferred the grace of adoption what He effected in the men who in the Acts of the Apostles received the same Spirit. Of these it is said that 'the multitude of believers had but one heart and one soul' (Acts 4:32). For the multitude of believers in God had been made to have but one heart and soul by Him who is the one Spirit of the Father and the Son, and with the Father and the Son is one God. Wherefore the Apostle says that this spiritual unity is to be carefully preserved in the bond of peace, exhorting the Ephesians in this fashion: 'I, therefore, a prisoner in the Lord, beseech you that you walk worthy of the vocation in which you are called, with all humility and mildness, with patience, supporting one another in charity, careful to keep the unity of the Spirit in the bond of peace; one body and one Spirit' (Eph. 4:1-4)."

[36] The primary meaning of the Apostle's statement is that the created charity

In like manner with the Son of God. The Son of God becomes the object of our happiness (in the future life, and with due proportion also in the present life) only because the Light of which He Himself is born, the Light of the divine nature and cognitive faculty, is irradiated in us as in Him, and produces a reflection of the Father's nature in us as, similarly, it does in Him. And conversely, this Light is irradiated in us only inasmuch as we know and perceive the Son as the mirror of the Father, and in Him the Father Himself. But, whereas the object of love is conceived as an attractive force, the object of knowledge must be thought of as illuminative and as stimulating the eye by its light. In a certain sense knowledge is effected by the illumination of its object; hence the Son of God must be regarded as an object that directs its beams toward us and invites our knowledge. Here, then, we have an indivisible irradiation of God's Son in our soul in His threefold character as prototype, as object, and as motive of our supernatural knowledge. This process, indivisible but still so profuse, this mission of God's Son to our soul, has been vividly described by the Apostle in the noble words previously quoted: "God . . . hath shined in our hearts, to give the light of the knowledge of the glory of God, in the face of Christ Jesus." [37]

Thus the two kinds of mission essentially involve and pervade each other, and combine so perfectly to form a single whole that the several parts of the organism are scarcely distinguishable. We might in general describe the complete mission thus: the mission of a divine person is effected in and by the fact that a rational creature participates in Him (this is the μετοχή κοινωνία, of the Greek Fathers). But to understand this participation properly we must carefully distinguish the assimilation to the participated person from the union with Him. Without an assimilation to the person sent the mission cannot be conceived at all; but the mission or real coming of the divine person to the creature cannot be formally comprised in the fact that He discerns an image of Himself in the creature. The real entrance of the divine person into the creature consists rather in His union with the creature in and by this assimilation, that is, in the

---

is imparted to us by the Holy Spirit, the personal uncreated charity, who is poured forth into us. But the words, "the Holy Ghost, who is given to us," can also be referred to our possession of Him by created grace.

[37] Cf. II Cor. 4:6.

astounding fact that He draws near to the creature as a seal, in order to assimilate the creature to Himself, and by such assimilation to offer Himself to the creature as the creature's own property, for his possession and fruition. According as we think of the presence of the divine person in the creature as principle or as goal of the assimilation, we have a mission of the first or of the second kind. But since the first kind of presence leads to the second, on account of the resulting assimilation, both kinds of presence contribute in indissoluble unity to form one sojourn and inhabitation that abounds in grace.

With this clarification we have gained a distinct and complete concept of the proper nature of the interior missions of the divine persons; we know the manner in which the proceeding divine persons can and will really, substantially, and hypostatically come to the creature along with sanctifying grace and exist in him.

But to characterize these missions adequately in their full course and to follow the scriptural view in smallest detail, we have still to consider two elements: the carrying out of the missions and their ultimate end, to which we must add some discussion of the relation between the mission of the Son and that of the Holy Spirit to each other and of both to the Father, who sends only and is not sent.

2. The mission of the divine persons or, better, their entrance into the creature, is carried out by a divine activity. According as this activity is attributed to the proceeding person Himself or to the person from whom He proceeds, we may say that the former person betakes Himself to the creature to whom He comes, or that the latter person sends Him. This activity considered in itself is not a *proprium* of the sending or of the sent person, but is only an *appropriatum*. We have already seen this; here we wish to repeat the matter only on account of its application. In virtue of this appropriation, the person sent is regarded as fulfilling the will of the sending person, although in reality He has the same will; and likewise He is frequently represented as effecting His union with the creature by Himself alone, although He can act only in and with the other persons. To the Holy Spirit especially is ascribed the carrying out of His own mission and also that of the Son, for the simple reason that the distribution of grace, with which the missions are so closely connected, is a work of the divine love, which is represented by the Holy Spirit, and also because the Holy Spirit, as the

term of the interior processions in God, is viewed as the natural channel conveying that love to the outside world. Thus even the execution of the Son's mission in the Incarnation (*conceptus de Spiritu Sancto*) is ascribed to Him; much more, then, the mission involved in grace.

3. Therefore, as concerns the decree and the execution of the mission, an activity that corresponds to their personal characteristics is appropriated to the sending and the sent persons; similarly an activity is appropriated to the persons sent, in their presence at the term of their mission, in order to bring out the fact that their coming is not merely hypostatic, but personal. So far as the persons sent are really in us according to their personal characteristics, they have no individual activity. They are merely the prototype of the effect of the divine activity, as well as the object and motive of the creature's activity. If without appropriation we call the Holy Spirit alone the Comforter, the Paraclete, we can do so only so far as He affords us consolation not by any activity, but by His interior presence in us and His possession of us. But when a divine person comes to us, He comes in reality with His power and activity, although He has these in common with the other persons; and we are led to believe that the person who is principally and especially active in us is precisely the person who comes to us. This is the way we think of the Holy Spirit particularly, for He is the person who chiefly comes to us in this life and is chiefly active in us, as the Comforter sent to us by the Father, as the life-giver, guardian, and friend of our soul; and we are all the more justified in this view, seeing that He is the representative of the divine love and in a special sense dispenses all of God's graces to the creature.

As we stated above, the end of the true mission of a divine person to the creature is not, strictly speaking, the activity which that person is to exercise there, because the activity is only an *appropriatum*, not a *proprium*; nevertheless this activity can be brought into harmony with the end of the mission. In carrying out His mission, the person who is sent is thought of as exclusively active in a twofold sense: first, so far as He Himself effects His union with the creature; and secondly, so far as, while sojourning in the creature, He puts forth an activity that corresponds to His union. But the appropriation of the activity does not negate the personal character of the mission, if we actually make the proper presence of the person who is sent the basis of this appropriation, and regard it as the center of the sending process.

In the scriptural and patristic treatment of this topic, we often find the appropriated activity closely associated with the real, hypostatic presence, in a way that resembles the connection between the two kinds of presence. This association is so close that sometimes we cannot distinguish them at all, as, for example, when the Savior says that He will send us the Holy Spirit as Comforter. If we analyze such expressions with sufficient care to fathom their full meaning, we shall discern all the pertinent factors and see them joined into one harmonious whole. Otherwise we run the risk of overlooking some elements in favor of others, and shall gain either a one-sided or a confused notion of the mystery which Sacred Scripture is intended to reveal to us.

If in the manner just indicated we include the appropriated activity in the concept of the mission, we see that the person sent is given by the sending person, and that He Himself comes, and that He comes to us not only to exist and abide in us, but also to act in us.

But the external divine processions cannot be regarded as finished when a divine person reaches the goal to which He has been sent. The entrance of a divine person into the creature can be effected only for this purpose, that, with the person to whom He is sent, He return to the person who has sent Him; or better, that He conduct and receive the created person to whom He is sent into union with the sending person, from whom He Himself never departs.

Owing to the περιχώρησις, the *circumincessio*, the mutual penetration of the several persons, one of them cannot enter into union with us unless the others, too, enter into union with us. To some extent this fact is expressed when we say that the sending person descends into our soul along with the person sent. But thus understood, our union with the sending person is not so clearly perceived to be a proper effect of the person sent, or as the result and goal of His mission. For in this case the person sent appears merely as one who is sent on ahead, as a precursor of the sending person. He appears as one coming to us first but without really effecting a union with the sending person by means of a special function, and without acting as intermediary between the two whom He is to unite.

But activity of this sort is what we ordinarily associate with the name of the person sent, an activity which Scripture and the Fathers ascribe especially to the Holy Spirit. According to the Fathers, a return movement corresponds to the processive movement of the divine persons; that is, by His coming, His sojourn, and His activity in our soul the Holy Spirit raises us up to a union with the Son, and through the Son with the Father. We are made partakers of the divine nature by the mission and the communication of the Holy Spirit. Thereby we attain to fellowship with the Son of God, who is born anew in us; with Him we enter into relationship with His Father, who thereupon becomes likewise our Father.[88] And when the Son is sent by this rebirth in us, the Holy Spirit also is sent in Him. Both conduct us to the Father who, as sending but not sent, is the first principle and the last end, and both unite us to the Father as His children. Our full entrance into the bosom of the Father, our complete union with the Father in which we behold Him face to face and have our beatitude in Him, and with Him the Son who dwells by nature in His bosom, take place only when the Son of God is reborn in us in His entire glory—in eternity. In eternity, in the eternal repose in God's bosom, the ultimate term of all movement is at length reached, but especially the term of the temporal missions and processions of the divine persons. There they will dwell in us, no longer that they may lead us to union with Him who has sent them, but to communicate to us, in fellowship with the Father as the object of our utmost beatific fruition, the divine peace of their unity.

The unfolding of the interior Trinitarian life in the productions and processions of the divine persons necessarily leads back to their unity in the possession of the one divine nature; and the Trinity terminates in the Triunity. So, too, the external unfolding of those processions in the missions comes to this, that the creature into whom they flow is taken up into union with the divine nature, in order to become one with and through the divine persons in a way similar to their oneness with one another. By the missions, therefore, the Triunity as well as the Trinity of God is manifested in the creature.

Much more could be said about the missions of the divine persons. But what remains does not lie within our scope. We refer

[88] Cf. St. Cyril of Alexandria, *De Trinitate dialogi*, IV, p. 530 (*PG*, LXXV, 905); VII, p. 644 (*PG*, LXXV, 1097).

whoever desires to know more about this matter to the theologians who have devoted special attention to it.[89]

Our aim has been sufficiently achieved. Our intention was to show that the mystery of the Trinity in its characteristic features, in the eternal processions which have an external prolongation in the missions, involves a most intimate and vital relationship to the mysteries of supernatural grace; furthermore, that it is the living root which puts forth the order of grace and intertwines its ramifications with that order; and lastly, that it acquires its greatest significance and most engrossing interest in and through the order of grace.

But beyond the external missions of the divine persons of which we have been speaking, there is another, an incomparably more sublime mission, that of the Son (and in Him also of the Holy Spirit) in the Incarnation. In this mission a divine person becomes present to a creature in His hypostatic individuality; and, by assuming a created nature to His hypostasis in hypostatic union, He actually becomes one with the creature, and by means of the assumed nature exercises not merely appropriated, but truly proper activities and functions. This is the mission of missions.

In this mission the mystery of the interior Trinitarian processions naturally acquires a still greater significance for the outer world, partly for the very reason that it is so closely interwoven with the other kind of mission, which it brings about and perfects. It is the point of convergence of an extraordinary, mysterious order of things, which in God's plan is constructed upon the basis of the Trinity, and springs up from it in glorious harmony as from a living root. It is the central point of a system which is the objective revelation and manifestation of the Trinitarian system, and therefore can achieve clarification only in terms of the Trinity.

We shall demonstrate this later, when we undertake to present in orderly fashion the entire doctrine of the mystery of the Incarnation.

---

[89] St. Thomas, *Summa*, Ia, q. 43. Among the commentaries on this question, see especially those of Suarez and Ruiz.

APPENDIX I TO PART I

A Hypostatic Analogue in the Created
Order for the Holy Spirit and His Origin [1]

▪▪▪

(As Supplement to p. 95)

W E have no reason to feel surprise if the second divine process
as hypostatic should have no analogue in the created order,
if God in His infinite fecundity should communicate Himself within
the divinity in a manner that would have no counterpart among
creatures, as is the case in His external communication of Himself
by creation. However, we are of the opinion that there is such a
counterpart, an image which partly by parallel, partly by antithesis,
in many respects throws clear light on the second divine procession,
and illustrates it not only by its difference from the first procession,
but also by its positive relationship to it. For the second production
in God does not differ from generation as though it ran independently alongside generation; it essentially presupposes generation, and its difference from generation lies precisely in its positive
relation to generation.

But where are we to find such an image?

1. When the Macedonians rejected the doctrine of the Holy
Spirit's procession from the substance of God, and argued that
no origin from a substance was conceivable except by generation,
the Fathers, especially St. Gregory of Nazianzus, pointed out that

[1] In this Appendix, Scheeben compares the position occupied by the Holy
Spirit in the Trinity with the place of the mother, especially of the virginal
mother, in the family. Theologians in general prefer to compare the Son of
God, as the Wisdom of the Father, with the woman in the family. Of course
all such comparisons are feeble and defective in the extreme. [Tr.]

181

a different mode of derivation is found even in human nature, namely, in the production of Eve from Adam's rib.[2]

This observation is generally taken as a mere subterfuge which disarms the adversary but does not shed any further light on the matter itself. We think otherwise. We are of the opinion that this example can brilliantly illustrate the dogma throughout its entire depth. Let the reader judge.

In deriving Eve from the side of Adam, God wished to bring about the procession of human nature in the representatives of family unity (father, mother, and child) from one principle, just as the divine nature is transmitted from the Father to the Son, and from the Father and the Son to the Holy Spirit. He wished to exhibit family unity in mankind as the truest possible imitation of the unity in nature of the divine persons. As in God, the Son alone proceeds from the Father, and the Holy Spirit is the fruit, the crown, and the seal of their unity, so in mankind the woman was first to proceed from the man alone, and the child was to be the fruit and crown of the union of man and woman. The differences which spring to mind in this comparison serve but to strengthen it.

In the human family the son appears as the third person, and his origin as the second procession; but in God the Son is the Second Person, and His origin is the first procession. But why? Duality, the twofold principle of act and potency, rules throughout creation; human nature, too, is split into two principles, one predominantly active, the man, the other predominantly passive, the woman. Therefore also generation, the supreme act of nature, results from the union of the members of the species. In God, on the contrary, in whom there is no partition into act and potency, who is the purest

---

[2] Cf. Gregory of Nazianzus, *Oratio theologica* V, nos. 10 f.; *PG*, XXXVI, 144 f. Gregory's adversary had challenged him to show how the same God could produce one person as a Son, and another who is not a Son; if Gregory could show him an instance of this, and also show that both were consubstantial with God, he would admit that both were God. Gregory replies that it is not always possible to find in the material universe an example which will illustrate divine truth. Nevertheless he adduces several instances from the animal kingdom, and finally from human nature: "What was Adam? An image of God. What was Eve? A segment of this image. What was Seth? The offspring of both. Do not the image, the segment, and the offspring seem to you to be [specifically] the same? Why not? Are they consubstantial or not? Certainly they are. Thus we must admit that beings which come into existence in different ways can have the same substance."

and most perfect nature, generation as the principal and most natural act of the divine nature must proceed immediately and exclusively from the First Person. With men generation is the *ultimum in executione* [last step in the order of execution], because it presupposes the difference between the sexes for its realization, while at the same time it is the *primum in intentione* [first objective in the order of intention], because the difference between the sexes exists only on account of it. But in God it must be absolutely the first production in every respect. For the very reason that generation in God is true generation, it must proceed from one person, not from two persons.

Nevertheless the Third Person in God functions as mediator between Father and Son, although in an incomparably higher sense than the mother does between father and child in human nature. As the mother is the bond of love between father and child, so in God the Holy Spirit is the bond of love between the Father and the Son; and as she brings forth the child in unity of nature with the father by transmitting the nature from the father to the child, so the Holy Spirit manifests the unity of nature between the Father and the Son, not of course by transmitting the divine nature to the Son, but because He Himself is the fruit of their mutual unity and love. In God, the Son proceeds from the Father as perfect Son without requiring the intermediacy of another person for His origin and constitution. The fecundity of generation in God requires as a consequence the bond of union which is a necessary condition for generation among human beings: although the Son has His origin from the Father alone, His supreme unity with the Father requires the production of a personal bond in whom the Father and the Son express their love for each other. The functions of the individual persons concerned in both cases are assigned in different sequence; but this change of order lies in the very nature of things, in the difference between divine and human nature.

So, too, in the very nature of things the production of the woman from the man corresponds to the production of the Third Person in God, although in the case of human nature that production precedes generation and presupposes no second person. (1) The production of the woman from the side of the man is not a natural, but a supernatural production, and therefore is not generation. The production of the Holy Spirit is not supernatural as regards God, but neither is it natural, in the sense of a production by way of nature, that is, of nature attesting and expressing itself. (2) The production of the woman from the man is a work of love, both of divine love, which drew her from the side of Adam, and of Adam's love, for he gave up his rib for her in the sleep of love. Eve did not spring from Adam by the exercise and actuation of his natural faculties, but was taken from the substance of Adam to be his help-mate in the propagation of nature by generation. Likewise the Holy Spirit is derived from the substance of the Father and the Son, and is given by them to each other in their mutual love, not as col-league of the Father for the generation of the Son, not as begotten by the Father along with the Son, but as the bond in which the oneness of nature between the begetter and the begotten is sealed. (3) And as Eve was taken from the side of Adam, from his heart, the seat of love, seeing that the material of her body was taken and given out of love, so we must say of the Holy Spirit that He proceeds not from the bosom, but from the heart of the Father and the Son.

2. If these notions of ours should seem too new and singular—and we confess that we have not found them in the Fathers and theolo-gians under this form—they are for all that quite ancient as presented in another and fairer guise. It is well known that the Fathers, fol-lowing the example of the apostles, regard Christ as the new, true Adam, of whom the first Adam was only the type. They also teach that the bride of Christ, the Church, as the new Eve, proceeded from the side of the new Adam somewhat as the first Eve proceeded from the side of the first Adam. For the divine vital principle which constitutes the Church the bride of Christ was drawn from the side of the new Adam, dying and sunk in the sleep of love. This vital principle is none other than the Holy Spirit who, as He receives His own essence from the divinity of God's Son, also enters into the Church through and from the Son's humanity, in order to im-pregnate it with the power of the Son of God. Further, the purifying and life-giving blood stream flowing from the heart of Christ over and into His Church is at once the vehicle and the symbol of the temporal, and consequently of the eternal, outpouring of the Holy Spirit. Thus the side of the first Adam, as type of the side or the heart of the new Adam, is likewise a type of the side or the heart of the Son of God in His divinity.

Scripture says that God formed the woman out of the rib taken

from the side of Adam; the Fathers teach that Christ formed the
Church out of the water and blood streaming from His side: in
like manner we may say that the Father and the Son have taken and
formed the Holy Spirit from their side, their heart. And as Eve can,
in a figurative sense, be called simply the rib of Adam, since she
was formed from the rib of Adam, St. Methodius goes so far as to
assert that the Holy Spirit is the *costa Verbi*, particularly since He
not only has His origin from the side of the Logos, but remains there,
and is thence communicated to creatures in order to form the bride
of Christ from Him. "By the rib," says St. Methodius, "we rightly
understand the Paraclete, the Spirit of truth; and they who are enlightened by drawing upon Him are reborn unto incorruptible life.
. . . For He, the septiform Spirit of truth, is quite properly called
the rib of the Logos; and after the ecstasy, that is, after the death of
Christ, God takes from Him and forms her [the Church] who is to
be Christ's helpmate." [8] However, since Christ does not give up, as
Adam did, a rib from His side, but His very blood for the formation of His bride, we shall do better to say that the Holy Spirit is
sprung from the heart's blood of the Father and the Son. In this
manner of expression His procession appears as substantial as in the
other figure, but in a more inherently true and vivid fashion, since
it is represented as arising immediately from the very source of love
and life, and directly implies love and life. Thus His production is
exhibited as an effusion rather than a formation, and so this analogy
is in fullest accord with the analogy previously derived from the
outpouring of the breath of life.

3. But why, then, the question will be asked, is the second production in God not designated by a special name, in conformity with
this figure? In answer we may observe simply that the figure itself
lacks a name of its own because it represents an act that has occurred
but once and is extraordinary by its very nature. We may add that
it is a reverse rather than an obverse image. But perhaps the similarity
of the image with the original, as well as its dissimilarity from the
original, is not without bearing on the naming of the Third Person
and His production.

The original name which Adam, enlightened by God, assigned
to the woman, was given to her with reference to her origin from
Adam: "She shall be called woman (הָאִשָּׁה), because she was taken

[8] St. Methodius, *Convivium decem virginum*, III, c.8; *PG*, XVIII, 73.

out of man (הָאִישׁ).'' Of course, even if the Third Person is to be named according to this analogy, the name of the woman need not be transferred to Him, any more than the name of the man is transferred to the Father and the Son. Indeed, in accordance with the basic concept of the analogy, this may not be done. If Eve was called "woman" because she was taken from "man," the Third Person in God must be named after the persons from whom He proceeds. He must be called Spirit, because He proceeds from the Father and the Son inasmuch as both are one Spirit; He is Spirit of Spirit, *Spiritus de Spiritu*, or *Spiramen*.

The very inflection of the term which in Hebrew means "woman" indicates that it is derived from the term which means "man," and hence that its object, too, is derived from the object for which the latter term stands, that it is essentially related to that object, and points to it. In the same way the name "Spirit" as the proper name of the Third Person, hence in the sense of *Spiramen*, necessarily points to the name "Spirit" as it pertains to the two other persons, and indicates that its object is derived from the object represented by the name "Spirit" in the latter sense. And as the Hebrew word for woman serves to show that the woman, who was taken from the side of the man, is joined to him most intimately as a companion and helpmate of like nature, so the name "Spirit" in the case of the Third Person in God indicates that He proceeds from the other two persons as their most perfect companion, and is united to them in the possession of their own infinite life.

Is not our analogy of great significance for the clarification of the name selected by revelation, and is it not in complete accord with what we have stated previously, following the doctrine of the Fathers, concerning the derivation and meaning of this name? And is not this harmony in turn the best justification of our analogy? Even the dissimilarity existing between the analogue and the original is not without bearing on the name assigned to the Holy Spirit; it corroborates negatively the name "Spirit," which is vouched for positively by the similarity.

The origin and the position of the woman among the three persons in whom the organization of human nature is represented, depend upon the fact, as do also the differentiation between the sexes and the transmission of human nature, that this is a corporal, or more significantly, a carnal nature. Among created spirits there is no substantial transmission of nature, nor is there among human beings to the extent that their nature is spiritual. The propagation of nature takes place only in the flesh and by the flesh. But the woman as wife and mother represents the imperfection inherent in this mode of propagation; that is, the need for the woman as secondary principle of generation brings to light the deficiency of the primary principle. Hence her name necessarily recalls all the imperfections that are implied in the relations of human propagation. Therefore, if we were to transfer the name "woman" to the Third divine Person, not only He but also the Father and the Son would be represented after the fashion of carnal beings; we should be led to think of a separation taking place in the divine substance, of mutual complementary functions between the several persons, of carnal appetite, and the like. This name and its basic concept cannot be simply elevated and purified as is the name of father. The latter expresses something that is predominantly active and perfect, whereas the name of woman, wife, and mother directly denotes a passive function.

But whereas in mankind the woman, the conjoining link between father and son, represents the carnal character of human nature and propagation, in God the person occupying the central position between Father and Son must represent the spirituality of the divine nature and its mode of propagation. He must be the flower, the consummation of the divine spirituality.

The propagation of nature among men is rooted in its carnal character; but the propagation of the divine nature arises from God's absolute spirituality. A communication of nature to another person takes place in God for the very reason that God is the absolute Spirit, that as such He intellectually conceives His essence and expresses it in a personal Word. Consequently, as in mankind the woman is the medium and representative of the carnal unity, the unity of flesh established between father and son, so in God the Third Person must represent the spiritual unity, the unity of spirit, of the spiritual nature between Father and Son; not indeed as its intermediary, but as its flower and culmination. Therefore, when we come to designate the character and position of this divine person, we may not transfer the name of woman to Him, but must rather designate Him as the exact opposite, as an absolutely spiritual bond or simply as spirit, as the issue and revelation of the spiritual unity between the Father and the Son. Because of its pure spirituality, generation in God is virginal; [4] hence the Holy Spirit must be the bond of union between the Father and the Son in virginal fashion.

The woman would represent the Holy Spirit not partially, but wholly, not merely in her origin but also in her nature, if without being wife and mother she could be the center of love between father and son in the family as a virgin. Hence, if we prescind from those relationships, we may to some extent regard the Third Person as the representative of feminine attributes, that is, of love and tenderness, among the divine persons.

But such relationships are so closely bound up with the notion of woman and her position in the family that they cannot be dissociated from her. They can be disregarded only where the woman, not in the human family, but in the supernatural divine family, in virginal espousals with the incarnate Son of God and as adopted daughter of His heavenly Father, becomes the representative of a heavenly love, of a love that is poured out into the hearts of all men, indeed, yet finds its most responsive flame in the hearts of virgins consecrated to God, and its most charming and beautiful expression in their contemplative and active life of love. Virgins consecrated to God are, as Cyprian so beautifully describes them, "the flower of the Church's buds, the luster and ornament of the Holy Spirit," [5] and as such are the most striking images of the Holy Spirit Himself, who stamps His own character upon them. This is true above all of the Virgin of virgins, who was made a mother in a supernatural manner by the power of the same Holy Spirit and who, through the Holy Spirit and with Him, is the bond of love between the Father and His Son become man, just as He is between the Father and the Son in the Godhead. And such too, modeled upon her, is the Church which, animated by the Holy Spirit, is in Him and through Him the spiritual, virginal mother of all those whom in the power of the Holy Spirit she presents to God the Father as His children, and incorporates in the incarnate Son as members of His mystical body.

But this idea of supernatural, glorified womanhood is not so much

---

[4] Cf. the beautiful poem of St. Gregory of Nazianzus, *Carmina*, II, "In laudem virginitatis" (*PG*, XXXVII, 523): "The Blessed Trinity is the first Virgin," etc.

[5] St. Cyprian, *De habitu virginum* (*PL*, IV, 443): "Flos est ille ecclesiastici germinis, decus atque ornamentum gratiae spiritalis."

a visible, independent image that leads us to a knowledge of the Third Person in God, as rather a reflection, invisible in itself, of His personal character, a reflection which can be conceived and understood only in and from the personal character of the Holy Spirit.

APPENDIX II TO PART I

The Appropriations of the Holy Spirit

▪▪▪

O N page 134, note 8, we promised to give a more protracted account of the activities and works appropriated to the Holy Spirit. We present this in the subjoined passages from the Fourth Book of the *Summa contra Gentiles* of St. Thomas, who has gathered most of them together in systematic order. However, we observe that the collection does not claim to be complete and that many of the scriptural texts quoted, as we have shown, can and must be understood not only of an appropriated activity but also of the Holy Spirit's hypostatic relations. St. Thomas is here concerned only with the activity of the Holy Spirit, and so in this supposition must interpret everything according to appropriation.

ST. THOMAS AQUINAS, *SUMMA CONTRA GENTILES*

BOOK IV

CHAPTER XX

On the Effects which Scripture Attributes to the Holy Spirit
with Regard to Creation in General

We must next treat of the effects which Sacred Scripture attributes to the Holy Spirit.

We have shown (Bk. I, chap. 75) that God's goodness is the reason why He wishes other things to exist and produces them by an act of His will. Therefore His love for His goodness is the cause of the creation of things. Hence certain of the philosophers of antiquity claimed that the *love of the gods* was the cause of all things, as we read in *I Metaphysics* (IV, 1); and Dionysius says (*De div.*

nom., chap. 4) that God's love did not permit Him to be without issue. In the preceding chapter we established the fact that the Holy Spirit proceeds by way of the love with which God loves Himself. Therefore the Holy Spirit is the principle of creation. And this is indicated in Ps. 103:30: "Send forth Thy Spirit and they shall be created."

From the fact that the Holy Spirit proceeds by way of love, and that love has a certain impelling and motive force, the power of movement with which God has endowed things seems rightly attributed to the Holy Spirit. But the first change induced by God in things is the production of the various species from formless created matter. Sacred Scripture attributes this work to the Holy Spirit; thus Gen. 1:2 states: "The Spirit of God moved over the waters." By the "waters" St. Augustine would have us understand the primordial matter over which the Spirit of God is said to move (I *de Gen. ad litt.*, c. 15); not that the Holy Spirit is in motion Himself, but because He is the principle of motion.

Further, God's government of creation is envisaged as a kind of movement, according as God directs and moves all things to their proper ends. If, then, impulse and motion pertain to the Holy Spirit by reason of love, the government and propagation of created beings is fittingly assigned to the Holy Spirit. Hence it is said in Job 33:4: "The Spirit of God made me"; and in Ps. 142:10: "Thy good Spirit shall lead me into the right land." And since the government of subjects is an act proper to a ruler, dominion is suitably ascribed to the Holy Spirit. Thus in II Cor. 3:17 the Apostle says: "The Lord is a spirit." And in the Nicene Creed we say: "I believe in the Holy Spirit, the Lord."

Finally, life especially is manifested in movement; for we say that things which move themselves live, and in general we ascribe life to all things that bring themselves to action. And so if impulse and motion are ascribed to the Holy Spirit by reason of love, life also is fittingly attributed to Him. It is written in John 6:64: "It is the spirit that quickeneth"; and in Ezech. 37:5: "I will send spirit into you, and you shall live." Likewise in the Creed we profess our belief in the Holy Spirit, the life-giver. This accords with the very name, "Spirit"; for even the bodily life of an animal is owing to the vital spirit that is diffused throughout its members by the principle of life.

CHAPTER XXI

On the Effects Attributed to the Holy Spirit in Sacred Scripture as Regards the Gifts Bestowed by God on Rational Creatures

With regard to the proper effects wrought by God in rational nature, we should note that, in whatever way we are conformed to a divine perfection, such perfection is said to be given to us by God. Thus wisdom is given to us by God according as we are in some way assimilated to the divine wisdom. Since the Holy Spirit proceeds by way of the love with which God loves Himself, as was shown in chap. 19, the Holy Spirit is said to be given to us by God, inasmuch as by loving God we are assimilated to this love. Hence the Apostle says (Rom. 5:5): "The charity of God is poured forth in our hearts by the Holy Ghost, who is given to us."

We must realize that whatever we have received from God is to be referred to God as its efficient and exemplary cause. God is the efficient cause inasmuch as an effect is produced in us by the divine operative power. He is the exemplary cause according as whatever we receive from God reflects Him in some way. Since the Father, the Son, and the Holy Spirit have the same power, as they have the same essence, everything that God effects in us must be wrought by the Father, the Son, and the Holy Spirit acting together as efficient cause. But the word of wisdom by which we know God and which God has implanted in us, is properly representative of the Son. Similarly the love with which we love God is properly representative of the Holy Spirit. And thus the charity that is in us, although it is the effect of the Father, the Son, and the Holy Spirit, is said to be in us in a special way from the Holy Spirit.

However, the effects produced by God not only have their origin in the divine operation, but are sustained in existence by it, as is clear from Bk. III, chap. 65. Further, a cause cannot operate except where it is present, since worker and work must actually be together, just as the mover and the things moved must (VII *Phys.*, II). Therefore, wherever an effect of God is found, God also must be there as cause. Wherefore, since the charity with which we love God is effected in us by the Holy Spirit, the Holy Spirit Himself must be in us, as long as charity remains in us. Thus the Apostle says (I Cor. 3:16): "Know you not that you are the temple of God, and the Spirit of God dwelleth in you?" Since, then, we are made lovers of God by the Holy Spirit, and every beloved object is in the lover as such, the Father and the Son necessarily dwell in us also, through the Holy Spirit. Hence our Lord says (John 14:23): "We will come to him," that is, to him who loves God, "and will make our abode with him." And in I John 3:24 it is stated: "In this we know that He abideth in us, by the Spirit which He hath given us."

It is evident that God ardently loves those whom He has made lovers of Himself by giving them the Holy Spirit; for He would not confer so great a good except through love. Hence Prov. 8:17 states, in the person of the Lord: "I love them that love Me"; and the beloved disciple adds (I John 4:10): "not as though we had loved God, but because He hath first loved us." But every beloved object is in its lover; and therefore by the Holy Spirit God is not only in us, but we are also in God. Wherefore we read in I John 4:16: "He that abideth in charity abideth in God, and God in him"; and in verse 13: "In this we know that we abide in Him, and He in us: because He hath given us of His Spirit."

One of the characteristics of friendship is that a friend reveals secrets to his friend. For as friendship unites affections and makes one heart, as it were, out of two, a person may be regarded as not having uttered outside of his own heart what he reveals to a friend. Thus in John 15:15 our Lord says to His disciples: "I will not now call you servants . . . but friends, because all things whatsoever I have heard of My Father, I have made known to you." Therefore, since we are made friends of God by the Holy Spirit, we may well say that the divine mysteries are revealed to men by the Holy Spirit. As the Apostle remarks (I Cor. 2:9 f.): "It is written: That eye hath not seen, nor ear heard, neither hath it entered into the heart of man, what things God hath prepared for them that love Him. But to us God hath revealed them by His Spirit."

And since a man's speech is based on his knowledge, he may fittingly be said to utter divine mysteries through the Holy Spirit, according to I Cor. 14:2: "By the Spirit he speaketh mysteries"; and Matt. 10:20: "For it is not you that speak, but the Spirit of your Father that speaketh in you." And of the prophets we read in II Pet. 1:21 that "the holy men of God spoke, inspired by the Holy Ghost." This is why the Creed makes mention of the Holy Spirit "who spoke by the prophets."

Besides the characteristic of friendship, which consists in the reve-lation of secrets on account of the union of hearts, the same union requires the sharing of one's possessions with a friend; for, since a man's friend is, so to speak, his other self, he will aid his friend as he would treat himself, by sharing his goods with him. And so it is held to be a mark of friendship to will and to do good to a friend, according to I John 3:17: "He that hath the substance of this world, and shall see his brother in need, and shall shut up his bowels from him: how doth the charity of God abide in him?" This is true of God above all, for His will is efficacious in the production of the effect He intends. And therefore all the gifts of God are with reason said to be given to us by the Holy Spirit, as is indicated in I Cor. 12:8: "To one, indeed, by the Spirit is given the word of wisdom; and to another the word of knowledge, according to the same Spirit"; and after enumerating many other gifts the text con-tinues, in verse 11: "But all these things one and the same Spirit worketh, dividing to everyone according as He will."

To reach the abode of fire, a body must evidently be made like to fire and become light, so as to acquire the motion proper to fire. In the same way, to attain to the happy state of divine fruition which is proper to God by nature, a man must first become like to God by the acquisition of spiritual perfections, and must then perform works that correspond to such perfections; and thus he will at length attain to the state of beatitude mentioned. But spiritual gifts are conferred on us by the Holy Spirit, as has been shown. And so we are made con-formable to God by the Holy Spirit; by Him we are rendered capable of performing good works; and by the same Holy Spirit the way to beatitude is opened up to us. The Apostle indicates these three stages in II Cor. 1:21 f., wherein he says that He "that hath anointed us is God, who also hath sealed us, and given the pledge of the Spirit in our hearts"; and in Eph. 1:13 f.: "You were signed [i.e., sealed] with the Holy Spirit of promise, who is the pledge of our inheritance." For sealing apparently alludes to the likeness of conformity to God; anointing, to man's capacity for the performance of perfect works; and pledge, to the hope which sets us on the road leading to our heavenly inheritance of perfect happiness.

Sometimes good will toward a person results in adopting him as a son, so that one's inheritance may fall to him. Therefore the adoption of the sons of God is fittingly attributed to the Holy

Spirit, as is stated in Rom. 8:15: "You have received the Spirit of adoption of sons, whereby we cry, Abba (Father)."

When a person becomes the friend of another, all offense is banished, for offense cannot stand with friendship; thus in Prov. 10:12 it is written: "Charity covereth all sins." Therefore, since we are made friends of God by the Holy Spirit, it is through Him that our sins are forgiven by God. And so in John 20:22 f. our Lord says to His disciples: "Receive ye the Holy Ghost; whose sins you shall forgive, they are forgiven them." This is the reason why forgiveness is denied to those who blaspheme against the Holy Spirit (cf. Matt. 12:31), because they lack that by which a man may receive forgiveness for his sins.

It is for this reason, too, that we are said to be renewed and cleansed, or washed, by the Holy Spirit, according to Ps. 103:30: "Thou shalt send forth Thy Spirit and they shall be created, and Thou shalt renew the face of the earth"; and Eph. 4:23: "Be renewed in the spirit of your mind"; and finally Isa. 4:4: "If the Lord shall wash away the filth of the daughters of Sion, and shall wash away the blood of Jerusalem out of the midst thereof, by the Spirit of judgment and by the Spirit of burning."

CHAPTER XXII

On the Effects Attributed to the Holy Spirit in His Guidance of the Creature Toward God

After this consideration of the effects which, according to Sacred Scripture, the Holy Spirit produces in us, we must next treat of the manner in which we are guided to God by the Holy Spirit.

In the first place, conversation with a friend seems to be a special mark of friendship. Man's conversation with God takes place in contemplation, as the Apostle stated in Phil. 3:20: "Our conversation is in heaven." As the Holy Spirit makes us lovers of God, He also makes us contemplators of God. Thus the Apostle says in II Cor. 3:18: "But we all beholding the glory of the Lord with open face, are transformed into the same image from glory to glory, as by the Spirit of the Lord."

Another trait of friendship is to delight in the company of a friend, to rejoice in his words and deeds, and to find comfort in him when in trouble; and so we fly to a friend for comfort especially when we are in sorrow. Since the Holy Spirit renders us friends of God and causes Him to dwell in us and us in Him, as has been shown in the preceding chapter, it is through the Holy Spirit that we have joy in God and consolation in all the afflictions and assaults of the world. Wherefore in Ps. 50:14 it is said: "Restore unto me the joy of Thy salvation, and strengthen me with a perfect spirit"; and Rom. 14:17: "The Kingdom of God . . . is justice, and peace, and joy in the Holy Ghost"; likewise Acts 9:31: "The Church had peace . . . and was edified, walking in the fear of the Lord, and was filled with the consolation of the Holy Ghost." This is why our Lord calls the Holy Spirit Paraclete, that is, Consoler, as in John 14:26: "But the Paraclete, the Holy Ghost," etc.

A further mark of friendship is acquiescence in the wishes of a friend. God's will is made known to us by His commandments. Hence the keeping of the commandments is part of our love for God, as we read in John 14:15: "If you love Me, keep My commandments." Accordingly, as we are made lovers of God by the Holy Spirit, it is by Him, too, that we are led to carry out God's commandments; this is the teaching of the Apostle in Rom. 8:14: "Whosoever are led by the Spirit of God, they are the sons of God."

We should note, however, that the sons of God are led by the Holy Spirit not as slaves, but as freemen. For, since he is free who determines the course of his own actions (I *Metaph.*, II, 9), we do freely what we do of our own accord, that is, of our free will. But what we perform unwillingly, we perform not freely but under compulsion. In this latter case the violence may be absolute, when the cause of an action is in the external circumstances and the agent contributes nothing (III *Eth.*, I, 12), as for instance when one is compelled to move by force; or it may be partly voluntary, as when one chooses to do or to suffer what is less opposed to his will, so that he may be spared what is more opposed to his will. But the Holy Spirit, by making us lovers of God, inclines us to act of our own free will. Thus the Holy Spirit leads the sons of God to act freely, out of love, and not slavishly, from fear. And so, in the words of the Apostle (Rom. 8:15): "You have not received the spirit of bondage again in fear, but you have received the Spirit of adoption of sons."

The will tends to what is truly good. Hence if a man turns from what is truly good on account of passion or an evil habit or disposition, he behaves in a slavish manner, inasmuch as he is swayed by some factor external to himself. This is the case if we consider the bent of the natural will. But if we consider the act of the will as tending to an apparent good, the person in question acts freely in following passion or corrupt habit. If, however, while still in the same disposition, he abstains from doing what he wishes to do through fear of the law which orders the contrary, he behaves slavishly. Therefore, since the Holy Spirit by love inclines the will to true good, which is its natural object, He obviates both the servitude whereby the slave to passion and sin acts against the right order of his will, and the servitude whereby a person acts in accord with the law but against the inclination of his will, as if he were a slave of the law, not its friend. Hence the Apostle says (II Cor. 3:17): "Where the Spirit of the Lord is, there is liberty"; and Gal. 5:18: "If you are led by the Spirit, you are not under the law."

This is why the Holy Spirit is said to mortify the deeds of the flesh; for bodily suffering does not turn us from the true good to which the Holy Spirit guides us by love; this is the doctrine taught in Rom. 8:13: "If by the Spirit you mortify the deeds of the flesh, you shall live."

PART TWO

The Mystery of God in the Original Creation

> This [divine] excellence, which tran-
> scends all our powers of comprehension,
> was once the portion of us men; and so
> much a part of our nature was this good,
> which passes all understanding, that man's
> own perfection seemed a most exquisite
> likeness and imitation of the original
> prototype.
>
> Gregory of Nyssa, *De beatitudinibus*, Or. III

CHAPTER VIII

Creation and Original Justice

▄▄

32. The Mystery of God in the Creature: Not the Creature as Such, but the Communication of the Divine Nature to the Creature

GOD as He is in Himself, in the Trinity of divine persons, God dwelling in inaccessible light, is the greatest and most sublime mystery of Christianity.

But much concerning God has been made visible in His works; and what is made visible is no mystery for us, at least not in the narrower, technical sense.

If the works of God reveal His invisible attributes and make them visible, they cannot be regarded as mysteries in the proper sense of the word. This is especially true inasmuch as these works come to our knowledge not indirectly but directly. We do not mean to say that we can fathom and understand all the works of God in their profoundest depths; such a notion would not occur to anyone. We see only the surface, not the center of things; only the phenomena, not their innermost substances; only the obvious effects, not their basic causes. We can probe into the interior, we can advance to reasons and causes only by inferential processes. Nevertheless we can thus advance; by the light native to us we can really come to know the natural world, although in an imperfect manner.

But according to Christian notions a true mystery in the created world must be something so sublime that by our natural light we cannot acquire even an imperfect and inferential knowledge of it. This mystery is hidden and unattainable, not because it lies so deeply imbedded in created nature, as if it were the innermost marrow and substance of things, but because it stretches so immeasurably high above the ultimate essence of created nature. Even if reason could succeed in perfectly grasping this essence, it would have made not the slightest progress toward the disclosure of the mystery placed by God in the creature.

This is not the case with our knowledge of God, as we have seen. If we knew His essence as it is in itself, we should straightway understand the mystery of the Trinity; for this mystery does not really and objectively extend above the essence of God, but rises above it only inasmuch as that essence is manifested in created nature. But on the created plane the natural is really distinct from the supernatural, and is not necessarily connected with it. The supernatural is added to nature as a new, higher reality, a reality that is neither included in nature, nor developed from it, nor in any way postulated by it. As God exhibits two kingdoms for us to contemplate, one plainly visible and one full of mystery, so, too, in the creature we discern two distinct kingdoms, as it were two worlds, which are erected one on top of the other, one visible and the other invisible, one natural and the other supernatural. The profounder reaches of even the first of these worlds is unfathomable for purely natural reason; the second is unattainable and unsearchable in every respect, and is therefore mysterious in the absolute sense of the word.

Everything that has existence outside of God must be a work of God. Hence, in the event that there is to be a true mystery outside of God, that is, in the creature, God's works must be of two kinds: visible (either for the corporal or for the spiritual eye) and invisible (for both of these faculties alike), natural and supernatural. The first kind of works is meant when we say that we acquire knowledge of God from His works, for only such works can lead us to a knowledge of God. Supernatural works, on the contrary, are not so well adapted to impart a knowledge of God to us, since they are not known to us in themselves; rather God makes them known to us by supernatural revelation. But, once revealed, they in turn manifest the majesty, power, and goodness of God in a far higher way than the works of the first sort usually do.

Consequently nothing can be more opposed to the sublimity and dignity of the exalted mystery which by faith we Christians discern in creatures than the refusal to acknowledge more than one kind of divine works. Nothing is thus more opposed than the mean view which would restrict God's activity to the production of non-divine beings, to mere concern for their natural development, and to the granting of extraordinary aids for the correction of any disturbances to this development that might arise. Yet it is not so long ago that this very notion found its way into many systems of thought.

Many thought that the great mystery of man which Christianity had revealed consisted in no more than this, that in Christianity man appeared truly as God's creature, and hence that he had a transcendental relation to God, that is, a relation which extended beyond man's nature as considered in itself and was imperceptible to reason.

Others, and to some extent these same thinkers, were of the opinion that the state in which God had created man was quite intelligible, on the ground that man's nature required that it be created in this state. Indeed they thought that such a state was so obviously intelligible and necessary that man, as he comes into the world now, stripped of the gifts of the original state, could not be understood at all, unless the loss of those gifts were ascribed to some common sin by which that loss was brought about. Accordingly it is precisely the present state of fallen man which was held to be a mystery, a mystery that could find clarification only in the mystery of original sin. "Without this mystery," says Pascal, "the most incomprehensible of all, we are incomprehensible to ourselves. The node of our present condition has its entanglements and complications in this abyss, so that without this mystery man is more inconceivable than the mystery is inconceivable to man." [1]

For my part, I should hold that in this view no mystery at all would remain. The original state is no mystery if it is so completely intelligible in itself; the present state in which we are born, and which is known by experience, is no mystery if its explanation necessarily requires original sin; even original sin itself is no mystery if it is postulated as the sole possible basis for the explanation of the actual and observable state of affairs, and hence is known by the unaided reason. At the most it could be called a mystery on account of the incomprehensibility of its nature. The incomprehensibility of original sin is so great in this theory that it arises not so much from the weakness of our intellect as from the absurdity of

[1] *Pensées*, Part II, a. 5, no. 4.

the thing, as will be shown later. But even if we grant that the incomprehensibility is only on the side of our intellect, we have no right to call original sin a mystery in a different sense from a thousand other, natural things, as, for example, the union of the soul with the body. Only the *how* is obscure to us in this theory; the *that* and the *what* are perceptible to our reason. And besides, in the event that the sin remains the sole mystery, has not this mystery entered the world through man, through the creature, as a work of man? What then remains of the mystery of God in the creature? We should have to restrict the mystery to a supernatural reaction of God against sin. But in that case it enters the world only incidentally, quite at haphazard. We shall see that even the Incarnation, if limited to this reaction, can scarcely retain its real sublimity, to say nothing of the possibility of displaying its entire grandeur.

Originally, prior to sin, a great mystery of God was lodged in the creature, particularly in man, a divine work that was mysterious and imperceptible to our reason. Only as a reaction against this mystery of God does sin appear as a mystery, with a character and range of malice that is as far beyond the reach of natural reason as is its opposite.

This mystery is a special, supernatural work of God. Hence it is by no means that relation of dependence in which man as creature stands to his Creator. Creation is the cause of non-divine beings and natures, which can come into existence only by creation. Dependence on God as Creator and the relations arising from that dependence are as essential and natural to every non-divine being as its own existence. On that account such matters are knowable not merely through supernatural revelation; the unaided reason can and must know them, even though it does not understand them completely. How, then, can anyone maintain that the relation of creature to Creator is a supernatural, specific Christian mystery? Undoubtedly it is difficult for reason, left to its own resources, to form a clear and distinct idea of creation from nothing. The very greatest philosophers of pagan antiquity did not succeed in formulating such a concept. But even they had some faint inkling of this truth, seeing that they thought of all non-divine being as dependent on God. In any case the fact of creation falls within the range of natural truths. Hence creation is not in any proper sense a transcendental truth that is unattainable for reason.

Unattainable for reason, truly supernatural, are those higher relations of dependence and union with God which are called forth in the creature by an action of God that is wholly and entirely distinct from creation. We say: by an action of God that is wholly and entirely distinct from creation, in order to distinguish it from that action which, though not in itself creation, that is, the production of a substance from nothing, is a necessary consequent of creation and is required for the continuation and completion of the order of things established by creation. As Creator, God cannot merely give sheer existence and nothing more to His creatures; He must so equip, sustain, and guide them that they can achieve their natural destiny and perfection. This activity of God and its necessary effects are self-understood in the supposition of creation. They are even less supernatural and suprarational than creation itself; they are included in the very notion of creature, of angels, of man.

But the higher activity which we were speaking of is neither creation itself nor its necessary accompaniment. It is an activity of a special, supernatural, and extraordinary beneficence and love, whereby God gives immeasurably more to His creature than the latter possesses in its nature or can claim for its perfection by virtue of its nature. It is an activity by which God builds upon the foundation laid in creation, and makes of it the substratum and basis of a higher creation, a higher order. It is, in a word, an activity by which God elevates the creature above its own nature and makes it participate in His nature.

The mystery of God in the creature is not the creature as such, even when he bears his natural relations to God clearly branded on his forehead. This, as has been stated, is not a mystery for the healthy natural reason. It is a mystery only for perverted reason, reason sunk in sense, reason which has smothered its own natural light and so can yield no norm for distinguishing the rational from the suprarational. The mystery of God in the creature is a supernatural ocean of light that wells up from God's bosom and pours over the creature to make him a sharer in the divine nature and glory. Consequently it is as enigmatic and mysterious for us as is the nature of God. It is a certain diffusion of the interior divine productions over the creature, and consists in the fact that God impresses the image of His Son on the creature in order to admit the creature to participation in His own nature, and thereby brings forth His own Son in the creature anew. It consists further in the fact that God once again breathes His own Spirit into the creature, thereby uniting the creature to Himself in closest supernatural fellowship of life and love. It is a re-birth and fellowship which, owing to their incalculable sublimity, are as mysterious and obscure for the creature as are the generation of the eternal Son and the spiration of the Holy Spirit. The mystery of God in the creature is the outpouring upon the creature of the secrets hidden in the bosom and heart of God. It is a raising up of the creature from his lowliness and remoteness to the bosom and the heart of God: to the bosom of God, that the creature may be reborn of Him, clarified by His light, and transformed into His image; to the heart of God, that the creature may be animated by His own Spirit, inflamed with His fire, and become fused with Him as one Spirit. This mystery is so sharply distinct from creation itself and from everything belonging to creation that it is, so to speak, the opposite of creation. It extricates the creature from the lowly position assigned to him by his origin from nothing in order to deify him, that is, to make him a sharer in the divine nature with all the majesty, sanctity, and beatitude of that nature. Therefore we must contrast it with creation in much the same way as we contrast generation and spiration in the interior of God with creation.

The difference between the only-begotten Son of God and the deified creature can but corroborate the mysterious, supernatural character of this deification. The eternal Word possesses the divine nature essentially and necessarily; the divine nature is inseparable from His personal character as God's Word, for He could not be the Word of God unless the Father expressed His own essence in Him and conveyed His own nature to Him. If, therefore, there is a Word in God, He must necessarily be of divine nature; He must be God. Creatures, on the contrary, because they are creatures, do not have part in the divine nature, and they can never become God. As creatures they are of other nature than their Creator. If their nature is in some respect similar to the divine nature, this similarity is not a specific similarity, and is not such that by virtue of the similarity it can be called divine. Hence participation in the divine nature can be neither essential nor necessary for creatures. It infinitely transcends the compass of their being and the dignity of their personality, and can be bestowed upon them only in consequence of a totally unlooked-for impulse of divine love, an inconceivable outpouring of divine omnipotence, as a sheer gift of overflowing divine grace.

What are we to infer from this? We conclude that the communication of the divine nature to creatures, although it is not so perfect or so sublime as the generation of the Word, is as inscrutable and mysterious from our point of view as this generation is. For, even though in the generation of the Word the divine nature is substantially communicated in its totality, we are as much struck with wonder at the thought that in His external works God should transmit a participation in His nature to creatures. True, the product of the eternal generation is infinitely greater. Still it is quite natural for God, and is intelligible even for us on the supposition of an interior production in God. This is so because, within the Godhead, God can communicate only His own essence, and that in its entirety.

Although in our case the effect of the divine activity is infinitely less, the distance of the creature from God is so immeasurably great that the suggestion that God could in any way grant a participation of the divine nature to creatures must strike us as inconceivable. Moreover, the communication of the divine nature to the Son of God is in reality objectively necessary. As has been shown, only the feebleness of our natural illumination is the reason for our failure to perceive its necessity and its product. But the communication of the divine nature to creatures is not at all necessary, not even on the supposition of creation; God has no need of effecting such a communication, nor have creatures the slightest right to it. The decree by which it is accomplished is an absolutely free act of the divine will. Hence for the creature it is an absolute mystery, which can be made known only by a revelation that on God's part is just as free.

Since, therefore, the communication of the divine nature to creatures is absolutely supernatural as far as they are concerned, we find joined in it the two characteristics of a true mystery which we have noted in the case of the Trinity. By reason of its supernaturalness this object is so sublime that of ourselves we cannot even surmise it, we can form no definite concept of it, to say nothing of the impossibility of a positive demonstration and comprehension of it. We grasp it only so far as we know that God "is able to do all things more abundantly than we desire or understand," [2] and so far as under the guidance of revelation we can form an analogous representation of it by comparisons and symbols taken from the natural world. Such a representation, indeed, can be made sufficiently definite and true; but it will always resemble more a silhouette than a clear, living image of the object.

Still less can we gain any knowledge of the reality of this object by our natural reason. A priori reasoning is ruled out, if only because the object is not necessary; and also a posteriori knowledge, such as is gained by personal experience of a fact or by conclusions drawn from a given fact, is impossible in this case. For an essentially supernatural fact can be the object only of a supernatural experience. We can no more be aware of participation in the divine nature, even if we actually possess it, by our natural illumination, than we can mediately or immediately perceive the spirituality of our soul by our senses and our organs of sense perception.

Whoever regards participation in the divine nature in man, along with its concomitant perfections, as obviously intelligible or as the object of natural experience, shows by that very fact that he does not understand it at all, that he has not the slightest notion of it. He confuses the higher with the lower, the supernatural with the natural, and so draws the former down from its celestial heights to the lowliness of the latter; or else he thrusts nature up to such an exalted level that the supernatural and the divine seem natural to it, and so he confuses nature with God. If we have a correct appreciation of the lowliness of created nature and of the infinite majesty of the divine nature, this sort of confusion is impossible; then we shall regard the communication of the divine nature to creatures as an infinitely sublime marvel of divine omnipotence and love, and shall know how to treasure it as such.

The more the possibility of a good among creatures is intelligible in itself, the less it arouses and merits our astonishment and admiration; we marvel only at the unexpected, the extraordinary, that which exceeds our notions and expectations. Theologians point out that the most correct and worthy idea of God is held by one who perceives how immeasurably all his notions and representations fall short of the greatness of this object. Similarly no one has a correct

[2] Eph. 3:20.

and worthy concept of God's supernatural grace unless he has arrived at the perception that in creatures no ground is found for the possibility of this great perfection or right for its realization. Such a person must also perceive that not even God's power and love which He manifests to us as our Creator allow us to reason to that higher power and love by which the communication of His nature is made possible and is realized in us; and that consequently this communication must be regarded as a true marvel of an exceedingly great power and love of God which remain hidden from our intellect. It is a marvel that has its like only in the generation of the Son and the spiration of the Holy Spirit.[8]

33. THE SUBSTANCE OF THE MYSTERY AS COUCHED IN THE LANGUAGE OF THE CHURCH AND OF REVELATION

If this mystery of God was so great in the first man, how are we to account for the fact that frequently it has not been esteemed at its full value? Certainly the reason is not that revelation and the teaching of the Church failed to impart sure knowledge of the realization of this great work. We know that by the grace of Christ we become adoptive children of God, participating in His nature. But we know equally well that Christ has but restored to us what we lost in Adam, and hence that Adam also was an adopted son of God and was deified, transfigured in soul by participation in the divine nature.

The above-mentioned lack of appreciation seems to have resulted from the fact that the expressions used in the teaching of the Church relative to Adam were not duly understood, and that information about this mystery was not sought in those scriptural passages where it is to be found.

In the teaching of the Church, as well as in the language of theology, the highest gift conferred on Adam is ordinarily designated by *iustitia et sanctitas*, "justice and holiness." If we regard these

[8] For a fuller development and vindication of the idea of sanctifying grace which is the point of departure for the present treatment, I must refer the reader to my earlier work, *Natur und Gnade*, and to my edition of Casinius' *Quid est homo*. [Cf. also Scheeben's *Dogmatik*, Bk. III, chap. 3: "1. Allgemeine Theorie des Uebernatürlichen und der Gnade; 2. Die konkrete Verwirklichung der übernatürlichen Ordnung."—Tr.]

terms superficially and merely in themselves, and associate with them the concepts to which they correspond in the language of natural reason, we may arrive at a faulty notion of "justice" and "holiness." By "justice" we may understand only the right orientation and disposition of man as such; by "holiness" we may understand that special attitude by which a man dedicates himself to God, and that internal harmony in which a person must be constituted in order to be a truly good creature, a good man. And in fact, if revelation had given us no detailed information about the first man, and if these expressions had acquired no higher theological meaning, we would have no other interpretation of them.

But we know from revelation that Adam was more than a merely natural man. We know that he was an adopted son of God. Therefore we also know that the terms "justice" and "holiness," applied to Adam as a child of God, must take on a new and higher meaning than they have of themselves in ordinary human speech. The justice that pertains to the child of God and that establishes him in the right order and disposition befitting his higher dignity and rank, must be a different and higher justice than that which establishes man as man in his rightful place. And can the holiness by which the child of God becomes a true temple of the Holy Spirit, be the same as the self-dedication and harmony of the servant of God?

The terms in question must be understood in this higher sense if they are to designate the noblest gift granted by God to the original man. They signify not human justice and holiness, but justice and holiness poured forth into the heart of Adam by the Holy Spirit, the Spirit of divine sonship. They signify the justice and holiness by which Adam was lifted up to childlike love of God and was made to share in the justice and holiness of the Holy Spirit: a divine holiness and justice corresponding to the divine dignity of a son of God.

The divine character of these gifts is well expressed in the very term "holiness." "Holiness" signifies the sublimity, purity, and inherent excellence, in a word the unique nobility, proper to divine goodness. It is only in imitation of this divine goodness and in relation to it that the creature is called holy. Of course a creature is holy by the very fact that he assumes the right attitude toward this goodness, esteems and honors it, and dedicates himself to it and its glorification. But in the full sense of the word a creature becomes holy only when he appropriates that divine goodness to himself, partakes of it and its exalted nobility, when the Godhead illuminates and glorifies the creature with its own holiness, and thereby communicates to him its own holy dignity as well as its own holy dispositions and sentiment. In the language of the Church, the holiness of the creature is nothing less than participation in the excellence of the divine nature, whereby the creature is raised above himself in dignity, glorified in state, bound to God in affection with the purest and most ardent love, indeed with filial love, and is ennobled and deified in all these relations. Taken in this full sense, holiness in creatures signifies without further qualification the sublimity and divinity of the goodness and justice imparted to them. Among the Greek Fathers especially, the term invariably denotes the outpouring and communication of the Holy Spirit.

The term "justice" is less well adapted by its root meaning to signify so high a perfection; it acquires such signification only by certain accretions. But it is a sufficiently definite and elevated term if it is used in conjunction with holiness, as when we say that Adam had justice and holiness. We are more correct when we speak of the justice of holiness, the *iustitia sanctitatis*, justice proportionate to holiness and associated with it, justice raised to the level of holiness. Only when thus regarded is Adam's justice an *admirabile donum*, an admirable gift of God, as the Roman Catechism calls it.[4]

Accordingly there is no doubt that the terms "holiness" and "justice" as applied to Adam in the language of the Church can and should mean a gift that is absolutely supernatural. It is likewise clear that holiness, at least if taken in its full comprehension, signifies more than the supernatural character of this gift. Considered even materially, it is not limited to the supernatural endowment and rectitude of the will. It denotes rather the supernatural consecration and divine nobility of the entire soul with all its spiritual faculties. But for that very reason we may feel some surprise at the frequent recurrence of these very terms in ecclesiastical and theological parlance for the description of the mystery in the first man. Even when Adam's grace is in question, the qualifying expressions "sanctifying" or "justifying" are employed. To be sure, this grace is often enough described also as the grace of adoptive sonship, of deification, of being destined to the intuitive vision of God; but these further modifications are not generally understood in their technical

[4] *Catechismus Romanus*, Part I, c. 2, q. 18.

meaning. Since it is precisely in this connection that many misunderstandings arise with regard to the sublimity and compass of the mystery, we must clarify the matter according to our standpoint.

The explanation would be very simple in the Scotist theory, which identifies sanctifying grace with *caritas*, the supernatural orientation of the will toward God. In this view the entire mystery consists in the supernatural rectitude and holiness of the will, and hence is adequately expressed by these terms. But this Scotist conception is the most attenuated that one can have and still remain within the stipulations of the dogma. It is not in accord with the concept of the profuse wealth of grace as briefly sketched above, which the Fathers insist is taught in Sacred Scripture. It can hardly vindicate in a scientific manner the supernatural character even of that one faculty which it has selected from the organism of the supernatural order. The holiness or supernatural excellence of love is conceivable only if a holiness or supernatural excellence has been conferred on the entire spiritual nature of man for its transformation. We must solve the difficulty in question not by applying the Scotist theory but by excluding it, especially since that very difficulty is invoked by the Scotists in favor of their own system. Our solution will consist in adducing reasons that will amply justify the use of the above-mentioned terms as understood in our view of the matter.

The Church and the theologians usually consider Adam's original state in opposition to the state of sin which followed upon it and blighted it. But the direct opposite of sin is justice and holiness; for sin is the reverse of justice and the destruction or profanation of holiness. Consequently the Church and the theologians had to regard and describe the original state primarily as a state of justice and holiness. They had all the greater reason for doing so since in the state of fallen man his misery and wretchedness are considered only in a secondary manner as compared with sin, and the sublimity and happiness of the original state of grace depended for its continuance on the preservation of his inherent justice and holiness.

Another reason for this point of view is implicit in the thing itself. Other expressions which might be employed here, such as glorification and deification, when understood in their full sense point rather to that state to which the grace of God destined the first man as to his end. They directly call up in our minds the idea of a stupendous glory and beatitude, and indicate the complete participation in the divine nature, the divine glory and beatitude which the first man was to attain only at the end of his life's course. The divine splendor and glory which Adam possessed from the beginning as an adopted son of God was but the hidden seed, whose full power was destined to unfold only in the next world. It existed not so much for its own sake as rather to set Adam on the path leading to the attainment of complete possession of the divine nature, to place him in the right relationship to this end. In this relationship to his ultimate goal in heaven is found the highest meaning of the supernatural transformation imparted to Adam already in Paradise. Therefore also its highest meaning is brought out in that expression which emphasizes it as the right orientation and tendency toward glorification in heaven and full union with God, that is, in the term "justice." The term "holiness" is no less appropriate here, although the viewpoint is somewhat different. It brings home to us that Adam was already a temple of the divinity, although as yet only a consecrated temple, in which the majesty of God was not to take up residence until later; for by consecration and sanctification the temple is made ready for the solemn entrance of God.

A third reason, connected with the second, would be the following. As a rule we assign names to things according to their activities, or with these activities in mind, rather than according to their innermost essence, since we know a thing's essence chiefly from its activities. What, then, is more natural than to designate the deifying grace of the first man according to the aspect wherein it is displayed as the principle of a specific action, that is, of the holy and rightly ordered act directed to a supernatural end? For that matter, we call even the grace of sonship sanctifying or justifying grace, in order to bring out the main significance it has for us.

Later we shall have occasion to mention a fourth and final reason.

But perhaps the scriptural account, even in the chapters specifically describing the creation of the first man and mentioning the gifts bestowed on him, is not the ultimate reason why many fail to attain to a worthy appreciation of the first man's mysterious state. Apparently some scholars were of the opinion that at any rate the most important of the privileges that God had conferred on the first man were expressly recounted in the first chapters of Genesis. Then they found further that all the terms occurring in those passages could be simply and reasonably interpreted as referring to man's natural endowment.

As a matter of fact, we are aware of no reason that would impel us to contest this view. When God says: "Let Us make man to Our image and likeness," [5] these words are sufficiently accounted for in the context if we hold that man is the image and likeness of God because of the spirituality of his soul. Although many of the Fathers incline to the view that "likeness" refers to something higher than "image," we may quite naturally understand it as a stronger expression parallel to "image." Similarly the statement which occurs in the following chapter, "And the Lord God formed man of the slime of the earth, and breathed into his face the breath of life, and man became a living soul," [6] signifies directly only the fact that God animated man's body in a higher way than He did that of the beasts, by breathing into it a vital principle like to Himself.

With St. Augustine we frankly maintain that only the creation of man's nature is explicitly narrated in Genesis, and with him likewise we deny that all the gifts which God showered on man are accounted for in these words. As we gather from the context, Moses merely intended to show how visible things came into existence, and how the production of man had to be the high point in the scale of creation. But concerning the mysterious benediction, the supernatural consecration that God spread over man, the sacred writer preserved a discrete silence, as the mystery was too vast to be understood by the people for whom he wrote. This folk was of too menial a frame of mind to have been capable of attaining a comprehension of the august dignity which is the portion of God's children. And in general the men of the Old Testament, before the grace and the Spirit of God's sonship had reappeared in Christ, were treated by God not as sons, but as slaves, and as stiffnecked slaves at that. For this reason also the mystery of the Trinity, which is so closely interwoven with the present mystery, was not distinctly revealed in the Old Testament. What was revealed of it was but dimly apprehended.

Nevertheless, since the entire Old Testament was a figure of the New, natural things could be made to serve as types of supernatural

[5] Gen. 1:26.
[6] Gen. 2:7.

things. So the spiritual sense of the words in which Moses relates the production of natural man suggests that the same words refer also to man's supernatural creation. As God makes man to His natural likeness by infusing a spiritual soul into the body as an image of His own spiritual nature, so He elevates man to His supernatural likeness by stamping upon his soul an image like to Himself, the image of His Son; and as God breathes a rational soul into man's body in order to give him natural life, so He breathes His own Spirit into the soul in order to impart to it His own divine life.

The words do not in themselves reveal this. Otherwise there would be no spiritual sense, no *sensus spiritualis*, such as is proper to Sacred Scripture. The types did not become manifest until the antitypes had appeared in the New Testament. Although in the present case the typified supernatural object actually existed in Adam, it could not be discerned in the words of Moses until the idea of this object had again become vivid in the New Testament. Pervaded and exalted by this idea, the Christian Fathers had no difficulty in unearthing the mystery hidden in those words. Especially in the forceful emphasis of the phrase "image and likeness" they discern a higher similarity of man with God than man could have or claim by virtue of his nature; and in the breath by which God animated Adam they descry the Holy Spirit Himself, who pours forth His own life upon man.[7] But to St. Augustine's mind the elevation of man to fellowship with the Holy Spirit, which changed him from an "animal man" to a "spiritual man" and afforded him entrance into a life of blessedness, is indicated in man's transfer to Paradise, whose surpassing material beauty was a reflection of the spiritual

---

[7] At times the Fathers appear to interpret the words, "and [God] breathed into his face the breath of life," as literally referring to the breathing forth of the Holy Spirit into man, and compare this action to the breathing by which the Savior conferred the Holy Spirit on the apostles. (Thus St. Basil, *Contra Eunomium*, V, and St. Cyril of Alexandria, *De Trinitate*, Dial. IV, in Kleutgen, *Die Theologie der Vorzeit*, II, 534 f.) Although we do not accept this interpretation, we see in it a proof that in the opinion of the Fathers the infusion of the Holy Spirit is at any rate in some manner obscurely indicated in the words of Moses. St. Augustine finds the same truth brought out in another connection: "Nondum tamen spiritualem hominem debemus intelligere, qui factus est in animam viventem, sed adhuc animalem. Tunc enim spiritalis effectus est, cum in paradiso, hoc est in beata vita constitutus, praeceptum etiam perfectionis accepit, ut verbo Dei consummaretur" (*De Genesi contra Manichaeos*, II, c.8).

glory and freshness of life which the Holy Spirit shed over the soul of the first man.

The words of Genesis do not exclude this supernatural mystery. Indeed, by refraining from explicit mention of it and by allowing it to remain in its obscurity, they manifest its grandeur and sublimity all the more clearly.

34. Second Mystery of the Original State: Integrity. Its Relation to the First Mystery

Certain other gifts which God granted to the first man and which were subsequently lost by sin, are more distinctly mentioned in Genesis and generally in the books of the Old Testament than the exceedingly august mystery of the sanctification and deification of the first man. Sacred Scripture relates how the concupiscence of the senses was awakened in man only after sin had been committed, and how the necessity of dying was inflicted on man only in punishment for sin. In this fashion it gives us to understand that freedom from concupiscence, from death, and from all other defects and sufferings that follow in the train of these imperfections, was, along with sanctifying grace, the proper lot of man prior to sin.

Without doubt exemption from such imperfections is not as great a mystery as the mystery of sanctification and deification. This is clear from the very fact that Moses could mention it expressly and still be understood. He who feels the stirrings of concupiscence, who experiences in himself the illnesses and afflictions that eventually lead to death, can form some general notion of what it means to be free from concupiscence and mortality. In particular, Adam himself could be aware of the presence of these gifts in his nature without special divine revelation, by purely natural perception; whereas he could be conscious of his dignity as child of God, even when he possessed it, only by faith and the light of grace. Again, the gift of exemption from concupiscence and death is far from being so exalted a gift as the gift of the divine sonship. The sonship of God is supernatural for the very angels, as in general for every created spirit; and it raises the soul of man in its highest spiritual perfection immeasurably above its natural condition, up to participation in the divine nature. On the contrary, the exemption we are speaking of does not elevate the human soul above itself. It merely makes the soul the absolute master of the body and of its own lower faculties. It merely effects the perfect harmony of the lower and higher faculties, prevents the former from disturbing the latter, and protects nature from every injury and from eventual dissolution. In a word, it effects and preserves the perfect unity, rectitude, and integrity of nature, and is accordingly called simply the rectitude or integrity of nature (by the Fathers it is often referred to as *incorruptio*, ἀφθαρσία).

There is no greater error than to confuse this integrity with the sanctity of the first man, and to hold that man's sanctity is nothing more than the excellent and comely order which integrity establishes in man. Sanctity is something incomparably more sublime than integrity; it is so great and glorious that the latter vanishes into insignificance alongside it.

But is not integrity a supernatural mystery? It would not, in truth, be so if it were present in sinless human nature as a mere matter of course, if it arose from the principles of nature, or at any rate pertained to the necessary equipment of human nature. For in that case it would involve nothing more obscure and mysterious than the nature of man itself.

With respect to the term "integrity," some thinkers are of the opinion that the presence of this perfection in the first man is self-understood, on the ground that God could not create a mutilated, disordered, vitiated nature. Certainly God cannot create a being without all its essential parts, and without endowing it with an aptitude sufficient for the attainment of its end, and hence without its integrity, as far as integrity consists in these two factors. But God can create a being that is imperfect, without giving to it the highest possible degree of unity and harmony, and without removing all obstacles to its development.[8] Thus God cannot create man without making his moral life possible for his soul, and without securing for him at least a political (today we should say constitutional) dominion over sensuality. But God need not endow the soul with an absolute, despotic control, so that man could deprive his sense faculties of all spontaneous movements and appetites. Although such autonomy of the sense faculties renders moral life more difficult, it does not make it impossible. Then, too, such absolute power of the soul by no means lies in man's nature; for according to the degree

[8] St. Augustine, *De libero arbitrio*, II, cc. 20, 22; *Retractationes*, I, c.9.

of their sensitivity the sense faculties by their very nature are more or less stimulated by their own proper objects, which are sensible things and goods. Likewise human nature does not have within itself the power to ward off suffering and eventual dissolution; and God is not obliged to preserve it from them. For man has no right to the perpetual preservation of his nature in its totality; of its own accord it naturally proceeds toward dissolution.

Therefore the integrity which the first man received from God, the integrity which consists in the complete and indissoluble unity and harmony between body and soul, and between the higher and lower faculties of man, was a great, supernatural marvel of God's power and love. It was a marvel of power, because by it God conferred on nature something that it could not in the slightest degree effect of itself. It was a marvel of love, because God did not owe this gift to nature, and granted it only through an extraordinary beneficence and grace.

So great a marvel can in no way be regarded as a self-understood natural endowment. It is extraordinary, unexpected; it is sublime and inconceivable in a special sense; it is a mystery in the proper meaning of the word. Whoever takes such a privilege for granted has a wrong idea of the nature of man; and what is more, he fails entirely to understand the greatness and value of this remarkable divine blessing. He does not reflect that this kind of integrity involves an elevation of man above his own nature to that of the angels. This is a wonderful elevation in virtue of which man, in spite of his corporality and sensuality, remains untroubled in his spiritual life, and even perceives that this corporality and sensuality are, so to speak, spiritualized: the body shares in the impassibility and immortality of the soul, and sensuality can stir only in accord with the regulations and commands of the spirit. He does not realize that this integrity, in St. Augustine's expression, was a marvelous state (*status mirabilis*) which was produced and conserved by a mysterious power (*virtute mystica*); [9] and that, according to the same holy doctor, a great grace of God had to be present where the earthy and sensual body was aware of no inordinate animal appetite. [10]

[9] St. Augustine, *De Genesi ad litteram*, XI, c. 31.
[10] "Gratia quippe Dei magna ibi erat, ubi terrenum et animale corpus bestialem libidinem non habebat" (*De peccatorum meritis et remissione*, c. 16, no. 21).

Thus there was a twofold supernatural mystery in the first man, that of the sanctification and deification of the spirit, and that of the spiritualization of sensual and corporal nature. By the latter his whole nature was endowed with a mysterious, supernatural integrity or rectitude. We must sharply differentiate between these two mysteries, even though they were most closely linked together in the first man; for the character proper to each determines the basis and manner of their connection.

Before we go on to explain this connection, we must give careful consideration to a detail in which both mysteries seem to coincide. Neglect of this detail inevitably leads philosophers and theologians to mingle and confuse them objectively.

The union of the soul with matter, as we have said, does not naturally admit of a full unity and harmony between both elements; rather it introduces a certain cleavage and discord into the soul itself. Not only do the spiritual tendencies come into conflict with the sensual tendencies; the spiritual tendencies themselves are drawn asunder in different directions. By nature the soul, under the guidance of reason, strives after moral good, after true happiness, after God, and is subjected to God. Because of its union with the body, the soul's spiritual cognition is dependent on sense perception, and becomes more obscure and difficult the more the soul raises itself above sensible and visible objects. If, then, inclination toward a good is proportionate to the clarity with which it appears to us, evidently the soul will more readily be drawn to those goods which, while not purely sensible, are nevertheless surrounded with sensible brightness, rather than to the higher, purely spiritual, and divine goods.

Thus it comes about that man has propensities to created things which, though not purely sensible, run counter to his tendency toward God and submissiveness to Him, because such propensities take no account of the relation of their object to God and His law. The suppression of these propensities and their cause, which is the excessive dependence of reason on sense perception, or in other words, the full harmony of the human spirit with itself, and the unruffled clarity of the intellect, in which an undivided inclination and submissiveness of the soul to God are included, evidently pertain to man's complete integrity. It is just as supernatural as the perfect harmony between sensuality and spirit. As the latter is a supernatural spiritualization of sensuality, the former is an emphatic witness of the workings of pure spirituality itself, although for that reason it is still poles apart from the holiness and divinization of the spirit.

The reason why integrity and holiness are sometimes confused lies in the fact that both gifts can be said to effect a supernatural union of the soul with God and its submission to God, as integrity in its lower function effects the harmony of sensuality with spirit and its submission to the spirit.

Actually the two gifts do exercise a mutual causality. But we must distinguish a twofold, essentially different kind of supernatural union of the soul with God and submission to Him. The first consists in this, that no inclination can hold sway in the soul against or even apart from the free will. Its object must in every respect harmonize with the will of God and His law; no tendency could induce the soul to transgress the divine law. It is a perfection that renders the harmony of the soul with God wholly pure, peaceable, and complete. But it does not transfer the soul to a higher fellowship with God, does not make its love a divine love, does not transmute its submission to God from a servile to a filial submission, such as a son has toward his father. This is brought about only by the sanctification, the divinization of the soul.

The sole function of integrity is to bring together, so to speak, the various elements of human nature into perfect harmony with one another and with the highest faculties that are directed toward God. It removes all obstacles to the serene, higher life, and cleanses nature of all the dust clinging to it, sprung as it is from matter. To nature thus in harmony with itself, sanctity then draws down the image of the divine nature. Into the nature thus freed of all corrupting and disturbing elements the Holy Spirit infuses His divine life; into this mirror purified of all tarnish, into this gleaming crystal, the Godhead pours its divine light, its divine fire. Integrity, even at its highest pitch of perfection, is but a disposition for sanctifying grace. It merely likens man to the angels; but by that very fact it enables him, along with the angels, to participate in the divine nature and to become like to God.

This observation not only indicates the difference between these two gifts, but also suggests the positive bearing of integrity upon sanctification and deification. Integrity was meant to prepare nature to be a pure and worthy receptacle for sanctifying grace. No doubt God can confer the grace of His sonship upon the nature of man just as it is in itself, and in fact He does thus give it to us through Christ. But He does so for special reasons, which we shall discuss later. In any case it was most seemly that, before participating in the divine nature, human nature should be made as pure as that of the angels, and that man, called to an ineffable fellowship of love with God, should encounter nothing in his nature to oppose God's law. It was highly fitting that he who was to receive divine life, should possess no disturbing, disruptive elements in his natural life. Thus grace was the end which God had in view in granting integrity, and the perfection for which He wished to prepare and dispose man by the gift of integrity.

On the other hand, grace was also the source from which the gift of integrity arose for man. This does not imply that integrity would have followed upon grace with absolute necessity—otherwise we should recover it along with grace; but the higher gift would very fittingly have drawn the lower in its train.

As God's chosen child, man was deserving of heaven and divine glory; all the more was he worthy while still on earth to be exempt from the natural imperfections of his earthly nature and to be made like to the angels. By grace he was raised to the bosom of God, invested with divine nobility, and called to the inheritance of God's riches. What was more seemly than that his entire being should be made heavenly and spiritual, and that his soul, completely freed from the servitude of matter, should dominate the whole of nature? The Holy Spirit through grace descended into man's spirit in order to breathe into it His own life. Could He not and should He not at the same time permeate the entire nature of man with His divine power, to guard it from all discord, from all disorder and ultimate dissolution?

Hence, although integrity and sanctity are distinct from each other, although they are separate gifts and are capable of separate existence, they were most becomingly and closely related in the first man, and mutually conditioned and complemented each other. These two mysteries were interlocked, and were woven together to form a single complete, complex mystery, which we are accustomed to call simply original justice.

35. The Two Mysteries of the Original State as Factors in One Complex Mystery: Original Justice

We shall find it worth the effort to consider more accurately the organic union of integrity with sanctity as forming one complete whole. The subject is of peculiar interest, and is of great importance for a clear and coherent understanding of many theological truths.

The composite supernatural state of the first man is called simply original justice, because this term suits the higher as well as the lower constituent of that state, while at the same time it indicates the way both elements combine to constitute a whole.

As we have seen, both sanctity and integrity place man in a supernatural order. The latter gift supernaturally binds the lower potencies and elements of nature to the higher, and subjects the lower to the higher. The former supernaturally attaches and subjects the higher part of nature to God, and thereby, as a matter of course, likewise subjects to Him all the dependent and subordinate parts of nature. Therefore, with reference to the supernatural union of the entire man with God and his subjection to God, sanctity and integrity form a single whole, the total supernatural justice of the first man. Thereby, without any unbridled attraction to creatures, and without being hindered by the encumbering ballast of his earthly body, he was enabled to cleave to God with divine love wholly and undivided, to belong to God, and to obey Him. In this respect sanctity and integrity supplement each other, imply each other, and are fettered to each other in solidarity. For God did not will merely the total effect of both; He gave the one gift only with reference to the other; He conferred both on Adam *per modum unius,* as two gifts which He intended to belong to each other, two gifts which, although absolutely separable, were to stand or fall together in Adam.

In the complex whole thus resulting, the two components naturally are not coordinated but subordinated, since the one is far inferior to the other and is to serve the other. Sanctity is the higher, predominant element, imparting its own essential character to the whole; it is the form, the soul of the whole. For the essential constituent of Adam's supernatural justice was precisely his union with God by filial love. So true is this that we can say that Adam's justice was restored to us through Christ, although integrity remains withheld from us; and the Roman Catechism regards original justice as coming to man only in the gift of sanctity. It is only through sanctity that integrity receives its higher consecration, its vital relationship to God as man's supernatural end, just as the body receives life through the soul. Or we should prefer to say that integrity is related to sanctity as the organization of the body is to the animating soul. On the one hand the organization of the body disposes it for the animating activity of the soul; but on the other hand this organization is caused and sustained by the soul itself. In like fashion integrity disposed man for the infusion and development of sanctity, and was bound to sanctity and dependent on it for its origin and for its continued existence.

Only after some such consideration can we rightly appreciate how well-founded and significant was the theory proposed by the ancient Scholastics, that sanctity or grace was the formal and principal element, whereas integrity of nature was the material and integrating element of original justice. This description is the more acceptable since it accounts for the diverse character of the visibility or invisibility pertaining to the two elements. Integrity, as the organic articulation of nature disposing it for the reception of the higher life of sanctity, is, in spite of its supernatural origin, naturally visible or perceptible, at least for its possessor, just as the organization of the body, although formed by an invisible principle and destined for the service of that principle, is visible to our bodily eye. Sanctity, on the contrary, the source of man's supernatural, divine life, remains invisible even for its possessor. It remains ever in its inaccessible divine light and mysterious concealment, as the soul remains invisible even when the body with its complete organization stands openly before us.

But can it not be contended that sanctity is at least indirectly perceptible in the gift of integrity, just as the soul animating the body is perceptible in the organism which it sustains in being and in the activity displayed by the body? The soul becomes perceptible in the body only so far as it manifests itself as the cause of the phenomena apparent in the body. If these phenomena could be explained without the soul, they would not point to the existence of the soul. And even when they thus point to the presence of the soul, they do not always reveal the soul in its proper nature, that is, if the soul does not manifest its proper nature in these phenomena; for example, the human soul cannot be inferred as a spiritual substance from its influence on the body. Such is the case with sanctity. Sanctity is the soul and form of integrity as, in due measure, the rational spirit of man is the soul and form of the body. Its essence does not openly appear in integrity. Its proper nature as the source of divine life is not displayed in the gift of integrity, but in the acts of the theological virtues, as the human soul does not reveal its spiritual nature in the organization and movement of the body, but in spiritual activities. Integrity is only a secondary effect of sanctity, its concomitant result. It is not even this in the sense that it can be defined and conceived only in terms of sanctity: first, because integrity can be granted to man independently of sanctity; secondly and particularly, because integrity was not a physical effect of sanctity in the actual order, nor can it be a physical effect of sanctity. We know this from the simple fact that we get back Adam's sanctity, and perhaps even in a higher degree than he had; but we do not actually recover integrity with it.

Therefore the absolute mystery of sanctity is by no means dissipated by considering it as the soul of integrity. Rather, when thus represented, its mysterious character is heightened to such an extent that it is communicated to integrity. Integrity, indeed, is a mystery in its own right, so far as it must be considered a marvel achieved by the supernatural power and the boundless love of God. But even though it is a marvel, it takes its place in the circle of naturally knowable truths, and hence is far less mysterious than sanctity. But by its union with sanctity it receives an absolutely mysterious character, a divine consecration, that is as far removed from natural perceptibility as the dignity which the human body receives from the spiritual soul informing it is concealed from the bodily eye. Of itself integrity serves only to facilitate man's pursuit and attainment of his natural end. But in union with sanctity it is designed to facilitate man's pursuit and attainment of his supernatural end, to mold his nature into an apt instrument for developing the life of grace, and to direct all its stirrings and movements in the most perfect way to the goal of the life of grace. Integrity becomes a member of an absolutely supernatural, mysterious organism, and consequently partakes of its divine character, as the human body partakes of the spiritual dignity of the soul which it serves and to which it belongs.

As far as the doctrine thus presented is concerned, it might in a certain respect seem almost a matter of indifference whether we assume that integrity and sanctity were both conferred together on the first man at the very instant of his creation, or whether at first integrity alone was given and sanctity later on, in response to man's free activity. The distinction and relation between the two gifts, as that of the lower to the higher, complementary, and perfective, almost appear more clearly in the latter supposition than in the former. It might even seem that the dependence of the earlier on the later gift is not broken off in this case. In any event, the dependence in question is only a moral one, not a physical dependence. It is a dependence of an effect not upon its efficient cause but upon the end which the efficient cause intends, and by which the latter is induced to produce the effect. Further, a thing that exists earlier in time can depend on a later thing with this kind of dependence; indeed, only in a case like this does the peculiar character of such moral dependence really appear.

But the kind of moral dependence by which a union of solidarity is established between the two gifts is entirely done away with in this supposition. If sanctity were imparted to man subsequently to integrity, we could say merely that God granted integrity to man so as thereby to prepare him for sanctity, but not because man was rendered worthy of integrity by reason of his sanctity. Sanctity, in the view we are criticizing, is indeed the end toward which integrity is ordained, but is not properly the motive that impelled God to grant integrity, and is not the condition to which He attached integrity and upon which He based its possession.

If integrity existed prior to sanctity, there is no reason why it could not have continued in existence without sanctity after the loss of the latter. In this hypothesis the union of both elements is lost sight of; the bond which fetters them is loosened, and their union of solidarity which, as we shall see later, is highly significant, is not at all brought out. We could then regard sanctity and integrity merely as two gifts, but no longer as one, that is, as given *per modum unius;* we could no longer regard them as two corresponding factors coalescing in one original justice.

And, in fact, the theologians who think that integrity and sanctity were communicated separately, at different times, restrict the term "original justice" to integrity alone, as the earlier gift, the gift lying closer to man's origin. In their view integrity is simply the right and complete ordering, or the justice, of man. Sanctity is only externally grafted upon this justice, in order to render man's activity and striving supernaturally pleasing to God, and hence meritorious for eternal life. The result is that later on, when they come to treat of original sin, which is *iniustitia originalis*, these theologians locate its center of gravity in the break-up of integrity, and hence chiefly in inordinate concupiscence.

The theologians we have here in mind are principally the representatives of the old Franciscan school: Alexander of Hales,[11] St. Bonaventure,[12] and to some extent Scotus.[13] We shall return to them later in connection with original sin.

Even St. Thomas, in one passage at any rate,[14] does not seem entirely hostile to this view. In the passage in question he calls integrity original justice, and describes the latter as an aid by which man is disposed for a higher aid that will conduct him to the vision of God. But in the answers to the objections (ad 13um) he declares that he holds it to be false that original justice does not include sanctifying grace.[15]

In the *Summa* he expressly describes sanctifying grace as the dominant factor in original justice. To his mind original justice is, in the first place, the supernatural ordering and subordination of man to God by grace; and this supernatural relation to God is the root from which proceed the supernatural order and harmony between the various elements and faculties of man himself, and to which are attached these latter as a subordinate member.[16] Further,

---

[11] Cf. IIa, q.91, membr.1, aa.1 et 2.
[12] *In II Sent.*, d.29, q.2, a.2.
[13] *In II Sent.*, d.29, q.unica.
[14] *De malo*, q.5, a.1.
[15] St. Thomas employs the term "original justice" in two senses. Occasionally original justice means no more than freedom from inordinate concupiscence or, more positively, perfect harmony and hierarchical subordination among the various human faculties. But employed in an ampler comprehension, original justice embraces, in addition to preternatural integrity, also the strictly supernatural gift of sanctifying grace, which indeed is its chief and formal element. Cf. C. Vollert, S.J., "Saint Thomas on Sanctifying Grace and Original Justice," *Theological Studies*, II (1941), 369–87 (esp. p. 384); "The Two Senses of Original Justice in Medieval Theology," *ibid.*, V (1944), 3–23. [Tr.]
[16] Cf. Ia, q.100, a.1 ad 2: "cum radix originalis iustitiae, in cuius rectitudine factus est homo, consistat in subiectione supernaturali hominis ad Deum, quae

besides being the root, sanctity is properly the seed, the substance, and the soul of original justice. This view is confirmed by the fact that, according to Christian ideas, sanctity is justice pure and simple, justice in the eyes of God, and in all truth makes us supernaturally pleasing to God, even if we do not possess integrity. Later we shall see that the most adequate and satisfactory concept of original sin results from this concept of original justice.

The Council of Trent did not wish to define explicitly that the first man was actually created in the state of sanctity and integrity, or at any rate that the gift of sanctity was not received subsequently to the gift of integrity, because it did not wish to stigmatize the adherents of the opposite view. But reasons adduced from Sacred Scripture and the Fathers speak overwhelmingly in favor of this doctrine. The opposite view can advance practically no positive arguments. To restrict the words, "God made man right," [17] to the harmony of the various faculties in man, is an entirely arbitrary limitation; "rectitude" means simply "justice," and in the scriptural sense includes everything by which a man is made pleasing to God.[18] Hence the Fathers as a rule state that grace, sanctity, the Holy Spirit, participation in the divine nature, and charity were given to man at the outset along with his nature.[19] St. Basil employs an expression that is very much to the point when he says that of old (at the creation of Adam) God breathed the Holy Spirit into man together with his soul, whereas now He breathes the Holy Spirit into the soul.[20] In view of this and many other passages of the Fathers, we must regard the doctrine that sanctity was conferred on the first man at the very outset along with integrity, as the only legitimate tenet, and find therein positive confirmation of the theory of St. Thomas regarding the close mutual relationship and solidary unity of the

---

est per gratiam gratum facientem, ut supra dictum est . . ." In q.95, a.1, St. Thomas had stated that original justice or rectitude, considered in its totality, consists in the subordination of the soul to God through grace, the subordination of the sense faculties to reason, and the subordination of the body to the soul; the first rectitude is the cause of the second and the third, and therefore must be given to man at the beginning along with the latter two kinds of rectitude. Cf. also *In II Sent.*, d.30, q.1, a.1, 3.

[17] Eccles. 7:30.

[18] Cf. Kleutgen, *Die Theologie der Vorzeit*, II, 500 ff.

[19] Cf. Suarez, *De opere sex dierum*, III, c.17; my *Dogmatik*, Bk. III, nos. 1164 ff.

[20] *Contra Eunomium*, V; PG, XXIX, 729.

two gifts. Not only is sanctity rightly to be considered justice as much as integrity is or even more so, but it is quite as original a dowry; and we are more entitled to signalize it alone rather than integrity alone as the original justice, as the Roman Catechism actually does.[21]

The elucidation and corroboration of this conception of original justice are greatly furthered if we regard it from another point of view, as a spiritualization of the whole of nature by the Holy Spirit who, in St. Augustine's words, transforms man from an "animal man" to a "spiritual man." Integrity, like sanctity, is a supernatural effect of God's Spirit breathed into man and pervading his entire nature. Just as sanctity and the divine life blossoming in it can be poured forth into man only by the Spirit of God, so integrity, the elimination of the corruptibility clinging to man's entire nature on its material side, can be explained only as an effect of the same vivifying Holy Spirit who purifies by His infinitely powerful fire. This divine Spirit permeated Adam's whole nature in order to spiritualize and transfigure it, that is, to make his spirit divinely spiritual, to fuse it in holy love with God to form one Spirit, and to conform the lower elements of human nature to the spirit thus elevated above itself. Although the Holy Spirit's activity manifests itself differently in the various parts of nature, the total effect must be conceived as a single unified effect. We do thus conceive it if we regard it as a supernatural rectitude and harmony, produced by the action of the Holy Spirit in human nature, with reference to God as its supernatural end. In other words, we conceive it correctly if we regard it as one supernatural justice. Thus both in their principle and in their end integrity and sanctity are seen to be joined in solidarity into one complete whole, and both together appear as simply the supernatural justice or the spiritualization of man effected by the Holy Spirit, as a great mystery issuing from the bosom of God and poured forth into human nature by His own Spirit.

[21] P. I, c. 2, q. 18.

CHAPTER IX

Original Justice in the Human Race and the World

▪▪

36. The Mystery in the Universality and Propagation of Original Justice

PRECISELY why is it that in standard theological terminology this justice is called original justice? May the reason be that it sprang from nature as a matter of course, or was to be naturally propagated at the origin of nature without further ado? Certainly not; thus understood the adjective "original" would do away with the supernaturality of that justice, and hence would destroy its mysterious character. The term must be explained on the supposition of this supernaturality and in accord with it. We shall undertake this explanation and thereby show that the adjective in question, far from eliminating the mystery, causes it to emerge greater and more profound than ever.

1. Because original justice is supernatural, it could not come to man by virtue of his natural origin, nor could it be transmitted to his descendants in a natural way by generation. Because it is supernatural, it is in no sense the product of the free, personal will of man, and therefore does not possess the character of personal justice, which is not communicable. Its existence does not depend on any previous cooperation of man's free will. It is exclusively the work of God; and therefore God could infuse this justice into the first man without the latter's concurrence at his origin, and could enact a law in virtue of which it was to be transmitted to his descendants along with nature at the generation of every human being. Although not included in nature or sprung from nature or postulated by nature, in a word, although not natural in itself, it could be imparted

to human nature as a dowry, which would begin to exist simultaneously with nature at its origin and be propagated along with nature. In the first man, accordingly, it would appear as his original capital, in his posterity as an inheritance. And since God actually did decide upon this very course, supernatural justice is with full right and most significantly called original justice, not exactly because it existed in Adam originally prior to his sin, but rather because, produced by God together with nature, it was also to be propagated along with nature, and because it was to be a God-given inherited property belonging to the whole of nature, to the entire human race.

This "originalness," if we may so speak, this linking of supernatural justice to the whole of nature, may most easily be grasped in the case of integrity. Integrity perfects human nature as a nature composed of spirit and matter, by suppressing the imperfections arising out of this composition. But human nature is communicable by way of nature, and is a specific nature, precisely because it is composite. A pure spirit can neither generate another spirit nor be generated; it cannot form a species along with other co-equals. We can readily see, therefore, that in communicating human nature the parent also communicates the integrity of his nature to his offspring; and this, if not a law of nature, is at any rate a law very much in keeping with nature.

Sanctity, on the other hand, directly perfects man's spirit as such. Like the spirit itself, consequently, it is not capable of being communicated by generation. But since integrity was, in God's plan, to be a disposition for sanctity, and at the time of generation this disposition would be propagated with nature in the manner explained, grace and sanctity would likewise be transmitted because of their connection with integrity. This process resembles that of human generation itself. By his own natural power the human father transmits only the material seed, which he disposes for the reception of the rational soul, whereas the soul itself is immediately created by God and infused into the body. Similarly in accord with God's supernatural law the communication of nature in the higher order is directly accompanied by integrity of nature, and it is only this gift of integrity that enables and disposes nature to receive the Holy Spirit in the gift of sanctity as the principle of its supernatural life.

If we attach too great weight to this function of integrity in the propagation of original justice, we stress the dependence of sanctity on integrity, but on the other hand we overlook the dependence of integrity on sanctity. Integrity is truly a disposition for sanctity; but we must not forget that it is just as truly a dowry, a hereditary good which pertains to the descendants of Adam, as to their progenitor, in virtue of their nobility as children of God, which they inherit from him. The transmission of this nobility from Adam by generation is like the transmission of earthly nobility among us men, but with this difference, that the former is hereditary by divine right, the latter by human right. However, the hereditary character of integrity is by no means purely physical, dependent on the physical power and nature of the generative act. Rather it is moral, and appeals to a divine law, in virtue of which God Himself, concurring with the physical act of generation, willed that integrity be transmitted from the progenitor to his posterity. On the part of its juridical basis and its productive principle, integrity in the case of Adam's posterity is communicated through sanctity. The Spirit of God, who produces it, first of all pervades the spirit of man in order to bestow on him the nobility of the children of God; and then, in conjunction with that nobility, the Spirit of God effects the entire supernatural equipment which the descendants of Adam are to share with him as heirs of his nobility.

2. Thus conceived, the hereditary transmission of original justice is envisaged as an activity of the Holy Spirit in the human race, a continued activity that goes along with natural generation. It is a continued activity that is closely connected with the propagation of nature but is not rooted in nature, and that is revealed as a great new mystery in its very connection with nature.

a) The Spirit of God wafts where He pleases, according to His gracious free will; but He is chiefly active in the distribution of supernatural gifts. He could have conferred supernatural justice on the first man for his person alone, reserving to His own good pleasure the further communication of the same gift to individual persons from among Adam's descendants. Or, if He willed to communicate the gift to all of Adam's descendants, He need not have made this communication dependent on the racial unity of other men with Adam, on their origin from him. The latter is what He actually decreed. He willed to communicate justice to other men precisely as descendants of Adam; and so He had to confer it on Adam as the progenitor of the rest of mankind. Therefore He dwelt in Adam as in a person especially endowed by Him with grace, but at the same time associated His spiritualizing, supernatural power of animation and generation with Adam's generative power, so that the effect of the former might be transferred to the product of the latter. He overshadowed Adam's natural fecundity with His own supernatural fecundity, so that the fruit of the former might issue from its originating principle immediately glorified and sanctified, as in similar fashion God accompanies man's generative act with His creative power in order to animate his material fruit with a spiritual soul. Was this not a new marvel of divine grace, a new, sublime outpouring of the Holy Spirit upon Adam, greater and more profuse than that by which He made Adam just and holy in his own person? Was it not a tremendous new mystery? Was it not a mystery approaching that by which the same Holy Spirit made the womb of the Virgin fruitful, so that she might give birth to the God-man?

b) The grandeur of the mystery shines forth more brightly still if we scrutinize its underlying idea more closely. By descent from Adam all men form one great whole, one body, which can and must be regarded as a development from Adam's body. To make this unity tighter and more complete, God willed that even Adam's helpmate for the work of generation should be taken and should proceed from his flesh and his bone. The great body of the human family thus arising had its unifying principle and its head in the progenitor from whom it issues. But this unity in one racial head was but a natural unity, a unity in nature and through nature. A supernatural unity is neither contained in nature nor can it proceed from nature; supernatural unity cannot be rooted in natural unity, but can have nature only for its substratum, its point of departure. This is accomplished when God pours forth His own Spirit as the supernatural principle of life into the body of the human race thus unified.

In this Spirit alone all the members of the body have a common supernatural bond, inasmuch as this Spirit, operating and dwelling in all individuals, embraces and pervades them all together, just as all the parts of the animal body find their unity in the unifying influence exercized by the animating soul. But if the unity is to be perfect and conformable to nature, the Spirit pervading the body as a whole must extend throughout the single parts inasmuch as they are formally members of the body, that is, according to the order and position they assume in the natural configuration of the body. Beginning with the head, He must pervade and animate all the other members, just as the soul, which exists and operates immediately in all the individual parts of the body, achieves the body's organic unity only by joining the influence which it exercises upon some parts to the influence which it exercises upon other parts, and by diffusing itself throughout all the members from the head down. The organization of the body and the union between the various members and the head depend on the natural procession of the former from the latter. In the same way the Holy Spirit, if He wishes to animate the body as a whole, must join His supernatural activity to natural generation. Thus the natural unity of the human race acquires a significance for its supernatural unity; thus fellowship in nature can become the basis for fellowship in grace and supernatural justice; thus the racial head of the natural unity of the race can become likewise the racial head of supernatural unity.

3. Adam's personal, exalted position as head of the human race and as the original possessor of original justice is at the basis of many important truths to be taken up later on. Therefore it merits special discussion, particularly as fresh light will thereby be reflected on what has already been established.[1]

We can and in fact must hold that Adam is the principle and head of the human race with respect to supernatural justice, because he is its principle and head by nature. But the former may not be regarded simply as the consequence of the latter, as if Adam automatically became the supernatural head of the race by the very fact that he is its natural head. His position as principle and head of nature did no more than fit him to be chosen and appointed by God as principle and head in the order of grace.

For, even though Adam received supernatural justice from God, the conclusion by no means follows automatically that his descendants also were to receive it with him, from him, and through him. Adam begot offspring by the powers of his nature, of his earthly nature, as an earthly man formed from the earth, as a man "of the

---

[1] The elaboration of this train of thought is one of Scheeben's great services to theology. It is important in preparing the way for the doctrine of original sin developed in sections 43 ff., and also for the theory presented in section 68, on the physical or dynamic character of the God-man's activity in behalf of the race. [Tr.]

earth, earthly," [2] and so could naturally transmit only this earthly nature of his, without integrity and sanctity. Supernatural justice is a free gift of God, which He need not give to every man. If He so chose, He could give it to Adam alone; and if He wished to give it to the rest of men also, He did not have to give it to them in dependence on Adam and through him. Indeed, in the strict sense of the word God could not give this justice to the rest of men through Adam, because Adam's justice did not virtually contain the justice of his posterity, in the way that his nature contains the nature of his posterity.

Even in a supernatural manner Adam could not become the principle of the justice of his descendants by reason of his own justice, in the way that he was the principle of their nature. To enable him to be such, grace would have had to be more than grace for him; it would have had to be his nature. For if what one possesses is itself only a trickle of grace, it cannot in any proper sense become a source of grace for others. Only the God-man, who possesses the divine nature essentially and in its overflowing fullness, who is a "heavenly man" by nature, on account of His heavenly lineage, can according to the Apostle be a "quickening Spirit," [3] that is, can fill others with supernatural life and preserve natural life from all corruption and dissolution. In the words of the same Apostle, Adam, as "man of the earth, earthly," was by nature only "a living soul," [4] and so could be no more than a principle of natural life for others. And not only was Adam unable to produce the supernatural gifts in his descendants, especially participation in the divine nature, but for the reason given he was unable to merit and acquire the same for them. For since the sonship of God was a pure grace for him, which he could not merit for himself, evidently he was still less able to merit it for others. He could do so neither in virtue of his nature nor by reason of the grace that had been imparted to him. The grace of divine sonship enabled him to merit a share in the inheritance of the children of God for himself, but by no means gave him the power to merit that others should share in the dignity and inheritance of the children of God along with him. Only He can merit that, who is

[2] Cf. I Cor. 15:47.
[3] Cf. I Cor. 15:45, 47.
[4] *Ibid.*

the Son of God not by grace but by nature, who on account of His natural, infinite dignity can claim everything from His Father, and hence can obtain for others a share in His dignity and His riches.[5]

In brief, descent from Adam, endowed though he was with supernatural justice, is not in itself an efficacious reason or an adequate juridical title for the transmission of supernatural justice to his posterity. In other words, fellowship in nature does not automatically establish fellowship in supernatural justice. It was rather in pursuance of a free, gratuitous, mysterious decree that God attached the transmission of grace to the transmission of nature, that He rendered fellowship in grace dependent on mankind's fellowship in nature, and made the propagation of nature, as it were, the vehicle of grace. It was a new grace for Adam that grace was intended not for himself alone, but also for his posterity as such, and consequently that he, who was the principle of nature, was also, to some extent, to be the principle of grace for the whole human race. However, he is principle of nature as the cause and source of nature in his posterity, whereas he is the principle of grace not as its cause or source, but as its first and original recipient, as the starting point from which God willed to diffuse it over the entire race.

If we wish to seek in the human race itself a true basis for this wonderful fellowship in grace that exists among men, we shall not find it in Adam or in any purely human being. We must look for it in the God-man, who can be and is the cause and fountainhead of grace for others and for all mankind. Only through the God-man does the race properly possess the power and the right to become children of God; only the God-man is properly the supernatural head of the race; and only through Him and with reference to Him dare we say that God endowed the natural head of the race with the exalted privilege of begetting not mere men but children of God. Adam was a figure of Christ, according to the word of the Apostle. He was a figure of Christ because his earthly fatherhood symbolized and presaged the heavenly fatherhood of the God-man; and it was precisely and solely for the reason that the power and dignity of the antitype reflected back upon the type, that the latter had some share in the supernatural fatherhood of Christ. Thus, too, the marriage of Adam with Eve was a type of the union of Christ

[5] Cf. St. Thomas, *De veritate*, q.27, a.3, esp. ad 21.

with the Church, from which the children of God are born; and so this marriage receives a supernatural fruitfulness by its anticipation of that marriage which it foreshadowed.

It is not without reason, therefore, that the Apostle calls Adam's marriage a great mystery on account of its relation to Christ and the Church. He speaks thus not only because this marriage presaged so great a mystery by its natural character, but surely also because it anticipated the supernatural power of that mystery, and because Adam and Eve, who were both earthly human beings by nature, were to generate children of God and a heavenly family.

But later on we shall come back to the relationship of Adam with the God-man. Even abstracting from it, we still have enough sublimity and mystery in the state in which man came forth from the hand of God.

We behold here a wonderful, supernatural blessing of God that is diffused over the human race, a blessing so rich and mysterious that even Moses did not venture to unveil it in all its grandeur. What was visible in original justice, namely, the perfect harmony and integrity of nature, was in itself so great and marvelous that Adam must have been lost in admiration at the extraordinary love of God revealed in it, and that we, who are fully aware of our native misery and poverty, must stand in still greater amazement at it. But what was best of all in it remained hidden from Adam's natural powers of perception; and this was the crown belonging to His own children that God placed upon his head, it was his reception into the fatherly bosom of God, his admission into the inaccessible light of the Godhead, and the divine glorification and sanctification of his soul. And what filled this cup of blessedness to overflow was the fact that God not only contrived for man a propagation of nature, as in the case of plants and animals, but joined to it a propagation and diffusion of those supernatural gifts. This supernatural blessing was the mystery of God in mankind, a mystery of His inscrutable power and goodness by which He elevated man above his nature and invested him with His own splendor, His own greatness and glory.

37. The Mystery in the Universe: Its Focal Point in Man

If we turn our gaze from the microcosm which is man and let it roam over the whole of creation, if we raise our eyes to the invisible spirit world and then lower them to the world of irrational nature, we shall find the mystery of God and His mystical consecration of creatures more or less spread throughout the entire universe.

1. Visible, material nature cannot in itself house the mystery of God in any proper sense, because it has no share in the divine nature. But in a wider sense the entire material world had a part in forming the body of man, whose corporal nature was derived from it and who was to be closely associated with it. The material world, like his own bodily nature and acts, was wonderfully subjected to man's dominion, and as represented in the tree of life was to contribute with mystic power [6] to the sustenance of his immortal life. Thus it partook of man's nobility; and by reason of the divine holiness imparted to man it was likewise, in him, a temple of the Holy Spirit. In man and through him it was destined to glorify God in a supernatural manner: the surpassing beauty and harmony shed over it reflected the divine glory enthroned in man's soul, much as man's body does when endowed with the gift of integrity.

As the natural head of the visible world, the man who had been raised above his own nature was in a supernatural and mysterious manner its prophet, who proclaimed the mystical praises of God for it and through it; its priest, who consecrated it to God along with himself as an offering made fragrant by the Holy Spirit; its king, who was himself to serve God and make it serve God by his enjoyment and use of it.

Thus the mystery which terminated in man thrust its widespread roots down into the whole of visible creation, and at the same time formed the crown in which the mystery of visible creation culminated.

2. But the mystery of God in His creation also towered above man himself into loftier, immeasurable regions. Far above visible creation, which terminates in man as its head, lies a higher and a purely spiritual creation, the world of the angels.

Since the angels are invisible to us human beings even in their

[6] "Virtute mystica," says St. Augustine. See above, p. 218.

natural existence, and are elevated high above all visible creation, they are to some extent supernatural from our point of view. Hence their existence and nature could in a sense be regarded as a mystery. In fact, rationalism repudiates the existence of the angels as it repudiates everything we number among the mysteries of Christianity; in opposition to the rationalists, the existence of the angels is commonly maintained as a supernatural truth.

In the strict sense of the word, however, the existence of the angels is not properly a mystery, because it is not properly supernatural. The supernatural as understood in Christianity does not mean precisely the superiority of one created nature as compared with another; rather it means the elevation of a nature above the natural limits of created existence to participation in the divine nature. Such participation is supernatural for the angels themselves, and hence was a true mystery for them prior to their glorification. Consequently the theological mystery in the invisible spirit world was sanctifying grace, which the angels possessed in common with the human race.

In the higher, angelic nature, which was closer to God in the scale of perfection, grace naturally unfolded its riches in far greater profusion than in the less lofty nature of man. But at the same time it necessarily brought man into a much more intimate relationship with the angels than was proper to him by nature. And grace raised man to a dignity immeasurably surpassing the natural eminence of the angels; it made both man and the angels heirs and fellow-intimates of God, and thus united him with them to form God's family.

3. Thus the mystery of grace spanned the whole of creation; the mystery of God permeated and animated creation in all its members, and drew them all together into a lofty, supernatural unity. This comprehensive view does not cause man's part in the mystery to melt into the background, but rather brings out its full significance. As by his nature man represented the connecting link between the spiritual and the material worlds, so in his supernatural endowment he was, so to speak, the focus of the supernatural light which God had diffused over all creation. The mystery dwelling in him was the reflection of the heavenly splendor of the angels, and the source and model for the heavenly glorification of the visible world. Later we shall see how the mystery in mankind, not in the first Adam, but in the second Adam whom he prefigured, became in

God's eternal plan the focal point of all mysteries in a still more exalted manner. This took place when the first-born of all creatures appeared in human nature with the fullness of His divinity. But this event was not to occur until another mystery, a mystery of darkness seeping down from the angels and spreading over mankind and the whole of creation, had obscured the sun of grace, devastated on all sides the mystical garden planted by God's love and, mocking the power and goodness of the Creator, called forth a second, greater mystery of His omnipotence and goodness.

PART THREE

The Mystery of Sin

The mystery of iniquity already worketh.
II Thess. 2:7

CHAPTER X

Sin in General

▀▀

38. Sin Rendered Mysterious by Reason of Its Relations to the Mystery of God in the Creature

THE Trinity of persons in God and the supernatural justice of the first man are mysteries, true mysteries. But they are mysteries of light and splendor, of holiness and blessedness. The mystical obscurity in them results from the superabundance and the sublimity of their light, which either remains remote from our sight or blinds it. They are mysteries of God, dwelling within Him, although outwardly manifested in His creation. They are an unfathomable, inexhaustible abyss of power, wisdom, and goodness.

But side by side with them Christianity shows us another mystery: a mystery of nothingness, of darkness, of evil; a "mystery of iniquity." And this mystery does not come from God; it comes from the creature which, wrested from nothingness and darkness by a divine act, rises up in rebellion against its Creator and extinguishes in itself the mystery of His grace.

In its own kind sin is a mystery, under all circumstances, wherever it is met with. Sin is disorder, annihilation of the good and true. Sin is opposition to all order, and to reason itself. Sin is a monster, aborted from the good works that God has wrought. Sin is not being, but non-being; and therefore it has no proper efficient cause, but a deficient cause (*causa deficiens*). Thus sin is essentially darkness, which appears blacker and murkier the more it is illuminated by reason; it is a darkness from which sound reason shrinks, which reason abhors and condemns. But on the other hand the more clearly this darkness is recognized in its true character of darkness and non-being, and the more reason shuns it and abhors it, the more does the mystery gain in light, and is fathomed, sounded, and seen through.

To the extent that natural reason is able to know and perceive the being or non-being of sin, the latter is of course not a mystery in the proper, narrower sense of the word. If sin is to be a mystery in that sense, it must in its own way be a supernatural mystery. But how is this possible? How can sin be supernatural? Would this not mean that it is raised above nature, whereas evidently it is nothing high and lofty at all, but is the deepest abasement and derangement of nature?

Let us examine the matter more closely. "Habit and privation," said the ancient philosophers, "are in the same genus." Things that mutually cancel and exclude each other, such as "to be" and "not to be," must lie within the same sphere. Sin is the privation, the exclusion of justice, an opposition set up against the moral order established by God. So far, then, as sin contradicts the order of nature and nature's natural relations and tendencies to good, it is contranatural, unnatural, as being the reverse of nature. But it is all this only because it contradicts nature and outrages the natural order alone.

Considered in this way, sin, like nature and the natural order itself, is an object of natural reason, and therefore of philosophy. Consequently sin can emerge beyond the horizon of natural reason only by setting itself against something higher than nature, by violating some order higher than the natural order, hence by invading a supernatural domain and working its havoc there. When this takes place, sin becomes doubly mysterious: it is no longer merely darkness and subversion, but rises in opposition to a supernatural, mysterious light, and ravages a supernatural, mysterious order. It becomes itself a supernatural mystery, because it comes into relations with one; it becomes an abyss of evil and corruption, an abyss which is as inscrutable and unfathomable as the mystery of good and grace which it extinguishes.

Although the exact position occupied by sin in the supernatural order may readily be determined, theologians as a rule devote but slight attention to the subject. Frequently the mystery of sin is sought only in original sin. But the truth is that original sin cannot be understood in its mystical character and be scientifically explained unless our search ranges further and we regard it as a factor in the great "mystery of iniquity" which has filtered down from heaven and has spread over the earth.

The mystery of original sin rests upon the relations between Adam's transgression and the mystery of original justice. To understand it we must keep in mind the relations of Adam's disobedience to the nature of original justice in its higher and lower elements, namely, sanctity and integrity, as well as to its hereditability by natural succession.

The first relation, that of sin to sanctity, is the most important. The mysterious character of sin is chiefly found here, since sanctity is incomparably a greater mystery than integrity. Since sanctity pertains also to the angels and has been restored to fallen man, and since, further, angels have no need of integrity and the same gift remains withheld from man, the mysterious character of sin as opposition to the gift of sanctity is seen to be common to all sin, and is not peculiar to the sin of the first man. It is also the basis of the connection between the "mystery of iniquity" in the angelic world and the human race. Let us endeavor to throw light upon this mystery from every possible point of view.

39. Mysterious Character of Sin Considered as Formal Opposition to the Mystery of God in the Creature

1. What is sin in general? It is an act by which the creature runs foul of the law laid upon it by God, and violates the order decreed by God; it is an act, therefore, by which the creature rebels against God and offends Him, refuses Him due subjection and love. This general description applies to the sin of the creature situated in the state of nature as well as to the sin of the sanctified creature. In both cases an obligatory order established by God is violated; in both cases sin is committed by the denial of due honor and love to God.

Yet there is an immense difference between the two. According to the dignity which the creature receives from God, it assumes a different position with regard to God, receives from Him a different law, and owes Him a different reverence and love. By nature the creature stands to God in the position of a servant, and in this quality is obligated to unquestioning reverence and love toward God. The infringement of this position and this duty is a monstrous, enormous evil, because it is a disparagement and affront offered to the infinitely great Creator and Lord. But there is something else, vastly greater. Through the grace of sanctity and deification the creature becomes a child of God; it approaches immeasurably closer to God than it did by nature, and is called to an ineffably intimate union with Him. But in proportion as the creature is raised by God and God stoops to the creature, the latter is bound to greater reverence and love toward God. If the creature does not fulfill this duty, there is no longer question of the servant offending his Master, but of the child offending his Father. The same difference that exists between the disobedience of a servant and that of a son exists here. The disobedience of a son is far more grievous than that of a servant; but it belongs to an essentially different order. It involves a different malice, a malice peculiar to it, just as the mutual relations upon which the duty of obedience and love rests are essentially different. If the creature is truly elevated by grace to the dignity of a child of God, the malice of his sin is as unprecedented and mysterious as is the position into which he had entered relative to God; it is a quite special, unparalleled malice, the depth of which the created intellect can no more plumb than it can comprehend the sublimity of the grace to which that malice runs counter.

2. Since the right relationship to God under all circumstances constitutes the creature's highest dignity and destiny, by sin the creature also dishonors and outrages himself. Nothing is more dishonorable and unnatural for a good servant or a good son than rebelliousness and lack of love toward his master or his father. The rebellion of a son is incomparably and essentially more disgraceful and unnatural than that of a servant against his master. Must not this difference hold for creatures in the natural and supernatural state? Is it not more dishonorable and unnatural for a creature in the state of God's sonship to disavow this intimate and exalted relationship, than for a creature to forget his Lord in the state of servitude? In the supernatural state the creature possesses a holy, divine dignity, with which his natural dignity can scarcely be compared. Therefore the profanation of that state involves a baseness so unworthy and unnatural that it is inconceivable in a profanation of the state of nature.

What a disparity between the malice of sin in the natural and supernatural order! How deep is the hell of malice into which faith affords us a glance!

3. Sin not only opposes the law of God, not only resists God as Lawgiver, not only besmirches the dignity and position of the sinner:

it runs counter to his own interior hunger and love for God and God's law, counter to his own interior justice and goodness.

In assigning a certain rank and destiny to His creature, God endows him with the power to live up to his position, and to attain his destiny; and together with the power He infuses a tendency, a desire for their realization. On His part God brings the creature into harmony with his rank and destiny, disposes the creature to submissiveness and love toward Himself and His law, and thereby makes the creature right and good. Therefore, when the creature demeans his rank and renounces his destiny, he opposes the goodness and justice dwelling within him, withdraws from their influence and guidance, and even perhaps seeks to banish them from himself.

All of this, of course, happens in the natural order quite otherwise than in the supernatural order, because goodness and justice themselves are entirely different in the two cases.

The necessary power and inclination for the realization of the creature's natural position and destiny are contained in nature itself. In the creature's own faculty of light, that is, the intellect, is inscribed the law which is revealed to him by God, his supreme Lord whom he must esteem and love. In the creature's will there exist a natural power and a natural aspiration toward good in general, and toward the esteem and love of the supreme Good in particular. This is the creature's natural goodness and justice, without which God cannot create him. When the creature thwarts this natural goodness and justice, he contradicts his own nature. But this opposition is not as sharp and brusque as that by which as child of God he disavows his supernatural goodness and justice.

For when God raises a creature to the dignity of His children and assigns a supernatural office and destiny to him, He likewise infuses into him a supernatural principle of life. He confers on the creature a supernatural power, and with it a corresponding disposition inclining him toward all that is involved in his new dignity, office, and destiny, but chiefly toward a filial esteem and love, based on supernatural knowledge, for God Himself as the Father of the creature who has been adopted by Him in grace and reborn of Him. In this power or virtue that is infused by the Holy Spirit lie the supernatural good and justice of the created spirit. It pertains essentially to the divine order, because it is based on a participation in the divine nature and fits the recipient for participation in the divine life.

Therefore it is divine goodness and justice, it is sanctity. And the inclination toward God and the fulfillment of His law is filial, divine love, which theologians call charity, a love which is breathed and instilled into our hearts by the Holy Spirit Himself. Hence the person who has been raised to this state but commits sin does not merely contradict the goodness and justice of his nature. He contradicts the goodness and justice of God, which had been communicated to him; he contradicts the Holy Spirit who dwells in him as a divine breath of life; he contradicts divine sanctity, which patently is infinitely less compatible with sin than is the creature's natural goodness. And this distinctive opposition of sin to supernatural justice brands it in the supernatural order with a special stigma of malice.

Thus from every angle sin assails the mystery of God in the creature and the entire order of grace. In its attack it advances against the very mystery of God in which the mystery of grace is rooted. Sinners rebel against the eternal Father who in His Son had also become a Father to them, and had taken them to His bosom along with His Son. They dishonor the Son of God within them, that Son whose image had been stamped upon them, and according to whose example they were to guard the most intimate, inviolable unity with the eternal Father. They resist the Holy Spirit dwelling and stirring in them, the Holy Spirit who joined them to the Father and the Son in living unity. They desecrate and outrage the profoundest and sublimest holiness of the Godhead in its most loving relations with creatures, and sever the bond which had joined it to creatures. They not only oppose the order of grace in itself and for itself, but also the all-holy, immutable order of the divine persons among themselves, as that order is externally reproduced and continued in the order of grace.

40. Mysterious Consequences of Sin: in Particular the Mysterious Nature of Habitual Sin

1. The character of sin's opposition to the order of grace, and especially to the soul's habitual goodness and justice in the order of grace, that is, to the soul's sanctity, is seen most strikingly in the fact that it actually excludes sanctity from the soul and effectively destroys that sanctity.

Contradiction tends in general toward the removal and exclusion of its opposite; and so in the natural order, too, man opposes and repels the goodness and soundness of his nature by sin. But he cannot effectively exclude and extinguish these natural properties, partly because he is unable to destroy his nature, partly because finite nature, while inherently inclined in the direction of good, is also inherently capable of defection and can co-exist with sin. Man may strip his natural bent toward good of all influence upon his free will, he may arrest its development, he may dull its power; but he will never annihilate it. And nature for its part will ever protest against sin; its very protestations show that it always remains essentially the same, even though its voice does not always come through audibly.

Matters are quite otherwise in the supernatural order. Sanctity, as divine light, stands in absolute opposition to grave sin; on the other hand, as a supernatural endowment of nature, sanctity does not necessarily belong to nature. Consequently holiness is not only negated but effectively extinguished and excluded when sin which contradicts it springs up in the soul. Supernatural virtue, the disposition and aptitude for supernatural good, is weakened and hindered in growth by every gravely sinful act; and it is even completely annihilated and torn out along with its root. Thus the habit of theological love, or charity, perishes whenever a grievous sin is committed, because all grievous sins are opposed to the love of God. The other virtues, for example, hope and faith, perish only when the sin committed is specifically directed against them, as despair is against hope, unbelief against faith, and so on. And since the divine virtues are the principles of the supernatural life, this life is not merely weakened, arrested, or wounded by grave sin; it is destroyed.

The question may be asked: How does the sinful act, the act that is opposed to supernatural virtue and justice, destroy them? A few Thomists have thought that this destructive power ought to be conceived as a sort of physical force, analogous to the power of the sword by which bodily life is destroyed. But it is highly improbable that a sinner could exterminate sanctity in himself unless God withdrew it. The destructive force of the sinful act lies in its absolute moral incompatibility with supernatural sanctity, which it negates. Owing to this incompatibility it expels and drives sanctity out of the soul, while God has no reason for preserving it against the sinner's thrust, but must rather withdraw it for the sinner's punishment.

2. Accordingly grievous sin is mortal sin—a concept and a term that have no proper application in the natural sphere, but are peculiar to the supernatural sphere known by faith. The concept is theological and therefore highly mysterious, and affords us a direct insight into the fearful abyss of evil laid open by sin as opposed to the mystery of divine grace. Thus grievous sin is suicide, incomparably more evil and frightful than that by which a person takes his bodily life; for it destroys and annihilates divine, supernatural life, which is immensely more precious than the soul itself, to say nothing of the life which the soul imparts to the body.[1]

Still more: this self-murder doubles and trebles the malice of sin. It doubles that malice, since sin is not only an act that contends against God, but in addition destroys the most glorious work of His supernatural grace in the soul, and snuffs out a life of which we can say with profound truth that God Himself lives it in us. It trebles the malice of sin, because the sinner, not content with perpetrating an unjust, inordinate deed, completely uproots the justice and conformity with our supernatural end effected in us by God, and because, further, the sinner not only turns from God in his iniquitous act, but forcibly rends the bond with which God had fettered us to Himself and dissolves supernatural union with Him. In a word, the sinner not merely fails to square his act with justice, but in consequence of his act strips himself of justice and thereby really perpetuates sin in himself.

3. That is to say, the eradication of the supernatural life-principle makes it possible for sin to survive habitually in the soul even after the actual sin has been committed, just as prior to the sin goodness and justice were habitually present.

After its perpetration, the sinful act can persist only in its consequences. In all cases it endures morally, as long as it is not retracted and redressed, that is, remitted; hence as long as the sinner remains accountable for his sinful deed in God's ledger. The effect of actual sin, in which effect the sin endures, is the guilt imputed to it on account of the fault (*culpa*); that is, it is the responsibility for

---

[1] J. Nirschl's *Gedanken über Religion und religiöse Gegenstände*, in spite of its unpretentious title, contains a wealth of excellent, deeply theological discourses adorned with all the graces of poetry and eloquence. In "Vortrag XV" it gives the most profound and graphic description of mortal sin that we have ever read.

the offense offered to God and the injury done to His honor by the sinful act, or the *reatus* in virtue of which the sinner as the perpetrator of this deed, becomes and remains answerable to God.[2]

In the natural order nothing further need be added to complete the description, except perhaps a weakening of the inclination to good, or a certain propensity to evil. But this may remain even after the retraction of the sin and the remission of the guilt, and therefore is not necessarily a sign that a man is a sinner. Generally speaking, we cannot say that some condition of interior depravity must be postulated in the sinner, if he is to remain a *reus*, a person to whom his sin is still imputable. Such a state would have to be an enduring sinful disposition, a lasting sinful will; but then the actual sin would endure precisely as actual sin.

Obviously this same sort of continuation or aftereffect of the sinful act occurs also in the supernatural order. Here too, until the act is retracted or redressed, the author of the act stands guilty of the act before God and is subject to retribution. But since the sinful act shuts out supernatural justice by its opposition to the latter, it has its aftereffect not only in the guilt with which it freights the sinner, but also in the exclusion of this justice. In the supernatural order, prior to the retractation and forgiveness of the sinful act, the sinner remains bereft of his habitual justice and tendency toward God, and by reason of his guilt continues to remain averted from God. And this culpable, self-inflicted privation of the habit of justice not only causes his sin to endure in God's memory, but stamps the brand of sin upon his soul. At the time of the sinful deed the author of it was a sinner because his act was destitute of justice; now he is a sinner because his offense strips him of the habit of justice by which he should be turned toward God. At the time of the deed he was unjust and a sinner inasmuch as he elicited an unjust and sinful act; now he is unjust and a sinner

---

[2] The words "guilt" and "fault" are usually employed interchangeably, since one implies the other. But for a deeper understanding of the nature of sin, we must carefully distinguish between them. The Latin *culpa* is properly the fault, whence arises the *reatus culpae*. Guilt is the *reatus* induced by the *culpa*. As long as the *reatus culpae* endures in its totality, it includes the *reatus poenae*. But if the *culpa* is retracted by the sinner, and friendship with God is restored, and hence the most radical element in the *reatus* is expunged, the debt of *satisfactio* or *satispassio* still remaining is called *reatus poenae* after its object, although this *reatus*, too, is based on the *culpa*.

because the extinction of habitual justice continues to remain imputed to him. Such is the theological distinction between actual and habitual sin. The habitual culpability is the impress of the culpable act in the soul of the sinner, a habitual deformity stemming from it; and this in turn is nothing other than the privation of a habit of justice which was once present and which still ought to be present, or the lack of a supernatural, habitual union with God and inclination toward God (*caritas*). The deficiency in question is caused by the sinner himself, and is the culpable privation of that justice which he had received from God and which he was bound to guard. Sin is not, therefore, the privation of grace as grace, for grace as grace is an indication of God's love for us and of its effect as such. When we sin, grace is withdrawn by God in punishment for our sins, and this withdrawal as inflicted by God cannot formally be sin. Sin is rather the privation of the justice effected in us by grace, so far as this privation is the result of our own expulsion or extinction of justice. However, since our supernatural justice is itself a grace of God and is inseparably bound up with grace in the technical sense, or the grace of divine sonship, the privation of supernatural justice in the sinner is at once sin and punishment for sin. It is sin so far as we expel supernatural justice by our sinful act; it is punishment so far as God withdraws this justice from us along with grace and in grace.

The usual terminology of many theologians, that habitual sin consists in the culpable privation of grace, we accordingly hold to be inaccurate. We should do much better to say that it consists in the culpable privation of sanctity, or more briefly, in culpable unholiness. For sanctity is a pregnant expression for the supernatural justice effected by grace, and so the proper character of habitual sin in the supernatural order is well described by saying that it consists in the extinction of sanctity. Hence we shall invariably employ the term suggested.

4. In the sense just explained, habitual sin is a condition inhering in the soul, caused by actual sin. Although this is only a negative state, consisting in the privation of the opposite, positive state (that of the infused habit), for this very reason the soul undergoes a real change by entering upon it. Henceforth the soul must be said to be in a quite different disposition from its previous disposition; for, besides its accountability for the sinful act, it bears in itself a real impress

of that act. If, now, instead of stressing the enduring deformity of habitual sin and the aversion from God which are caused by actual sin, I place the emphasis on the debt of guilt contracted with God, then habitual sin is habitual not as a sinful state (*habitus* in the sense of *qualitas quae habetur*), but as an enduring relationship, or more exactly as a want of right relationship to God (*habitus* in the sense of *modus quo aliquis se habet ad aliquid*). In virtue of this wrong relation I am under the obligation of returning to God in repentance and of rendering satisfaction, or else I shall have eventually to sustain His hate and anger. With respect to the guilt, habitual sin is an injustice so far as the guilty party, after his infringement of God's right, has not yet recovered his right relationship to God by retractation and satisfaction. With respect to its deformity, habitual sin is injustice so far as the latter consists in the reverse of the habit of justice or of the right ordering of the will to God.

Both views are equally warranted in the supernatural order. We should err if, as so often happens, we were to insist on one of them at the expense of the other. According to circumstances we can prefer one to the other. For example, when there is question of the remission of sin, the reference is not to the habitual deformity, but to the debt of guilt. If, on the other hand, we speak of the sanctification of the sinner, we have directly in mind his abiding deformity. Other expressions, such as deletion of the sin, or justification of the sinner, refer equally to the liquidation of the debt and the removal of the habitual deformity.

5. This fact indicates that the guilt and deformity of habitual sin are very closely connected. We believe that, with their difference and in their difference, they form an organic whole, in which both their distinction and their unity are noteworthy.

To be explicit: the guilt or *reatus* follows immediately from the culpability of the sinful act as an offense against God. Although I can also conceive of the habitual deformity as produced directly by the deformity of the sinful act, yet it is likewise an effect of the guilt induced by the culpability of the sinful act, inasmuch as it results from the deserved withdrawal of grace, as has been remarked above. But so far as the habitual deformity is directly induced by the deformity of the sinful act and is its impress, it is as culpable as the deformity of the sinful act itself, and so by reason of its culpability becomes a debt of guilt contracted with God.

In this guilt the culpability of the transitory act becomes the culpability of a permanent deformity and aversion from God. Thus by reason of the second culpability the first culpability acquires a lasting hold on the soul of the sinner, as also does the debt of guilt which it contracts with God. Even more than this: the debt acquires a new title besides. Although the first title, the culpability of the act, amply suffices to account for the guilt, the culpability of the depraved state which ought not exist is at least as adequate a title for the guilt. For if actual opposition to the demands of the love and veneration due to God can burden us with guilt in God's eyes, why should not the rending of the bond that fetters us to God in love and veneration do so still more? And do we not incur a special guilt because of the obligation to recover this bond and to render special satisfaction to God for having severed it? However, since the second culpability can stem only from the first and is virtually included in it, we shall do best to say that the first culpability terminates in the second, and that the first guilt is completed and consolidated through the second.

Hence, although the guilt as a result of the theological sin can and must be conceived as in a certain respect independent, alongside of and outside of the habitual deformity of sin, in its totality and in the concrete it presupposes the culpability of this deformity and essentially implies it. And conversely, although the habitual deformity can in a certain respect be regarded as a consequence and punishment of the guilt (namely, that guilt which is incurred by the act), it is also, on the other hand, a factor whereby the guilt itself is conditioned, completed, and consolidated in its totality.

Therefore the full concept of theological, habitual sin must bring into prominence both of these factors in their organic connection. According as we put one before the other, the *reatus* or the *pravitas*, we shall say either that sin is the guilt deliberately incurred in God's sight on account of the act and state opposing His will, or that it is the state enduring as the imprint of the sinful act in the soul, by which the soul's imputability before God is completed and consolidated.

6. It follows from this that the deformity of theological, habitual sin, and also its guilt possess a mysterious character. This guilt has such a character because, in the first place, it is contracted not before God as Creator, but as Father, and results from the criminal outrage

done to that love and veneration which the creature owes to God as his adoptive Father. Another reason is that it is a consequence of the sundering of the bond which joined the creature to God as his adoptive Father. Therefore the guilt has its foundation in the mysterious change of condition which takes place in the subject laden with imputability for the sin.

Reason can no more gauge the enormity of the guilt burdening the sinner than it can comprehend the nature of the sin. If even in the natural order the sinner's guilt is in a certain sense infinite, with reference to the person offended, it is evidently much more so in the supernatural order. For, by participating in the divine nature, the sinner had stood incomparably closer to God's infinity, and had had a much clearer knowledge of it; nevertheless he has torn himself away from it, has disdained it. If only for this reason, the guilt is incalculable on the part of the sinner. Furthermore, the sinner cannot by his own efforts again bind himself to God in supernatural love, nor can he by himself ever regain the point of vantage, the state of the sonship of God, from which he might to some extent offer satisfaction. In no way at all can he regain that state unless God first condones, at least partially, the guilt by which the sinner has forfeited this grace.[8]

Thus, until the sinner's state and relationship to God are changed by an utterly gratuitous intervention on God's part, he merits God's hatred and wrath, a hatred and a wrath that correspond in exact proportion to the sublime love and benevolence which were showered upon him in the state of charity and the grace of adoption. The sinner not only deserves the loss of the supernatural goods to which he was summoned by charity and grace, but he calls forth from God a reaction against himself that is as fearful as the attack of the adopted child against his Father was disgraceful and abominable.

From the unremitted, and humanly irremissible, debt of guilt contracted with God, arises the obligation of enduring the effects of His hatred and anger, His punishments; the *reatus culpae* begets

[8] The gravity of sin is also dependent on the sinner's realization of his act, and on his own nature, not only on the dignity of the offended person. The reason why man can be redeemed by God is that he is not capable of a purely spiritual sin. In the following paragraphs the analogous character of such expressions as God's "hatred," "wrath," and "reaction" should be borne in mind. [Tr.]

the *reatus poenae*, the latter of which, in the case of theological sin, has as mysterious an aspect as the former.

But we shall have to come back later to a more detailed study of the mystery of God's punitive justice. For the present we wish merely to clarify one more term. It is an expression we usually employ to illustrate the nature of habitual sin. I say "to illustrate" rather than to define in concept; for the expression in question does no more than suggest a sensible image, which we may not substitute for proper concepts; indeed, we must use the concepts to determine the applicability of the figure.

7. Actual sin as well as habitual sin is called metaphorically a stain on the soul, a term which has a definite meaning in the supernatural order. We prescind here from the problem to what extent sin considered as a turning to creatures (*conversio ad creaturam*), whether in the act itself or in the habit induced by the act, stains the soul in the matter of man's inordinate craving for creatures. We wish to confine our attention to sin regarded as a turning from God (*aversio a Deo*).

What concept underlies this metaphorical stain? How is it connected with sin? Actual sin is something in the soul that conflicts with its inherent inclination toward God, its harmony with God, something that disturbs right order and tends to annihilate it, and that renders the soul displeasing in God's eyes. What actual sin does at the instant it is committed, is perpetuated in the guilt incurred and not yet remitted, as long as the disturbance of the order and the offense to God caused by sin are not repaired, and as long as the author of the sin remains responsible for this disturbance and offense.

That which disfigures material things and makes them appear disgusting is called a stain. This same term is fitly transferred to sin and guilt, by which the soul is disfigured and rendered odious in God's sight. Thus far this spiritual defilement is no particular mystery. Anyone who has a notion of justice and sin must regard sin as a disfigurement and degradation of God's image. After the act itself has passed, the defilement is nothing real and physical in the soul, but is a moral entity flowing from the act, a wrong relationship of the soul to the moral order and to God; it is, so to speak, the shadow which the sinful act casts over the soul in guilt.

This sort of defilement stains the soul in the supernatural order, too. But in that order it is not only far more portentous in itself; it results in, or rather implies, a stain of a different kind.

We have already seen that the sinful act, regarded as opposition to the supernatural order, is far more odious, and disgraces and dishonors its author much more, than in the natural order. We likewise saw that as long as the enduring guilt encumbering the sinner has not been canceled and remitted, it makes him incomparably more displeasing and detestable to God than does guilt in the natural order. Thus both the act, at the moment of its actual perpetration, and its aftereffect, the shadow of the act present in the guilt, must defile the soul of the sinner and make it repellent to a degree that reason cannot surmise or conceive.

This sort of defilement has a certain mysterious character. Nevertheless, considered in itself, it is only a moral stain, which remains habitually in the guilt incurred by the sinful act. Regarded in this sense the notion of defilement in the supernatural order is by no means exhausted, at least as concerns mortal sin; for with venial sin the concept of moral stain suffices. In the supernatural order there is another kind of defilement of the soul, which not only covers its countenance with filth, but eats into it like a corroding poison, and thoroughly disfigures and devastates it by altering its state.

Endowed with grace and supernatural justice, the soul possesses a supernatural radiance, a heavenly harmony with God, and a divine beauty, which stand in the same relationship to sin as light to darkness. This radiance, this harmony and beauty, are not merely to some slight degree disfigured or beclouded by sin, but are annihilated, completely extinguished. The soul which through grace shone in the light of the divine sun like a bright star in the heavens, is suddenly changed by sin into a dark, somber orb. Like a black cloud, sin (the sinful act) comes between the soul and the divine light of grace, so as to shut the soul off from that light and bar all access to it. Actual sin, both at the instant of the deed and later, as long as the act continues to exert its efficacy, is this cloud which robs the soul of its radiance and beauty, and thus defiles it or rather completely blackens it.

Actual sin by itself is a stain, in the sense explained. But its effect is a much greater stain, although it would not be a real defilement at all if it were not the result of a sinful act. For, if by God's will the soul were not to possess the splendor of grace and sanctity, or if it lost this gift otherwise than by its own culpability, it would indeed be less pleasing to God by reason of its lack, but it would not on that account be positively displeasing. In order that the absence of sanctity and justice truly defile the soul and render it displeasing in God's sight, it must be more than some indeterminate consequence of the sinner's culpability. If we think of this lack, as in fact we can, as incurred in consequence of the sinful act, as a result and punishment of the guilt contracted through the sinful act, then it is not the lack but rather the act and the guilt alone which make the soul displeasing to God. Thus this lack is a blemish that pertains not to sin but to punishment, and merely shows how repellent the soul has become through the sinful act and the guilt.

The real blemish in the case of permanent sin is the guilt which moves God to take away the jewel of His grace from the besmirched soul. If, on the other hand, we think of this lack of grace as directly and immediately caused by the deformity of the act, and therefore in the proper sense as culpable, then the culpability of this lack completes the guilt burdening the soul. Thus the lack itself has an essential part in constituting both the sin and the basis for the repulsiveness of the soul in God's sight, and hence in constituting the sinful defilement.

Since the repulsiveness of the soul in God's sight consists in the moral continuance of a passing act, and also in a real, culpable alteration and disfigurement of the soul, manifestly the notion of defilement is realized in its full force in the supernatural order alone. But the stain thus produced is also a true mystery, not so much because we cannot perceive it with our natural vision, as rather because it involves the extinction of a supernatural radiance, the annihilation of the supernatural likeness of God in the soul. This notion of defilement is on a par with that of mortal sin. The natural likeness of God in the soul can be tarnished and disfigured, just as the soul's natural principle of life can be obstructed and weakened. But only the supernatural likeness of God, the seal of the Holy Spirit, the impress of the divine nature, can be destroyed, as also only the supernatural principle of life can be killed in its root.

If the doctrine which envisages habitual sin as the privation of sanctity is not adequately grasped and proposed, the sinner may wrongly be represented as sinking from his supernatural height only to the level of nature after he has committed the sin. But in reality the burden of guilt connected with that privation forces him as far beneath his nature as the gift of sanctity had raised him above it; for now he is hated by God and thrust away from Him in the measure in which he was formerly loved by God and drawn close to Him. Further, since sanctity not merely clothed nature like a garment, but grew up with it like a living limb engrafted to it, or better, like its own vital principle, the withdrawal of sanctity must leave nature in a state differing as much from the state of pure nature as the state of a corpse bereft of life differs from the state of a body that had never been alive. And as the will in withstanding grace displayed a greater malice than would have been possible outside the order of grace, so likewise the tendency to a repetition of the act, which is usually engendered in a greater or lesser degree, becomes a far more evil thing than in the mere order of nature. This evil tendency is engendered especially when the sinner directly and formally desecrates grace, and so transforms its heavenly sweetness into the most virulent poison, as we shall explain more fully further on. All of this, however, is applicable only to personal sin, not to original sin; for the supposition is that the guilt burdens the subject with its full gravity and in its entire compass, and that the sinful act comes into conflict with grace in the same subject. Neither of these suppositions is verified in the case of a person laden with original sin.

41. The Element of Mystery in the Origin and Course of Sin

The true, mysterious character of the conflict into which sin enters with the goodness and justice given by God in the supernatural order, and with the sanctity of him who commits sin, must manifest itself not only in the consequences of sin but also in its origin. By the act that opposes his goodness and justice, as we said above, the sinner tends to destroy or at least to repel these gifts. But since the God-given goodness and justice precede sin, and on their part incite to good and restrain from evil, a creature cannot commit a sinful deed unless he withdraws from their influence. Only thus does sin become possible.

The creature, to be sure, is by nature free, and has the free choice of taking a stand for God or against God. But this freedom is not an absolute indifference and detachment. The will necessarily receives from its Creator the power of determining itself in favor of God, and such self-determination is a law for it, and a duty, a moral bond. But God does not let the matter rest there. He Himself introduces into the will a disposition and tendency to good, which impels it, directs it, and as it were binds it to good, so that the will, if it decides in favor of sin, must cut itself loose from this bond in a violent and unnatural way. It is in this withdrawal and defection that we have to look for the origin of sin. Let us note how utterly different is the manner in which this shapes up in the natural order and in the supernatural order.

There is present in nature itself, as has been repeatedly remarked, a tendency toward love of God and subjection to God, a tendency that is designed to impede all turning away from God and deviation from His law. But created nature is of itself so remote from God and is so engrossed in its own interests, that defection from God is not automatically and completely out of the question. Though from God, the creature is likewise from nothing, and is essentially frail; and so defection from God by sin does not appear to be particularly exceptional and mysterious.

On the other hand, the creature's supernatural goodness flows immediately from God and is a participation in the divine goodness and holiness, which stand in as stark a contrast to sin as fire does to water or light to darkness. The connatural tendency of this supernatural goodness is to make the creature as sinless as God Himself. And in fact, once participation in the divine nature completely floods the creature, once the creature is fully reborn of God in the luminous state of glory and is wholly united to God, then sin is utterly excluded and cannot approach even from afar; then defection from God and aversion from God are absolutely unthinkable; the frailty of nature is wholly and entirely consumed by divine holiness.

But are not supernatural grace and justice, as given to us here on earth, and as once given to the angels during their period of trial, likewise a participation in the divine nature and holiness, an anticipation of the holiness and union with God which we shall receive in the state of glory, and must they not likewise tend and serve to make the creature sinless? No doubt such is the case; nevertheless

St. John says: "Whosoever is born of God committeth not sin; for His seed abideth in him. And he cannot sin, because he is born of God." [4] Because the seed of God abides in the soul, and hence as long as it abides there, no grievous sin can be committed. The soul cannot sin except at the instant when the seed of God, which is holiness and grace, retires from it, when the soul struggles free from the bosom of God in which it was born, and disengages itself from the arms of God which held it in close embrace, when it violently cuts itself loose from the bonds of love which wonderfully fettered it to God. But the soul can do this only because here on earth the seed of God has not yet fully sprung up in it and has not yet entirely pervaded and animated it, because the divine ardor of sanctity has not yet completely absorbed and transformed it, because union with God is not yet wholly perfected and achieved. But in any case the origin of sin in the sanctified creature is incomparably more mysterious than in the unelevated creature. If it is universally true that even in the mere creature apostasy from God is inexplicable and unnatural, the dissolution of supernatural union with God, or the sin of the creature despite its mysterious sanctity, is singularly incomprehensible and inscrutable.

But perhaps we may succeed in casting into this abyss a few rays of light that will afford us a deeper insight into the factual origin of sin and its development, and that especially will explain the terrible malice and violence with which it rages through the world. We shall not be able to illuminate the abyss completely, but we shall discover in it the foundation of that terrifying kingdom of sin, the baffling maze of whose outermost pinnacles, bristling grimly in the distant mist, the peering intellect here on earth barely discerns.

How in general are we to conceive this defection, this separation from God? Secession from God can arise only from union with God, not as from a cause, but as from a presupposed state; for where there is no union, there can be no separation. If a being were of itself entirely dissociated from God, either because it did not depend on God or because God had not placed it in relationship to Himself, it could not turn away from God, because it had never been turned toward Him. And since sin cannot have its origin in sheer nothingness, it must proceed in every case from the good which God has implanted in creatures. This is what happens when the sinner, in-

[4] Cf. I John 3:9.

clining to this good and turning toward it, turns his back on God. Every good which the creature possesses comes from God, and has been given by God with freely willed munificence. The creature ought to see in this good a motive for thanking God, for loving Him in return, for using it according to God's will. Since he himself has his entire being from God, he ought wholly to subject and surrender himself to God. The creature of himself is nothing, whereas God of Himself is everything; and so the creature ought to rejoice that God is everything of Himself and hence can draw him from nothing; he ought to be glad and thank God that out of free love He, the Creator, has communicated Himself to His creature. And the greater the good which the creature has received from God, the more liberal is the love whereby God has given it to him, and the greater, too, should be the creature's joy over God's infinity and his gratitude toward Him; but the greater also and the more marked is the utter dependence in which the creature stands to God.

It is this very dependence that should impel the creature to turn to God and surrender himself to Him unconditionally. But the same dependence is also the point of departure for the creature's defection from God and resistance to God. It becomes the occasion of the creature's fall if he begins to feel mortified at the thought that what he is and has is not of himself; when he longs to use and enjoy the good he has received according to his own arbitrary pleasure, as if he had not received it; when, finally, he demands more than God with loving liberality has assigned to him; in a word, when he wishes to be like God. The greater the good which he has received from God, the easier it is, on the one hand, to thank God for it, but on the other to desire to have it of himself, to be able to enjoy and use it at will, and to acquire still more. It is precisely at this stage that dependence on God and the sense of obligation toward God most irritatingly prick the sensibilities of him whose ambition is to be like God.

This is especially the case with supernatural grace. When God proclaims to the creature that out of pure, overflowing love He wills to raise him from the depths of servitude which was his lot by nature to the honor of His own children, the creature must be most keenly aware of his nothingness before God, and his utter dependence on Him. He is humbled by the very hand that would raise him; and if he refuses to submit to this humiliation, he insolently spurns the hand of God so lavish of graces, turns his back, and in the inflation of his ego prefers to cut himself off from God rather than enjoy in God's bosom and receive at His hand the happiness of His children.[5]

Let us imagine a similar case among us men. A prince takes a man from his lowly station and adopts him. This is an unparalleled kindness, and should enkindle in the recipient a most heartfelt love of his benefactor. But it can also give rise to hostile relations between the two, which otherwise perhaps would never have occurred. If the person in question had remained in his own class, he would perhaps never have thought of setting himself on a par with his prince and of supplanting him. But now he suddenly beholds himself raised to a dizzy height. He is delighted to occupy this pinnacle, becomes intoxicated at the prospect, and would enjoy it fully and completely. He would like to be able to call all this his own; but at the same time he is necessarily aware that his own origin gives him no right to it, that it was conferred on him out of sheer bounty and charity. He is to reign, but only as a vassal, in full dependence on his adoptive father, under the latter's tutelage, led by his hand. Considering the matter from one point of view, he is elated; but looking at it from another, he feels himself grow small, like a foundling infant adopted out of kindness. Pride awakens, and with it a rage that no one could have foreseen. Black jealousy and savage hate take the place of devoted, grateful love. The sweeter the beneficence, the bitterer is the poison into which it turns.

It is in some such way that we have to represent the fall of the angel. Holy Scripture itself portrays him emerging from the ecstasy produced in him by the dizzy height and glory to which God had raised him. Because he was so very like to God, because he was called to closest fellowship with God, he wished to be entirely like God. His exceedingly lofty position inflated his heart, so that he laid claim to goods which otherwise he would not have thought of; no longer content with sheer grace received from the hand of God, simply on his own account he craved to be more than befits a creature of God.

[5] This is by no means a theological fiction. The history of modern times bears abundant witness to the craving for autonomous self-assertion in purely naturalist and humanist spheres. The apostasy from God manifests itself positively in an exclusive preoccupation with man on the natural level, and negatively in a rejection of Christ's revelation. [Tr.]

Some theologians of antiquity went so far as to think that without a supernatural elevation of the angel his fall would not have been possible at all. This is undoubtedly excessive; else the angel would have been incapable of sin by nature, and would have become so only by grace, whereas it is precisely grace that is intended to make the naturally peccable creature partake of the sinlessness of God. But this much is to be admitted: in actual fact the angel found the impetus to his fall in his supernatural elevation, and this, too, is why it was so deep, so terrible, and so fearful a fall.

When we wish to express the extreme degree of malignity and evil in a sinful act, we are accustomed to say that it is a diabolical sin. This word directly implies that the sin is committed not out of weakness or ignorance, but with open eyes and full deliberation, out of sheer malice, as was the case with the fallen angels, and that consequently the evil is willed as such with a vigor and decisiveness like that of the angels, as once and for all eternity they plunged into evil with their whole being. But the blackest depths, the uttermost hell of demonic malice, is not yet reached. This abyss is plumbed only when we reflect that the angel desecrated God's own supernatural grace, that he turned the sweetness of the Holy Spirit into foulest poison, that while dwelling in the very bosom of God he rebelled against Him and, so to speak, ventured to root up the innermost being of God. This bottomless evil affects the devil's act and disposition not only objectively, so far as the act results in a violation of the supernatural order of grace, as happens with us in sins of weakness or ignorance, but touches his act subjectively in its core, because its malice is ignited at the very fire of God's grace. Hence that unfathomable, raging hatred of God which characterizes the devil's sin, that frightful obduracy and malevolence which could never have arisen on the basis of mere nature, and which appears among men only at rare intervals and to a limited degree, in sins against the Holy Spirit. It is this unfathomable hatred of God, this obduracy and malevolence, which brand the sin of the devil with that distinctive, mysterious character that we have come to describe as demonic.

A further interesting fact follows from this. Sin in the supernatural order, at least when it is committed with out-and-out malice, has a terrible reaction on the sinner's nature. The real malignity of sin in this supposition does not pass over to the nature without leaving a trace, as though it did nothing but fling off grace while leaving the nature uninjured. By going counter to grace and steeling his heart against it as the supreme good of nature, the creature perverts and deranges his nature in a way that would be otherwise impossible. The will becomes perverted, malicious, and poisoned in a manner that is unthinkable in a mere rebellion against the natural order. Herein, apparently, is found the ultimate reason why a change and conversion of the will to good, even to natural good, seems an impossibility with the fallen angels, as also with men who sin against the Holy Spirit, unless a great miracle of divine omnipotence intervenes. This impossibility of conversion among the fallen spirits is, to be sure, explained by theologians on the basis of the natural condition of their will. But as the natural goodness of creatures receives its sanction in grace and thus becomes holiness, so the perversion of the creature by opposition to grace becomes more deeply rooted, more heinous, and more irremediable.

But our chief concern is with the sin of man, and specifically of the first man. As man is constituted now, actual sin usually has its origin in his defective knowledge of good and in the earthly or carnal inclinations of his nature. But this condition of weakness and ignorance was not the original state. Owing to the gift of integrity, man was originally immune from the darkness of the understanding and the lower tendencies of his concupiscible faculty. The supposition that Eve, or Adam also, for that matter, was tempted to sin by sensible craving for the fruit, betrays a complete failure to comprehend the nature of the original state. No sort of craving for a forbidden good could arise in either of them without a preceding assent of the will, which would itself be a sin. The sensible attraction that Eve experienced for the fruit when she gazed upon it was not the beginning of the sin, but the consequence of a sin already committed in her soul. The first sin of Eve and Adam could be nothing but pride, and according to all appearances was in reality that sort of pride which directly assaults the grace of God, a pride similar to that which took place in the fallen angel, who sought to trap them both into his own sin.

Was not pride clearly the motive whereby the devil sought to entice Eve when he asked her: "Why hath God commanded you that you should not eat of every tree of Paradise?" [6] and promised

[6] Gen. 3:1.

her that if they ate of it they would be as gods? Did he not thereby depict God to Eve as a tyrannical Lord who wished to make them keenly aware of their utter dependence on Him? Did he not challenge her to claim an independence of God which was absolutely impossible for her as God's child, and to declare her independence of God as a child that has come of age? In giving heed to this voice and desiring to be like God in her own right instead of through the grace generously dealt out to her by God, Eve flung God's grace from her as though it were a harsh, oppressive yoke, and so succumbed to the impetus which caused her to fall from the dazzling heights to which God had raised her and where she could stand only while clinging fast to God's hand. She fell as the evil angel fell, and with her fell Adam, undoubtedly in the same way; either he, too, hearkened to the words of the serpent, or else Eve did not delay to lay before her husband the motives that had led her to fall.

According to the Apostle, Adam's sin was even greater than Eve's, because it was more deliberate. He points out that Eve was deceived by the serpent (and hence, although inexcusably, gave credence to the serpent's words), whereas Adam was not deceived (and hence sinned with full consciousness of the folly and malice of his deed).[7]

Nevertheless the greatness of the malignity in the sin of the first man differed notably from the sin of the angels. Man's understanding, although less bound up with the sense faculties than now, was in any case not so clear and lucid as that of the angels, and his will was not so energetic and powerful as theirs. For this reason, too, the recoil of sin upon his nature was quite otherwise; it manifested itself, as we shall see later, especially in a derangement of nature resulting from the loss of integrity, and in an acutely painful sense of wretchedness, which on the one hand could go on fostering the seed of malice, but on the other could incite man to acknowledgment and repentance of his wanton deed.

Through this temptation the sin of the angels was transmitted to man, and in its own proper character. In both cases the flame of opposition to the order of grace was ignited, if I may say so, at the heavenly fire of grace itself.

Might we not add that fellowship in sin between the angels and man, this mutual traffic in evil, has likewise its strongest and deepest foundation in the order of grace?

[7] Cf. I Tim. 2:14.

A union and commerce between angels and men, in good as in evil, is conceivable even in the natural order, on the basis of the natural unity of both prevailing in their common creation. However, in view of the great difference between the two natures, that unity alone is not sufficient to account for the intimate fellowship and lively commerce in both good and evil that revelation actually describes. In grace, which is imparted to men as to angels, the contrast between their natures recedes. When raised to God's fatherly bosom and clothed with the divine nature, both angels and men acquire equal rank and are united into one great family in the house of their heavenly Father. Hence the intimate intercourse with the good angels, who make every effort to keep men loyal to their common Father and to associate them one day with themselves in the beatific vision of His countenance. But thence, too, the fury of the fallen angels, who envy man the heavenly treasure which they themselves have lost, and who seek to enmesh him in their insurrection and their fall, so that he may not succeed to the place in heaven from which they were ejected. Hence the savage malice of the infernal serpent, as it stalks the heavenly Dove in man (the Holy Spirit), which with its tender love had retired from the rebellious angel and had settled down upon the head of man. Hence the terrible, invisible, and mysterious battle between heaven and hell, between light and darkness, between holiness and godlessness, supernatural grace and devilish malice, with mankind the object and scene of the battle. Hence the tremendous and fearsome mystery of iniquity, which unremittingly works against the mystery of God's grace, and is explicable only in terms of this opposition.

That "mystery of iniquity" which the Apostle specifically mentions [8] is nothing else than the persistent effort of the devil in the midst of the human race. He labors to destroy grace, and with grace nature, too. By his pestiferous breath he hopes to evoke in man himself an estrangement and rebellion against grace, such as will recoil upon nature in the most frightful and pernicious manner. This mystery of iniquity operates in the world like a subterranean volcano, to the depths of which we cannot descend, but the appalling effects of which enable us to judge the might of the destructive force and fury raging in it. Countless manifestations in the realm of evil astound us by the distinctive character of their malignity. The sys-

[8] Cf. II Thess. 2:7.

tematic war against all that is good and holy, the bottomless hatred against the Church and its officials, the service of Moloch and the unnatural vices among the heathen, all these are facts which are scarcely explicable as products of human passions. They point to a dreadful abyss of sin and darkness yawning under our feet; but to descend to its depths, to perceive the true form of the sinister powers reigning there below, exceeds the capacity of reason. Only faith, which reveals to us the august, heavenly mystery of grace, light, and love, can afford us a glance into the hellish chasm of sin, darkness, and hate. We have as much cause to fear the latter mystery as we have to hope in the former.

42. The Theological Opinion about the Origin of Sin as Arising from Rebellion against the God-man

The doctrine thus far presented about the mystery lying in the origin and history of sin and its specific malignity, does not preclude another profound view accepted by many theologians. The two theories are capable of organic conjunction.

According to a rather commonly propounded view, the angels before their fall had received a revelation of the future incarnation of the Son of God. This theory has its firmest foundation in the supposition, otherwise not very generally held, that the incarnate Word, who according to the Apostle is the head of all principalities and powers and the first-born among all creatures, was from the very beginning predestined in God's plan for the universe to be the head and king of the angels, and as such was to have been the source of supernatural grace and glory for them, too. Later, in treating of the mystery of the Incarnation, we shall discuss the speculative merits of this hypothesis.

For the time being we may assume the plausibility of this view. Then the consequence would necessarily follow that the angels had to adore as their God the Son of man thus presented to them in human form. Moreover, in the bearer of a human nature, in a man, they were obliged to acknowledge and revere the source of the grace and glory intended for them, just as those among them who remained loyal had later, according to the Apostle,[9] to adore the first-born upon His entrance into the world.

[9] Heb. 1:6.

Of course this was a great humiliation for the angels. Elevated as they were by nature high above man, they had nevertheless to behold him so markedly preferred to them that human nature was raised above their own in dignity. They had to acknowledge that in spite of their sublime natural perfections they had no claim to the divine sonship, and that they could be members of God's household only as strangers who had been received with gracious condescension. Besides, they had to rest content that the only-begotten of God, who willed to communicate His divine dignity to them as the first-born of all creatures, did not take up His abode among them, but erected the throne of His grace in human nature which was so far beneath theirs, and would speed forth the rays of His divine glory to them from that lower stratum. More, they had to thank God for having united Himself so intimately to mankind, for having located the sun of grace there, and for having singled it out as the central point of the universe.

Can the sin of the angels be more naturally explained, and the malice of their insurrection more profoundly represented, than in this hypothesis? If an angel, especially the most brilliant of them all, Lucifer, became absorbed in the contemplation of his glorious nature, and conceived the idea that God preferred human nature to this lofty nature, and even made him dependent on a man for his own highest and noblest prerogative, must he not have held himself scorned by God, must not his natural exaltation have turned to grievously wounded pride, must he not have been wroth that God had passed his nature by, must he not have burned with envy of the favored human race, and above all must he not have been consumed with ungovernable hatred against the Son of man, to whom he had to pay homage, whom he was bid to adore? We need not assert, as some theologians do, that Lucifer in his pride went so far as to claim the hypostatic union for himself. Such a supposition is contrary to all likelihood; he would have had to give up his own personality, whereas pride is wholly immersed in one's own ego. If, as Scripture indicates, Lucifer craved in his insane rashness to be like the Most High and to set up an empire of his own against Him, the simplest explanation is to be found in his resentment at the thought that any created nature, and especially human nature, should be exalted above him and that he should be made subject to it. Wrath at the exaltation of human nature, and at the fancied slight to his own, seems to have been the original form of his pride, which also included envy of men who had been preferred to himself and of their head, the Son of man, and rebellion against God who had contrived this arrangement so hateful to him.

The doctrine proposed by several of the Fathers, who place the angel's sin in envy of man, can be accounted for only on this hypothesis. For at his creation man had received and could have received no privilege capable of arousing the angel's envy, whether in the order of nature or in the order of grace; nothing could have provoked such fierce resentment except the fact that a member of the human race had been singled out for elevation to the dignity of hypostatic union with the Son of God, and hence to headship and kingship over the angels. The view of these Fathers, although not worked out in detail, can well be regarded as lending positive support to the theory advanced.

If the revelation of the incarnation of the Word furnished the impetus to rebellion against God for Lucifer and his angels, who preferred to subject themselves to one of their own kind in a war against God rather than submit to a man, even though He were really God, then sin takes on a new, more terrible and appalling character of malice than we have heretofore found. Since this pride and this hatred toward God were occasioned by opposition to the most sublime mystery of divine love, we have here a doubly unfathomable hell of venomous malice. The will of the rebel does not merely aim at wrenching itself free from God's dominion; it strives formally and primarily to slay, to destroy the Son of God in His mortal, human nature, in the conviction that only thus can redress be gained for the affront at which it recoils. The most monstrous and the blackest of all crimes, and at the same time the most inconceivable of all, deicide, resulted inevitably from the angel's rebellion, and accounts for the frightful malignity manifested in its purpose.

This appalling mystery of sin considered in its origin becomes in turn a beacon which serves to throw light on the entire subsequent course of sin. It permits us to peer into the depths of hate with which the devil pursues man. He persecutes man not only because man is destined to succeed to the glory which he himself has lost, but much more because man is a member of the body of God's Son. He persecutes mankind on account of its head, and in turn persecutes the latter because He has joined Himself to men as their head. He does not rest or halt until he has likewise destroyed the human race, until he has set up his reign, the reign of death on earth, until he has treacherously enticed men to pay homage to him instead of to the Lord's Anointed, to adore him, to bring him offerings, offerings of death, of ignominy, and deepest degradation. More fiercely still does he persecute the human race in the person of those who, after Christ's incarnation, join His colors, and who seek to destroy the empire of hell in themselves and in others. And since it was a woman, a mere human being, who as Mother of the God-man was to become Queen of the angels, hell's hate had to turn especially against this woman, as well as against her entire progeny.

Do not the awful atrocities of heathendom, particularly the human sacrifices, and the cult of foul vice in its most unnatural forms, as also the systematic attack against Christianity with all the weapons of falsehood and calumny, thus find their fullest explanation? The passions of men would never, at least on such an enormous scale, lead them to rage so ferociously against themselves, and to attack the most exalted ornament of their race; they can be brought to such a pass only by the craftiness and deceit of him who envies them. But in giving heed to his promptings they can, and actually do, arrive at such extremities that once the incarnation of the Son of God is laid before them, and the command to adore Him as their God, their King, and the source of their happiness is issued to them, they too break into fury, rise against their heavenly King with super-human malice, vaunt themselves above Him, and seek to destroy Him together with His kingdom. Thus in their day the Jews joined in with the devil's schemes for the murder of God and allowed themselves to be used as the devil's tools. Thus for a century and more hell's agents have been shrieking forth their "écrasez l'infâme!" Since the incarnate Christ is beyond their clutches, they hound His mystical body with diabolical frenzy.

The scandal which the mystery of the God-man is to the fallen angels and the men who follow them results in their refusal to accept God's truth with the love and reverence due to His word, and in their rejection of faith in the proper sense of voluntary belief. But unbelief that repudiates belief for the sole reason that its object arouses resentment, does not diminish culpability; it increases culpability, it lays bare the full range of the malice involved in persecuting the good that is proposed for belief. Unbelief can partially excuse only where some uncertainty creeps in. Since the revelation of this mystery does not force itself upon men with the same clarity as it does upon the angels, especially when men are deluded by the powers of hell, men's guilt and malice never come up to the guilt and malice of the angels. Yet men can share in the malice of the devils to a high degree; in point of fact, modern unbelief is largely a demonic unbelief.

At any rate, the conclusion cannot be escaped that the "mystery of iniquity" has in the course of time taken shape as formal hatred and conflict against the mystery of the Incarnation, and hence that the abyss of its malice can be grasped only in terms of this mystery. Since the malice which it occasioned is essentially more heinous than any other, and we cannot readily suppose that the prince of darkness in establishing his kingdom would neglect to lay its foundations on the bedrock of evil, what is more natural than the assumption that from the very outset he would have wished to set up his kingdom in direct opposition to the kingdom of the Son of God made man?

However, we propose this whole theory about the origin and history of sin only for what it is worth, as a serious theological opinion that is not strictly deducible from the data of revelation, but that has a strong intrinsic probability.

CHAPTER XI

Original Sin

▀▀▀

43. The Sin of the First Man in Its Relationship to the Lower Element of Original Justice

LET us undertake a closer study of the sin of the first man, for it is this sin that has proved so disastrous for us. With Adam's sin the "mystery of iniquity" has descended from the angels to men, and through it that mystery has been transmitted to the whole human race.

We have already spoken of its mysterious origin. Whether there may be any probability in the supposition that this sin, too, was in some way occasioned by the mystery of the Incarnation, we do not choose to discuss. We think not. In any case, it had a truly mysterious character, inasmuch as it did violence to the order of grace, so that man thereby entered into opposition with the supernatural sanctity that had been conferred on him, and expelled it from himself.

It had this character and this consequence in common with the sin of the angels and with the sin of men of our own time, who in their sinful acts negate and destroy the sanctity restored by Christ. Opposition to sanctity and the destruction of it constituted, in any event, the chief element of mystery in Adam's sin.

But, since the supernatural original justice of the first man contained, besides holiness, another and a lower element, we cannot fully understand the present mystery unless we also consider the opposition of his sin to this lower element.

In the original justice of the first man the gift of sanctity effected a supernatural orientation or turning of the soul to God (*conversio supernaturalis in Deum*), whereas the gift of integrity produced a supernatural detachment or turning from creatures. This detachment was a certain condition of the faculties of the soul in virtue of which these faculties did not, in pursuit of their natural bent, gravitate toward created goods without and against the decision of the free will, and hence could not entice the will to turn away from God.

In direct opposition to justice, sin, in the well-known definition propounded by theologians, is at once a turning from God and a turning to creatures. As a turning away from God, actual sin is incompatible with sanctity, expels it from the soul, and thereby induces a state of habitual aversion from God. Similarly, as a turning to the creature it must come into opposition with the state of detachment of the soul's faculties from created goods. By reason of this incompatibility it must destroy that state, and consequently evoke a habitual inclination of the soul to creatures.

This observation is of extreme importance. A full appreciation of its meaning is impossible without a searching analysis.

By its very nature the actual turning of the will to an object more or less engenders an enduring, habitual propensity toward it, in much the same fashion as the repeated bending of a sapling to one side produces a permanent slant in that direction. As in this example, so also in the case of the will, not any sort of bending is sufficient to produce a permanent inclination, especially if it contradicts the natural uprightness of the will. To engender an abiding tendency, the bending must be effected once with tremendous energy or it must be repeated many times. The former is the case with the angels, as accords with their nature; the latter is the case with men. Since the angels are pure spirits, their energy of will is incomparably greater than that of men.

This habit or propensity is the direct and natural effect of the act of the will, and therefore can gradually be rectified again by a reversal of the will. Manifestly it is rooted chiefly in the will itself, and in other faculties only so far as they were repeatedly and forcefully directed by the will to one object. Therefore evidently it is limited to those objects to which the will has deflected itself and other faculties.

The view has sometimes been maintained that the unruly tendencies which arose in the first man in consequence of his actual inordinate turning to a creature are the natural result of this act. But even on the supposition on which this contention is based, namely, that integrity was a natural good of man, this is utterly impossible. For if man was entirely free from unruly tendencies by nature, a single sinful act, be it ever so energetic, could naturally engender only one inordinate tendency, a tendency toward the object of his sin and to other objects of a similar sort; and by a single opposed act he could have recalled that tendency. How, then, in consequence of Adam's sin could carnal concupiscence immediately surge up in him, which he had done nothing to foster, and indeed with such vehemence that Adam had to hang his head in shame at his powerlessness against it?

Do we, then, absolutely deny that Adam's inordinate tendencies to created and sensible goods were in any way the natural consequence of his sin? By no means; the opposition of sin to the harmony of nature brought about by integrity had necessarily, and to this extent naturally, to destroy integrity; but only because integrity was a supernatural, mysterious gift of God. Sin exterminated this gift as it did the gift of sanctity. As the mystery of sin in Adam consisted primarily in opposition to sanctity and the suppression of sanctity, so it consists secondarily in the negation and suppression of integrity.

Sanctity linked man's will to God in supernatural fashion; in like manner integrity supernaturally linked all the faculties of the soul to the will which was turned toward God. God laid this bond upon the soul's faculties in order that they might not forestall the will, in order that they might never hurry the will along with them to a point where their objects would be forbidden by divine law, and catch up the will into their movement, which rushes on uncontrolled by a higher law. If, nevertheless, the will of its own accord decides to turn to what is prohibited, it opposes the supernatural order and justice established by God, breaks through the bonds laid upon it, and in breaking through rips them apart, bursts them asunder. It severs these bonds in the same way that by its defection from God it rends the tie of supernatural love which fettered it to God. If they were natural bonds, the will could loosen them or stretch them back, but it could never burst them or cast them off. But they are supernatural bonds; and although they were not produced by nature, but were laid upon nature by divine grace in a manner that surpasses our understanding, they can be thrown off from nature by man's sin and depravity. And because this supernatural bond embraced in solidarity the whole of nature with all its powers, because it subjected all the faculties as one unit to the will and made them dependent on the will in their activity, the bond snaps apart in all the members simultaneously if one of its links is broken; or better, it is cast off not in part but throughout its whole length if the will turns inordinately to creatures at a single point.

Thus at one stroke are aroused all those stirrings and inclinations which, rooted in the various faculties of human nature, had been held in check by the gift of integrity. Like the tendrils of a creeping plant that have been plucked out of the trunk in which they had been growing in beautiful order, they now shoot up rankly in a wild tangle, each following its own bent; like unbridled horses they plunge forth in mad haste, so that the will cannot hold them together, and can scarcely assert itself against them. Dissolved is the harmony in which formerly all the faculties were in accord, thanks to the gift of integrity; and with it disappears that unsullied, undisturbed healthy state which previously had made the life of nature so pleasant with amicable peace and order. This state of sound health is succeeded by a condition of decrepitude, of discord, of dissolution, which can aptly be called illness. Like a sharp sword, sin cleaves the original unity by which all the parts of nature were firmly tied to one another and closely united in one another. It inflicts on nature a wound that deprives the will of the free, unhampered use of all the parts and powers of nature, and that results not only in the aforesaid illness, but in the eventual dissolution of nature.

Briefly, by the sin of the first man the impediment which kept nature from adhering to created and material goods independently of and against the free will was removed. In freely turning to such goods, the will cast off the bond that held it and all the other faculties back from them. And so man slipped into a permanent, habitual condition of dependence on creatures, into a condition which he could no more surmount by his own efforts than he could restore his supernatural union with God once he had severed it. In both cases he renounces a grace of God, which he can indeed lose and fling away, but cannot by his own power regain.

The view of the dissolution of integrity here proposed does not receive much light from theologians. The direct production of this dissolution by sin considered as inordinate deflection to creatures is more often, but only in shadowy outline, described by those who postulate a corruption which sin effects in nature, a downright,

positive poisoning of nature.[1] On the contrary, those who regard
integrity as a supernatural endowment of nature, generally hold that
its destruction is effected not immediately and directly by sin, but
mediately and indirectly, in the sense that the sinner expels sanctity
by his reaction against it, loses sanctifying grace, and in consequence
deserves to incur the loss of integrity which is connected with
grace.[2] This is the way St. Augustine usually represents the matter.[3]
The matter undoubtedly works out this way, owing to the firm
mutual connection between sanctity and integrity. In any case,
privation of integrity is punishment for actual sin, and a very fitting
punishment; for the spirit that rebels against God cannot be more
justly and grievously chastised for its pride than by the loss of
dominion over its lower faculties and by their rebellion against it.
Indeed, so far as integrity is regarded not as governing the faculties
of sense cognition and sense appetite, but as constituting the happy,
impassible state of bodily life, this view of the matter is decidedly
preferable. But so far as integrity is regarded as regulating those
faculties, and hence constitutes a certain justice, the material element of original justice, our view must take precedence; otherwise
the concupiscence which springs to life as soon as integrity is lost is
merely punishment, but in no sense forms part of the sin by which
punishment is merited. All those who in some manner or other include concupiscence in original sin, can do so only by holding that
integrity is directly and immediately abrogated by the culpable act,

[1] These are the Jansenists, who with Baius reckon the gift of integrity
among man's natural endowments. [Tr.]

[2] Note carefully that in our conception also the inclination to creatures, or
concupiscence in the widest sense, is to some extent caused indirectly, since it
is not, like an acquired habit, produced by a positive impression which the
sinful act leaves in the soul's faculties, but by the removal of the bridle which
restrained concupiscence. But inasmuch as the liberation of concupiscence
coincides with the removal of the bridle, and this removal is directly and
immediately effected by the sinful act, unbridled concupiscence may itself be
regarded as the result of the sinful act.

[3] *De Genesi ad litteram*, XI, c.31, no. 41; PL, XXXIV, 446: "Mox ut ergo
praeceptum transgressi sunt, intrinsecus gratia deserente omnino nudati, quam
typho quodam et superbo amore suae potestatis offenderant, in sua membra
oculos coniecerunt eaque motu, quem non noverunt, concupierunt."
De civitate Dei, XIV, c.17; PL, XLI, 425; CSEL, 40.2, 39: "Patebant ergo
oculi eorum, sed nondum erant aperti, hoc est attenti, ut cognoscerent, quid
eis indumento gratiae praestaretur. . . . Qua gratia remota, ut poena re-
ciproca obedientia plecteretur, extitit in motu corporis quaedam impudens
novitas, unde esset indecens nuditas."

in such wise that the unleashing of concupiscence is regarded as the effect of the sinful act, that it is evoked and awakened by this act, and hence by the sinner himself. In any other interpretation concupiscence is not caused in man by man himself, and therefore it is not a factor in his sin, but is only punishment for his sin.

An objection might perhaps be raised at this point, namely, that it is impossible to see how the negation of integrity by a deliberate, inordinate deflection of the will to a created good could of itself effect the actual destruction of the gift. Without doubt, if God wished integrity to endure notwithstanding the will's opposition to it, the act of the will could not extinguish it. In itself, such opposition is purely in the moral order, not in the physical order. But it is precisely in virtue of this moral opposition that the inordinate act of the will tends toward the disruption of the restraining bond of integrity, and God has no motive for conserving His supernatural gift against the press of the will. Accordingly, if in consequence of the will's opposition God withdraws the gift, the will is the cause of its expulsion from man and its destruction, although at the same time the gift is withdrawn by God in punishment for the refractoriness of the will.

Against this reply the further protest has been made that for all his sinful concupiscence the first man could not have had the intention of extinguishing his freedom from concupiscence; and that the Fathers and theologians tend to view the unleashing of concupiscence precisely as a thoroughly disagreeable punishment which is quite contrary to man's wishes. But the intention formally to effect the extinction of integrity is not in the slightest degree necessary; there is no more need for such an intention than there is need for the sinner, who destroys the gift of sanctity in himself by grave sin, to intend this effect. In order to be accountable for this effect, the sinner need do no more than foresee it as something resulting automatically from his act.

Hence the opposition of the first man's sin to the mystery of integrity was no less instrumental in making it an "ineffably great sin," in St. Augustine's words, than was its opposition to sanctity. In the unbridled hankering for creatures which characterized Adam's sin according to its lower aspect, the sin perpetuated itself and left its mark upon its author, when thus considered in its lower aspect, in the same way that, when considered according to its higher aspect, it perpetuated itself and left its impress in the dissolution of sanctity. This propensity was a habitual deformity resulting from the sinful act, a disorder caused by man and opposed to the supernatural order intended by God; hence it pertains to Adam's habitual sin conceived in its fullness. I say, it pertains to Adam's sin. For in itself it is no more, indeed it is less, a formal sin than is the tendency which results from acquired habit. Like the latter, this propensity originated from actual sin, inclines to actual sin, and can be linked to what is properly habitual sin so as to form a whole with it. In a word, it can be associated with what is properly sin as its consequence, its source, or its material component. Therefore if it is called sin, this is always in a metaphorical sense, never in a literal sense. An inordinate inclination toward creatures can persist as the consequence or virtual cause of an actual sin even though no habitual sin here and now encumbers the subject; but it can be the material component of sin only when actually linked to what is properly habitual sin. In that case, however, it really pertains to habitual sin, so far as I understand by this term the entire habitual deformity which is induced by the sinful act. We shall return to this later.

From the point of view of *conversio* (similarly as from the point of view of *aversio*), the state of sin caused by the sinful act further produces a state that may be aptly described by the figurative term "defilement," which however is quite different from the stain or defilement produced by the *aversio*.

In actual sin the turning to a creature is the positive factor, as the turning from God is the negative factor. Hence the former implies a positive defilement of the sinner, as the latter implies a negative defilement, which is the privation of previous beauty and splendor. As has been stated, however, the guilt which accompanies the privation can in some sense be regarded also as a positive defilement. By turning to a sinful object and lovingly embracing it, the will enters into spiritual contact with it and is stained with its foulness. This is a positive defilement, which lasts as long as the will yields its love to the degrading object. As long as this attachment to a creature endures in a free act of the will, or at any rate in man's conscious awareness, the defilement in question is formally sinful, and indeed is the sin itself, since it involves a formal turning away from God.

Spiritual contact with ignoble or degrading objects [4] likewise obtains in the case of habitual propensities that manifest themselves in indeliberate actual cravings. Such propensities are engendered by frequently repeated actual sins or, in the present case, result from the dissolution of integrity. Therefore in this instance too, in due proportion, the contact must stain and defile the soul. But in itself this defilement is not formally sinful, and is not a stain which simply makes man repulsive in God's eyes. Of course it cannot be pleasing to God, especially when man has brought it upon himself by his own guilt, and still less when it is connected with the stain of guilt and of the privation of grace. But in itself the defilement resulting from the extinction of integrity is a natural imperfection which pertains to human nature by virtue of its natural principles, owing to the union of spirit with matter. It is an imperfection which takes on the character of shameful defilement in man chiefly because he was endowed originally with a superhuman, angelical perfection, and because he expelled the principle of this perfection from himself by his freely willed sinful contact with creatures, thereby uncovering the imperfection.

We are now in a position to present a more adequate survey of the sin of the first man. It consisted in this, that man by his sinful act destroyed and expelled from himself the whole of that supernatural justice which is known as original justice, both in its higher element, sanctity, and in its lower element, integrity. Accordingly he was a sinner not only because he turned from God and toward the creature in his sinful act, but also because in consequence of this act he deprived himself of that state of union with God and detachment from creatures by which he had stood in the right supernatural relation to God. The relation of Adam's sinful act to the dissolution of the mystery of justice, and the privation of this justice in relation to the sinful act as its cause, constitute the mystery in the iniquity of the first man. In its totality this mystery was peculiar to the sin of Adam. As we shall see directly, however, it necessarily entailed another mystery, equally distinctive.

[4] An object is "ignoble" or "degrading" only because of sinful attachment to it, not in itself. [Tr.]

44. The Mystery of the First Man's Sin in Relation to the Hereditary Character of Original Justice. Original Sin

Scarcely any object proposed by supernatural revelation has been held to be so obscurely and unfathomably mysterious as the doctrine of original sin. At the same time there is scarcely a mystery whose mysterious character is so often grievously misunderstood. Some scholars locate the mysteriousness not in the obscurity of the object itself, but in the absolute incomprehensibility of that object, and contend that, whereas reason can perceive the existence of original sin, it cannot free the concept of original sin from all contradictions.

In our opinion the exact opposite is true. Reason cannot perceive the existence of original sin, for this sin involves assumptions that are absolutely supernatural, and hence are impervious to the unaided reason. On this account original sin is a true mystery. But on the basis of these assumptions, once they are revealed, the concept of original sin can be clearly and definitely formulated, and hence freed from all contradictions. The darkness surrounding original sin vanishes in the supernatural light of original justice. Original sin admits of clarification, but only in terms of another mystery; and therefore, in spite of all the illumination we can shed over it, it does not cease to be a true mystery for the intellect.

But what is the nature of this clarification? If we consider sin exclusively from the standpoint of natural man, we can hardly conceive the notion of a transmission or inheritance of sin in any proper sense, in such wise that, as Catholic doctrine demands, the descendants would truly and interiorly be sinners. In fact, the notion seems to us quite inconceivable and preposterous. In the natural order sin can be fully and formally ascribed as a real, interior sin to no other person than to him from whose will it issued forth. For sin in this case is no more than an act, which does not destroy the inherent justice and goodness of nature, and continues only morally in God's imputation of it to the offender; nor does it entail any inordinate tendency other than that engendered by habit. Hereditary sin would be possible in the natural order only on the supposition that God would impute the guilt of him who performed the sinful act to his posterity also, and would regard the action of the progenitor as an action perpetrated by the entire race represented by him.

But in the first place this supposition would not really place a sin in the descendants; secondly, such imputation would itself be unjust, if on account of it God were to withdraw from the descendants goods to which they had a natural, personal right, and in respect to which they could not purely and simply be made dependent on their ancestor without injury to their personal dignity. Likewise the propensity to sin engendered by habit is not properly injustice; and even if it were, it is something purely personal, and naturally affects only those who have brought it about in themselves. Reason and experience teach this sufficiently; and if evil tendencies are sometimes transplanted from parents to children, they are tendencies that arise from the natural temperament of the parents or, if they result from habit, they have not remained merely habit, and have exercised a positive influence upon the temperament, the physiological side of human nature.

But when faith reveals to us the presence of a supernatural original justice in the progenitor of the human race, the matter shapes up quite differently.

This justice was supernatural; therefore Adam's descendants had no right to it either by nature or as persons, and so God could ordain that they should receive it from their progenitor, and hence should be dependent on their progenitor with regard to their possession of it. On the other hand, God really bestowed this justice on the first man not as a personal good, but as the common good of the whole of human nature, of the entire race stemming from Adam, so that all members of the race were to receive it through Adam and from Adam. If Adam preserved it, it was to be preserved for all; if he destroyed it in himself and discarded it from himself, it was in consequence to be taken away from the whole race. In other words, Adam represented the entire race with regard to the preservation or rejection of original justice. As original justice itself was a common good and a hereditary good of the entire race, so also the sinful act by which Adam lost it, and the loss itself, had to be a common evil and a hereditary evil of the whole race. As original justice was to have been transmitted to all Adam's descendants according to God's decree, so the loss of it had in actual fact to be transmitted to all.

Let us explain this somewhat more in detail. The sin of Adam as a sinful, perverse act was physically committed by him alone and pertained physically to him alone; therefore he alone had the full and original responsibility for it. But with respect to supernatural justice as the common good of the whole race, Adam's act had to avail for all other men. Since Adam was the trustee of this common good, he acted with reference to it as the family head of the entire race, and his deed had in this connection to count as the act of all, in the way in which generally the act of the head is imputed to the whole body that is dependent on the head. Consequently we must say: in Adam, who physically placed the sinful act, the entire race morally placed it, owing to the race's fellowship with Adam, precisely so far as that act had to do with the good belonging to the community—about in the same way as that in which we are accustomed to say and have to say that not only has Christ satisfied for us, but we ourselves in Christ as our new Head have rendered satisfaction to God for our sins.

This by itself is not yet sufficient. The statement that we all have part in the one sinful act committed by Adam means, in the last analysis, only that it is imputed and accounted to us as ours, much as the Protestants teach that Christ's merits are imputed to us. We can be called sinners in this sense, but only by a purely external denomination and not by reason of any injustice and sinfulness inhering in each one of us and proper to each one of us.

But the progress made thus far is not in vain. It is the preliminary condition for a second step which automatically follows from the first. Precisely because Adam's sinful act is imputed and imputable to us in its relation to original justice, because it must be regarded as our act in this connection, it extinguishes original justice in us, and by it we extinguish original justice in ourselves, just as Adam extinguished it in himself so far as the act pertained to him personally. The whole race stands before God as one moral body, which in Adam, its head, rejected and lost supernatural justice for all its members, and expelled it from all its members. Every individual human being, by the mere fact that he becomes a member of the race stemming from Adam, that is, by being generated from Adam, forfeits the justice which he was to receive from Adam. He stands in the sight of God as one who, not indeed by his personal act and culpability, but by reason of an offense common to all the members of the race, is destitute of the justice he ought to have; as one who, through racial guilt, has lost his supernatural attachment to God and is turned in the direction of creatures in a manner opposed to God's original plan. He stands before God as a sinner, not indeed as one who has sinned personally, but as one who is a sinner by heredity.

Accordingly original sin itself admits of a double definition, as act and as state of sin. If we regard it as an act, it is the sinful act of Adam, so far as it not only expelled supernatural justice from Adam himself, but also excluded it from his posterity (*peccatum originans*). If we regard it as a state of sin, it is the privation of supernatural justice in the descendants of Adam, a privation inherited from him, so far as this privation is brought about by the progenitor's act which is likewise imputed to all his posterity (*peccatum originatum*). Without relation to Adam's act as a joint act of the race, privation of supernatural justice would be simply a lack of justice, but not a sin, for sin is a culpable lack of justice. Similarly, Adam's sinful act would be neither a joint offense nor the cause of an interior injustice in his posterity, if it were not regarded as related to the supernatural justice which was to be the common possession of all through Adam. The extent to which the habitual state of original sin involves a *reatus* which likewise could be termed habitual sin, we shall see immediately, as we proceed to a more detailed study of the various factors that enter into original sin, and determine the proper position occupied by each.

45. FAULT, DEFORMITY, AND GUILT IN ORIGINAL SIN, ACCORDING TO THEIR DISTINCTION AND RELATIONSHIP

Sin in general always includes two factors, both essential, either one of which can, according to preference, be stressed and placed in the foreground. These two factors are the fault committed and the resulting deformity. The first is no more conceivable as sin without the second, than the second is without the first. Sin is either the culpable cause (voluntary placing) of a deformity, or a deformity that is culpable (voluntarily placed or incurred). Even in the sinful act I can distinguish the fault from the deformity discerned in the act and inhering in the act. However, this distinction appears more prominently in the contrast between actual and habitual sin. Habitual sin is primarily a state of deformity, of injustice, but this state is formally sinful only inasmuch as it is caused and rendered culpable by a sinful act. The sinful act, on the other hand, appears mainly as the factor which renders the habitual deformity culpable, as the cause effecting and producing this deformity, which it effects by stamping its own character on the habitual state it engenders.

In original sin, too, we must distinguish these two elements. In fact, it is here that the distinction appears in its full significance.

Adam's descendants are not truly sinners unless the deformity attaching to sin is interiorly present in them and becomes each one's own; and this takes place as soon as each individual becomes a member of the race, when he is found to be destitute of the state of obligatory justice. But the culpable cause of this deprivation of justice need not be inherent in the individuals, for the fault as such does not pertain to the guilty person as a state, and moreover it cannot be inherent in them, since Adam's descendants have not personally committed the sin. The fault attaches to Adam's act, which avails for all; it is this act of Adam. It continues and is transmitted in the enduring imputation of the act in God's eyes, an imputation which passes over to all of Adam's progeny.

Hence in original sin these two factors (the deformity and the fault) are widely separated. If the one is emphasized, original sin appears to be internal; if the other is stressed, it appears to be external. But in the nature of things and in the language of the Church and of theologians, the former mode of expression is to be preferred; therefore what is ordinarily called original sin must be designated simply as internal. Especially the Latin *peccatum* (misstep) connotes chiefly the deformity involved in sin and induced by the fault. Moreover, by original sin we mean directly that which is transmitted by Adam to his descendants as something inhering in them, that which is produced in them by their origin from Adam; and this is precisely the deformity which consists in the privation of obligatory justice. Or, as theologians are accustomed to say, original sin simply as such is the so-called *peccatum originatum*, the deformity resulting from the sinful act and offense of the progenitor, not the offense of the progenitor which gives origin to this deformity, that is, the *peccatum originans*. "The voluntary sin of the first man," says

St. Augustine, "is the cause of original sin." [5] But this relation of the deformity to its cause, the culpable act, may not be regarded as a purely external relation, as if the relation of the deformity to the fault did no more than account for the existence of the deformity, without being necessarily required to impart to it the character of true sinfulness. The Church has expressly condemned the proposition of Baius which advances this view.[6]

Further, we cannot sufficiently stress the truth that if the privation of justice is to be termed sin and not merely an evil, it may not be represented as being only demeritorious by reason of the fault committed by the head of the race, that is, as an effect of the guilt contracted by Adam's act before God, for himself and his posterity. In that case it would be no more than punishment. It must also be conceived as the immediate effect, as the impress of the deformity contained in the culpable act. Only thus does the deformity appear as incurred by the race itself in its head.

This observation prepares the way for a more accurate examination of the manner in which the idea of guilt or *reatus*, that is, of the liability and obligation before God resulting from the fault, receives application in original sin. In personal sin, as we have seen, this guilt can be conceived independently, alongside and outside of the culpable, habitual deformity; it is already sufficiently accounted for by the culpability of the iniquitous act, and is merely consolidated by the iniquitous state that ensues. But in original sin guilt before God rests exclusively on the culpability of the habitual deformity or injustice, and consists in nothing else than in the responsibility of the race for not having the justice which it ought to have, owing to the fault of its head. For the culpable act of Adam was a joint act, availing for the race, only so far as he effected the abrogation of the justice common to all.

For the violation of order and the affront to God which the act itself brought about, the author of the act is alone responsible. Consequently he alone has to sustain the full odium and the full punish-

---

[5] "Voluntarium peccatum hominis primi originalis est causa peccati." *De nuptiis et concupiscentia*, II, c. 26, no. 43; *PL*, XLIV, 461; *CSEL*, XLII, 297.

[6] Prop. 46: "Ad rationem et definitionem peccati non pertinet voluntarium, nec definitionis quaestio est, sed causae et originis, utrum omne peccatum debeat esse voluntarium." Prop. 47: "Unde peccatum originis vere habet rationem peccati sine ulla relatione et respectu ad voluntatem, a qua originem habuit." (Denz., nos. 1046 f.)

ment due to it. In this connection others, no matter how close their relationship to him, cannot properly be called to account.

Nevertheless descendants can suffer punishment for a sinful deed of their parents, so far as goods are withdrawn from them to which they had claim only by right of succession, not by any personal right of their own. God, particularly, who as supreme Lord of His gifts can in any case withdraw all goods from His creatures, even natural goods such as bodily life, can also withdraw such goods in order to punish parents in their children, or in order to exhibit to mankind the enormity of the guilt with which the parents are laden. In this case, however, the sin as such does not really encumber the children, but the parents alone, and it is only metaphorically that we can say that the children have forfeited the lost goods in their parents. The children have no real fellowship of guilt with their parents. This would be the case only if they imitated the sin of their parents. And although they are drawn into fellowship with their parents in suffering punishment or the effects of divine wrath, they do not on that account bear God's wrath against their own person, or stand in a wrong relationship to God. A true fellowship in guilt, without the active cooperation of one of the parties concerned, can take place through simple communication from one person to another only when and to the extent that the culpable act of one passes over to another who is dependent on him, and counteracts justice in and for this other. In such a case it might be held that the latter is the culpable cause of his own injustice by reason of his connection with the former, and consequently that he is responsible for his privation of justice in and through the former. Catholic teaching requires no more and no less to account for the character of guilt in original sin.

The race is responsible before God and is called by Him to account, so far as through the sinful act of its head it has relinquished (*deseruit*, not merely lost) the justice which according to God's will it ought to have, and has taken upon itself (not merely received) the deformity which according to God's will ought not disfigure it. Only for this reason does each individual member enter into a wrong relationship with God, only for this reason does God's wrath fall upon the head of each, only for this reason can the evil inflicted on each be regarded as true punishment; it is only for this reason and to this extent that not merely the evil which is punishment, but also the sin and guilt of the progenitor, and hence punishment as deserved, become the property and inheritance of his posterity. And although the privation of original justice itself must be looked upon as punishment for original sin, it is such only so far as God withdraws it from man not in punishment for the sinful act as such, but for the negation and expulsion of original justice which is caused by the act. Privation of original justice is both sin and punishment; but it is the latter only because of the former.

Accordingly, if the deformity which consists in the privation of original justice in its relation to the fault of the head of the race constitutes original sin (*peccatum originale* in the strict sense), and the latter in relation to the former establishes original guilt (*reatus originalis*), all that is lacking for a complete exposition of the doctrine of original sin is a consideration of this deformity itself according to its various aspects.

46. The Nature of the Culpable Deformity which Disfigures Man in Original Sin

Since original justice consists of two elements, so that in consequence the privation of it must likewise comprise two elements, we must see how these two elements are related to each other and to the whole, if we would arrive at a more accurate appreciation of the habitual deordination present in original sin.

Original justice is composed of sanctity and integrity. Sanctity, the supernatural attachment to God as the ultimate end, is its predominant, formal, and essential element. From this it follows that original injustice, if I may thus term it, must predominantly, formally, and essentially consist in the privation of sanctity. This is so all the more inasmuch as the essence of sin lies in aversion from God, hence in the negation of conversion to Him. So true is this that we could speak of an original sin in the proper sense even if man had never lost original integrity or had never possessed it at all; as also, according to the teaching of the Church, that which truly and properly has the character of sin in original sin can be taken away without integrity being restored.

If, on the contrary, the first man had possessed only the gift of integrity and had lost merely this gift by his sin, we could not in any proper sense refer to his posterity as interiorly sinful. This follows from what has just been stated. Integrity does indeed confer a certain justice on man; but not a justice such as unites man to God or turns him to God in a special way. It is a rectitude that effects nothing more than good order and harmony among the various faculties and appetites of man; it merely prevents any natural power from directing itself to creatures apart from and against the judgment of the reason. Its privation is doubtless a certain kind of deordination, deformity and, if one will, also injustice. But even if this privation is brought about by man, it is no true sinfulness, since in itself it does not turn man from God or place him in a wrong relationship to God. Consequently if Adam had lost only integrity for us, we could say merely that a grievous blight induced by the progenitor's sin had descended upon the race, the effects of which manifest themselves in an interior disorder and confusion of nature; but we could not say that nature is interiorly laden with original sin on account of this disorder. At most we should have an inner injustice in an improper sense, which would indeed render man in some respect displeasing to God, in an analogous way, as venial sins do, but which would no more destroy our friendly relations with God than it would counteract our tendency toward our last end.

Culpable privation of integrity could make men sinners interiorly only if it involved a formal aversion and separation from God. But it does not of itself involve such aversion and separation; otherwise man in the state of pure nature would be formally cut off from God, not only as from his supernatural end, but as from his natural end. It entails no more than a disposition toward a separation from God which would be effected later by actual sin. If this propensity is assumed to be simply invincible, the virtual aversion from God implied in it would have to be equated to a formal aversion; but in the case of a formally invincible proclivity of this kind, the subsequent act would not be a formal sin. Actually, however, concupiscence is no more than a greater or lesser impediment to steadfast and persevering devotedness to God; with natural man and with man in original sin this difficulty could and would, with God's ready assistance, be sufficiently counteracted. For man who has been stripped of integrity not by personal sin but by racial guilt continues to retain his natural destiny, and with it also his claim to God's assistance, which is unconditionally necessary for its attainment.

However, among the relationships now being considered, there is a notable and intrinsic connection between the privation of integrity and the privation of sanctity. In original justice integrity was the complement of sanctity, in order to constitute man's complete supernatural justice. Therefore the privation of both constitutes man's complete injustice, in which the privation of integrity is the complement of the privation of sanctity. By reason of the latter privation, man is turned away from God; by reason of the former, he is turned toward the creature. Thus from every point of view the state of injustice is the true image of the sinful act by which it was induced, which was the first act to be known as sin, and which consequently is the type of all that is called sin or sinful. The sinful act is inordinate conversion to the creature and aversion from God; similarly the sinful state of fallen man is a state of aversion from God and of conversion to creatures. It becomes the former because the sinful act, as aversion from God, dissolves the habitual union with God effected by the gift of sanctity; it becomes the latter because the same act, as inordinate conversion to creatures, negates and annuls the detachment from creatures effected by the gift of integrity.

Both these factors are integrally connected in the sinful act; for no one can with full deliberation turn inordinately to a creature without turning his back on God, and vice versa. But in the sinful state of fallen man the two factors are joined only for this reason: that on the one hand God had originally conferred sanctity and integrity on man in solidary union; and on the other hand man reacted equally against both by his sinful deed; by expelling them he stamped and impressed the two sides of his act upon his habitual state.

Hence if we desire a composite picture of the state of original sin, or more accurately, of the culpable deformity attaching to man in original sin, we must represent it as a whole made up of two parts that differ as night from day but are nevertheless closely articulated; we must conceive it as the reverse of original justice in its full sense. Original sin consists exclusively neither in the privation of sanctity nor in the privation of integrity or the unbridled concupiscence it entails, but in the privation of original and hereditary justice as composed of sanctity and integrity. However, these two privations are not of equal import. The privation of sanctity is the formal, decisive, primary, intrinsic, essential factor, as it were the soul and kernel of the whole; whereas the privation of integrity is the material, subordinate, extrinsic factor, the factor which pertains merely to the completeness of original sin, and is, so to speak, the body and shell of the real essence. Man's essential and substantial deformity is wrought by the loss and forfeiture of his ordination to his supernatural end. This deformity suffices by itself to constitute original sin; but the turning to an opposite end is joined to it as an integrating part. However, this second deformity is branded as sinful only because of its connection with the first deformity.

To place original sin exclusively in one of these factors, or to locate its center of gravity in the subordinate factor, is to distort the truth. If the primary factor is stressed to the exclusion of the other, the resulting one-sided view has no further consequence than the inadequacy and defectiveness of the concept, since the essence of the whole is comprised in this element. But if we stress the second element, we can easily fall into a grievous error, by ascribing to it a significance which it can have only by reason of its connection with the first element. Of itself and by its own nature the secondary element of original sin cannot cut man off from God and make him displeasing to God.

Such a lopsided view of original sin arises necessarily from a lopsided view of its opposite, original justice. All who are acquainted with the history of theology will readily be convinced of this. Those theologians who make original sin consist exclusively, not merely primarily, in the privation of sanctity or of charity and grace, likewise represent charity and grace alone as constituting the entire essence of original justice, without heeding its connection with integrity. But those who place original sin exclusively or predominantly in concupiscence perceive nothing but integrity in original justice, either to the exclusion of sanctity, which they confuse with integrity, or in loose association with it. If we once concede that the intrinsic deformity of the person stained with original sin consists in the culpable privation of original justice, and if we cannot deny that original justice essentially and primarily consists in sanctity, obviously that deformity cannot be sought exclusively, or even predominantly, in concupiscence, for in that case we should have to assume that concupiscence of itself, or at any rate what is usually called its dominion, entails the abrogation of sanctity.

The latter has actually been maintained, and in recent times this view has been proposed *ex professo* in a monograph on original sin.[7] St. Bonaventure, too, seems to have been of this opinion. If one treats this view seriously, and attempts to show that an exclusion of sanctity is brought about by the dominion of concupiscence with physical necessity, the theory seems utterly inadmissible, at any rate from a scientific standpoint. For the dominion of concupiscence is nothing else than a vigor so irresistible that in the face of it the subject's will cannot long continue on its straight course to God.[8] Prescinding from the fact that the deformity involved in the sway of concupiscence over the will would be nothing more than a weakness in the will which could issue in separation from God, or an illness which in the course of time could have death as its consequence, but is not a formal, present, already effected separation from God, this weakness still remains in us, if only in limited degree, even after the restoration of sanctity. According to Catholic teaching, however, even the justified person cannot, without God's special assistance, resist the more savage assaults of concupiscence with only the strength that is received in sanctification. But if the dominion of concupiscence can as a matter of fact coexist with grace, then we do not see how it can be held to exclude grace; this becomes even less apparent if the sway of concupiscence is regarded as resulting from the privation of sanctity.[9]

[7] F. Schlünkes, *Das Wesen der Erbsünde nach dem Konzilium von Trient unter gleichzeitiger Berücksichtigung der Heiligen Schrift und der Väter der Kirche, insbesondere der heiligen Augustinus, Thomas von Aquin und Bonaventura* (Regensburg, 1863). We believe that the author's view really accords, in the main, with that of St. Bonaventure, and to that extent can claim to be of some theological value. We wish to omit discussion of St. Augustine, who never succeeded in achieving a complete, scientific analysis of original sin. But we cannot allow Schlünkes to retain St. Thomas and the great majority of theologians, whom he cites in his favor. Especially we cannot surrender Bellarmine to him.

[8] The formal and actual domination of concupiscence does, to be sure, consist in the fact that the will really follows its beck and call. Hence it involves an actual, formal sin in the will. But in the case of habitual concupiscence, particularly that which is considered in connection with original sin, there is no question of an actual consent of the will on the part of him who is afflicted with it. Therefore it has only a virtual dominion, which consists in its power of eventually forcing the will to accompany it.

[9] This point is often completely misunderstood in descriptions of habitual sin. The formal domination of concupiscence, such as entails the will's acquiescence, cannot exist in the sanctified. Its virtual sway, the predominant force

The objection will perhaps be made that it is not precisely concupiscence itself or its dominion, but culpable concupiscence and the *reatus* clinging to it as a result of this culpability, that excludes sanctity. However, since concupiscence does not of itself cut us off from our last end, its culpability, especially when it is not caused by our own personal will, can hardly freight us with a guilt that would render us unworthy of sanctity. But even assuming that it could burden us with such guilt, the privation of sanctity, the separation and estrangement from God would be no more than punishment for the guilt, and an effect of the demerit involved in the guilt. In that case what is manifestly the chief factor in sin (the separation and estrangement from God, the interior injustice and deformity properly so called) would not be accounted sin, but only punishment.

Estrangement from God, which constitutes the essence of original sin as of every sin, is not therefore to be regarded as effected by concupiscence or as proceeding from it, but as occurring alongside and above it, as being contemporaneous with it or even prior to it. Hence concupiscence can be considered apart from such estrangement, without any alteration of its nature or its dominion. Why, in the case of original sin, should we conceive aversion from God as caused by a habitual conversion to the creature, seeing that the former is as much an immediate result of the sinful act according to one aspect as the latter is according to another aspect? In the case of personal sin it would occur to no one to think of the privation of sanctity as dependent on the persistence of propensities induced by habit and as caused by such propensities. Why, then, should this take place in original sin?

The notion that the extinction of sanctity is wrought by concupiscence and that the center of gravity of original sin is to be sought in concupiscence, is accounted for chiefly by an excessively

---

of inordinate propensities, not only can exist alongside the weakness of the will which shrinks back from it, but usually does. In general the justified have only this advantage over the unjustified, that they are firmly resolved to resist temptations to grave sins, and that, owing to their possession of supernatural virtues, they can more easily resist temptations, and have a stronger claim to such further divine assistance as is necessary. But the right to strength from without does not constitute inner strength, nor does it imply an interior ascendancy of good over evil tendencies. Consequently such ascendancy cannot be one of the constitutive elements of justice, nor can the want of it constitute injustice in any proper sense.

physiological phantasm of its hereditary transmission. We shall return to this point presently.

For the nonce we content ourselves with one further remark. We assume in the paragraph immediately above—and for that matter we believe that we have previously justified the assumption—that outside of guilt nothing else encumbers the person in original sin than that deformity which consists in the culpable privation of sanctity and integrity, or results from these factors alone. Hence we also contend that this deformity is purely relative, that is, it can be conceived as such only in terms of opposition to the supernatural state through whose destruction it has come into being, and that consequently it involves no deordination which, materially considered, could not arise in man otherwise than through sin and guilt, and whose presence of itself would cause man to appear not merely in an imperfect state, but in a morally evil state.

For the proof of the contrary, appeal has been made to experience, and the assertion has been advanced that as a matter of fact there exist in man evil propensities which cannot be explained on the grounds of the imperfection of his nature, or which positively distort the nature of man.

As concerns the first argument, we could concede that in the heart of man there are certain proclivities that do not find their explanation in his natural passions, the imperfection of his knowledge, etc.; but thereupon we should have to ask for proof that such propensities really arise from some interior principle in man, from the interior depravity of his nature, and are not rather actuated from without through the agency of evil spirits. It would be difficult to show such proof, particularly since, according to the universal teaching of Scripture and the Fathers, the influence of the devil is incalculable, and the pestilential breath of hell surrounds man on all sides like a poisoned atmosphere. If only for the sake of the honor of our nature, we should trace all the genuine viciousness that springs up in our hearts back to a root lying outside of us, that seeks to cast its seeds into our breasts. But if such evil propensities seep into our nature from without, they do not materially or formally constitute the deformity and corruption inherited from nature, for it was their culpable presence in us that first subjected us to the servitude of the devil.

Propensities of this sort, like all other inclinations which incite to evil only indirectly, cannot absolutely and by themselves make man appear evil or wicked or displeasing to God. In themselves they are as much an occasion of meritorious striving as of an ignominious fall, and can therefore go on existing with their full inner force even in the sanctified man.

47. The Transmission of Original Sin

The transmission of original sin from father to son is often envisaged according to the analogy of generation. Although generation is basically a simple act, its primary function is to dispose the matter of the newly begotten being for the reception of the soul. In like manner original sin is represented as propagated primarily according to its material element, which then draws the formal element after it. Generally this is expressed by saying that a father stained with original sin generates a body likewise stained, and then this body infects the soul, which it implicates in its own defilement.

First of all, it must be observed that in the propagation of original sin there is not only question of the way the evil or perverse state it involves is transmitted by heredity from Adam to his descendants, but of the way it passes over to them as a culpable state, hence as entailing guilt. Participation in Adam's culpability, and consequently in the responsibility for the culpable deformity which pertains to the individual in original sin, is not, properly speaking, transmitted through the medium of the corruption and deformity of nature; rather, such deformity can be accounted sin and guilt only because of that participation. A share in Adam's culpability is transmitted simply for the reason that nature laden with guilt in Adam passes over to his descendants, and the soul of each of the latter, although directly created by God, enters into a member of Adam's progeny and becomes a part of him. As soon as a new bearer of human nature proceeds from Adam, or a soul created by God enters into Adam's progeny, the shadow of Adam's act, which avails for the whole of nature, falls upon this bearer and his soul, invests him with responsibility for Adam's act which passes for his own act too, as far as its relation to original justice is concerned, excludes this justice from him as from Adam, and thus causes the deformity and corruption in question.

Accordingly the responsibility and guilt to be transmitted in

original sin can be conceived as passing from body to soul only so
far as the soul by union with a body stemming from Adam enters
into his posterity, but not so far as the body is first represented as
their subject—that is altogether impossible.

Hence the view mentioned above can at most explain a transmission of corruptness from body to soul, without regard to the character of guilt clinging to it. Let us see to what extent the notion is
admissible at least in this respect.

Integrity, we said, was given by God to the first man as a disposition to sanctity, a disposition which, by God's free ordination, was
to be the *conditio sine qua non* for the possession of sanctity. Sanctity
was linked to integrity, and consequently could be transmitted only
to those persons who received integrity. Moreover, integrity, which
perfected man according to the lower side of his nature, and hence
as a being capable of propagation by generation, was more closely
bound up with the sexual propagation of nature than sanctity, and
consequently could be regarded as a gift which was directly to be
transmitted by generation and was to be followed by sanctity.

Naturally, the very same relationship must obtain in the privation
of integrity and sanctity. Along with the abrogation of integrity
as the necessary disposition for sanctity, sanctity too, as attached to
integrity, must be abrogated; and so whoever has received from
Adam a nature destitute of integrity, cannot have sanctity as his portion. And since integrity, as immediately attached to nature, was immediately to have been transmitted in the propagation of nature, so
now when nature is propagated the privation of integrity must be
conceived as preceding the privation of sanctity and as being followed by this privation.

Further, since integrity in the last analysis comes to this, that the
body, subjected to the spirit in the most perfect manner and governed by the spirit, is prevented from directly or indirectly causing
any disruption or disorder in the human soul, we may say that the
transmission of integrity or, as the case may be, of its privation, is
proximately linked up with the generation of the human body. If
the body is formed under God's supernatural influence as an instrument of the soul, tractable for any employment and in no wise impeding its operation, then the soul receives its full purity, harmony,
and order, and in consequence also its supernatural union with God,
through the gift of sanctity. But if at the production of the body this

supernatural influence of God is lacking, the body, freighted with the natural imperfections proper to matter, remains an intractable and a frequently obstructive instrument of the soul. In that case the soul does not obtain the purity, harmony, and order required as a disposition for the reception of sanctity, and so it does not obtain the gift of sanctity itself. Burdened with the heavy weight of the body, the soul is attracted to material things and to creatures in general, and hence is not directed to God by the gift of sanctity, but remains turned away from God. In this manner and this sense it is true that the body infects the soul and draws it down to sin, that the flesh begotten in concupiscence does not enter into full harmony with the soul and so does not permit the soul's supernatural harmony with God to arise, and that finally the defilement of the body or generally of the lower part of human nature entails that of the soul, that is, so far as the nature stripped of integrity no longer possesses the purity and harmony which were to dispose it for the reception of the heavenly splendor of sanctity.

For all that, we must avoid looking upon the privation of integrity as though by its very nature it necessarily involved the privation of sanctity or aversion from God; for sanctity can exist in nature by itself without integrity, as is now the case with us. The reason why they stand and fall together is the union of both in solidarity, as originally willed by God.

But even so we may not attach too great importance to the above-mentioned relationship between the two elements pertaining to the deordination of original sin. For not only is the character of guilt clinging to this deordination forced into the background when viewed from the standpoint of this relationship, but what is essential in the deordination itself is made to seem a mere consequence of what is accidental, and the formal element appears as the effect of the material element. The two factors stamping the deordinate state of Adam's descendants, namely, guilt and aversion from God, must be immediately transmitted to the descendants by virtue of their origin from Adam, since everything else inherited by the person born in original sin depends on the fact that he inherits the sin itself in its proper essence. It is only because we inherit the sin that we inherit also its consequences; it is only because we inherit the sin itself in its proper essence that we inherit also its subordinate elements.

We should do better to invert the relationship and regard integrity as a grace conferred on man for the sake of sanctity, although in reality it is a disposition for sanctity. The matter would then be represented as follows. Adam was to be the progenitor of grace and sanctity for all those whose natural progenitor he was; along with nature he was to diffuse the light of sanctity over all his descendants. But after Adam had blocked off the light of sanctity from himself by his sinful deed as by a dark cloud, the shadow of that sinful deed had at once to fall upon all those who received their nature from him, for the very reason that they did receive nature from him. The inevitable result was that he destroyed and shut out the light and splendor of sanctity from all his descendants as he did from himself, and in this way interiorly contaminated all of them, with a contamination that was sinful, since it involved a culpable aversion of the soul from God. But if sanctity was thus lost, loss of integrity had to follow, since integrity was given for the sake of sanctity. Thus, with the defilement of the soul through the extinction of the light of its supernatural splendor, of its supernatural contact with the all-pure fire of the Godhead which pervaded and transfigured it, the other defilement had to make its appearance because of the contact with creatures, seeing that the soul, bereft of integrity, was inordinately propelled toward creatures.

Thus when the matter is viewed from various angles, the transmission of the privation of integrity is seen to involve the transmission of privation of sanctity, and vice versa, although it is true that both factors can be regarded as simultaneous and parallel. For, after all, nature is not generated successively; the human body becomes a human body only when it is informed by a rational soul, and original sin is a portion of the inheritance of a complete nature, not of the body alone or of the soul alone, but of both so far as they belong to each other and to the complete nature. Thus the share which the two components have in the original catastrophe falls to them both alike and simultaneously. On the other hand Adam's sinful act directly and immediately excludes both sanctity and integrity, from himself as well as from the nature of his descendants. Consequently the privation of integrity in Adam's descendants is not only a result of the privation of sanctity, but is in itself directly induced by the racial guilt, and hence comes into existence in Adam's descendants simultaneously with the privation of sanctity, as soon as they are numbered among his posterity and are placed under the shadow of the racial guilt.

Sometimes the transfer of original sin is conceived as a physical transplanting, like that of diseased matter, and not as a simple juridical transmission by inheritance. In following out such a train of thought, one easily gets embroiled in a labyrinth of contradictions and obscurities, and above all is unable to reconcile original sin with the origin of the soul through immediate creation by God. This whole theory is in itself utterly inadmissible. It contradicts the ethical as well as the supernatural character of original sin. It contradicts the ethical character, because original sin is not merely something corporal, but is predominantly spiritual, and especially its transmission involves the transmission of guilt to us. It contradicts the supernatural character of original sin, because this sin can be transmitted in no other way than the way its opposite, original justice, was to be transmitted. Original justice was to be communicated to Adam's offspring not exactly by the physical act of generation, but rather with reference to it and in conjunction with it. Hence the transmission of original sin must without any reservations be reduced to simple juridical inheritance. Then all the difficulties derived especially from creationism vanish. God creates the soul immediately, but in connection with the generative act placed by Adam, and infuses it into a body stemming from Adam. The soul thereby becomes an essential component of a being begotten by Adam, and in this being becomes likewise the heir of the dowry which, either as a result of divine grace or as a result of Adam's culpability, belongs to the latter's posterity.

48. Metaphorical Expressions for Original Sin and Its Transmission

The view of original sin and its transmission which we have developed does not at first sight seem to be in full accord with the doctrine proclaimed in the customary language of the Church and of theologians. At any rate a host of expressions occurs which, it is often alleged, would lead one to understand that original sin, conceived as a state of Adam's posterity, is to be represented not as a mere privation of supernatural justice, that is, of sanctity and integrity of nature, but as something positive or as something which corrupts nature as such. A stain, it is observed, is something positive, not purely negative. The infliction of a wound must do more than merely divest nature of its supernatural gifts; it must interiorly harm and lacerate nature. Original sin is a poison which makes nature ill, and hence again is something positive and injurious to nature itself.

What have we to say to all this? We must take these expressions for what they are, that is, as figurative expressions; and the figure must be interpreted in the sense which has already been proposed in our theological analysis.

The stain in original sin is to be taken in the same sense as in personal sin. It consists first of all in the liability for the sinful act committed, or better, in the guilt resulting from the culpability and encumbering the person in original sin. It consists further in the disfigurement of the soul through the annihilation of the supernatural beauty which it ought to have, and in the laying bare of the native imperfection of human nature. It is neither necessary nor possible to apprehend anything else in the stain. Whoever insists on reading more into it must give up the idea of attributing a definite meaning to the metaphor.

Adam's actual sin is also a sword that rends the supernatural union of the soul with God and violently severs the bonds with which the gift of integrity had held all the faculties and tendencies of nature together in perfect accord. The lack of this accord permits the various faculties and tendencies to go their own way, and thus introduces into nature a cleavage which was not originally present. But this cleavage is no more than the result of the loosing of the supernatural bond with which God had enveloped and vested nature.

But what of that infectious, pestilential poison that exudes from Adam and seeps down upon his descendants? This poison also is Adam's sinful act, which cannot be transferred to his descendants, but which, enduring morally in its aftereffects, is able, like a noxious gas, to stifle and expel the supernatural life-principle in them as in Adam himself. So far as this act also pertains to Adam's descendants, it dries up the source of supernatural divine life, and corrodes the supernatural principle of health (the gift of integrity) whereby nature was preserved from every corporal disorder arising from its native frailty, or from derangement of its faculties and parts. Consequently all those phenomena had inevitably to appear which we call diseases or corruption of nature, and which end with the eventual dissolution of nature in physical death, which is preceded by the death of the soul (that is, sin) as cause and prototype. To account for this sickness no real, positive *morbida qualitas* must be assumed. St. Augustine, from whom the expression is taken, means thereby a condition of physical life which man has in common with brute animals, inasmuch as man, like them, possesses a material body that is derived from the earth. Hence the infirmity in question is natural to man in virtue of his origin, and was held in check and repressed only through God's supernatural grace. For the resurgence of its baneful influence, nothing else was needed but the withdrawal of this gift.[10]

Accordingly there appears no reason for interpreting these expressions in the sense that original sin as habit or state was a positive quality inhering in man and added to his nature. What really constitutes original sin and attaches to nature is the privation of the supernatural quality that ought to be present in nature. Although it is not a positive entity, we can well say of it that it is a quality, that it flows over from father to son, that it is propagated and inheres in the son, just as we say of darkness, in spite of the fact that it is only a privation of light, or even because of that very fact, that it inheres in an object, encases it, covers it, or is diffused over an object. We are fully justified in using such expressions inasmuch as the privation in question has positive consequences in the unfettered propensities and appetites of the lower faculties of nature which, because they are unrestrained, operate in a destructive and subversive manner.

This being so, we can perceive only one difference between the state of the man laden with original sin and the state of the purely natural man who has never been endowed with any supernatural grace: the latter has never possessed supernatural justice and was not under any obligation to possess it, whereas the former has possessed it in his first ancestor and ought to possess it in his own person, but actually does not possess it, since Adam's sinful act has caused it to be excluded and withdrawn from him. What distinguishes the man born in original sin from the natural man is not properly a positive or a negative quality. It is the relationship to the sinful act

[10] See my edition of Casinius, *Quid est homo,* c.4.

of the progenitor of the race, and to the supernatural justice violated by him, a relationship by which every descendant of this progenitor becomes a sharer in the culpability of that act, and by virtue of which this act itself pertains to Adam's offspring, not physically but morally, in the guilt induced by it; the act casts its shadow upon him. Without this relationship the withdrawal of supernatural justice would merely be an absence, not a privation of a perfection which ought to be present, nor a subversion of an order established by God. Since it would not be a culpable privation and subversion, it would not be an imputable deformity and deordination, and therefore would in no way be sinful. But because of this relationship it is both; it is deformity and culpable deformity, and hence sin in the full sense of the word. Therefore, too, it makes man abhorrent in God's sight, since man no longer conforms to God's original idea, and thus makes him a child of wrath, whom God repels from His bosom and thrusts out of His kingdom. But the hereditary guilt which brands this privation as sin does not degrade man beneath the level of his nature as personal guilt does, and does not draw any punishment upon him except to deliver him over to the full wretchedness of his nature, from which grace had snatched him.[11]

[11] The notion of original sin which we have here reported was by and large, naturally with many variations of shading in details, that of the whole of Scholasticism from the time of St. Thomas on, although individual factors to which we have attributed greater weight, particularly the relation of habitual to actual sin, have not always been sufficiently stressed in the terminology taken over by us. This alone is enough fully to justify our view. Moreover, we do not believe that Scholasticism finds itself at odds with St. Augustine in this matter; rather we are of the opinion that Scholasticism has but brought to maturity the seeds planted by St. Augustine. Especially in this doctrine, which had been fully treated by him alone, St. Augustine was the principal source of the theology of the Scholastics, and they drew upon it with a conscientiousness that often appeared almost scrupulous. St. Thomas furnishes us with the best example of this. Whoever studies his procedure carefully will find that he was at any rate most eager to present no other than the Augustinian doctrine of original sin, which of course he developed and integrated. Today one could scarcely hope to have a greater enthusiasm and a greater aptitude for understanding the Augustinian doctrine than St. Thomas had. One can always go back to St. Augustine; but one ought first to examine whether Scholasticism has really failed to grasp the gist of his teaching. That in the development of his central thesis certain items, pertaining not to the substance of the doctrine but to the imperfection and indefiniteness of its first formulation, have been discarded, will surprise no one who has any knowledge of the laws that operate in the evolution of science. Hence we are in complete accord with the plea of a highly esteemed

49. THE TRUE CHARACTER OF THE MYSTERY
INVOLVED IN ORIGINAL SIN

In view of all these explanations, how can original sin still be a mystery? How can it be a mystery if it passes over the natural condition of fallen man without leaving a trace, if it does no more than strip him of supernatural goods? What remains of the obscurity which according to universal acknowledgment veils its nature and renders it the "philosophers' cross"?

I should hold that it is precisely in this respect that original sin is represented as a genuine mystery. If the condition of fallen man is in itself such that it can be conceived apart from any association with inherited guilt, then this inherited guilt itself and the character of sinfulness which thereby pertains to man's condition, is something hidden from reason and inscrutable, something that can be known only through divine revelation, hence a true mystery. On the other hand, if we insist on discovering in fallen man a condition that is not explainable in terms of a mere imperfection of nature, or that implies some positive corruption of nature, such a condition must lead at least to the idea of an inherited guilt or of some indwelling, hereditary sin. But would this inherited guilt or original sin then be something altogether hidden?

Further, in our exposition original sin is understandable only on the supposition of three great mysteries: the elevation of the first man to the sonship of God by sanctifying grace, the spiritualization of his earthy nature to a peak of perfection wherein it resembled the angels of heaven, and finally the wonderful privilege in virtue of which the first man was to transmit these supernatural blessings along with nature to his posterity, so that he was to beget not merely earthly men but men deified and made like to the angels. If a person perceives no mystery in these matters, we can have no further discussion with him; our explanation is not designed for him, for it rests wholly and entirely on the supernaturalness of the gifts mentioned. But if these truths are conceded to be mysteries, and great, supernatural mysteries, then original sin, too, is a mystery, because

theologian who urged in *Katholik* (1864, p. 200), that we should give up saying, "Here St. Thomas, and there St. Augustine," and should rather say, "Patristics and Scholasticism, Scholasticism and Patristics." To this we add that he honors Scholasticism only in the letter and not in the spirit who does not know and appreciate it in its development from patristic theology.

it can be known and conceived only in terms of other mysteries and in relation to them. Evidently original sin cannot be better known and more profoundly conceived through this relationship than are the mysteries in terms of which it is known and conceived.

The fact that when it is known and conceived in this manner it stands forth in very clear light, does not detract from its mysterious character. Once mysteries have been revealed by God, they should become clear, luminous truths, they should shed light on one another. By means of this light the obscurities and seeming contradictions, which they exhibit when inadequately apprehended, should be dispersed and cleared up. This is the case in an especially high degree with original sin.

Let it not be said that when viewed in such a light original sin loses the somber, fearsome character that we all attribute to it. No, it is this very light that displays to us the vastness of the abyss into which original sin has plunged us, and the fearful darkness which constitutes its essence. Is not man's fall from his supernatural height, his severance from the bosom of God, his nature's divestiture of its angelic splendor, an appallingly horrible thing? Is this not incomparably worse than all other taints and infirmities of his nature? As sin in general is seen to be an unspeakably monstrous evil only in its opposition to grace, so original sin is an *ineffabiliter grande peccatum* for the very reason that it razes to the ground the entire glorious temple which the Holy Spirit with His infinite power had erected for Himself in human nature, and destroys it not merely for one individual, but for the whole race.

But when original sin is viewed from another angle, the light shed over it can and should relieve it of the sinister aspect with which it confronted us at first sight. It can and should banish the contradictions that are associated with a superficial acquaintance with original sin. Especially it can and should make clear to us how the implication of the whole race in the sin of its progenitor and in the consequences of that sin is opposed neither to the mercy of God nor to His justice.

In fact, the hereditary character of original sin, in the view we have presented, is so far from contradicting the mercy of God that it finds its explanation in a most extraordinary act of divine mercy; and it is so far from contradicting the divine justice that, on the supposition of this act of mercy, the divine justice must take heed of the hereditary character of the sin. The harmony between divine justice and mercy here appears in so resplendent a light that original sin even becomes an indirect proof of the infinite mercy of God.

"What can more aptly serve to demonstrate the greatness of God's goodness and the plenitude of the grace He accorded to Adam," says St. Anselm, "than the fact that, as Adam had the power to impart to his descendants the nature which he himself possessed, so likewise he had the free option of begetting them in the justice and happiness which were his? This privilege was granted to him. But because, situated as he was at the very summit of so great a grace, he deliberately relinquished the goods he had received in trust for himself and for them, the sons lost what their father deprived them of by not keeping it, although he could have handed it over to them if he had kept it." [12]

It was the wealth of the grace, the superabundant wealth, which was to be handed over to his descendants, and hence the greatness of the divine mercy bestowed on Adam and his posterity, that made the hereditary transmission of the sin possible. On the supposition of this grace the divine justice had necessarily to look upon Adam's posterity as implicated in his guilt, once the grace had been forfeited.

The overturning of an exceedingly great, mysterious deed of God into its opposite by man's agency: that is the easily perceptible mystery of original sin. It is a mystery, however, which by that very fact is made known in all its appalling enormity.

Before we leave the subject, we wish to subjoin the following remarks, which we believe are required for a more adequate appreciation of its mysterious character.

When treating of the mystery of the original state, we observed that it was not as mysterious when viewed according to its lower side as when viewed according to its higher side, since the gift of integrity is not supernatural to the same degree that the gift of sanctity is; hence it falls within the realm of naturally knowable truths. Similarly the lower, material element of original sin is naturally knowable and is even taken for granted in unadorned nature. Hence materially considered it is no mystery at all; it is, so to speak, the visible body in which the invisible mystery of the sin is incorporated. Formally considered, however, when regarded precisely as pertaining to the sin, as the fruit of a sinful act and integrating ele-

[12] *De conceptu virginali et originali peccato*, c. 23; *PL*, CLVIII, 456.

ment of the truly sinful deformity produced by that act, it remains obscure and mysterious. In this respect it is knowable only on the supposition of the original state and its connection with the higher element which accompanies it. A knowledge of this latter element is not deducible from the visible element, which consequently does not afford us a view of the whole. Indeed, knowledge of the visible part's function in the whole is completely dependent on our knowledge of the other, invisible part.

But the presence of this higher element, namely, the loss of an absolutely supernatural, ineffable union with God which obtained originally, is quite beyond the reach of direct natural perception.

Nevertheless it can be said that the sad predicament and history of a mankind stained with original sin may lead indirectly to a shadowy, indefinite suspicion that some such evil exists.

In the case of personal sin, we have already observed how its violation of the higher order of grace necessarily reacts upon nature and induces a depth of malice and depravity that cannot be explained and understood from a natural standpoint. Such a reaction cannot take place in original sin in the same degree and manner as in personal sin, for the person born in original sin does not expel sanctity from himself by an act intrinsic to him; he is not even stripped of his natural tendency toward God as the *finis naturae*, and of course there is no question of any deterioration of his nature in the direction of diabolical malice. However, in consequence of the privation of sanctity which was rejected by the racial guilt, he finds himself in a relationship to God and His providence other than that of the purely natural man, who would have been originally created without a supernatural destiny. He has forfeited the true destiny actually assigned to him by God. We are not obliged to assume—and I even believe that we may not assume it—that God would entirely deny him the assistance absolutely necessary for the attainment of his natural end and for the avoidance of grievous personal sins. Yet it is plain that, once the riches of divine grace have been frittered away, God need no longer provide so generously for the attainment of this end as in the supposition that the wealth of grace had never been granted.

On account of original sin, therefore, the help which God gives man against the surge of concupiscence will prove less abundant than reason would otherwise expect in view of God's wisdom. Concupiscence will become a dominant force; by and large mankind will succumb to it. Actually, outside the circles influenced by Christianity and its grace, the moral corruptness existing among men is so terrible that reason does not easily admit the possibility of such a condition on the hypothesis of an unsullied, untarnished relationship of mankind to God at the beginning, or at least would prefer to seek the explanation in some guilt on the part of the human race rather than in neglectful treatment at the hands of Providence.

Hence reason can readily surmise the existence of some such untoward relationship between God and man. But it is by no means able to infer this truth with certitude, nor to establish definitely its real character. Not the former, because reason cannot maintain with certitude that God really refuses man sufficient grace for the avoidance of fully deliberate grave sins, or that even from the standpoint of pure nature He could not allow many men to fall short of achieving full moral growth. The second alternative is ruled out, because the character of the supernatural relationship to God which was dissolved, too greatly transcends all the concepts of natural reason.

Even more strikingly than in the dominion of concupiscence, the "mystery of iniquity" prevailing among men manifests itself in the evident sway of the devil over mankind.

It is a tenet of faith that, owing to original sin, mankind has fallen into the captivity and slavery of the devil.[13] As mankind in its totality was overcome by the devil in Adam, or better, by freely following the whispered suggestions of the devil was in its head torn loose from its union with God, it is now subjected to him, belongs to his kingdom, and constitutes his kingdom on earth. Mankind is so firmly shackled to the devil that of itself it can in no way recover the lost freedom of the children of God, and can in no way recapture the lofty position from which he has cast it down. From this standpoint, man's imprisonment, prescinding from redemption through the God-man, is absolute and total. But this captivity is nothing else than the culpable privation of the supernatural gifts of the original state, so far as the will of the devil in man's regard is fulfilled in this privation, which man has drawn upon himself by reason of his fellowship with the devil. Accordingly this captivity and the corresponding dominion of the devil over mankind coincide with the

[13] Cf. John 12:31; I John 3:8; II Cor. 4:4; Heb. 2:14; II Pet. 2:19. See also Council of Trent, Decree on Original Sin; Denz., 788. [Tr.]

mystery of original sin itself. It does not formally involve any special, positively corruptive activity perpetrated by the devil upon his captives, and therefore cannot be looked upon as a visible manifestation of the mystery.

In addition to this, however, experience and revelation teach us that in consequence of the racial guilt God has delivered the race up to a positive dominion of the devil. God permits him in many ways to injure mankind in soul and body, to harm mankind morally and physically and, in order that man's ambition for self-deification may find its true punishment, to work for the end that men may adore the devil and his minions instead of the true God. But this dominion of the devil over man does not necessarily mean that man is reduced to full slavery; the slavery is not as absolute as the captivity. For by original sin man does not lose his natural as well as his supernatural liberty; not only is his natural liberty retained in substance, but it is not even completely suspended, as it is in the actually damned. It is only curtailed to such a degree that without God's special assistance man is not capable of steadfast resistance to the devil's influence over a long period of time.

A dominion of the devil over mankind of the sort that comes to light in countless instances, is not in itself, materially considered, absolutely unthinkable even in a race not laden with guilt. God could expose even a guiltless man, for his probation, to so formidable an influence of the infernal power, provided that at the same time He granted him the necessary help to stand firm against it, or did not assign an eternal punishment for the defeat suffered without grave personal sin. We must, in fact, assume such a help of God for the person constituted in original sin, since after all he retains at least his natural destiny, and consequently a title to the means absolutely necessary for its attainment. But for all that, reason can argue and find it more in accord with God's goodness and wisdom that man should not be surrendered to the devil's powerful ascendancy without guilt on his part, although here, too, it cannot pronounce upon the cause of man's sad plight with any certitude and definiteness. Therefore in reality the lamentable slavery to sensuality and to the devil in which our race was wasting away is an effect of the culpable rebellion of its representative against supernatural grace. If we view the slavery in this manner, we are enabled to grasp its real nature and the ultimate reason for it. But if we look at it only as it is in itself, we can do no more than vaguely conjecture what the reason is.

We are unable to share the conviction of those theologians and apologists who believe they can demonstrate with certitude the existence of some guilt encumbering the race, if not alone from concupiscence and the temptations of the devil, at any rate from the monstrous power of both which actually appears in the appalling moral depravity of mankind. We cannot approve of this attitude because we think it preposterous that the members of the race, who as persons with their personal rights do not simply merge with the community, should in consequence of non-personal guilt lose titles and goods to which they have a personal claim by nature. This view of ours need not give way before the powerful array of facts cited. In no case can we maintain that this vast corruption is explicable only in terms of a deficiency in moral strength on the part of man such as could not occur except on the hypothesis of his guilt. As a matter of fact, this corruption is found in mankind, and to some extent in the Church itself, in spite of the certain doctrine taught by the best theologians that truly sufficient help for the attainment of their supernatural salvation is offered to all adults without exception. Besides, is it not manifest that God, for the sake of His Son, loves the whole human race infinitely more than He hates it on account of sin? [14] Should He not therefore bestow upon it in all its members at least as great a good as it could lay claim to by nature?

Therefore the fact must find its explanation in the ever just, but ultimately inscrutable, decrees of God. Who knows how much personal guilt slips in when individual men do not lift themselves out of their helplessness by grasping God's hand? Who knows to what degree God holds the individual accountable for his depravity, and what He does with him in the hour of judgment? Who knows what wise designs God has when He suffers His creature to struggle and contend in a conflict that is so painful and fraught with danger?

One of these designs we know: it is the manifestation of the utter wretchedness into which the creature plunges when He abandons God and is abandoned to his own resources. This is a revelation which, owing to the enormity of the contrast, is to serve for the greater glorification of God in the re-elevation and restoration of man. God permits hell to rage, permits it to unfold its full might, in order later to demolish its works all the more gloriously, in order to

[14] Cf. Rom. 5:20: "Where sin abounded, grace did more abound."

celebrate all the greater triumph over it, in order to snatch victory from its grasp and to make its defeat all the more shameful at the very moment when it believes it alone remains master of the field. Thus did God vanquish hell the first time, when He allowed it to pierce even His Anointed with its sting; it lost the sting, and sank powerless at the feet of Him whom it ventured to destroy. Thus at the end of time He will once again give free rein to the "mystery of iniquity." He will permit the prince of darkness to set up a rival to God's Anointed in the man of sin, and will suffer him for a brief hour to lord it over the Anointed One's kingdom with plenary power, according to outward appearance. But then, too, with a bolt of lightning from His mouth He will hurl the devil down from His lofty throne and bury him forever in the pit of nethermost darkness.[15]

[15] Cf. II Thess. 2:3–8.

PART FOUR

The Mystery of the God-man and His Economy

And evidently great is the mystery of godliness which was manifested in the flesh, was justified in the spirit, appeared unto angels, hath been preached unto the Gentiles, is believed in the world, is taken up in glory.

1 Tim. 3:16

CHAPTER XII

The God-man

▀▀▀

50. NATURE AND CONSTITUTION OF THE GOD-MAN

THUS far we have examined three mysteries: the mystery of God, or the Trinity of divine persons; the mystery of man in his supernatural union with God and sanctification by God; and the mystery of man's separation from God in the dissolution of his supernatural fellowship with God through sin. The mystery of the God-man stands in closest and most sublime relationship with all three. In Him we find the most perfect prolongation and revelation of the interior productions of the Godhead, the restoration and re-establishment of man's supernatural union with God, and finally full compensation for the extirpation and obliteration of sin.

The mysterious character of the Incarnation is more commonly acknowledged than that of any other mystery. And indeed, where should we look for the mystery of Christianity if Christ, its foundation, its crown, and its center, were not a mystery? Besides, the general recognition of this fact is easily accounted for. The Trinity, although a still more exalted truth than the Incarnation, is nevertheless a necessary truth, which some have thought they could, if not conceive, at any rate demonstrate, on account of its objective necessity. With regard to the other truths, which refer to justice and injustice, beatitude and wretchedness, and generally to the good and evil states of man, one may easily come to look upon them as quite intelligible, if care is not exercised to distinguish sharply between natural and supernatural states. The Incarnation, on the contrary, appears to be a supernatural, extraordinary work of God under all circumstances, at least in some respect. But the full grandeur and sublimity of this work, both as regards its nature and particularly as regards its function and significance, have often been grossly misunderstood, or at least have not been sufficiently appreciated. In their endeavor to gauge its value and significance by the norm of natural reason, some have pulled it down from its supernatural eminence and have thereby jeopardized its object, if they have not altogether destroyed it.

This we shall see in due course. To rectify this abuse at the very outset, so as not to be led astray concerning its nature by a pre-conceived, one-sided, or erroneous notion of the import or necessity of the Incarnation, we wish first of all to fix our attention on its nature as faith proposes it to us. After that we shall examine its function and significance in the order of things, and determine the sense in which necessity may be predicated of this mystery.

The God-man is the new, heavenly Adam, of whom the first, earthly Adam was only the figure, or rather the reverse image. Sacred Scripture itself presents Him to us in this guise, and we believe that the mystery of His nature and His meaning cannot be set forth in a better, more adequate, and more profound way than by this comparison. The sequel must show whether we err in this conviction.

Even the first Adam was no ordinary man. He was elevated to a superhuman dignity, indeed to a dignity that simply surpassed the capabilities of all creatures, and was adorned with supernatural gifts and qualities. He was an adopted child of God, and therefore had a share in the divine nature. He was united to God in an ineffable manner, and God Himself dwelt in him, not as He does in mere creatures, but as in His own special sanctuary, through His own Spirit, whom He poured forth into him. The first Adam, although earthly and a creature by nature, was made heavenly, nay divine, by a wonderful grace of God.

As a result of God's grace, Adam himself was an incomparably greater and more sublime mystery than that which the rationalists have fashioned for themselves in their notion of the God-man. The very men who have no true concept of the one person in Christ, and who imagine two persons joined together in Christ, likewise fall short of ascribing a real participation in the divine nature to the human person in Adam or in Christ. They would have it that Christ occupied a unique position in God's favor and was intimately associated with Him, that He acted as God's envoy and worked in special harmony with Him, that He kept His human will exquisitely attuned to the will of God. But these are all merely moral and purely external relationships, such as can be procured even among men by adoption. By themselves they do not establish any real communication and unity between man and God. They do not even suffice for the idea of true divine adoption, in which the creature not only receives definite rights from God, but by the communication of the divine nature participates in the divine life and the divine holiness, and becomes a supernatural likeness of God.

Conversely, he who cannot rise to the notion of the deification and the supernatural sanctification and glorification of the first man, or at any rate fails to grasp this idea in its full purity and precision, blocks the way, so far as in him lies, to a correct conception and appreciation of the still higher mystery of the Incarnation. If with upright faith he accepts the doctrine taught by the Church, he can indeed still grasp and hold fast to the idea of the God-man. But he can do so only by making a leap; with a sudden spring he vaults straightway from a low level to the very highest, without traversing the intermediate stages. Through faith he undoubtedly arrives at the summit; but if he does not pass through the intervening steps he will not be able so accurately to gauge the immeasurable distance between the summit and the base. It is for this reason that we have premised the idea of the first man's supernatural dignity and nobility, so that it may serve as the starting point and the point of intersection leading to the idea of the God-man. Great was the mystery of the first Adam; all the greater and more sublime must the mystery of the second Adam appear when compared and contrasted with it.

The union and conformity with God involved in the mystery of the first Adam are so inconceivably and inexpressibly great and unprecedented that, even with the aid of the many concepts and comparisons at our command, we can gain only a faint inkling of the truth. The holy Fathers vie with one another in proposing the boldest expressions and metaphors, so as in some degree to illustrate it and make it intelligible. We are not surprised that, when subsequently they seek to describe the unity of the God-man, they can scarcely find any new expressions and figures to characterize it in its contradistinction to the union of Adam with God.

Even when discoursing on grace they state that God thereby dwells in man as the soul dwells in the body to which it communicates its own life, or that the creature is engulfed and consumed, permeated and transfigured, by God as iron is by fire, as a drop of water by a great quantity of wine.[1] They are unable to find stronger, more striking illustrations for the Incarnation.[2] But this circumstance, far from betraying us into confusing the hypostatic union of the God-man with the union which grace effects between man and God, must rather induce us to regard the former as a superlatively great and doubly sublime mystery. For the fact that we are obliged to employ the same images to illustrate the most diverse supernatural objects, is to be ascribed only to the deficiency of our intellects and the baseness of the natural things from which we derive our concepts and figures.

Is, then, all perception of the difference between the hypostatic union and the union effected by grace to be withheld from us? By no means. As under the guidance of revelation we are able to form an analogous concept of man's grace and sanctity from ideas and images of natural things, so under the guidance of the same revelation, by employing another analogy, a comparison of natural things according to another point of view, we can form a distinct, although ever analogous and hence imperfect and dim notion of the Incarnation. Let us endeavor to do so.

By grace the first man was deified, but he was not made God or turned into God, if we may so speak. It is only in a figurative sense that the Fathers refer to the deified man as God, that is, as a different God by similarity, not by identity, but only in the sense in which we are accustomed to speak of the so-called parhelion or mock sun as the sun.[3] When man, the original bearer and possessor of a purely human nature, became also the possessor and bearer of a share in the divine nature through grace, he did not become another, but remained the same person. He did not lose himself; he continued to belong to himself. By participation in the divine nature he only acquired a new possession, a new, higher, supernatural character, by

---

[1] See my edition of Casinius, *Quid est homo*, art. 6 *passim*, esp. pp. 248 f. and 285 f.

[2] Cf. St. Cyril of Alexandria, II, 107 (*Thesaurus de sancta et consubstantiali Trinitate*, asser. XII; *PG*, LXXV, 177).

[3] Thus St. Basil, *De Spiritu Sancto*, c.9, no. 23 (*PG*, XXXII, 109): "Hence arises a similarity with God and, summit of sublimity, you become God." St. Gregory of Nyssa, *De beatitudinibus*, Or. III (*PG*, XLIV, 1225): "So much a part of our nature was that divine good . . . that it seemed to be a new human good, an exquisitely perfect likeness and imitation of the divine good."

which he was transformed into God's image, was made like to God in a supernatural manner, and in consequence of this resemblance necessarily entered into a most intimate union and unity with his divine Exemplar. Accordingly God dwells in him as the soul in the body, but only so far as the soul communicates of its life to the body, not so far as it really constitutes one essence with the body. Hence man is immersed in God as iron in fire, as a drop of water in wine, but only to the extent that the fire by its penetrating propinquity communicates of its flame, its brightness, and its heat to the iron, and the wine communicates of its color, its aroma, and its taste to the drop of water, not to the extent that the flame-emitting body acually merges with the fire-shot metal, or the wine actually merges with the water to form a single whole. All this is extraordinarily marvelous, supernatural, and mysterious; but, that a God-man may come into being, a marvel of a wholly different order is required.

For in this case it is not sufficient that a human nature merely lay aside its natural imperfections and be endowed with a likeness of the divine nature. The nature must cease to possess itself, to be its own, to belong to itself; it must be inserted and, as it were, incorporated in a divine person, a subject that is by nature a bearer and possessor of the divine nature, so that the bearer and possessor of the divine nature becomes likewise bearer and possessor of a human nature. Only in this case do we have a subject that is at once possessor of a divine and a human nature, and hence can be called both God and man; a subject that makes its appearance not only as deified man, but as God become man, as God-man. God must clothe Himself with human nature, must put it on, as in the deification of man the man must put on the form and character of God. In this event humanity is engrafted in a divine person, as in the other case a shoot of divinity is, so to speak, engrafted in man.

Both cases are utterly astounding, supernatural, and mysterious: that a human person share in the divine nature, and that a divine person assume a human nature. St. Peter Chrysologus, in a flight of ecstatic wonderment at God's ineffable love for us men, even fancies that the first is more marvelous than the second.[4] This is perhaps true

[4] "God's condescension toward us is so great that the creature does not know at which to marvel the more, at the fact that God lowers Himself to the level of our servitude, or that He raises us to the dignity of His divinity" (Sermo 72; PL, LII, 405). This is only a comparison between the two marvels; but in the sixty-seventh homily he states (PL, LII, 391): "Which is the

so far as in the first case an elevation of man to a dizzying height, whereas in the second a descent, a climbing-down of God, is the first thing to strike our attention. But if we consider the elevation of the human nature in both cases, this is beyond comparison more amazing and sublime in the case in which the human nature ceases to belong to itself, in which it is not merely clothed with divine splendor but becomes literally a nature of God, a nature belonging to God, and in the person to whom it belongs constitutes one being with the divine nature and essence, in which consequently the divinity not only gives of its life to the human nature, but combines with it to form one substantial whole, as the soul does with the body, or the wine with the drop of water.

This union is absolutely miraculous and supernatural and hence mysterious if only for the reason that two extremes which are separated by so immeasurable a distance as the finite and the infinite combine to form one whole, and that the lowest joins with the highest in the closest fashion conceivable. But it is unprecedented and supernatural also because of the particular way it unites the two substances. For it unites them in one personal, hypostatic whole, without at the same time merging or fusing them into one nature. Body and soul in man are joined not only in unity of person, but also in unity of nature; or better, they constitute one person only so far as they also constitute one nature. Among natural things, which are accessible to our reason, we nowhere find a personal or hypostatic union apart from union in nature. Only when two substances constitute a single complete nature, can both belong to a personal or hypostatic whole and be possessed by it. Obviously, however, the divine nature cannot descend so low as to merge with a created nature to form a third nature; this contradicts the absolute simplicity, immutability, and independence of the divine nature. Consequently, if the divine nature unites itself with a created nature

---

more awesome mystery, that God gave Himself to earth, or that He gives you to heaven; that He Himself enters into the society of carnal beings, or that He admits you into the fellowship of divinity; that He takes death upon Himself, or that He rescues you from death; that He Himself is born into your state of bondage, or that He begets you as His children; that He accepts your poverty, or that He makes you His heirs, and coheirs with Himself alone? Surely the more impressive mystery is that earth is transferred to heaven, that man is altered by divinity, that the bondsman acquires the rights of dominion."

to form one whole, the resulting union must be a purely personal, purely hypostatic union, which neither presupposes nor involves a union in nature. It can only be a union by which the divine nature, without losing its independence, draws the created nature to itself and makes the latter its own, and by which, accordingly, it forms a whole with this created nature without itself becoming merged in the whole; rather, the divine nature manifests its own absolute independence in its possession and domination of the assumed nature.

Such a purely personal or purely hypostatic union is without parallel or comparison in created nature, for the simple reason that no created substance is so independent or is so much the master of its independence that it can completely draw another substance to itself and make it its own without reciprocally being drawn to it and becoming merged with it. If a union of this sort is possible at all, it is possible only with God and by God's power. But since what is possible only with God and by God's power is positively known only from what actually takes place among creatures, this union must be viewed by us as being so sublime and transcendent that our reason of itself cannot so much as suspect its possibility, let alone demonstrate it positively.

Hence the God-man is an absolutely supernatural mystery for two reasons: first, because the human nature in Him is not joined to another created essence, but is elevated above all the boundaries of the created world and united to the divine substance far more closely than it could be through grace; and secondly, because this kind of union is not a union in nature, nor is it a union such as could be found in the sphere of created nature at all, but is an absolutely unique, supereminent union.

Therefore whoever would define and appraise this mystery according to the natural concepts of his reason must inevitably distort it. He does one of two things. He comes to an abrupt halt before the infinite chasm separating the finite from the infinite, and also sees his speculations brought up short when confronted with the natural autonomy and personality which rational nature implies; and then he will be able to think of no union of the finite, human nature with God that would bridge that chasm and raise the human nature to be a nature of God. Or, with the aid of faith, he apprehends the incredible intimacy of the union, but perceives it under the concept of a union in nature, in which case he lowers the divine nature as much as he raises the human nature. Neither of the two, neither the Nestorian nor the Eutychian, rises to a true concept of the supernatural, towering elevation of the human nature without debasing the divine nature. The former rejects the elevation of the lower nature, whereas the latter, in elevating the lower nature, cannot retain the sublimity of the higher nature; but this must endure undiminished in the very union.

To attain to a notion of the mystery we must, therefore, suffer ourselves to be led by revelation and soar above the circle of rational concepts, and thus discern in human nature a potency for union with God and perfectibility through the agency of God which our reason cannot in the remotest degree uncover or even surmise. We must then represent this union and perfectibility not according to the norm of that hypostatic union which is implicated in or based upon a union in nature, but as an eminent and purely hypostatic union purged of all the imperfections that accompany a union in nature.

Since the concept of Christ's supernatural union is formed only by analogy, by purifying and transforming natural concepts of a hypostatic union, and besides is asserted in a sphere in which the autonomy and immeasurable distance of the extremes to be united seem to preclude every union other than that of mutual converse, it must remain obscure, vastly more obscure than the idea of natural union from which it is derived.

For the latter, too, is obscure and mysterious in its own way. Indeed the correct notion of the union between soul and body is one of the most profound and difficult problems of all philosophy. Whoever has reflected upon this problem even slightly, or has cast but a glance at the muddle of views on it, will easily be convinced of this. Those who have attempted to clear up every last bit of obscurity in it have destroyed the true union of nature and hypostasis, by assuming only a certain mutual interchange, a mutual operation, and a reciprocal harmony between soul and body, as between two autonomous substances. Hence we cannot take it amiss if these philosophers, in explaining the hypostatic union of the Logos with human nature on the analogy of the union between soul and body, have in this case hoped to find the matter wholly comprehensible. But if the soul as the substantial form of the body constitutes one nature and hence also one hypostasis with it, we have before us a marvelous reality that is couched in severely accurate language, but is for all that unfathomable in its essence; and so we have to regard the higher union in Christ as a still more unfathomable mystery.

But as the notion of the hypostatic union in Christ necessarily shares in the obscurity of the notion of the union between soul and body in man, an obscurity that must increase in proportion to the former's elevation over the latter, so on the other hand the former must receive more light the more sharply we mark it off from the latter's limitations and the more decisively we divest it of all the latter's imperfections. The concept of the purely hypostatic union stands here in the same relationships as the concept of the purely hypostatic distinction in the Trinity. If we assert it, all the contradictions that reason with its natural concepts would discern in the dogma vanish automatically; they vanish so completely that the foundations on which they might rest contribute to their extinction. For example, the infinite gap between the finite and the infinite is so far from standing in the way of the hypostatic union, that the latter essentially presupposes an infinite preponderance of the one element over the other, since otherwise it could not make that other completely its own.

The natural totality of a rational nature, which makes every substantial union with a superior nature impossible, is not absolute, and hence admits of a domination, even an unconditional domination and appropriation by Him on whom it is in any case wholly dependent together with all that it is. This is all the more readily perceived inasmuch as this nature not only loses nothing by being thus assumed, but rather is incalculably enriched. On God's part, finally, purely hypostatic union with a created nature, far from entailing any imperfection, nowhere more splendidly manifests His infinite perfection than here. For God can draw a created nature so powerfully to Himself, permeate it so deeply, and clasp it to Himself with so unalterably firm an embrace that He can call it His own without in any way being subjected to it, only because He is the absolutely independent, the absolutely simple, and the absolutely immutable being.

To be sure, it might appear that the Son of God, even when considered as the suppositum or bearer of the human nature, would be debased and composite. But when we say that He sustains the human nature and makes Himself the bearer of it, we do not mean to imply that He takes it to Himself as something higher or complementary. Rather we mean that He, as the nobler and as infinitely perfect, begins to possess in a uniquely perfect way and to rule with absolute authority that which is lower and which originates from Him with all the perfection it has. The assumption of the lower to the higher, or rather the absolute dominion of the lower by the higher, whereby the former becomes the exclusive property of the latter: such is the notion of the purely hypostatic union. Far from losing any of its nobility, the superior hypostasis can exercise such dominion only because of its sublime dignity and divine personality.

Thus in the case of the Incarnation, no less than in that of the Trinity, if only we accommodate our ideas to their sublime objects and have regard for the supernaturalness of the latter, or better, if we view the object from the right distance, we can succeed in forming a notion which, although faint and imperfect, dispels all the clouds that could disfigure or distort its object. Here again it will be true that a conscious awareness of the darkness that surrounds our eye will cause the object of its contemplation to stand forth the more clearly and distinctly.

51. The Attributes of the God-man

The elevation of a human nature to the status of a nature of God, the engrafting of it on a divine hypostasis, the organic incorporation of it in a divine person whose living flesh it becomes: that is the heart of the supernatural mystery of the Incarnation. But besides this infinitely august dignity and nobility which the human nature receives in Christ, or rather in very consequence thereof, the mystery hidden in Christ's humanity shelters still further supernatural, mysterious things within it.

1. In the first place, the hypostatic union between the human nature and the Godhead immeasurably transcends the union of a human person with God by grace, and essentially excludes a fusion of the divinity with the humanity to form one nature, which is the natural function and result of a hypostatic union. But we should fail to have a full appreciation of its force and significance were we to overlook the fact that by virtue of and because of the hypostatic union between the humanity and the divinity, the humanity participates in the nature of the divinity.

The perfection with which God can equip and adorn the nature of a mere man by grace when He adopts him as His child, cannot be wanting in the human nature of Him who is His natural Son. The humanity of God's Son not only can, but must possess the endowment and perfection which God presents to the children of His grace, precisely because it is to become or has become the nature of God's Son. The humanity hypostatically united in the highest conceivable union with the divinity in the person of the Son must, if any nature, and in a measure equalled by no other, participate in the nature of God, must be pervaded, shot through, transfigured by it, vitalized by it, must be made conformable and like to it, must be fashioned in its image; in a word, the divine humanity, the humanity which belongs to God, must be deified to the full capacity of its own condition. Is it conceivable that God, whereas He raised to His own level the first Adam who stood so remote from Him, in order to communicate to him of His own life through His Spirit, would not do the same for the humanity which is embodied in His Son and is united in the closest way to the source of divine life as the body is united to the soul? Is it thinkable that God, who set a mere man on fire with the flame of His own nature, clothed him with His own glory, and filled him with the aroma of His own sweetness, would not do all this for that humanity which in the most intimate of all unions is plunged into the fire of the divine sun, and is absorbed like a drop of water in a river of wine?

Surely not. That union and glory which could and did become the portion of a mere creature's nature, could not be wanting to the humanity of Christ which was joined to God in a special and unique manner, and in the highest possible manner. The hypostatic union does not exclude the perfection which is become the portion of the nature of a mere man. On the contrary, it implies the presence of that perfection in itself, it requires and demands it, calls it forth. Therefore the difference between the supernatural condition of the first Adam and that of the second Adam consists precisely in this, that the first Adam possessed it not of himself, not by reason of the power and right of his person, but out of sheer grace, whereas the second Adam possesses it of Himself, that is, by the power and right of His person, and hence by nature. The splendor of the divine nature was for the first Adam only the raiment of an adoptive child of God, freely granted from without as a grace. But in the case of

Christ's humanity it bursts forth from the divine person, who thereby manifests even in His humanity the dignity and power dwelling in Him by nature. The divine life flowed to the humanity of the first Adam from a source widely separated from it, situated outside it. The humanity of Christ receives that divine life from a source interiorly united to it, just as life is conveyed to the members of the body from the head, or to the branches from the vine to which they are joined.

In itself the humanity of Christ, according to its substance and nature, was like that of the first Adam. To this extent there were included in it no greater privileges than in the nature of the first Adam. All the privileges transcending Adam's nature also transcend Christ's humanity, and are supernatural with respect to it. The humanity of Christ was not holy, or free from inordinate concupiscence, suffering, and death by virtue of its nature; all the prerogatives of sanctity and integrity were gifts added to it by God. But because it was united to God in so extraordinary a manner, the right to these privileges and the source from which they sprang were embodied in it by virtue of this union. The God-man had essentially in Himself the right and the power to endow His humanity with all the wealth of sanctity and integrity that it was in any way capable of. Indeed, since His dignity is the highest possible, and since on the other hand His humanity also must possess an endowment in keeping with this supreme dignity, this endowment must differ in compass and wealth from the endowment of all mere creatures as heaven differs from earth. And since, further, the humanity of Christ draws its wealth immediately from the divine source abiding in it, that wealth must be so abundant that it surpasses beyond comparison the supernatural riches of all creatures combined, as a mighty torrent surpasses the tiny rivulet that drains off from it. And so, although this wealth is not absolutely infinite, it cannot be gauged by the amount apportioned to mere creatures. Hence, as contrasted with the latter, it appears infinite. In a word, it is so abundant that it is the very fullness of grace and of all supernatural gifts.

2. Accordingly, though Christ is certainly a true man, we may not think of His person, as bearer of the humanity, and of this humanity itself, in too human a fashion. All the wonders and mysteries that are discerned in Christ's humanity are nothing in comparison

with the hypostatic union, and follow as a matter of course once this is supposed. Even in the case of the first man, we may not gauge the greatness of his privileges according to the norm of his nature, because the love of God was more generous toward him than his nature was. Much less in the case of Christ should we be hesitant in expecting great and incomprehensible things for His humanity from the infinite dignity and power of His person.

As has been stated, the first Adam possessed all his prerogatives of sanctity and integrity only by virtue of the extraordinary love and liberality of God. Since he was called to the sonship of God by grace alone, as we also are, God gave to him, as He does to us, only the dignity of His sonship in the first instance, together with the power to work in the state of this dignity for the attainment of his inheritance. He was united to God in a supernatural manner, but was not from the outset admitted to the glory of the children of God and to the face-to-face vision of God. Called as he was by grace, he was for a time to remain in an intermediate stage, at a transition point between the rank of God's servants and that of His fully reborn children.

With the God-man such a period of separation is inconceivable. He was the Son of God by nature. As God, He possessed the divine nature wholly and essentially, and therefore had from the beginning the right and power, even as man and in His humanity, to enjoy the full sonship of God, to heap up all its goods in His humanity; hence not only those which we receive in the state of sanctifying grace, but also those which we await in the state of glory. Therefore His soul's participation in the divine nature meant not merely holiness and grace; it meant fully achieved glory and beatitude from the very first instant. Not only could this be so, it had to be so, unconditionally. It is unthinkable that the Son of God would not from the beginning have stood in closest and highest union with His Father even in His human nature, and that He would have strengthened and perfected this union only by degrees. But such would be the case if He had not from the first instant looked upon His Father face to face, if He had had to stand afar off like a stranger, and if, as a result, He had not been able to embrace His Father with that love in which the blessed in heaven are consumed. As there is no closer union with God than hypostatic, personal union, there can be no kind of union with God by knowledge and love that did not exist from the beginning in consequence of the hypostatic union of Christ's humanity with the Son of God. Owing to the hypostatic union, that humanity from the moment of its conception was present in God's bosom, to which creatures are raised only gradually and imperfectly; and in God's bosom it had also to gaze upon God's countenance, and to embrace God not with a love of longing and striving, but with a love of possession and fruition. Hence, as far as union with God is concerned, there was no *status viae* for Christ's humanity, as there is for us. From the very beginning Christ stood at the end of the road, at the summit of the mountain, which we must strive to gain by degrees, and to which we have to be raised by the grace of God. Christ is a *comprehensor*, as the theologians say. He is not only holy, but also in possession of divine glory and happiness; He is transfigured and beatified.[5]

With this there is connected another, equally sublime privilege of Christ and His humanity. The first Adam, and the same is true of every creature, does not by virtue of his natural origin stand in indissoluble union with God; even grace, by itself, does not raise creatures to such a union. Grace is sanctifying, grace is divine holiness, and repels grave sin to the extent that it cannot coexist with grave sin in one and the same subject. But so long as it is not yet joined to the immediate vision of God, so long as it is not yet transformed into the light of glory, it does not take possession of the human will and prevail upon it to the extent that the will cannot withdraw from its influence, it does not fetter man so firmly to God that man cannot tear himself loose from God. It is only heavenly glory that perfects sanctity; and so Adam, so any creature in the state of grace, could sin in spite of his sanctity.

But Christ was in the state of glory from the beginning, and hence in the state of perfected holiness. Accordingly sin was utterly impossible in Him. And it had to be impossible; for if Christ's humanity had sinned, the sinful act would have had to be ascribed to the divine person to whom the humanity belongs. Since all the actions of Christ's human nature were under the control of the divine person,

---

[5] Theologians propose many other arguments to prove Christ's beatific vision, drawn chiefly from His relation to creatures and from His offices. Cf. especially Suarez, *De Incarnatione*, disp. 25; Petavius, *De Incarnatione*, lib. XI, c.4; Legrand, *De Incarnatione Verbi divini*, diss. 9, c.2, a.1, in Migne, *Theologiae cursus completus*, tom. IX; Melchior Canus, *De locis theologicis*, lib. XII, c.14.

the impeccability of that nature is founded upon and postulated by the hypostatic union alone, and is also in some degree explained and conceived in terms of it. But that impeccability is perfectly clarified and understood only when we perceive that not only must the divine person ward off all sin from the humanity assumed by Him, but also that in consequence of the hypostatic union the humanity itself is the recipient of a condition and transferred to a state that necessarily excludes all thought of the possibility of sin, and does away entirely with the need of an immediate interference on the part of the divine person for the prevention of sin. For if Christ's humanity enjoys the vision of God, it is thereby placed beyond the possibility of sinning; sin simply cannot arise, and so does not have to be prevented by any higher, positive influence.

Thus the humanity of Christ, owing to the hypostatic union, was joined to God by a union which in manner and degree was supremely perfect from the beginning, and so could be neither strengthened nor dissolved; or, what comes to the same, Christ's soul, so far as it was orientated toward God, was in the state of the most perfect supernatural sanctity, glory, and beatitude. In highest measure and richest fullness it participated in the divine nature with all the latter's own sanctity, glory, and beatitude, and thereby proved itself to be a humanity belonging to the Son of God and worthy of Him.

3. But what was the situation with Christ's humanity regarded according to its lower side, in relation to the body and the lower faculties of the soul, and also in respect to the higher faculties in their dealings with creatures; briefly, in the sphere in which the gift of integrity operated in the case of the first man?

Without doubt the right to all the goods of the gift of integrity and the power to realize them dwelt interiorly in the God-man, in the humanity united to the Son of God. This fact by itself alone gave to the God-man an incalculable advantage over the first Adam, who possessed these goods not by right, but by grace, not by his own power, but by influx from without. But there is much more to be said. The God-man had in Himself the right and the power to adorn His humanity with the most perfect integrity from the very outset, and also to glorify and beatify it from every point of view, that is, to diffuse throughout His whole nature the supernatural immortality, glory, and beatitude which transfiguration by divine fire shed over the higher reaches of His soul. Consequently from the first moment, at His very entrance into the world, He had the right and the power to appear in the same splendor and glory into which He actually entered only after His resurrection.

The gift of integrity and the glory of the body stand in a relation to each other like that between grace and the glory of the soul. During this life the soul is placed in supernatural harmony with God by grace, and is thereby made ready to be filled with God's glory by transfiguration. In the same way the first man's body was placed in fullest harmony with the soul by the gift of integrity, in order one day to be wholly pervaded and completely spiritualized by the power and glory of the soul. These two stages came to the first Adam successively, because both were supernatural with regard to him, and hence God at His good pleasure could separate the inchoate from the consummate grace. But in the case of the second Adam, who is not earthly but heavenly by nature, the two stages could coincide.

In the same way that Christ did not attain to glory of the soul through the gift of sanctity alone, He did not necessarily require the gift of integrity as an intermediate stage leading to glory of the body. Indeed, the glory of the soul of Christ, if it were left to exercise its connatural influence, would have had to pervade and transfigure His entire nature, and hence establish His body in the state of glory from the first moment of its existence. If this did not occur, if Christ restrained the divine fire into which His soul was plunged so that it did not lay hold of His entire nature and transfigure it, that very fact is a miracle of the most exalted kind and a new, great mystery whose import we shall consider later. It is a self-renunciation by which Christ withheld from Himself a glory which He could lay claim to and effect in Himself, which He did not lack for the reason that He was as yet unable to have it, but which rather He voluntarily denied Himself; a self-renunciation which accordingly bore witness to His power over the glory of His body even more than the actual possession of it would.

In reality, however, Christ not only did not glorify His whole nature from the beginning; He did not, in fact, even confer upon it all the gifts of integrity that had been imparted to the first Adam. Hence His humanity, though immensely superior to that of the first Adam in holiness, was far inferior to Adam's humanity as regards integrity. But this lesser perfection of the second Adam's humanity as compared with that of the first is only apparent. The essence of integrity, its innermost substance, was just as perfect in Christ as in Adam, or even more so. For in what does the essence of integrity consist? Does it consist in this, that the nature cannot suffer at all, that it cannot be disintegrated? By no means. In spite of integrity, Adam could still suffer, and he could also die. The incapacity to suffer and die belongs to the state of the glorified body, as incapacity to sin belongs to the state of the glorified soul. Adam's integrity rather consisted in the fact that by a special divine ordinance his lower faculties could not be stimulated apart from and contrary to his will, and consequently, as matters stood, that suffering and particularly death could not effect an entrance against his will. But is this not the case with Christ in a far higher degree? Not only by a special grace and ordinance of God, but in His own right and by His own power Christ was able to impede any modification of His nature that did not accord with His will, and so He was also able to keep all suffering and death at a distance from Himself. He suffered and died not because He had to, or because He could not prevent it, but because He willed to. He could have warded off suffering and death even if all the external causes which are of a nature to produce suffering and death had rushed upon Him; according to the more probable opinion of theologians, Adam could not have done this. Therefore He really possessed integrity in its essence, that is, the inviolability and invulnerability of nature. He had it by right and in His power; and having it by His own right and with an inborn power to procure it, He possessed it more perfectly than Adam did. But He made no use of it, as far as suffering and death are concerned, because He could will and love suffering and death as a most excellent good, because He could manifest Himself and willed to manifest Himself as true Son of God in suffering and death as well as in impassibility and immortality.

But from another angle He had of necessity to assert uncompromisingly His absolute dominion over His nature. Whereas He could forgo immunity to suffering and death, He could in no way permit propensities and appetites to rise in Him which would contradict the absolute holiness and the dignity of His person and His human nature. He could not allow inordinate cravings for sinful objects to agitate Him, or let concupiscence of the senses in any way strive against the judgment of His intellect or even anticipate it. In this we observe again an incomparable superiority of the integrity of the second Adam over that of the first Adam. To be sure, Adam, too, had perfect dominion of will over all his proclivities and appetites, a dominion which he should not give up, but which he actually could give up, inasmuch as it did not pertain to him necessarily, but was dependent on the continuing uprightness of his will. But Christ possesses such dominion necessarily, because of His personal dignity and power. Besides, His will is unalterably holy; so holy that it cannot even admit the presence of an opposing inclination, even though it would be able to suppress it or hold it in check. Therefore in this respect Christ is incomparably more inviolate and invulnerable than Adam, and possesses an incomparably more perfect integrity, both virtually and formally.

4. Still more impressively, if we may speak thus, do the dignity and power of the divinity residing in Christ's humanity manifest themselves in another way. Not only does this humanity experience the operations of the divine person's dignity and power dwelling in it, but by virtue of the hypostatic union it is called to share in the divine power and activity of the person. In its own actions the humanity becomes the *instrumentum coniunctum* of this divine person, and these actions themselves thereby receive an infinite dignity and efficacy, in a word, an infinite value.

By his participation in the divine nature even the first Adam received a power which, in a certain sense, was infinite, because it immensely surpassed all natural power, and further because it rendered him capable of knowing and loving the infinite God, and of meriting the possession of God. But the infinity of this power was purely relative, and was restricted to his own personal development. This power did not enable him to perform external works like those of God, nor did it enable him to merit all of God's goods simply, but only for himself, and according to the measure of grace apportioned to him.

But the humanity of the God-man operates on the basis of the fullness of the divinity residing in it, not merely on the basis of a participation in the divine nature. Therefore its activity, although finite in itself, is of infinite dignity and value, because it is backed up by the dignity of an infinite person. Consequently God can be infinitely honored by this activity, and an adequate satisfaction can be offered to God's offended majesty. Further, all the goods of God and the possession of God Himself can be purchased and merited by it, not only for the God-man in His own person, but universally, for all other persons.

Because of this same plenitude of the divinity and its power, the humanity of Christ is able to operate in a supernatural manner within itself, and also to perform acts which are of supernatural benefit to all creatures and to achieve much that in itself can be effected only by the infinite power of God. Thus the humanity of Christ can communicate to others the supernatural life which it possesses itself.

In brief, the hypostatic union enables the humanity of Christ to acquire for others without numerical restriction, and to produce in them its own supernatural prerogatives. The grace conferred upon it for its own endowment is an overflowing, fruitful, self-communicating grace, which was not the case with Adam. Adam could serve only as a point of departure from which the Holy Spirit transferred to others the grace bestowed on him. The God-man, on the contrary, in His very humanity is a profuse source of grace in the proper sense of the word.

Thus in Christ's humanity we distinguish a threefold supernatural mystery, a threefold elevation above its natural condition, a threefold reception of the divine nature, a threefold deification and sanctification. The first of these mysteries is the foundation of the other two. The initial mystery is the hypostatic union with the person of the Logos, whereby the humanity is deified as a nature belonging to God. Secondly, springing from this union and rooted in it, come the transfiguration of the humanity and its assimilation to God by grace and glory, wherein it participates in the nature of the divinity. Finally, there arises the relation of the humanity to the Logos in virtue of which it becomes the latter's instrument in His supernatural activity. All this immensely transcends our ideas of the capacity of human nature, and indeed the entire range of our natural powers of comprehension.

5. All three mysteries may be synthesized under the notion of the anointing by which the man in the God-man becomes Christ, that is, the Anointed.[6] The fact that the humanity is anointed is no mystery for us; it is something natural. But the ointment which is

[6] In the Old Testament the future Redeemer is described chiefly as the "Anointed" (Messias). Cf. especially Ps. 2:2; 44:8; Dan. 9:24; Isa. 61:1. There

poured over it and into it is a mystery far greater than the mysteries wherein the angels and saints are anointed by the grace of the Holy Spirit.

For the anointing of Christ is nothing less than the fullness of the divinity of the Logos, which is substantially joined to the humanity and dwells in it incarnate, which so permeates and perfumes it with its fragrance and life-giving force that through the humanity it can extend its influence to others and imbue them also with its power and its fragrance. When the Fathers say that Christ is anointed with the Holy Spirit, they mean that the Holy Spirit has descended into the humanity of Christ in the Logos from whom He proceeds, and that He anoints and perfumes the humanity as the distillation and fragrance of the ointment which is the Logos Himself.[7] Properly, however, only God the Father can be regarded as the source of the ointment poured out upon Christ, because He alone communicates to the Son the divine dignity and nature with which the humanity that is assumed to the Son's person is formally anointed. As this ointment imbues the humanity with the fullness of the divinity, it raises the humanity to the highest conceivable dignity and sets it upon God's own throne where, borne by a divine person, it becomes worthy of the same adoration as that paid to God Himself.

This is the divine ointment which, flowing down from the well-spring of the Godhead into the creature and submerging the creature in God, constitutes not merely a deified man, but the true God-man. This is the mystery of Christ par excellence. He is anointed not merely by divine deputation for the discharge of an office, nor

is no question of a material anointing, such as the Israelite kings received. In Luke 4:21 the Savior applies Isa. 61:1 to Himself. In Acts 4:27 the Father is said to have "anointed" Jesus, and in Acts 10:38, to have "anointed Him with the Holy Ghost and with power." [Tr.]

[7] Not so much the Holy Spirit in Himself, as rather the source from which He issues, but including, besides this source, all its wealth and its overflow, is the unguent with which Christ is anointed. In other words, the ointment is not the *Spiritus Sanctus spiratus*, but the *Spiritus Sanctus spirans* together with His *spiramen;* it is not the latter's operation through the former, as with the saints, but the former's operation through the latter, that produces the Saint of saints. Moreover, the execution of the hypostatic union, which is the reason why the dignity of the Son of God pertains also to the Son of man, is ascribed to the Third Person, the representative of the divine love, only by appropriation.

even merely by the outpouring of the Holy Spirit in His deifying grace, but by personal union with the principle of the Holy Spirit. Hence the divine ointment is contained in the very make-up of Christ's being, and constitutes Him a divine-human being.

Accordingly "Christ" and the "God-man" mean one and the same thing. Both names, the one figurative, the other without any figure, express in different forms the august and incomprehensible mystery residing in the person of Jesus.[8] The name "Jesus" directly signifies the person according to the function which He was to exercise in behalf of men here upon earth, but not according to His inner being and constitution: it signifies the latter only indirectly, so far as the function of the Redeemer presupposes the divine-human constitution of the person to whom it is committed. The mysterious make-up of the person Himself is indicated directly by the name "Christ," which thereupon enables us to apprehend in their mysterious character the significance and the range of the function which Christ as Jesus is called to exercise. And thus the Apostle speaks of the "mystery of Christ" [9] into which he had been initiated, and of "the unsearchable riches of Christ" [10] which he proclaims to the nations, riches that have an inestimable greatness decreed in the wonderful anointing of Christ, riches that are poured forth upon Christ along with the fullness of the divinity, and are thence spread over all those who by their union with Christ become Christs them-

[8] Gregory of Nazianzus, Or. X; PG, XXXV, 832: "The Father of the true and genuine Christ, whom He imbued with the oil of gladness above His fellows, anointed the humanity with the divinity that He might make both one." St. John Damascene uses language that is even more pointed, De fide orthodoxa, lib. III, c.3; PG, XCIV, 989: "Christ is the name of the person; but the name also signifies the two natures. For He anointed Himself: He anointed as God, and was anointed as man. He Himself is both one and the other. The ointment of the humanity is the divinity." The saint speaks similarly in lib. IV, c.14; PG, XCIV, 1160: "He who is the Son of God and is God incarnate was born of the Virgin; He is not merely a man bearing God, but is God made flesh. He is anointed not by any action, as a prophet is, but by the presence of the anointing person, so that He who anointed has become man, and that which was anointed has become God, not by any mutation of nature, but by a union according to hypostasis. He who anoints is the same person as He who is anointed." On the name "Christ," as the name which discloses the essence of Jesus, see my Dogmatik, Bk. V, sect. 222.
[9] Eph. 3:4.
[10] Eph. 3:8.

selves and are one Christ with Him. Later we shall return to the significance which the idea expressed by the name "Christ" has for the position and the influence of the person of Christ with regard to the universe.

CHAPTER XIII

Our Knowledge of the God-man

▲▲▲

52. THE INCARNATION NOT KNOWABLE FROM THE EXTERNAL APPEARANCE OF THE GOD-MAN

THE notion of the anointing, exaltation, and transfiguration by which He who bears the humanity of Jesus becomes the Christ in the noblest sense of the word, is so sublime that it lies quite outside the circle of our rational concepts. Even in a limited manner it can be rendered intelligible to us only by an elevation and sublimation of our natural ideas. Accordingly, as must be self-evident, without formal divine revelation and faith the fact that the Incarnation has actually occurred is likewise impenetrable to our reason. Hence the second condition requisite for a theological mystery is fulfilled.

However, the importance of the matter makes a further discussion of this point imperative.

There are two ways in which a process of reasoning can convince us of the actual existence of a thing: *a posteriori*, that is, by the appearance of the thing in itself or in the effects which enable us to reason back to it; and *a priori*, that is, from its causes, particularly its final cause, the fact that certain ends have been established which demand the realization of a thing and therefore imply its existence. Neither of these methods can be employed to make the reality of the mystery of Christ known to reason. This indemonstrability rests upon the same objective foundation as the previously mentioned incomprehensibility, namely, upon the absolute supernaturalness of the object, and is therefore so closely bound up with the incomprehensibility that the one entails the other.

An *a posteriori* demonstration that the God-man really exists would require that He appear visibly as such either in Himself or in His effects. This supposition implies our ability to form a purely rational concept of Him whose reality we behold. Consequently it would no longer be true that the idea of the God-man lies outside all the concepts we can form from objects available to natural reason. In like manner the end that would supposedly enable us to perceive the necessity of the Incarnation would have first to provide us with a concept of it.

However, as we shall show, the supernatural character of the God-man excludes both methods of demonstration. Therefore any knowledge of Christ's existence necessarily depends on divine revelation.

We begin with the invisibility of the God-man.

The man, or better, His human nature, was of course visible to the people who saw Him with their natural eyes. But the divine dignity and personality of this Son of man, the hypostatic union of His human nature with the person of the Son of God, the fullness of the divine being dwelling in Him and the wealth of divine glory and sanctity streaming therefrom, were hidden from every earthly eye, from every created intellect. Christ's humanity, although visible in its natural constitution, was, with regard to the supernatural perfections abiding in it by reason of the hypostatic union, caught up into the inaccessible light of the Godhead in whose bosom it reposed and with whose majesty it was filled. But we do not on this account contend that Christ's humanity was itself a mystery; it was visible, it harbored the mystery within itself, and concealed the mystery by its own natural visibility. For, since the external appearance of Christ was like that of other men, no one could conjecture that interiorly He was much more, infinitely more, than merely a man.

Perhaps it will be thought that the miracles which Christ worked outside Himself, or those which He wrought within Himself, as at His transfiguration on Thabor or at His resurrection, would have manifested His higher, divine nature. Indeed Christ Himself appealed to His miracles against the Jews, that they might know that He was the Son of God. But Christ's miracles in themselves merely showed that God worked through Him in a supernatural manner, and hence that God was in Him and with Him in some special way. In themselves they did not prove that He Himself was God in His own person, and that God the Father was in Him and with Him as with His own Son by nature. Other men, too, mere men, have worked miracles, and the Savior Himself said that those who believed in Him would perform even greater wonders than He performed. Those very miracles which were wrought visibly in Christ Himself, such as the Transfiguration and the Resurrection, have occurred to some extent in other men, and will one day be repeated in all the elect. Therefore neither class of miracles, considered as miracles, warrants the conclusion that Christ is God. Such would be the case only if we could further perceive that Christ worked these miracles not by power derived from another, but in the plenitude of His own power. But we are not able to do so, since in these miracles we perceive only the effect that is produced, but not the manner in which it is brought to pass.

Hence the miracles do not by themselves reveal to us either the divinity of Christ or the God-man as such. They do no more than show that God is with this man in a special way, that God wills in a special way to call attention to Him, to glorify Him, and to accredit Him as His envoy. In particular they authenticate the words with which Christ describes His union with God as that of a natural Son with His Father, and solemnly proclaims that He performs miraculous works in the plenitude of His own divine power. Christ's divine dignity is revealed not by the miracles alone, but by the word proceeding from the mouth of Christ as of one sent by God, the word whose truth the miracles attest. It is only by belief in His divine word that we can apprehend this dignity.

What we say of the physical miracles is just as true of the moral miracles that are visibly manifest in Christ, miracles such as the majesty of His whole demeanor, His acts of superhuman love and surrender, and the magnetic force with which He drew hearts to Himself. In stating this we are not ignorant of the fact that the impression which He made upon men, and in which He was revealed to them as the Son of God, is to be ascribed not so much to His outward appearance as to the inner workings of grace. It was not flesh and blood, it was not the natural eye, that made the apostles recognize the Son of the living God in the Son of man; it was the heavenly Father who revealed this truth to them by His enlightening grace and the word of His Son.

Accordingly the divinity of Christ, no matter how dazzlingly it shines forth from the veiling cloud in isolated flashes of lightning, remains concealed in its obscurity that is inaccessible to reason: it is a true mystery.

53. The Objective Motivation of the Incarntion Not Discoverable within the Sphere of Reason

By processes of natural reasoning we can neither conceive of the God-man as such, nor conclude from His outward appearance that He is divine as well as human. But with the purely natural reason can we not perhaps infer His existence in a general way, as the existence of a being necessary for the perfection or the restoration of the natural world-order, or of the human race? In other words, arguing from the objectives which the Incarnation is meant to attain in the world, from the motives which determine its realization, is it not perhaps possible to demonstrate its actuality, or at any rate to explain it and give an account of it? We join the second question to the first, since in part it admits of solution from the same principles, and also since moderate rationalism desires in the case of the Incarnation, as in other instances, not so much to prove its real existence a priori, as rather to conceive of it from its internal grounds.

But even this is impossible, because the same sublimity of object which a posteriori is seen to be the reason why our mystery is incomprehensible and its existence imperceptible, places it beyond the range of the purely natural reason in every respect, and cannot permit the motive for the actualization of its object to be situated within so low a sphere. Whoever claims the opposite draws the mystery down from its lofty position, and will not be able to raise it up again by any process of reasoning.

If we proceed logically, inferring from purely rational truths and starting out with purely rational ideas, we will never arrive even at the concept of the Incarnation, to say nothing of its actuality. In place of the ideal presented to us by revelation, we would thus set up a caricature that has nothing in common with the truth.

In this connection it makes almost no difference whether we hope to hit upon the idea of the Incarnation after abstracting from all historical knowledge of it, or whether, presupposing this knowledge, we wish from a purely philosophical standpoint to allege reasons that will explain the idea and account for its necessity, as the adherents of Günther's school in particular have presumed to do. In this way, too, we would be shifting the standpoint which reason must take in view of the sublimity of the object, and we would be forcing the object into so narrow a system that its greatness must necessarily suffer impairment, because it simply does not fit into such a system.

To be able to demonstrate the Incarnation along these lines, natural reason would have to discern some purpose lying within its own horizon. This purpose would have to be one that could not be attained otherwise than by the Incarnation, and for its realization the Incarnation would have to be absolutely necessary. That reason cannot rise to such heights would be easy to prove. But we go still further and contend that within the purview of the intellect there is no good which would be worthy of the Incarnation, no good whose attainment would represent the Incarnation as appropriate at any rate, if not necessary, and could give an account of its actuality that would in any way be satisfactory. To be sure, there are natural goods which can be brought about by the Incarnation (for example, a greater clarity and certitude in our natural knowledge of God), and for the procuring of which the Incarnation seems appropriate from the viewpoint of our nature. But there are no natural goods which would be deserving and worthy of the Incarnation, which because of any intrinsic, high value could counterbalance so tremendous a work and make the execution of it appear appropriate from God's viewpoint or justify it in His eyes, which appraise all ends according to their true value. For not every good effect that a thing can produce is of such a nature as to supply motives for its real existence. The appropriateness in question has two meanings, which must be carefully distinguished. Only in the latter sense (i.e., from God's viewpoint) can it enter into consideration here; and with regard to such appropriateness, as with regard to the necessity of the Incarnation, we contend that reason, when restricted to its own standpoint, cannot perceive it.

Let us take our stand at the viewpoint of the purely natural reason, without any suppositions derived from faith. Further, let us consider reason at the level of culture it has actually acquired with the aid of revelation, and with all the material that can be supplied to it from the natural course of history. But let us also determine the domain in which alone it can move about. This domain is limited to the natural order of visible creatures, to their nature and their natural end, as well as to everything which in a necessary or naturally perceptible manner has been ordained by God for the attainment of this end, or which perceptibly obstructs progress toward this end.

Accordingly, to demonstrate that the idea of the Incarnation is acquired by reason alone, and to show its necessity or even its appropriateness in the sense explained, we would have to prove that without the Incarnation man could not realize his natural destiny at all, or at least could not repair the derangement of the natural order brought about by his guilt, that is, by sin.[1]

1. Let us first take up the question of man's natural destiny, leaving sin out of account, and let us begin by considering its subjective aspect, the natural perfection and happiness of man.

a) Why should man not be able to attain his natural perfection and happiness without the Incarnation of the Son of God? Indeed, if man had a natural destiny, would not the Incarnation seem inappropriate? Man's claim to all the goods necessary for his natural happiness is sufficiently cared for by his nature and the natural providence of God. Furthermore, man has the principles of his spiritual and moral life within his own nature; and if he stands in a more special need of God's external and internal assistance, internally for the stimulation and strengthening of his faculties, externally by education and instruction, this too lies within the sphere of God's natural providence. There need not be, and there cannot be, any thought of an incarnation of God for this end. What would be the relationship of this greatest supernatural miracle of the divine power and love to its end, if this end contained nothing that is not already amply provided for by the nature of creatures and their natural relation to God? Why the personal entrance of the Son of God into human nature, if He is to let it remain on its own natural level, and is to advance humanity only within the circle of its natural life, wherein it is already revolving without Him? For the full moral education of natural man a positive revelation of God is necessary only in a relative sense, to the extent that God does not choose to avail Himself of other means. But even if we grant the necessity of such a revelation, there would be no adequate motivation for the Incarnation.

As in the Old Testament God spoke to His people by the mouth

[1] The following exposition may seem to go into excessive detail. The reason for such full development is the supreme importance to theological science of a clear understanding of this point.

of His servants, so He could impart the revelation in question through any of His servants, without sending His only-begotten Son. The personal sending of His Son has meaning only if God no longer wishes to treat us as His thralls and servants, only if He wishes to speak to us with the greatest familiarity, in most tender intimacy, as His friends and children, and to elevate us to the dignity of His friends and children. Less still could the Incarnation be necessary or appropriate from the standpoint of giving us God's only-begotten Son as our model and example of virtue, as long as we remained in our natural relationship to God. This would be like setting up a royal prince to be the pattern and model from whom the king's servants might learn their menial duties and manners. No, the Son of God can be sent to men to be their ideal and model only if they are no longer to serve God as menials, but, as true children of God, they are to learn divine habits and are to become perfect, as their heavenly Father is perfect.

All things considered, then, if man is to retain only his natural dignity and position, and is not to be raised to a higher rank by the Incarnation, if he is merely to develop his natural life and is not to be transferred to a higher, supernatural region of life, and lastly, if he is to achieve only the perfection and happiness designed for him by nature, there is not the slightest reason, to say nothing of any necessity, why our thoughts should mount to an idea of the incarnation of God's Son.

Therefore, if we view the matter from the standpoint of reason alone, as the rationalists do, we must hold it to be not merely quite comprehensible, but necessary and inevitable, that the rationalists refuse to understand how and for what purpose the Incarnation could take place, and since they do not acknowledge the Incarnation, that they consider the dogma irrational and inadmissible. And those who, whether theologians or philosophers, accept the Incarnation as Christianity has proposed it, as a fact, but who consistently appraise its character according to the viewpoint of natural ends, will fail utterly to scale the heights of the dogma. They will explain it away or water it down; they will reduce the God-man to a man standing very near to God, a man singled out and sent by God, a man who is joined to God not in real union of person, but only by an especially intimate moral relationship. Presently we will discuss this point further.

b) Hence others, with Malebranche at their head, have convinced themselves that, if they were to preserve the dogma in its true character and mount to its high level, they must hit upon some higher road. They connect the Incarnation not with the natural development, perfection, and happiness of creatures, but with the glorification which God must demand and receive from His creatures. The glorification, they say, which God must seek and find in His creatures, can be perfect and commensurate with His dignity only if it is infinite. But God can receive an infinite glorification only through the Incarnation. Such glorification can be rendered only if a created nature is invested with the dignity of a divine person and itself becomes worthy of adoration, in order to offer to God a homage proportionate to His dignity.

Of course God can obtain an infinite glorification of Himself from creatures only through the Incarnation; and actually this glorification was the chief end of the Incarnation. But, as is likewise manifest, this glorification is absolutely supernatural. It is supernatural inasmuch as no created nature, not even the totality of created nature, can supply it; and it is also supernatural inasmuch as no creature by virtue of its origin and its nature owes it to God. How could God exact from nature something that it is not able to provide? But this glorification, since it is supernatural, must remain an absolute mystery for the understanding of a mere creature. With our reason we do indeed perceive that the honor we render to God by our natural efforts falls infinitely short of the honor due to His majesty. But we also perceive that God is under no necessity of demanding more from us than we can give. What we do not perceive is how God can receive from without an honor that is commensurate with His greatness. We should comprehend this only if with our reason we could conceive the possibility of the Incarnation. But this work is so transcendent, so great and divine, that we cannot fully understand its possibility even now, after it has been revealed to us. And this glorification of God would not be so sublime, it would not be divine and infinite, if it could be even so much as conjectured, and much less so if it could be conceived. As for its necessity, God needs no external glorification at all. Even if He does wish it, He is not obligated to obtain it in the highest possible degree. As far as the creature is concerned, the infinite glorification of God is an utterly gratuitous, privileged vocation and elevation, rather than the discharge of a debt attaching to the creature by nature.

Accordingly whoever hopes, by following this course of reasoning, to light upon the idea of the Incarnation and to demonstrate its actuality, deludes himself. Perceiving how much in keeping with nature is the mystery which, according to revelation, has been vouchsafed to the creature, he then fancies that from the nature of the creature he may infer what in reality God has placed and hidden in nature with an unprecedented, gratuitous condescension that transcends the whole natural order.

2. More often attempts to account for the Incarnation and to infer it from the standpoint of natural reason proceed according to the second method indicated above. The Incarnation is regarded not as a complement physically necessary for the natural perfection of innocent, unsullied nature, but as a necessary remedy for the restoration of a nature stained with sin and arrested in its development. Let us see whether this undertaking is more successful and more appreciative of the sublimity of the dogma.

This procedure has in its favor an important point: once a derangement has occurred in nature, a special, supernatural intervention of God may appear appropriate or even necessary, an intervention that would not appear appropriate or necessary without such a derangement. However, it will be shown that an intervention of God by means of the Incarnation can never be fittingly motivated and logically deduced from this viewpoint alone.

A strict a priori inference of the actuality of the Incarnation is out of the question. With regard to creatures' attainment of their end, God is not bound to remove obstacles that have arisen through the creatures' own fault. If God pleases to come to the help of man in order to take away his sin and its consequences, this is an act of pure mercy. The point at issue is whether, in the readily presumed case that God wills to take pity on guilt-laden man and to restore him to the state that existed before the sin, the Incarnation is the only sufficiently motivated or the only adequate means for this purpose.

In sin there are three things to consider which bring man to an abrupt halt in the pursuit and attainment of his end, and which require reparation: the affront that man offers to God by rebelling against Him, the separation from God that ensues when man turns his back on Him, and the resulting inner ruin and depravity that render man less fit for the pursuance of good, and solicit and draw him to the perpetration of evil. All these factors must be understood in the sense in which they are naturally involved in sin in the natural order; otherwise we abandon the standpoint of the unaided reason.

a) The most grievous and decisive factor is manifestly the affront, the *iniuria*, offered to God. When man sins, as in fact he has sinned, he is said to offer God an infinite affront, because he offends the infinite Good which is deserving of infinite honor, and contemns God's infinite dignity, on which His sovereignty over us rests. That this infinite dishonor may be redressed, an atonement of equally infinite value must be rendered to God. Consequently a person of infinite dignity must undertake the atonement.

Undoubtedly, if God insists that adequate satisfaction be rendered to Him for the affront offered Him by the creature's sin, no one less than the God-man can give it to Him. But how will the intellect which supposes only the natural order of things arrive at the conviction that God demands this infinite satisfaction? Perhaps for the reason that God could not condone and remit man's sin without such satisfaction? But this is false, utterly false; practically all theologians are in agreement on this point. They regard as an evident, established truth that, if the deed is retracted, God in His infinite mercy can acquit wretched man of the debt with which sin encumbers him, and can remit it without exacting full payment.[2]

---

[2] Suarez, *In Illam Partem*, disp. 4, sect. 2, states that this doctrine is "common, and of such high certitude that it cannot be denied without rashness and without compromising the faith." St. Augustine, *De agone christiane*, c.11, no. 12 (*PL*, XL, 297; *CSEL*, XLI, 114) had affirmed before him: "They are stupid who contend that God in His wisdom could not have saved man otherwise than by assuming a human nature." Satisfaction by the God-man was necessary only on the hypothesis that man's deliverance was to be achieved not through sheer mercy, but by meeting all the requirements of justice. We cannot maintain that justice unconditionally obliged God to exact such satisfaction. St. Thomas, *Summa*, IIIa, q.46, a.2 ad 3, is well worth listening to on this point: "This matter of justice depends on the divine will, which exacts satisfaction for sin from the human race. If God had willed to free man from sin without imposing any satisfaction, He would not have acted against justice. A judge cannot in justice simply dismiss a crime without imposing punishment if there is question of an injury committed against another, for example, against another man, or against the whole state, or against a ruler who is his superior. God, however, has no superior above Him, but is Himself the supreme and common good of the whole universe. Hence if He should remit sin, which is culpable for the reason that it is committed against Him, He does wrong to no one; just as any person who forgives an offense committed against himself without demanding satisfaction acts mercifully and not unjustly."

God is not obliged to vindicate His honor before creatures in its entire infinite dignity. He is no more bound to require infinite atonement after sin has been committed than He is to claim infinite honor prior to sin. As soon as God demands infinite atonement from sin-laden man, and makes it possible for him to offer it, He does not thereby merely restore man to a previous natural state of innocence, but raises him immeasurably above his nature, by the very fact that He enables him to pay infinite honor to God through such atonement. By demanding infinite satisfaction, God cannot restore the natural order of things without changing it to a supernatural order, without assigning to man a high, supernatural destiny, namely, the destiny of glorifying God in a manner commensurate with His infinite dignity. This destiny is far in excess of man's natural destiny, which required him in his own way to render finite honor to God.

Hence, if there is question only of a restoration of the natural order, without the establishment of a new, supernatural order, the mind will never be able to conceive the idea of infinite satisfaction, and still less the idea of the true Incarnation. The Incarnation is motivated and is conceivable only if God in His mysterious decrees wills externally to vindicate and manifest His infinity; if God chooses to display not merely His mercy, but to place man on a level of equal rank with His infinity and to bring it about that, even in view of the infinity of the one offended, man can come forward with a payment that fully discharges his debt, and if, consequently, God wills to raise man to an infinite dignity. But such a decree on the part of God is so exalted, so stupendous, that natural reason cannot soar up to it, or even grasp its meaning; in its own right it is an exceedingly profound, obscure mystery which, far from impairing, confirms and emphasizes the mysterious character of the Incarnation.

Strictly speaking, all this holds true even with regard to the dishonor which man as God's adopted child does to Him by sin. In this case, however, the need for an infinite satisfaction is considerably more manifest. For this dishonor, taken in itself, is incomparably greater than the dishonor done to God by the mere creature. With much greater propriety it can be said to be infinite, since the creature had stood far closer to the infinite God, had had a much clearer understanding of His infinite dignity, and had scorned and repelled God who with all the riches of His own being had given Himself to the creature for his possession and enjoyment. But, whereas man's state of grace thus increased the gravity of the sin and certainly required a greater satisfaction, on the other hand this greater satisfaction, such as would be commensurate with God's dignity, is rendered impossible by sin. If man had retained the dignity of God's sonship after committing grievous sin, and had remained in the state in which he sinned, he would have been able to offer to God a satisfaction that would not indeed be commensurate with the infinite rank of the offended person, but would at any rate be consonant with the state of the offender. However, by grievous sin he forfeits the grace of sonship, and so loses his hold on the position which alone could have given him some right to atone for the offense offered to God. Therefore, even if God did not require of man an adequate, but only a real satisfaction of some sort, He would in any case have to call some truly supernatural institution into being. Hence it becomes understandable, though it is by no means demanded, that the natural Son of God should make amends for the crime of God's adoptive children.

But this title to satisfaction through God's Son is itself a supernatural mystery. And so it remains ever true that natural reason knows nothing of the God-man; because He is so great, natural reason cannot even surmise His existence. Hence those rationalists, whose judgment concerning the plan of redemption that has actually been contrived is based on man's need of restoration after his sin, on his need of deliverance from guilt, cannot lightly be charged with inconsistency if they find that the incarnation of a divine person is not necessary, and indeed is not even suitable for the purpose, and if they fail to form the sublime notion of the person of the Redeemer which Catholic teaching proposes. God could, they rightly contend, blot out the sin simply by gratuitously remitting it, consequent upon man's repentance; He had only to send an envoy who would lay before men the enormity of their sin, rouse them to repentance, and in His name promise them merciful forgiveness of the repented sin. And if need be, God could have such an envoy intervene by interceding for the sinners, lead the way before them by his self-sacrificing example, and put heart into them. A God-man is not required for all this; a blameless human being, a man specially favored by God, suffices. Proceeding in this way, rationalists, both ancient and modern, could literally never arrive at the idea of the Incarnation. Almost all the heresies that have debased the notion of the Incarnation have come to their error along this path. This is manifest with the Socinians, and highly probable with the Nestorians.

Thus reason, starting from its own point of view and remaining true to it, cannot arrive at the idea and deduce the necessity of the Incarnation by arguing from the need of an adequate, infinite satisfaction, since such satisfaction lies outside the entire natural order. Still less successful is the attempt which is based on the other factors that have to be considered when dealing with sin, that is, the separation from God and the inner ruin and corruption of the man who sins.

b) Let us continue to take our stand within the natural order, as indeed we must, in accordance with our supposition. On this hypothesis we can account for the sinner's separation from God only by perceiving that he has diverted his love from God by his sinful act, and that, as long as he does not repentantly redirect his love to God, or at least does not turn again to God as his last end, he remains in this morally enduring state of aversion from God. At the same time God on His part withholds His love from man and hates him, as long as man refuses to make himself again worthy of that love by repentant conversion. Must the Incarnation be brought in to effect a reconciliation after such a separation, or even, can it be brought in? By turning from God does man lose the absolute possibility of returning to God? By sin does he annihilate the principle of his conversion to God, does he cut off his union with God at its very root? He does not, any more than by an act of his will he can annihilate his nature. On our hypothesis his previous attachment to God proceeded from his nature; it was an activity of his natural free will; and if this is not lost by sin, man is able to actuate it again after his sin, and to actuate it by retracting his sin and turning again to God. Certainly this will be more difficult after the sin than before. If great sins have been frequently repeated, it will become very difficult, terribly difficult. But it will never become absolutely impossible, particularly as a result of a single, simple sin; in this case, indeed, it will not even be very hard for him. Since he always has within him the root of his union with God, he will be able, at least to some extent, by his own efforts to recover this union, to enter into it again. At all events he can begin to detest the sin and again to gravitate toward God. In sensing the great difficulty of arriving at his goal by himself alone, he will beg God for assistance in order that he may carry out his good intention and again come close to God.

God, to be sure, is not obliged to give this assistance and, if He so chose, could attach it to the condition of an adequate satisfaction. But if there is question of no more than the restoration of man's previous union with Him, with the same mercy as led Him to hold out to man the prospect of such a recovery He will suffer Himself to be prevailed upon to grant to man who pleads for reconciliation with Him the assistance necessary for it.

Where do we find a place for the Incarnation in all this? The Incarnation does not even appear suitable, much less necessary. In this reunion of man with God, the Incarnation could serve only to recover its principle after it has been lost, or to merit for man the help necessary for a complete conversion. But the principle of man's natural union with God (that is, the union proper to the natural order) was never lost, and cannot be lost; how then could it be restored? And as far as His assistance is concerned, God can grant it without any special meriting of it, out of merciful regard for the need of the sinner and his prayers. Surely there would be some wastage, some undervaluation of the infinite dignity of the God-man, if God should wish to call upon the infinite merits of His incarnate Son exclusively or primarily before conferring so slight a benefit as that which is required by man for the same union with God as is determined by nature. There would be no place at all for the merits of the God-man in the present case, because, on the supposition that God wills to restore man to his previous natural position in spite of his sin, all the earlier claims and rights of nature revive; hence also God's natural providence again takes effect for man's benefit.

Accordingly we can but repeat what we stated before about the implications of the Incarnation with regard to man's natural destiny. Only in the event that by sinning man has severed his supernatural union with God and is to be received back into this union, is the Incarnation in place. For, on the one hand, the sinner rends the last fiber of the bond that had joined him to God, so that he no longer has within him any starting point from which he can set out to effect reunion with God. Consequently he cannot achieve this reunion by himself either easily or with difficulty. On the other hand, this union is so high above even sinless human nature, that of himself man is not able to initiate the slightest motion toward its attainment. In this connection the question can well arise, whether subsequent to sin God wills without condign merit to give back to man the precious bond that has been lost. On account of the infinite value of that bond, by which God takes man into closest fellowship with Himself, such merit can be the merit only of the God-man.

c) By the disruption of his union with God, man plunges from the heights upon which it placed him, and thereby falls into ruin within himself. Hence, it is argued, this fall and ruin points to the Incarnation as the adequate, and the only adequate, means of raising him up again. But once more we repeat: from the standpoint of pure reason, and with reference to the natural order of things, there can be no question of such a conclusion.

In what do this fall and this ruin actually consist, when thus viewed? When man sins he does not merely come to a halt in the road leading to his natural end, he does not merely suspend his advance and development; he blocks all advance and development and, so long as he remains in sin, makes them impossible. By sin he deviates from the upward course leading to God, turns his steps downward to himself, to creatures, and hence blunders into a path that lies far beneath his natural destiny and is unworthy of his natural nobility. In freely clinging to creatures, he gives a new weight, a new impetus to his natural hankering for creatures, which quite apart from that is already strong enough, and can be held in check only by the resolute counterpull of the will. In the case of great and repeated sins particularly, he sinks so low and becomes so interiorly corrupt that only with the utmost difficulty will he be able to right himself, pursue the higher, nobler course again, and gain control over the seductive inclinations impeding his progress.

Obviously, without the special, merciful assistance of God he will not be able to raise himself up from this fall which has plunged him so far beneath his natural level and perfection. Ought not this help be looked for in the Incarnation? We should note carefully that the sinner's fall is but a fall beneath human nature, and his corruption is but a corruption occurring in human nature as such. Or we should do better to say: the fall is a deflection from the higher route which man, to be true to his nature, ought to pursue toward his natural end; and the corruption is a derangement, perversion, and debasement of his nature with respect to its capacity for achieving its natural development. Hence man has only to re-enter the road that leads upward, abandon the wrong road, and bring his downward course to a halt or at least so control his lower tendencies that they can no longer impede his upward course.

Certainly man can return to the higher road by himself, because it is natural to him, and neither his nature nor its natural yearning has been lost by sin. Similarly he can retard and abate his downward course, if only partially and gradually, to the extent that it is the product of his own activity. It is only the complete freedom to follow the upward course, and the absolute power to break off the downward, that he cannot achieve by himself. Therefore in this case also man needs no more than God's energizing and sustaining assistance in order to rise from his fall and collapse, and so regain his natural level. But such assistance alone would by no means be an end worthy of the Incarnation and its grandeur; there is no proportion between a restoration of man to his natural height and the incalculable sublimity of the Incarnation. It is inconceivable that God should equip a man with His own dignity and take him to His bosom as His own Son by nature, just in order to restore the rest of men to their full human dignity.

No, if the God-man is to come in order to raise the rest of men from their fall, then the height from which they had sunk must be a superhuman, supernatural height, it must in its own way be a divine height and dignity. And if the corruption from which the God-man is to rescue man cannot be merely the depravity of his nature, it must be the corruption of a divine life in man, of a life that is rooted not in man himself but in God who, as He alone conferred it in the beginning, alone can reconstruct it after its collapse.

What has been said thus far chiefly concerns the personal sins of individual men. We have prescinded from original sin, for in its proper character it lies beyond the horizon of reason. As to that aspect of it which belongs to the domain of reason and is naturally perceptible, namely, the actual lack of integrity and the consequent actual inability of man to attain even his natural end without God's special help, the matter has already been settled, so far as it is pertinent to the present question.

Nevertheless, let us append the following consideration. It is interesting to observe that nearly all the rationalist schools, which generally reject or distort the supernatural mysteries of Christianity, followed a like procedure in their rationalistic conception and distortion of original sin and the Incarnation. We find the first and most revealing example in Nestorius and his school. In the spirit of Theodore of Mopsuestia and Pelagius, he represented the first man in the state of pure nature, without assigning to him any supernatural principle of divine life. Consequently he could not admit a real hereditary guilt that would be transmitted from Adam to his posterity as true sinfulness. Sin could not involve a true death of the soul, an extinction of a supernatural principle of life (grace), either in Adam or in his descendants. Sin could have no other result than a darkening of the intellect, particularly with regard to knowledge of God, and in connection with it a weakening and stifling of moral life which, as was expressly pointed out, entailed a certain lethargy of the spiritual sense and so might be compared with death, or even be called the death of the soul. According to Theodore of Mopsuestia, not even bodily death was properly a consequence of sin. Nestorius, however, at any rate in his letter to Pope Celestine, ascribed death to a *debitum poenale* with which nature was encumbered. All in all, there was no evil in man except for a certain infirmity and frailty of nature.[8]

To cure this disease or at least to render it innocuous, Nestorius required only a physician, but no Giver of life equipped with divine power. He required only a man, who would be endowed by God with extraordinary wisdom and virtue, in order by his doctrine, his example, and his prayer to recommend himself to mankind as God's envoy, and also in some degree to act as mediator between God and man. What need was there of a God-man, of a hypostatic union of a human nature with a divine person, if a man surrounded by divine prestige and luster, if a moral union of a man with God, sufficed? Is not the connection clear between this lowly, erroneous view of the Savior's office or function, and the disfigurement of His august, divine-human character?

This relationship did not escape St. Cyril of Alexandria, the main adversary of Nestorius. Hence, to safeguard and inculcate the

---

[8] Cf. J. Garnier, S.J. (ed.), *Opera Marii Mercatoris*, Appendix ad part. II, diss. 2, sect. 3 (contained in Migne, *PL*, Vol. XLVIII).

exalted doctrine of the true Incarnation, he seeks to bring out its sublime implications.[4] To him the Savior is not a mere physician, He is the dispenser of divine life, the mediator who negotiates a supernatural union between man and God, the source whence the Holy Spirit, with the entire fullness of His divine gifts, is diffused over the human race, the foundation of our adoption and rebirth as God's children, the victim by whose death sin is most perfectly taken away not only in its natural, but also in its supernatural effects, and so on. Occupying such a position, the Savior must inevitably be recognized as truly divine and truly human; He appears in all His greatness. Hence the Savior's healing influence upon nature is not misunderstood. He who can do the greater can also do the lesser. But the very influence which Christ exercises upon nature is regarded by Cyril in a way that reveals the Savior's divine power. The Savior does not, indeed, give integrity back to us; as long as we are in this life, He leaves us in the corruptibility of our nature, merely paralyzing its noxious influence upon the soul. But by the power of His Spirit He will one day rescue us, God's children, from all decay, and will elevate us again to an immortal, glorious life, in which corruptibility will be swallowed up by incorruptibility; to do this, He too must possess a truly divine power and must be a divine person. Later we shall return to this thought, which St. Cyril shares with many other Fathers.

54. The True Motivation for the Incarnation Found in the Supernatural Sphere

If we gather together the various points that have been established, we perceive that, for the perfecting or restoration of the natural order as such, no good is discovered that would be sufficiently important and estimable to motivate the Incarnation and make it appear justified. Still less is any end indicated that could not be attained except through the Incarnation.

Accordingly the idea of the Incarnation immeasurably transcends the whole sphere of natural reason and the natural order, so much so that the latter can no more provide a sufficient motivation for its

---

[4] He does so especially in his commentary on St. John, in which he embodies his vast theological erudition. In the course of this section of our book we shall have occasion to quote some of the more striking passages.

realization than it can furnish an adequate comparison to illustrate its character. The nature of the Incarnation, as an absolutely supernatural work of God, is and remains inconceivable in every respect. Likewise its realization is both a priori and a posteriori indemonstrable with regard to its real and logical motivation. Hence it is a mystery of faith in the fullest sense of the word.

Nevertheless reason rightly inquires into the motivation and significance of this supernatural work. It cannot rest content with a simple acceptance by faith of the fact and its import. It wishes to account for the fact and its import. That it does not find an explanation within its own province, should not at all appear strange to it. Indeed, strict science demands that the questing intellect betake itself to the region to which the object which is to be accounted for belongs.

Accordingly we should follow the example of St. Cyril and seek the reasons for the Incarnation in the domain of the supernatural, in motives which are themselves mysteries for the unaided intellect. If the motives enabling us to perceive the appropriateness or necessity of the Incarnation are likewise mysteries, it loses nothing of its mysterious character by virtue of its connection with them, although an understanding of this connection will shed a brilliant light over its nature and significance.

The mystery which thus confronts us as calling forth the Incarnation is exhibited in Scripture, the Fathers, and the theologians as consisting primarily in original sin.

If we represent original sin to be something pertaining to the order of nature, then according to the doctrine previously established we can no more conceive it to be a true original sin than we can envisage its counterpart, the redemption, as a true incarnation of the Logos. But if we regard it as it really is, as a supernatural mystery, as a common guilt of the race with respect to the privation of supernatural original justice, that is, of the sanctity and integrity which were the initial stage leading to the divine glorification of man in soul and body, then redemption must consist in the extinction of this common guilt and in the re-establishment of the supernatural sanctification and glorification of the race. In this case we also find place for the divine-human dignity and majesty of the Redeemer.

But even so, an adequate motivation or a true necessity for the Incarnation is not an inevitable consequence. Even in this case

God is not obliged to exact adequate satisfaction for the sin. He could remit the sin upon the mere intercession of the Redeemer. And as concerns restoration to the supernatural state, God could constitute the new Adam, as He did the first Adam, a mere point of departure for the conferring of supernatural grace, in such a way that the new Adam, as God's legate, could offer grace to men in the name of God, while men could attach themselves to Him by faith in His word in order to become sharers in the same grace with Him.

But on this supposition the restoration of the race would not properly have its basis in the race itself; the race would not be elevated by itself, as it had fallen by itself. If the race is to be raised by itself, it must do more than obtain release from the debt contracted by its original head through the intercession of its new head, it must pay the debt. It must not only have the grace which was lost in the old Adam restored to it, but must merit this grace and acquire a new title thereto through its new head. In the concrete this can take place only if the new head of the race is a person of infinite dignity, so that He can pay an infinite debt and purchase a good of infinite worth.

Evidently under such circumstances God pursues immensely higher ends by means of the Incarnation than a simple restoration of the supernatural order in the human race. By the Incarnation He elevates the race to an immensely higher plane than that on which it stood prior to its sin. Grace no longer flows into the race merely from without; the race receives a right to it, and nurtures its principle within itself. By reason of its union with its new head it receives an infinite dignity, which enables it to discharge its debt to God in full, and also to offer Him an infinite glorification.

Only in the realization of these truths does the mystery of the Incarnation appear in all its grandeur, in its full sublimity, which is not in the remotest degree perceptible by reason. The God-man is not merely a supplement, a substitute for the first Adam, with the function of being for us what Adam should have been by nature or grace but was not, of supplying for the deficiency caused by Adam. He is a complement to the first Adam, preordained by God in His mysterious decrees and made ready from all eternity, as one who should be and do infinitely more for the race than the first Adam, whether by nature or by grace, could be or do even before his sin.[5] To be sure, He was also a supplement to Adam, because He was to repair the havoc wrought by Adam in himself and the race, and to supply for the deficiency that thus arose. But this function is absorbed in His higher, more comprehensive function as complement. Since the God-man can and should be and effect immensely more for us, He can and should make good what Adam lost, and supply for the deficiency brought about by Adam's fall.

If we wish to appreciate the mystery in its proper and highest meaning, we should not begin with a consideration of purposes that lie outside it, such as would point to it as something required by creatures. There is no absolute need in the created world, not even in the order of grace, to say nothing of the order of nature, which could not be provided for by God without the Incarnation. Only if God has decided to employ no other means for the satisfaction of existing needs, if He directs creatures exclusively to the Incarnation for this purpose, is the need in question referred to the Incarnation. In that case the Incarnation takes care of the need not merely sufficiently, but superabundantly. Providence has actually ordained matters thus; in actual fact, both in the order of nature and in the order of grace, we are referred to the God-man for the alleviation of our wants. Apart from Him we really cannot find complete deliverance. But, from the fact that God directs us to the Incarnation in this matter, we cannot conclude that the Incarnation is primarily motivated and accounted for by our distress. The truth is rather that God, in order more perfectly to attain the higher objectives He purposes in the Incarnation, has referred us to it with all our deeply felt wants that we might bind ourselves more closely and lovingly to the God-man, and so by our union with Him do our part to bring to fruition the wonderful plan that God wished to realize through the Incarnation.

[5] This is beautifully expressed in the exordium to the dogmatic bull on the Immaculate Conception: "God, the Ineffable . . . foreseeing from all eternity the tragic ruin of the whole human race that would be brought about by Adam's transgression, and decreeing in the mystery hidden from the world to complete the first work of His goodness by a still more hidden mystery, through the Incarnation of the Word, so that . . . what had fallen in the first Adam might be more blessedly raised up in the second Adam. . . ." (Bulla *Ineffabilis Deus* of December 8, 1854; *Col. Lac.*, VI, 836.)

Therefore in order to form a true notion of the motivation or necessity of the Incarnation, and in order to grasp its ruling and determining idea, we must mount above the natural order of things, and even above the order of grace as considered in itself, and think of the Incarnation not as a factor in another order, conceivable apart from it, but as the basis of its own proper order, of a special and altogether sublime order of things, in which the orders of nature and of grace are absorbed. We must soar up to the heights of the immeasurable power, wisdom, and love of God, which in an extraordinary, extravagant manner, such as no creature can surmise and apprehend, are revealed in this work and lay open the uttermost depths of the divinity, in order to submerge creatures in it and to flood the world with its illimitable riches.

Only from this summit, which we scale in faith, may an opinion of this mystery be formed and an account of it be given. To grasp its underlying idea, to perceive the plans that God could have in this mystery, and to know how the mystery is worthy of these designs, and how the designs are worthy of the mystery, we need merely fasten our gaze upon its import as revelation lays it before us. This approach is to be preferred to every other, because thus we do not begin by limiting our horizon, but reserve room for setting forth the entire fullness of the doctrine contained in the mystery. A clear knowledge of all that is effected by the Incarnation and of the entire divine economy based on it, is not less interesting and necessary than a perception of the reasons that motivate the Incarnation itself. The objectives which the Incarnation is intended to achieve are most impressively revealed to us by a general survey of the whole divine economy which rests upon it, and which is not conceivable without it.

CHAPTER XIV

The God-man in His Relations with the Trinity, the Human Race, and the World

••

55. RELATIONS OF THE GOD-MAN WITH THE TRINITY

TO unfold the true, mysterious significance of the Incarnation, let us first contemplate the God-man as He is in Himself, then in His function with regard to creatures, especially the human race. In both respects we shall best succeed in keeping the exceeding sublimity of the mystery clearly in mind if we continue, as before, to contrast the God-man with the first Adam.

1. What was the purport of the first Adam's supernatural endowment? It meant that God willed to attain the two objectives which He intends in all His external works (the communication of His goodness outside of Himself and the extrinsic glorification of Himself), in a supernatural manner, and hence in a way incomparably more perfect than could be realized through the nature of man. If this endowment is truly supernatural and mysterious, it must be a manifestation of a supernatural, mysterious love of God for man, and an organ of a supernatural, mysterious glorification of God. It means, further, that God wills to be an adoptive Father to man, and as such wishes to be honored and glorified by man as by His adopted child. It means that God, not content with His natural relations to creatures and with those of creatures to Himself, wills to establish a far more intimate and tender relationship, from which a higher beatitude should arise for His creatures, and a wholly new glorification for Himself. And since all creation, both spiritual and corporal, is represented in man, God's supernatural, mysterious cosmic plan is centered in man, not in the angels.

But great and mysterious as the communicative love and the

glorification of God appear in man, His adopted child, this communicative love is not infinite, any more than the glorification of God is. We have here only a feeble imitation of the interior communication that takes place in God, and a faint reflection of the internal glory of God. But God willed that the interior communication of His nature and essence should be projected and continued outside of Himself in all its infinity. He willed that a bearer of created nature, and in particular of human nature, which is the epitome of all others, should also be the bearer of His own divine nature and essence. Since this could be done in no other way than that the Son, who had received the divine nature from Him, should assume a human nature, He willed that a bearer of the divine nature should become also a bearer of human nature. Thus God extended to a man the relationship of natural fatherhood in which He stands to the Son of His bosom, in that He begot His Son not only in the interior of His bosom, but also in the outer world, in a created, human nature. He communicated Himself outwardly in so high a degree, in so mysterious a manner, that even He could behold His natural image in a man, and all creatures had to exhibit divine honor and adoration to this man.

Moreover, since the external glorification of God mounts in proportion to the communication of Himself to the outer world, God attained an infinite glorification of Himself in this infinite communication. Mere creatures, being finite in nature, can honor God only in a finite way; creatures endowed with grace honor God far more perfectly with the homage of adopted children. But only the Son, identical in nature with the Father, is able to honor and glorify God in His entire greatness. He alone, as the Father's essential Word, can express the entire majesty of the Father; He alone, as the Father's substantial image, can manifest the Father; and He alone can return the Father's infinite love with equal love. So if God is to be infinitely glorified from without, this inner Word must step forth into the created universe, and this image must impress itself substantially upon a created nature and outwardly manifest both its own infinite greatness and that of its original; in a word, the natural Son of God must honor and adore His Father in a created nature. And if all created nature, spiritual as well as corporal, was to take part in this infinite homage and glorification, the Son of God, as the instrument of all, had to assume not the purely spiritual nature of the angels, but a human nature, in which the spiritual and the corporal are joined.

The interrelationship between the mystery of the Incarnation and the mystery of the Trinity is obviously very close. The former has its explanation and its source in the latter, while the latter has its external prolongation and its highest meaning for the outer world in the former.

Holy Scripture gives expression to both mysteries when it describes the Incarnation as a mission of the Son. If a divine person enters the world as one who is sent, His procession from another person is thereby presupposed, and this procession is externally continued by the entrance into the world of the person in question. The internal production which takes place in God, whereby He communicates and glorifies Himself within the Trinity in an infinite manner, becomes an external production in the sending of the produced person, so that the internal, infinite communication and self-glorification are projected into the outer world.

If there were no interior, infinite communication and glorification in God Himself, the substructure for the incarnation of a divine person would be lacking, not merely because there would then be only one person in God, but chiefly because there would be no basis, no point of departure for the idea of an infinite communication and glorification of God within Himself. There would be no organism from which the idea of the Incarnation could be derived, into which it could be fitted.

According to the teaching of revelation, however, an infinite communication and self-glorification actually does take place in God; and on this supposition nothing appears more appropriate or more natural than that the same situation should obtain, and the same communication and glorification should be achieved, also in the external works of God. Of course God is perfectly free thus to crown His external works, and to communicate Himself to the outer world in so marvelous a manner. But if God's entire greatness is to shine forth outwardly, the Incarnation appears not as an extraordinary event, but as the flower springing from a root buried in the Trinitarian process, as the unfolding of a kernel contained therein, as the surging forth of a boundless stream that wells up in the Trinitarian production.

2. For the realization of this idea of the external prolongation of

the Trinitarian process, it was not necessary for both of the proceeding persons, the Son and the Holy Spirit, to be sent forth into the outer world by hypostatic union with a created nature. It was sufficient, indeed it was appropriate and altogether according to the nature of things, that only one of the two proceeding persons should assume a created nature, and that this should be the Son.

a) There are two productions in God, and of these each has its own exclusive product. As has been shown, however, these two productions are not parallel: the second has its basis in the first, and the first virtually includes the second. The Son has the first, the initial procession from the Father, procession by generation, by the impress of the Father's image. The procession of the Holy Spirit is possible only through the procession of the Son; it is a secondary procession, serving for the fulfillment of the first, so as to join to the Father the Son who proceeds from the Father.

Therefore if the Son enters the outer world, the primary process in the Trinity is thereby continued externally; the second process also, which depends on the first and is based on it, is virtually continued in the primary process. For inasmuch as the person of the Son descends into a created nature, He brings with Him into this created nature the Holy Spirit who proceeds from Him; consequently the Holy Spirit is sent in the Son and through the Son. But on the supposition of an incarnation of the Holy Spirit, the latter alone would be sent, because He would bring with Him the Son not as a person proceeding from Him, but only as the person from whom He himself proceeds, as in actual fact the Father, who is not sent in any sense, descends into the humanity along with the Son. But if the Holy Spirit should assume a created nature alongside the Son, the external juxtaposition of the two persons would obscure their interior, harmonious relationship, and so the intrinsic character of the Trinitarian process would not be appreciated in all its unity by those who view it from without.[1]

---

[1] The Holy Spirit is regarded, but only by appropriation, as the cause of the hypostatic union, which is a work of love. The substantial Word of God makes His appearance in a way that recalls the outward expression of our intelligible word. Our external word is formed through the agency of the breath streaming from the heart, and is propelled by love, which induces us to communicate our thoughts outwardly. But when our inner word, our thought, begets true and living love in us, our external word, too, bears this love within it, and breathes forth love. The pulsating of the Holy Spirit, by

The external prolongation of the Trinitarian process in the person of the Son conforms especially well to its double basic significance, repeatedly mentioned above: the communication of the divine nature, and the resulting infinite glorification of God.

b) The first and most natural communication of nature is that from father to son. Accordingly if God wills to extend the interior communication of His essence into the outer world, this must take place in the person of the Son, who is the rightful heir of the Father by virtue of His personal position, and who is initially called to the copossession of the Father's nature, whereas the Holy Spirit enters into possession of the divine nature only as the bond of union between the Father and the Son. Owing to His double function, the Son partakes both of the Father, whose heir He is, and of the Holy Spirit, to whom He gives of His own. Hence the divine nature is communicated to the outer world most perfectly in Him. Furthermore, as heir of the divine nature He is pre-eminently called, in the name of His Father and on behalf of the Holy Spirit, to take possession of the entire created world as the head and king of all creatures and, as will be shown later, to pour out the riches of the divine nature upon the creatures to whom He has united Himself through the Incarnation.

c) Again, the Son is precisely the person whose incarnation most fittingly gives outward expression to God's interior glorification of Himself. As the Word and image of the Father, He is quite literally the expression and reflection of the Father's glory. At the same time the glory of the Holy Spirit is expressed and represented in this infinite Word, because it streams forth and issues from Him. Hence when the Son becomes man, God the Father in a true sense formulates the full expression of His glory in the humanity assumed by Him; the personal Word of God personally appears in the outer world and is externally uttered forth. The divine Word takes shape and is manifested in an incomparably more real and substantial fashion than our thought shapes and reveals itself in audible sounds. Therefore the incarnation of the Son most magnificently and impressively extends and reveals to the outer world God's glorification of Himself in the Trinity.[2]

---

which the incarnation of the Logos is effected, and His pulsating within the incarnate Logos, are interconnected in a similar manner.

[2] The fact that of the three persons in the Trinity it is precisely the Son

Such is the exalted, mysterious significance that we apprehend in the Incarnation at the very first glance, when we contemplate its connection with the greatest of all mysteries, the mystery of the Trinity. The two mysteries mutually illuminate and emphasize each other. The Trinity appears greater and more glorious the greater is the mystery that springs from it; and the Incarnation shines forth in more brilliant light the more we penetrate into the depths of the abyss into which its roots are sunk.

3. As the infinite communication and self-glorification of God, which consist in the Trinitarian productions, are best prolonged in the mission of the Second Person, so it pertains to the perfection of this prolongation that the Son of God take to Himself a human nature rather than any other.

a) That God's communication of Himself to the outer world may be realized to the full, all created nature must be represented and have a share in it. Created nature is divided into two opposing categories, into spiritual and material nature. In man both elements enter into a union of nature and personality. Man is the microcosm, the world in miniature; his nature is the epitome of the two opposites, the focus in which they are brought together.

Therefore if the mission of the Son was to be the prolongation of the eternal production which takes place in God, or, more accurately, the introduction of it into His creation, it had to be directed to human nature as the center of God's external works. This is human nature which, regarded from below, has its roots in the material world, but regarded from above projects into the spirit world and assumes in the universe a double position analogous to that of the Son of God Himself in the divinity, inasmuch as He proceeds from the Father and is the principle of the Holy Spirit. By being directed to human nature, the mission of the Son also reaches the two natures that are related and united in human nature according to its diverse elements.

If the Son's mission were directed solely to a purely spiritual nature, the communication of the divine nature would be confined

---

who becomes incarnate, is closely connected with other aspects of the Incarnation, which we shall discuss later. The Fathers and theologians have amassed a host of other reasons which are not to be contemned, but which are more remote and are not so decisive. Cf. Thomassinus, *Theol. dogm. de Incarn. Verbi*, lib. II, cc. 1 et 2.

to the latter and would not be extended to material nature. But by His union with humanity the Son of God admits both spiritual and material nature to participation in His divinity; although He thus passes over the angels, He does not omit them, since their nature is in a sense comprised in the spiritual element of human nature.

b) Likewise the introduction of God's infinite glory into the world is brought about most perfectly and universally by the incarnation of the Word. For in the incarnation the Word is not merely conveyed externally in the usual way, but is literally equipped with a body, so that the infinite anthem ringing forth in Him is both intellectually and sensibly perceptible, and the image of the Father shining forth in Him is rendered visible to the spiritual and also to the material eye. Moreover, by His assumption of a human nature, the whole of created nature represented in it, the spiritual as well as the material, is gathered up into the glorification which He who bears it, the eternal Word, offers to His Father.

c) Along with its central position human nature has this further advantage over purely spiritual nature, that all its individuals, owing to their specific unity, constitute a single great body, an immense whole. This is the reason why all its individuals can assemble in a unique association under a single head. This is the reason, too, why the God-man, by entering into human nature, can closely unite the whole race in Himself to form His mystical body, and so can most perfectly and universally carry out the idea of His mission in this body as in His own. This objective is attained by the fact that the communication of the divine nature is extended to the entire body as to one solidary whole, and this body in turn is gathered up in its totality into the infinite oblation of the Son of God.

4. This thought carries us over to a consideration of the significance which pertains to the God-man in His relation to the universe.

For in all that has been hitherto said, we have not yet exhausted the vast significance of the Incarnation, or rather of the Incarnation and the Trinity regarded in their interrelationship. We have been considering the Incarnation only as the culmination of a special process. But it is at the same time the root from which an immense, mysterious tree grows, the center round which revolves a new, wonderful order embracing the whole world. The God-man, in whom are focused the rays of the Trinitarian process in its external unfolding, necessarily becomes a sun for the entire world, a sun which draws all creatures to itself in order to shed over them all the beams of the divine goodness and glory that are concentrated in itself, in order to confer the riches of the Trinitarian communications upon the whole world, and thereby also to admit the world to participation in the Trinitarian unity. The God-man is associated with all creatures into whose society He has entered, and must on His part catch up all creatures into the mystery of the divine Trinity and Triunity.

Accordingly we have next to consider the God-man in His relation to creatures, and in the significance which pertains to Him conformably to this relation.

56. THE MYSTERIOUS POSITION OCCUPIED BY THE GOD-MAN WITH REFERENCE TO THE HUMAN RACE

The God-man is the head of all creation, and of the human race in particular. With these words is expressed the entire mystery of His place in the world, a whole series of the most lofty and sublime mysteries. He is the head of the human race in an exalted sense that can be predicated of the God-man alone. Let us endeavor to gain at least a somewhat more adequate notion of the greatness of this mystery.

1. The first and most necessary condition for applying the term "head" to anything, is that it be a member, and indeed the most eminent member of a whole.

All creatures together constitute a great whole, to which the God-man belongs by virtue of His created nature, and in which He is the noblest and most distinguished member. For this reason He is called the first-born of all creatures and the head of the heavenly powers, which in itself makes Him immensely superior to Adam, who is merely the head of the human race. In a narrower and stricter sense, however, He is, like Adam, the head of the human race, but in a much more eminent way.

The human race forms a whole in a fuller sense than the totality of all creatures does. This it does because all its individuals possess one and the same nature in common, but especially because this one nature passes to all from one principle, the possession of it being transmitted from one ancestor to all the rest. Thus they are not only quite similar to one another on account of the unity of their nature; they are not only one species, but are one race. They are related to one another like the branches of a giant tree: since all the branches spring from one root, they form a single whole, a single vast body, which is made up of really interdependent parts, because of their connection with the root.

The first man, from whom human nature is propagated, is obviously the first member of the body, the principal member in the proper sense, because the rest depend on him as their root, and are brought into unity in him and through him. He is the natural head of the race precisely because he is the root principle of the entire nature.

The God-man cannot be the head of the race in this sense; the propagation of human nature does not have its origin in Him. Rather He Himself takes His nature from the already established race, and is Himself a fruit of the race, not a natural, but a supernatural fruit, which springs from the race through a miracle wrought by the Holy Spirit. He does not found the race in its natural unity; it is already there, and His existence presupposes it. For as the supernatural in general presupposes the natural, so the supernatural head of the race supposes the existence of a natural head as a preliminary condition. If men did not already constitute a whole on the basis of nature, and if the God-man merely appeared on the scene like one of them without entering into the one body as a member, He could not become their head in the full sense of the word. That the God-man may become such, men must form a truly interconnected race, a single great body by descent from a single natural ancestor, and hence must already be joined in unity under one natural head.

2. By what means, then, and in what manner does Christ, the God-man, become head of the race if He is not, like Adam, its principle? We could state simply: because He is by far the noblest, the most distinguished, and the worthiest member of the race. But if this were all, the God-man would seem to be the crown, the noblest, fairest flowering of the race, rather than its head. The head, in the proper sense of the word, is not only the summit, the most prominent member of the body, but is further what the root is to the plant, what the vine is to the branch. The head is that by which the whole body is held together, that to which the body is attached. It is that which acquires, possesses, and rules the whole body. Lastly it is that in which the entire body is, so to speak, summed up. Adam occupied

this position because the whole race proceeded from him and, in proceeding from him, remained united to him. The God-man occupies a like position for the reason that, although the race did not proceed from Him, He took it to Himself by His entrance into it, united it to Himself, and made it His own. Adam was the head of the race because he was the cause of its natural unity and to the extent that he was so. The Son of God, exerting the infinite attractive force of His divine person, took to Himself the race thus unified and made it His own throughout its entire compass. This He did by making His own and assuming to His person a member of the race that is ontologically connected with all the other members. Thereby He becomes the new head of the whole race, its natural head included.

This is a tremendous, an astounding mystery. It is as great a mystery as the Incarnation itself, upon which it is based and from which it issues. The union into which we enter with Christ as our head, and the nature of our dependence on Him, are so extraordinary that we could not enter into such a relationship with any other than the God-man. No mere human being, not even Adam himself, can so tower over the whole race that by virtue of his elevated position he could draw all the members of the race to himself, make them his own, and subject them to himself. Adam stands wholly and entirely within the race; and although he stands at its beginning, he is absorbed in the race. Christ stands absolutely above the race, because His divine person is not the parent, but the Creator of the race. The personality of Adam is limited by his possession of human nature; the personality of Christ is independent of it. Christ's person makes a human nature His own in order to rule it, to embody it in His own personality. Therefore, by taking complete possession of a member of the race, He can draw the entire race to Himself, incorporate it in Himself, and rule it. In this connection the Fathers express a beautiful thought when they say that, by incorporating a human nature in Himself and making Himself its hypostasis, bearer, and proprietor, God has in a wider sense incorporated the whole race in Himself and has made Himself its hypostasis, bearer, and proprietor. They explain that God does this, not as if He had united all the members of the human race to Himself in the way that He has taken to Himself that member in which He became flesh; the reason is rather that because of the intimate, solidary union of this one member with all the rest, He has made all the other members His own through this one and in this one.[8]

The whole human race becomes the body of the Son of God when one of its members is embodied in the Son of God. Indeed, it becomes one body with Christ in a far higher and fuller sense than it does with Adam. This is so because it belongs to Christ more than

---

[8] St. Hilary of Poitiers, *In Psalmum 51*, nos. 16 f. (*PL*, IX, 317 f.; *CSEL*, XXII, 108 f.): "The Son of God assumed the nature of flesh common to all; and having thus become the true vine, He contains within Himself the entire race of its offspring." And a little further on: "It is manifest to all that they share in the body and kingdom of God; for the Word was made flesh and dwelt among us, that is, He took to Himself the nature of the whole human race." In the *De Trinitate*, lib. II, no. 25 (*PL*, X, 67), he says: "He by whom man was made had no need to become man; but we had need that God be made flesh and dwell among us, that is, that He dwell within the flesh of all by assuming the flesh of one."

St. Leo the Great (*Sermo 10 de Nativ.*, c.3; *PL*, LIV, 231) observes: "The Word was made flesh and dwelt among us: among us, certainly, whom the divinity of the Word joined to Himself; we are His flesh, that was taken from the womb of the Virgin. If this were not really our flesh, that is, human flesh, the Word made flesh could not be said to dwell in us. But He did dwell in us, for He made His own the nature of our body." In *Serm. 14 de passione Domini* (*Sermo 12*, c.3; *PL*, LIV, 355) he says: "There is no doubt that human nature was assumed by the Son of God in so intimate a union that one and the same Christ is not only in that man who is the first-born of every creature, but also in all the saints."

The words of the Lord, "That they all may be one, as Thou in Me, and I in Thee," are explained as follows by St. Athanasius, *Or. III contra Arianos*, nos. 22 f. (*PG*, XXVI, 372; the latter part is not a literal rendering): "That, borne as it were by Me, they may all be one body and one spirit, and may combine to form a perfect man . . . so that, made divine, they may be one in Us." Cf. St. Cyril of Alexandria, *In Ioan.*, lib. V, c.2 (*PG*, LXXIII, 749-93), and often elsewhere.

In other passages the Fathers, following the Apostle's lead, compare the union between Christ and the race with the union between bridegroom and bride, which also is a union in the body. Thus St. Fulgentius, *Ad Thrasam.*, lib. I, c.10 (*PL*, LXV, 234), says: "Gathering up the first fruits of nature, the Lord received the body of all the faithful in His body, and the souls of all the faithful in one soul, through the unity of nature and the grace of justification. Thereby He took to Himself the whole Church in a marriage of perpetual incorruptibility." And St. Augustine states, *In epist. Ioannis*, tract. I, no. 2 (*PL*, XXXV, 1979): "The nuptial chamber of the bridegroom was the womb of the Virgin, for in that virginal womb were the bridegroom and the bride, namely, the Word and flesh. . . . Therefore now they are not two, but one flesh. . . . To that flesh is joined the Church, and thus arises the whole Christ, head and body."

it belongs to Adam, because Adam himself is taken up into Christ, and as the natural head of the race belongs to Christ along with all its members, and so must acknowledge Christ as his own supreme head. Further, Adam carried the race in himself only so long as it had not yet proceeded from him, and hence is merely the point of departure, not the real bearer of the race as expanded in its individuals; Christ, on the contrary, takes the race to Himself precisely as it unfolds in each member.

Therefore the whole human race is related to the person of the Son in a manner analogous to the way in which the humanity assumed by Him is related to Him. Christ's humanity is usually called the flesh or body of the Word, to signalize it as the Son of God's own body. Apart from other reasons, this designation is chosen mostly because it clearly expresses the fact that this humanity belongs to a superior person; but its racial unity with the rest of men is also brought out. The race itself is styled "all flesh," to emphasize its racial character. The whole race is a solidary mass; if one of its parts enters into union with the person of the Word, the race as a whole is taken up into Him. This principal part is united to the Word in a way that is unique, in absolute unity of person; it is absolutely and *per se* the flesh and body of God's Son. Since it is the first fruit of the mass, it is the favored, privileged part; but being the first fruit, it does not break off its continuity with the race. In it and through it the whole mass is taken up by the person of the Word.[4] The entire race likewise becomes the body and flesh of the Word, not in a purely moral sense, but as truly and really as the union of the race with the humanity of Christ, and the union of this humanity with the divine person, are true and real.

Consequently the whole race truly belongs to the person of Christ as His body, although not in so close a relationship that the independence and personality of the other members are completely absorbed in the person of the Word, as is the case with the first fruit of the race. The other members keep their personal autonomy. But since the racial unity persists in spite of this personal autonomy and

---

[4] "From the whole of human nature, to which was joined divinity, arose, as the first fruit of the common mass, the man who is in Christ, by whom all mankind was united to divinity." St. Gregory of Nyssa, *Or. de verbis 1 Cor. 15:28* (PG, XLIV, 1313).

along with it, and since this autonomy is not isolated or completely blocked off, the persons pertaining to the race can be taken up in a higher person who mysteriously dominates the whole race, can be assimilated to the personality proper to this higher person, can be embraced and pervaded by Him. Thus they belong to Him more than to themselves, and in a larger sense form one person with Him, somewhat as Christ's own humanity, which is entirely stripped of its autonomy, forms one person with the Son.

The race is usually styled the mystical body of Christ, and Christ's own humanity is known as the real body of Christ, just as the union of the race with Christ is termed a mystical union, and that of His own body with His divine person is called a real union. This mode of designation is undoubtedly justified; but it is employed for want of better expressions, and must be carefully explained and circumscribed, if no misunderstanding is to result.

As the distinction stands, the adjectives "mystical" and "real" must be taken as opposites that mutually exclude each other. If such were actually the case, the union of Christ's humanity with His divine person would not be mystical, that is, mysterious and supernatural, and Christ's body would not be the body of God's Son in a mystical and mysterious manner. But how is this conceivable, since there is no more sublime, more wonderful, more mysterious union and unity than that between the Son of God and His humanity? And is it not true that the mystical character of the union of the race with Christ is based precisely upon the mystery of the hypostatic union? Conversely, too, the union of the race with Christ is real and objective, and is based on the real, internal unity of the race; further, it participates not only in the mysterious character, but also in the reality of the hypostatic union, without of course attaining to the full perfection of the latter.

That the full hypostatic union is immensely more real, firmer, and closer than the union of the race with Christ, is the truth pointed out by the distinction just enunciated and the fact that has given rise to it. The word "mystical," as occurring in this pair of opposites, is not employed in its full meaning, to indicate something mysterious, but rather in a figurative, metaphorical sense, as contrasted with the literal, concrete sense. When I refer to the whole race as the body of Christ, I am actually, to some extent, using figurative language. This figure, however, does not rest on a simple resemblance, but on a profound, objective reality, which harbors a great mystery.

3. In the view of Sacred Scripture the union of the human race with the Son of God is so intimate that, as regards the predicates applied to it, the race is represented as being one person with Him. Even in the Old Testament the people of Israel was called God's son on account of its close connection with Christ, not as a mere type of Him, but because it was His own people by kin and formed one person with Him.[5] The Apostle says still more clearly that Christ has as many members in Himself, that is, in the race, as a physical body has. As the Son of God is Christ because He anoints and pervades His own humanity, so too, according to the Apostle, He is Christ as the Son of God who takes the entire race to Himself and consecrates it with the ointment of His divinity.[6]

And Sacred Scripture does not merely allude to this kind of union in passing, but carries it through consistently in a great variety of ways.

We are to keep our own persons and our own bodies holy and unsullied, since they are members of Christ, since they belong to Christ and are sanctified by the nobility of His person.[7] A profanation of our body is henceforth not only a profanation of our own, but of Christ's person.[8] And in general it is not only we who suffer, but Christ suffers in us, with sufferings that resemble those He sustained in His own humanity.[9]

On the other hand, Christ's lot, His sufferings and activities, are ours, on account of our union with Him. Christ dies and is buried: we die in Him and are buried too.[10] He rises from the dead and ascends to heaven: we rise from the dead in Him and mount up to heaven with Him. God, says the Apostle, "hath quickened us together in Christ (by whose grace you are saved), and hath raised us up together, and hath made us sit together in the heavenly places."[11] St. Chrysostom remarks on this passage that, if Christ

[5] Osee 11:1, in conjunction with Matt. 2:15.
[6] Cf. I Cor., the whole of chapter 12.
[7] Cf. I Cor. 6:15.
[8] *Ibid.*
[9] Col. 1:24, according to the best exegesis.
[10] Rom. 6:4, 6.
[11] Eph. 2:5 f.

our head is raised from the dead, we, too, arose at the same time; and if the head is seated, the body, too, is seated. Further, if Christ is obedient to His Father, we, too, obey the Father in Him; if He renders satisfaction to the Father, we also give satisfaction to the Father in Him, just as in the first Adam we offended Him and ate the fruit of the forbidden tree.[12]

Moreover, as Christ, our head, suffers in us, and we suffer and act in Him who is our head, so Christ must act and live in us. Not all our actions, however, are on that account to be ascribed to Christ as our head, just as not everything that the members of our body effect can be ascribed to the head or to the whole man. To the head and to the whole man pertain only those acts that proceed from the head and the whole man. Christ, too, can act and live in us only with regard to those acts which proceed from Him, and which are elicited and carried out by the power flowing from Him as the head, by His own Spirit. Such are the acts about which the Apostle's statement is verified, that it is no longer he that lives, but Christ lives in him.[13] Even with reference to Christ's own humanity, we can say that the Son of God lived and acted in it only so far as the acts performed in it and by it proceeded from His divine Spirit, and hence were performed not only by its natural power, but by the divine power of grace of the predominating person.

Briefly, owing to our incorporation into His divine person and our union with His own humanity as the head of the mystical body, a *communicatio idiomatum* (interchange of properties) takes place between us and Christ similar to that which obtains between His own humanity and the divine person. And this interchange of properties is the best proof of the wonderful, mysterious union existing between the human race and the Son of God, who has entered into its midst.[14]

[12] Rom. 5:19.
[13] Gal. 2:20.
[14] This communication of idioms is referred to by the Greek Fathers countless times in their conflict with the Arians, and is employed in their explanation of those scriptural passages in which something is predicated of Christ that does not apply to Him as the Son of God. It was appealed to in connection with and according to the analogy of that interchange which takes place between the divinity and the humanity; thus with Athanasius in numberless instances, with Gregory of Nazianzus, Cyril, and others. The whole idea of the mystical union of head and body is treated with predilection by St. Augustine, especially in his commentary on the Psalms. We quote one of

4. However, this union of body and person obtaining between Christ and man may most easily be illustrated by that union which the Apostle so vividly proposes as the figure of the union between Christ and the Church, namely, the union between man and woman in matrimony. For here the distinction between the persons is rigorously observed. Nevertheless the union of the persons is so intimate and complete that henceforth they seem merged in one whole. Husband and wife are not merely morally one with each other by reason of their harmony of disposition and mutual love; this moral oneness has a real, physical basis on account of its relation to the oneness of body. Hence, too, their personal oneness is not a mere moral union, as between two friends, but is so real and thoroughgoing that the wife almost yields up her independence in favor of

---

the finest passages, from *Enarr. in Psalm. 62*, no. 2 (*PL*, XXXVI, 748 f.): "This psalm is uttered in the person of our Lord Jesus Christ, both head and members. For that one person, who was born of Mary, and suffered, and was buried, and rose from the dead, and ascended into heaven, and now sits at the right hand of the Father and intercedes for us, is our head. If He is the head, we are the members: His entire Church, which is spread throughout the world, is His body, of which He Himself is the head. Not only the faithful who are now on earth, but also those who preceded us, and those who are to come after us until the end of time, pertain one and all to His body: and of this body He is the head, who has ascended into heaven. We now know the head and the body, He being the head, we the body. When we hear His voice, we ought to hear it as proceeding both from the head and from the body; for whatever He has suffered in the body, we too have suffered, just as whatever we suffer in ourselves, He too suffers. If the head suffers any pain, can the hand say that it does not suffer? Or if the hand suffers, can the head say that it does not suffer? Or if the foot suffers, can the head say that it does not suffer? When one of our members suffers, all the other members hurry to aid the ailing member. Therefore if, when He has suffered, we too have suffered in Him, and if He has already ascended into heaven and sits at the Father's right hand, whatever His Church suffers in the troubles of this world, in temptations, in trials, in tribulations (for thus the Church must be proved, as gold is purified by fire), He suffers. We prove this truth, that we have suffered in Him, from words of the Apostle: 'If, then, you be dead with Christ . . . why do you yet decree as though living in the world?' [Col. 2:20.] And again he says: 'Our old man is crucified with Him, that the body of sin may be destroyed' [Rom. 6:6]. If, then, we have died in Him, we have also risen with Him. For the same Apostle states: 'Therefore if you be risen with Christ, seek the things that are above, where Christ is sitting at the right hand of God' [Col. 3:1]. Accordingly, if we are dead in Him and are risen in Him, and He died in us and rises in us (for He is the unity of the head and the body), rightly we may say that His voice is our voice, and also that our voice is His. Let us, therefore, listen to the psalm, and let us understand that Christ is speaking in it."

her husband, takes over his name, and has him as her natural head and protector, while at the same time she shares in his honors and merits.

Prior to the appearance of Nestorianism, some of the Fathers and ecclesiastical writers, such as Novatian, St. Augustine, and Cassian, spoke also of a marriage of the Logos with His own human nature. The comparison is, in fact, pertinent in a number of points. But since it does not bring out the complete unity of the hypostasis, the later Fathers ceased to employ it in this connection. They do, however, declare that, because of the perfect hypostatic union of a member of the human race with the Logos, the whole of human nature is wedded to Him in a very expressive sense of the word, and has become His bride. The Logos, by assuming flesh from the flesh of the race and by making it His own, has become one flesh with all the other persons of the race. The womb of the Virgin has become the bridal chamber wherein human nature has celebrated its ineffable nuptials with Him, and on account of its first fruit has been accepted by Him as His bride, has become united to Him.[15] That member of the race in which and through which the Logos has wedded the whole of human nature, had necessarily, of course, to be joined to Him in an infinitely closer and firmer union than the other members; it had to be completely taken up into His person; and if the Logos was to become one flesh with the other members, He had Himself to become flesh in this one member.

[15] Cf. Thomassinus, *De Incarnatione*, lib. III, c. 24; St. Augustine, *Serm. 12 de temp.*; *Confess.*, lib. IV, c. 12; Cassian, *De Incarnatione Domini*, lib. V, c. 12; especially St. Gregory the Great, *In Evangelia*, lib. II, hom. 38, no. 3 (PL, LXXVI, 1283): "God the Father prepared the nuptials for God the Son when He united the Son to human nature in the womb of the Virgin, when He wished Him who was God before all ages to become man at a later age of the world. But although such a union ordinarily requires two persons, be it far from our thoughts to suppose that the person of God and our human Redeemer, Jesus Christ, is made up of two persons. We do indeed affirm that He is made up of two natures and exists in two natures; but the belief that He is composed of two persons, we avoid as a heresy. Hence, speaking more plainly and safely, we may say that the Father arranged the marriage of His kingly Son by joining to Him the holy Church through the mystery of the Incarnation." See the last group of quotations in note 3 above; also St. Augustine, *In epist. Ioannis*, tract. II, no. 2 (PL, XXXV, 1990): "The spouse of Christ is the whole Church, whose principle and first fruit is the flesh of Christ: there the bride is joined to the bridegroom in bodily union."

Apart from the fact that this conception of bodily union between the God-man and human beings is quite biblical and patristic, it has the further advantage that it strongly emphasizes the form and the significance of the union of the race with its second head, the heavenly Adam, and also of the union with its first head, the earthly Adam. Stronger and closer ties bind human nature to the new Adam than to its earthly progenitor; for here, too, the injunction holds good: a man shall leave father and mother, and shall cleave to his wife. Mankind belongs to this bridegroom so completely because He is its supreme and sovereign Lord, to whom even its father is subject, and also because, by its nuptials with Him, not only is it to receive back the nobility it lost in its father but, raised above its natural rank and above all that is earthly, even above the vast heaven itself, it is to be introduced into the bosom of His heavenly Father.

However, concerning the meaning of these nuptials and this bodily union, we shall have to speak at greater length presently. We wish merely to remark that so far as the bodily union between God's Son and the human nature wedded to Him resulted immediately from the Incarnation, it is to be thought of primarily along the lines of the union which existed between Adam and Eve inasmuch as Eve was derived from Adam's side, but not according to the analogy of the union effected by their marriage as formally contracted or consummated. The latter kind of union is not established between Christ and us except by baptism and the Eucharist. But just as the derivation of the woman from the man's side served to prefigure and prepare the way for their marital union, and this union had its basis in their destiny for each other, so likewise the assumption of human nature from the midst of the race is the foundation of the formal nuptials of God's Son with the human race by baptism and the Eucharist. It is, so to speak, a virtual marriage, owing to which the Son of God could straightway pour forth His heart's blood in behalf of human nature, as a bride already belonging to Him in reality, in order to make her pure and undefiled, to render her fit for the holy alliance with Him, and so in due time to nourish her with His own flesh and blood.

This observation forestalls, in some degree, an objection that could be alleged against us here. The objection might be worded as follows: it is not the human race as such, but those of its members who have entered into a special union with Christ by faith or baptism, that is, the members of the Church, that form the body of which Christ is the head. Who could deny that men become members of the God-man in the narrower sense only by faith and baptism? Truly, it is only by faith that their oneness with Christ becomes a living union, since it is only by faith that the Spirit of the head begins to function in them, and that they on their side cling to the head and are orientated toward Him. And it is only by baptism that the relation of men with Christ becomes an organic union, a union which is outwardly visible to men as well as inwardly existent; by baptism Christ sets the seal of His proprietorship on them, and thereby confers on them the full possession and enjoyment of the rights and privileges which are theirs as members of His body. But faith and baptism do not establish the simple union of the body with Christ; rather they presuppose its existence. If faith makes this union a living union, some material, lifeless union must already be present as that which is to be vitalized. The Spirit of the head cannot flow into us unless we already pertain to His body in some respect; and on our part we cannot lay hold of Christ our head and clasp Him firmly unless He is already our head in a true sense, and unless we are already joined to Him in some way.

Further, since faith, and indeed complete oneness of life with Christ can be present in us prior to baptism, some sort of bodily union with Christ must precede even baptism. Baptism merely perfects, seals, organizes, completes, and consummates this union; but its foundation had been laid previously. The basis for our common sharing in Christ's goods and graces is His general relationship with the race as such. But our actual admission to the enjoyment of this fellowship has in the New Law been attached by Christ to baptism as its ordinary organ. In the Old Law this fellowship was not in any way attached to baptism, either to actual baptism or to the intention of receiving it; and still Christ was basically the head of the race in the Old Testament as well as in the New.[16]

Hence we have no reason for abandoning our view of the matter; on the contrary, we must unconditionally hold fast to it in its essentials. We shall see how this conception brings out the tremendous and mysterious significance of the Incarnation.

[16] Cf. St. Cyril of Alexandria, *In Ioannem*, lib. VI, ad verba, "Et cognosco oves meas" (John 10:14), pp. 653 f.; *PG*, LXXIII, 1045 f.

57. First Significance of the God-man as Head of the Race: Communication of Divine Nobility; Foundation and Consummation of the Divine Sonship

The position which the God-man, or the Son of God in His humanity, occupies with reference to the human race, is a mystery that excites our wonder. No less so is the significance which attaches to Him by virtue of this position.

In His position as supernatural head of the race, the God-man was able, as is evident, to repair the damage caused by the first head of the race. By his solidary unity with the race, the first Adam burdened it with an incalculable debt which it could not pay. But the new Adam, whose union of solidarity with the race was still greater, so that His own infinitely valuable merits belonged also to the race, could discharge this debt, and assumed the obligation of doing so. Without payment of that debt the race could not recover from God the supernatural justice that had been forfeited. But it could, and was meant to, reacquire this justice by the liquidation of the debt through the good offices of its new head.

Thus the new head was a substitute, a supplement for the old.

But we should have a mean notion of the exalted, supernatural dignity of our new head, if we were to think of Him as merely supplying for a deficiency in the race. The supplying of this deficiency can be no more than a subordinate factor in His mission and significance. The essential characteristic revealed in the assumption of the human race to the person of the Son and its incorporation in Christ, is not one of compensation, but of elevation and enhancement. As head, the God-man raises the whole race up to a height of nobility, life, and activity that is immeasurable and inconceivable; and this height to which He elevates the race enables it to fill up all the gaps and make good all the defects that have ever made their appearance either because of its natural baseness or in consequence of its culpable fall. Liquidation of the debt by payment in full is a natural result of the exalted dignity thus imparted to the race; but the guilt is extinguished in this fashion only for the purpose that that race may be raised untrammeled to the plane which is intended for it by the Incarnation, and may abide there securely.

The significance and the influence which the God-man is to have with regard to the whole race must, in line with what has previously been laid down, be ascertained in accord with the norm of the significance and influence which the divine person has with regard to His own humanity,[17] due allowance, of course, being made for the difference between the two cases. "The Christian is another Christ," said one of the ancient Fathers of the Church. "What man is," St. Cyprian declares, "Christ wished to be, that man in turn might be what Christ is." [18] That is, Christ's divine dignity and power, which anointed His own humanity and constituted Christ by their union with it, must be applied to the whole race in all their grandeur and sublimity, in order to elevate, transfigure, and deify the members by uniting them to the head.

Let us see this more in detail.

1. By the hypostatic union Christ's own humanity was invested with the divine dignity of the Son of God, who assumed it to Himself; and to such an extent, indeed, that even in His human nature the God-man had to be adored by all creatures, and loved by His Father with the same infinite love with which He is loved in His divinity. In consequence of this dignity, that human nature had to be endowed with the sanctity and splendor of the divine nature, so that it might possess an equipment conformable to its infinite dignity.

If, then, the human race, in analogous fashion, likewise becomes the body of Christ, and its members become the members of God's Son, if the divine person of the Son of God bears them in Himself as His own, then, with due proportion, must not the divine dignity of the Son of God flow over to men, since they are His members? Must not God the Father extend to these members the same love as that which He bears for His natural Son, must He not embrace them in His Son with one and the same love, inasmuch as they belong to

---

[17] St. Gregory of Nyssa had drawn up this norm, *Contra Eunomium*, lib. XII (*PG*, XLV, 889 f.): "What took place in the human nature assumed by Christ is a grace granted to all men of faith. For, just as when we see that a body which naturally tends downward is lifted to the heavens through the air, we believe according to the words of the Apostle that we 'shall be taken up . . . in the clouds to meet Christ, into the air' [I Thess. 4:16], so, when we hear that He who is the true God and Father is become the Father and God of the first fruit of our race, we can no longer doubt that He has also become our Father and God, for we have learned that we shall go by the same road," etc.

[18] *De idolorum vanitate*, c. 11; *PL*, IV, 579; *CSEL*, III, I, 28.

Him? [19] Must He not communicate to the Son's mystical members the same divine holiness and splendor with which He adorns the human nature of His Son? Must He not raise them to infinite heights and place them next to His Son on the latter's own throne? [20]

Yes, the divine dignity which falls to man's portion by his incorporation in Christ, gives him a right to deification, that is, to a divine transfiguration of his nature that corresponds to this dignity. Such a sublime union with the Son of God would be futile and meaningless unless human nature were really meant to share in the divine nature. What is the purpose of this incorporation in God's Son, if man is to be left standing on the level of his own poor nature?

No, say the holy Fathers, following the lead of Sacred Scripture: if the Son of God becomes man, He does so only for the purpose of deifying man. "God has become man," says St. Augustine, "that man might become God." [21] St. Hilary declares: "If God laid hold of us by means of our bodily nature, by being born as man and becoming what we are, at a time when we were far removed from His nature: so now it is incumbent on us to endeavor to become what He is,

---

[19] "That the love wherewith Thou hast loved Me may be in them, and I in them" (John 17:26). "Who hath blessed us with spiritual blessings in heavenly places, in Christ, as He chose us in Him before the foundation of the world . . . unto the praise of the glory of His grace, in which He hath graced us in His beloved Son" (Eph. 1:3-6).

[20] No one has more brilliantly described the exaltation of human nature in Christ than St. Leo, in his first sermon on Christ's ascension. His primary concern is with the outward glorification of the body; but this is only the reflection of the inner elevation and transfiguration of the whole of nature: as with Christ, so with men. "And truly, great and unspeakable was the reason for rejoicing, when in the sight of that saintly throng a nature pertaining to the human race was raised beyond the rank of all the heavenly creatures, to pass above the angelic orders, to ascend above the heights of the archangels; nor was there any measure to its exaltation until, admitted into the company of the eternal Father, it was made to share in the glorious throne of Him to whose nature it was joined in the Son. Since, therefore, the ascension of Christ is our elevation, and whither the glory of the head has gone before, there the body is called to be in hope, let us exult, dearly beloved, with becoming gladness, and rejoice with pious thanksgiving. For today we are not only made secure in our possession of paradise, but we have reached the very pinnacle of heaven in Christ. We have obtained more by the ineffable grace of Christ than we lost by the envy of the devil. For we, who had been cast out of the happiness of our first home by our villainous foe, have been made one body with the Son of God, and by Him placed at the right hand of the Father" (Sermo 73, c.4; PL, LIV, 396).

[21] "Factus est Deus homo, ut homo fieret Deus" (Sermo 13 de temp.; Sermo 128; PL, XXXIX, 1997)

in order that our eager striving may penetrate into that splendor and thus grasp that whereby we were seized, by acquiring the nature of God, seeing that God has shown us the way by acquiring the nature of men." [22] "As the Lord became man by putting on our body," says the great Athanasius, "so shall we men be deified, assumed by His flesh." [23] St. Leo declares: "The Son of God came to destroy the works of the devil; and He so united Himself to us and us to Him, that the descent of God to the human level was at the same time the ascent of man to the divine level." [24] St. Peter Chrysologus speaks more beautifully still; he marvels, as at an indescribable wonder, that so intimate an interchange could suddenly take place between heaven and earth, between flesh and God, that God should become man and man God, that the Lord should become a servant and the servant a son, and that a close and eternal relationship should spring up between divinity and humanity in so ineffable a manner.[25] Similarly St. Maximus Martyr: "The Word of God, become man, has again filled with knowledge the nature which had been emptied of the knowledge committed to it, and fortifying it against corruption, has made it divine, not in substance but in quality. He has sealed nature with His own Spirit to preserve it against its defects, just as one mixes water with the quality of wine, to enable it to share in the latter's strength. He became man in all truth, in order to make us gods by grace." [26]

2. In general the Fathers regard the elevation of man to divine dignity and glory as the counterweight corresponding to the infinite condescension of God, and hence as an objective worthy of

[22] Scheeben is here quoting St. Hilary rather freely. Related passages are found in De Trinitate, lib. I, no. 13; lib. II, no. 24; lib. VI, no. 44; lib. VIII, nos. 14, 21; lib. IX, nos. 3, 9, 11, 13 f., 38–41, 49. [Tr.]

[23] Or. III contra Arianos, no. 34; PG, XXVI, 397.

[24] Sermo 7 de Nativitate Domini, c.2 (PL, LIV, 217 f.): "Quae hoc sacramentum mens comprehendere, quae hanc gratiam lingua valeat narrare? Redit in innocentiam iniquitas, . . . in adoptionem veniunt alieni, et in haereditatem ingrediuntur extranei, . . . de terrenis incipiunt esse coelestes. Quae autem est ista mutatio, nisi dextrae Excelsi? Quoniam venit Filius Dei dissolvere opera diaboli, et ita se nobis nosque inseruit sibi, ut Dei ad humana descensio fieret hominis ad divina provectio."

[25] Hom. 72; PL, LII, 404 f.

[26] Cap. Theol. Hecatont., II, c.26; PG, XC, 1229. Cf. the Office for the Feast of Corpus Christi, the first lesson of the second nocturn: "The only-begotten Son of God, wishing to make us sharers in His divinity, took our nature to Himself so that, having become man, He might make men gods."

the latter. As a rule they express this by saying that the Son of God has become the Son of man in order to make the children of men children of God; and that the natural consequence of the Incarnation is to confer on men the right and power to become the children of God. Sacred Scripture had pointed out this truth to them in explicit words. "God sent His Son, made of a woman," the Apostle said, "that we might receive the adoption of sons."[27] And in his magnificent description of the genesis of the mystery, the disciple who more than any other had been initiated into the secrets of the God-man, emphasizes as its chief effect that the Logos, in coming unto His own, gave to all who received Him the power to be made the sons of God.[28]

Thus in his day Irenaeus could teach: "The Word became man for this reason, that man by accepting the Word and receiving the grace of sonship might become the son of God."[29] And again: "In His immense love He became what we are, in order that He might make us what He is."[30] St. Cyril of Alexandria explains in more ample detail: "Through the Word, who joined human nature to Himself by means of the flesh united to Him, but who is by nature joined to the Father . . . servitude is raised to sonship, being summoned and elevated by its participation in the true Son to the dignity which pertains to Him by nature."[31] We could adduce countless passages which bring out the same doctrine, especially from St. Cyril.[32]

We wish to set down only a few more, which accurately stress the way the communication of Christ's perfections takes place in the human race, considered as His body. St. Cyril interprets the words of the Evangelist, "and [He] dwelt among us," as follows: "He [the Evangelist] fittingly remarks that the Word dwelt in us, and thereby made known to us this great mystery, namely, that we are all in Christ, and that the totality of mankind comes to life again in Him. For He is called the new Adam because by sharing in our

---

[27] Gal. 4:4 f.

[28] John 1:12.

[29] Apud Theodoret., *Eranistes seu Polymorphus*, dial. I (from *Adversus haereses*, lib. III, c.2; *PG*, LXXXIII, 85).

[30] *Adversus haereses*, praef. ad lib. V; *PG*, VII, 1120.

[31] *In Ioan.* (lib. I, c.9, no. 24; *PG*, LXXIII, 156).

[32] Cf. Petavius, *De Incarnatione*, lib. II, c.8; Casinius, *Quid est homo,* pp. 236 ff., in my edition.

nature He has enriched all unto happiness and glory, as the first Adam filled all with corruption and ignominy. Thus by dwelling in one, the Word dwelt in all, so that, the one being constituted the Son of God in power, the same dignity might pass to the whole human race according to the Spirit of holiness, and that through one of us these words might have application for us, too: 'I have said, You are gods, and all of you the sons of the most High.' In Christ, therefore, servile nature truly becomes free, by being raised to mystical union with Him who bears the form of a servant; in us it becomes free by imitation, and by our resemblance to that one, on account of our kinship according to the flesh. Why else did He take to Himself, not the nature of the angels, but the seed of Abraham, wherefore it behoved Him in all things to be made like unto His brethren, and to become truly man? Is it not clear to all that He lowered Himself to a menial condition not to gain anything for Himself by so doing, but to give us Himself, so that we, raised to His own inexhaustible wealth by our resemblance to Him, might be rich by His poverty, and be made gods and sons of God by faith? For He dwelt in us who is Son and God by nature. And that is why in His Spirit we cry: Abba, Father." [33]

St. Peter Chrysologus says: "After the Son of God, like rain falling on fleece, had poured Himself into our flesh with all the ointment of His divinity, He was called Christ, by reason of the unguent. And the sole author of this name is He who was so flooded and filled [*superfusus et infusus*] with God that man and God were one God. This name, derived from unguent, He then conferred on us who, after Christ, are called Christians." [34] But the unguent of

---

[33] St. Cyril of Alexandria, *In Ioan.* (lib. I, c.9, no. 24; *PG*, LXXIII, 161). No less beautiful is another selection from the same Father (*Thesaurus de sancta et consubstantiali Trinitate*, assert. XX; *PG*, LXXV, 333): "Christ is glorified and anointed and sanctified for our sake; through Him grace comes to all, and is even now conferred on nature and granted to the whole race. The Savior Himself indicates this in the Gospel according to St. John [17:19]: 'For them do I sanctify Myself, that they also may be sanctified.' Whatever Christ has, that becomes our portion, too. For He did not receive sanctification for Himself, seeing that He is the Sanctifier, but that He might acquire it for human nature; and so He has become the channel and principle of the goods which have flowed into us. This is why He says: 'I am the way,' that is, the way by which divine grace has come down to us, exalting and sanctifying and glorifying us, and thus deifying human nature in the first Christ."

[34] *Hom.* 60 (*PL*, LII, 367): "Postquam Dei filius sicut pluvia in vellus toto divinitatis unguento nostram se fudit in carnem, ab unguento nuncupatus est

divinity, as St. Augustine observes, flows over us because Christ, "by incorporating us in Himself, has made us His members, so that in Him we, too, might be the Anointed." [35] Similarly St. Leo: "In Christ 'dwelleth all the fullness of the Godhead corporeally, and you are filled in Him.' The entire divinity fills the entire body; and just as nothing is lacking in that majesty by whose habitation the domicile is filled, so there is no part of the body which is not filled with its indweller. But as for the statement, 'and you are filled in Him,' our nature is of course meant, since we should have no share in that repletion unless the Word of God had joined to Himself both a soul and a body derived from our race." [36]

Accordingly the truth is well established in the teaching of the Fathers that the head of the race, who as the only-begotten Son of God has been anointed with the fullness of the divinity, can and will transfer His divine dignity to His members, and with it a corresponding splendor and holiness.

3. Even without the Incarnation, God could have adopted us as His children and made us brothers of His natural Son, by conferring grace on us. For we are children of God by the very fact that we are like to the only-begotten Son of God by participation in His nature. But without the Incarnation this dignity would have lacked

---

Christus: et huius nominis exstitit solus auctor, qui sic Deo superfusus est et infusus, ut homo Deusque esset unus Deus. Hoc ergo unguenti nomen effudit in nos, qui a Christo dicimur Christiani; et impletum est illud, quod cantatur in Canticis Canticorum [1:2]: Unguentum effusum est nomen tuum."

[35] *In Psalm.* 26, enarr. 2, no. 2; *PL*, XXXVI, 200.

[36] *Serm. 10 in Nativitate Domini*, c.3 (PL, LIV, 231): " 'Verbum caro factum est, et habitavit in nobis.' In nobis utique, quos sibi Verbi divinitas coaptavit, cuius caro de utero virginis sumpta nos sumus. Quae si de nostra, id est, vere humana non esset, Verbum caro factum non habitasset in nobis. In nobis autem habitavit, qui naturam nostri corporis suam fecit, aedificante sibi Sapientia domum, non de quacumque materia, sed de substantia proprie nostra, cuius assumptio est manifestata, cum dictum est: 'Verbum caro factum est, et habitavit in nobis' [Ioan. 1:14]. Huic autem sacratissimae praedicationi etiam Beati Pauli Apostoli doctrina concordat, dicentis: 'Videte ne quis vos decipiat per philosophiam et inanem fallaciam secundum traditionem hominum, secundum elementa mundi, et non secundum Christum, quia in ipso habitat omnis plenitudo divinitatis corporaliter, et estis repleti in illo' [Col. 2:8-10]. Totum igitur corpus implet tota divinitas; et sicut nihil deest illius maiestatis, cuius habitatione repletur habitaculum, sic nihil deest corporis, quod non suo habitatore sit plenum. Quod autem dictum est: 'et estis repleti in illo,' nostra utique est significata natura, ad quos illa repletio non pertineret, nisi Dei Verbum nostri sibi generis et animam et corpus unisset."

a basis in us, and would have been less perfect in its value for us. It is too high above us; so much so that of ourselves we could not have even the slightest prospect of ever possessing or acquiring it. It is pure grace, motivated exclusively by God's overflowing kindness: and by itself alone this grace would not be powerful enough really to usher us into the personal relationship of the Son of God to His Father, in such wise that in Him and through Him this Father would in very truth be our Father also.

By the Incarnation, however, we are in all truth embodied in the person of God's Son and have become His members. God looks upon us no longer as situated upon the low level proper to our own persons; He sees us in His Son, and His Son in us. He beholds us substantially united to His Son, and kin to Him. Consequently we are perfectly worthy, and not merely worthy in some indefinite way, to be adopted as His children. Indeed, the very fact of our union with His only-begotten Son virtually confers this sonship on us.

Because of Christ this sonship is no longer a mere adoptive sonship, since we receive it not as strangers, but as kinsfolk, as members of the only-begotten Son, and can lay claim to it as a right. The grace of sonship in us has something of the natural sonship of Christ Himself, from which it is derived. Because we are not mere adoptive children, because we are members of the natural Son, we truly enter into the personal relationship in which the Son of God stands to His Father. In literal truth, and not by simple analogy or resemblance, we call the Father of the Word our Father, and in actual fact He is such not by a purely analogous relationship, but by the very same relationship which makes Him the Father of Christ. He is our Father in somewhat the way that He is Father to the God-man in His humanity by the same relationship whereby He is Father of the eternal Word. Therefore we are not mere brothers, or comrades admitted to the majesty and eminence that belong to the eternal Word by nature, but are in some sense one single son of the Father in the Son and with the Son. Because of this oneness we become like and conformable to Him in His glory.

This difference has been formulated by St. Cyril in all its sharpness: "The same person," he remarks, "is the only-begotten and the first-born. He is the only-begotten as God, and the first-born inasmuch as He has dwelt among us and many brethren as a man intimately united to us, that in Him and through Him we also might be made children of God according to nature and grace: according to nature, in Him and in Him alone; but according to grace through Him in the Spirit." [37]

We shall be able to gain a clearer idea of this great mystery if we revert to the special character of the corporal union between us and Christ, and again have recourse to the analogy of matrimony. Does not the wife of one's real son become the daughter of her husband's father in a far higher sense and in a more perfect manner by her union with her husband, than a stranger who is simply adopted by this same father? The relationship of the latter is purely extrinsic, formed only according to the analogy of real filiation; but that of the former is closely connected with real filiation, and is actually based on it; it is but an extension and expansion of this same relationship. Let this be applied to the relationship into which the human race has entered with Christ's Father by means of the Incarnation.

4. Thus the incarnation of the Son of God is the real basis for the divine adoption of the human race, and likewise conducts that adoption to a consummation that is unique in its sublimity. It is the bridge leading to the extension of the divine Trinitarian fatherhood to the race. This fatherhood is not merely imitated in God's relation-

---

[37] *De recta fide ad Theodosium*, no. 30; PG, LXXVI, 1177. Cf. Naclantus, *In ep. ad Ephes.*, c.1, and *Tractat. de regno Christi*; also Cardinal Bérulle, Opusc. 84. In his *De regno Christi*, quoted by Thomassinus, *De Incarnatione*, lib. VIII, c.9, no. 18, Naclantus says: "We have received the Spirit of adoption, and by Him we have not only been made brothers and coheirs of Christ, but have been transformed into branches and members of Him and, if the expression be allowed, have been absorbed into Him. Therefore He not only lives in us: 'I live, now not I, but Christ liveth in me;' He not only speaks in us: 'Do you seek a proof of Christ, that speaketh in me?' He not only suffers is us: 'I fill up those things that are wanting of the sufferings of Christ, in my flesh,' and 'Saul, Saul, why persecutest thou Me?' He not only is clothed, harbored, and fed in us: 'As long as you did it to one of these My least brethren, you did it to Me'; but we are reputed to be one and the same person as He, and we receive His throne, as He once promised, that where He is, we also may be, as He begged of the Father, and could not but be heard for His reverence. And thus at last, from having been adopted sons, we become in a sense natural sons, and we call to the Father not alone by grace but, as it were, by natural right. Accordingly the Holy Spirit not only cries to the Father in the hearts of the sons, but breathes the name of the Father in a sigh, saying, 'Abba, Father,' thereby giving testimony that He is our Father in both ways."

ship to man, out of sheer grace, but is joined to man substantially; and it is only as a result of this substantial union with man that its imitative force can come into play. The Incarnation sets up a real continuity between the Trinitarian process and the human race, in order that this process may be prolonged in the race. The Incarnation raises the human race to the bosom of the eternal Father, that it may receive the grace of sonship with all its implied dignities and rights by a real contact with the source, rather than by a purely gratuitous influx from without.

In a similar way, as members of the Son of God we enter into a closer, more excellent, and more personal relationship with the Holy Spirit than would be possible by grace alone. We saw previously [38] that along with the grace of sonship the Holy Spirit is given in His hypostasis as the seal of this dignity of ours, seeing that in Him we enter into a relationship with the Father that is analogous to the Son's relationship with the Father. But here He becomes our very own property, for we, being the body, possess Him as the Spirit of our head. Here He seals the relationship in which we stand to the Father not only alongside the only-begotten Son, but in Him as one Christ. Here He is given to us, or better is *ipso facto* our own, as the pledge of the fatherly love with which the Father loves us in His only-begotten Son as His members, and as the pledge of the Son's love for the Father, which love the Son offers to the Father in behalf of us too, since we are His members. Hence the relationship whereby the Holy Spirit dwells in us as the *Spiritus Christi* is a hypostatic relationship through and through; and it would be hypostatic even if grace would not by itself place us in a hypostatic relation with the Holy Spirit. Moreover, it is the foundation and the crown of the divine sonship contained in grace itself: the foundation, because our right to the pledge of God's fatherly love must draw down upon us the effects of that love; and the crown, because it so closely interlaces the adoptive sonship with natural sonship.

All the scriptural passages concerning the hypostatic mission and inhabitation of the Holy Spirit, which we endeavored to explain above [39] in connection with the grace of adoptive sonship, receive their fullest and deepest meaning in terms of the Incarnation. The Holy Spirit is placed in a more personal and hypostatic relation to

[38] See pp. 161 f.
[39] Cf. sections 29 and 30.

us in the Son's mission through the assumption of human nature than by the Son's purely spiritual rebirth in our soul. Proceeding as He does from the hypostasis of the Son, He descends with the Son in His hypostasis into the real and mystical body assumed by the Son; as the Spirit proceeding from the head and belonging to the head by virtue of this procession, He dwells in that body by a real prolongation of His eternal procession.

Although the Holy Spirit does not, like the Son, join a human nature to Himself, or rather, because of that very fact, we can say that He is hypostatically sent along with the Son in the latter's mission. Manifestly this mission is fulfilled in substance by the very entrance of the Son into the human race. It is only the vitalizing possession and fruition of the Holy Spirit that are later imparted to the race after Christ's resurrection, that is, after Christ had manifested His entire divine splendor in His own body and had appeared as the glorious Son of God even in His flesh.

5. We perceive, then, how high the new, heavenly head of the race towers above the first Adam. The first Adam was himself only an adopted child of God. By nature he was no more than the rest of men. Therefore the fact that he stood at the summit of the race did not enable him to give to the other members of the race or to acquire for them a higher dignity than they themselves had from nature. Neither his natural rank nor his works enabled him to become the principle of supernatural goods and of a supernatural order for himself or for his posterity. He was chosen and commissioned by the grace of God to be no more than the point of departure from which the dignity of divine sonship was to be extended to his posterity. He could not give it, because it was not his own; he could only lose it. The race had in him an unstable head, as far as the supernatural order is concerned. The God-man, on the contrary, is the principle of the supernatural order in virtue of His personal and natural dignity. Grace belongs to Him essentially as His own, and through Him it truly belongs also to the race as its own. Therefore He is truly constituted the depositary of grace for mankind; not only can He give it, but He cannot lose it, either for Himself or for others.

Accordingly the God-man must be regarded as a supplement whose function was to make up for a defect brought about by Adam's sin. But He is also a complement to Adam, with respect to

what Adam could and should have been. That is, He must be regarded as the one who was to be the true and unshakable foundation
and principle of grace in mankind, whereas Adam of himself could
be no more than the principle and foundation of nature.[40] Only by
thus being complementary to Adam could He, after Adam (and in
him the race) had fallen from the heights of grace, become supplementary to Adam, so as after the Fall to elevate the race again to that
height.

But since Adam, besides the grace of divine sonship, had possessed
also the gift of integrity as subsidiary to the first gift and as the
seed of the future glory of his whole nature, we should be guilty
of undervaluing the dignity which the race receives through the
God-man if we failed to perceive that the right to this gift is inter-
linked with that dignity. Inasmuch as it is the God-man's body, the
race must become conformable to its head not only in its union with
God, but also in the supernatural transfiguration and elevation of
its entire nature. This truth does not imply that even in the present
life the race must receive through the God-man all the prerogatives
which it actually possessed in the first Adam before his fall. Christ
Himself did not endow His own humanity with all of these. But
this much is true, that these gifts henceforth do not, as formerly,
transcend the dignity of the race, and that, if this dignity is to be
realized in all its splendor, they must be allotted to the race sooner
or later. As a matter of fact, we do recover integrity. During this
life we do not, indeed, receive the imperfect gift, whose function
is to preserve nature from dissolution. But in the life to come we

[40] St. Cyril of Alexandria, *Thesaurus* (assert. XXV; *PG*, LXXV, 405): "He
is the only-begotten according to nature, for He alone proceeds from the
Father as Son, He alone is God of God, Light of Light. But He is the first-
born on account of us, in order that every creature may be inserted in Him
as in an undying root, and may grow forth from Him who is forever. For all
things were made by Him, and exist, and are preserved by Him." Similarly
in *De recta fide ad Theodosium* (no. 20; *PG*, LXXVI, 1161): "The human
soul, after He had made it His own, and had imbued it with the firmness and
changelessness of His nature, as one dyes wool with solid color, was declared
by Him to be superior to sin. . . . Thus the soul, once it had been made
His who knows no sin, straightway acquired a condition of firmness and
stability in all goods, and a great power over sin. Christ . . . therefore was
made, so to speak, the root and origin of all those who in the Spirit are reborn
to newness of life and bodily immortality. For that unshakable constancy,
which comes from divinity, He transferred to the whole human race by
communicating grace to men."

shall receive integrity as the perfected gift in the glorious state of transfiguration, when it will restore the nature that had fallen into dissolution, and will make nature henceforth incorruptible in divine beauty. But precisely this is a proof of the greatness of our dignity, which gives us a claim to so marvelous a restoration and transfiguration of our entire nature.

Thus the dignity which the human race receives on account of its connection with its new, divine-human head, is so great that all supernatural goods, which in themselves immeasurably transcend its natural dignity, become connatural and proper to it. Because of His personal, divine dignity, the God-man merits for the race the entire series of supernatural gifts which the race could not merit in any other way. This is the first meaning which the Incarnation has for the race. Even if there were no other, this alone suffices to show its unique excellence.

The reader may notice with some surprise that we are here speaking of a merit that is based simply on the dignity of Christ's person, not on His free activity. And indeed by merit we understand at present only the dignity of a person, and the rights emanating from that dignity. A person could possess such a dignity by virtue of his origin, without the performance of any definite works, and could communicate it to other persons because of their connection with him. Indeed, the original, personal dignity is what imparts to his works the value by which they are rendered meritorious. Later we shall come back to this question and see how Christ's merit is consummated in deeds. This much is certain, that the Son of God can merit supernatural goods for His own human nature and also for His mystical body without being restricted to particular activities, although as matters actually stand God has made the communication of these goods dependent on the meritorious activity of Christ. The prerogatives of Christ's humanity accrue automatically to the rest of the members by an extension of privileges.

It is in this sense that the Apostle affirms: "Even when we were dead in sins, [God] hath quickened us together in Christ, . . . and hath raised us up together, and hath made us sit together in the heavenly places, through Christ Jesus." [41] St. Gregory of Nyssa explains this very beautifully in connection with Christ's resurrection and ascension: "From no other source than from our midst was

[41] Eph. 2:5.

taken that flesh which God assumed and which was raised at the resurrection along with the divinity. Hence, as in our body the activity of one of the members is shared by the whole which is joined to the part, so the resurrection of a part affects the whole, as if the whole of nature were one organic being, extending from the part to the whole on account of the continuity and unity of nature." [42] St. Chrysostom has something similar: "When [Christ] our head was raised from the dead, we also were raised. . . . And when the head takes His place [at the right hand of the Father], the body also is seated there." [43]

58. SECOND SIGNIFICANCE OF THE GOD-MAN AS HEAD OF THE RACE. COMMUNICATION OF DIVINE LIFE

The relation of the race to its divine-human head has a still deeper significance.

1. The head does more than communicate its dignity and rights to the members joined to it; it is also the source of life for the other members, since they are destined to share in the life proper to it.

The first Adam was constituted by nature the source of the natural, transitory life of the race. The second Adam, endowed with heavenly, divine power, must become the source of a heavenly, divine, everlasting life.

When the Son of God joined His own humanity to His divine person, thus effecting a union like that between body and soul, He planted in it the seed of divine life, substantially united the divine vital energy to it, and so transformed the life of His humanity into a supernatural, divine life.

[42] *Or. catech. magna*, c.32; *PG*, XLV, 80.
[43] *In epist. ad Ephesios*, hom. 4, no. 2; *PG*, LXII, 32. A like view is given by St. Maximus of Turin, *Hom. 6 in Pascha*: "In the Savior we have all risen, we have all been restored to life, we have all ascended into heaven. For a portion of the flesh and blood of each one of us is in the man Christ. Therefore, where a portion of me reigns, I believe that I reign; where my blood rules, I conceive that I rule; where my flesh is glorified, I know that I am glorious. Although a man be a sinner, let him not lose trust in this communion of grace. For even though sin forbids our approach, our substance demands our presence; and though our own crimes shut us out, the community of our nature does not drive us away. The goodness of divinity requires that our Savior love us with a special affection; for, as our God is in Him, so, too, our blood is in Him."

Since, however, the whole human race became in a wider sense the body of God's Son through His humanity, the divine life-stream could not remain dammed up in His own human nature. Through the latter and in it, that life-stream had to flow to all the members of the body, and had to fill up and pervade all the members. It had to encompass and transfigure the whole of natural life with its divine energy, so that the soul might share in God's own vital activity, and the body might be freed of all the corruptibility and weakness of its natural life.[44]

Ordinarily the Fathers designate the higher, divine element, by which the creature's life is transfigured, as ἀφθαρσία, that is, incorruption or immortality. This term is used chiefly to denote the transformation of animal and vegetative life in man. But we have seen [45] that this transformation is but a consequence and manifestation of the divine vitalization of the naturally incorruptible spirit which, when it is sanctified, participates in the immutable purity and sublimity of the divine life; and the Fathers regard it in this light too, when they represent incorruption as a factor in man's deification, or as this deification itself. We must keep this in mind if we wish properly to understand the passages quoted in these pages, as well as those to be quoted later on.

Adam also had possessed supernatural life; but it could not strike root in the race through his instrumentality. The root of this life lay outside and above the race, in God. Only in the God-man, in the new Adam, is this root implanted in the race itself, through the hypostatic union. Only the God-man, in whom the race which proceeded from Adam according to nature is implanted, can truly be the heavenly vine from which the divine life flows into the branches engrafted on it. Only through Him does this life become the true and inalienable property of the race.[46]

[44] St. Athanasius, Or. III contra Arian., no. 33 (PG, XXVI, 393): "After the Word has been made man and desired that whatever belonged to the flesh should become His own, these defects [corruption and mortality] no longer affect the body, on account of the Word who has taken up His abode therein; nor do men remain any longer sinful and dead by reason of their evil dispositions but, restored to life by the power of the Word, endure forever, immortal and incorruptible. . . . Hence we do not, like that which is of earth, return to the earth but, joined to the Word, who is of heaven, we are borne aloft to heaven by Him."

[45] See section 35.

[46] In spite of the inspiration of grace Adam ever remained an "animal man,"

The Fathers employ a great variety of comparisons to illustrate this radication of the divine life-energy in the heart of the human race. "If," says Theodore Abucara, "you sow a melon seed that has been soaked in honey, the sweetness of the honey will pass over to the fruit. Thus Christ has assumed our nature without flaw or stain, as it was in the beginning, and as it had been created; He has dipped it in the honey and sweetness of the Godhead, that is, in the power of the Holy Spirit, the Paraclete, and has made us sharers in its sweetness, just as the melon seeds pass on their sweetness to the fruit that grows from them." [47] Many of the Fathers compare Christ to a leaven which frees the mass of the race from all impurity and pervades it with divine holiness and vital energy, seeing that Christ, and in Him the Godhead itself, is mixed with it. St. Gregory of Nazianzus and St. Gregory of Nyssa speak in this strain.[48] Similar is the metaphor of the lily which, when planted in the depths of the race, wafts its stimulating fragrance over it. St. Cyril of Alexandria discusses this point in his *Scholia;* we shall come back to this idea later. Here, lastly, belongs the figure of the glowing coal, by which the same Cyril represents Christ: for, since the communication of divine life to the creature takes place through a transformation and transfiguration of natural life, this vitalizing flame of the divinity or of the Holy Spirit must lay hold of the entire race in the first-born of the race, and through Him must take the race to itself and thus pervade it with its energy.

2. The communication of divine life to the creature and to man-

---

since the divine life-faculty merely exercised influence upon him, but did not have its root in him. Prudentius, in his *Apotheosis*, sings words that are much to the point: "An animal man had he been; but the Spirit planted in him a nature sprung from better seed, infusing God Himself, who gives life to mortal beings." Athanasius, too, asserts that God did not wish the second Adam to possess grace by a mere outward title, like the first, but willed that He bear it incorporated in His body, so that the race could never lose it again.

[47] *Opusc.* VI (Abu-Qurra; *PG*, XCVII, 1524).

[48] St. Gregory of Nazianzus, *Or.* 30 (no. 21; *PG*, XXXVI, 132), says that God became man "to sanctify man, and to be, as it were, a leaven for the entire mass; and by joining to Himself what has been condemned, to free the whole from damnation."

St. Gregory of Nyssa, *Or. de verbis I Cor. 15-28* (*PG*, XLIV, 1313), says: "The pure divinity of the only-begotten, knowing naught of corruption, was in human nature, that was mortal and subject to corruption. But from the whole of human nature, to which was joined divinity, arose, as the first fruit of the common mass, the man who is in Christ, by whom all humanity was united to divinity."

kind is further to be regarded as an extension and continuation of that communication of life which is transmitted from the Father to the Son in God. Absolutely speaking, this can take place apart from our entering into continuity and closer union with the Son of God. But manifestly this is brought about most perfectly if we come into a union of continuity with God's Son as His body.[49] For then the divine life passes from the Father into the Son, in order to be transferred to us in the Son and through the Son. Then the divine life-force does not merely trickle down upon our earthly nature like a heavenly dew, but a great river of life flowing from the Father as the source into the Son enters into our race through the Son and with the Son, and thus floods all the members of the race in fuller abundance. This is the profound meaning of the Savior's words: "As the living Father hath sent Me, and I live by the Father, so he that eateth Me, the same also shall live by Me." [50] By partaking of Christ's flesh we are united to Him in the closest way so as to be a single body with Him; but since we are one body with Christ even without this partaking, the Savior's statement remains true although this particular condition should not be fulfilled.[51]

[49] The Fathers often affirm that natural man, or man deprived of the original infusion of the Spirit by sin, can achieve a full, unalterable life only by a real union with God. Thus Irenaeus, *Adversus haereses*, lib. III, c.19 (*PG*, VII, 939), says: "No otherwise could we take on incorruption and immortality than by being joined to life and immortality. But how can we be joined to incorruption and immortality unless incorruption and immortality first become what we are, so that what is corruptible may be swallowed up by incorruption, and what was mortal, by immortality?" Similar expressions occur again and again in St. Athanasius and St. Cyril. Athanasius remarks pertinently, *Or. de Incarn. Verbi*, no. 44 (*PG*, XXV, 176), that mortality cannot be fully eradicated unless life becomes one with the body, so that the body, impregnated with life, expels death.

[50] John 6:58.

[51] Cf. St. Cyril of Alexandria, *In Ioan.*, lib. IX; *PG*, LXXIV, 280. Although this passage does not give unmistakable evidence that the topic has been completely thought through, we cannot resist the inclination to quote it in full, since it shows how powerfully St. Cyril was occupied by the ideas we have been pursuing.

"Man, being corruptible by nature, could not escape death unless he received that grace bestowed of old, and became a partaker of God, who sustains all things in being and gives life to all through the Son, in the Spirit. Therefore the only-begotten Word became a partaker of flesh and blood, that is, He was made man who is by nature life and by nature is born of life, that is, of His God and Father; and He joined Himself to flesh that is by nature corruptible, in an ineffable and mysterious manner known to Himself

3. The energy of divine life surges and culminates in the Holy Spirit, and hence the communication of it to creatures must be regarded and characterized as a communication of the Holy Spirit, the Spirit of divine life. This Spirit can move in the creature and fill him with divine life even without the incarnation of the Son; but to be communicated in such wise as to become truly the creature's own Spirit, is possible only through the Incarnation.

In the Incarnation the Son of God brings to His real and His mystical body the Holy Spirit who proceeds from Him and who, because of this procession, is His own Spirit.[52] As this Spirit is the

---

alone, so as to recall it to His own life and make it a partaker, through Himself, of God His Father. For He is the Mediator of God and men, as it is written, naturally joined to God His Father, as God and proceeding from God, but also to men as a man, having, however, the Father in Himself, and Himself existing in the Father. For He is the figure and the brightness of the Father's substance, by no means separated from the substance of which He is the figure and from which He proceeds as its brightness, but dwelling therein, and possessing it in Himself, and us too, inasmuch as He bore our nature, and the body of the Word was the same as our body. For the Word was made flesh, according to the witness of John. He bore our nature, to reshape it to His own life. But He is also in us: for we have truly been made partakers of Him, and we have Him in us, by the Spirit. Thus, being made partakers of the divine nature, we are called sons; and we likewise have the Father in us, through the Son, as Paul testifies: 'And because you are sons, God hath sent the Spirit of His Son into your hearts, crying: Abba, Father' [Gal. 4:6]. For the Spirit is not something different from the Son, that is, from the standpoint of identity of nature. With these matters thus explained, let us bring out the sense of the text we are considering, and accommodate it to our Savior's words. 'In that day,' He says, 'you shall know that I am in My Father, and you in Me, and I in you.' I live, He says. For I am by nature life, and I have shown that My temple is a living temple. But when you see that you, too, who are by nature corruptible, are living, that is, in imitation of Me, then you will clearly perceive that I, who am by nature life, have through Myself joined you to God My Father, who is likewise by nature life, and that I have made you in a certain sense sharers and partakers of His immortality. I exist in Him naturally (for I am the fruit of His substance and His true offspring), and I have existence from Him, and life from His life; but you live in Me, and I in you, inasmuch as I have appeared among you as a man; and I have made you partakers of the divine nature, conferring My Spirit on you. For Christ is in us through the Spirit, changing what is by nature corruptible into incorruption, and from death transferring it to immortality. Hence Paul says: 'He that raised up Jesus Christ from the dead shall quicken also your mortal bodies, because of His Spirit that dwelleth in you' [Rom. 8:11]. For, although the Holy Spirit proceeds from the Father, He comes through the Son, and is the Spirit of the Son; for all things are from the Father through the Son."

[52] The Fathers frequently come back to this point, especially in con-

Son of God's own Spirit, He now becomes the body's own Spirit. As He moves in Christ's own humanity, He must also move in the race, since this race is the body of Him to whom the Spirit belongs and from whom He proceeds. "The body of Christ," says St. Augustine, "is animated by the Spirit of Christ." Inasmuch as the race is Christ's body, it must be animated by no other spirit than the Spirit of God's Son. It has a right that this Spirit live and work

---

troversy with the Arians, when they have occasion to explain how the proposition that Christ receives the Holy Spirit is to be reconciled with the proposition that He breathes forth and gives the Holy Spirit. Thus Athanasius, *Or. 1 contra Arian.*, nos. 46 f. (*PG*, XXVI, 108): "Although the Savior was God, and had reigned from eternity in the kingdom of His Father, and was Himself the giver of the Holy Spirit, He is now said to be anointed. As man He was anointed by the Spirit so that, as He put it in our power to be exalted and raised from the dead, so He made us the abode and home of the Spirit. This is borne out by the Lord's own words, as reported in the Gospel according to St. John [17:18 f.]: 'I have sent them into the world; and for them do I sanctify Myself, that they also may be sanctified in truth.' In these words He implies that He is not sanctified, but sanctifies. For He is not sanctified by another, but sanctifies Himself, in order that we may be sanctified in truth. But He who sanctifies Himself is the Lord of sanctification. How this is brought about may be represented as follows: I, who am the Father's Word, give the Spirit to Myself as man, and in Him I sanctify Myself made man, so that in Me, who am Truth (for 'Thy Word is Truth') all may be sanctified. If, then, He sanctifies Himself on our account, and does so after He has become man, it is clear that the Spirit, in descending upon Him at the Jordan, descended upon us also, since He bore our body. Nor was this done to effect any improvement in the Word, but for our sanctification, that we might be made partakers of His anointment, and that it might be said of us: 'Know you not that you are the temple of God, and that the Spirit of God dwelleth in you?' [I Cor. 3:16.] For when the Lord, as man, was washed in the Jordan, we ourselves were washed in Him and by Him. And when He received the Spirit, we were the ones who were made worthy to receive the Spirit through Him."

St. Cyril of Alexandria remarks further, *In Ioan.* (lib. II, c. 1; *PG*, LXXIII, 205): "Since the first Adam did not preserve the grace entrusted to him, God the Father ordained that the second Adam should come down to us from heaven. . . . But when the Word of God was made man, He received the Spirit from the Father, as if He were one of us, not receiving anything particularly for Himself—for He was the giver of the Spirit—but that as man He might keep the Spirit He had received for our nature, and that, as He who knew no sin, He might again establish in us the grace that had departed. It was on this account, I think, that the holy Baptist added for our instruction: 'I saw the Spirit coming down as a dove from heaven, and He remained upon Him' [John 1:32]. For the Spirit had departed from us on account of sin; but He who knew no sin became man like one of us, so that the Spirit might remain permanently in us, seeing that in Christ He had no

in it; and not only has it the right, but in Christ it is so closely united to the latter's Spirit in a wonderful and ineffable way that the Spirit truly and substantially dwells in it with the power of His divine life, as the soul dwells in the body, and must manifest His divine energy to it and in it. He dwells in us not merely as in the adopted children of God, but as in the members of the natural Son of God. And as He is the pledge and seal of the dignity of those members, He is the principle of the divine life which is theirs by reason of this dignity. He is our own somewhat in the way that the vital sap flowing from the trunk naturally belongs to the tendrils that sprout forth from the vine. Thus the Holy Spirit is nothing less than the life-sap welling from the divine heart of the Logos, and His life-blood.[53]

Is this not some indication of the dazzling, divine heights to which the Incarnation raises man? Is not the Incarnation, when thus viewed, evidently the basis and the crown of the fellowship in life which man has with God, with the persons of the Holy Trinity? Without the intermediacy of the Incarnation, only grace could cause a brooklet of this life to flow to man. But a real and full fellowship of life, a fellowship which draws man into the circuit of divine life, enabling him in the Son and through the Son to derive that life from the Father, and enabling him likewise in the Son and through the Son to receive the personal Spirit of the Son as his own Spirit—such a fellowship is effected only by the Incarnation. The Incarnation places man, in Christ, upon God's throne, inaugurates his fellowship of dignity with the divine persons, and ushers him into relations with

---

reason to betake Himself hence. Therefore He received the Spirit on behalf of us, and restored to the race its ancient treasure." And again St. Cyril says (*In Isaiam*, lib. II, tom. I; *PG*, LXX, 313): " 'And the Spirit of the Lord shall rest upon Him.' In the beginning the Spirit had been given to the first fruits of our race, that is, to Adam; but he, grown careless and remiss, did not observe the injunction laid upon him and violated the command. . . . In due time the only-begotten Word of God was made man, not ceasing the while to be God. And He was like to us, but was not ensnared in sin; and the Holy Spirit settled down upon the nature of man, in Him first of all, as it were in the second first fruits of the race, so that He might thereupon take up His abode and remain within us, and dwell with delight in the souls of the faithful."

[53] When treating of the Trinity, we saw how the material blood of Christ represents the Holy Spirit, and how wine, as the blood of the vine, as the purest and noblest fluid for the nourishment of life that the vegetable kingdom affords, calls to mind by a remarkably suggestive relationship the blood of Christ and the Holy Spirit. We shall make this thought clearer when we come to the Eucharist.

the Trinity. It transports him to the bosom and heart of God, so that he may enjoy with the divine persons their own life in most real and close union with them, as belonging to their company.

In this respect, too, we perceive that the God-man is not merely supplementary, but complementary to the first Adam. We behold Him not as the principle of natural fellowship of life among men, but as the principle of men's supernatural fellowship of life with God, and hence also with other men. We apprehend that it is He who has changed the human race into a divine race, which Adam could not do. Lastly, we come to understand that in His hypostatic mission He has most perfectly and universally extended the Trinitarian communications to beings outside of God.

59. Third Significance of the God-man as Head of the Race. Vocation to the Infinite Glorification of God

The sublime meaning of the Incarnation is not yet exhausted. The divine dignity and the divine life flowing to the race through the Incarnation, which is a continuation and extension of the Trinitarian communications taking place in God, enable the race also to continue and extend that mysterious, infinite glorification of God which God attains in His interior productions, and prolongs exteriorly in the Incarnation.

It was remarked above that even in His humanity the Son of God honors and glorifies His Father as the latter's natural Son, and that He thus continues in the outer world to render to the Father the honor which as the eternal Word He renders within the Godhead. Since He communicates His own dignity and power to His mystical body, the human race, the latter is enabled and summoned in its supernatural head to glorify the eternal Father with infinite honor.

As long as man is confined to his own nature, he cannot give infinite honor to God, because of his finite rank and limited powers; still less can He glorify God in His infinite fatherhood, because he stands in no relationship to it. Even the grace of adoptive sonship, considered as such, cannot raise him to such exalted heights. Grace does indeed impart to man a dignity that is incomparably greater than the dignity he has by nature. Still that dignity is not infinite, any more than man's power is. Besides, grace confers on him only an analogous, not a literal, relationship of son to the Father. Only God's natural Son can glorify His Father with infinite honor.

But He does so even in His humanity. For, although the power conferred on this humanity of loving God and of performing works in God's honor is not in itself infinite, it rests on the infinite dignity and power of Christ's person, and on that account its acts are infinitely pleasing to God. In a similar way Christ can glorify His Father infinitely in His mystical body; and so far as He is able to do this in us as in His members, we are able to do the same in Him.

We have this power, in the first place, because the actions of Christ Himself, as our head, belong to us too, inasmuch as we are His members. In virtue of our solidarity with Christ, the prayers that He wings aloft to the Father, His works, His filial obedience, His sufferings borne for the honor of the Father, are also ours. As we enter into Christ's personal relationship with the Father because of this connection of ours with Him, we can infinitely glorify the eternal Father in His fatherhood through Christ's prayers, His works, and His sufferings.

We are enabled thus to glorify God, in the second place, by the prayers, works, and sufferings we perform or endure, provided that we perform or endure them not as from and for ourselves alone, but as members of the God-man, in His name, in His Spirit, in His power. For in this case our works, although finite themselves, are sustained and elevated by the infinite dignity and power of the head whose members we are, and we honor God by them from the standpoint of the relationship in which we stand to Him through Christ. This is a relationship with God considered not only as our adoptive Father, but as Christ's natural Father, to whom we are kin through Christ in the character of natural sons. Obviously this is not true of natural works, for we do not perform these through power flowing into us from our head. It is true only of supernatural works, the works of the divine life within us, and of these only so far as the energy of divine life streams into us from Christ as our head. Only if this condition is verified, can we say that Christ, the only-begotten Son of God, lives and acts in us; only then are our works also His works in us; only then are they informed by His divine dignity and power, and glorify God with infinite honor in the mystery of His natural fatherhood.

60. SUMMARY VIEW OF THE ELEVATING INFLUENCE EXERCISED
BY THE GOD-MAN AS HEAD OF THE RACE. RELATION OF
THIS INFLUENCE TO HIS RESTORATIVE FUNCTION

We are now in a position to present some kind of survey of the essential meaning which the Incarnation has for the human race. Through the God-man the fullness of the divinity, which dwells corporally in the head, also dwells in the race, of which the head forms part, in order to elevate and deify it in every respect. The fullness of the divinity is the unguent with which the head of the race is anointed as the Son of God, so as even in His humanity to possess divine dignity and power, and to glorify God as His Father. By this anointing He is the Anointed simply as such, the Christ. But all the members of this head, who form one whole with Him, must also be one Christ with Him. The unguent of the Godhead must flow from the head to all His members, so that they too, imbued with divine dignity and power, may in union with their head become what their head is, a kingly priesthood: kings, who with Christ and in Christ share in the royal majesty and beatitude of God, as His children; priests, who in virtue of a divine consecration are to have part in the exalted priesthood of the Son of God, by which God is honored and glorified in His Trinitarian majesty.

This sublime significance of the Incarnation, as is crystal clear, is conceivable only in terms of its relationship with the mystery of the Trinity in God and the mystery of supernatural grace in the creature. The Incarnation takes its place in the middle, between these two mysteries, in order to join them together and to fit them to each other. The infinite communication and self-glorification of God in the Trinity are continued and prolonged in the Incarnation, and are effected not only in the God-man but also in His entire mystical body. The mystery of grace has a firm foundation and receives its highest fulfillment in the Incarnation. The twofold communication of the divine nature, in the Trinity and in grace, combines in the Incarnation to constitute one organic process, and the twofold supernatural glorification which God the Father wills to receive from His natural Son and His adopted children merges into a single harmonious, divine hymn.

In its function as connecting link between two such august mysteries, of which it presupposes the one and effects the other, brings the one to full revelation and completes the other, has the one as its root and is the principle and sustaining cause of the other, the Incarnation becomes known to us both in itself and in its significance as a most eminent and elevating mystery. Viewing it thus, in its full grandeur, we perceive that it is the basis of an absolutely supernatural elevation of mankind, and the organ and center of an inexpressible, inconceivably intimate union of mankind with God.

When we thus regard it, how its glory shines forth differently from the way it does if we look upon it merely as an organ effecting an elevation of the race after its fall, or as a medium restoring the union with God that had been severed by sin!

Of course this conception, as was observed previously, is fully justified, if it is not insisted upon in too one-sided a manner, and if it is related to the other factors.

How is such a relation to be represented? First, by conceiving the fall of the race as a plunge from a height which the race could not reach by its own efforts, and its separation from God as the rending of a union with God which the race could neither effect originally nor repair subsequently. If we thus view the matter, we perceive that the re-elevation of the race is an absolute elevation which properly can be effected only by the God-man, and that the reunion of the race with God is a supernatural union which can be achieved and can culminate only in the God-man.

In the second place, the relation in question is rightly represented by taking account of the fact that the liquidation of the debt which mankind and men had contracted with God is not a mere cancellation, but a payment in full. In the full payment of such a debt the race emerges from its lowly state and is elevated so high that it can meet God's infinite demands by calling upon its own resources. However, the infinite payment exacted by God has its explanation not so much in the nature of the debt, as rather in the fact that God wills to be glorified in an infinite way by men, and that He wills to confer an infinite dignity on the race for this end.

In conceiving the restoration from the fall and the extinction of the debt according to this point of view, we do not at all disparage the sublime meaning of the Incarnation. Indeed, only thus do we allow its full splendor to shine forth. For the God-man comes forward as the bearer of supernatural gifts, and also as the infinitely powerful conqueror of all evil and iniquity. He does more than give to innocent man the right and power to become a child of God, and as such to glorify God and be happy in Him, for in His infinite might He frees man from his guilt, and takes away the unworthiness and helplessness which resulted from sin. Finally, as He annihilates the measureless distance that nature itself had interposed between man and God, and introduces man into the presence of God, indeed into God's very bosom, so He is able to fill up the bottomless chasm that sin had blasted open between God and man.

We may well dare to say that, in order to display the full greatness of the God-man from all sides, God sent Him not only to elevate the race, but to rescue it from its fall and free it from its guilt. If the race had originally, prior to its sin, received its supernatural goods from the God-man, then the truth would not have been so manifest that He, and He alone, is and can be the source of these goods. For that which has been lost and for a long time missed, points much more emphatically to its source, once it has been found again, than that which has uninterruptedly been possessed in peace. And if the God-man had had no evil to combat in the human race, and particularly if He had had no evil so formidable as sin to vanquish, His divine, all-conquering might, operating only in the silent distribution of graces, would have lacked a theater ample enough for the full range of its activity. However, as matters actually are, the God-man stands forth clearly as God. For in every respect He accords to the human race and to the whole universe all the perfection it lacks by reason of its natural penury and in consequence of its own fault. Despite sin and in the midst of sin He confers a truly priceless perfection and nobility upon the universe.

If the greatness of the mystery is to be preserved from all impairment, this priceless perfection of the universe, and the infinite glorification of God implied in it, must be regarded as the proper, determining objective of the Incarnation. This is the standpoint from which the Incarnation must be viewed. Once this is done, the mystery itself and the whole supernatural world-order are clearly illuminated.

61. Mystical Position and Significance of the God-man as Head of the Entire Universe

Although the God-man primarily enters into union with the human race, through His humanity as the microcosm, He is placed in relationship with the entire cosmos, as was pointed out above.[54] The two halves of the universe, spiritual and material nature, come together in human nature, which is the connecting link joining them both into a whole composed of differentiated members. The fact that the God-man is the head of mankind makes Him directly the head of material nature, whose natural head is man. At the same time He becomes the head of the angels, since in His divine dignity He towers infinitely above them. Moreover, He enters into union with them not, indeed, by unity of race, but by similarity of nature and the organic unity of the universe: He is "the head of all principality and power." [55] "The first-born of every creature" [56] unites in Himself and around Himself the whole of creation in one mystical body and one holy temple of which He, and in Him the Father and the Holy Spirit, take possession, seeing that all things in heaven and on earth are comprised in Him as the head of all. As God, He is before all things, and all things hold together in Him, inasmuch as He, the Word of the power of God, upholds all things, and hence, according to the Apostle, in His humanity He is the head of His body, the Church. Consequently the Church, which is built upon Him in His humanity, must embrace all things that are sustained by His divine power, so that it can be said that even according to His humanity all things hold together and repose in Him, that by His hypostatic union with a created nature He is become the hypostasis of all creation and bears it upon His shoulders,

[54] See St. John Damascene, *Hom. in transfig. Domini*, no. 18 (*PG*, XCVI, 573): "The gracious will of the Father has effected the salvation of the whole world in His only-begotten Son, and has brought all things together in Him. For, since man is the microcosm, joining in himself every nature, the visible as well as the invisible, the will of the Lord and Creator and Governor of all things ordained that the union of divinity with humanity, and thereby of every creature, should be accomplished in His only-begotten and consubstantial Son, that thus God might be all in all." This discourse in general contains many a flash of brilliant insight into the depths of the mystery of Christ.

[55] Col. 2:10.
[56] Col. 1:15.

that the whole of creation is joined to Him and is let down into Him as its root.[57]

Therefore the entire exalted meaning which the God-man has for the human race in particular as its head must pertain to Him, with due proportion, also as regards the whole of creation. Creation receives its ultimate and most august consecration through Him, seeing that the ointment of its head flows down upon it. Hence creation in its entirety becomes a temple of the Holy Spirit in a unique manner, for He is the Spirit of its head; it becomes a sharer in the glory and beatitude of God's Son, who comes to it as the source of divine light and life; it becomes, finally, an endless hymn in praise of the eternal Father, whose eternal Word merges with its tones and brings all its voices together in Himself to form one harmonious chord.

Material nature, which had possessed the root and the crown of its supernatural luster in the sanctity of the first Adam, is raised still higher by the new Adam, who by Himself, by the power of the divinity residing in Him, is the true principle of its supernatural splendor and, in His own body, glows as the most precious pearl in it. Material nature had fallen from its height in the first Adam; but in the second Adam its supernatural destiny is secured with unshakable firmness. For He lays hold of it with so powerful a grip and elevates it so high that neither the sin which He found upon His arrival can hinder Him in the execution of His mission, nor the sin which rises in rebellion against Him after He has established Himself can stem the mighty onrush of His influence.

The angels, purely spiritual natures, did not have the first Adam as their head; they were superior to him. But the second Adam towers above them, and is their head at least so far as He is their king. No Catholic theologian denies this. Can we not go further, and assume that the idea of the head is verified in a still richer sense in Christ's relations to the angels? Is this not suited to the dignity of the God-man and to that of the angels? Is it not in the highest degree fitting that the God-man, as the first-born of all creatures, should be, by power and right, the principle of the supernatural dignity and consecration, grace and glory, of the angels as their head? Do not the angels, too, acquire a much higher dignity, a

[57] See Colossians, the second half of the first chapter, together with the exegesis of Cornelius a Lapide.

closer union with God, by this dependence on Christ, than they would have in virtue of the simple grace of divine sonship?

Not without reason has the Vulgate translated the Greek ἀνακεφαλαιοῦσθαι (Eph. 1:10) by *instaurare*.[58] The angels were not to recover lost grace through Christ; the good angels had always possessed it, the evil spirits were never again to receive it throughout all eternity. Hence the re-establishment of the angels, which was accomplished when the Incarnation actually took place, can mean only that their sanctity was now deeply and firmly rooted in the foundation which God had preordained from eternity, and was adorned with the crown by which it was to receive its final consecration. We are impelled to think of this re-establishment in connection with the void left in heaven by the departure of the fallen angels. This void was to be replenished by the infinite wealth of the divine head: on the one hand, by His making reparation for the dishonor done to God by the sin of the angels; on the other hand, by His ushering men into the places that had been vacated. But, since this *instaurare* must correspond to the Greek ἀνακεφαλαιοῦσθαι, and the Apostle speaks of a re-establishment of all things in heaven as well as upon earth, it must be referred to a perfecting of the good angels, and this is brought about by the fact that Christ became their head.

Accordingly the mysterious import of the Incarnation comes to this, that the God-man, as the Christ par excellence, and as the noble head primarily of the microcosm which is mankind, and thereby also of the macrocosm which is the universe, realizes the highest aim and the most sublime idea that God can have in His

[58] The term ἀνακεφαλαιοῦσθαι implies more than the finishing touch effected by placing the highest and most precious part in its proper position upon the completed whole. We can best clarify its sense by the example of a Gothic building. The placing of the finial upon the pinnacle is a coronation of the edifice. This ornament is the loftiest portion of the building, the last detail that crowns its beauty; but the structure itself is in no way dependent on it. On the other hand, the keystone of a cross-arched vault gives the structure its inner stability; the building is as dependent on it as on its foundation. Even though we be reluctant to admit that grace and glory were originally granted to the angels on the basis of Christ's merits, and hold that the primordial structure of the supernatural order rested on pure grace, we can well suppose not merely that subsequently this edifice received its crowning ornament in Christ, but that He was the keystone imparting inner stability to it. This is quite conceivable in itself; and apparently, according to the Apostle's statement, this is the way we must conceive the matter.

external works. This is the idea of the highest and most comprehensive communication of Himself to creatures, and the idea of the highest and most extensive glorification of Himself through creatures.

Of this idea we can say that it dominates and determines the mystery of the Incarnation; but it is likewise an utterly supernatural, mystical idea, which pure reason can neither conceive nor postulate. It is "the mystery of His will, according to His good pleasure," [59] whence issued the Incarnation itself, which in its own right is the mysterious "dispensation of the mystery which hath been hidden from eternity in God." [60] So far as the Incarnation corresponds to this idea and is determined thereby, we can account for it on the basis of faith; and since the perception of this motivation permits us to catch a glimpse of the most sublime and wonderful plans of divine Providence, it accords to our thirst for knowledge an immensely greater satisfaction than if with our natural reason we had hit upon some other motives pertaining to a lower order of things.

[59] Eph. 1:9.
[60] Eph. 3:9.

CHAPTER XV

Mystical Position and Significance of the God-man as Mediator Between the Trinitarian God and the World

62. THE MEDIATORY FUNCTION OF THE GOD-MAN

TO acquire a deeper and more adequate understanding of the God-man's sublime and universal plan, we must contemplate Him from another angle, which is essentially connected with the view of Him hitherto gained, but affords us many a new insight into His functions.

Thus far we have been regarding the God-man chiefly in His relation to man and the universe, as their head. But at the same time He necessarily occupies a middle position between God and creatures. Or better, He is mediator between God and creatures in His capacity as the supernatural head of the universe in general, and of the human race in particular. The notion of this mediatorship, when viewed in its inmost nature and its vast compass, serves excellently to place the whole supernatural significance of the Incarnation in its proper perspective.

1. When Christ's mediatorship is mentioned, we at once think of His conciliatory function, the intermediacy of reconciliation between sinful mankind and God. But this function is only a single subordinate factor in the idea of the God-man's mediatorship. The mediation in question is essentially the negotiation of an ineffably noble and surpassingly intimate union and intercourse of God with the creature and of the creature with God, although it includes the reconciliation of the creature with God, and indeed a reconciliation unparalleled in its kind.[1] Such is the notion we gain from a simple

[1] St. Cyril of Alexandria, *De Trinitate*, dial. I (*PG*, LXXV, 692): "B. Is, then, the only-begotten to be regarded as mediator for the sole reason that

analysis of the nature of the Incarnation and its relation to God and man.

The God-man is the product of the personal, hypostatic union of divinity with humanity; He is in truth God and man. As man He is at one with the whole human race, indeed, with the created world, for He is its head. As God He is united in the most real and intimate fashion possible with His Father, from whom He proceeds, and with the Holy Spirit, whom He breathes forth. Though in the world and at one with the world, He reaches into the innermost recesses of the Godhead, is God Himself, and is one with the Father and the Holy Spirit. Consequently in His person He raises the world up to the closest proximity, the most intimate union, with the eternal Father; on the other hand, the union which He has with the Father, He extends outside of God, and conveys to the entire world. He links God and God's creature together in so close a union and mutual relationship that all separation of the creature from God caused by the creature's defection, and also the infinite distance

---

He has banished sin, which kept us from God's love and friendship, and has restored us to our pristine state, with all enmity abolished? If there is any other reason, pray tell me at once, for I am most anxious to know. A. I shall do so, and without delay. I wish to point out, however, that in His human nature He did truly do away with all enmity, as it is written [Eph. 2:16]. He came among us as a depositary, so to speak, and a mediator. Although we had wandered far from the love of God in our eagerness for worldly pleasure and our perverse worship of creatures instead of their Creator, He offered us up to God His Father and, having justified us by faith, gained us for God. Still we do not assert that He is our mediator on account of this action alone; the name of mediator, fully justified by fact, belongs to Him for another reason that is secret and mystical. . . . Although He was the unsullied beauty and form and image of God His Father, yet God the Word, who is from the Father and in Him, emptied Himself to the point of self-effacement, not forced thereto by anyone, but voluntarily carrying out the will of His Father. He became man, preserving His natural dignity absolutely whole and unimpaired, but assuming a human nature by His incarnation. He is one Son, and we know Him as such, but He is made up of two elements: for the divine and the human nature came together and were joined in unity, in some indescribable and mysterious manner that exceeds our understanding. . . . Hence He is held to be a mediator in this sense, too. By showing that there were joined and united in Himself elements that are naturally very remote and separated by an immense gap, namely, divinity and humanity, He also united us, through Himself, with God His Father. He is of the same nature as God, because He is from God and in God; and He is of the same nature as ourselves, for He is from us and in us. For, as far as His humanity is concerned, He is not different from us, but is like to us in all things, sin alone excepted, our Emmanuel."

which nature itself sets up between the creature and God, even abstracting from the creature's fall, are surmounted and abolished.

Thus through the sublime miracle of His personal union, Christ is the substantial and supremely real bond which marvelously associates the most widely separated opposites. The immediate effect of this bond is a union of the creature with God, a union that is willed for its own sake and is substantial, a union by which the substantial unity between the Father and the Son is to be communicated to the creature and glorified in such communication. The inspiring words of the Savior: "that they may be one, as We also are one: I in them, and Thou in Me; that they may be made perfect in one" [John 17:22 f.], are here perfectly fulfilled.

St. Hilary explains these words in the sense of a substantial union whereby the oneness of nature between the Son and the Father is to be transmitted to us, when in referring to Christ's union with us he brings in the Eucharist: "If the Word is truly made flesh and we truly partake of the Word made flesh in the bread of the Lord, must we not conclude that He abides in us by nature, since He, born as man, has inseparably taken to Himself the nature of our flesh, and has joined the nature of His flesh to the nature of eternity [i.e., the divinity] under the sacrament of His flesh which is to be distributed to us? For all of us are thus one, since the Father is in Christ and Christ is in us. . . . Therefore He is in us by His flesh and we are in Him, for what we are is with Him in God." "And so," continues St. Hilary later, "we are taught that a perfect unity is established through the mediator. For, while we abide in Him, He abides in the Father; and while abiding in the Father, He abides in us. This is the way we mount up to unity with the Father." [2] "The divine Logos," says St. Cyril of Alexandria in like vein, "wishing to confer a great grace, nay, in some sense an infinite grace, upon the human family, draws all together into a certain oneness with Himself. By assuming a human body He has taken up His dwelling in us; but He has the Father in Himself, being His Word and reflection." [3]

By the union with the Father which Christ achieves in His person, "we are lifted up to oneness with the majesty of the Father," [4] we

[2] *De Trinitate*, lib. VIII, nos. 13–15; *PL*, X, 246–48.
[3] *Thesaurus*, p. 122 (assert. XII; *PG*, LXXV, 204).
[4] St. Hilary, *In Psalm.* 67 [no. 37]; *PL*, IX, 469.

are made substantially akin to Him as a truly divine race; we share in the manner of the Son's union with the Father, and also in its power.[5]

For such a union of man with God the Father is unthinkable unless we were meant to participate in the prerogatives and the life of the divine nature, just as the Son participates in the majesty and life of the Father by His substantial oneness with the Father. This living union, the root of which is substantial union, can be nothing else than participation in the divine nature by the grace of sonship. How could the Father take us, in His Son, to His bosom, if He desired merely to enter into a simple relation of peace with us, but not into the intimate friendship and fellowship of life? This substantial union can be necessary or appropriate only if another union, measuring up to it, a supernatural oneness of life, of glory, and of beatitude, is to be established and sealed by it.

St. Athansius was aware of this when he explained the necessity of a mediator who would be truly human and divine: "Man would not have experienced deification by union with a mere creature, unless the Son of God were truly God; nor would man have been brought nigh to the Father, if it had not been the true, substantial Word of the Father who assumed flesh. And as we should have been freed neither from sin nor from damnation if the flesh assumed by the Word were not really and essentially human flesh—for with a thing foreign to us we have nothing in common—so man would not have been deified if it had not been the Word substantially proceeding from the Father, the Father's own true Word, that took our flesh. For this union was contrived that the true and, so to say, substantial divinity might bind the true and natural man to itself, and that the welfare and deification of man might be made to endure." [6]

[5] St. Cyril of Alexandria, *In Ioan.*, lib. VI; *PG*, LXXIII, 1045.

[6] St. Cyril, who follows in the footsteps of St. Athanasius throughout, describes the necessity and significance of Christ's mediation in a way that recalls his predecessor (*In Ioan.*, lib. XI, c.12; *PG*, LXXIV, 564): "The bond of our union with God the Father is manifestly Christ, who has joined us to Himself as man, but also to God, seeing that as God He is naturally in His Father. For a nature that is subject to corruption could not be raised to incorruption unless a nature that is free from all corruption and mutability had come down into it, elevating to its own condition of perfection the nature which ever remains inferior, extricating the latter, so to speak, from the limitations proper to the creature by joining and associating it with itself, and changing to conformity with itself the nature which inherently is not such." In another passage (*Contra Arianos*, Or. IV, no. 6; *PG*, XXVI, 476), Athanasius himself, like Cyril, explains the mediation of the Word made flesh

From the standpoint of its activity, the substantial mediatorship of Christ may be conceived in a twofold way: first, in a more physical sense, as a bridge [7] or channel that establishes contact between God and creature, and so we have been regarding it thus far; secondly, as a certain reciprocal and real pledging of God and the creature, by which the most intimate, noble, and changeless friendship and love are inaugurated and made secure on both sides. Thus Irenaeus stated that the Logos has brought God to man through the Father's Spirit (whom the Apostle calls the pledge of our inheritance), and conversely has inserted man in God by the assumption of human nature, and thus has truly and lastingly conferred incorruptibility on us.[8] In another passage he remarks that the Son of God, by making Himself like to us and us like to Him, has brought it about that man became dear to the Father (and was thus assured of the Father's love).[9] Tertullian designates the mediatorship as the function of a depositary, a guarantor of pledges. "He [Jesus], called the depositary of God and of man because of the deposits of

---

as a transfer of those goods which the Logos possesses in His own right, but which man can lay no claim to: "The Word was made flesh that He might transmit to us the gifts which had been granted to Him. Simple men would never have been worthy of these goods. And the Word as such had no need of them. Wherefore the Word was joined to us; and then He gave us to share in His power, and raised us to the heights. For the Word who existed in man elevated man, and man received the Word who existed in man."

[7] This is the name St. Paulinus of Nola applies to the God-man in a passage (Epist. 33 [alias 13]; PL, LXI, 222) in which he also alludes to an idea of Tertullian's, which we shall call attention to shortly. "By Christ we are joined to God and incorporated in Him, so that upon earth we may cling to the pledge of God, the Holy Spirit, whom He gave to us, and in God may have the pledge of ourselves, the flesh of Christ. For He closes that tremendous gap which separates mortal things from divine, by His mediation and common link with both. He is, if I may say so, a bridge between the two, and the road which joins earth to heaven."

[8] Adv. haer., lib. V, c. 1, no. 2 (PG, VII, 1121): "Suo igitur sanguine redimente nos Domino, et dante animam suam pro nostra anima et carnem suam pro nostris carnibus, et effundente Spiritum Patris in adunitionem et communionem Dei et hominis, ad homines quidem deponente Deum per Spiritum, ad Deum autem rursus imponente hominem per suam incarnationem, et firme et vere in adventu suo donante nobis incorruptelam, per communionem, quae est ad eum, perierunt omnes haereticorum doctrinae."

[9] Ibid., lib. XVI, c. 16, no. 2 (PG, VII, 1167): "Tunc autem hoc Verbum ostensum est, quando homo Verbum Dei factum est, semetipsum homini, et hominem sibimetipsi assimilans, ut per eam, quae est ad Filium, similitudinem pretiosus homo fiat Patri."

both parties entrusted to Him, guards the deposit of the flesh in Himself as the pledge of the whole sum. For as He has left us the pledge of the Spirit, so He has accepted from us the pledge of the flesh, and has taken it up to heaven as the earnest of the whole sum that is one day to follow after. Rest assured, flesh and blood: you have taken possession of heaven and the kingdom of God in Christ." [10]

We need no longer call attention to the fact that the mutual friendship, love, and kindness which rest upon so excellent a pledging cannot be purely natural, or a mere restoration. This pledging is of such a sort that in it God bestows on us and makes our own His most precious and His dearest possession, the Spirit of His heart in His Son, and that He must love the assumed flesh as His own, and consequently must love us, too, as belonging to Himself. With right, therefore, the Fathers agree with the Apostle in basing upon the pledge of the Holy Spirit the hope for the inheritance of the children of God, and upon the possession which God takes of our nature the confidence that He, treating it as His own, will lavish His everlasting love upon it.

2. The meaning of Christ's substantial mediatorship is not exhausted by the supernatural union of the creature with God which it formally establishes and seals. At the same time it makes Christ a born mediator in His activity; it is the foundation for His active mediatorship. We may no more concentrate on the former without the latter than we may on the latter without the former. However, it is manifest that the latter as well as the former, to be appreciated in its full import, must be conceived as an instrument effecting an absolutely supernatural unity and union of the creature with God.

In His active mediatorship Christ negotiates a certain interchange between God and the creature: God's activity with regard to the creature, and the creature's activity with regard to God.

In the concrete: Christ first appears as God's emissary to creatures. Proceeding from the Father while nevertheless remaining

[10] *De resurrectione carnis* [c. 51] (*PL*, II, 869; *CSEL*, XLVII, 105): "Hic sequester Dei atque hominum appellatus ex utriusque partis deposito commisso sibi, carnis quoque depositum servat in semetipso, arrhabonem summae totius. Quemadmodum enim nobis arrhabonem Spiritus reliquit, ita et a nobis arrhabonem carnis accepit, et vexit in coelum, pignus totius summae, illuc quandoque redigendae. Securae estote caro et sanguis, usurpastis et coelum et regnum Dei in Christo."

with Him, and bearing the fullness of the divinity in Himself, He comes to the creature not as a mere authorized agent with delegated authority, but as the personal representative of God, anointed by the unguent of the divine nature and essence as one endowed with divine activity.

It is clear that the divine activity, to the exercise of which this legate is appointed, must be most extraordinary. For He proceeds from the interior of the Godhead, is equipped with unheard-of power, and in Him God approaches so very near to the creature. In drawing so near to us, in descending so far to us, in sending the Son of His bosom to us, God must unlock the depths of the Godhead and deliver over to creatures the fullness of its riches in the person of His own Son who comes to us. The Son of God made man must transmit to creatures the divine light, the divine truth, of which He is the incarnate Word, and by which creatures are raised to a participation in divine knowledge. As the only-begotten of the Father, as "the Son of His love," [11] He must transmit the grace of the children of God, by giving to all who believe in Him the power to be made the sons of God. He must deliver to creatures a new, higher kingdom of divine dominion, by taking special possession of them in the name of God, and by bringing it about through the power proceeding from Him that God may live and hold sway in them and make them reflect His splendor as the body reflects the soul united to it. In short, anointed with the ointment of His divinity, He is destined by His procession from the Father to be prophet as the mediator of supernatural enlightenment, to be priest as the mediator of supernatural graces, and to be king as the mediator of the supernatural divine kingdom.

But He is also mediator of men, and of creatures in general, at the court of God. By bringing God so close to creatures that God, as it were, pours Himself into creatures and lives in them, He brings creatures so close to God that in their offices to God they attain to God's infinity, otherwise unapproachable for them. He acts in creatures as their head, and they conduct themselves toward God in His name. Thus, as mediator of creatures to God, He can and should offer to God the hymn of an acknowledgment and praise proportionate to His majesty. Thus He can and should bring it about that in Him and with Him creatures pay to God a tribute of adoration

[11] Col. 1:13.

and satisfaction which is worthy of God's infinite eminence, and which counterbalances the affront done to Him by sin. Thus, finally, He can and should subject creatures so completely to God's dominion that in Him and with Him creatures serve their Lord with a kingly service, and their homage is no longer that of slaves but of royal personages summoned to joint rule. As He represents God among men in the capacity of prophet, priest, and king, so He represents men at the court of God as a prophet who in their stead sings God's praises as they are unable to do, as a priest who in their behalf gives to God the supreme tribute which they are wholly incapable of supplying, and lastly as a king who in place of them and through them renders to God the noble, free service of a Son.

The functions of the God-man's mediatorship are manifestly summed up in His priesthood. When He brings God's grace down to us, it is clear that at the same time He is acting as prophet to convey to us the light of truth which is implied in this grace, and in which this grace and its author are known; and that He is a king who founds and rules the kingdom of God, for this is nothing other than the kingdom of grace. And on the other hand, if He alone is able in the creature's name to pay worthy tribute to God, then He, and He alone, will be in a position to render to God the praise and obedience which His infinite majesty demands.

Indeed, the entire mediatorship of Christ is at bottom nothing but a priesthood, just as His priesthood is nothing but a mediatorship between God and man. But Christ's priesthood is a unique, superhuman, heavenly priesthood, which brings God down to creatures and raises creatures up to God in a supernatural, mysterious intercommunion, for it is the organ of a supernatural activity of God in man's behalf, and of a supernatural worship which man pays to God. However, we shall arrive at a complete notion of Christ's priesthood and mediatorship only when we come to consider the effects and inner relationship of the two functions that thus meet in the God-man.

Owing to the fact that in the God-man God draws so amazingly near to us with the power of His grace and works His influence upon us, there is abolished the immeasurable chasm that separated the creature from God, whether on account of the creature's natural lowliness or on account of his guilt; and in the grace of divine sonship, together with the extinction of the guilt, a supernatural union of the creature with God is inaugurated. But God's plan is not that the God-man should simply bring this oneness with God down with Him from heaven; rather He is literally to purchase it, earn it by His religious subjection, and so draw it down from heaven. For its firmer foundation and strengthening this oneness is to be achieved in a way that obliges God on His part to establish and effect it. But God can be thus obligated only if the creature offers Him an infinitely valuable price through the cult instituted by the God-man.

Consequently the sacerdotal mediatorship of the God-man must culminate in the fact that, by the worship He offers to God in the name of creatures, He purchases and merits the union with God which He is appointed to accomplish as God's instrument.

Even as substantial mediator the God-man sets up between God and the creature a bond that can and must result from the union of both in grace, seeing that God draws near to the creature with the power of His grace, and that the creature becomes worthy of union with God by grace, because of his relation to the God-man as his head. But this bond is strengthened and sealed only by the active or moral mediatorship exercised by Christ in His priesthood, since it is only in such mediatorship that an interchange of counter-balancing offices takes place.

If man is brought into union with God through the mediation of the God-man, then the God-man, who is the mediator in the acquisition of grace, becomes also the mediator in the gratitude owed for this gift. Surely gratitude for a gift, if it is to be adequate, must be as great as the price for which the gift was bought. By himself the creature can no more return due thanks for his supernatural union with God than he can merit it by himself. Only the God-man, and the homage He renders, is sufficiently worthy and valuable for this end; by His oblation He must crown and perfect the union of the creature with God, a union which He had founded.

How Christ actually realizes the worship which He offers to God, and the bond which He draws between God and man, and in particular how His moral mediatorship thereby becomes a thoroughly real and substantial mediatorship, so that He not only performs works in God's honor but also presents to God a substantial gift of infinite value, we will show later when we treat of the sacrifice of Christ.

Such, in outline, is the idea of the exalted mediatorship of the God-man. Clearly it is not reducible simply to the satisfying of some need grounded in nature, but evinces an exceedingly lofty, supernatural character, and has as its essential effect not only the restoration of a natural unity that had been sundered, but also the foundation and perfecting of an absolutely supernatural, mysterious union between the creature and God. Consequently it must be an august mystery in itself.

In the concrete, of course, Christ is mediator for the restoration of a unity that had been severed, and therefore His mediatory activity has necessarily the character of atonement. This atonement, however, is intended not only to extinguish sin, but to set up an ineffably close and tenacious bond between the parties to be reconciled, such as prior to sin could be neither claimed nor surmised, at least not by natural man.

Christ's mediatory office with regard to material creatures and to the angels might be explained in a similar manner. But we should merely have to repeat in other words what we have already stated about the significance of Christ as head of the entire universe.

Accordingly we conclude this section with the reflection that the significance of the God-man as mediator is no less sublime and mysterious than His significance as head. The mysterious character of the Incarnation is not at all destroyed by this significance, or by the appropriateness and necessity of the Incarnation which it implies. On the contrary, such considerations accentuate the mystery.

63. SUBJECTIVE SIGNIFICANCE, FOR GOD AND MAN, OF THE INCARNATION AND ITS ECONOMY

The purposes that we have listed as determining and dominating the idea of the Incarnation in God's sight are entirely objective in character: they are found in an order of things which was established by the Incarnation and is to be crowned by the Incarnation, in the continuation of the Trinitarian communication and self-glorification of God to the whole outside universe, and in the foundation and perfecting of a most sublime, supernatural union of the creature with God.

All the other aims and effects of the mystery are of a more subjective nature, as regards both God and creatures: as regards God, who in carrying out the project and achieving its objective, intrinsic ends (the *finis operis*) intends to assert and reveal those of His attributes that cooperate in its execution; as regards creatures, who receive great spiritual profit from their knowledge of the origin, nature, and effects of the mystery.[12]

Thus in carrying out the Incarnation, God displays His power by the production of so noble and arduous a work; His wisdom, by the temperate yet effective disposition of means leading to the highest goal; His goodness, by wishing to communicate Himself to creatures in so unparalleled a fashion that He incorporates them in His only-begotten Son, and gives Him to them as the pledge and purchase price for their liberation from guilt and acquisition of grace; His sanctity and justice, by willing to extend outside of Himself the glorification which He receives within the Godhead, and to remit sin only after condign satisfaction. The manifestation of these attributes we call God's subjective aims (*finis operantis*), because they do not determine the intrinsic character of the object willed, but presuppose it as determined according to its idea, and follow more from the relationship of the effect to its cause than from the nature of the effect as such. Therefore these aims may always be mentioned when explaining the origin of the Incarnation, but they do not disclose the proper, intrinsic motive of the effect as it is in itself, and do not lead to an understanding of the idea of it; rather, in order to be fully understood, these aims presuppose the understanding of the idea.

Whoever would be satisfied with these aims would be like the art critic who, in accounting for the existence of a painting and its beauty, would say no more than that the artist wished to reveal the whole of his genius and skill in this creation. The art critic would satisfy us only if he explained the inner motive which inspired the artist and guided him in executing the painting, and by the under-

---

[12] The expression, "subjective significance," or "subjective end," will perhaps not meet with universal favor. But from the nature of the case all such terms are ambiguous. As stated, by the objective significance of the Incarnation we here mean the significance attaching to the object as it is in itself; the subjective significance is the meaning which the Incarnation has for the subjects concerned, in the sense that by their activity they either effect it, or in some way occupy themselves with it. So far as the subjective significance is rooted in the objective significance, and is not arbitrarily connected with the latter by the Author of the work, it also is undoubtedly objective.

standing of which alone we can appreciate how the picture is really so beautiful, and how, consequently, it could have inspired the artist and shows forth his art. In the same way theological science does not give a full account of the tremendous work which the Incarnation is, unless it discloses the great idea that underlies it, and consequently shows how God was able and willed to reveal His power, His wisdom, His goodness and holiness, in carrying it out. The inner motive here is the wonderful extension of the Trinitarian productions to the whole outside universe, as well as the surpassing union of creatures with God that is thereby brought about.

In like manner the subjective meaning which the Incarnation has for the man who contemplates it lies outside its proper idea, although it automatically follows therefrom, and in any case was comprised in God's plan. To the objective idea of the Incarnation belongs the fact that man is raised to the status of a member of Christ and to the sonship of God, in order through Christ to glorify God in a supernatural manner and to be happy in God. Whence it follows automatically, and God also intends this, that man is roused to the practice of good and the avoidance of evil by his knowledge of the Incarnation, that in Christ he beholds the model he is to imitate, that this intimate union of God with him strengthens his confidence, makes an awareness of God easy for him, and enkindles and inflames his love. But all these subjective effects of the Incarnation are conceivable only on the basis of the objective effects. That is, they presuppose that we are called to be members and brethren of Christ by the objective power and significance of the Incarnation. This bearing which the Incarnation has on the guidance and stimulation of our life, so as to make it pleasing to God, enables us to give an account of the Incarnation only because it has called us to so high an estate.

Such an account would be quite impossible if by a life pleasing to God we should understand no more than the development of our nature—as we have previously seen—although the fact that the Incarnation is of supreme importance for the ravages and needs of nature is not excluded. It has a closer connection with the unfolding of man's supernatural life.

We desire here to call attention to some profound but seldom applied thoughts of St. Thomas, which enable us to see this relation in its proper perspective.

In the *Summa contra Gentiles* (lib. IV, c. 54), St. Thomas shows how admirably the Incarnation is adapted to the purpose of rendering easy for man the pursuit of his supernatural end, that is, the vision of God.

In the first place, he points out, man might doubt his ability to attain to so marvelous a union of his intellect with the divine essence as is necessary for the beatific vision, because of the immeasurable disparity between the two natures. But the still higher, hypostatic union of a divine person with human nature shows us that the lesser union must be possible, and hence strengthens our hope for its consummation. Moreover, it strengthens our hope all the more since it brings the excellence of our nature home to our consciousness, and shows us that we, elevated as we are above all creatures, can and ought to achieve perfect happiness in closest union with God.[18]

If man is destined to the immediate vision of God, and hence to a participation in the knowledge proper to God, with regard to the road leading to this goal he can have no other teacher than God Himself. That this instruction which man receives from God may take place in a manner befitting man's nature, it appears suitable that God Himself should come to him in visible form, that God's own Word should personally communicate such participation in the divine cognition, and that the Son of God should usher us into the bosom of His Father. Thus the Incarnation of the Logos is admirably adapted to the formation of supernatural faith in us.

Further, the intimate love for God, by which we are to tend to supernatural union with Him, cannot be better roused and inflamed than by the love which God Himself displays most perfectly by assuming our nature and wishing to become our brother. The closer God draws to us and the more He comes down to our level, the more tender and trusting will be our love for Him, and the more ardently our love must long to be united with Him also in His divinity.

It is apparent that these reasons which St. Thomas advances are not derived from the corruptness of our nature or the sinfulness

[18] Similar is the following thought of St. Maximus Martyr (*Cap. theol. dogm.*, cent. I, c.62; *PG*, XC, 1204): "A firm pledge of hope for deification is given to human nature by the incarnation of God, which makes man divine in the same measure as that in which God was made human. For He who became man free from all sin will deify human nature without changing it into divinity, and will exalt it as much for His own sake as He has humbled Himself for man's sake."

clinging to it, but from the elevation of nature above itself. We are so insistent in stressing this point because of the general tendency to explain the appearance of the Son of God in the flesh exclusively on the basis of our nature's inclination to sensuality. Certainly the Incarnation is, and must be, a means whereby man lifts himself out of the servitude of sense to all that is spiritual. But more important is the visible appearance of God in the flesh as a pledge that He will one day reveal Himself to us in His essence. The visible appearance of God can be recognized as a suitable means for raising us up out of sensuality only in view of our destination to the immediate vision of the divine essence. If we were not thus raised, but were merely to be freed from servitude to sensuality, this means would be disproportionate.[14]

64. Justification and Further Development of the Doctrine about the Meaning and Motivation of the Incarnation. The God-man in Every Respect the Focal Point and Center of Gravity of the World

1. In explaining, as we have done, the meaning and motivation of the Incarnation and its relation with its end, have we not come into conflict with the view which, if not dogmatically established, is commonly held in the Church? Does not the Church teach us that the Son of God became man on account of us men (*propter nos homines*), and indeed to save us from sin? Is not the doctrine of the Fathers fairly constant, that it was precisely the need and the wretched estate of the human race that prevailed upon Him, who otherwise would have had no reason for doing so, to come down from heaven? Is it not the common opinion that the Incarnation is

[14] In chapter 25 of the *Manuale*, erroneously ascribed to St. Augustine [found in *PL*, XL, 962, where it is chapter 26], the author rightly describes the visible appearance of God as a good parallel to the spiritual intuition of Him and corresponding to it, for by it man's corporal nature is united to God in the same way as his spiritual nature is united to God in the beatific vision: "God became man for the sake of men . . . so that both of man's perceptive faculties might be beatified in Him: namely, that the eyes of the soul might be filled with His divinity, and the eye of the body with His humanity. Thus human nature, created by Him, feasts upon Him, whether absent from Him or in His presence." St. Bonaventure frequently quotes this passage and develops its underlying thought.

in itself an abasement unworthy of God, so that the Son of God not only would not have become man, but could not have done so, if sin had not made it necessary? Accordingly does it not seem that the motivation of the Incarnation is to be sought not so much in the lofty regions where we have located them, as in man's dire need resulting from sin?

Well and good. But have we denied that the Son of God became man for the sake of us men, and to save us from sin? Not at all. We have expressly taught that the Incarnation is pre-eminently for the benefit of us men, and hence that God willed it out of indescribable love and benevolence toward us. Indeed, this love shows itself greatest of all by not merely releasing man in the most complete manner from sin and its consequences, but by willing further to raise him to an astounding sublimity and glory that surpasses all understanding.

Again, have we denied that the Incarnation is designed precisely to free fallen man from his sin, and that consequently God's love, which is the motive of the Incarnation, is a merciful love? We deny only that the wealth of this love is limited to the claims of compassion, and that the principle and motive of the Incarnation can be found in such limitation. This motive can be no other than the boundless love which God displays after man's sin, contrary to all expectation and beyond all our notions. And further, we deny that the elevation of fallen man was the only end or at any rate the highest end, and that love for man was the only motive or the highest motive of the Incarnation. The glory of Christ and of God Himself is the highest aim, and the love of God for Himself and for Christ is the highest motive of the Incarnation. Often as the holy Fathers assign the necessary restoration of fallen man as the end of the Incarnation, and God's mercy as its motive, no less often do they insist that God in His overflowing love has decreed to give us incalculably more, and to elevate us incomparably higher after the Incarnation than He had done before. "Since the fullness of life enjoyed by the human race," says St. Leo, "had collapsed in our first parents, God in His mercy willed, through His only-begotten Son Jesus Christ, to come to the assistance of the creature made to His likeness, in such wise that the repairing of nature should not come from outside that nature, and that its second state should advance beyond the dignity of its own origin. Happy the nature, if it had not fallen from that state which God had ordained; happier, if it remains in that state which God has restored. It was a great thing to have received its form from Christ, but it is a greater thing to have its substance in Christ." [15]

If, then, the Fathers make it a rule to stress the forgiveness and extinction of sin as the end of the Incarnation, this is explained quite simply from other reasons, without assuming that this aim is objectively the ultimate purpose of the Incarnation.[16] They usually portray that side of the Incarnation which appears to the human race from the standpoint of the actual plight in which it finds itself;

[15] St. Leo the Great (*Serm. 2 de resurr.; PL*, LIV, 390): "Collapsa in parentibus primis humani generis plenitudine, ita misericors Deus creaturae ad imaginem suam factae per unigenitum suum Iesum Christum voluit subvenire, ut nec extra naturam esset reparatio naturae, et ultra propriae originis dignitatem proficeret secunda conditio. Felix, si ab eo non decideret, quod Deus fecit; felicior, si in eo maneret, quod refecit. Multum fuit a Christo recepisse formam, sed plus est in Christo habere substantiam. Suscepit enim nos in suam proprietatem illa natura, quae nec nostris sua nec suis nostra consumeret." St. Chrysostom goes into greater detail in a passage which, as is well known, has been grievously mishandled by the Pelagians. "For this reason the Apostle does not here say grace, but abundance of grace. For we did not receive merely so much grace as was necessary to do away with sin, but much more. We have been freed from punishment, and have put off all iniquity, and have been regenerated from above and, leaving the old man in the grave, have risen. We have been redeemed and sanctified and admitted to adoption. Moreover, we have been justified, have been made brothers of the only-begotten and coheirs with Him, have been fashioned into one body with Him, are accounted members of His flesh, and have been joined to Him no less closely than the body is joined to the head. All these blessings Paul calls an abundance of grace, thus indicating that we have not merely received a medicine that is capable of healing our wounds, but in addition health, beauty, honor, glory, and dignities that vastly surpass our natural condition" (*In epist. ad Rom.*, hom. 10, no. 2; *PG*, LX, 477). Similarly Isidore of Pelusium, lib. III, ep. 195; *PG*, LXXVIII, 880. Among recent theologians, Dieringer has given special prominence to this point, in his *Lehrbuch der katholischen Dogmatik*, 4th ed., p. 464.

[16] That the Fathers do not really intend their words to be taken in an absolute and categorical sense when they set forth redemption from sin as the end of the Incarnation in terms which seem to exclude every other purpose, is clear from the many passages we have already cited. At times they employ similarly exclusive expressions with regard to other objectives. Thus, for instance, St. Bernard (*Serm. 1 de vig. nativ.; PL*, CLXXXIII, 88): "Why did the Son of God become man, except to make men sons of God?" St. John Chrysostom speaks in the same way, *In Matth.*, hom. 2, no. 2 (*PG*, LVII, 25). In any case we may not lose sight of the truth which St. Augustine mentions in *De Trinitate*, lib. XIII, c. 17, no. 22 (*PL*, XLII, 1031): "There are many points in the incarnation of God's Son which we will do well to inspect and study."

they emphasize that effect which is most indispensable to us and which is at the same time the preliminary condition for all the higher effects. They behold in it especially the means of banishing the evil which burdens the race, without thereby denying or even losing sight of the incalculable goods which it is meant to convey to us. Otherwise why should they call Adam's sin happy, for the reason that it has brought us such and so great a Redeemer, if they thought that Christ was merely to do away with sin, without conferring any higher good than existed before the Fall?

Hence the effacement of sin must be regarded as a subordinate objective, and the sin itself as an occasion which God awaited in order to manifest His love to men in so astounding a manner, and to give the God-man an opportunity to display His inexhaustible power on all sides, in the conquest of evil as well as in the inauguration of good.

Thus when we profess in the Creed that the Son of God became man *propter nos homines*, we do not thereby signify that love for us men was the first and highest motive of the Incarnation. Love for creatures is never the highest motive for God's external works. The phrase, "God acts out of pure love for creatures," means, wherever employed, that God's external operations are not motivated by personal need or performed for His own utility. Manifestly God loves creatures only in Himself, and hence wills to glorify Himself in them. In the present case God could not will the God-man out of sheer love for creatures, seeing that the God-man Himself is worth infinitely more than all mere creatures. Consequently creatures exist for Him and are loved for His sake even more than He exists for them and is loved and willed on their account. Hence God's love for Himself, by which He wills the external manifestation of His Trinitarian glory, and His love for the God-man, to whom He wills to communicate Himself in an infinite way, as He does to no creature, is the motive for the Incarnation even more than is the redemption and elevation of creatures. We by no means exclude this, but rather suppose it as self-understood, when with grateful hearts we so often proclaim that the Son of God has become man for the sake of us men.

So, too, the angels, in the hymn by which they announced to men the birth of Emmanuel and sang of its joyous fruits, placed the glory of God ahead of the peace which was thereby to come to men. True, we are accustomed to look upon ourselves as the goal and the motive of the Incarnation, and accordingly we lay stress on God's love for us. But we do so in order to impress on ourselves the truth that God was not compelled to the Incarnation by any sort of necessity, least of all by any need on His part, and that the whole benefit arising from it can accrue only to us. We do so in order to excite our wonder at the purity and disinterestedness of the love which gave us Christ, and thus to discharge the first and highest duty which so great a benefit lays on us, the duty of gratitude. We might add that as a rule we emphasize that aspect of a thing which is of prime importance and interest to ourselves.

These reasons likewise explain why Sacred Scripture itself almost always depicts the Incarnation as ordained to our salvation and benefit. Furthermore, just as God's love for us, whereby He loves us in Himself and for Himself, appears infinitely purer, holier, and greater than if He loved us merely for our own sake, so the love with which God gives us Christ out of love for Him is more precious and valuable for us than if He had given us Christ only for our own sake, loving us on account of ourselves.

However rightly we may raise the question, whether Christ would have become man in case Adam had not sinned, at any rate this much must be held, that even then the main ends of the Incarnation could have motivated its realization. The relations of the Incarnation to the founding and perfecting of the order of grace, to the perfecting of the universe in general, and to the infinite glorification of God, would have been pertinent in that case also. Thus, for example, St. Thomas, who answers the question in the negative, or rather declines to treat it, in other passages suggests many reasons for the Incarnation which are entirely independent of sin and the Fall, and have to do exclusively with the institution of the supernatural order.[17] To have any meaning, the question must seemingly inquire whether some of the aims actually intended by God are sufficient to motivate the Incarnation, if sin is left aside. In reality and in the concrete the Incarnation is envisaged together with the Fall, but without doubt in such wise that God has associated the permission of the Fall itself with the decree of the Incarnation.

Hence we must categorically reject as untenable the opinion that

[17] See the preceding paragraphs. [Cf. *Summa*, IIIa, q. 1, a. 3; *In III Sent.*, d. 1, q. 1, a. 3.]

the Incarnation would have been unworthy of God apart from the anguish of mankind that resulted from the Fall, and that God could not have been induced to effect it unless He had been, as it were, forced thereto by man's distress.

2. In proceeding with a refutation of this view, we shall be preparing the way for a vindication of the idea of the absolutely supernatural character of the Incarnation at the precise juncture where the God-man most completely humbles Himself.

In the first place, is there any need on man's part which God could not alleviate in any other way than by the abasement of Himself? Nearly all the Fathers and theologians declare themselves decisively against such a view, and contend that many other means were at the disposal of God's wisdom and omnipotence, not only to free man from his sin, but even to restore him to his supernatural union with God.

But even supposing that the Incarnation were the only means: would God have been able to abase Himself to please man, to make a sacrifice of Himself for man? Does God exist for men's sake, or man for God's sake? And although God embraces man with an infinite love, this love is infinite only because God loves man in Himself and loves Himself in man. If, then, the Incarnation really involves an abasement of God, this could not be justified by any need on man's part.

However, does any such abasement of God really take place? God stoops down to man's level by becoming man, without however quitting His exalted position; this condescension is precisely the truest and most perfect proof of His greatness. God descends to the lowliness of humanity; but He thereby raises humanity, which He assumes, to His own level, to His own majesty. When the Son of God becomes man, the Father prolongs the eternal generation into the outside world, utters His infinite Word from the interior of the Godhead to the exterior, and by this very utterance gains the greatest glory which He can attain in His external works. And so the Incarnation could have taken place without man's sin; there is no reason why it could not have occurred on this supposition, since its very highest goal, the infinite glory of God, could have been attained.

The Apostle's words, "He emptied Himself," cannot be applied to the Incarnation as such. Otherwise the Son of God even now in heaven would have to be in a state of self-divestment, self-emptying —which has never been maintained by anyone.

The Son of God has divested, emptied (ἐκένωσεν) Himself [18] not by the very fact of assuming human nature, but by assuming human nature in its condition of lowliness, imperfection, and passibility, just as it is possessed by mere men, and by not pervading and filling it with His divine glory and happiness from the beginning, and particularly by allowing Himself, like any other man, to appear in its lower and more external aspect ("in habit found as a man," that is, mere man), and not as the God-man. In short, He divested and emptied Himself in the sense that as man He waived claim to the glory and happiness which were His due as Son of God, and did not transfigure and glorify the "form of a servant" in the way in which per se it should have been transfigured and glorified as belonging to the "form" of the Son of God, and in the way in which it actually was transfigured and glorified after His resurrection.[19]

But at any rate was not this state, so far short of the dignity of the God-man, an abasement which He could take upon Himself only on account of man's need? If the God-man could not have taken this self-emptying upon Himself for other reasons than the crushing distress of man, for which on our hypothesis no other relief was at hand, He could not have done so for this purpose either, at least He could not have done so purely for man's sake. Man's plight is explained only by the demands of God's offended honor; and just as God could have forgone an adequate satisfaction if He had so willed, so He would actually have had to forgo it if the self-emptying of the God-man had been something intrinsically unworthy of Him.

But suffering and death are not in themselves ignominious; they are such only when they freight the subject with a compelling necessity, in consequence of nature or of sin, and against his will. When voluntarily assumed or accepted they are, according to circumstances, the highest honor and ornament. No one, to be sure, as long as there is question only of his own well-being, will prefer suffering to impassibility, death to life, mortality to immortality. We take

[18] Phil. 2:6 f.

[19] What we here state is so true that theologians commonly distinguish a *status exinanitionis* and a *status exaltationis* in Christ. If the *exinanitio* referred to the substance of the Incarnation, this distinction would be meaningless.

suffering upon ourselves only to gain a greater good. But a person suffers for others not only to relieve a need or to acquire a good for them, but also for the sole reason that he shows his love and esteem better by suffering than by all the deeds he performs for their benefit or by all the goods he gives them. Suffering thus undertaken is obviously an act of the purest self-sacrifice and the most sublime virtue, and hence is more honorable and lovable than impassibility.

If we apply these considerations to Christ, we perceive that He could have taken suffering and death upon Himself out of love for man, to redeem him, but still more out of love for God, to restore to Him the honor of which He had been robbed and the exactions of which gave rise to man's need of redemption. This material abasement involved no moral abasement, since suffering and death, arising from Christ's free will and undertaken for the noblest motives, were most honorable for Him, much more honorable than immunity to suffering.

Upon looking more closely into the matter, we see that what makes suffering honorable is not the distress or the need of him for whom one suffers; rather it is the freedom and the noble motive of the sufferer. Consequently suffering is the more honorable the greater the freedom of the person concerned, and the less he is limited in his love to the bare need of the beloved. Hence we should be disparaging Christ's honor if we were to hold that He had allowed Himself to be subjected to suffering merely because, in consequence of sin, God had some need of the restitution of His honor, or the sinner had need of redemption. Christ appears most majestic in His suffering, if from boundless love for God and man He suffers more than the need strictly requires, and at the same time suffers not only to relieve the need, but by His suffering to give to God the highest possible glory, and to creatures the proof of a love which is worth incalculably more than the aid He accords them in their wretchedness, more even than all the benefits which He can confer on them.

This is demonstrable particularly with reference to God's glory, which is the highest and worthiest objective both of the Incarnation as a whole and of the suffering experienced in the assumed humanity.

God is in general honored by the fact that the creature subjects himself to Him in acknowledgment of His supreme majesty, and makes an oblation of himself to God. This oblation does not necessarily require that the creature suffer and annihilate himself for God's sake; only propitiatory sacrifice in reparation of violated honor is essentially bound up with suffering and renunciation. But it would be a grievous error to think that God could demand a sacrifice of renunciation, and the creature offer such, only in atonement for sin. Nothing is more opposed to the spirit of Christianity. It is precisely by renunciation and self-abdication that we offer God the greatest honor, and attest our unreserved adoration and boundless love for Him in the most noble and excellent manner. Otherwise why do the saints love suffering so much, and nothing more than suffering? Because they thereby satisfy for their own or others' sins? No, but because they place their supreme happiness and honor in magnifying and glorifying God by the abasement of themselves. They love suffering and death because they thereby become like the God-man, who had in fullest measure glorified His Father and Himself in this very way. As the adoration and love of the God-man are of infinite value on account of the dignity of His person, they had to be proven and carried through in the most perfect manner by His endurance of the greatest sufferings, such as no mere creature has ever undergone. This overflow of suffering was not needed to satisfy for man's sins; a single drop of Christ's blood, even a single tear, would have fully sufficed. Only because Christ was to glorify God so perfectly that no higher degree is conceivable, did the measure of His suffering have to be in keeping with the infinite dignity of the offerer, and the infinite value of the sacrificial Lamb.

Regarded from this standpoint, the voluntary abasement and self-renunciation of the God-man constitute the greatest triumph, indeed an infinite triumph, of God's honor and glory. But Christ also celebrated His supreme triumph therein; for He is greatest when He most glorifies God. Hence His abasement is not an abasement unworthy of Him. By divesting Himself of the glory that is His as the Son of God, He proves most magnificently that He is God's true Son, who wishes to glorify His Father in every possible way, and in the absolutely highest way. In His suffering and death He appears even greater and nobler than He does in His glorified, impassible body after His resurrection. Even in His glorified body the marks of His voluntary suffering are the most beautiful pearls that adorn Him, and make Him far more attractive than the brilliant light that encompasses Him.

This glorification of God, procured through the most extreme self-annihilation, such as was impossible in a purely spiritual nature, was the worthiest objective the Son of God had in assuming a created nature, a human nature capable of suffering. The infinite love which the Son bore for His Father and which in His divinity He could manifest only by the co-possession and co-fruition of the Father's glory, impelled Him to glorify His Father by the perfect surrender and divestment of Himself in a nature subject to pain. This love also impelled Him to associate the members of His mystical body in the same project and for the same end. Are these conclusions an exaggeration? May we not make bold to add that this self-annihilation, so far as it was achieved in the name of creation and for the benefit of creation, was intended to make it possible for creatures to offer God the most sublime homage, and that thus it was destined to acquire and assure the highest favor and grace for them from God's side? Are we out of joint with the sense of Christianity, or do we not rather express its very soul, if we assert that not only was the world's sickness to be cured, but the world itself was to be raised to the summit of honor and glory, by no other means than Christ's suffering?

No, the death of God's Son on the cross does not have to be justified by the necessity of the Cross. We believe rather that God has connected the restoration of the world with the cross of His Son in order to glorify the Cross. Therefore, if the abasement of the God-man would not have taken place except in consequence of sin, sin was not merely a ground for its necessity, but was also and to a greater extent an occasion, distinct from the dishonor to God and the ingratitude of men contained in it, for showing forth the glory of God and His love for Himself and for men in so imposing a way. Indeed, the revelation of God's glory and love reaches its peak in the employment of sin as an instrument, so to speak, for the attainment of its ends. By the very fact that Christ satisfies for sin, God's honor is not merely saved, but is further glorified according to a new aspect. This is all the more true if He compels sin in the midst of its supreme triumph to take part in the conquest of itself. Sin celebrated its triumph when it strove and actually contrived to slay God's Anointed. But at the very moment that Christ seemed to succumb to it, He performed the supreme act of adoration and glorification of God. That act did more than merely compensate for sin. It drew the most precious honey from the poison of its sting, forced sin to achieve an effect opposite to its intention, and deeply humiliated sin in a way that not even the everlasting punishments of hell could equal, thereby securing for God a triumph that would not have been possible without sin.

Although not motivated by sin alone, Christ's suffering, as the Incarnation in general, remains in fact connected with sin as with its occasion and a reason for its necessity. The predominant concern of Sacred Scripture and the Fathers in presenting Christ's Passion under this sole aspect is explained by their desire to depict the greatness of the benefits it has brought to us.

Accordingly we have no reason for thinking that the Incarnation, or even the abasement of the God-man unto the death of the cross, is justified only as a means motivated by the purpose of exterminating sin or compensating for sin. Indeed, we demean the God-man if we regard the humiliation implied in His incarnation and death merely as a means for the attainment of ends which are far below Him, such as the salvation of men, or are incidental to the order of the world, such as the compensation for sin which had been rendered necessary.

The infinite dignity of the God-man makes it impossible for Him to play a subordinate, secondary role in God's plan. All that He is and does cannot exist exclusively for the sake of man or on account of sin. In everything He is willed essentially for His own sake and for God's sake. If He is given to men and delivered up for men, men at the same time belong to Him more than He belongs to them; and as His surrender conduces to their advantage, so it redounds to His own honor and to the glorification of His Father. As He and His activity are ordained to the salvation of men and of the whole world, so men and the whole world are ordained to Him as their head and king who, in freeing them from the servitude of evil, makes of them His kingdom, and along with Himself lays them at the feet of His heavenly Father, that God may be all in all.[20]

In the divine plan, with the Incarnation as an organic part, the Incarnation itself is the first and most essential member. Around this everything else revolves, to this everything else is joined and subordinated, through this everything else receives its definite position and meaning.

St. Anselm's question (*Cur Deus homo?*) has an immediately

[20] "All are yours; and you are Christ's; and Christ is God's" (I Cor. 3:22 f.).

practical aspect: Why did we stand in need of the God-man and His suffering? But we may also grasp the question scientifically according to its entire range: What, in God's eyes, was the end proportionately adequate to this infinite project? If we consider this latter aspect, we must seek the answer in the mysterious regions of an order that is wholly supernatural, in the design of a most extraordinary communication and glorification of God. This is an order in which every other world order is taken up as in a higher and more universal order. The answer to the question *Cur Deus homo?* is then also an answer to the question *Cur mundus?* or *Ad quid mundus?* What direction is given to the world by the Incarnation? This question, although ordinarily too little noted in theological science, is as much in place as the first question.

God alone can give us the answer to both questions. He can do so either explicitly or implicitly, that is, by revealing to us the mystery of the Incarnation, and then leaving it to our reflection to infer the end to which He has destined this work, and the end to which He has destined the world with reference to it. But the second question admits of solution only in terms of the first, not vice versa, since in the last analysis the world is not the ultimate end, but Christ is the ultimate end of the world. This second way of proceeding is as fruitful and illuminating as the first is fruitless and one-sided.

Pursuing this second method, we understand at the outset that Christ is both the end and the beginning of the way mapped out by the Lord at His creation of the world. We perceive why, from the outset, God had diffused a supernatural splendor over the whole of creation, and particularly why He communicated grace to the human family as a solidary body, in the person of its progenitor. All this pointed to the king whose realm the whole world was to become, and whose body the human race was to become. We gain an insight into the origin and the frightful malice of the sin of the angels, and perceive it in its entire mysterious profundity. We apprehend the basic reason why God could allow the angels to fall, and why He could permit all mankind to fall through their instigation: because He not only knew that the havoc thus wrought would be repaired, but wished to utilize it for the supreme revelation of His goodness and glory.

Thus the mystery of the God-man, when grasped in its mysterious sublimity, diffuses the clearest rays of light over all the other mysteries, since they are all related to it. It sheds light not only over those mysteries which flow from it after its realization in the fullness of time, but also over those which God had previously summoned forth or permitted in view of it. As it is the central point of the entire supernatural order of the world and its history, so too, despite its obscurity, it is the beam of light which, under the guidance of faith, enables us to penetrate that order down to its deepest abysses.

Like the sun in the midst of the planets, Christ stands in the midst of creatures as the heart of creation, from whom light, life, and movement stream forth to all its members and toward whom all gravitate, so as in Him and through Him to find their rest in God. According to outward appearances and in practical life, the sun is regarded by us only as an abundant source of aid designed for the well-being of the earth. In the same way we are accustomed to think of Christ as the helper and liberator sent to us by God, as our Jesus from whom we have everything to hope for. But just as science in the course of time has demonstrated that it is not the earth which attracts the sun, but the sun which attracts the earth, so scientific theology, if it is to apprehend Christ in all His meaning, must forge ahead to the point where it will consider Him as the center of gravity of the entire world order, and hence grasp the full sense of the words: "I will draw all things to Myself." [21] It must learn to know Him as the Christ, the Anointed par excellence, in whom are concentrated the supreme union and the most intimate friendship between God and the creature. And this realization will become eminently practical, especially if we do not regard the priesthood of Christ merely as an office which He discharges at the court of God in our behalf. We should rather perceive that we must attach ourselves to this High Priest, so as in Him and through Him to render to God the honor which He expects from His creation. We will presently come back to this point.

[21] John 12:32.

CHAPTER XVI

Activity of the God-man in the Execution
of His Divine Plan

▪▪

65. Nature and Latreutic Character of Christ's Mystical Sacrifice

FROM the God-man's relation to the mysteries of the Trinity and grace we have discerned the mysterious significance and mission motivating His existence and character, as well as the nature of the divine economy founded on Him. The mystical character of the activity by which He is to realize His destiny results from this exalted mission and the organization of His economy.

The most sublime function of the God-man is the infinite glorification of God, which He is to achieve in Himself and in His mystical body. The discharge of this task is the central point around which all His activity revolves. By carrying out this mission He procures for men their reconciliation and pardon with God, but in such a way that, once men have been reconciled and pardoned, they are to join Him as His living members for the purpose of glorifying God.

The most perfect and effective glorification of God consists admittedly in sacrifice. Therefore, if the God-man is to promote the infinite glorification of God in the most effective and perfect manner, as He can, He must offer to God a latreutic sacrifice of infinite value.

I say, a latreutic sacrifice; for in latreutic sacrifice the full capabilities and highest meaning of sacrifice are realized. All other kinds of sacrifice are contained in it, are based on it, and are subordinate to it. Latreutic sacrifice achieves all the effects that can be attained by other species of sacrifice. The several kinds and forms of symbolic sacrifice were introduced only to signify more clearly certain special aims and results, particularly the reaction of the sacrifice upon the offerer. In the case of Christ there is only one form of oblation; hence this must be a latreutic sacrifice.

The latreutic character of Christ's sacrifice is not, as a rule, greatly stressed. Even Sacred Scripture exhibits it usually as a propitiatory sacrifice, but evidently only in the sense in which Scripture is accustomed to view the service of God in relation to the goods to be attained thereby. Although the service of God does indeed procure from God a reward for the creature, it is not the happiness of the creature but the glory of God that is the supreme end of the service of God and of the beatified creature himself. In the same way the sacrifice of Christ is directed to the reconciliation and pardon of the creature. But this does not prevent it from being a latreutic sacrifice on its own account, decreed for the glorification of God. It is precisely in this feature that we must discern its deepest essence and its most august meaning. Indeed, we are of the opinion that even the propitiatory and impetratory character of Christ's sacrifice can be fully appreciated only if its latreutic character is duly weighed.

Accordingly our task is to point out how the mysterious character of Christ, who is the Anointed and Priest par excellence, is enabled by His sacrifice most effectively and perfectly to realize the idea of the infinite glorification of God. We shall see that the nature and form of His sacrifice are thoroughly supernatural and mystical, in spite of the fact, or rather on account of the fact, that it is the realized ideal of all that sacrifice in general, even as it is offered in the natural order, strives to attain and represent.

By sacrifice in the widest sense of the term we understand the surrender of a thing to another person, in order to manifest to him our love and esteem. This is in general also the notion of the sacrifice that is offered to God. However, since God is deserving of infinite love and esteem, and since we are dependent on Him in our entire being, we should surrender and sacrifice to Him not merely other things, but most of all ourselves.

In this sense sacrifice is conceivable even in the spirit world. In general every act of religious worship directed to God is a sacrifice, because it is an acknowledgment of our dependence on God and of His supreme, infinite excellence.

But in a stricter sense we understand by sacrifice a special act of worship and surrender to God. The first distinctive feature of this act consists in the fact that there is a certain real distinction between the offerer and his gift, owing to which the oblation can be conceived as particularly expressing the interior disposition of the one who offers sacrifice. In the case of spiritual sacrifice, the distinction between such a disposition and the oblation expressing it is entirely in the ideal order. For the love by which the creature cleaves to God is likewise the bond by which he already belongs to God and is subject to Him as His property. The real distinction in question can be found only in a being composed of spirit and body. Where this obtains, the spirit gives expression to its love and submission toward God by surrendering to God the body that belongs to it. And as man can do this with his own body, so likewise he can signify his love and submission toward God by surrendering to Him any material being that is related to him and is subject to his dominion.

The second characteristic of sacrifice in this sense flows from the first. It consists in this, that man's complete surrender of the object to God can and should be accomplished and made manifest by a real and visible alteration wrought in the object. In proportion as this alteration, and the withdrawal of the object from human use effected by the change, and the occupying of it by God, are more real and perfect, the sacrificial ideal is more effectively and fully realized.

Many difficulties can arise with reference to the significance and necessity of the real change to be wrought in the sacrificial gift. We believe that the following points may throw some light on the problem.

As an irreducible minimum, sacrifice requires an externally manifested dedication of the object to God, and a prayer for its acceptance which must be at least tacitly implied in the dedication. Obviously the sacrifice has a higher degree of reality in proportion as the surrender to God is really expressed or achieved by the sacrificial act.

If in making this surrender the emphasis is placed on the alienation of the gift on man's part in order to express his utter subjection to God or his atonement for sin, the change to be effected in the sacrificial victim consists in its destruction and annihilation, and most of all in slaughtering it. Such annihilation is often regarded as pertaining only to the sacrifice offered in expiation of sin; and, in fact, it is essential in this case. But it can also, apart from any sense of guilt, proceed from the vivid appreciation of one's own nothingness and from fervent love and reverence toward God; hence it pertains also to the perfection of latreutic sacrifice.[1]

On the contrary, if the stress is laid upon the donation of the object to God, the transfer of it to His possession, the alteration of the gift must consist not so much in its annihilation as in a transfiguration and ennobling of it. This is accomplished by means of the fire which transforms the oblation, and makes it ascend heavenward as the flame or smoke of sacrifice. One might object, indeed, that fire annihilates the oblation even more than slaughtering does. But in the view of Sacred Scripture and the Fathers, of whom we shall soon have more to say, fire is here considered inasmuch as it effects a transformation of the object into something finer and nobler, by resolving the victim's flesh into flame and smoke.[2]

It follows as a matter of course that the first type of alteration must terminate in the second, and that the second presupposes the first, and finally that both suppose that the object which thus undergoes change is offered to God.

As long as the sacrificial gift is but an external thing belonging to man, the sacrifice is purely symbolic in character. The value of this external oblation consists essentially in the disposition with which it is offered, not in the thing itself; the presentation of it to God cannot afford Him any special pleasure, since the object does not acquire any intrinsic nobility. But if man could thus offer to God his own body together with his own corporal life, the gift would have a special value in itself. For man's body and corporal life, united to the rational soul which was made to the image and likeness of God, share in the soul's excellence. This is true particularly if the soul has been raised to the sonship of God. Thus the Apostle ex-

---

[1] This point has already been mentioned in the preceding paragraphs. Here we wish merely to observe that even in the common theological definition a latreutic sacrifice is "an oblation made to God as the Lord of life and death." Since God's dominion over us is not based on our sins, but on our nothingness in comparison with Him, we could attest our submission to Him by means of a sacrifice in which the victim is destroyed, even if we were wholly sinless.

[2] The meaning thus expressed by the sacrificial fire, and the entire theory of sacrifice connected with it, are fully developed, demonstrated, and defended in my *Dogmatik*, III, sect. 270 ff.

horts us to present our body to God as a living, holy, unblemished sacrifice,[3] whereas He rejects all sacrifices of animals as quite worthless in themselves.[4] The material sacrifice, if it is to have objective value and not merely a symbolic meaning, must be an oblation of him who offers it. The victim must pertain to the person who offers the sacrifice and must be one with him, so as to be ennobled by its union with him and to enable him to make a real surrender of himself. If the idea of sacrifice is to be perfectly realized, the victim and the offerer must be joined in one person, so that one and the same person may be both the offerer, through his spiritual disposition, and the victim, in that part of his being which is actually immolated.

This is the third factor entering into the idea of a genuine sacrifice.

There is no doubt that sacrifice in this sense is the most efficacious expression of worship. It is, to be sure, only an effect of the interior sacrifice, and must suppose it. But it is not on that account a mere symbol, a mere reflection of the interior sacrificial disposition. In the most perfect manner possible it is the real and concrete consummation and execution of the interior sacrifice.

If all three conditions mentioned are to be fulfilled, no mere man is capable of offering a sacrifice. The sacrifice of external objects has no more than a symbolic worth. The sacrifice of himself, of his own life and body, is not suitable for man, in view of his nature. For, on the one hand, God has not given him the right to dispose of his own body and life; on the other hand, although man can deprive himself of life by the destruction of it, he cannot actually donate it to God; he is able, indeed, to destroy it, but he cannot make it ascend to God as a living holocaust. The sacrifice of himself would be no more than a sacrifice of death; but death in itself would be merely a suffering or a punishment for man, and is not the most perfect worship of God, who is a God of the living,[5] and wills to be adored as such.

According to its highest notion, sacrifice, as the most effective and perfect form of worship, is realized only if God receives from the creature a worship that is absolute in its value, that is, if the offerer is of infinite dignity, and the victim of infinite worth. The

[3] Rom. 12:1.
[4] Heb. 10:1-8.
[5] Matt. 22:32.

God-man, as the High Priest placed over all creatures, has, in virtue of the infinite dignity of His person, conferred an infinite dignity on His human soul and its sacrificial disposition, and an infinite value on His body and blood. Because of the omnipotence of His person, He has the power to lay down His life and to take it up again, and in the resumption of His body to transfigure it by the fire of the Holy Spirit, to deliver it up to God, and to make it a temple of the divine Majesty. For the very reason that Christ, as the Lord's Anointed, can and must be a priest par excellence in the most proper and perfect sense of the word, He could and should in His bodily life be also the Lamb of God par excellence, the sacrificial Lamb which is offered to God in the most literal and perfect manner, as the tribute of perfect worship, a worship that is worthy of God.

How the first act of latreutic sacrifice, the destruction of His life, is accomplished in Christ's sacrifice, we need not delay in explaining here. But we must insist on the fact that His resurrection and ascension actually achieve in mystically real fashion what is symbolized in the sacrifice of animals by the burning of the victim's flesh. Christ's resurrection and glorification are often conceived merely as the fruit of His sacrifice on the cross. And such it is in all truth, but not that alone. In the idea of God and of the Church, it is also a continuation and fulfillment of the first act. According to the Apostle's teaching, the carrying of the blood of the sacrificed animal into the holy of holies, whereby it was appropriated to God, was a type of the function of Christ in heaven, whereby He constantly appropriates His body and His blood and offers them to God. The Resurrection and glorification were the very acts by which the Victim passed into the real and permanent possession of God. The fire of the Godhead which resuscitated the slain Lamb and, after consuming its mortality, laid hold of it and transformed it, caused it to ascend to God in lovely fragrance as a holocaust, there to make it, as it were, dissolve and merge into God.[6]

---

[6] ". . . the substance of the body is changed into a heavenly quality, as was signified by the sacrificial fire which, so to speak, swallows up death in victory" (St. Augustine, *Contra Faustum*, lib. XXII, c.17; *PL*, XLII, 409; *CSEL*, XXV, I, 605). St. Augustine frequently reverts to this idea and carries it further, as we shall see later. "Then did He offer the solemn sacrifice, when in heaven He showed Himself to the eternal Father in His glorified body" (St. Gregory the Great, *In lib. I regum*, lib. I, c.1; *PL*, LXXIX, 42; this is not Gregory's work; the author is unknown). The sacrifice of Christ con-

Consequently, in accord with God's plan, the entire life and existence of Christ were essentially devoted to His sublime sacrificial worship. By taking possession of His human nature He made His own the object He was to offer, and by uniting it to His person He invested it with an infinite value. By His Passion and death, which He had in mind during His whole earthly career, He accomplished its immolation. By His resurrection and glorification He made it a holocaust. Finally, by His ascension He transferred it to heaven, and placed it at the feet of His Father, that it might be His as the eternal pledge of perfect worship.

But Christ's sacrifice is not purely personal; it is truly sacerdotal. It is the sacrifice of the head of the whole human race and of the born mediator between God and man.

A priest is a person deputed by society or appointed by God Himself to sacrifice, and is to offer his sacrifice to God in the name of that society. Taking his place between society and God by the act of sacrifice, he offers the worship of the community to God, and then transmits the fruit of the sacrifice from God to the community. Therefore, as the priest must represent the community, and to represent it must belong to the community and have his origin from it, so the sacrificial gift must be presented to him by the community; and as the priest offers himself at least symbolically in his sacrifice, so also the community must make an offering of itself by participating in his sacrifice.

All this takes place in an eminently beautiful manner in the sacri-

---

sidered in its totality is, therefore, essentially a "paschal sacrifice," or a "sacrifice of passover, that is, to God," as St. Bernard so beautifully explains: "Resurrection, passover, transmigration. Christ did not succumb on this day, but rose: He did not return, but passed over; He did not merely come back, but was transformed. The very feast we celebrate, the Pasch, means not a return, but a passover; and Galilee, where He who rose from the dead promised He would show Himself to us, signifies not a mere coming back, but a transmigration. . . . If, after the consummation of His death on the cross, our Lord Christ had again taken up mortal existence and the tribulations of this present life, I should say that He had not passed over, but that He had returned; that He had not been transformed into something nobler, but had resumed His prior state. But since He has passed over to newness of life, and invites us to a like passover, He summons us to Galilee. For in that He died to sin, He died once; but in that He liveth, He liveth not unto flesh but unto God [cf. Rom. 6:10]" (*Serm. de resurrect.*, no. 14; *PL*, CLXXXIII, 281). Death to one's own life, and transition to life in God and for God, represent the very ideal of sacrifice.

fice of Christ. We have seen that Christ as the head of the human race is truly a priest, the representative of all His members in the worship of God. Hence He offers His sacrifice as head of all His members, primarily in the name of the human race, secondarily in the name of the entire universe.

He became the representative of the race by taking human nature from its midst, by proceeding from it. Thus it was from the midst of the race that He took the body and the blood which He was to sacrifice to God. The flesh and blood that He immolated and that, glorified by the fire of the Holy Spirit, He gave over to God, was at the same time our flesh and blood. Therefore it was not alone Christ Himself, but the whole human race that in Christ's flesh and blood took from its own substance and offered to God the pledge of an infinite worship, and sent it up to heaven.[7]

On the other hand, the human race not only can and should offer Christ in His own body as a sacrifice to God, but conversely Christ can and should consummate the sacrifice of Himself both in Himself

---

[7] "We were crucified with Him when His flesh was crucified; for in a sense it contained all nature, just as when Adam incurred condemnation the whole of nature contracted the disease of his curse in him" (St. Cyril of Alexandria, *In epist. ad Rom.*, c.6; *PG*, LXXIV, 796). "The cross of Christ contains the sacrament of the true altar announced of old, where by the saving Victim the sacrifice of human nature is celebrated" (St. Leo the Great, *Serm. 4 de pass. Dom.*; *PL*, LIV, 324). St. Augustine speaks still more explicitly (*Enarr. in Psalm.* 129, no. 7; *PL*, XXXVII, 1701): "He received from you what He offered for you, just as the priest receives from you the gift that he offers for you, when you wish to appease God for your sins. The sacrifice has already been offered, and it has been offered thus. Our Priest took from us what He offered for us: He took flesh from us; and in this flesh He was made a victim, He was made a holocaust, He was made a sacrifice. He was made a sacrifice in His passion; and in His resurrection He renewed what had been slain, and offered it to God as your first fruits, and He says to you: Now all that is yours has been consecrated, seeing that such first fruits have been given to God from you. Hope, therefore, that what has taken place in your first fruits may be realized in you." No less to the point is the statement of Ferrandus the Deacon (*Ep. ad Anatolium*, no. 4; *PL*, LXVII, 892): "It behoved Him, as priest, to receive from us what He offered for us. If He did not receive the material of His body from Mary, He did not receive anything from us that He might offer for us. And in that event how could He discharge His office of eternal Priest? It was incumbent on us to give to our Priest the victim that was to be immolated to God: the only-begotten Son of God the Father, become our Priest in mortal flesh, offered not gold or silver or the blood of goats, but His own body. The Victim is ours, the body is His. And if He received His body, assuredly it was from us that He received it; and He received it when blessed Mary conceived Him."

as the head, and likewise in His entire mystical body. His entire mystical body is to be sacrificed through His power and according to the model of His real body. As His sacrifice is by no means purely symbolic in character, but is utterly real, so too, when considered as the sacrifice of the community, it must not merely represent what the community of itself could and should achieve for the honor of God, but should be the efficacious ideal of the real sacrifice which the community ought actually to offer.

This is why Christ continues the immolation and glorification of His own body in His mystical body. By their union with Him the bodies of His members attain to a higher, mystical consecration. Furthermore, they receive thereby a freedom from death in virtue of which they undergo death not so much as a natural necessity or punishment, but rather, after the example of their head, take death upon themselves for the honor of God. This they do by allowing Christ, to whom henceforth their life belongs, to immolate that life. The bodies of Christ's members have necessarily the destiny to be one day awakened from death as His own body was and, transfigured by the fire of His glory, to be stationed by Him before the face of God for all eternity.

In this sense the Apostle desires to fill up in his body what is still lacking of the sufferings of Christ.[8] In this sense Christ suffers and sacrifices in all the faithful who endure their sufferings in His spirit, and especially in the martyrs who, in the form and cause of their suffering and death, are most of all like their head. By the immolation of their bodies and their earthly life, effected in all the sufferings, mortifications, and toils of this life and crowned in death, by the immolation which takes place in Christ's members in the spirit and power of Christ, the members are made ready as a fragrant holocaust to enter with Christ into the presence of God in their glorified bodies, and to be received by God. After the general resurrection the whole Christ, head and body, will be a perfect holocaust offered to God for all eternity, since Christ Himself, not only in His personal being, body and soul, but also in His entire mystical body, will be a truly universal, total holocaust offered to God through the transforming fire of the Holy Spirit.[9]

[8] Col. 1:24–29.
[9] St. Augustine is very partial to these ideas. In his commentary on the Psalms especially he comes back to them again and again. We quote here

Meanwhile He has gone on ahead as the first fruits of this grand holocaust, as the first gift which our nature and the whole world surrenders to God and sends up to heaven. "He was offered to God the Father," says St. Cyril, "as the first fruits of our mass, since He was the first-born of the dead, and ascended into heaven as the first fruits of the resurrection of all. For He was taken from us and was offered by all and in behalf of all, that He might give life to all and

several of the finest passages. " 'I will go into Thy house with burnt offerings.' What is a burnt offering, a holocaust? A whole victim burned up, but with divine fire. For a sacrifice is called a holocaust when the whole is burned. The parts of a sacrifice are one thing, a holocaust is another thing: when the whole is burned and the whole is consumed by divine fire, it is called a holocaust; when a part, it is called a sacrifice. Every holocaust is a sacrifice, but not every sacrifice is a holocaust. He promises holocausts; the body of Christ is speaking, the unity of Christ is speaking: 'I will go into Thy house with burnt offerings.' May Thy fire consume all that is mine; let nothing remain of mine, let all be Thine. This will take place in the resurrection of the dead, when this corruptible is clad with incorruption, and this mortal is clad with immortality; then shall come to pass what is written: 'Death is swallowed up in victory' [cf. I Cor. 15:53 f.]. Victory is, as it were, divine fire; when it swallows up our death too, it is a holocaust. Nothing mortal remains in the flesh, nothing culpable remains in the spirit; the whole of mortal life will be consumed, that in eternal life it may be consummated (and that we may be preserved from death unto life). Such, therefore, will be the holocausts" (*Enarr. in Psalm.* 65, no. 18; *PL*, XXXVI, 798). " 'Oblations and whole burnt offerings.' What are holocausts? A whole victim consumed by fire. When a whole animal was placed upon the altar of God to be consumed with fire, it was called a holocaust. May divine fire wholly consume us, and that fervor entirely enfold us. What fervor? 'And there is no one that can hide himself from His heat' [Ps. 18:7]. What fervor? That of which the Apostle speaks: 'In spirit fervent' [Rom. 12:11]. Let not only our soul be consumed by that divine fire of wisdom, but also our body, that it may merit immortality therein. May it be lifted up as a holocaust, that death may be swallowed up in victory" (*Enarr. in Psalm.* 50, no. 23; *PL*, XXXVI, 599). " 'And a vow shall be paid to Thee in Jerusalem.' Here we vow, and it is a good thing that we pay there. . . . For there we shall be whole, that is, entire in the resurrection of the just; there our whole vow will be paid: not only our soul, but the very flesh also, no longer corruptible, because no longer in Babylon, but changed into a heavenly body . . . when death shall have been swallowed up in victory. . . . At the present time, how violent is our conflict with death! For thence come carnal pleasures, which suggest so many unlawful things to us. . . . I will pay my vow. What vow? A holocaust, so to speak. For when fire consumes the whole victim, it is called a holocaust. . . . Therefore let fire lay hold of us, a divine fire in Jerusalem. Let us begin to burn with love, until all that is mortal in us be consumed, and what is opposed to us go up in a sacrifice to the Lord. Whence it is said elsewhere: 'Deal favorably, O Lord, in Thy good will with Sion, that the walls of Jerusalem may be built up. Then shalt Thou accept the sacrifice of justice, oblations, and whole might be offered to God the Father the first sheaf, as it were, from the threshing floor." [10] For the very reason that He is offered from the midst of all and in the name of all, He is also offered as the first fruits in behalf of all, so that the sacrifice which is to be offered to God in all the others is pledged in Him.

That is to say, the immolation of Christ's flesh is a pledge to God that all flesh will be immolated to Him. St. Augustine, discoursing on the words of Job, "All flesh shall come to Thee," asks: "Why will all flesh come to God? Because He has assumed flesh. Whither will all flesh come? He took the first fruits thereof from the womb of the Virgin; and now that the first fruits have been taken, the rest will follow, so that the holocaust may be complete." [11]

But the sacrifice of the first fruits which God took to Himself is also a pledge that God will receive the whole together with its head as an acceptable sacrifice, and will bless it and make it conformable to its head through the entire course of His sacrifice, from the Incarnation to the Ascension. Thus the sacrifice of Christ becomes the real pledge, the real purchase money for all the supernatural goods by which man becomes like to the God-man and is consecrated as a sacrifice to God. It purchases for him, first of all, the remission of the sins that made him displeasing and unclean in God's sight, and

---

burnt offerings' [Ps. 50:20 f.]; 'A hymn, O God, becometh Thee in Sion, and a vow shall be paid to Thee in Jerusalem'" (*Enarr. in Psalm.* 64, no. 4; *PL*, XXXVI, 775). St. Gregory the Great (*In Ezech.*, hom. 22, no. 4; *PL*, LXXVI, 1060) is in full agreement: "Holy Church has two lives, one which it leads in time, another which it receives in eternity. . . . And in each of these lives it offers sacrifice: here a sacrifice of compunction, there a sacrifice of praise. Of the sacrifice on this earth it is said: 'A sacrifice to God is an afflicted spirit' [Ps. 50:19]; of the sacrifice in heaven it is written: 'Then shalt Thou accept the sacrifice of justice, oblations, and whole burnt offerings' [*ibid.*, 21]. Of which again it is said: 'To the end that my glory may sing to Thee, and I may not regret' [Ps. 29:13]. In each of these sacrifices flesh is offered: here the oblation of the flesh is the mortification of the body; there the oblation of the flesh is the glory of the resurrection in praise of God. For there the flesh is offered, as it were, in a holocaust, when finally, transformed in eternal incorruption, it will have no more of contradiction or mortality; because, wholly consumed once and for all by the fires of God's love, it will persevere in praise without end."

[10] *In Ioan.*, lib. IV, c. 2; *PG*, LXXIII, 569.
[11] *Enarr. in Psalm.* 64, no. 5 (*PL*, XXXVI, 776): "Ad te, inquit, omnis caro veniet. Quare ad illum omnis caro veniet? Quia carnem assumpsit. Quo omnis caro veniet? Tulit inde primitias de utero virginali; assumptis primitiis caetera consequentur, ut holocaustum compleatur."

unworthy to appear before His countenance. It purchases for him the grace by which he is sanctified as a victim, the power by which he conquers death in all its forms so that he can live for God, the right after the death of the body to see it awakened to life again and to behold it, in union with the soul, filled with God's splendor, and finally, the prospect of eternally praising and glorifying God in heaven in this transfigured form.

But all that makes man an agreeable sacrifice in God's eyes is at the same time man's own highest honor and greatest happiness. Remission of sin and sanctification with all its consequences are, therefore, to be regarded as a reward that God gives to the human race in return for the sacrifice that Christ offered to Him. By accepting the sacrifice of the first fruits, God binds Himself to receive the race back into favor and grace, to exonerate it of the curse of its guilt, and to bless it with every spiritual benediction.[12]

Accordingly, with reference to the human race, Christ's latreutic holocaust takes on the character first and foremost of a propitiatory sacrifice: it effects the removal of guilt and the reconciliation of man with God. For the holocaust, which involves the most complete surrender to God and the most complete self-renunciation, contains everything that is necessary for the restitution of God's violated honor and hence for counterbalancing sin. Christ's holocaust, being infinite in value, effects this reconciliation not only by way of petition, but also by way of justice through real and equivalent satis-

[12] St. John Chrysostom, *Hom. de ascens. ad coelum*, no. 2 (*PG*, L, 445): "What takes place in teeming fields of wheat, when one makes a tiny sheaf of a few ears and, offering it to God, blesses the whole farm with that small quantity: that Christ did when by His single body, our first fruits, He called down God's blessing on our race. But why did He not offer the whole of nature? Because if the whole is offered, the first fruits are not offered; whereas if a small portion is offered, the whole is consecrated by that little. But, some one will say, if there was question of offering the first fruits, the very first man to be created should have been offered; for the first fruits are those which are first plucked and which have first sprouted. But surely, my dear friend, no one will say that we offer the first fruits if we offer the first scanty and drooping blade that may appear, but only if we offer full and perfect fruit. And that is why that other fruit, even though it was the very first, was not offered, for it was defiled by sin. But this fruit was free from sin, and so it was offered, although it appeared later. For He is the first fruits. . . . So He offered the first fruits of our nature, and the Father looked upon the gift with favor. And on account of the rank of the offerer and the excellence of the gift, the Father received it with His own hands, and placed it next to Himself, saying: 'Sit Thou at My right hand'" [Ps. 109:1].

faction, and therefore in its eternal duration it avails in God's sight as a thankoffering for the remission that is granted, as well as its guaranty.

With reference to the creature, this one sacrifice, which is an infinitely perfect holocaust in every respect, is also an impetratory sacrifice of infinite efficacy. It wins for us and vindicates for us all the supernatural goods of divine grace and glory, indeed the possession of God Himself, for which we could have no claim on the basis of nature, even if there had never been question of sin. But as the latreutic sacrifice is more than a symbolic expression of inner worship, since it is a real donation of infinite value, so also in its impetratory power it is not a mere prayer, a mere expression of a desire, but is a request based on the surrender of a real, equivalent value, a true merit. In its eternal duration it is both the surest guaranty for the permanent possession of those goods and an adequate thanks for the reception of them.

Thus in His high-priestly sacrifice Christ verifies the notion of the most exalted, eternal mediatorship between God and man. As He brings God and man together in intimate, indissoluble union by His twofold nature, so in His sacrifice He seals the mysterious compact that God wills to form with humanity: He secures for man God's richest favor and grace, in such a way that sin leaves no barrier between God and man, and nature need not be timorous on account of its lack of a claim to so astounding a friendship. In the same way He secures for God the infinite gratitude which man owes Him for such great love, and unites mankind redeemed by Him to Himself in an eternal holocaust, which in fullest measure realizes the supreme end of creation, the perfect glorification of God.

Having proceeded from the bosom of the eternal Father as the reflection of His splendor, He is also a priest forever according to the order of Melchisedech. Equal to His Father in majesty, He is anointed and called by nature to offer to God in His creature the supreme glorification. This He offers by deeply humbling Himself, as only a creature can, and He takes the matter of His sacrifice from that nature which alone is capable of true self-renunciation, but which also, as the junction of the spiritual and the material world, represents all creatures. By His resurrection, in which He preserves the distinctive marks of His self-renunciation, He stands eternally before the eyes of God as the Lamb slaughtered in the beginning, and so makes eternal the sacrifice that was offered in the fullness of time. Thus He officiates in His sacrifice as a priest in the absolute sense of the word, reproducing in the creature, by the mutual surrender of boundless love, that mutual surrender which necessarily takes place between the Father and the Son.

If we do not restrict Christ's sacrifice to atonement, but rather see in it the formation of an indissoluble covenant between God and mankind, and the noblest latreutic worship that God can receive, and if consequently we behold in it the supreme act by which the creature approaches God, we are naturally led to ascribe to that sacrifice a universal significance for the whole of creation. This creation includes more than the material creation, which is, as it were, the extension of man's body; it includes also the spirit world. What is more natural than to suppose that this supreme sacrificial act, which is offered in the heart of creation and enables it to achieve its ultimate purpose, is performed in the name of all creatures, and that creation in its totality shares in it? Does not the dignity of Christ, head of all the heavenly powers, require this? Does not the honor of the angels themselves require it, since otherwise they would have no part in the most exalted homage that is offered to God? To be consistent, must we not further assume that the sacrifice of Christ is a universal, corporate sacrifice offered for all creatures? Should not this include the angels, not indeed that it reconciles them to God after sin, but in the sense that the Lamb which was slaughtered in the beginning stands eternally in God's sight to merit and secure supernatural grace for them also? In the controversy over Mary's Immaculate Conception, the champions of both sides regarded it as a special glory of the ever-blessed Virgin and her Son that grace was imparted to her through the merits of her Son. Why should we deny this privilege to the angels, and this honor to Christ with respect to the angels? Apart from this dependence on Christ's sacrifice, so honorable for them, the angels do not fully belong to His kingdom, in particular to that kingdom which Christ has purchased with His blood. Surely this blood, which was sufficient to purchase the entire world, may not be limited in its operation and power to the lower portion of the world.

We have intimated more than once that Christ's sacrifice, adequately grasped, must be regarded as the perfect effusion and the most exalted outward representation of the eternal love which Christ bears for the Father as the Son of God. We find this suggested in the Savior's words: "That the world may know that I love the Father. . . . Arise, let us go hence." [13] We believe that we can enlarge on these thoughts in the following way, and can present Christ's sacrifice in the very form in which it was actually offered, namely, in the shedding of His blood to the last drop, as the highest expression of the Trinitarian relations and the most perfect vehicle of their extension to the outer world.

In the Godhead the mutual love of the Son and the Father pours itself out in the production of the Holy Spirit, who issues from their common heart, in whom both surrender their heart's blood, and to whom they give themselves as the pledge of their infinite love. In order worthily to represent this infinitely perfect surrender to His Father, the Logos wished in His humanity to pour forth His blood from His heart to the last drop, that blood in which and through which the Holy Spirit gave life to His humanity, the blood that was pervaded, sanctified, and scented with heavenly loveliness, and so ascended to God with such pleasing fragrance. The Holy Spirit Himself is portrayed as the agent of this sacrifice. He is the agent in this sense, that in His capacity of *amor sacerdos* [14] He urges on the God-man to His sacrifice, and brings the oblation itself into the presence of the Father, uniting it to the eternal homage of love, which is He Himself.

Since the Holy Spirit proceeds from the love of the Father for the Son, and through the Son is to be poured out over the whole world, nothing is more appropriate than that the Son in His humanity, as the head of all creatures, should represent and effect this outpouring of the Holy Spirit in the outpouring of His blood, and that this latter outpouring should become the real sacrament of the other outpouring. Is not the shedding of the blood of Christ's heart the truest pledge that He and His Father will, in their own Spirit, share with us the innermost character, so to speak, of their divinity? Is not the blood with its purifying, warming, life-giving energy the sacrament of the corresponding activities of the Holy Spirit? And is not the mystical body and corporal bride of the God-man formed from the blood of Christ's heart by the power of the Holy Spirit

[13] John 14:31.
[14] This title occurs in the hymn *Ad regias Agni dapes*, sung at Vespers during the paschal season. [Tr.]

dwelling in Him, just as the Spirit of the Father and the Son and their partner in love springs forth from their divine heart? [15] At bottom, the heart's blood of Christ is the bond between God and the world, the bond in which heaven and earth are brought together, just as in the Trinity the Holy Spirit, the outpouring of the mutual surrender of the Father and the Son, is the eternal bond which joins these two persons with each other and with creatures.

Thus the idea of Christ's sacrifice thrusts its roots deep into the abyss of the Trinity. As the Incarnation itself was to be the prolongation and extension of the eternal generation, and can be adequately comprehended only from this viewpoint, so the sacrificial surrender of the God-man was to be the most perfect expression of that divine love which, as God, He shows forth in the spiration and effusion of the Holy Spirit.

We realize that these thoughts are rather mystical in character.

[15] The parallelism and inner relationship between the shedding of Christ's blood and the outpouring of the Holy Spirit can be carried very far merely on the basis of Sacred Scripture. Consider the following texts. "The sprinkling of blood which speaketh better than that of Abel" (Heb. 12:24). "The Spirit Himself asketh for us with unspeakable groanings" (Rom. 8:26). "The blood of the covenant"; "the blood of the testament" (often). The Spirit "is the pledge of our inheritance" (Eph. 1:14). "Unto the sanctification of the Spirit . . . and sprinkling of the blood of Jesus Christ" (I Pet. 1:2). "You were signed with the Holy Spirit of promise" (Eph. 1:13). "My blood is drink indeed" (John 6:56). "In one Spirit we have all been made to drink" (1 Cor. 12:13). "You who some time were afar off, are made nigh by the blood of Christ" (Eph. 2:13). "By Him we have access both in one Spirit to the Father" (ibid., 18). "In whom you also are built together into a habitation of God in the Spirit" (ibid., 22). "Almost all things . . . are cleansed with blood" (Heb. 9:22). "Blessed are they that wash their robes in the blood of the Lamb" (Apoc. 22:14). "How much more shall the blood of Christ, who by the Holy Ghost offered Himself unspotted unto God, cleanse our conscience from dead works?" (Heb. 9:14.) "But you are washed, but you are sanctified, but you are justified in . . . the Spirit of our God" (I Cor. 6:11). The blood of Christ is the blood of the Lamb; but Christ in turn is the Lamb of God par excellence, the tender, pure, and altogether lovable Lamb that is so pleasing to God, because in Him dwells the Holy Spirit. On account of these same attributes, the Holy Spirit is symbolized by the dove, and descended upon Christ under the form of a dove, to show Him to the world as the Lamb of God. The divine dove instills into the blood of the Lamb that wonderful loveliness and excellence by which it is made a balm that brings grace and peace. As is evident, the symbolism of Sacred Scripture remains quite consistent, and is a pregnant, forceful presentation of rich and profound ideas.

To the phlegmatic inquirer they may perhaps seem to be of little moment and significance. We acknowledge that they parade before our own mind in very shadowy outline. But they are suggested often enough in the Fathers, and may afford to such souls as are not in eternal quest of the stark austerity of intellectual concepts rich matter for lofty and loving contemplation. We shall return to these considerations on another occasion.[16]

66. The Mystery of Free Will in the Sacrifice and Merits of Christ

Several theologians, or rather philosophers, of modern times have held that, to render the meritorious character of Christ's sacrifice intelligible, freedom of choice between good and evil must be predicated of His will. Certainly, if Christ's merit had to consist in His subjection to a probation that would counteract Adam's probation, in the sense that He would freely decide in God's favor as Adam had decided against God, then such freedom would be necessary. But then, too, Christ would have had to be pure man, and could not be the God-man. If our redemption was to be effected by the God-man, the latter simply could not have any choice between good and evil. In fact, however, the God-man did not have to undergo such a real, counterbalancing trial. His task was to destroy the consequence of the failure of Adam's trial, that is, the violation of God's honor, and to merit and restore the grace forfeited by that failure. This objective required a free activity on the part of the God-man, but not an election between good and evil. There was need of a

[16] If we may hazard a practical remark, we should like to point out that the devotion to the Sacred Heart of Jesus, as the altar of divine love, is closely connected with the devotion to the Holy Spirit, as the divine representative of that love, and must naturally result in a more general practice of the latter devotion. The need of such a devotion is widely felt, and we sincerely hope that God, in the gracious dispensations of His providence, will call it to life against the indifferent, frivolous spirit of our time, just as several hundred years ago He stirred up devotion to the sweetest Heart of His Son against the bleak heartlessness of Jansenism. The longing for a richer devotion to the Holy Spirit is growing in the Church. It is manifested in a deeper understanding of the liturgy as a visible representation of the unified operation exercised by our divine Lord and the Holy Spirit, and in the desire for a more fitting celebration of ecclesiastical functions both interiorly and exteriorly. [Tr.]

freedom that rested on the basis of absolute holiness; for only in that case could its activity be of infinite value, such as was necessary in order to satisfy for sin and merit grace.

Indeed, I should go further and maintain that the freedom upon which Christ's merit was based had to be the liberty not of a *viator* but of a *comprehensor*. In other words, Christ could merit for us only so far as He Himself was not merely in the state of grace, but also in the state of glory. Theologians discern in Christ's beatific vision a tremendous difficulty against the meritorious character of His activity, and regard the reconciliation of the two as an exceedingly obscure mystery. We acknowledge that it is indeed a most sublime mystery, but one that is illuminating in its very sublimity. How is the matter to be explained?

When there is question of a person meriting for himself, the natural assumption is that he does not yet possess what he is to merit; he is to acquire it by his merit. Therefore he must first be on the road that leads to the good which he is to merit, he must be *in statu viatoris*. During our mortal life this is our condition with regard to heavenly glory in the bosom of our heavenly Father, who is the goal of our pilgrimage. Christ, on the contrary, was in the bosom of God as His natural Son from the first instant of His conception, and hence even in His humanity had to be united to God by the immediate vision of God and a love corresponding to that vision, the *amor beatificus*. He could not be a wayfarer on the road leading to God; as God's Son He had to possess God from the outset; He had to be a *comprehensor*, in the language of theology. Only that love which flows from the intuition of the Father was fittingly the love proper to God's Son, a filial love worthy of Himself and of His Father. From this love had to proceed all those works which He performed as God's Son, and which, as works of God's Son, were to have an infinite value; from this love they received their high consecration and their proper, unique efficacy. And what is stated of His works in general, holds true particularly of the sacrifice by which the Son of God made man was to glorify His Father.

What were these works to merit? Evidently they could not increase the love from which they proceeded, or unite the Son of God, if only in His humanity, more intimately with His Father and bring Him closer to the Father; and so they could not heighten the glory and beatitude which flow to the soul from the vision of God. But inasmuch as the God-man showed Himself in these works to be the true Son of God, indissolubly linked to the Father, they served all the more to merit for Him that immense glory and beatitude which were His from the beginning, but which He had withheld from Himself out of love for His Father, desiring to glorify Him the more. As these works gave evidence of the interior glory and beatitude uniting the soul of Christ to the Father, so likewise they merited that this same glory and beatitude should spread from the highest part of the soul to all its faculties and to the body. Thus in different respects Christ was simultaneously *comprehensor* and *viator*. He was not simply a *viator* as he is who struggles and strives for a remote, unattained goal, but as he who already has one foot upon the goal, and is drawing the other after it. Therefore He was a *viator* in a vastly more perfect way than we are, because He was at the same time a *comprehensor;* and His merit as *viator* is more genuine and more perfect in proportion as it was based upon His *comprehensio*.

This feature of Christ's merit stands out still more prominently if we turn our attention to the meritoriousness of His works for us. Since these works do not merit grace and glory for Christ Himself but for others, there must be a great difference between the principle of His merit and that of creatures. Creatures can merit an increase of grace and glory for themselves, and exclusively for themselves; hence the principle of their merit cannot be the full grace and glory which they are to attain. Therefore, if Christ is to merit grace and glory for others, if His merit is to redound upon others, it must proceed from, and be based upon, the overflowing plenitude of the grace and glory which is His already, not a plenitude that is still to be acquired. If Christ is to lead us men to grace and glory, then it is impossible that He must first seek and strive after them along with us. To draw us after Him to their attainment and to lavish them upon us, He must possess them in their fullness from the outset. As He can merit for us the adoptive sonship of God with all its rights only because He is the natural Son of God, so too the principle of this merit must be that union with God which pertains to Him as the natural Son of God: namely, the love which flows from the immediate vision of God, and in which He mounts to the pinnacle of holiness and sinlessness.

But this love, it will be objected, is not a free love, and only by a love that is free can we merit with God. Without doubt this love is not in itself free. How could the Son of God have a free choice between loving His Father and not loving Him? If it were free in itself, the Son of God would not be necessarily and essentially holy. In that case He would have to strive for holiness and union with God. But then, could He be the source of our holiness?

How, then, shall we account for the freedom of Christ's will? Not according to the norm of freedom in creatures, but according to the norm of God's freedom. Every free act of God proceeds from the necessary love which He bears for Himself. If God did not love Himself necessarily, He would not be able freely to will anything outside Himself. Everything external to God that is freely willed by Him is a free manifestation of His necessary love for Himself, and has an infinite value precisely because it proceeds from an infinite love. So too with Christ. He loves God necessarily, with a love that cannot be exceeded in a created nature. But He is not obliged to give expression to this love in any predetermined way; herein lies His freedom. If He does give expression to it in this or that way, His free act derives its value from the necessary love from which it emanates.

The free activity of Christ's love for His Father consisted in the fact that from the motive of this love He performed works for the glorification of His Father which He need not have performed, and that in particular for the greater glory of His Father He renounced the glory of His body and took upon Himself the greatest sufferings along with the bitterest death, although He could have been immune to all suffering and had the fullest right to be thus immune. In view of this right of His Son's, God could not absolutely exact suffering and death from Him by a strict command; at any rate the dignity of the Son of God which Christ possesses even in His humanity required that He could either secure release from such an obligation, or by petition obtain a dispensation from it. Besides, the command in question was imposed by God only so far as God intended to attain a free glorification of Himself and the redemption of the human race through Christ's merit. Consequently the command had to be such that it would leave ample room for the play of Christ's free will, notwithstanding His necessary love for God, and that Christ would not be forced to its fulfillment by His love for the Father. Thus Christ, as God's Son, was not simply subject to the command like mere creatures, who are free only so far as they can transgress the command; He was superior to the command; yet in fulfilling it out of love for His Father, He fulfilled it with a freedom still more perfect than that with which Adam, who was subject to the command, transgressed it. It is this peculiar character of Christ's free will that endows His actions with their distinctive, supreme meritoriousness.[17]

The reason why freedom is required for the meritoriousness of actions is that we can expect a reward from another only if we do for him something that is in our power. Hence a simple creature can merit with God only so far as the performance of the good acts which are intended to please God depends on the creature; but this depends on the creature only so far as the latter can actually omit the performance of the acts. For God, the absolute Lord of the creature, has an absolute right to the actions themselves; and although He does not always vindicate this right by enjoining the acts in question, He has the right to demand them if He so wills. The mere creature can give God nothing that is his absolute property and is completely dependent on him. This is one of the reasons adduced by theologians to prove that a creature cannot satisfy for sin in strict justice: for such satisfaction must be made *ex alias indebitis*, that is, from goods which are not already owed in virtue of some other title.

The God-man, on the other hand, in humbling Himself even unto the death of the cross, renounced a good that was His full property, and He performed a service for God that He was quite free to omit, simply because He was not bound to perform it. Whence theologians infer that Christ has satisfied perfectly *ex alias indebitis*. We conclude, then, that Christ has merited with perfect freedom, from the fact that He rendered something to God which He did not have

---

[17] The theory here advanced may seem somewhat new and singular. Nevertheless it has been proposed, in more or less developed form, by many theologians of first rank. In justification of this assertion we cite the following: Peter Paludanus, *In III Sent.*, d. 12, q. 2, a. 3; Victoria, in manuscripts cited by Medina, *Expositio seu scholastica commentaria in D. Thomae Aq. III parte*, q. 47, a. 2; Salmeron, *Commentarii in Evangelicam historiam*, tom. X, tract. 2; Ribera, *In Ioannem*, 10:18; Pallavicinus, *Cursus theologicus de incarnatione*, c. 8; Petavius, *De Incarnatione*, lib. IX, c. 8, no. 6 sqq.; Viva, Wirceburgenses, etc.; A. Rayé, *Opusc. in Thesaur. Zachariae*, tom. IX.

to give. Is there not greater liberty and merit when something not owed is offered to God out of pure, indefectible love, than when something owed is offered out of defectible love?

For all that, the meritoriousness of Christ's works is a mystery, because it rests upon mysterious, supernatural principles. But these same principles, if they are logically and adequately developed and are apprehended in the fullness of their supernatural character, may in turn throw considerable light on the question. However, we do not in any way claim that we have banished all obscurity. Rather we are convinced that scarcely a more perplexing problem is to be found in the doctrine of the Incarnation, and perhaps in all theology, than the endeavor to give an intelligible account of human freedom in the divine person of Christ.

67. The Mystery in the Propitiatory and Meritorious Value of Christ's Sacrifice, or in His Moral Causality

We stated above that the meritorious and expiatory power of Christ's sacrifice is based on its latreutic character. This latreutic character may not be regarded as a subordinate factor. It is the primary and most important element. It is willed not merely for the sake of the effects to be achieved for creatures, for the sake of pardon and reconciliation, but also for its own sake, namely, that the Son of God may manifest in His external mission, by a real and perfect surrender of Himself, the honor which He is to give to His Father.

Atonement or redemption from sin, taken in itself, may by no means be looked upon as the most important effect which this sacrifice has procured for creatures, as if the sacrifice were necessary, and actually took place, primarily on their account. Still less may the factor of merit be lost sight of in preoccupation with the aspect of atonement, as has more or less been the case in some modern views of the theory of redemption.

Those who are exclusively concerned with this element do not reflect that by the same price of blood by which Christ paid our debt and bought us off from the slavery of sin, He has also purchased our admission into the sonship of God. Christ has not only regained for us the grace of the children of God, which we had forfeited by sin, in the sense that He has wiped out the sin and thereby enabled the original grace of God to return to its rightful place; for in that case grace would ever remain pure grace, and would not have been positively purchased by Him. No; just as, by the satisfactory efficacy of His sacrifice, He has absolved us of the infinite debt which we had incurred with God, so by the meritorious power of His sacrifice He has made God our debtor; that is, He paid Him so high a price that God no longer bestows upon us that great benefit, the grace of divine sonship, out of sheer, gratuitous kindness and free love, but now confers it upon us as our due. It is here above all that we gain some insight into the meaning, so sublime and mysterious, which the sacrifice of Christ has for us.

For the grace of divine sonship demands an infinite purchase price, quite as much as the debt of sin demands an infinite ransom. By himself a mere creature cannot in any proper sense merit the grace of sonship, either for himself or for others, any more than he could satisfy for sin. In the latter case there is question of restoring to God the honor of which He has been deprived; in the former case the finite creature is to share in the infinite greatness and majesty of God: the creature is to possess and enjoy God as He is in Himself, and receive Him as the portion of his inheritance. To purchase the grace of divine sonship is as much as to purchase God Himself, and no man, no angel, can do this; only the God-man can do so. If all men together were to shed all their blood for one single individual, with the intention of procuring for him but the minutest share in the divine life of the children of God, all this blood would fall infinitely short of the value of that good. Nothing less than the divine blood and the infinitely precious life of the only-begotten Son of God is valuable enough to pay for this treasure.

Which is the greater or nobler achievement: to free men of their debt to God, or to make God their debtor; to rescue men from the slavery of sin, or to raise them from the servitude of God to the sonship of God; to ransom souls from God's wrath, or to purchase for them the friendship and the sonship of God, and with it God Himself? In which respect does Christ's blood appear more precious, more valuable, more powerful: when it washes men clean of their guilt and slays sin, or when it showers them with divine splendor and floods them with divine life? It is equally necessary in both cases, that is, it is alone sufficient; but in the latter case it is incomparably more fruitful and effective. At any rate we shall account for only half of its value if we acknowledge that it is effective in the first regard alone, and overlook the second or allow it to merge with the first.

As a rule, the distinction between these two aspects of Christ's achievement is so neglected because in reality they are in exceedingly close contact. But a careful examination of their point of contact sheds clear light on the importance of the difference between them.

In the first place, Christ's task is to efface sin as it actually presents itself, that is, as an obstacle to the supernatural grace which it expelled from mankind. Therefore if sin is thoroughly eradicated, its result, the expulsion of sanctifying grace, must cease and grace itself must return. Nevertheless, to destroy the obstacles to the readmission of grace after sin, is one thing, and actually to usher it in, to acquire it, to merit it, is another thing; to remove positive unworthiness of grace is quite different from conferring a positive worthiness, or rather a right to grace.

In the second place, Christ's satisfaction and merit coincide in the manner in which both were effected. For by His Passion and death Christ has both satisfied for our sins and merited grace and glory for us; and His Passion and death drew their satisfactory and meritorious power from one and the same source, the divine dignity of the person of Christ. But Christ could have merited grace and glory for us without suffering for us, whereas suffering is essentially required for satisfaction. For without self-renunciation, self-denial, self-abasement, God's ravaged honor cannot be restored; merit, on the other hand, rests simply on the performance of some service for the honor and glory of God out of love for Him. However, as self-surrendering love is most resplendently manifested when one delivers oneself up for the beloved, and as, further, the most perfect adoration of God consists in man's real effacement of himself before God, so also Christ's merit actually culminates in His Passion and death. To purchase for us the supernatural, divine life of the children of God, Christ offered to His heavenly Father His blood and His natural, corporal life.

Wonderful dispensation of divine Providence, which decreed not only to destroy death by death, but to make death itself the source of life, and ordained that we should receive supernatural life in exchange for the death of nature! In making us His children, God gives us Himself along with His entire divine glory and beatitude;

and so He willed that we, too, on our part, should surrender ourselves entirely to Him in and with Christ, and should annihilate ourselves for His glory, that by this unreserved surrender of ourselves to Him we might become worthy of the unrestricted communication of Himself to us. Thus viewed, death loses the appearance of punishment, even of penance; it takes on the guise of the greatest honor that man can render to God. No longer does it seem a harsh, physical necessity; nature's very weakness and frailty are to be the door to supreme glorification. Christ has drawn the sting from death, ever since the time that He Himself suffered death for us, in order to merit life for us. And ever since that time we too, in union with Him as His members, offer to God by our death the noble sacrifice that brings down upon us the fullness of divine glory.

In this respect, too, the order of grace established by Christ is more wonderful and splendid than that of the first Adam. As Adam had not merited grace, so he was not to have purchased the state of glory by suffering and death. God exacted of him no true sacrifice as the price of glory. Although the painless manifestation of tender love for God could avail as merit for glory, still for Adam heaven was given rather than bought, since it cost him nothing. The new Adam, on the contrary, has purchased grace itself for us by a true sacrifice; and although we do not recover integrity through Him along with grace, yet we are summoned to battle and sacrifice in order to storm heaven and thus win it. Are not this battle and this sacrifice more noble, more glorious, more sublime than the tranquil state enjoyed by Adam, seeing that he received his happy life entirely from the goodness of His Creator, without meriting it by a worthy return of service in the immolation of himself?

68. Physical or Dynamic Character of the Causality Exercised on the Race by the God-man

By His satisfaction and merit the God-man is the moral cause of man's restoration to the sonship of God; that is, He moves God, He begs God to forgive us our sins and receive us back into grace. This moral causality is a great mystery in its own right. It supposes that Christ is truly the God-man and the real head of the human race. Christ's merit is infinite only if He is the God-man, and He can give the race the benefit of His acts only if He is its head. Christ merits, the theologians say, by the *gratia capitis*, that is, by His superabundant grace which is of infinite value on account of the hypostatic union, the grace that abides in Him in His capacity as head of the race.

Does this moral efficacy entirely exhaust the mystery of Christ's significance to the race? Many theologians proceed no further in their speculations. They are content to let the matter rest there, because they fear to stress the mysterious element unduly. We believe with St. Thomas that we must go further. The grounds on which Christ's unexampled moral causality rests demand that we admit a physical causality, or better a hyperphysical causality, analogous to the physical, exercised by Him upon the human race. In other words, the very reasons that enable the God-man to act for us with God require that He also act dynamically upon us as the bearer and channel of the power of God's grace.

1. If Christ is the God-man and at the same time the true head of the human race, He must be able to do more than appear before God, in the name of all the other members, with an activity that is of infinite value, for the purpose of thus obtaining grace and life for them. As supernatural head He must exercise a direct influence upon His members. From His own interior, from His own fullness of life, He must flood His members with grace and life. While it is true that as the primal source of grace and life He merits both gifts for us, He must actually convey them to us from God. The causality exercised by God must pass through Him. Otherwise He would be head of the race in a very imperfect sense. He would not have the full significance for the race that the head has for the members of the body, whereas Holy Scripture carries through these parallels with striking emphasis and complete consistency. Further, He would not be the supernatural head of the race in as full a sense as that in which Adam is its natural head; for we receive our nature from Adam as from its physical principle, its source. If Christ is truly to be the new, heavenly Adam, we must receive our heavenly grace-nature not only on account of Him, by virtue of His merits, but from Him and out of Him as its source.

And actually the God-man bears in Himself the grace that He merits for us; He Himself can communicate it to us, and God wills to convey it through Him. Why else does Sacred Scripture, in the very texts where the significance of the God-man is most profoundly

and clearly expressed, state: He was "full of grace and of truth
. . . and of His fullness we have all received"? [18] Why does the
Apostle assert that in Christ dwells the fullness of the Godhead
bodily,[19] if not to point out that this fullness is poured forth from
Him over the whole race? How would Christ in His humanity be
truly the vine and we the branches, if merely by His merits He
drew grace down upon us like a dew from heaven, and did not pour
virtue and life into us from Himself, as the Council of Trent says? [20]
How could the Savior Himself say that those who believe in Him
and partake of Him receive life from Him, as He does from the
Father, if He had done no more than merit it for us? In particular
how could He state with such pronounced emphasis that the Father,
as He has life of Himself, has also granted to the Son to have life
in Himself, if He did not wish to intimate that the Son in His humanity, in which He is united to us, not merely obtains life for us,
but also gives and produces it? [21]

2. These reasons, which bepeak a physical or dynamic causality
on the part of the God-man, also point the way, if more closely
examined, to a clearer notion and explanation of this causality.

We cannot maintain that Christ's humanity is in itself the cause of
grace; for although it is endowed with an immeasurable fullness of
grace and glory, it does not have this fullness of grace from itself,
and therefore cannot communicate it. It is universally true that
nothing created can of itself effect the participation in the divine
nature which is comprised in grace. God alone can do this; and
therefore He alone is the real source of grace, and the principle by
which grace is produced. Whatever is created can be no more than
an organ or instrument in this regard, and that, too, only so far as it
transmits God's operation to the subject to which it is directed.

This is the sense, then, in which the humanity of Christ is the
cause of grace in us: it is the organ of the Godhead, the channel and
conductor of the divine causality; but it is such in a unique and
most striking way. It is an instrument that is hypostatically united
to the divinity as the body is to the soul, an instrument in which

[18] John 1:14, 16.
[19] Cf. Col. 2:9.
[20] Sessio VI, cap. 16 (Denz., 809): ". . . ille ipse Christus Iesus tamquam
caput in membra [Eph. 4:15] et tamquam vitis in palmites [Io. 15:5] in ipsos
iustificatos iugiter virtutem influat. . . ." [Tr.]
[21] Cf. John 6:57 f.

God's power is ever active, and this for the reason that God Himself is substantially joined to it in closest unity. It bears the Son of God Himself and the entire fullness of the Godhead substantially within it. Accordingly, as the sacred humanity is itself transfigured, glorified, and in highest measure made to participate in the divine nature by the power of the divinity, it conveys this same power to all men who are in union with it; or better, the power of the divinity is extended through the sacred humanity to all the members of the body of which it is the head. And because this power does not pass through the sacred humanity without affecting it, that is, without filling it with grace, since this power is primarily operative in that humanity and is active in the rest of men only secondarily, the humanity of Christ appears as a teeming channel, as a second source of grace, which renders it essentially different from all other means instituted to conduct grace. Thus in individual men grace is actually an outpouring, a derivation from the grace of the head, the *gratia capitis* in Christ, as theologians say, with the first chapter of St. John in mind. However, the created grace with which Christ's soul is endowed must not be regarded as the *gratia capitis* abstractly in itself, but in conjunction with the hypostatic union; for it is only in virtue of the hypostatic union that the power of communicating grace to other subjects, like the power of meriting grace for others, resides in the soul of Christ.

Therefore when we speak of physical causality in connection with Christ's humanity, we regard that humanity not as the principle, but as the organ of the activity exercised by the divine Logos. In an absolute sense, we can ascribe that activity only to the concrete subject, the God-man. But then we have to add that as God He physically or hyperphysically produces grace in us through His humanity. Moreover, He is the cause of the supernature in us just as truly as Adam was the cause of nature, or even in a still more perfect way. He begets us unto supernatural life even in a truer sense than Adam has begotten us unto natural life. Adam is the cause of our nature, although he does not produce the vital principle of our nature, the rational soul. He is the cause only of the body and the formation of it which is a necessary disposition for the reception of the soul and which calls for the infusion of the soul. Thus his generative activity is at bottom only an instrument by which God causes the way to be prepared for the infusion of the soul, an instrument that conducts God's life-giving activity to a definite subject.

The second Adam, on the contrary, the God-man, has in Himself, as God, the power to confer supernatural life on man, and this power passes through His humanity, to which it is substantially united, over to the rest of men. His humanity in itself does not do so much, or rather does nothing at all, to produce man's supernature, whereas Adam does contribute something of himself for the production of nature. But this deficiency is richly compensated by the fact that the sacred humanity bears within itself the very source of the supernature and is its channel in the fullest sense. By His divinity in His humanity the God-man is, according to the expression used by the Apostle, a *Spiritus vivificans*, a "life-giving Spirit," [22] who fills men with divine spirituality, with divine life. His divinity is the fire that is to pervade, illuminate, and transform the whole human race; but His humanity is the glowing coal [23] in which the fire dwells and from which it is diffused over the whole race. The coal does nothing of itself to kindle fire in other substances; but since it bears fire within itself, it brings this fire to all objects coming into contact with it. Therefore the effect produced belongs

[22] Cf. I Cor. 15:45.
[23] This figure of the glowing coal is one of the commonest, but also one of the deepest and richest, used by the Fathers to illustrate the nature of Christ and His activity. St. Cyril of Alexandria is very fond of it, and employs it especially in his polemical writings against Nestorius. He has a chapter on the topic in his *Scholia de incarnatione Unigeniti* [c.9; *PG*, LXXV, 1377], part of which we quote here. "Blessed Isaias narrates: 'And one of the seraphim flew to me, and in his hand was a live coal, which he had taken with the tongs off the altar. And he touched my mouth, and said: Behold this hath touched thy lips, and thy iniquities shall be taken away, and thy sin shall be cleansed' [Isa. 6:6 f.]. We assert that the coal is a figure and image of the Word made man; if it touches our lips, that is, if we confess faith in Him, He will cleanse us of all sin and will deliver us from our former iniquities. Furthermore, in the live coal as in an image we may perceive the Word of God united to His humanity; not that He has ceased to be what He is, but rather that He has transformed the assumed or united nature into His own glory and power. When fire is applied to a log, it penetrates the wood, lays hold of it and, although it does not drive away the nature of wood, changes it into the appearance and energy of fire, and carries on its own activities in the wood, and seems to be but one thing with it. This is the way you are to think of Christ. For God, in uniting Himself ineffably to humanity, preserves that humanity in its own proper nature, and He Himself remains what He was. But once the union is effected, He seems to be one with that nature, taking as His own what belongs to it, but at the same time bestowing on it the activity of His own nature."

more to it than to other causes which merely prepare objects for the reception of fire. Must we not, then, ascribe to the God-man, even in His humanity, an even greater efficacy in the production of supernature, than we attribute to Adam in the generation of nature?

3. The objections which can be raised against the physical causality of the God-man and His humanity have already been anticipated in the foregoing exposition. They may be reduced to two categories.

a) In the first place it is stated: In effects which can be brought about only by divine power and in which nothing created can co-operate, the creature cannot be an instrument. For the essence of an instrument lies precisely in the fact that it contributes something of itself to the effect intended by the principal cause. But grace is so very supernatural and divine that no created agent can contribute to its production. Consequently not even the humanity of Christ can serve as an instrument in the production of grace.

We concede that such is the ordinary meaning of instrumental cause. No one, for instance, would use a hammer unless the power inhering in it, its weight and its hardness, lent itself to the attainment of the effect. But the formal character of the instrument always consists in the fact that it transmits the power and energy of the user to the subject in which the effect is to be produced; and if the instrument adds something of its own power, it is not merely an instrument, but is to some extent a proper, independent cause. It is purely instrumental only if its activity is entirely absorbed in that of the principal cause, and if it works only so far as the principal cause works through it.

But, it will be asked, what purpose is served by instruments that contribute nothing of themselves to the effect? They serve to establish a connection between the efficient cause and the subject to which the efficacy of the cause is to pass, whether such connection cannot otherwise be established, or whether the efficient cause chooses to work in this way. They serve to transmit the power of the efficient cause to the substratum upon which it is working, by bringing the cause into a certain contact with this substratum. They convey the effect of that force to the subject which is to receive it, and cause it really to enter into the subject. Or, if one will, instruments serve in general to prepare the way for the transmission of the power of the principal agent to the subject that is to receive its effect. This can take place in a twofold manner, either in such a way that the instrument by its own power disposes the subject for the reception of the effect intended by the principal agent, as the hammer disposes the iron for the reception of the form intended by the craftsman; or simply in such a way that the instrument effects a juncture between the principal agent and the subject of the effect, as, for example, a handle by which one grasps an object in order to drag it away or push it aside.[24]

Let us transfer these general notions to instruments employed by God. Since God is all-powerful and is everywhere present with His substantial power, He nowhere is in need of any created instrument to produce His effects. And where as yet there is no existing subject upon which He intends to act, it is not even possible for Him to employ an instrument, for then the idea of an instrument is absolutely ruled out. This is the case with creation. In all other cases it depends wholly on God's will whether He elects to avail Himself of an instrument or not. If He so chooses, He can employ an instrument in the twofold manner just indicated: first, to dispose the subject that is to receive an effect in keeping with its nature. Thus He makes use of man to produce a new man by way of generation, in which man produces dispositions in a body for the reception of a soul. In this way, too, Christ acts as an instrument for God's redemptive work, when by His human activity He satisfies and merits for the race, and thus renders it worthy of grace. Secondly, God avails Himself of a creature as an instrument in order to have His power pass over to a subject simply through a creature, and thus to effect by means of a creature what He can effect alone. It is in this sense that He produces grace itself in us through the humanity of Christ, since that humanity, as the chief member of the race, brings its inherent power into contact with all the members of the race, and is thereby able to transmit the effect of its power to these members. Yet it remains true that the production of grace is a purely divine work, proceeding exclusively and entirely from the Godhead. But the entrance of grace into man is at the same time the work of Christ's humanity as the organ of the divinity.

Very well, the rejoinder will be made, let it be granted that Christ's humanity becomes an instrument for the infusion of grace by bring-

[24] The function of a catalyst in chemical reactions suggests a pertinent analogy. [Tr.]

ing the real cause of grace into contact with the recipient; but then, will it not be necessary that the humanity itself come into real, physical contact with the rest of men; and can this be admitted without postulating at least a relative ubiquity for it?

b) This is the second class of difficulties which we indicated above. By wishing to save ourselves from the first set of objections, we fall into the second; we escape from Scylla into the arms of Charybdis. Must we then relinquish our position? Certainly not. Is there, then, such a real, physical contact of Christ's humanity with us? What else is sacramental Communion but such a real contact, or rather, a substantial union of our humanity with that of the Son of God? Cannot the humanity of Christ be the organ of the divinity and the vehicle of its activity in the realm of grace at least here? Even were this all, the principle is saved, that Christ's humanity can and should be the physical organ of the divinity. It is a different question whether grace always and in all instances flows to us physically through the humanity of Christ, that is, even outside of sacramental Communion. To maintain and explain that such is the case, many theologians speak of a spiritual contact with the humanity of Christ, to whom we attach ourselves by faith and love; or they have recourse to an indirect contact established by sacramental rites. But I must confess that physical contact is not at all made clear in such theories. The spiritual contact in question is in itself a purely moral contact, and in the alleged indirect contact it still remains to be explained how the humanity of Christ is physically joined to the sacramental rites, so that by means of them it is physically united to us. In both theories some essential, supplementary element is lacking. Where are we to look for it?

We need merely revert to what we stated at the outset about the manner in which Christ is head of the race in His humanity; for it was through this idea of the head that we arrived at the thought of Christ's physical influence. By the very fact that the human nature of Christ is drawn from the substance of the race and remains in the substance of the race, it is joined in real, physical continuity with all the other members of the race, and forms with them not merely a moral, but a real, physical body. Our union with Christ in Communion is, as we shall show later, only the perfected expression, the seal of that other, but just as real union which we have with Him as members of the same race. Consequently, if the first mode of union suffices, as it undoubtedly does, to bring us into so close a contact with Christ's humanity that it can act upon us as the organ of the divinity, the second mode of union must also suffice for the same purpose, at any rate to some extent.

This is all the more evident in view of the fact that the divine power residing in Christ's humanity is able, on account of its infinity, to extend not only to whatever is immediately united with it, but also to everything that is in any way at all, even remotely, joined to it. Christ's humanity is like a source of electricity which enables not only those bodies which immediately touch it, but all with which it is connected by any kind of suitable conductor, to receive the effects of the electrical energy residing in it. It is an incandescent coal placed in the midst of the human race, a coal which by reason of the fire of the divinity pervading it is capable of illuminating and warming the entire race which is joined to it.[25] In brief, the humanity of Christ is in real, physical continuity and contact with all men, in Communion by substantial presence, outside of Communion by the real union which is grounded upon the physical unity of the race; and this is sufficient to make it the conductor of the divine power dwelling in it.

The spiritual contact which some theologians speak of and which, as has been remarked, is in itself purely moral, is supplemented by this physical contact. It cannot and ought not be substituted for the physical contact, but should be added to it, as actually happens

[25] A clearer and more appropriate illustration of this point is furnished by the figure of the lily, which diffuses its perfume all about it and scents the whole atmosphere. St. Cyril devotes a chapter of his *Scholia* [c. 10; *PG*, LXXV, 1380] to this image, which he applies to Christ: "In the Canticle of Canticles our Lord Jesus Christ is introduced as saying to us: 'I am the flower of the field, and the lily of the valleys' [Cant. 2:1]. An odor, to be sure, is an immaterial thing, but its body, so to speak, is that in which it inheres; still, the lily is seen to be a single thing composed of both these elements; it is no longer a lily if one of them ceases to be, seeing that fragrance is in a body. Thus, too, in the case of Christ we perceive that the divine nature, which diffuses its most excellent majesty throughout the world like a delightful fragrance, is in the humanity as in its subject; that which is by nature immaterial, I should almost say, has been made material by the union wrought for our salvation, since He wished to manifest Himself by means of a body. For it was in a body that He worked divine signs. Therefore what is immaterial can readily be apprehended in its body, as fragrance is perceived in the flower; both the fragrance and the flower are styled lily." See also the selections from the Fathers quoted above, in section 58, and the figures therein employed.

where (in Holy Communion) Christ's humanity is substantially present. Through it we on our part draw near to the God-man, who already is close to us and is present to us with His divine power by His entrance into our race, in order to make ourselves responsive to the workings of this power, or actually to receive it into ourselves. By this approach from our side we could not make the power of the God-man physically present to ourselves if it were not so already; we can do no more than avail ourselves of the power already present.

What then of the sensible, indirect contact with Christ in the sacraments? Such contact has meaning only if Christ is virtually present in the whole human race even apart from the sacraments. For how else would Christ be in the sacraments themselves, the Eucharist excepted, and also in the ministers of the sacraments? How can they bring Him near us? Christ has no more need of these new organs than God has need of the humanity of Christ in order to act on us in a supernatural way; otherwise grace could not be given outside the sacraments, without the actual reception of them. Yet as a rule Christ wills that His influence should flow to us by way of these visible media; and He shows that He is present with His infinite power to all of us by the very fact that He can choose any apt instrument He pleases for the exercise of His activity.

Before we leave the mystery of the God-man, we ought to turn our eyes for a moment to the Blessed Virgin, from whom He received His human nature, and in whose womb He wedded the human race and became one body with it. Especially we ought to show how the heart which is at the center of the race, that heart from which the divine head diffuses His sanctifying and life-giving energy throughout the body, had itself to be free from the universal sinfulness and disease.[26] It had to be free in such a way that this im-

[26] This thought is by no means new; the Jesuit Ballerini, in his *Sylloge monumentorum ad mysterium conceptionis immaculatae Virginis Deiparae illustrandum*, has brought to light a hymn that apparently dates back to St. Ambrose. It expresses our point in noble verse:

Rerum misertus sed sator, inscia
Cernens piacli viscera virginis,
His ferre mortis crimine languido
Mandat salutis gaudia saeculo.

The stanza may be rendered thus:

The merciful Creator of the race
Then chose the Virgin's womb that knew no stain,

munity was an effect produced by the same head and the same sanctifying, life-giving power whereby the race was to be freed from the sin and mortality actually contracted. That is to say, if the new Eve, after the model of the old, was to become the mother of the race in its heavenly birth, she had to proceed in her heavenly nature from the side of her bridegroom, and had to issue from the sacrificial outpouring of His heart.[27] Thus we should have to stitch in many threads by which the mystery of Mary's Immaculate Conception is interwoven with the mystery of the Incarnation. This demonstration would be all the more important in view of the statement made some years ago by one of our most distinguished theologians, to the effect that there is practically no speculative content in that dogma. But this would take us too far afield. Besides, in recent times so much has been written on the subject that the utterance of the theologian referred to will certainly have met with but slight approval. In any case, we shall come back to the meaning typified by the Virgin Mother of God when we take up the doctrine of the Church and of justification.[28]

And bade it bear the Joy of saving grace
To men whose crimes deserved eternal pain.

[27] Whatever we may think of the "debitum incurrendi peccatum originale" in Mary's case, the Church holds fast to the truth that the Blessed Virgin's privilege is a fruit of Christ's sacrificial death, without, however, condemning the denial of such a *debitum*, as some have erroneously maintained in commenting on the bull *Ineffabilis Deus*. The one proposition is not a necessary consequence of the other. Cf. p. 444.

[28] We take this opportunity of calling attention to the rich theological content revealed in the work of A. Nicolas on the Virgin Mary, *La vierge Marie et le plan divin* (4 volumes, Paris, 1852 ff.). The first volume especially is to be recommended.

PART FIVE

The Mystery of the Eucharist

The Mystery of Faith.
Words from the consecration of
the chalice.

CHAPTER XVII

The Real Presence and Transubstantiation

▄▄

69. MYSTICAL NATURE OF THE EUCHARIST

FROM the mystery of the Incarnation we pass immediately to the mystery of the Eucharist. Our main reason for proceeding thus is that the relationship of the two mysteries is so close that they serve to complement, illuminate, and clarify each other. Starting from them as the central point of Christian life, we hope to prepare the way for a deeper and more comprehensive discussion of the Church, the sacraments, justification, and all the other mysteries.[1]

When set forth according to the norm of the Catholic faith, the Eucharist, like the Incarnation, is manifestly an astounding, supernatural work of God. It is a work hidden from the intellect, and is quite beyond our understanding. It is a true mystery. Its mysterious character is so readily acknowledged that the Eucharist is often referred to simply as the mystery par excellence.

What does faith teach us about the Eucharist? It teaches us that by the consecration of the priest the substance of the body and blood of Christ becomes present under the appearances of bread and wine, in place of the natural substances corresponding to these appearances.[2] It teaches further that the substance of Christ's body and blood remains actually, truly, and essentially present as long as

---

[1] Two of the best among recent German theologians have preceded us in following a like order, inasmuch as they treat of the Eucharist, if only from the standpoint of sacrifice, prior to the other sacraments. We have in mind Dieringer and Schwetz in their dogmatic textbooks.

[2] Later we shall have occasion to speak of the nature, and discuss the meaning, of transubstantiation as an action that brings about the Eucharistic presence. At this point we are speaking only of the mystery which the Eucharist actually is, not of the mystery by which it becomes what it is.

the appearances endure, yet in such a manner that it is present whole and indivisible under each species, as well as under any part thereof.

The very wording of the dogma bears witness to its mysterious character. For the substantial presence of the body and blood of Christ under alien species is plainly a fact at which we cannot arrive by reason alone, because we are naturally able to know substances only by their accidents and their outward appearance. According to the ordinary laws of thought, reason is quite justified in inferring a substance from the accidents that are naturally associated with it. Reason will not be led to affirm the presence of Christ's body by following its natural course; on the contrary, reason will pronounce without hesitation that it is not present. Faith is required, not only to assist reason by leading it further, but to bring its natural course to a halt. The fact of the mystery is utterly cut off from unaided reason, because it is a supernatural fact, one that is wrought not upon the surface of things, but in their innermost core.

The reality of the presence of Christ's body under the sacramental species is undiscernible and, in a higher sense, the nature of that presence is inconceivable. That is to say, its supernatural character places it beyond all natural concepts, and even beyond the natural conceptive power of the intellect. This is the second distinctive note of a supernatural mystery.

The concepts of substance and accident, considered from the standpoint of their inner nature and in their reciprocal connection and relation, are full of obscurity for our natural cognition, even when left undisturbed in their natural existence. We are unable to comprehend them in all their aspects, and to fathom them in all their depths. But our reason can at least form some idea of them. Natural substances, along with their accidents, are the direct objects of our apprehension, and metaphysical philosophy has much to say concerning their essence and mutual relationship. Although our concepts of substance and accident are obscure, they are at any rate formed directly from the things that confront us. They are not mere analogies; hence their object is not a mystery in the higher, theological sense.

But the Eucharist is a mystery in the theological sense. There the substance of Christ's body exists in a way that is not natural to it, but supernatural. We cannot form a direct concept, but only an analogous one of this supernatural mode of existence. For to form a concept of the mode of existence of Christ's body in the Eucharist, we must transfer to it our notions of the natural existence of other substances. Herein precisely is the miracle and the mystery: in the Eucharist the body of Christ exists supernaturally in a way that only substances of an entirely different kind can exist naturally. Although material in itself, the body of Christ exists after the fashion of a spiritual substance, so far as, like the soul in the body, it is substantially present whole and indivisible in the entire host and in every part of it, and is beyond all sensible perception. Moreover, the existence of the body of Christ in the Eucharist is analogous to the existence of the divine substance. That is, it exists in a way that is naturally impossible even to a created spiritual substance, since it is present not only in a single place, but in numberless separate places. But while it thus exists in the manner of higher, immaterial substances, it also exists, to some extent, in the manner of a material substance specifically distinct from it and inferior to it, inasmuch as it takes the place of that substance and, with reference to its accidents, takes over their functions, at least in part.[3]

This body, which exists after the fashion of other substances—spiritual and divine substances, and the substance of bread—must continue in its own proper existence. Hence the mode of existence of these other substances can be appropriated to it only on the condition that its own material, created, and specific nature is not thereby jeopardized. Therefore the Eucharistic mode of existence must be apprehended in terms of concepts derived from other existences; and these alien concepts themselves, because they are alien, may be applied to the body of Christ in the Eucharist only proportionately and analogously. Thus the obscurity we encounter in the concept of the Eucharistic existence of Christ's body is not only that which confronts us whenever we penetrate deeply into the nature of things, but is a quite other and more profound obscurity, such as is exclusively proper to supernatural things.

As we have remarked more than once, we must be extremely careful to attend to the peculiar type of obscurity that emanates from

---

[3] We will subsequently explain in detail what we hold on this point. We believe that the doctrine as we will outline it is the simplest and most natural account of the sacramental presence, and especially that it is most conformable to the dogma of transubstantiation.

supernatural objects. Only then shall we clearly perceive that mysteries are inaccessible to our scrutiny not because of any confusion or lack of light on their part, but because their very greatness and splendor dazzle us and compel us to remain at a respectful distance. And so we must again come back to the supernatural character of Christ's mode of existence.

This supernaturalness does not consist merely in the impossibility of naturally effecting Christ's mode of existence in the Eucharist. Such impossibility could well obtain even if this mode of existence were not higher and more exquisite than that which is natural to Christ's body as it is in itself. Is not the state of the damned supernatural in this respect, seeing that they cannot naturally suffer from material fire, at least so long as they lack bodies? Their condition cannot be the result of natural forces. Their state is not, of course, an exaltation of nature, but an inconceivably disgraceful abasement, which is the more degrading as it is the product of a supernatural miracle of divine omnipotence. We must insist strongly on this difference, since Christ's sacramental mode of existence might at first sight appear to be nothing but a supernaturally effected degradation.

One may, if one cares to, concentrate upon the concealment of Christ's glory and majesty, which is a necessary consequence of His sacramental mode of existence, and regard it as an abasement of Christ. But such a view touches only the surface of the mystery, and does not reach down to its inner nature. It does not follow that the manner of Christ's existence in the Eucharist is not, in itself, most sublime and mysterious. On the contrary, we must hold that the body of Christ retains its supernatural glory even in the Sacrament, but that in the Sacrament it takes on a supernatural mode of existence which does not appear outwardly any more than His glory does. As the hypostatic union does not cease to be a superlatively great mystery because the full magnificence of the divinity does not pierce through the humanity, so the sacramental existence is no less glorious for the body of Christ for the reason that it does not stand forth in all its splendor.[4]

[4] Ascetical writers particularly often thus regard the Eucharistic form of existence as a humiliating debasement of Christ's body. Certain theologians, for example, De Lugo and more recently Franzelin, my esteemed teacher in Rome, even attempt to find in this abasement the reason why the body of

Is there any sense in which we may say that the sacramental existence of Christ's body is more glorious than the mode of existence natural to it? The sacramental existence is evidently the nobler inasmuch as the body of Christ in the Eucharist exists after the manner of higher substances, namely, the spiritual and the divine: the spiritual, because it is present whole and undivided in the entire host and in every part of it; the divine, because it is present in countless places, wherever the bread is consecrated. But the divine substance is also spiritual, and the privilege of the created spirit here appears indissolubly joined to the prerogative of the uncreated Spirit. Further, the indivisibility of the presence of Christ's body reaches so far that even after the division of the host His body continues to exist in every part of it, unlike the soul which, after the dismemberment of the body, can go on existing only in one of its parts. For these reasons we can say simply that the body of Christ is present in the Eucharist in a way that transcends its own nature and the nature of all bodies: it exists in a spiritual manner, indeed in a divinely spiritual manner, and shares in the mode of existence proper to God.

But the body of Christ also exists in the manner of another, and a lower, material substance, which it replaces. Can we say that this mode of existence, too, is in itself something higher, nobler, and supernatural? If the accidents of bread informed the body of Christ and inhered in it, so that it would become their material substratum, as the substance of the bread was, then of course the body of Christ would suffer degradation by taking the place of that substance, since it would be subjected to the accidents of a less perfect body as their material cause. In that case the body of Christ would be more material in the Eucharist than it is in itself, whereas, as we have just seen, it is precisely in the Eucharist that it takes on the existence of a spiritual substance, indeed of the divine substance. And in fact, if we look at the matter closely, we shall discover that the body of

Christ exists in the Sacrament as a victim. But the humiliation which the ascetics ponder and use for practical ends is something purely external as far as the body of Christ is concerned; it is no more than the absence of all outward splendor, and the possibility of a purely exterior dishonoring. The sacrificial character of the Eucharist cannot, it seems, be found in such humiliation, if only for the reason that this humiliation, regarded as a moral annihiliation, would renew the death and immolation of Christ, and hence also His meritorious activity, instead of merely representing them.

Christ, even in succeeding to the place of the substance of bread, does not forfeit the spirituality and divinity of its mode of existence, but triumphantly vindicates it. The body of Christ takes the place of the substance of bread not in any ordinary sense, but in a quite eminent way. That is to say, it succeeds to the perfection of that substance, not its imperfection; to its active, not to its passive function relative to the accidents.

For the substance of bread has a twofold relation to the accidents. It is the source, the principle, from which the accidents flow and have their stability. But at the same time the substance is informed, completed, and perfected by these accidents. The body of Christ cannot take the place of the substance of bread in this second respect. What need has it of being thus informed by alien accidents, since it is complete in itself and supremely perfect? But to replace the substance of bread in the first of these two relations is a mark of tremendous energy and power. The accidents corresponding to the specific nature of an object can arise naturally only from that substance whose nature is manifested in them. If this substance is withdrawn from existence, its accidents must naturally perish with it. Only God, who is the absolute cause of substances and accidents alike, can in such an event supply for the energy of the substance in question by His absolute power and omnipresence, preserve the accidents in being, and save them from annihilation. If, therefore, the body of Christ replaces the substance of bread in the Eucharist, it can keep the accidents in being only by acting as the organ of the Godhead. Yet by the very fact that it serves as the instrument of an exclusively divine operation it shares in the omnipresence of God, which penetrates to the deepest essence of things, interiorly sustains that essence, and hence is able to supply for its entire causality. Accordingly, is it not once again clear that Christ's sacramental mode of existence is utterly supernatural, seeing that it is a participation in a mode of existence proper to a higher substance, indeed the very highest, the divine substance?

A created analogon of the relationship of Christ's Eucharistic body to the species of bread is naturally found where a created image of the divine omnipresence is forthcoming, namely, in the relation of the spiritual soul to the accidents of the body which it animates. The soul is the cause, or at least the co-cause, of many of these accidents, but it is not their substratum, because it is not informed by them. At any rate the relationship of Christ's body to the Eucharistic accidents is spiritual, that is, it is a relationship that by nature is proper only to a spirit. But in a natural way the soul can be the cause of the accidents of the body only so long as it is united to the substance of the body to form one nature. Separated from the body, the soul can no longer sustain those accidents. Hence the soul is not able to do as much as the body of Christ in the Eucharist. And so it remains true that even in its relation to the accidents the mode of existence proper to Christ's body in the Eucharist is not only spiritual, but partakes of the divine.

Thus it is clear that the supernatural and mysterious character of the Eucharistic presence of Christ's body consists in the fact that this body enjoys a higher mode of existence than is conferred on a body by nature: it exists in the manner of a spiritual substance, even the divine substance. We might say that the mystery lies in the spirituality and divinity of that body's existence. Yet the meaning of the expression "spiritual presence" must be carefully determined, so as to preclude all error. Rightly understood, this term expresses the intrinsic nature and the highest reality of the presence of Christ, and consequently renders the supernatural grandeur of the mystery prominent. But wrongly understood, it can dilute and destroy the reality of the mystery, and is actually employed to signify the exact contrary of the real presence of Christ. It is wrongly understood if spiritual presence, as opposed to physical contact, indicates no more than a presence for the spirit, or for the eyes of the spirit contemplating it. In this sense Christ could be spiritually present to us in the Eucharist even though the latter were only a sign instituted in memory of Him, and did not really and substantially contain Him.

The phrase is correctly understood only if spiritual presence is taken to mean a presence according to the manner of spirits, namely, in the way that spirits themselves, and they alone, are present in a place or in an object. Real presence is not thereby excluded; in fact, real presence is emphasized, since spirits can be present in a place or an object in a more real, intimate, and perfect manner than bodies can. However, since the term "spiritual presence" is always ambiguous and, furthermore, does not perfectly and adequately express the character of Christ's presence even when used in its legitimate sense, we must further clarify and complete it by adding "divine presence," or "divine, Godlike mode of existence," as we have done above.

Even expressions such as these are in need of a more detailed explanation and justification. It is well known how the Lutherans, to escape the necessity of accepting transubstantiation in the Eucharist, or of admitting any objective efficacy at all in the words of consecration, were driven to uphold the real presence of Christ's body by postulating for Christ's humanity a certain ubiquity that arose from the hypostatic union. From the undeniable fact that the God-man, that is, the person of Christ, is everywhere present, they argued that all parts of His person, not only the divinity but also the humanity, were everywhere present—a manifest and egregious non sequitur. Not everything that pertains to the person of Christ by reason of one nature is attributable to Him also according to the other nature; and not everything that is predicated of the person can be predicated of every part of Him. Otherwise we should have to say that the humanity of Christ is God and His divinity.

Accordingly, when we ascribe a divine mode of existence to the body of Christ, we do not mean formally to appropriate to it, on the basis of the hypostatic union, the mode of existence proper to the divine nature and person. We say no more than that it shares in certain of the properties characteristic of the mode of existence enjoyed by the divine person and nature, somewhat as our soul shares in the life and glory of God through grace. For all that, it is ever true that this unique, supernatural participation in the divine mode of existence predicated of Christ's body, like the grace and glory of His soul, is not formally but virtually based on, and flows from, its hypostatic union with the person of God's Son. Because the body of Christ is the body of the Son of God, it receives through the power of the divine person inhabiting it the unique privilege, similar to the prerogative of the person Himself, but in limited measure, of being present indivisible and undivided in many places and in the innermost recesses of things. Not formally through the hypostatic union, but still because of it and on the basis of it, the Son of God raises the body He has assumed to a share in the simplicity, universality, and pervasive power of His divine existence.[5]

---

[5] Alger of Liége remarks rather boldly, but pertinently: "If the bodies of the saints are to be endowed with such great agility that their cumbersomeness will not at all hinder them from carrying out the directives of the spirit,

He does so particularly for the weighty reason that as head of the human race He wills, by means of His body, to establish the closest contact, and enter into the most solid union, with all the members of the race. He wishes to use His body as the instrument of His all-embracing activity, reaching down into the hearts of beings and deifying their natures.

Thus the mystery of the Eucharist is ontologically joined to the mystery of the Incarnation, just as the mystery of the Incarnation is joined to the Trinity. The Incarnation is the presupposition and explanation of the Eucharist, just as the eternal generation from the bosom of the Father is the presupposition and explanation of the

---

what is to be thought of the body of Christ, our head, who not only possesses agility, so as not to be hindered from doing what He pleases, but also says of Himself, 'All power is given to Me in heaven and on earth'? Thus He can do all things with God because of His personal unity with Him. If our bodies are to be spiritual because personally joined to a spirit, what is the body of God but divine, since it is united to God? Certainly we do not claim that the divine flesh is substantially the same as God. But since the Apostle says that all things are subjected to Christ, except Him who subjected everything to Him, and since the Son of God Himself testifies that all power is given to Him, we believe that this flesh is so joined to God in unity of person that what God possesses by nature, His flesh possesses by grace. Therefore we are to have the power already enjoyed by the angels, who with exceedingly great speed can traverse any distance at all in almost no interval of time. They do not, however, possess the power of remaining in the place whence they have withdrawn. Only the flesh of Christ, which has been exalted above every creature, possesses this extraordinary privilege over and beyond every nature. In virtue of the omnipotence given to Him in heaven and on earth, He is present whole and entire and substantially in heaven and on earth wherever and in what manner He pleases, not by passing from place to place, but by remaining where He is, and existing elsewhere also, just as He chooses" (*De sacramentis corporis et sanguinis dominici*, lib. I, cap. 14; *PL*, CLXXX, 782). Peter de Blois, *Epist.* 140 (*PL*, CCVII, 420), has a similar doctrine: "The same body is among us in widely separated places. . . . Although [the body of Christ] is limited to one place by reason of its corporal nature, it is in many places by virtual power and in a spiritual way. For so close is the union of divinity and flesh, which has been made wholly divine and glorious, that out of the fullness of the Godhead which, on the testimony of the Apostle, dwells there corporeally, that body, although it is corporally and naturally in one place, is in many places by divine and spiritual power. And as God Himself is, according to a certain personal mode of existence, present in one place, namely, in the man assumed by grace, although virtually and essentially He is in many places, indeed in every place, so He ineffably renders to His body the attributes of divinity, in such wise that by virtue of the union the Word is in one man, whereas the incomprehensible sacrament of His body and blood is in many places."

Incarnation, regarded as the stepping forth of God's Son into the world. These mysteries disclose a remarkable analogy and relationship with one another. All three show us the same Son of God: the first in the bosom of His eternal Father, whence He receives His being; the second in the womb of the Virgin, through which He enters the world; the third in the heart of the Church, where He sojourns by an enduring, universal presence among men and unites Himself to them. Yet He remains ever hidden from the natural eye of body and soul. In all of God's visible creation we cannot find the generation of His Son; nor in the humanity of the Son can we discern His hypostatic union with the divinity; nor under the Eucharistic species can we discover the body of Christ spiritually present. In all three forms only supernatural revelation, and only belief in that revelation, can enable us to recognize the Son of God. And this is a faith by which we do not simply grasp some object lying beyond the reach of our reason, but must break through the barriers thrown up by our natural concepts.

In a natural way we have a notion only of one person in one nature, of one nature in one person, and of the existence of a substance under its own proper accidents, and vice versa. But in order to apprehend these mysteries, we must hold that there is more than one person in the one divine nature, that there are two natures in the one person of Christ, and that in the Eucharist the body of Christ is raised above the accidents of extension and spatial limitation natural to it, and is joined to accidents belonging to another substance. In these mysteries the very foundations of all categories, suppositum and substance, substance and accident, take on relationships and meanings wholly different from those they have when they are looked upon by the eye of unaided reason. Consequently these mysteries do not at all fall under the metaphysics of pure reason, under philosophical metaphysics. They erect a system of a new, supernatural metaphysics, which is almost related to natural metaphysics as the latter is to physics: a rich and harmonious system, in which the roots of all categories appear in a new light under viewpoints of a most astounding variety, and where one member essentially completes and clarifies the other.

As all three mysteries are supernatural and mysterious in the extreme, their meaning for us must be correspondingly supernatural and mysterious. And as they are intimately connected with one another, so that the one invariably appears as the prolongation and continuation of the other, they not only must be in accord with one another as regards their supernatural meaning, purpose, and operations, but must mutually support, promote, and explain one another. These are the points we must further develop and demonstrate.

70. Mystical Purport of the Eucharist. General Aspects

The tremendous and exalted function of the Eucharist in the system of Christian mysteries, and especially the meaning it has for us men, is as a rule more readily understood and more accurately grasped than that of the Trinity, or even that of the Incarnation. Every Christian looks up to the Eucharist as the miracle of an unspeakable, inconceivable love of God for us human beings, the love of God who desires to unite Himself to us in the closest possible manner. In the thoughts and feelings of every Catholic the idea of a supernatural union with God is inseparable from belief in this mystery. In the case of the Incarnation, on the other hand, as we have seen, the idea of a mere cessation of an unnatural separation from God may at times prevail; and with regard to the Trinity, scarcely any reference to a union with God is forthcoming.

But we cannot have a clear idea of the full force and significance of God's supernatural union with us in the Eucharist, or of the nature and sublimity of the unspeakable divine love which is the source of that union, unless we take into account a number of other factors. That is, we must understand the supernatural import of the Incarnation and the Trinity and, on our part, must be aware of the fact that we are destined to an absolutely supernatural life, which is a participation in the divine nature and the divine life.

For how could we account for this ineffable miracle of divine love in the Eucharist, if it were God's intention to treat us merely as His servants, and if it were not His will to raise us above our nature and take us to His fatherly bosom? Whence comes this heavenly, divine nourishment, and to what end is it directed, if we are not born to a supernatural, divine life? Why this stupendous, substantial union of the new Adam with man, if He wishes to do no more than offer satisfaction for our sins, or merit God's assistance for us, and does not intend, as supernatural progenitor of the race, to recharge our nature with divine energy, and to be for it the seed of a life that is not only humanly good and just, but divinely holy and blessed? Why, I repeat, this substantial union of God with us, unless it is to be a communication and an image of that inexpressible union which in the Trinity binds the Father to the Son in the Holy Spirit? Why all this, if Christ does not purpose to pour out upon us, along with His substance, His own divine life, just as the Father, in communicating His substance to the Son, floods Him with His own life?

We are quite prepared to maintain that if the idea of man's elevation to a true participation in the divine nature, and in connection therewith the supernatural import of the Trinity and the Incarnation are abandoned, the Eucharist appears as an isolated, insufficiently motivated, and inexplicable work of God. In such case, too, it becomes impossible to convince any thinking person of the appropriateness of the Eucharist, to say nothing of its necessity. If we consider the matter thus, we will involuntarily be led to deny the Eucharist outright or at any rate to disavow its mystic reality. The Protestants, both the old and the new, afford the best proof of this: the old, because they regard grace as a mere covering over of sin, without any interior renovation; the new, because they think of grace as a state pleasing to God, brought about by a simple change of will.

The Nestorians, in league with the Pelagians, were if not the first at least the most logically consistent rationalist school of antiquity. It is interesting to note how, once they had rejected the supernaturalness of grace, they were forced to attack the true notion of original sin, then the true and solid basis, as well as the true nature, of the Incarnation, and so finally the real presence of Christ in the Eucharist.[6] So true it is that the mysteries involve one another, and that one supernatural mystery can keep its meaning, and hence vindicate its nature and reality, only as a link in a chain, as a mem-

---

[6] It is impossible to show with certainty that Nestorius did not believe in the Real Presence and transubstantiation. St. Cyril says only that he denied the power and the significance of the Eucharist, inasmuch as he deprived the flesh of Christ of the *vis vivificatrix*. But there is only one step from this to the denial of the Real Presence. Besides, many adherents of the school of Theodore of Mopsuestia, to which Nestorius belonged, expressly denied the entire mytsery of the Eucharist. Even Theodoret, the schoolmate of Nestorius, at times expressed himself indistinctly and ambiguously on the subject of both the Incarnation and the Eucharist. Cf. J. Garnier, *De haeresi Nestorii*, dissert. I, cap. 6, no. 5; *PL*, XLVIII, 1163–68.

ber in an organism of related mysteries. Wrested from this chain, deprived of their position in the supernatural organism, the mysteries, as we have insisted over and over again, turn into obscurities, and can scarcely be detected by blind faith, despite the most earnest searchings of reason. But when strung on this chain, when integrated in an organism, the dead members spring to life, the darkness turns into light, and, as though an electric current were suddenly switched on, brilliance and life stream from them.

We shall see this fact verified anew in the case of the Eucharist.

In what does the supernatural organism of the mysteries of Christianity consist? In this, that the mystery of the Godhead, the inner communication of the divine nature, prolongs and reproduces itself exteriorly. It is projected into the outside world so far as the Son of God assumes a created, human nature, and imparts to it, in His person and as belonging to Him, the substantial union and unity that He Himself has with His Father. Not only this one human nature, however, but the whole human race, is to enter into closest union with God. To bring this union about, the Son of God, made man, unites Himself to us in His humanity in the most intimate, substantial fashion, to form one body with us, as He Himself is one Spirit with His Father. And as He Himself has the same nature and life as the Father, by virtue of His spiritual oneness of essence with the Father, so by His ineffable union of body with us He wishes to make us share in His divine nature, and to pour out upon us the grace and life that He has received in their entire fullness from the Father and has communicated to His humanity. Thus by a prolongation of His eternal procession from the Father, the Son of God goes forth from the Father and enters into the human race as a real member thereof. As a result, we enter into a most perfect union of continuity with the Father, the ultimate source of divine life. Consequently there is formed in us a perfect replica of the unity of God's Son with the Father. Our substantial union with the God-man is an image of the substantial unity between the Son and the Father. Thus our participation in the divine nature and divine life becomes a reproduction of the fellowship in nature and life which the Son of God has with His Father, as their supreme, substantial oneness requires.

Such is the general idea of the supernatural organism in which the Eucharist has a structural function. At the very first glance it is seen to be, if not an essential member, at least an integrating member, required for the finished perfection of the whole. The Eucharist logically emerges from the idea of the whole, and in turn corroborates the truth of this idea.

For, as we know, the God-man desired to give the highest degree of inner cohesion and the firmest possible basis to His fellowship of life with the individual members of His mystical body. The continuity and real union of each individual man with Christ as the channel, and with the eternal Father as the wellspring of supernatural life, were in every respect to be carried to perfection. Finally, the union of the race with Christ was meant to be an adequate representation of His substantial oneness with the Father. These reasons make it altogether fitting, and even in a sense necessary, that the seed, the leaven of the higher life, should be substantially implanted not only somewhere in the midst of the race, but likewise in each of its members. In this way a more real and more interior union, a substantial union, would be added to that union of individual men with the God-man which results from racial union, or even the union which is engendered by baptism. In such a union the members would become one body with their head by reason of kinship or organic connection and also by a substantial reception of the substance of their head. As a result, the divine-human head would not merely, like the head in the physical body, be virtually and indirectly joined to each member, but, like the soul which informs the physical body, would enter into the individual members with His own substance, thoroughly pervade them, and fill them with His divine energy and splendor.

Therefore the significance of the Eucharist comes to this, that the real union of the Son of God with all men is ratified, completed, and sealed in it, and that men are perfectly incorporated in Him in the most intimate, real, and substantial manner, so that, as they are His members, they may also partake of His life. The concept of our real and substantial incorporation in Christ is the fundamental idea of the mystery of the Eucharist. It is from this basic idea that we may trace out the relationship of the Eucharist to the mysteries of the Trinity, the Incarnation, and grace.

Let us, then, examine more closely the nature and implications of this incorporation.

71. THE INCORPORATION OF CHRISTIANS IN CHRIST THROUGH THE EUCHARIST AS THE KEYNOTE OF ITS ENTIRE MYSTIC SIGNIFICANCE

1. That Christ unites Himself to us in the Eucharist in such a way as to become one body with us, is the clear, decisive teaching of Holy Scripture and the Fathers. The essential function of any food is to combine with the one partaking of it in the formation of a single substantial whole. Hence the Fathers employ the strongest terms in speaking of an assimilation and fusion of Christ's body with ours. Specifically, they insist that our union with Christ is more than simply a moral union; it is a real, physical, substantial union. Later we shall quote from some of their writings in which they refer to this union as an imitation of the Son's consubstantiality with the Father.

Of course this union is not to be regarded in every respect as on a par with that which takes place between natural food and the body of the person who eats it. There is question here not of the union of a lifeless body with one that has life, but of a living body with another living body. In this union the substance of the one is not consumed by the other for the latter's sustenance, but the one is intended to share its life with the other and to fructify the other. The best natural analogy for this union of bodies is provided by the union which obtains in marriage. The Apostle himself proposes the latter as the true exemplar of the relation of Christ to the Church and to each member of the faithful.[7] Besides, as we have seen, this analogy brings out the difference, as well as the similarity, between bodily union as based directly on the Incarnation alone, and its consummation in the Eucharist. By the entrance of the Logos into our race we became flesh of His flesh; but only in the sense that Eve became flesh of Adam's flesh by the fact that she was taken from his side. In the Eucharist, however, our body is again joined to the body of the Logos, and so we become flesh of His flesh a second time; but we now become flesh of His flesh in so perfect a way that the first union,

[7] Theodoret, *In Cant.*, cap. 3 (*PL*, LXXXI, 128): "By eating of the members of the Spouse and drinking of His blood they will attain to nuptial communion with Him." Vasquez too (*In Illam Partem*, disp. 204, no. 36 f.) employs the analogy of marriage to illustrate the habitual corporal union that remains after the actual partaking of the body of Christ.

as was the case with our first parents, is by comparison no more than the foundation and type of the second.

Another difference between natural bread and the body of Christ follows from this. Bread is changed into the body of him who eats it. But Christ, who is incapable of such change, takes the partaker to Himself, not by transforming his substance, but by joining him substantially to Himself as a member that belongs to Him and is to be animated by Him. This is exemplified in the union which takes place in marriage, where the wife, whose function it is to receive, is joined and subjected to the husband, whose function it is to impart, as her head. According to outward appearances, the body of Christ is received into us under the form of natural bread; but in reality He takes us to Himself as branches into the vine. And therefore He is not divided up among many partakers, but gathers the partakers to Himself to form one body and one bread, in the words of the Apostle.[8] With Him, our head, we grow together into one body. We become His body in a far more literal and fuller sense than the sense in which we are His body by the fact that He has virtually assumed the whole race in assuming His own body, or has accorded us access to His life through baptism or faith.

Hence arises a last difference between natural food and Eucharistic food. The former is nothing more than a means of sustaining and augmenting the body that has been formed and brought to life by procreation. The Fathers often remark that, as the child must be nourished on the substance of the mother that gave it birth, so Christ, once He has begotten us to supernatural life, must feed us with His substance in order to sustain and strengthen that life. But if we go a little deeper into the matter, we see that the procreation of

---

[8] "For we, being many, are one bread, one body, all that partake of one bread" (I Cor. 10:17). Baader's treatise *Sur l'eucharistie*, the work of a brilliant theologian despite its many peculiarities and errors, reveals, besides many another flash of light, a deep grasp of the Apostle's words. The following lines repeat in lively and graphic manner the ideas we have developed. "The light shed by this glance at the known words of Christ becomes brighter when we recall that He refers to Himself as the head and the heart of that body which men, united in Him and by Him, are to form, and consequently that there is question here of the nourishment of an organic system by its center or sun, and not of the nourishment of an isolated individual by the remains of another individual. The latter is a gross concept of feeding which the Jews wished to read into Christ's words, and which many Christians condemn, without being able to discern a truer and more worthy meaning in these words so full of spirit and life."

Christians in the supernatural order is not a going forth from Christ, but an engrafting in Christ. We receive life from Christ only so far as we are His members. Substantial union with the body of Christ in the Eucharist means more than a nourishment which supports the life that has been brought into being. It signifies a deeper insertion of that life into its root, and a firmer attachment of it to its source by a bond that is essentially intrinsic. By comparison, the communication of that life outside such substantial union almost seems to be no more than a preparation for it.

Consequently we would notably debase the idea of Eucharistic union with Christ if, after the analogy of natural food, we were to regard the body of Christ as no more than a means for strengthening and sustaining the life that is already present. We must rather see in the Eucharist a deepening and intensification of the general union inaugurated between the God-man and human beings by the Incarnation, or even by faith and baptism. Commenting on the Apostle's words, "The bread which we break, is it not the κοινωνία ("communion") of the body of the Lord?" [9] St. Chrysostom remarks appositely: "Why does he not say, 'partaking'? Because he wished to express something greater, and to indicate a very intimate union. For we enter into fellowship with Him not only by eating and receiving Him, but also by becoming one with Him. For, as that body is united to Christ, we also are united to Him by this bread." [10]

2. With this notion of incorporation presupposed, the relations of the Eucharist with the mysteries of the Trinity, the Incarnation, and grace are easily set forth. Obviously, its connection with the Incarnation should be treated first.

As regards our real incorporation in Christ, as brought about by this sacrament, we may say with profound truth that the Eucharist is a real and universal prolongation and extension of the mystery of the Incarnation.

The Eucharistic presence of Christ is in itself a reflection and extension of His incarnation, as the Fathers so often observe. The changing of the bread into the body of Christ by the power of the Holy Spirit is a renewal of the wonderful act by which, in the power of the same Holy Spirit, He originally formed His body in

[9] Cf. I Cor. 10:16.
[10] *In epist. I ad Cor.*, hom. 24; *PG*, LXI, 200.

the womb of the Virgin and took it to His person. As He effected his first entrance into the world by this act, so by that other act He multiplies His substantial presence over and over again in space and time.

But this presence is multiplied only that the body of Christ may grow and spread throughout the members which He attaches to Himself and fuses with Himself.[11] For this reason alone the true body of Christ is reproduced at the Consecration, that He may unite Himself with individual men in Communion and become one body with them, so that the Logos may, as it were, become man anew in each man, by taking the human nature of each into union with His own.

For, if the Word is made flesh by assuming flesh, is He not to some extent incarnated anew when He makes those who partake of Him in the Eucharist His members, and as such takes them to Himself? We have just heard the statement of St. Chrysostom: "As that body is united to Christ, we also are united to Him by this bread." So completely do we become one with Christ that we can say with deep truth that we belong to the person of Christ, and in a sense are Christ Himself. "Christ is the Church," says St. Hilary, "bearing it wholly within Himself by the sacrament of His body." [12]

Let us inquire into the meaning and the effect of this real continuation and extension of the Incarnation. After that we will take up the inner relationships of the Eucharist to the mysteries of grace and the Trinity, which are so closely connected with the Incarnation.

3. If it is true in general, as we saw in dealing with the mystery of the Incarnation, that our embodiment in Christ must have the aim and effect of making us share in the privileges of our head, and of raising us to His divine dignity, glory, and beatitude, must not the same be the case, and to a still higher degree, in this wonderfully intimate incorporation? "Nothing else," says St. Leo, "is aimed at

[11] "Do not doubt that the Word of the Father, which is flesh, and which once was made, is daily made so again, inasmuch as the flesh and blood become our food, to the end that we, too, may be His body." Paschasius Radbertus, *De corpore et sanguine Domini*, cap. 12; *PL*, CXX, 1311.

[12] "A dominatu enim vitiorum animam liberavit, anteriora delicta non reputans, et nos in vitam novam renovans et in novum hominem transformans, constituens nos in corpore carnis suae. Ipse enim est ecclesia, per sacramentum corporis sui universam eam continens" (*In Psalm.* 125, no. 6; *CSEL*, XXII, 609; *PL*, IX. 688).

in our partaking of the body and blood of Christ, than that we change into what we consume, and ever bear in spirit and flesh Him in whom we have died, been buried, and have risen." [13] "By the food of His body," remarks another estimable writer, "we are embodied in Him, and so it is necessary that we be lifted up to where Christ is." [14] This ineffable union of body, which knows no limits and transcends all our notions, must inevitably give rise to an equally exalted fellowship in goods and life between man and the Son of God. Without such fellowship the union is unthinkable.[15] If anywhere, surely here we must become the object of God's supernatural, infinitely fruitful love, a love that embraces us in Christ as God's children, and clasps us to its bosom: for the only-begotten Son of God is in us, and we are in Him.[16] We must be overwhelmed with the fullness of the Godhead; we must be deified. We must share in the glory that the Son has received from the Father; [17] and this

[13] *Sermo* 14 de passione Domini [*Sermo* 63; PL, LIV, 357]: "Non enim aliud agit participatio corporis et sanguinis Christi quam ut in id, quod sumimus, transeamus: et in quo commortui et consepulti et conresuscitati sumus, ipsum per omnia et spiritu et carne gestemus."

[14] Auctor elucidarii apud Anselmum, lib. I, cap. 28 [apparently Honorius Augustodunensis, who lived in the first half of the twelfth century; PL, CLXXII, 1129]: "Sicut esca in comedentem vertitur, ita quisque fidelis per comestionem huius cibi in corpus Christi convertitur. Igitur per fidem mundi vitiis et concupiscentiis Christo concrucifigimur, et in baptismate Christo consepelimur, ideo et ter immergimur: per cibum corporis eius ei incorporamur, et ideo necesse est ut illuc, quo Christus est, pertransferamur."

[15] Alger of Liége stresses this repeatedly: "Christ has truly and perfectly given Himself to us, even visibly uniting and incorporating the Church in Himself by the wonderful sacrament of His body and blood. So signal is the grace He has conferred that He is the head of the Church, and the Church is His body, not in name only, but in all truth embodied in His very body. There can be no cleavage of grace in that body with which the sacrament of singular unity has consolidated us. Thus it is certain that with Him and through Him we shall obtain a like glory of dignity in eternal life, if with Him and through Him we strive to preserve a like grace of innocence in this life" (*De sacram.*, lib. I, cap. 3; PL, CLXXX, 747). And again: "Once He, who is the priest, has been made the sacrifice, He is united to all who die with Him, so that by becoming one with Him they may be in Him where He Himself is" (*ibid.*, lib. II, cap. 3; PL, CLXXX, 816).

[16] "I in them and Thou in Me; that they may be made perfect in one, and the world may know that Thou hast sent Me, and hast loved them, as Thou hast also loved Me. Father, I will that where I am, they also whom Thou hast given Me may be with Me" (John 17:23 f.).

[17] "And the glory which Thou hast given Me, I have given to them; that they may be one, as We also are one" (John 17:22).

is what really takes place through sanctifying grace and the glory in which it culminates. And if the Fathers indicate the deification of man as the goal of the incarnation of God's Son, this must be true in fullest measure with regard to the Eucharist as the continuation of the Incarnation.

Thus, for example, the Council in Trullo declares: "God, who is offered and distributed for the salvation of souls and bodies, deifies those who receive Him." [18] Similarly St. Cyril of Jerusalem: "When you partake of the body and blood of Christ you are made one body and one blood with Him. Receiving His flesh and His blood into our members in this way, we become Christbearers. And so, according to Blessed Peter, we are made partakers of the divine nature." [19] This participation in the divine nature is at the same time a replenishing of man with the Holy Spirit and a fellowship with Him. Since the Holy Spirit dwells in the body of Christ in a quite singular way by a very real union, He must also pour Himself out upon those who have been joined to Christ in one body. That we are filled with the Holy Spirit,[20] that the Eucharist becomes a fellowship with the Holy Spirit for those who partake of it,[21] and that we are all joined to one another in the fellowship of the one Holy Spirit,[22] we find indicated in the ancient liturgies as the aim and effect of the Eucharist. St. John Damascene, too, points out with considerable emphasis that we are to be inflamed and divinized in partaking of the Eucharist, by our sharing in the divine fire (the Holy Spirit, dwelling in the Eucharist).[23]

Our fusion with the God-man into one body, of which the Fathers speak in such bold terms, is conceivable only if we are filled with His divine Spirit, with the vital force of His divinity, and if we are wonderfully fused with His divinity into one Spirit. We must become one Spirit with God in as true, profound, and real a sense as Christ is perceived to be one body with us in the Eucharist.

[18] Praef. can. ab initio.
[19] *Catechesis mystagogica*, IV, no. 3; PG, XXXIII, 1100.
[20] Liturgy of the Apostolic Constitutions.
[21] Liturgy of St. Chrysostom.
[22] Liturgy of St. Basil.
[23] *De fide orthodoxa*, lib. IV, cap. 13 (PG, XCIV, 1149): "Let us approach Him with burning desire and . . . let us lay hold of the divine coal, so that the fire of our desire, fed by the flame of the coal, may sear away our sins and enlighten our hearts. Let us be enkindled by our contact with that great divine fire, and come forth gods."

An exclusively moral relationship of our soul to God by the subjection of its will and by conformity of disposition, is not sufficient for this union. For in such a case we behold no more than two spirits that somehow meet, react upon each other, and stand in a certain reciprocal relationship that is purely external. The union of the spirit with God which is produced and represented in the Eucharist, must be based upon a real penetration of the human spirit by the divine. God must lower Himself into the soul with His innermost essence, flood it with His own life, and take up His abode within its deepest recesses. He must seize upon the soul like a consuming fire, in order to permeate it with His own light and warmth and to clothe it with His glory. Only when our spirit lives of God and in God, and appears to be swallowed up in the torrent of divine life that encompasses it, is it one spirit with God as truly as it becomes one body with Christ in the Eucharist.

We could never, in all eternity, attain to such an intimate, spiritual union with God even by the most perfect development of our natural spiritual powers, and by the conformity of our natural life with the divine will. This union is contained only in the supernatural grace of divine sonship, which makes us, as children of God, partakers of His nature and His life. And so we infer that, without reference to this mystery of grace, the meaning of the Eucharist cannot be apprehended at all.

But in connection with this mystery the Eucharist appears in its full beauty, as the foundation and seal and crown of our union with God that is effected by grace. In the Eucharist the truth is realized that the Son of God does more than produce an imitation of His divine life in us; He actually continues it in us. In the Eucharist He brings us into closest contact with the divine source of that life, most generously guarantees our stability and perseverance therein, firmly binds us to God in living union, and secures the union with His most sacred seal.

4. The mystery of grace, however, is but an imitation and continuation of the mystery of the Trinity, with which it is connected by the Incarnation. Hence the Eucharist, as the extension of the Incarnation, must also bring us into close relationship with the Trinity.

The grand mystery of these sublime relationships will be laid before us later by St. Cyril, in his commentary on the majestic prayer which Christ addressed to His Father at the Last Supper to secure our union with Him and the Father.[24] Since his exposition is somewhat lengthy and forms a complete unit in itself, we have placed it at the end of Part V, where it can serve as a sort of recapitulation of the whole mystery of the Eucharist. At the present time we wish to outline the briefer, but no less profound commentary of St. Hilary of Poitiers on the Savior's words. The passages we have selected are taken from his work on the Trinity.

The saint undertakes to show that the unity between the Father and the Son in God cannot be a mere moral union, a mere harmony of wills, seeing that it is proposed as the model and root of our union with Christ and His Father. To this end he remarks that the nature and the cause of the unity which is mentioned in the words: "That they all may be one, as Thou, Father, in Me, and I in Thee; that they also may be one in Us," [25] must be determined from the following verses. Thus the Savior immediately adds: "And the glory which Thou hast given Me, I have given to them; that they may be one, as We also are one." Whereupon Hilary observes: "They are all one in glory, because no other honor is given than that which was received, and it was given for no other reason than that all might be one. And since all are made one by the glory that was given to the Son, and by Him shared with the faithful, I ask: How can the Son have a glory different from that of the Father, seeing that the glory of the Son gathers all the faithful together into the unity of the Father's glory? The language of human hope may well seem bold here, but at least it is not unbelieving. For, although it is venturesome to hope for such a favor, it is impious not to believe, since the author of our hope and our faith is one and the same." [26]

"Still," continues Hilary, "I do not yet understand how the glory that has been given makes all one." But this, too, our Savior explained clearly, when He added: "I in them, and Thou in Me; that they may be made perfect in one." "Some hold that there is only a unity of will between the Father and the Son. I ask them: Is Christ in us today by the reality of His nature, or by a mere harmony of will? If the Word was truly made flesh, and if we truly partake of the

[24] John, chapter 17.
[25] John 17:21.
[26] Hilary, De Trinitate, lib. VIII, no. 12; PL, X, 244.

Word made flesh in the food of the Lord (*cibo dominico*), how could anyone think that He does not remain in us with His nature? For when He was made man He took the nature of our flesh inseparably to Himself, and in the sacrament of His body, which is to be given to us, He joins the nature of His flesh to the nature of His eternal divinity. And thus we are all one, because the Father is in Christ, and Christ is in us." [27]

This natural, or essential, substantial union of men with Christ, and through Christ with the Father, is necessarily connected with the union of glory. Hilary, however, does not develop this point, which would be outside his scope. But the connection is obvious. In any case Hilary indicates it clearly enough when he states that we, who are joined to the Father through Christ, "ought to press on to union with the Father." [28] If this is to be not a dead, but a living, fruitful union, it can be nothing else than the union of glory and of life which the Son of God possesses by His substantial oneness with the Father, and which is transmitted to us by a similar substantial oneness of the Father with us. It is transmitted to us in two ways; for, as Hilary so beautifully says, Christ is in us by His flesh, and we are in Him; and all that we are is with Him in God. [29]

We observe that, in speaking of the Eucharist, St. Hilary pursues the line of thought which we, following his lead, used as the groundwork of our discussion of the God-man's substantial mediatorship. And rightly so. Christ's mediatorship is essentially bound up with His position as head, and is based on it. Therefore, as it is only in the Eucharist that Christ perfectly becomes our head, so it is only in the Eucharist that He can perfectly become the mediator of our union with God. Paschasius Radbertus, in commenting on our Savior's words: "He that eateth My flesh and drinketh My blood abideth in Me, and I in him" [John 6:57], expresses this idea very well: "As God the Father is in the Son by the nature of the Godhead, so God the Son, made man (*Dei Filius homo*), is rightly said to be in us by the humanity of His flesh. He is celebrated as the mediator between God and men because we have fellowship of

[27] *Ibid.*, no. 13; PL, X, 246.

[28] "Ut ad unitatem Patris proficeremus" (*ibid.*, no. 15; PL, X, 248).

[29] "Est in nobis ipse per carnem, et sumus in eo, dum secum hoc quod nos sumus in Deo est" (*ibid.*, no. 14; PL, X, 247).

union with God through Him. Although He remains in the Father,
it is asserted that He also abides in us." [30] On this account the Eucharist itself is called Communion, a fellowship of the highest degree,
for in itself it is a most intimate and real bond. It joins man to Christ,
and in Christ unites man on the one hand with the Trinity, and on
the other with all men who partake of the Eucharist.[31]

5. This wonderful fellowship with Christ and His Father is most
gloriously manifested by the fact that it makes us children of God
in the most perfect manner. As was noted above, we are accustomed
to regard the Eucharist, on the analogy of natural bread, merely as

---

[30] "Qui manducat meam carnem et bibit meum sanguinem in me manet
et ego in illo. Vere igitur, sicut per naturam Deitatis Deus Pater in Filio est,
ita Deus Filius homo per humanitatem carnis in nobis esse iure dicitur, ac
per hoc mediator Dei et hominum praedicatur, quia per eum communionem
unitatis habemus ad Deum, dum ipse, in Patre manens, et in nobis quoque
manere dicitur" (*De corpore et sanguine Domini*, cap. 9; PL, CXX, 1296).

[31] This notion of *communio* is found also in the Greek Fathers; for example,
in Pseudo-Dionysius, *De ecclesiastica hierarchia*, cap. 3, no. 1. We give the
sense of the passage according to the commentary of Robert of Lincoln
[Robert Grosseteste]: "The Eucharist is perfection [*teleté, perfectio,* 'a good
perfect and perfecting,' as Dionysius calls the Eucharist], the most excellent
and the greatest of all perfections, on account of the most excellent and the
greatest thing contained therein. For, as Blessed Ignatius says, there is present
in the Eucharist the flesh of our Savior Jesus Christ, that flesh which suffered
for our sins, and which the Father in His great love lifted up. Every other
perfection has its power of uniting, of leading back to fellowship with God,
and of perfecting, from this perfection, which is primarily and of itself capable of uniting us to God and bringing about fellowship with Him. For in
this perfection is contained the true flesh of the Savior, which He took from
the Virgin, and in which He redeemed us by His suffering. It is not separated
from His soul nor from the divinity, but is inseparably united thereto. And
so in that perfection is the Son of God, perfect God and perfect man who, assuming our humanity, joined us together and made us fellows with Him in
one nature. He gave us His excellent flesh to eat and joined us to His excellent
person, so that we might all be one in Christ, made perfect with His perfection, and united in fellowship with Him. Rightly, therefore, the name of
Communion is pre-eminently assigned to this perfection. For primarily and
principally it joins us to God, and establishes and perfects our communion
with Him, giving other perfections their efficacy by its own inherent power."
[The theology of Pseudo-Dionysius is not free from all taint of Monophysit-
ism.] St. John Damascene speaks in similar vein (*De fide orthodoxa*, lib. IV,
cap. 13; PG, XCIV, 1153): "It is called Communion and truly is so, for by it
we are made fellows of Christ, and receive of His flesh and divinity; indeed,
by it we are also united and made one with each other. For since we partake
of the one bread, we are all made the one body and one blood of Christ; and
inasmuch as we belong to the one body of Christ, we are also made members
of one another."

a food that is worthy of the children of God, and that serves to sustain and strengthen their divine life. But if this food makes us substantially one with the only-begotten Son of God in the way explained, it must do more than sustain and gradually augment the dignity and the life of the children of God. It must provide a deeper basis for this dignity and life, and bestow on them an essentially higher beauty than they would otherwise have had.

As a result of the Incarnation we are no longer merely adopted children of God. Through the sacred humanity we are received into the natural, only-begotten Son of God as His members, and as His members share in His personal relationship to the Father, somewhat as His own humanity does. But by the Eucharist we are bound to Him much more securely, and become His body much more perfectly; for He has not only taken His flesh from our flesh, but has returned to us the flesh that He assumed. "Since He is in us, and we are in Him, all that we are is with Him in God," we heard St. Hilary say. Thus in the eyes of the eternal Father we are members of His natural Son. And the Father extends His hypostatical fatherhood to us, not only by some imitation of it, but as it is in itself, just as He does to Christ's own humanity. For greater clarity we might here again bring in the analogy of marriage [32] in which, especially once it is consummated, a real, and not simply a juridical, kinship arises between the bride and the father of the bridegroom.

Further, we may say that, even as regards the divine life bestowed on us in sanctifying grace, we are not merely adopted by God—in the way, that is, in which adoption takes place among men—but are in a sense begotten of Him. But the ultimate factor in generation, the substantial connection between the begetter and the begotten, would be lacking if the Son of God did not unite Himself to us in His substance and take us up into His substance. Both occur in the Incarnation, which is continued in the Eucharist. In the Eucharist we receive life from God; and we receive it by substantial union with His Son, inasmuch as we become bone of His bone and flesh of His flesh. Indeed, our substantial connection with Him is more enduring than that which exists among men between parent and child. For in this latter case the substantial union ceases with birth; but in the Eucharist it can and should be continually renewed and strengthened. And so in virtue of the Eucharist we not merely re-

[32] See above, pp. 483 f.

ceive our life from God, as children do from their earthly parents, but we live in God; we have our life from His substance and in His substance. Eucharistic Communion with God has the double function of begetting and nourishing the children of God.

Can we conceive a more exalted and effective continuation and extension of the divine productions that take place within the Trinity, particularly of the divine generation? Can we imagine a more intimate reception of the creature into the unity of the Trinity? Is not the Eucharist a necessary element in the full unfolding of that majestic organism of the Christian mysteries whereby the underlying idea of the Incarnation is carried out and perfected?

6. Lastly, let us examine from still another angle the meaning which the God-man has as head of the human race. Here, too, we shall see that the Eucharist continues and completes the idea of the Incarnation.

As head of the human race, we recall, the God-man has a real influence on its members, inasmuch as He is the principle of their supernatural life. More than this: as head He also represents all the members of this vast body before God. And as He offers Himself in His own person to God as an infinitely perfect and agreeable sacrifice, so He associates His entire mystical body with Himself and in Himself in this consecration, and His mystical body in turn is to offer the God-man, and itself in Him, to God as one great sacrifice. Thus the sacrifice offered by the individual men in whom the God-man is harbored likewise becomes infinitely precious and agreeable in God's sight. As Christ the head continues His divine life in His members, so He is also to continue His divine sacrifice in them.

For the continuance and perfection of His sacrifice, as for the continuance and perfection of His life in His members, Christ had truly and substantially to dwell among those members, within the bosom of the human race. He had to continue to be really and substantially present in the midst of His body, in order that men might unceasingly offer and immolate Him to His Father. Two things were especially needed for this purpose: first, that He continue to re-enact in Himself the immolation once accomplished on the cross; secondly, that He dwell among us in a way that would make a real association in His sacrifice possible for men. Both conditions are splendidly and admirably verified in the Eucharist.

The God-man makes His appearance among us under the separate forms of bread and wine. Under the species of bread He is present directly with His body, and under the species of wine directly with the blood He shed for us. Thus He appears in our midst under the symbols of His immolation, as the Lamb slain for the honor of God. As such He comes before our eyes; as such He also comes before the eyes of His heavenly Father. He vividly exhibits Himself to God and to us in His sacrificial death, that we may offer Him to the heavenly Father in our own midst.

By adopting this mode of effecting His presence, He makes it possible for us to unite ourselves closely with Him in His capacity as the true sacrificial Lamb. If Christ were not actually present in the Eucharist, or if He were not present as the sacrificial Lamb, we could not associate ourselves with Him in one sacrifice except by a moral union, a union of affections. We could not even share in the fruits of the sacrifice by any real, true participation. But as matters actually stand, we quite literally and most intimately partake of the sacrifice by receiving its fruits during the sacrifice itself and by drinking in the merits welling up in it from their very fountainhead. Moreover, since we are embodied in the sacrificial Lamb by this partaking, and become one whole, one body with Him, we are also made one sacrifice with Him by the most intimate and real union that may be conceived.[33] Therefore we also truly take part in the infinite glorification which the Son of God gives to His Father. God receives this glorification from us too, because we offer Him Christ as our head, and because Christ who dwells within us presents us to the Father as His members.

Here again the idea of man's incorporation in Christ stands out as the distinguishing note in the significance of the Eucharist. But

[33] Döllinger says very beautifully, *Christentum und Kirche*, p. 254: "The Eucharistic bread, which veils the body of the Lord, nourishes many unto one body. And thus the Church, as the body of the Lord, which has been fed by Him on His bodily substance and has been brought together in all its members, is presented to God along with His own natural body. The Eucharistic sacrifice is the product of this unity of head and members. At the same time, however, in Communion it is the means of sustaining, nourishing, and strengthening this unity." In general the entire presentation of the doctrine concerning the sacrifice of Christ, as given by Döllinger in accordance with the teaching of St. Paul, is among the best of such treatises written in recent times. This is especially true of his treatment of the unity between the Eucharistic and the heavenly sacrifice (pp. 255 f.).

the full, mysterious import of this incorporation will be grasped only if we regard its effect and its goal as absolutely supernatural, and if we clearly realize that, as the life it confers is absolutely supernatural, so too the glorification of God which it aims at and achieves must be infinitely great.

We do not fully comprehend this greatness so long as we have in mind no more than the glory which the creature can and ought to render to God in virtue of his natural capacities. Nor shall we rightly view it if we regard Christ's immolation, with which we are to associate ourselves, exclusively as a propitiatory sacrifice offered in atonement for our sins; for sin must be eliminated before we can really take part in this sacrifice by Communion. We appreciate it only when we perceive that the glorification which man must render to God is a continuation and extension of that infinite glorification which God, not as Creator, but as Father, receives within the Godhead from the Son who is equal to Him in nature. Such glorification could be imitated by creatures provided they were called by grace to participation in the nature, the dignity, and the love of God's Son. But it is continued and extended only if the creature, already endowed with grace, is incorporated in the Son of God. And since this incorporation could be directly effected only in a nature assumed by the Son of God Himself, and could be extended to other creatures only indirectly by the real union of the Son of God with them, the Eucharistic presence and the union of the God-man with us constitute the sole foundation and prerequisite of the worship and glorification which God expects and demands of us.

Accordingly is it not true, as we pointed out in the beginning, that the Eucharist is closely bound up with the Incarnation and the Trinity? Do not these three mysteries explain and complement one another? Does not the mystery of the Eucharist take its rightful place in organic connection with these other, supremely supernatural mysteries? And, as the Eucharist throws light on the meaning of these two mysteries, does it not in turn receive light from them? The import of all three mysteries comes to this: by admitting man to participation in the divine nature they make him supernaturally happy and enable him to glorify God in a supernatural way. They are the substantial revelations of the infinite, supernatural divine love which pours forth the divine substance into the Son, the Son into a human nature, and the human nature thus divinized into the whole human race, in order to flood mankind with the torrent of divine glory and beatitude. But, as the divine love is substantially poured out from the bosom of the Father, so the infinite glorification of the Father must, in inverse order, return to Him in a manner no less real. The human race must be substantially united with its head, its head must be substantially one with the eternal Word, so that the whole of creation, its myriad voices blending in triumphant harmony, may join in the hymn in which the infinite Word celebrates the greatness and the glory of His Father.

72. NATURE AND MEANING OF TRANSUBSTANTIATION

To acquire a more adequate understanding of the nature and meaning of the mystery of the Eucharist, we must attend to the several factors that are involved in the substantial presence of Christ or that accompany it, as well as the real incorporation of His mystical body in His physical body. Such factors have as weighty a significance in the organism of the supernatural order as the substantial presence itself.

1. The first problem we encounter in this discussion is transubstantiation, or the fact that the body of Christ becomes present in the Eucharist not by being combined with natural bread, not by being enclosed in the bread as in a container, but by taking the place of the substance of the bread under the accidents of the latter. This process is not to be understood in the sense that Christ's body expels the substance of bread by its entrance, but rather that it is, as it were, produced anew from the bread, that it is made present by the conversion of the bread into it.

At the very least the concept of transubstantiation requires that the substance of the bread cease to exist, and that the body of Christ, succeeding to its place, take on its substantial functions, at any rate the active ones, with reference to the accidents. I dare say that this notion of the transition of the one substance into the other would well satisfy the conception of transubstantiation as rigorously defined by the Church. Thus conceived, however, transubstantiation appears to be an interchange of one substance with another, or a substitution of one for another, rather than a conversion of one into the other. The presence of Christ's body would be effected in the form of an adduction, a bringing of it down from heaven upon the altar (without, of course, involving its departure from heaven), but not in the form of a production or reproduction of it from the bread. Consequently the actual advent of Christ's body would not be the term or result to which the act of transubstantiation is directed, but rather the point of departure, or at any rate a causative factor in the process itself. A good deal of effort is required to make all this square with the language of the Church, the liturgies, and the Fathers.

Certainly this view has clarity of conception in its favor. For evidently there can be no question of a production of Christ's body in the sense of natural conversion, so that the material of the bread would pass over into the body of Christ, or that the body of Christ would be made present by transformation of the bread. The bread simply ceases to exist as to both form and matter; and the body of Christ existed in its own proper nature even before the consecration, without receiving any accretion from the bread changed into it, or in any way becoming a new body.

But although the two factors mentioned essentially differentiate this supernatural conversion from natural conversion, the ideal comprised in the latter must be retained and applied to the former, and thus a deeper and more vivid conception of what takes place in transubstantiation be acquired.

According to the language sanctioned by ecclesiastical usage which, it seems to us, St. Gregory of Nyssa has plumbed to an extraordinary depth,[34] the Eucharistic conversion of bread into the

---

[34] *Oratio catechetica*, cap. 37; *PG*, XLV, 96. St. John Damascene has made good use of Gregory's idea in his discussion of transubstantiation, *De fide orthodoxa*, lib. IV, cap. 13 (*PG*, XCIV, 1144): "To the divinity is truly united the body that was born of the Blessed Virgin, not in the sense that the body which ascended into heaven comes down again, but in the sense that the bread and wine are changed into God's body and blood. If you ask how this takes place, it is sufficient for you to know that it is done by the Holy Spirit, in the same way that our Lord took flesh from the Holy Mother of God and made it subsist in Himself. We apprehend and understand no more than that God's word is true and efficacious, and can do all things. But the way it was done is simply beyond our powers of investigation. This much may be said without misgiving: just as bread by eating, and wine and water by drinking, are naturally changed into the body and blood of him who eats and drinks, and do not become a body different from the living body that existed before, so the bread that had previously been placed on the table, and also the wine and water, are converted into the body and blood of Christ by the invocation and coming of the Holy Spirit, in a manner

body of Christ is to be represented along the lines of the change by which the bread which Christ ate during His earthly life was converted into His body. The latter change was effected by the natural warmth and vital energy of His body; the former is brought about by the supernatural, spiritual fire and vital energy of the divine Spirit of Christ, the *calor Verbi*,[35] who also made ready for Him the initial existence of His body in the womb of the Virgin. By the consumption of natural bread the human body receives, so to speak, its second substance, an enlargement of its previous existence. In a similar way the body of Christ in the Eucharist receives an expanded existence, not of course in the form of material increment,[36] but in the form of a reproduction of its original substance,[37] in so far as its existence in the Eucharist requires an act fully as powerful as that by which its existence in heaven is sustained. For the same reason it is not enough for the substance of the bread, if it is to be kept from augmenting Christ's body with its material content, merely to receive a different form for its matter; it must totally, matter as well as form, be consumed by the fire of the Holy Spirit, so that nothing but the body of Christ with its entire being may exist under the appearances of bread.[88]

---

that exceeds the powers of nature. Once this action has been performed, there are no longer two substances, but one and the same."

[35] In the hymn *Iam Christus astra*, sung at Matins on the feast of Pentecost.

[36] This notion, taught by Rosmini, has been condemned by the Holy See [Prop. 29-31; Denz., 1919-21].

[37] Such is the sense of certain expressions used by the Fathers, as when they say: "corpus Christi conficitur, efficitur, creatur in altari." Cf. Lessius, *De perf. div.*, lib. XII, cap. 16; Suarez, *In Illam Partem*, disp. 50.

[88] The following description of the notion of conversion and transubstantiation, which we take from Franzelin's synopsis, should aid toward a clearer and deeper grasp of the subject: "For the concept of conversion it seems to be necessary and sufficient (a) that there be a twofold term, *a quo* and *ad quem*, the former ceasing to exist, and the latter succeeding to it in a way that will vary with different kinds of conversion; (b) that between the cessation of one term and the succession of the other a mutual connection and order obtain, whereby the succession requires the cessation of the prior term, and the cessation is ordered to the succession of the other term; (c) moreover the concept of conversion, not excepting transubstantiation, is at any rate more properly verified if some common third element persevere in both terms; together with the formal term this third element would constitute the total term, and thus we could truly say that 'what is, is changed into what it was not before' (Ambrose, *De mysteriis*, cap. 9); (d) lastly, although the production of the formal term *ad quem* is not required with the

Perhaps the divergence between the view of transubstantiation first mentioned and this latter conception lies more in the exposition than in the thing itself. However that may be, the latter explanation gives a deeper, more vivid, more reasonable account of the doctrine, and in particular throws brilliant light on the significance of this remarkable action. And this is our next concern.

2. If the body of Christ were merely present *in* the bread, and did not replace the substance of the bread, Christ would not be incorporated in us by our reception of the Eucharist, nor would we be incorporated in Christ. In that case we should have to assume that the substance of the bread is hypostatically united to Christ's body, although even then we would not in any proper sense become one body with the living body of Christ. We become so only if the substance of the bread, which is naturally capable of passing over into our body, has been changed into the body of Christ, and if Christ, taking the place of the bread, unites Himself to us as closely as though He were the bread itself.

It was not only to give some sensible indication of His presence that Christ has attached the real union of His body with us to the condition of our partaking of the consecrated bread, as we might suppose if the union itself were to be purely spiritual in form. He had a much higher purpose in mind: to effect a union that would be not simply the presence of His body in ours or a contact between the two bodies, but would be an organic connection between them. That our bodies may be assumed into His body and become one with it by being united to it, He takes that substance which naturally can and does become one body with us, and changes it into His body by conversion. To fuse our bodies with His body by the fire of the Holy Spirit, He melts down the food proper to our body by that same fire and changes it into His own body. We are virtually taken up into the body of Christ by the very changing of the bread into His body, seeing that bread represents the bodies which draw it into their substance for their nourishment. In the bread, an element

---

same insistence as the cessation of the term *a quo*, it seems, in accordance with the explanation of the Fathers, to be postulated for a conversion strictly so called, with respect even to Eucharistic conversion, that the positing of the term *ad quem* be analogous to production rather than to adduction, and hence that it be an action equivalent to production; this action we might call replication." Cf. Lessius, *De perfect. div.*, lib. XII, cap 16.

necessary to the life of our bodies, our bodies themselves are, as it were, changed into the body of Christ.

That Christ might become a member and the head of our race, it was not enough for Him to assume a human nature like ours; He had to take His nature from the very midst of the race. Similarly, to perfect the organic bond which is to bind us to Him, He wills not merely to bring the substance of His body into contact with us, but to implant Himself in us, or rather us in Him; He wishes us to strike root in Him, just as He took root in our race at the Incarnation. This He does by changing into His body the food that nourishes our body; in this food and by means of it He inserts our body in Himself as a branch is engrafted on a vine.

Accordingly transubstantiation is as necessary a condition for the perfect carrying out of the sublime idea of our incorporation in Christ as is the substantial presence of His body in general; perhaps even more so. It confirms the existence of this idea in the divine scheme, and is in turn illuminated, clarified, and vindicated by this idea.

3. The same relationship appears when we consider transubstantiation with regard to the double import of the incorporation itself. As we have repeatedly observed, there is a twofold significance: first, the communication of the life and glory of the head to the members, and secondly, the union of the members with the head in a sacrifice that is infinitely pleasing to God. In both respects the transubstantiation of the bread into the real body of Christ produces and prefigures a supernatural and very remarkable transformation of Christ's mystical body by assimilating it to its head. This transformation, as it is the most brilliant reflection, the most splendid revelation and outgrowth of that first miracle, is also the sole justification for it.

a) Let us begin with the relation first mentioned, that of transubstantiation to the communication of the life and glory of the head to His members.

Möhler makes the profound observation that all who refuse to acknowledge that the Eucharist effects a deep-seated and thoroughgoing transformation in man, for whom it was instituted, cannot appreciate the import of this astounding work of God, and hence must render it utterly incomprehensible.[89] His remark is aimed pri-

[89] *Symbolik*, 6th ed., pp. 318 f.

marily at the Reformers who, in view of their theory about the radical, essentially incorrigible viciousness and depravity of human nature that entered with sin, could not ascribe any really efficacious and genuinely restorative power either to the grace of redemption itself, or consequently to the sacraments which confer that grace. But the point he makes may with full right be scored also against those who, while not regarding nature as fundamentally vicious and depraved, assign to the grace of redemption only a purifying, healing, and reinforcing energy, but not a power that can absolutely elevate and transform nature.

As has been shown, a true elevation of Christ's human nature to real union with a divine person is neither necessary nor appropriate if nature is merely to be freed of its infirmity and disorder. On the same supposition, no real changing of the substance of our natural food into the life-giving flesh of the God-man is necessary; it is not even reasonably conceivable. This is the case still less if, with some recent theologians, we restrict the effects of the Eucharist to the so-called natural side of man, his sentient and animal life. That miraculous conversion of bread into the body of Christ must correspond to another conversion, likewise absolutely supernatural and mysterious, which takes place within man's interior. As we have explained and contended throughout the course of our exposition, only the absolutely supernatural elevation of human nature to participation in the divine nature stands in proportion to the elevation of Christ's humanity to hypostatic union with the divine Word, as to its exemplary and efficient cause. In the same way it is only the sublime and mysterious transformation of our nature resulting from that elevation which is proportionate to the conversion of bread into the body of Christ, as to its model and its efficient cause.

The change effected in our spiritual substance is not such as to deprive it of its essential being. Our substance undergoes no destruction, but a glorification, a transformation from glory to glory.[40] The same Holy Spirit who upon the altar changes earthly bread into heavenly bread changes us from earthly men to heavenly, deified men. Operating on the principle of transubstantiation, the Holy Spirit fuses us with Christ by His divine fire, not only morally, but *naturaliter*, as the Fathers express it, that is, physically, so that we

[40] "But we . . . are transformed . . . from glory to glory, as by the Spirit of the Lord" (II Cor. 3:18).

form one body with Him. So also, operating on the same principle, He brings about within our interior not only a moral conversion, or a new juridical relation to God, but an altogether real, physical assimilation and union with God. By the reception of grace our soul takes on a higher nature; that is, with regard to its interior condition, its faculties, and its activity it is transformed into the image of the divine nature, is raised to an incomparably higher life, and according to the teaching of the Fathers is, in a certain true and exalted sense, divinized.[41]

This is an amazing transformation, and is one of the greatest and most mysterious works of God, as theologians commonly aver in connection with the doctrine of justification. It has a fitting ideal in that change whereby the substance of bread, to the annihilation of its own essence, passes over into the infinitely higher and more perfect substance of Christ's body. Here, surely, we must perceive how powerfully, how deeply, and with what unbounded generosity the divine love invades the world of God's creatures to rescue them from their lowliness and, so to speak, to consume them entirely with its divine fire down to the innermost reaches of their being. For, as the Apostle says, the whole of created nature, the spiritual as well as the material, sighs for its redemption and glorification.[42] And particularly men, endowed with grace and adopted by God as His children, shall be pervaded, body and soul, by divine fire, and shall be wholly taken up into God as a drop of water into an ocean of wine; all their natural weakness and baseness, in the words of the same Apostle, are to be absorbed, so that God may be all in all.[43]

Consequently if man, body and soul, is to be nourished for the leading of a life that is not natural, but is supernatural and divine, the bread which has to feed him unto eternal life must be a heavenly

[41] To preclude all danger of misunderstanding, we should note that the term "nature" as used by the Fathers does not ordinarily have the Aristotelian sense in which it is employed by Scholasticism, namely, to indicate an essence, so far as it is the intrinsic principle of an individual's activity. Again, the Fathers do not regard grace and the workings of the Holy Spirit from the standpoint of the Aristotelian category of physical accident. Consequently they do not sharply distinguish, in the manner of scholastic and post-Tridentine theology, between nature and a so-called "supernature." They look upon the world as renovated by Christ and brought by Him to a new unity. This is what they ingenuously call "nature." [Tr.]

[42] Rom. 8:19-23.

[43] Cf. I Cor. 15:28.

food, not indeed according to outward appearance, but in substance. It can be no other than the true body of God's Son, the giver of life, who, as He Himself states and as the Fathers proclaim countless times, is the seed of immortality, of incorruption, and of eternal, supernatural life for the whole race. This bread, we say, must be a heavenly food in substance; for according to appearance and outward aspect it must continue to resemble earthly and natural bread, just as the supernatural transformation of man, real and thoroughgoing though it be, is mainly interior and hidden during our present existence. For the most part it affects only the soul in its spiritual character, not the body and the life of sense. "We are now the sons of God"; interiorly, according to "the inward man," we are transformed into God. But "it hath not yet appeared what we shall be"; [44] and so according to the outward man we are like other, natural men. As our life, in the Apostle's words, is still "hid with Christ in God," [45] the bread which nourishes our life must remain concealed under its natural veil. This veil will be snatched away when the veil covering our weakness and frailty drops, when Christ will no longer be content to sow and coax forth supernatural life in the infirmity of our nature, but will pour out His divine life upon us in its entire fullness, make our body conformable to the body of His glory, and bring our souls into the immediate presence and vision of the divine essence, which is not only the vehicle, but the source and the true food of everlasting life. [46]

[44] Cf. I John 3:1-2; Eph. 3:16.
[45] Col. 3:3.
[46] Hence the interior conversion, with which transubstantiation is connected, is also a motive for the credibility of the mystery, just as in general the mysteries bear witness to one another. St. Caesarius of Arles has developed this thought beautifully in his celebrated seventh homily on Easter [PL, LXVII, 1052, where it is the fifth homily]: "The authority of heaven confirms Christ's statement: 'My flesh is meat indeed, and My blood is drink indeed.' Therefore let all waverings of unbelief cease, since He who is the author of the gift is also the witness of its truth. For the invisible priest, by the hidden power of His word, changes visible creatures into the substance of His body and blood, saying 'Take and eat.' . . . At the nod of the commanding Lord, suddenly the vaults of heaven, the depths of the seas, and the vast reaches of the earth succeed to nothingness. The power of the Word issues commands with equal authority in spiritual sacraments, and the effect follows. That the power of the divine blessing bestows extraordinary benefits, and that it ought not appear strange and impossible that earthly and mortal things are changed into the substance of Christ, you yourself can bear wit-

b) With respect to the Eucharistic sacrifice, too, the mystery of transubstantiation is full of meaning.

Sacrifice, understood in its most comprehensive sense, involves a certain destruction of the victim. This idea has led some theologians to seek the sacrificial character of the Eucharist in an annihilation of the substance of the bread and wine effected by transubstantiation. This is an evident illusion; for it is not the bread that we immolate in the Eucharist, but Christ, or His body, into which the bread is changed. The bread is immolated only so far as it is changed into the sacrificial Lamb. Further, the destruction of the bread is not an end in itself; the bread is annihilated only to make way for a higher substance. Hence its destruction is part of the process of conversion, and has its meaning only in this process.

This meaning is found especially in the fact that the body and blood of Christ, which are no longer to be presented to God in their own forms, but under alien species, would not really and truly be offered under these appearances if the latter, instead of being sustained by the substance of Christ's body and blood, continued to inhere in the substance natural to them. The impanation theory alone was enough to oblige Luther to deny the sacrificial character of the Eucharist.

Furthermore, the meaning under discussion is found in the fact that the supernatural conversion of the bread and wine into the sacrificial body and blood of Christ procures and typifies our super-

---

ness, who have been reborn to Christ. For a long time you dwelt in interior exile, with no part in life, a wanderer from mercy and from the way of salvation. All at once you were introduced to the laws of Christ, and initiated into the saving mysteries; you passed into the body of the Church, not beholding but believing, and from a son of perdition you deserved to become an adopted child of God in hidden innocence. Though remaining in your ordinary visible stature, you were made greater than yourself. You were still the same person as before, but you became quite different in the ways of faith. Nothing was added externally, but your whole inner life was changed. Thus the man was made a son of Christ, and Christ was formed in the soul of the man. Unperceived by the body, your past defilement was washed away, and you suddenly put on a new dignity. And as you did not see with your eyes of sense, but believed in your heart that God healed your wounds, cured your infected sores, and wiped away your stains, so when you go up to the holy altar to be filled with its food, behold the sacred body and blood of your God by faith, marvel at it with reverence, taste it with your soul, grasp it with the hand of your heart, and consume it with a draught that is above all interior."

natural union with the immolation of the God-man. Without such conversion this would not properly be the case.

Transubstantiation procures our union with the victim: for if the gift we offer to God in the Eucharist were to remain what it had been, instead of truly and substantially becoming the oblation of Christ, then in partaking of the species we would not really and immediately unite ourselves with the body of Christ as the victim; and hence we would not become one sacrificial body with Christ. Transubstantiation typifies our union: as the bread is really changed into the sacrificial body of Christ, so we too, not of course by substantial conversion, but by substantial union with Christ, reproduce in ourselves His sacrificial life and death. As the fire of the Holy Spirit consumes the substance of the bread and substantially changes it into the highest and most sacred holocaust, so the fire streaming forth from the oblation which is united to us lays hold of us and consumes us too, makes us a living holocaust that melts away in supernatural, divine love and is wholly transferred to God and, scented with the sweetness of the Lamb of God, sends up a heavenly fragrance pleasing to God. And as the bread becomes something nobler than it had been by its destruction, so we, dying to nature in Christ and through Christ, rise to an infinitely higher life in virtue of the same grace by which we renounce and slay our nature.

We believe that we can gain a still deeper insight into the function of transubstantiation in sacrifice; that is, transubstantiation formally constitutes the real sacrificial action proper to the Eucharistic sacrifice.

In the opinion of many theologians transubstantiation pertains to the Eucharistic act of sacrifice only with reference to its term; that is, it vividly presents Christ as the true sacrificial Lamb in the bosom of the Church, and represents Him under the visible symbols of the immolation once accomplished in Him. In all truth these two factors are absolutely essential, since on the one hand it is not the bread but Christ that is properly the victim to be offered, and on the other hand Christ is not really to be immolated anew, but His former bloody sacrifice is to be offered in an unbloody manner by symbolic representation. Particularly the second factor explicitly presupposes transubstantiation. But for that very reason, in this theory, the Eucharistic act of sacrifice does not consist formally in transubstantiation. We maintain that it does.

This view of ours is not new,[47] nor does it require any elaborate process of deduction. In the first place, the transubstantiation which occurs at the holy Sacrifice of the Mass is called in ecclesiastical language the Consecration, or simply the *actio* (that is, the sacrificial action). The reason is not so much that it renders the Holy One present, but rather that it consecrates the bread and wine to God by the conversion of them, makes them an agreeable offering to God, and by means of their transubstantiation carries the gift offered by the Church up to the altar of God in heaven, at the hands of the angel of sanctity, the Holy Spirit.[48] Every sacrificial action is at bottom a consecration, a dedication and surrender of a gift to God, especially when the gift itself is consumed and transferred to God. This particular consecration is all the more a sacrifice inasmuch as it puts forth a most sweet odor by the very absorption of the gift, and changes the first gift into another which need not mount up to God, since it stands ever present before the eyes of God in His own bosom.

In the second place, even if the Eucharistic act of sacrifice consisted formally in the sole representation in vivid fashion of Christ's sacrificed body, doubtless the fruits of Christ's sacrifice could be applied to the Church, and the Church could include itself in this sacrifice. But the sacrifice would not appear to be taken from its midst, and the Church would not be offering itself to God in what is objectively the sacrificial act, but only with it. The sacrifice of Christ, it seems, rises to God from the bosom of the Church only if His sacrificed body is not merely brought into the Church, but

---

[47] Cf. Suarez, *In Illam Partem*, disp. 83, sect. 2; Lessius, *De iure et iustitia*, lib. II, cap. 38, dub. 2; also *De perfectionibus moribusque divinis*, lib. XII, cap. 13.

[48] Such is undoubtedly the meaning of the sublime oration, "Supplices te rogamus," in the Roman Canon of the Mass, as Dr. L. Hoppe has shown with great erudition in his highly esteemed work, *Die Epiklesis der griechischen und orientalischen Liturgien und der römische Konsekrationskanon* (Schaffhausen, 1865), pp. 166 ff. This work, the fruit of comprehensive and exhaustive researches, gives a foretaste of the rich treasures of profound theology to be found in the various ancient liturgies.—Scheeben's equation between the "angel" of the prayer "Supplices" and the Holy Spirit is far from being a settled issue, from the standpoint of liturgical history. For example, in the *De sacramentis* apparently written by St. Ambrose the passage in question reads: ". . . et petimus et precamur, ut hanc oblationem suscipias in sublimi altari tuo per manus angelorum tuorum, sicut suscipere dignatus es. . . ." The plural, *angelorum*, seems to exclude Scheeben's interpretation. [Tr.]

is taken from among the gifts of the Church by the conversion of the bread it offers. And the Church presents itself to God in the body of Christ only if it changes into the body of Christ the bread which, as the noblest food of its members, represents their bodies, and by this consecration of the bread dedicates and consecrates its members to God. Not the bread, but the body of Christ, is the proper sacrificial victim of the Church, as it is of Christ Himself. But the body of Christ truly becomes the sacrifice of the Church only on the condition that the Church makes an offering of that body to God from its own midst by changing the bread into it, and by this same conversion pledges and effects the surrender of itself to God. And if this oblation is to be more than a simple offering made to God in connection with a sacrificial act already accomplished, and is to be offered in a new, genuine act of sacrifice, the conversion of another gift into this gift must be brought about.

Therefore we may not seek the essence of the Eucharistic act of sacrifice in the sole representation of Christ's body, any more than in the sole annihilation of the bread. We find this essence exclusively in the total conversion, with reference simultaneously to the *terminus a quo* and the *terminus ad quem*, or in the real consecration of the bread by its transubstantiation into the most sacred body of Christ.

In the third place, this idea finds confirmation in the fact that it alone furnishes us with a real sacrificial action in the Eucharistic sacrifice, a real and visible mutation of the offered gift, whereby the gift is conveyed from man to God.

Although remaining constant in its root idea, that of the delivery of the object to God, the change effected in the sacrificial gift, or the real sacrificial action, fulfills that idea in various ways according to the manner and specific character of the sacrifice itself. Therefore we are not justified in forthwith transferring the form in which it occurs in one sacrifice to all others.

In the present case such mutation has two characteristics that notably set it off from the mutation which takes place in other sacrificial actions. First, the proffered gift is not merely altered in such a way that something is done to it, but its entire essence is changed into another gift, and in this gift is transferred to God and accepted by Him. Hence the value of the sacrificial action is not gauged by the value of the gift undergoing change, but by the value of the gift into which it is changed. But this latter gift, on which the value of the action depends, is not in any way to be altered by the sacrificial act. For there is no question of giving Christ anew to His Father as His own, but of exhibiting and ratifying the union of the Church with the gift of Christ that has already been handed over to God.

The second characteristic is this: the mutation effected in this sacrifice is in itself invisible, because it goes forward within the inner-most hidden depths of the gift that is offered. But the action whereby it is accomplished, the words of Consecration, which not merely signify but also cause what is taking place, is perceptible to the senses; and this suffices to make us aware that a real mutation is being effected during the sacrificial action, even though the true nature of this action must remain wholly mysterious.

Since the sacrificial action consists in a mutation by which the lower gift is changed into the higher, it has, from the viewpoint of its essential character, greater similarity with the execution of the hypostatic union and the resurrection of Christ's body than with the immolation of that body on the cross. Of old the flesh derived from Mary's womb was consecrated as the body of the Lamb of God by the hypostatic union, and the body of Christ lying lifeless in the tomb was consecrated as the temple of the Holy Spirit by the Resurrection. In the Mass the bread which represents the natural side of the mystical body of Christ is changed into the hallowed and glorified body of Christ; under the veil of the sacramental species the Holy Spirit re-enacts the miracle that He once wrought in the womb of Mary, and again in the darkness of the sepulcher. By the celebration of the sacrificial act which takes place on this earth, the Church is to enter directly into union with the heavenly sacrifice Christ offers in the body that is glorified in a manner commensurate with His hypostatic dignity. The Eucharistic act of sacrifice bears the stamp of the immolation consummated on the cross, and re-enacts it vividly in its form and power, only so far as in the heavenly holo-caust the immolation of the cross is exhibited and offered in God's eternal remembrance, and this remembrance is visibly depicted to us in the separation of the blood from the body in the Eucharist by the difference between the species.

According to the conception of the ancient liturgies, the Eucha-ristic act of sacrifice is effected by the fire of the Holy Spirit which, called down by the Church, falls upon the bread that represents mankind. From this bread it forms the body and blood of the true sacrificial Lamb,[49] as once it formed Him in the womb of the Virgin, thereafter to offer Him on the cross and in the resurrection as the perfect holocaust. As Christ was conceived of the Holy Spirit, so in the Holy Spirit He offered Himself to God undefiled on the cross, and by the power of the same Holy Spirit He rose again to incorruptible life, in which He eternally displays and guards the value of His sacrificial death. That this sacrifice, thus brought to pass in the Holy Spirit, may be embodied in the Church and the Church in it, the bread and wine are changed, by the power of the same Holy Spirit and in a renewal and continuation of the mystery of the Incarnation, into the body and blood of the Lamb already immolated and existing as an eternal, perfect holocaust. In this way Christ, as one who has already gone on ahead by reason of His death and resurrection, is offered to God from the midst of the Church as its sacrifice.

Such seems to us to be the deepest and most adequate conception of the Eucharistic sacrifice. The form of the sacrificial action is simply that of the holocaust. It has this distinctive characteristic, however, that the spiritual fire produces the victim and presents Him to God in His glorified state by one and the same action, and further that no new slaying of the sacrificial Lamb occurs; the sacrificial Lamb is offered to God by the re-enactment of the immolation that took place of old. It is a holocaust of the noblest and most sublime kind, in which the fire that rushes forth from the heart of God Himself consumes the victim, and fuses the Church represented therein with the eternal holocaust of the Lamb.

Hence the symbolic representation of the sacrificial act by the consecration of the sacramental species does not consist solely in the vividly portrayed separation of the blood from the body as exhibited in the difference between the species. Just as essential is the representation of the union of the Church with the sacrifice of Christ, and of the transition of the sacrifice of the Church into His

---

[49] Cf. L. Hoppe, *op. cit.*, pp. 268 ff. The *Pontificale Romanum* says expressly (De consecra. alt.): "Domine sancte, Pater omnipotens aeterne Deus, . . preces nostrae humilitatis exaudi et respice ad huius altaris holocaustum, quod non igne visibili probetur, sed infusum Sancti Spiritus tui gratia in odorem suavitatis ascendat." St. John Chrysostom compares the priest with Elias, who called fire down from heaven to consume the victim.

sacrifice. This, according to the Fathers, is supposed in the fusing of the grains of wheat or the grapes into one whole and their combining to form a nobler substance, as brought about by material fire in one case, and by fermentation in the other.[50] It is clear that in this connection not only the outward species, but also the elements naturally corresponding to them, are interwoven into the symbolism of the sacrificial action.

[50] Of the many patristic passages that we could cite to illustrate this point, we quote the following from the seventh homily of Caesarius of Arles [PL, LXVII, 1055]: "By the very fact that, as we know, the bread is made of innumerable grains of wheat, it is clear that the unity of the peoples is designated. The wheat, after it has been carefully cleansed, is ground to a white mass by the mill; it is then mixed with water, kneaded into a single loaf of bread, and baked. Similarly the various nations which subscribe to one faith make up the one body of Christ; and the Christian peoples, like innumerable grains of wheat, are separated from the idolatrous nations by the cleansing and sifting power of faith, and are gathered into one, while the infidels are rejected like cockle. As the wheat is prepared by the work of the two millstones, the Christian populace is purified by the two Testaments. By its inherent sanctity it is restored to the dignity of its primal origins, and by the waters of baptism, or the fire of the Holy Spirit, it is made the body of that eternal bread. Accordingly, as the grains cannot be separated from their union once the bread has been made, and as water cannot return to its own proper state once it has been mixed with wine, so the faithful and the wise, who know they have been redeemed by the blood and passion of Christ, ought like inseparable members so to cling to their head by the consecration of themselves and their fervent religious life, that they cannot be torn from Him either by their own will, or by compulsion, or by ambition for any earthly good, or finally by death itself."

CHAPTER XVIII

Significance of the Eucharist

▸▪▪◂

73. THE MYSTERIOUS EXISTENCE OF CHRIST'S BODY IN THE EUCHARIST

TURNING from our study of transubstantiation, by which the body of Christ becomes present under the sacramental species, we shall next consider the meaning of the peculiar mode of existence proper to Christ's body in the Eucharist. As we have seen, this existence is twofold, or even threefold, in manner: it is spiritual, divine, and sacramental. Perhaps we shall do better to say that it is divine-spiritual and divine-sacramental.

1. What significance do we perceive in the divine-spiritual existence of Christ's body and blood?

a) We have noted that Christ makes His appearance in the Eucharist as the supernatural head of mankind. His intention is to deify humanity and associate it in a great sacrifice for the honor of God. As the supernatural head of the race, Christ must especially be the principle of real unity for His members. Hence, without becoming separated from Himself, He must really and substantially be present in all. Accordingly He must exist in such a way that, like the soul with respect to the body, He can enter undivided into all the members of His mystical body, not only as regards His power, but as regards His substance. This is why He is present whole and entire in many different hosts. But He cannot, of course, be subject to the limits of the space and extension of each one of them, particularly as He must be the principle of unity, and consequently must pervade and encompass the entire being, of each person to whom He unites Himself in the host. In a physical body the several parts are held together for their common benefit by a higher, spiritual principle. In like manner the body of Christ, which as the organ of His divinity brings us together in supernatural unity with itself and all the other members, must be endowed with a supernatural, spiritual unity that springs from the same divine power by which it clasps us to itself. Moreover, this unity must be such as to combine the greatest extension of presence with the greatest indivisibility. At the same time it must keep its bodily, corporal substance intact, because it is to join all men into one body, and not, formally, into one spirit. The Spirit of God abiding in us, which is also the Spirit of Christ, brings us together in one spirit. Since, however, the Spirit of Christ is operative only in the body of Christ, we must be one with this body, so as to share in the energy residing and functioning in it.

b) What effect does this energy produce in us? It is meant to spiritualize and divinize our whole being, to transform and glorify us. The body of Christ is to be our spiritual food, and so it must exist in the Eucharist in a spiritual manner. What is the meaning of the assertion: the body of Christ is to be our spiritual food? Do we mean to do away with its material nature or its substantial presence, as in the theories proposed by Protestantism and rationalism? Not in the remotest degree. The meaning is that the body of Christ is a nutriment not only for our corporal life, but first and foremost for our spiritual life. The meaning is, further, that in giving life to us the body of Christ does not perform the function of purely material food, which does no more than supply the stuff of life and hence is changed into the substance of the eater. Its relation to us is rather that of the soul, which permeates and animates the body into which it enters, not by being assimilated by the body but by dominating it. This heavenly food nourishes us as light nourishes our eye, by impressing upon the retina the images of the objects from which it radiates. It is received into us as fire is received into iron, not thereby to become merged with it, but to change the iron into itself and to impart its own qualities to the iron. The body of Christ, to be sure, or for that matter the entire humanity of Christ, is not properly the soul of our supernatural life, nor the light and fire by which we are glorified and transformed into the supernatural image of God. But on account of its hypostatic union with the Son of God, the animating, spiritualizing, divinizing power of the Godhead dwells in it; and so, as the organ of the divinity, it also animates, spiritualizes, and divinizes.[1] The body of Christ

[1] Cf. St. Cyril of Alexandria, *In Ioannis Evangelium*, lib. IV, c.3; *PG*, LXXIII, 565, 601-4.

houses within it the divine energy of life, the divine light, and the divine fire; it is precisely in this capacity that it is to nourish us in the Eucharist. Accordingly it is our nourishment no less truly and substantially than natural food. Indeed, it is incomparably more so. It comes into no less intimate contact with us than natural food does, and at the same time animates us and imparts life to us in a far higher sense.

Thus the body of Christ nourishes us in a spiritual way. As the organ of the highest spiritual and spiritualizing force, it directly affects our spirit, not merely our body. And it does this not by being absorbed into us, but by changing us into itself. Hence it need not, in fact it cannot, exist and be received into us in a carnal manner. If we were to partake of this food as we eat ordinary food, it would be destroyed, it would be changed into us, it would nourish only our body, not our soul. If along with our body it is to nourish our soul and our entire being, it must stand on the same plane as our soul, and come to our spirit in a spiritual way. If it is to transform us into its immortality and glory, it cannot itself come to us as a perishable, corruptible substance; it must come as an immutable, imperishable, insoluble substance. If, finally, it is to act upon us not by its material content, but by the divine energy residing in it, what purpose could be served by its dismemberment and dissolution? Rather, since it harbors within itself the divinity in its totality, since, further, as the vehicle of the Godhead it must bear itself accordingly, and since like a live coal,[2] gleaming and molten with the divinity, it is to enkindle a divine fire and splendor in us, it must itself be a body thoroughly spiritualized and in the highest degree glorified by the divinity.

More than this: in a certain respect the body of Christ in the Eucharist must be endowed by God with a higher mode of existence than it possessed in its state of divine transfiguration and glorifica-

---

[2] Ἄνθραξ (*pruna*, coal) is a term frequently occurring in the ancient liturgies and the Fathers to describe the body of Christ in the Eucharist, inasmuch as the sacred body houses the fire of the Holy Spirit, which purifies and transforms our souls and bodies. A reference was implied to the glowing coal with which the seraph cleansed the lips of the prophet Isaias. Cf. L. Hoppe, *Die Epiklesis*, p. 259, note 565, where this question is treated with the comprehensive erudition that marks the entire work. One of the finest passages in patristic literature (from St. John Damascene) has been quoted above, p. 488, note 23.

tion even after the Resurrection. For in the glorified state pertaining
to it for its own sake it is animated and transfigured by the divinity;
but in the Eucharist it animates and transfigures others, and so shares
in the spiritualizing and life-giving power of the Godhead. In its
own glorified state the body of Christ is, so to speak, the wheat
living by the power of the Holy Spirit; in the Eucharist it is the
bread baked by the fire of the Holy Spirit, whereby the power of
the Holy Spirit confers life on others.[3] In its glorified state it is related to the divinity as the body to the soul; in the Eucharist it partakes of the divine attributes, so that its relation is that of the soul
itself to the body which it animates.[4] In the former case, despite its

[3] Baking not only makes the nutritive powers of the wheat available in the
form of bread, but confers on the wheat itself a different mode of existence.
In some such way, according to expressions employed by the Fathers, the
body of Christ is, as it were, baked by the fire of the Holy Spirit, so that it
can enter into the substantial union with us which is necessary for our utilization of its life-giving energy. Cf. below, p. 521, note 11.

[4] Cf. Guitmund, *De corporis et sanguinis Christi veritate*, lib. I, med. (PL,
CXLIX, 1435): "St. Augustine proves convincingly that our soul, though
weighed down by the corruptible body, is not split up into parts throughout
the various members of the body, but is contained whole and entire in every
portion. Why cannot He, who gave to our soul the power of existing whole
and entire at one and the same time in each little particle of its body, give
to His own flesh, if He so wishes, the dignity of simultaneously being present
whole and entire in the various members of that body of His which is the
Church? For, as our soul is the life of the body, so by an even greater title
through God's grace the flesh of the Savior is the life of the Church. It is
through the soul that the body has temporal life; and it is through the Savior's
flesh that the Church has eternal life in all blessedness." Immediately preceding
this passage Guitmund employs another analogy, which is no less to the
point. In the Eucharist the subsistent divine Word is to be distributed to all
men in the flesh wherein He came forth from God: "We are aware from
everyday experience that our thought, that is, the word of our mind, can
in a certain way be clothed with sound, so that the thought which was concealed in our mind and was known to us alone can be uttered, and thus
manifested to others. Even while it remains wholly in our own mind, it can
be wholly made known to a thousand persons through the agency of the
sound it has assumed, so that it not only simultaneously illuminates the minds
of them all, but at the same time, still whole and entire, strikes the ears of
all with the sound in which it is embodied. If, then, God has conferred such
power on the human word that not only the word itself, but the sound wherewith it is clothed, can at the same time reach a thousand people without any
cleavage of its being, no one ought to refuse to believe the same, even if he
cannot understand it, of the only and omnipotent and coeternal Word of
the omnipotent Father, and of the flesh in which He is clothed, so that the
Word Himself may be made known to us. Neither can we understand the
matter as regards the tenuous and fleeting word of a man, and the sounds

glorification, Christ's body can be present only in one place at any one time, and is not exempt from corporal extension or from commensuration with the place it occupies; but in the latter case, the universality and sublime nature of the activity it exercises as the organ of the divinity necessarily entail its participation in the universality and simplicity of the Godhead.

This account, if we are not completely mistaken, throws a good deal of light on the Eucharistic discourse of the Savior (John, chapter 6), the context of which otherwise presents so many difficulties; in turn, our explanation receives strong corroboration from this discourse.

The Jews had begged the Savior to give them bread from heaven, as Moses had done. The Savior replied that He would give them the true bread from heaven, a bread of which the manna was no more than an empty symbol, a bread which by its inherent power would really nourish men unto a heavenly, immortal life. He Himself, He said, was this bread, which had literally come down from heaven, from the bosom of God, and therefore contained the energy of divine life, and so was a truly heavenly bread. The heavenly power to nourish possessed by this bread, its chief characteristic as a heavenly bread, derives from the divinity of Christ, from His origin out of the bosom of the heavenly Father, with which His supernatural origin from the womb of the Virgin is connected, to the exclusion of all dependence on a human father. The Jews denied His divinity, they denied His origin from God the Father, and held Him to be an ordinary son of man, a son of Joseph; and so they denied that He was the true bread from heaven.

More and more the Savior insisted that He really was so, and demanded that they believe the fact. He showed them that faith was necessary if they wished to be nourished on this strength-giving bread. He pointed out that such faith was as much a gift from the Father as the bread which the Father gave them in His Son. Undeterred by the Jews' lack of faith, which was to be ascribed to their stiff-necked obstinacy and nothing else, He went on to set before them the mystery of the bread from heaven. He specified the way He intended to give Himself as the bread of everlasting life, and

which scarcely hover in existence for a second, and yet we accept it on the basis of daily experience."

stated that He would give us His flesh and blood for our nourishment. Through the medium of His flesh we were to be united to His person, and through His person to the Father, so that we might have life from Him, as He Himself has life from the Father. The Jews were still less willing to believe this, and even some of the disciples were perplexed. "This saying is hard, and who can hear it?" [5] The statement seemed hard to them because they thought that Christ meant to give them His flesh to eat and His blood to drink in a crudely literal and bloody manner.

But the ultimate reason why they held so fast to this idea and could not rise to a loftier notion was that the Jews did not believe at all in the divinity of the Savior, and the faltering disciples believed only faintly. Had they believed firmly and unshakably like Peter, they too, like him, could have perceived with the aid of grace that the flesh and blood of Christ had their nourishing strength not from His fleshly nature, but from the Godhead dwelling in that nature, and hence that there could be no question of a cannibalistic repast.

It is from this angle that the Savior undertakes His answer. He does not overlook the cause of the error. Still less does He explain away His words in the sense of a purely ideal partaking of His flesh and blood by faith. He grasps the error by its roots. "It is the Spirit that quickeneth," He said; "the flesh profiteth nothing. The words that I have spoken to you are spirit and life." [6] That is, My flesh, as mere flesh like any other, can be of no help to you whatever; it imparts life not by being torn to pieces and devoured, but by the Spirit, the divine energy residing in it. It gives life not as a dead and bleeding corpse, but as living flesh, permeated by the Spirit of God. What I said of the flesh is to be understood with reference to this life-giving energy present in the flesh. Therefore whoever believes that My flesh is not an earthly but a heavenly bread, into which a divine strength has come down from heaven, and which because of this same divine strength belongs to heaven and will ascend thither, cannot see anything objectionable in My words. Such a one will not fear that he has to eat My flesh in a bloody manner. For he knows that the same divine power whereby My flesh gives life

[5] John 6:61.
[6] John 6:64.

enables Me to offer it for consumption in a way different from the way people eat natural meat.[7]

Generally speaking, add the Fathers in this connection, we should beware of regarding the flesh of Christ in too carnal a fashion. It is, to be sure, flesh of the same substance as our flesh. It was even derived from the womb of a daughter of Adam; not, however, in the way of ordinary flesh, but in a spiritual way, by the power of the Holy Spirit, who overshadowed the Virgin. "The flesh of the Lord is life-giving Spirit," says St. Athanasius, "because it was conceived of the life-giving Spirit; for what is born of the Spirit, is spirit." Although it possesses the true nature of flesh, it cannot be disfigured by the defects of flesh, especially since the Spirit of God abides in it, and the Son of God, from whom the Spirit proceeds, has taken it to Himself as fire takes iron. This indwelling Spirit did not, it is true, actually preserve it from death, but guarded it from dissolution and decay; and once death had embraced it, the Spirit called it back, in a way that was all the more miraculous, to a new, immortal life. This same Spirit brings the flesh of Christ, as the organ of His spiritual might, upon the altar, there to unite it to the flesh of the faithful.[8] Are we, then, to be surprised that the Spirit endows it with qualities which are primarily spiritual, and that He permeates it with His own spirituality, so that it seems to be spirit rather than flesh?

c) Thus Christ unites Himself to us in the Eucharist as the spiritual nourishment of our soul and our whole being. Even more than this: He is also, in our very midst, to be a spiritual sacrifice to God, and by His union with us is to include us in this spiritual sacrifice. This is another reason why He must exist in the Eucharist in the manner of a spirit.

As the Apostle teaches, the priesthood of Christ is a priesthood according to the order of Melchisedech, not by any law of carnal succession, but by virtue of an indissoluble life.[9] The new High Priest, who is also the sacrificial Lamb, had to deliver Himself up to death. But He could not lie forever subject to death. As He gave up His life, so He could and had to take it up again by His own

---

[7] Cf. St. Augustine, *In Ioannis Evangelium*, tract. 27 (*PL*, XXXV, 1616–18); St. Cyril of Alexandria, *loc. cit.*

[8] Cf. St. John Damascene, *De fide orthodoxa*, lib. IV, c.13; *PG*, XCIV, 1140–5.

[9] Heb. 7:16.

power, thenceforward to stand at the throne of God, living ever-more as priest and victim, so as by the efficacy of His death to lead men from death to life. Even on the cross His sacrifice was more spiritual than corporal. For Christ offered Himself unspotted to God through the Holy Spirit; [10] and the sacrifice, although accomplished in the flesh and in a bodily fashion, was carried out in flesh that was incorruptible, inseparable from the Son of God, and hallowed by this union. Moreover, this flesh was more than mere flesh: it was imbued with the spiritual dignity and the divinity of Him to whom it belonged. More than ever did the flesh of Christ have to become a spiritual sacrifice after its triumph over death; for now the Lamb, slain from the beginning of the world before the eyes of God, has to stand before God as an eternal holocaust burning with the fire of the Holy Spirit.

In point of fact, the Apostle teaches that Christ could die only once, and that He was to offer His sacrifice in the weakness of the flesh only once. The perpetual sacrifice which He offers is nothing but the triumphant commemoration of the sacrificial death of old, which endures in the body of Christ that has been liberated from the weakness of its flesh and has been spiritualized and transformed by the Spirit of God. The glorious immortality of Christ's body after its resurrection, far from being an impediment to the continuation of His sacrifice, is the very condition without which the sacrifice once consummated could not avail as a sacrifice that is to endure for all eternity.

This is the sense in which we speak of Christ's spiritual sacrifice in heaven. We do not mean to imply that the flesh of Christ is not the victim there, but we wish to insist that it is the flesh of Christ as glorified and spiritualized by victory over the death once suffered in the infirmity of the flesh. Here on earth there is all the greater reason why the flesh of Christ must be the object of sacrifice in its spiritualized and deified state, inasmuch as here in the midst of mankind it is to be offered in countless places and at all times, and is to associate individual men with it in a grand holocaust by a real union with them. If it were to remain among us in the manner of natural flesh, it would also retain the limitations of the flesh, and so could not be really present everywhere, nor could it everywhere apply anew the inherent power of its sacrificial death. Again, it could not

[10] Heb. 9:14.

unite itself to us wholly and entirely, nor could it fuse us with itself. Particularly its oneness with the glorified, spiritualized victim in heaven would not be apparent, and Christ would not appear among us, as He does in heaven, as the conqueror of death, and as He who is to lead us in triumph from earth to everlasting life.

A further consideration is that the flesh of Christ is made present in the Eucharist and is offered as the sacrifice of the Church through the fire of the Holy Spirit, which consumes the bread. Here precisely, by the distribution of the spiritual graces won in its immolation and resurrection, is manifested the priceless value which the sacred body possesses in virtue of its hypostatic union with the Son, and in Him with the Holy Spirit. On the cross the flesh of Christ had to be offered in its earthly nature, as otherwise it could not suffer. At the resurrection it had to be glorified, in order to complete the holocaust. But in the Eucharist it must display its efficacy as the holocaust already consummated by death and resurrection, together with the power that has wrought full regeneration in the midst of redeemed mankind. Its value and its efficacy come from the "odor of sweetness" emanating from Him who bears the flesh and penetrating the flesh itself; and this is no other than the sweet aroma of the Godhead, the Holy Spirit. Must not this sacred flesh, even as regards the manner of its existence, enter into the highest possible kind of unity and conformity with the Spirit that fills it with fragrance? Must it not be, as it were, wholly consumed by the Spirit's fire, mount up in spiritual incense, and present itself in the guise of a spirit?

One more point presents itself for our reflection. The flesh of Christ is to nourish us not as mere natural flesh with a view to the life of flesh, but as flesh steeped in the Spirit of God, unto a life that is at once divine and spiritual. Similarly, it has the function of not only offering an external sacrifice of the flesh, but of prefiguring and effecting a spiritual oblation of our soul. The sacrifices of flesh in the Old Law serve merely to symbolize the sacrifice that we offer to God in our spirit and along with our spirit. Such sacrifices of flesh, worthless in themselves, become spiritual and take on value only if they are directed to God and are sanctified by the sacrificial disposition of the person offering them, and thus avail to express the interior oblation. Quite different is the case with the sacrifice of Christ's flesh. Made godlike by the hypostatic union and steeped in the Holy Spirit, it is this flesh which is to arouse a truly spiritual disposition of sacrifice in us, and pour forth the consuming fire of love into our souls. It is from this flesh that we are to draw the strength to offer up our souls to God; and in union with that flesh, which reposes on the bosom of the Godhead, we are to lay our souls as a worthy and sweet-smelling sacrifice before the throne of God. The flesh of Christ must scent our souls through and through with the sweet aroma of the Holy Spirit, with which it is filled itself, so that they may become truly spiritual and divine, and may send up a most pleasing incense to God. This flesh was conceived of the Holy Spirit because it was to be thus sweetly scented by Him, and is again and again made present on our altars by the same Holy Spirit.[11] And so it must come upon our altars truly and in its own nature, but in a spiritual form.

Lastly, in union with the sacrifice of Christ, we should offer not only our souls but also our bodies as a sacrifice to God. But the very sacrifice of our bodies should become a spiritual sacrifice, so far as the spirit offers itself with its body. Furthermore, it should become spiritual because our flesh can be a sacrifice acceptable to God only by ceasing to be carnal, by being pervaded, ruled, and purified by the spirit. But even this spiritualization of our flesh is a sacrifice truly pleasing to God only if the body, like the soul itself, is sanctified and transfigured by the Holy Spirit, the Spirit of God. Hence, if Christ's immolated flesh is to be the model and inspiration for this oblation of our bodies, it must be purified and ennobled in the highest degree by the Holy Spirit, and the divine energy housed within it must be raised above all the limitations and defects of material and corporal nature.

Therefore the body of Christ in the Eucharist is a spiritual food and a spiritual sacrifice. It is spiritual in the power imparted to it by the divinity dwelling within it; it is spiritual in its effects upon our souls and bodies; hence it is spiritual also in the manner of its existence and substantial presence.

2. If the body of Christ existed for us and became united to us

[11] Rupert of Deutz, *In Exod.*, lib. II, c. 10 (*PL*, CLXVII, 617): "The Virgin conceived Him of the Holy Spirit, who is eternal fire; and through the same Holy Spirit He offered Himself, as the Apostle says [Eph. 5:2], a living victim to the living God. Hence on the altar He is immolated by the same fire. For it is by the operation of the Holy Spirit that bread becomes the body, and wine the blood, of Christ."

in this spiritual way alone, the conditions necessary for its union with us and its activity in us would, indeed, be fulfilled. But its relations to us would be wholly internal and spiritual, and would not be effected by an external, physical bond. Its oneness with us would not have the character of a bodily oneness that is outwardly apparent, and that serves as the vehicle and expression of spiritual unity.

That it be so is an integral factor in the organism inaugurated by the Incarnation. The Eucharist is meant to be the continuation of the Incarnation. In the Incarnation the Son of God clothed Himself with natural, visible flesh, to confer on us the union He envisaged and to manifest it outwardly. Accordingly, if this union is to be carried through to its appointed end, Christ's body may not be entirely withdrawn from the sphere of the natural and the visible. The presence of Christ in the Eucharist is primarily spiritual in character; but His body must be made manifest to us under the form of some external medium and image assumed by it.

Upon this fact rests the sacramental mode of existence of Christ's body in the Eucharist. As the elevating and transforming power of the Incarnation is continued and perfected in the spiritual mode of that body's existence, so the union of the invisible with the visible, of the divine with the human, which we observed in the Incarnation, is distinctly brought out in its sacramental existence.

The sacramental mode of existence enjoyed by Christ's body is the chief element in the rich, sacramental organism wherein the Incarnation is prolonged. We shall regard it as such later when undertaking a comprehensive survey of the whole doctrine, and shall seek then to fathom its full meaning.

Even at this stage we could show how the nature and significance of the Eucharist are most clearly and strikingly expressed in the sacramental medium chosen by Christ. However, this is not so essential to our immediate purpose, and would necessitate numerous repetitions. For that matter, we have already touched on this point.

74. Mysterious Significance of Our Reception of the Eucharist

Reception of the Eucharist, or Holy Communion, especially effects our incorporation in Christ, and consequently all that is naturally involved in such incorporation. We have already pointed out that the Eucharistic Christ, as the vine into which we are set, is infinitely more than a mere food on the analogy of natural bread. Nevertheless it accomplishes all that natural food does, although in a higher way. For "My flesh is meat indeed; and My blood is drink indeed." [12] As the Savior says that in virtue of the Eucharist we abide in Him, so He also states that He will abide in us.[13] We propose at present to regard the Eucharist in this latter respect, according to which Christ is received by us and is taken into us as the object we partake of.

Concerning our reception of the Eucharist, as of any food, two aspects may be distinguished. We take food and make it a part of ourselves to draw new energy of life from it, and to derive refreshment and enjoyment from it. In the case of natural food the latter factor is quite subordinate, as food is desirable not as an end in itself, but as means to an end. Further, since it loses its own nature when utilized for this end, enjoyment of it for its own sake is of no value for rational man. The case is quite different with the Eucharist. We should desire not merely to derive vital energy from the God-man, but to possess Him in His person within us and to enjoy Him. Indeed, it is precisely in virtue of the vital energy He bestows on us that we are to clasp and possess Him in living embrace.

1. The first function of this partaking is clear from what has been said about the effect of our incorporation in Christ. We saw that the body of the God-man is given to us as the vehicle or organ of the life-giving and transforming power of the divinity. We receive it as such in all truth if this power proves operative in us, and if in consequence of sufficient preparation on our part we draw from it a genuinely divine life and transformation, and are confirmed and more deeply grounded in supernatural union of life, in spiritual unity with God. In this case reception of the Eucharist is

[12] John 6:56.
[13] John 6:57.

a partaking that truly confers life on us; otherwise it is a poison that works our ruin.[14]

What feeds and nourishes us in the Eucharist is properly the divine energy of the Logos inhabiting Christ's flesh. But if, in order to give us life, the Logos unites His body to us in so astounding a fashion, we must conclude that He unites His divinity to our souls in a way that resembles the union of His flesh and blood with our bodies. Our partaking of the God-man's human flesh and blood is the real sacrament, that is, the sign and instrument signifying our reception of the flesh and blood of His divinity, if I may so express myself.

What meat and drink are to the body, that the light of truth and glory, and the fiery torrent of love are to the soul. The human flesh of Christ corresponds to the brilliant aura of glory that suffuses Him in His divine nature, and His human blood corresponds to the river of life and love that gushes forth from His divine heart.[15] Thus by

---

[14] An analogy that well brings out the difference between a dead and a living reception of the Eucharist, suggested by Alger of Liége, should not be overlooked. The passage is from his *De sacramentis corporis et sanguinis Dominici*, lib. I, c.21 (*PL*, CLXXX, 801): "As a word is a sound that signifies and contains thought, so the species of bread is a sacrament that signifies and contains Christ. And as a word is both heard and understood by some, and thus is received in every way, but is only heard without being understood by others, and thus is received externally by the ear, as far as the sound goes, but not internally by the mind, as regards its sense, although it conveys sense, even if not understood, just as much as it gives forth sound, even if not heard: so the unbeliever or the sinner receives the sacrament externally by mouth under the form of bread, but does not receive the body of Christ internally into his heart in true unity and conformity. Nevertheless the Sacrament is no less the body of Christ as regards its real substance when received by the wicked, than when it is received both in its real substance and in the truth of spiritual grace by the good."

[15] This notion is very ancient. "The blood of the Lord is twofold," says Clement of Alexandria (*Paedag.*, lib. II, c.2, no. 19; *PG*, VIII, 409; *CB*, I, 167). "The one is bodily blood, whereby we have been redeemed from ruin; the other is spiritual blood, whereby we have been anointed. And to drink of the blood of Jesus means no less than to share in the Lord's incorruption. For it is the Spirit that gives vitality to the Word, just as blood conveys energy to the body." In the sacrament of Christ's blood the Spirit of divine life, gushing from the Logos like the blood from His bodily heart, pours into our souls as the blood of divine life, to anoint them and to allay their thirst. In the Eucharist we draw the Savior's own divine life, as it were, from His very side. If we can thus speak of a twofold blood of the God-man, why should we not speak of a twofold flesh? Is not the flesh, the bodily veil and frame of Christ, likewise the sacrament of the radiant form of His divinity,

partaking of His flesh we are illuminated by the light of eternal truth, and are transfigured and transformed by its glory; and in His blood the ocean of eternal life and divine love floods our hearts. By the divine power inhabiting the Lord's flesh we are transformed in soul into the image of His divine glory, and in body into the image of His own glorified body, just as by the power of the Holy Spirit coursing in His blood our souls and our bodies are filled with immortal, divine life. The hunger and thirst of our souls are assuaged by the fullness of the divinity just as really as our bodies are nourished by suitable food and drink. Indeed, this takes place in such a way that our lives become homogeneous with the divinity, and hence divine.

So long as this partaking of the divinity is confined to the sacramental medium and is conferred by it, the divine life thence arising is only inchoative and embryonic. But this same sacrament is at the same time a pledge and guaranty that the seed will some day flower into full beauty, that the Logos will irradiate and transform us with the plenitude of His light, and that He will completely flood us through and refresh us with the torrent of His love and His life, so that in knowledge and love our lives will appear as the full expression and outpouring of the divine life.

Whoever can grasp the meaning of the statement that at present our soul is imperfectly nourished and refreshed with the fullness of the divinity, but that some day its hunger and thirst will be perfectly satisfied, will no longer look upon the Eucharistic repast as a wonder; for he will learn to regard it as the prelude and preparation for a still more marvelous banquet. In the words of St. Augustine, as tender as they are profound, the Eucharistic food is but the milk into which the heavenly bread of eternal life was changed in Mary's breast, so as to accommodate itself to our feebleness, and thus to

---

which is reflected in the flesh? And is not our soul's advancement furthered by the enlightenment and transfiguration imparted to it, as the body is perfected by the reception of Christ's flesh? However, we are not accustomed to employ the word "flesh" in this higher sense, for in scriptural language it is ordinarily used to indicate whatever is opposed to the spiritual. But for that reason we can the more justifiably, in keeping with the sense of Scripture, refer to the divinity of the Logos as bread. Indeed, His divinity is truly the *panis superessentialis* (as some of the Fathers render the ἄρτος ἐπιούσιος of the Lord's Prayer) which is concealed under the substance of the body present in the Eucharist.

prepare us for partaking of the heavenly bread itself in the greatness of its proper nature.

2. Thus when we partake of the Eucharist it nourishes us by conferring upon us the energy of divine life. Further, in conferring the energy of this life, it furnishes us with the object which we are to lay hold of in the Eucharist and clasp in strong embrace.

In receiving the Eucharist we unite ourselves, in closest and most substantial fashion, primarily with the God-man's body, which enters into our inmost being, there to be the object of our loving and rapturous possession. But in this body and through it, He who bears it, the only-begotten Son of God, comes to us in order to deliver Himself personally into our possession with all that He is. It is this substantial possession and partaking of a divine person that makes the mystery of the Eucharist so delightful and blissful.

However, as the sacramental nourishment of our soul can be thought of as the prelude and type of a still greater nourishment bestowed by the divinity itself, so the substantial possession and partaking of the God-man in His humanity necessarily points to a possession and partaking of God Himself, a possession and partaking of God in His divine substance. The Eucharist cannot be conceived and appreciated apart from this relationship.

The God-man gives Himself up to us in His human substance, and through it in His divine substance, in order some day to confer His divine substance upon us as the object of our possession and fruition, just as really as He now gives us His human substance. This takes place in the beatific vision. By the fullness of light with which God floods and strengthens His creature in the beatific vision, He enlarges the creature's powers of comprehension in such a way that the creature is able to apprehend God as He is, in His own nature and substance, and so can revel in the sight and love of God. A mere image radiating forth from God, or an impress emanating from Him, would not enable the soul to perceive God in His essence. Such an image or impress would serve only as a food that would stimulate the flowering of the soul's vital activity. No, it is the immediate, intimate presence of the divine substance itself in the soul that enables the soul to embrace God in knowledge and love, and thus to unfold its own godlike life. In the beatific vision the divine substance is received into the soul as a factor in its life as really as bodily food substantially enters into the organism of bodily life.

Or better still, the divine substance becomes wedded to the soul and descends into the depths of the soul, there to supply food and drink for the unfolding of the soul's activity. This takes place in somewhat the same way that an image radiating from an external object, though not the object itself, combines with the visual power of the eye.[16]

The fact that God has invited us to the sublime banquet in which we are given His divine substance, enables us once again to understand why in the Eucharist He confers His human substance upon us. Partaking of the Eucharist is, let us repeat, but the figure and pledge of the promised enjoyment of the divinity. The Eucharist is, as it were, the milk in which the divine food is adapted to our present powers of reception; some day it will be given to us in all its greatness.

Whether we regard this food from the standpoint of its power to nourish, or in terms of the blissful, intimate, and substantial possession which it accords, the Eucharist is the type, the pledge, and the prelude of a magnificent replenishing of our soul with the fullness of the divinity, and its mystery is seen to be vitally and naturally connected with the mystery of our supernatural destiny. It is quite properly the food of God's children, who in Christ are called to closest fellowship of life with God. So marvelous a bread is the right food for them in their infancy, since a still greater awaits them in the fullness of their maturity.

75. Connection of the Eucharist with the Other Mysteries, Especially with the Mission of the Holy Spirit

Again our attention has been drawn inevitably to the close and harmonious connection existing among the mysteries of Christianity, and to the remarkable organic relationship whereby any one of these profound truths recalls the others. The mystery of the Eucharist reminds us of the mystery of grace and of heavenly glory, for it is their connatural cause, prefigure, and inauguration. The mysteries of grace and glory in turn postulate the mystery of the Eucha-

---

[16] Cf. Scheeben, *The Glories of Divine Grace*, Bk. II, chap. 6, pp. 141 ff.; also the charming and profound explanation there quoted from St. Francis de Sales' treatise, *The Love of God*, Bk. III, chap. 11.

rist as their foundation and type. And, as the mysteries of grace and glory are inextricably interwoven with the mysteries of the Trinity and the Incarnation, the same is necessarily true of the Eucharist.

As concerns the Trinity, we have already remarked that the oneness of substance and life existing between the Father and the Son is transmitted to us and reproduced in us most perfectly by the Eucharist. In particular, the Eucharist is the agency that effects the real and perfect mission of the divine persons to the outer world.

Above all it crowns the Son's mission to us on this earth. For in the Eucharist the Son unites Himself to us in the most perfect way, to give us in general the power to become sons of God, and also to make us one Son of God by incorporating us in Himself.

In the Eucharist we likewise perceive the real and intimate mission of the Holy Spirit. For, since the Holy Spirit, the Spirit of the Son, is really united to the Son's body, in which He reposes and dwells, He also comes to us in this same body, to unite Himself to us therein, to communicate Himself to us, and to give Himself to us as our own. In the body of the Logos, which is filled with the Holy Spirit, we receive the Holy Spirit Himself, as it were, from the breast and heart of the Logos, whence He proceeds. Like the blood flowing from the heart into the other members, the Holy Spirit flows forth from the real body of the Logos into the members of the latter's mystical body, inasmuch as they are substantially united to Him.[17] He joins Himself to us and pours Himself into us in the two kinds of mission that we discussed earlier: first, as the breath of divine life and holy love, which reaches its apex in this sacrament wherein we are so closely united to the heavenly Father through the very real union we have with the Son; secondly, as the pledge of the divine love for us, which is offered to us for our enjoyment and as the seal of our sonship and union with God, which here attains its full perfection.

As pointed out above, the mission of the Son, in its difference from and its relation to the mission of the Holy Spirit, is expressed in the Eucharistic species themselves. The species of wine, as the symbol of blood, with its fluidity, its fiery ardor, its bouquet at

[17] With characteristic tenderness St. John Chrysostom calls the Eucharist the breast of the spiritual mystery (that is, of the mystery of the Holy Spirit), from which, like infants, we drink in the grace of the Holy Spirit (*Hom. de S. Philogonio;* ed. Montfaucon, VIII, 890).

once heady and delightful, and its life-giving power, suggests to us the Holy Spirit, whose procession is a welling forth from the heart of the Father and the Son, whose mission is an outpouring, and who is in Himself the flood and fragrance of the divine life. It sets Him before us as the wine gushing from the divine grape-cluster, the Logos; [18] as the wine of ardent love, of refreshment, of life, of the ecstatic happiness poured forth over the world in the sacred blood that was pressed from the human heart of the Logos by the force of His love, and is now poured into us in the Eucharistic blood.

The relationship of the mission of the Holy Spirit to the mission of the Son in the Eucharist presents so many facets, and yet is so harmonious in its multiplicity, that a fuller study of the question will well repay us.

Although the Holy Spirit is sent by the Son and comes to us in the Son, He is, by the strongest of all appropriations, also the channel through which the Son is brought to us. As the aspiration terminating the Son's love, He urges the Son to deliver Himself up to us in the Incarnation and the Eucharist. As the flame issuing from the mighty ardor of the Son in His work of sanctification and unification, in the womb of the Virgin He brings about the origin, the hypostatic union, and the resulting holiness of the Son's human nature, and in the Eucharist effects the conversion of earthly substances into the Son's flesh and blood. After the hypostatic union and transubstantiation have been wrought, He lives on in the Son's flesh and blood with His fire and His vitalizing energy, as proceeding from the Son, and fills the sacred humanity with His own being to sanctify and glorify it. Particularly in the Eucharist He glorifies and spiritualizes the Son's human nature like a flaming coal, so that it takes on the qualities of sheer fire and pure spirit. Straightway He makes use of the Eucharist as an instrument to manifest His sanctifying and transforming power to all who come into contact with it, and as a channel to communicate Himself to all who receive it and feast upon it. The body of Christ, as a spiritual gift which God presents to us and which we offer in sacrifice, has its origin from the fire of the Holy Spirit; it is permeated and encompassed by the Holy Spirit, who so transfigures and spiritualizes it that both the fire and the coal which the fire pervades with white heat seem to be one and the same

[18] "The Word is a great cluster of grapes, pressed out for us," says Clement of Alexandria.

object; and, finally, it is flooded with the Holy Spirit, thus yielding up His fragrance in sacrifice, and His vitalizing energy in Holy Communion.

All these relationships of the Eucharist to the Holy Spirit are beautifully expressed in the figure of the glowing coal, which the Eastern Fathers and liturgies are so fond of employing in describing the Eucharist. The very word "Eucharist" indicates these relationships. For it signifies the eminently good gift, the gift conferred by the Holy Spirit as the eternal *donum per excellentiam,* the gift which contains the Holy Spirit Himself with His essence and His power. How striking and well devised was the ancient usage of reserving the Eucharist in a receptacle symbolic of the Holy Spirit, in a vessel fashioned in the form of a dove—in the so-called *peristerium!* How beautifully the Holy Spirit was thus symbolized as He who brings and fashions the gift contained in that receptacle; as He who, encompassing and permeating that gift as fire does the coal, dwells therein with His essence and His power!

76. The Eucharist and Related Mysteries according to St. Cyril of Alexandria

We have mentioned several times that St. Cyril, the champion raised up by God to do battle with Eastern rationalism, had an extraordinarily clear insight into the meaning and connection of the cardinal mysteries, and pressed home his views with vigor. We will here set down a somewhat lengthy passage from his masterly commentary on St. John's Gospel,[19] which comprises the gist of his vast theological erudition.

He is undertaking an explanation of the words of the Savior: "And not for them only [the apostles] do I pray, but for them also who through their word shall believe in Me; that they all may be one, as Thou, Father, in Me, and I in Thee; that they also may be one in Us." [20] He begins with the remark that the Savior's prayer may not be limited to the apostles alone, but must extend to all men, since all have need of the grace of redemption. In proof of this he continues:

"It would in a sense be unbecoming that sentence of condemna-

[19] Ed. Aubert, pp. 995 ff.; *PG,* LXXIV, 553–61.
[20] John 17:20 f.

tion should pass to all men through the first man, I mean Adam, and that those who did not sin when our first parent violated the command laid upon him should bear the dishonorable image of earthly men, and yet that at the coming of Christ, who appeared among us as the heavenly man, those who were called by Him to justice, the justice of course that is through faith, should not all be molded to His image. The distorted image of the earthly man, we say, is seen in a form and figure marred by the defilement of sin, the infirmity of death and corruption, and the impurity of carnal lusts and worldly thoughts. But, as we know, the image of the heavenly man, that is, Christ, shines forth in purity and integrity, and in perfect incorruption, life, and holiness.

"However, it was impossible for us, who had once fallen away through the sin of the first man, to be restored to our original glory, unless we were admitted to an ineffable fellowship and union with God; for thus the nature of men upon earth had been ennobled at the beginning. But no one can attain to union with God except by participation in the Holy Spirit, who implants in us the sanctity proper to His own person and forms anew to His own life the nature that had been subject to corruption, thus bringing back to God and to His likeness those who had been deprived of so great a glory. For the Son is the exact image of the Father; and the Spirit is the natural likeness of the Son. For this reason He transforms the souls of men as it were into Himself, stamps them with the divine likeness, and molds them into the image of the Most High."

Therefore, according to Cyril, our need of redemption is not based primarily on the view that our nature was in itself deranged, but on the fact that through original sin we had fallen away from that indescribable, mysterious, utterly supernatural, and not human but divine beauty and likeness to God which we had originally possessed by the grace of God, and which we are now to recover. Thus he explains the mysterious significance of the pristine state and of original sin, and, incidentally, of the Trinity also. For he associates our supernatural likeness to God through the Holy Spirit with the natural likeness of the Son to the Father, and of the Holy Spirit Himself to the Son.

He next goes on to explain the oneness which Christ begs for us from the Father, and for which He proposes His own oneness with the Father as model. He observes that this union must first of all be a moral union, that is, a union of mutual love and concord, and further of conformity in godliness, in obedience of faith, and in love of virtue. But this moral union, which later toward the end he calls ἕνωσις κατὰ σχέσιν ("union by relationship"), falls far short of an imitation of the ideal, and does not completely exhaust the profound sense of the Savior's words: "as Thou, Father, in Me, and I in Thee, that they also may be one in Us." And so he continues:

"We rightly stated above that the union of the faithful in concord of mind and heart ought to imitate the manner of the divine unity and the essential identity of the Holy Trinity and the perfect connection of the persons with one another. At present, however, our endeavor is to show that this unity is also in some respect a physical unity [that is, a real or true unity: physical only as opposed to moral, but hyperphysical as opposed to a union that is naturally real], by which we are joined to one another, and all of us to God," not excluding even unity of body, at least with reference to our mutual connection, although the numerical distinction between our bodies may neither be denied nor destroyed.

"Taking, then, the physical oneness of the Father, the Son, and the Holy Spirit as admitted by all . . . let us inquire how we too are bodily and spiritually one, both among ourselves and with God.

"The only-begotten Son, proceeding from the very substance of God the Father, and bearing His begetter completely within His own nature, was made flesh according to the Scriptures, joining Himself, so to speak, to our nature [ἀναμιγνύς, a term which expresses the reality and closeness of the union] by an ineffable union and conjunction with this body of earth. Thus He, who is by nature God, truly became a heavenly man, both in name and in reality, not as a man who bears God within him, but as one who is at the same time God and man. This He did in order that, combining as it were in Himself things widely separated by nature and averse to fusion with each other, He might enable man to share and participate in the divine nature. For the fellowship and abiding presence of the Holy Spirit has passed to us, beginning with Christ, who as man like us was anointed and sanctified [by the Holy Spirit], but as true God, inasmuch as He proceeds from the Father, first sanctifies His own temple [His human nature] with His own Spirit [who proceeds from Him], and through Him all creatures capable of sanctification. Thus the mystery that is in Christ has been, so to speak, a beginning and a way admitting us to participation in the Holy Spirit and to union with God."

Accordingly the mystery of the Incarnation, of the real, hypostatic union between humanity and God, has a mysterious significance for us. It means that we are most intimately united to God, and are raised to a supernatural relationship with God, to participation in the divine nature, and to the specifically divine holiness that is proper to the Holy Spirit.

Further, by the same mystery we are made supernaturally one body with Christ and one spirit with God. St. Cyril proceeds to develop this point:

"That we might attain to union with God and with one another, and, in spite of the individual differences that separate us, that we might be joined and united in body and soul, the only-begotten devised a special plan in the wisdom proper to Him and by the counsel of His Father. With one body, that is, His own, He blesses those who believe in Him through the mystic partaking of Him [Holy Communion], and makes them one body with Himself and with each other. For who will separate those who are joined to Christ in unity by that one sacred body, and detach them from the real union which they have among themselves? For if we all partake of one bread, we are all made one body.[21] Christ cannot be divided. On this account the Church is called the body of Christ, and we are His several members, according to the teaching of St. Paul.[22] For if we receive the one and indivisible Christ into our own bodies, and are all united to Him through His sacred body, we owe the service of our members more to Him than to ourselves. . . . This is the great mystery which Paul speaks of when he says: 'Which in other generations was not known to the sons of men, as it is now revealed to His holy apostles and prophets in the Spirit, that the Gentiles should be fellow-heirs, and of the same body, and co-partners of His promise in Christ Jesus.'[23] And if we are all one body among ourselves in Christ, and not only among ourselves but also with Him who is in us through His flesh, are we not all plainly one with one another and in Christ? For Christ is the bond of union, since He is at once God and man.

[21] Cf. I Cor. 10:17.
[22] Cf. I Cor. 12:27; Eph. 5:30.
[23] Eph. 3:5 f.

"With reference to spiritual unity we shall say, following the same course of inquiry, that in a way we are all fused with one another and with God by the reception of the same Spirit, that is, the Holy Spirit. Individually, it is true, we are many, and Christ causes the Spirit of the Father and His own to dwell in each one of us; yet the Spirit Himself is one and indivisible, and through Himself He joins into unity the spirits that are distinct from one another inasmuch as they exist individually, and makes them appear as one in Himself. For, as the power of His sacred flesh makes those into whom it comes to be one body, so likewise the Spirit of God, who dwells in all, brings all together into spiritual unity. For this reason St. Paul again urges us: 'Supporting one another in charity, careful to keep the unity of the Spirit in the bond of peace: one body and one Spirit; as you are called in one hope of your calling; one Lord, one faith, one baptism; one God and Father of all, who is above all, and through all, and in us all.' [24] For if the one Spirit sojourns in us, the one Father of all, God, will be in us through His Son, joining into unity with one another and with Himself all that partake of the Spirit.

"That we are united to the Holy Spirit by participation is made clear from the following consideration. If, giving up our natural way of life, we once allow the laws of the Spirit completely to reign over us, is it not evident beyond all question that, abandoning as it were our own lives, and taking upon ourselves the transcendent likeness of the Holy Spirit who is united to us, we become almost transformed into a different nature, and are known no longer simply as men, but as children of God and heavenly men, since we are made partakers of the divine nature?

"Accordingly we are all one in the Father, and in the Son, and in the Holy Spirit; one, I say, in unity of relationship [of love and concord with God and one another], . . . one by conformity in godliness, by communion in the sacred body of Christ, and by fellowship in the one and Holy Spirit [and this is a real, physical union]."

Thus we perceive that the three mysteries of the Trinity, the Incarnation, and the Eucharist are connected with one another in perfect harmony. They represent three kinds of supernatural and supremely real unity: that of the divine persons with one another

[24] Eph. 4:2 ff.

by identity of nature, that of the Second Person with the humanity assumed by Him, and that of the sacred humanity with the rest of men. The latter two kinds of unity are the organs by which, in the mystery of the grace of the Holy Spirit, we are to be raised to imitation of the first unity, in oneness of spirit with God.

PART SIX

The Mystery of the Church and the Sacraments

> This is a great mystery—I mean as
> pointing to Christ and to the Church.
>
> Eph. 5:32

CHAPTER XIX

The Mystery of the Church

••

77. GENERAL NOTION OF THE MYSTERY

BY becoming man the Son of God has called the whole human race to fellowship in His body. That which was remote, that which was far from God and vastly below Him, He has brought near in His person, and has joined in one body, His own body. Upon Himself and in Himself He has established a great community and society of men. He is at once the head and the foundation of this society. In it He wills to continue His activity and His reign. Through it He wishes to unite men to Himself and to His heavenly Father. This society is the Church.

The Church is a great and stupendous mystery. It is a mystery in its very being, a mystery in its organization, a mystery in the power and activity it exercises. Let us endeavor first of all to determine the perspective according to which it is to be viewed.

When we assert that the Church is a mystery, do we intend to do away with its natural visibility? By no means; the Church is visible in its members, in its external organization, and in the relations existing between its superiors and subjects. It is as visible as any other human society.

I venture to make an even greater claim: the Church is visible not only as it actually stands at present, but in its divine foundation and institution.

The astonishing origin and the no less astonishing continuance and growth of this society, the numberless moral and physical miracles marking its course throughout the centuries and in every quarter of the globe, prove that it is no mere work of man. They prove that it is a work of God, that God has instituted it and continues still to acknowledge and uphold it as an organization that He Himself has founded.

The Church is visible in the very way that its historical founder and head, the God-man Himself, was visible. The God-man was visible both as a real man, and as a man sent by God and standing in a unique relationship to God. Similarly the Church is visible both as a society of men, and as a society founded and sustained by God.

The likeness of the Church to Christ is carried out even in its invisibility and its mysterious character. Despite the visibility of His humanity and its unique relationship to God, the proper character of Christ as true God and true man lay hidden beneath the visible veil in the depths of the Godhead. So too, the inner nature of the Church, the sacred bond which envelops its members and links them together, the marvelous power which holds sway in it and energizes it with life, the heavenly goal which it pursues—all this, notwithstanding the visibility of its external organization and its divine origin, is simply impenetrable to the natural eye of man, and hence is incomprehensible and inconceivable. It is only by belief in divine revelation that we can conceive and know the true nature of the God-man, head of the Church. Likewise it is only by acceptance of this same revelation that we are able to grasp the true inner greatness which marks the Church because of the divine-human character of its head.

The inner nature of the Church is absolutely supernatural, as is that of the God-man. This is the reason why it is so hidden and mysterious; this is the reason why the Church, although conformable to other human societies in its outward organization, differs essentially from these in its innermost character; and this is the reason why its unity, its power, and its organization are so matchless, sublime, and inconceivable.

Concerning the nature of the Church, the temptation might arise to form a notion that has regard only to externals, on the analogy of other societies that exist among men, and to account for its radical difference from these only by the fact that it is a religious community founded by God. Such it is, no doubt; but this alone would not place it so high beyond the range of our minds. In the same way that men organize themselves for other purposes, they could also band together for common worship; there is nothing supernatural in this. Indeed, by a positive ordination God Himself could decree the formation of such a society, assign laws to it, bestow special rights and privileges on it, and, on the other hand, bind men to it and refer them to it for the fulfillment of their religious obligations, as was done through the Mosaic institutions of the Old Testament. A society of this kind would not come into existence without a supernatural, extraordinary intervention on God's part. But this circumstance would not make it supernatural and mysterious in its very nature. The worship of God would be purely natural, except that it would be regulated and conducted according to fixed norms. And if God were to attach a special efficacy to the priestly and jurisdictional functions of this society, so that remission of sins and other graces would be granted through the former, and subjects would be guided with full certitude in the conduct of their religious life by the latter, this indeed would be quite extraordinary. It would be the effect of a special, gratuitous Providence; but it would not be genuinely mysterious and supernatural. If such were the case, the entire Church as an institution would be reduced to a mere system of education and guidance directed by God, and a legal code regulating man's dealings with God; its unity and activity would be only something moral, after the analogy of other human societies.

Faith shows us that there is vastly more to the Church than this. Faith enables us to see in the Church not merely an institution established for the education and guidance of natural man, but one that confers on man a new existence and a new life, a wholly new, supernatural rank and destiny, and that is designed to support, strengthen, and direct him in his striving for this destiny. To the eyes of faith the Church is not merely a society founded and approved by God or a divine legate; but it is built upon the God-man, it is made an organic part of Him, it is raised to His level, it is upheld by His divine power and is filled with His divine excellence. The Church is the body of the God-man; and all who enter it become members of the God-man so that, linked together in Him and through Him, they may share in the divine life and the divine glory of their head. Lastly, as seen by faith, the Church is more than a handmaid of God or of the God-man, a servant who would aid in bringing about a certain limited intimacy between God and man. As the mystical body of Christ, the Church is His true bride who, made fruitful by His divine power, has the destiny of bearing heavenly children to Him and His heavenly Father, of nourishing these children with the substance and light of her bridegroom, and of conducting them beyond the whole range of created nature up to the very bosom of His heavenly Father.

In brief, the Church is a most intimate and real fellowship of men with the God-man, a fellowship that achieves its truest and most perfect expression in the Eucharist. If the God-man dwells in the Church in so wonderful a manner as to associate Himself with all its members to form one body, then evidently the unity in which He joins them is so august and mysterious that no human mind can conjecture or understand it. And if through the agency of this unity He draws the members of the Church up to and into Himself in order to permeate them with His divine power and glory, to offer them in Himself and with Himself as an infinitely pleasing sacrifice to God, this also is a mystery surpassing all human understanding and all human notions. This mystery induces in us the realization that we can never think too highly of the nature and importance of the Church.

78. THE MYSTERY OF THE CHURCH IN THE FELLOWSHIP OF ITS MEMBERS WITH CHRIST AS HEAD AND BRIDEGROOM

If the mystical nature of the Church, as the fellowship of men with the God-man, culminates and receives its fullest expression in the Eucharist, we cannot better study the Church than by regarding it from the standpoint of the Eucharist, its very heart. Let us begin with a consideration of that fellowship with Christ which is common to all the members of the Church.

The Eucharist, whether regarded as sacrament or as sacrifice, is the sacred and mysterious bond encircling all the members of the Church. Fellowship in the Church attains its full perfection in the actual partaking of the Eucharist, and in actual participation in the Eucharistic sacrifice. The right to participate in the Eucharist as sacrifice and sacrament is the chief factor that determines membership in the Church. Faith and baptism truly initiate us into the Church, but only for the reason that they qualify us for participation in the Eucharist. Indeed, by faith and baptism we spiritually anticipate the power conferred by the Eucharist, and are made members of Christ's body in proportion to our dignity. But this membership looks forward to a closer, substantial fellowship in His body that is to be effected later.

Hence to be a member of the Church is to be a member of Christ's body. In a wider sense man is a member of Christ's body by the very fact that he belongs to the human race, but only so far as he is thereby called actually to attach himself to Christ and to enter into the organism of His body.

On the one hand man is to move toward his head by faith in His dignity and power, and on the other hand he is to appropriate to himself the signature and the seal of his head, so as to belong to His body in the stricter sense, to become a member that will be responsive to the influence emanating from the head and will stand in organic connection with the head. The first step is made by faith, the second by baptism. Faith and baptism together make man a member of Christ in the organism of the Church instituted by Christ Himself.

What high, supernatural dignity is attained by man when he becomes a member of the Church, how astounding the union into which he enters with Christ, and through Christ with God, and at the same time with all his fellow members in the Church! What a tremendous mystery lies even in simple membership in the Church! It is a mystery as great as the mystery of the mystical body of Christ, as the mystery of the Eucharist in which it culminates, as the mystery of the Incarnation upon which it is based, as the mystery of grace which is its fruit.

To conceive of the integration of all members of the Church in Christ under the notion of a mystical marriage with the God-man, as the Apostle does,[1] is merely to express the truth in another way. By the Incarnation Christ has assumed our nature in order to yoke Himself with us. The Fathers view the Incarnation itself as a marriage with the human race, inasmuch as it virtually contains everything that can lead to the full union of the Son of God with men. But the relationship of unity it sets up comes to full fruition only in the Church. Man is to attach himself to his divine bridegroom by faith; and the bridegroom seals His union with man in baptism, as with a wedding ring. But both faith and baptism are mere preliminaries for the coming together of man and the God-man in one flesh by a real Communion of flesh and blood in the Eucharist, and hence for the perfect fructifying of man with the energizing grace of his head. By entering the Church every soul becomes a real

[1] Eph. 5:22-33.

bride of God's Son, so truly that the Son of God is able, in the Apostle's words, not only to compare His love and union with the Church and her members with the unity achieved in matrimony, but can even propose it as the ideal and model of the latter. Is not such unity an ineffable, stupendous mystery, which infinitely transcends all the notions of natural man?

If the Church in all its members is thus the body of Christ and the bride of Christ, the power of its divine head, the Spirit of its divine bridegroom, must be gloriously operative in it. In all its members the Church is a temple of the Holy Spirit, who dwells in it as the soul in its own body, and manifests His divine and divinizing power in it. He is active in the Church not only in the way in which, as the Spirit of eternal wisdom and order, He guides and directs all well-regulated societies, not merely by sustaining with special assistance individuals and the entire community in its religious pursuits, by granting the remission of sins, and by helping to heal our moral weaknesses and infirmities. No, He must be active in the members of Christ's body as He is in the real body of Christ, namely, by filling them with the plenitude of the divinity. He must overshadow the bride of Christ as once He overshadowed Mary's womb, so that in her the Son of God may be reborn in His divine holiness and majesty. With His divine fire He must gloriously change Christ's bride into the image of the divine nature, transform her whole being by adding splendor to splendor, and pervade her with His own divine life. All this He must do so radically and powerfully that it may be said of her that she does not herself live, but God lives in her. He must make her so like her divine head and bridegroom that she seems to be Christ Himself.

When it is asserted of other societies that the member joining it becomes like a plant that is transplanted in a new soil, or grafted onto a new trunk, the figure is to be taken in a very diluted and weakened sense. For in such cases the soil and the trunk of the society can do no more than give a new bent to the member's growth, and aid him in the developing of existing aptitudes. These societies cannot transform the new member's innermost being and nature, or the root of his life. All that is possible is a moral suasion by moral influence. But when a person becomes a member of the Church, he is taken up to the bosom of God in Christ and through Christ; he is planted in a heavenly soil, and grafted on a divine trunk;

he enters into a new, supernatural sphere where his nature is transformed and transfigured. A wholly new life is infused into him, and this new life is nourished and cultivated under the sun and dew of a new heaven. The Holy Spirit, it is true, reigns in the members of the Church by guiding, assisting, and healing them. But such aid is granted only on the basis of that elevation and transfiguration of man beyond his nature which is effected by the Holy Spirit. Its purpose is to inaugurate and foster the divine life which must first be implanted in human nature by Him, and to furnish and adorn the divine temple which must first be built by Him.

We shall see later how the Holy Spirit gradually unfolds His activity in the individual members of the Church. Here our object is to make clear that the presence and activity of the Holy Spirit in the members of the Church, as the members of Christ, must be intimate and mysterious to a high degree, inasmuch as it is the emanation and the continuation of that presence and activity with which He dwells in the humanity of the Son of God. Since the Holy Spirit Himself proceeds from the Son of God and as such belongs to Him, He necessarily enters into the Son's humanity and into His whole mystical body, and belongs also to the latter. This is true all the more inasmuch as in the Eucharist the Son of God dwells bodily and essentially, with all the plenitude of His divinity, among His members in the bosom of the Church. In the Son and through the Son the Holy Spirit dwells there also, personally and essentially. He is the very Spirit and, as it were, the soul of the Church.

Thus the great mystery of the Eucharistic Christ is the center around which is grouped the noble community of Christ's faithful. This community we call the Church. It is a fellowship that is a great mystery in its own right, because it elevates all its members in a mysterious way, and operates in them in a mysterious way.

79. The Mystery of the Church in Its Maternal Organization

With all this we are still far from appreciating the mystery of the Church in all its greatness. The God-man had no intention of making the members of the ecclesiastical community His members simply in order to act in them as their head. He willed further to appoint some of them as representatives and organs of His own activity, so that His mystical body might be equipped with an internal organization, which would, however, find expression in external signs. As bridegroom He had a higher object in view than merely to be yoked with all the members of the Church so that they might benefit their own persons by sharing in His dignity and honor. In a part of its members the Church, as His bride, was meant to be a true mother to the children who were to be reborn to Him as bridegroom, so that the heavenly rebirth of the human race might correspond to its natural generation, and the organization of the God-man's family might conform to the family of earthly man. To this end He weds a part of the members of the Church in a special way, entrusts to their keeping the mystical resources belonging to the Church in common, and overshadows them beyond all others with the power of the Holy Spirit, so that they may bear Him children and bring them into closest fellowship with Himself.

This is the great mystery of the maternity of the Church in her priesthood. In general the priesthood of the Church functions as intermediary between Christ and His children, much as the mother does between father and children. But the similarity between this twofold intermediacy must be adequately understood.[2]

In accordance with its office the priesthood must bring Christ to birth anew in the bosom of the Church, both in the Eucharist and in the hearts of the faithful, by the power of Christ's Spirit reigning in the Church. Priests must build up the organism of Christ's mystical body, as Mary, by the power of the same Holy Spirit, brought forth the Word in His own humanity, and gave Him His physical body. The miraculous conception of Christ and His birth from the womb of the Virgin is the model and also the basis of the further spiritual conception and birth of Christ in the Church through the priesthood. And this priesthood stands in a relationship to the God-man similar to that of Mary to the Son of God who descended into her and was born of her. The two mysteries are complementary; they illuminate and set off each other.

As Mary conceived the Son of God in her womb by the over-

---

[2] The close connection between the sacerdotal dignity and the sacrifice which Christ has bequeathed to His "beloved bride, the Church," has been pointed out by Pius XI in his encyclical *Ad catholici sacerdotii* (December 20, 1935, no. 1). [Tr.]

shadowing of the Holy Spirit, drew Him down from heaven by her consent, and gave Him, the Invisible, to the world in visible form, so the priest conceives the Incarnate Son of God by the power of the same Spirit in order to establish Him in the bosom of the Church under the Eucharistic forms. Thus Christ is born anew through the priesthood by a continuation, as it were, of His miraculous birth from Mary; and the priesthood itself is an imitation and extension of the mysterious maternity that Mary possessed with regard to the God-man. The priesthood is for the Eucharistic Christ what Mary was for the Son of God about to become man.

With this maternity which the Church in her priesthood exercises over Christ who is to be received into her bosom, is connected, or rather from it proceeds, her mysterious motherhood over her individual members. Christ is brought into the Church in the Eucharist because the Church is to be joined with Him in one body, because He is to be reborn in her members. For this reason also the priesthood has the power, through the overshadowing of the Holy Spirit, to bring forth Christ anew in the hearts of the faithful, and the faithful in Christ, in order to effect a substantial union between them and Christ in His real body, and to nourish them with His own flesh and blood in their new, supernatural life. As the priesthood gives rebirth to Christ, the head of the Church, so it must also impart new birth to the members of the head.

The underlying idea and the essential functions of the sublime motherhood that we must ascribe to the Church in her priesthood consist in making the real body of Christ present in the Eucharist for union with His mystical body, and in building up this mystical body itself. Hence this maternity is no empty formula, it is not a weak analogue of natural motherhood. It implies more than the fact that the Church has the attitude of a loving mother toward her members by caring for them, nourishing them, instructing them, and rearing them like children. All such activity exercised by the Church and its priesthood has its basis and receives its true meaning and character from the fact that the priesthood is supernaturally related to the children of the Church with a relationship no less real and true than that of a natural mother to the children she has borne. In its own way this relationship is as real and objective as the real presence of the God-man in the Eucharist which is effected through the cooperation of the priesthood, or as the new, supernatural existence and life of the children of God which is brought into being through the agency of the same priesthood.

Hence the priesthood itself is as great and mysterious as the two effects with which it is associated. Inexpressibly sublime is the dignity imparted to the priesthood, and in it to the Church: to be the mother of the God-man in His sacramental existence, and of men in their higher, divine existence. Incomprehensible is the fruitfulness which the Church reveals in this maternity, unspeakable the union with the overshadowing Holy Spirit, who in her bosom and through her brings about marvels similar to those that took place in the most pure womb of Mary. This supernatural motherhood is the central mystery of the Church as an organically constructed society. For it is this motherhood by which the ecclesiastical fellowship is made a soundly constituted society, wherein the children are linked to the Father through the mother. By it the body of the Church, the mystical body of Christ, is developed and extended by a process of growth from within; by it the real presence and the real union of the head with His members is sustained and perfected. Finally, this maternity is the basis of all the other social relations and activities which regulate and shape the Church in the unfolding of its life. It imparts to these a supernatural, mysterious stamp which they would lack apart from union with the Church.

The activity of the priesthood in the Church, to use the Apostle's words, amounts to this: to fashion Christ in its members, to unite them to Christ, to conform them to Him, to build them up to the full measure of the stature of Christ.[8] Because of this end the activity of the priesthood receives, to a greater or less extent, a higher, supernatural significance wherever it is exercised. The sublime motherhood of the Church leaves its mark upon all the functions of the priesthood.

As a heavenly mother, the Church nourishes her children with heavenly bread, the flesh of the Son of God. With this same flesh and blood of God's Son she places in their hands a gift by the oblation of which they can offer a perfect sacrifice to their heavenly Father. In this oblation they can also offer themselves to Him in a fitting manner, so as to honor Him as He deserves, to thank Him, to make satisfaction to Him for all their sins, and to obtain abundant gifts from Him. As heavenly mother she stamps on their forehead

[8] Eph. 3:14–19; 4:11–16.

the seal of the Holy Spirit in the sacrament of confirmation, to equip and strengthen them for strife and battle. As heavenly mother she washes her children clean from the filth of sin, and after the disastrous separation from their heavenly Father leads them back into His arms. As heavenly mother she cures and heartens them in their illnesses of body and soul, particularly at that decisive hour when in the midst of harsh conflict their very entrance into the joys of their heavenly Father is at issue. As heavenly mother she reproduces herself in the persons of the priests who bear her maternal dignity, and with her blessing accompanies those of her children who, animated with her dispositions and by virtue of the Holy Spirit's consecration imparted to them, join in wedlock for the bodily propagation and multiplication of her members.

In all these activities the Church operates on the basis of her motherhood, with an ever-growing manifestation of the marvelous fertility she possesses by reason of her union with the Holy Spirit. But, since she is a mother, she must do more than prove herself fruitful in her children by the communication or renovation of an increasingly intimate fellowship with Christ and His heavenly Father. She must also guide and regulate the activity which her children are to undertake for the purpose of entering into that fellowship; or, when in it, of making it known and further developing it. She must teach and educate them. She must instruct her children especially concerning those supernatural, mysterious truths which the Son of God has brought down to her from His heavenly Father. She must initiate her children into the mysteries of God and of their own supernatural nobility and destiny. She must teach them with an authority and infallibility which correspond to the dignity of Christ's bride who occupies the place of God, and to the sublimity of the faith which is to be engendered in them. And she must so guide and rule her children that, led by her hand, they may with certainty and confidence set out toward the mysterious, supernatural goal which, in the person of her divine head, she has long since anticipated and taken into possession.

The power to teach and educate, even when exercised with a certain infallibility, may perhaps not seem to be a very great mystery. But at any rate there is a great mystery in the teaching and educating power which the Church possesses as the heavenly mother of the human race, and which is inseparably bound up with that motherhood. For this power supposes that the priesthood of the Church is truly the bride of Christ and the organ of the Holy Spirit. This Holy Spirit, by the glorious presence and union whereby He imparts to the priesthood its sublime fruitfulness, enables Christ's bride to keep alive and cultivate her fruit in the faithful, and to make that fruit beneficial and salutary to the faithful through their obedience in matters of faith and conduct.

80. Relation of the Sacramental Maternity to the Jurisdictional Organization of the Church

The maternity of the Church, which is represented by a specially favored number of its members, comprises two functions: the power to confer grace, and the power to direct the use or acquisition of grace. A clearer understanding of the relationship between these two functions is indispensable for a deeper insight into the mystical organization of the Church.

This distinction coincides with the distinction familiar to theologians of a former age, between the power of orders and the power of jurisdiction, as two powers essentially different and even separable in those who possess them. In more recent times the distinction has repeatedly been assailed; the contention has been advanced that it is inadequate because it excludes the teaching authority, and that it sets up too great a cleavage between the powers which it distinguishes. It may well be that many theologians have given occasion for such strictures, owing to a superficial appreciation of the purport of the distinction. But at bottom it is a profound concept, and is rich in most weighty consequences.[4]

By the power of jurisdiction we must here understand not only external legislative power in the ordinary sense, as it is found in other societies, but especially the power by which the Church authoritatively directs and regulates the activity of its subjects, and by which it establishes and enforces the norms for that activity. But the Church does precisely this and nothing else even in the exercise of its teaching power, since in virtue of its divine authority it rules and regulates outward actions and also their inner principle,

---

[4] Scheeben defends this distinction against the division, current in his day, into "regal, sacerdotal, and prophetical power," and gives the dogmatic bases for it in his *Dogmatik*, Bk. I, sec. 10, nos. 109-26. [Tr.]

and the inner attitude of those who perform them. By jurisdiction we usually mean no more than disciplinary power over external actions and over the external order prevailing in a society, since it is only in such cases that an external code of laws, or jurisdiction in the narrower sense, can be administered. But the Church has judicial competency even in matters of faith; although it can pass no judgment concerning the fact of interior belief, it can at least determine the obligation of believing. Were it not for this competency, we could well forgo the expression "power of jurisdiction," and substitute "pastoral office" for it. This is the term used by the Savior Himself; it implies the competence which the Church possesses with regard to the guidance and education of its children, an office to be discharged by feeding and leading them. The Church feeds its children by setting up norms for their belief, and guides them by setting up norms for their conduct. At the same time this term tones down the opposition of this power to the power of orders, that is, the priesthood, and clears the way for an understanding of the connection between them.

Despite such connection, we must hold fast to the truth that the pastoral power is not formally bound up with the power of orders, since there can be priests and bishops without actual jurisdiction. In virtue of its higher "order," the priesthood constitutes, so to speak, the nobility in the Church, a nobility whose higher dignity and control of the society's supernatural goods in the realm of grace set it apart from the other members. On account of its rank it is called upon, as a body, to wield the pastoral power in the Church. As the spiritual mother of the rest of the faithful, the priesthood is also the natural custodian of the educational authority over them. Moreover, since the priesthood is so closely related to the God-man, and since the Holy Spirit resides in the sacerdotal order with the rich fruitfulness of His graces, it is the organ by which the same Holy Spirit wills to lead the Church to all truth and to guide it to all good.

This is not to say that the pastoral office is entrusted wholly or in part to any individual simply because of his priestly rank. Nor do we assert that any individual has, without further consideration, even the right to exercise his sacerdotal fruitfulness, or to dispose of the treasures of grace contained therein, either for himself or in behalf of the faithful; for this disposal does not belong to the sacerdotal power as such, but to the pastoral power. In virtue of the title by which the pastoral power has the exclusive right to guide and to regulate the ecclesiastical activity of the rest of the faithful, it has the right to govern and to regulate those activities by which the Holy Spirit distributes His graces. In general, of course, the Holy Spirit entrusts the guidance and government of His Church to His priestly organs, as is in keeping with their position. But if the great number of these organs is to prove no detriment to the union and order of the Church, He must regulate the exercise of their sacerdotal power and the transmission of the pastoral office to them according to a definite hierarchy, and place it under undivided control. Hence the organism of the Church, which is based on the segregation of Christ's priestly organs from the lay members, must be carried on and be brought to perfection by the organization of its governing power.

Therefore the unity of the Church in its social life depends in a special way on the unity of the pastoral power. This unity of the pastoral power must be a clear sign that the Spirit of the Church operating in many organs is a single Spirit, who brings all these organs together in one whole, and causes them to exercise their activity in an orderly manner conformable with the unity of the whole. The members and organs of the Church form one body of Christ and assemble around the Eucharist as the source of their common life, and they are called to image forth the highest unity of all, that of the Trinity. In the unfolding of their life and activity, these members and organs constitute a closely knit whole, in which the unity and harmony of external social life is the faithful reflection of its true, internal, mysterious unity. This fact must be manifested by the unity of the pastoral power.

This unity of pastoral power in the Church is guaranteed by the revealed doctrine that the entire plenitude of such power is in one supreme pontiff. Moreover, this power is so vested that the whole flock of the Church and even the priests and high priests are entrusted to his care and are subject to him, and that all these high priests and priests can obtain and exercise their pastoral office in the Church only in dependence on him and in union with him. The entire social structure of the Church rests on him as its foundation. The pastoral power passes from him to the other pastors of the Church as rays proceed from the sun, brooks from their source, branches from the tree. Owing to the fact that the plenitude of the pastoral power resides in him, and that no such power can be envisaged in the Church as independent of his, the Church is made truly and perfectly one, not only in its summit, but in its deepest base—and from the base up; not only in its topmost branch, but in its root—and from the root up. Any other, lesser unity in the Church is unthinkable, unless the structure of its social organization is to be quite at odds with its inner nature.

Prior to the Vatican Council many theologians could not rise to this lofty idea of the position of the papacy in the Church. One of the reasons for this failure, and not the least, is the fact that they did not sufficiently know or view the Church in terms of its supernatural, mysterious nature, which is reflected and expressed precisely in the papacy. The Church, although founded by God, was made to conform too much to the pattern of natural societies. In natural societies the undivided ruling power, even when the form of government is monarchical, is never more than representative of the common interest; the unification of power in one hand does not pertain to the essence of such societies, but constitutes only a special mode of their existence and structure. Hence the monarch is the pinnacle of the society rather than its base or an essential condition of its existence. The Church, on the contrary, is formed around an already existing, supernatural center, namely, Christ and His Holy Spirit, and this center must, by intrinsic necessity, manifest itself in the social organism in the person of a single representative, a single organ. The Church does not project this central point from itself; nor is the center set up by God merely for the purpose of completing the Church as an undivided whole. Rather it is intended to be the foundation upon which the Church is constructed, by which the Church rests upon the God-man and the Holy Spirit, and by which the unity of the Church is not incidentally brought about or crowned, but is essentially procured. The Church, as a society, is held together in this central point, as it is in Christ; through it the Church is in Christ, because it is only through it that Christ Himself, as the supreme head of the Church, is in the Church with His pastoral power.

If such is the true notion of the unity of the pastoral power in the Church, and of the unity of the Church which stands or falls with the unity of the pastoral power, the infallibility which is associated with it or, rather, is intrinsic to it, must evidently reside in him who possesses the pastoral power in its plenitude. The pastoral office must involve infallibility, at least with regard to the regulation of faith and morals, since otherwise it could not with absolute reliability guide those who are subject to it. It is so in fact, because they who possess it administer it as representatives of Christ and organs of the Holy Spirit. Consequently he who has this power in its plenitude, who therefore is the fully qualified representative of Christ and the spokesman of the Holy Spirit, must possess infallibility, so far, of course, as he acts in virtue of his full power and asserts the full range of his authority. Through him Christ wills to bring all the members of the Church together in unity of faith and love; through him and in him all the faithful are to attach themselves to their supernatural head and permit themselves to be guided by the Holy Spirit.

This supernatural infallibility of the pastoral power in the pope is, like the radical unity of the same power in his person, the reflection of the inner, mysterious character of the Church. Hence it is itself a supernatural mystery, which the Church in its divine greatness offers for our contemplation. A mere infallibility of the whole— that is, of the whole Church, or even of the entire episcopate, as resulting from the agreement of individuals—would be only an imperfect, deliberately planned measure of expediency, unworthy of the sublime activity which the Holy Spirit unfolds in the Church. On the other hand, its center of gravity would be withdrawn from the direct influence of the Holy Spirit, and would be shifted to a natural basis. If none other than the Holy Spirit is to gather the many together, why should He not group them organically, by assigning them to a common center? Surely, where such agreement in matters of faith actually exists among the faithful or their pastors, it must be referred to the Holy Spirit, who operates in all. But their infallible certitude would at the same time have a predominantly natural cause and warrant in the fact that the constant agreement of so many men could not otherwise be procured than by the objective truth of the matter agreed upon.

An explanation thus based on natural causality obviously weakens the mystery of infallibility. Those who acknowledge the root of the Church's infallibility only in such accord, show only too clearly that they shy away from whatever is supernatural or mysterious in the Church, and cannot reconcile themselves to these qualities of the

Church. Indeed, they undermine even the external organization of the Church, which rests essentially upon supernatural foundations. If this view is justified, the Church is lacking in an organ to produce such accord among the faithful, when it is not already present; the pronouncement of the pope is no more than an official witness of the existing agreement, and the pope himself is but the spokesman of the community, and only in this sense is also the spokesman of the Holy Spirit who abides in the community. His faith, therefore, would not be the basis of the faith of the community; and instead of upholding the community, in accord with the words of the Savior, his faith would be upheld by the community.

But why should we be reluctant to admit a mysterious foundation for the external organization of this structure, whose entire being is a mystery? Why should not the Holy Spirit, who dwells in the priesthood with His marvelous fruitfulness in order to distribute His graces in the Church through its agency, be able so to dwell, and why should He not actually dwell, in the central point of the Church's social structure, in the bearer of His pastoral power? Why should He not bring the whole flock together in faith and love from that point, and through it impart unity and stability to the structure? Such union of the Holy Spirit with the head of the Church would be a tremendous wonder; but it ought to be precisely that. The Church is throughout an awe-inspiring, divine edifice. What wonder that its foundation should be so remarkable? The Church is the bride of the God-man. What wonder that it should be so closely united to Him through its head, and be so marvelously guided by Him through its head?

Only in terms of the mystery of the fullness of the pastoral office in the head of the bishops, can we form an adequate notion of the mystery of the sublime maternity of the Church, as it has been described above.

The motherhood of the Church in the strict sense pertains not to the whole community, but to those persons endowed with the fruitfulness and the pastoral power by which the children of the Church are begotten, reared, and guided.[5] In a word, it belongs to the fathers

---

[5] Such motherhood can be ascribed to all the members of the Church only in an analogous sense. They cannot be the ministers of the sacraments by which grace is conferred, or acquire grace by offering the Holy Sacrifice of the Mass, or guide others authoritatively. But they can implore grace by

of the Church. We call them "fathers" because of their natural sex character, which in conformity with propriety is demanded by Christ for the carrying out of the higher offices in the Church. But if their function in the Church is considered formally according to its supernatural side, and if attention is focused on their dignity rather than on their persons, they obviously have a maternal character. Thus viewed, their persons are seen in a special way to be wedded to the God-man in His Holy Spirit: they are persons through whom the God-man begets, rears, and educates His children, as the father of the family does through the mother. In this particular respect the multiplicity of their persons does not enter into consideration, but rather the unity of their relationship to Christ and to the Holy Spirit; and even in the external organism this unity is represented by the dependence of them all on him who possesses the pastoral power in its fullness.

In virtue of this double union (internally with Christ and the Holy Spirit, and externally with the representative of both), the priests constitute the one bride of Christ. Christ Himself renders them fruitful for the purpose of begetting and nourishing the children of the Church, and He crowns their head with His pastoral power. Thereby they are likewise made the one mother of the faithful. They possess this dignity when all of them are taken together as a unit, whereas their head, the pope, possesses it by himself alone. So far as they proceed and act in virtue of their double connection, the qualities of their individual personalities do not enter into consideration. Whether such personality is good or evil, Christ acts through them as through His organs. This activity is ever fruitful, or infallible according to the nature of the case; no account is taken of the personal condition of the organs. They are fruitful in the exercise of the sacerdotal power, and infallible in the exercise

---

prayer and by personal sacrifice, and lead others to good by their personal influence. This common fruitfulness and activity of all the members does not at all exclude the aforesaid motherhood in the narrower sense. Indeed, the former can exist only in close dependence on the latter, as the latter can successfully realize its fruitfulness and activity only in connection with the former. The two kinds of motherhood are intimately related, and must support each other. The justification and significance of the general motherhood rest on the fact that all the members of the Church are the brides of Christ, and as such are made fruitful by His Spirit, and so are called to bear fruit to their bridegroom both in themselves and in the community to which they belong, and to contribute to the building up of His mystical body.

of the complete pastoral office, with regard to faith and morals. This is the concrete sense of the words that are often understood but vaguely: the Church as such cannot err; the errors of her members and of him who holds authority do not touch the Church herself. Her womb remains ever undefiled and immaculate, for it is the abode and vehicle of the fructifying and ruling power of the Holy Spirit. And so, too, the children of the Church, so far as they are begotten of her and are reared and guided by her in the power of the Holy Spirit, are unstained and holy: they are children of God in their very being and in their life.

But since even those who are endowed with the glorious maternity of the Church do not always personally measure up to their dignity, and since the children of the Church do not always conduct themselves as such, but thwart the fruitfulness of their mother and withdraw from her guidance, the outer countenance of this heavenly bride is often stained and disfigured. In her womb, but not from her womb, rankly grows many a weed that casts a shade over her heavenly blossoms. And although often enough her inner majesty and greatness are manifested in luminous rays, these brilliant signs are not sufficient to disclose the entire wealth of her grandeur. The true glory of the King's daughter is from within; it lies hidden within the wonderful power with which the Holy Spirit acts in her and through her. That glory will be completely unveiled only when it will have completely purified, sanctified, transfigured, and deified all her true children. The less that glory can be perceived and grasped from without, the greater and more sublime it is; and the less the sordidness clinging even to the Church can tarnish or destroy her inner glory, the more divine must that glory be. These reasons show the august mystery that is the Church; a mystery calling forth a vigorous divine faith that will soar above whatever is visible and natural, but also providing that faith with an inconceivably lofty object.[6]

[6] During the period of the Kulturkampf and the following decades German theology paid less attention to such ideas as developed by Möhler and Scheeben than to pointing out the notable achievements of Catholic culture. Scheeben did not by any means, however, overemphasize the spiritual character of the Church. Rather he suggests elements for a new exposition of the moral and cultural contribution made by the visible Church. The value of this contribution stands forth as prominently in the chaos of the modern world as during the greatest spiritual periods of the Church's long history. [Tr.]

CHAPTER XX

The Sacraments of the Church

▴▴

81. The Sacramental Mystery in Christianity

THE mysterious character of the Church is most clearly evinced in its sacraments, as can readily be inferred from what has been said. The inner, supernatural organism of the Church is built up through the sacraments and in relation to them, and in turn manifests its supernatural power principally through them.

Before undertaking a more comprehensive study of the nature of the sacraments, or rather, to gain a higher vantage point for this study, we wish to discuss in greater detail an idea that runs through the whole of Christianity, the idea of sacramental mystery in general, an idea lying at the bottom of the sacraments considered in the stricter sense.

1. In its original meaning, the term "sacrament" can be synonymous with "mystery"; at any rate the terms involve no opposition to each other. In the language of the early Church the two expressions were used in a parallel sense. The Latin Fathers regularly use the word *sacramentum* as equivalent to the Greek μυστήριον. The difference pointed out later, that *sacramentum* connotes something visible, μυστήριον something invisible or hidden, does not originally appear. The Latin Fathers call entirely invisible things, such as the Trinity, *sacramenta*, while the Greeks refer to visible things, for example, the seven sacraments, simply as μυστήρια, because of the mysterious element in them.

But in the course of time *sacramentum* came to mean, for the most part, visible things which in some way or other involve a mystery in the narrower sense, and which therefore are mysterious despite their visibility. In such things the mystery, the hidden element, was linked with the visible element, and the whole composed of both

558

elements shared in the character of its two parts: it could appropriately be called a sacramental mystery. Indeed, the two parts thus joined share in the character of each other, so far as the one is related to the other. In particular the mystery hidden in the sacrament could be called sacramental mystery, owing to its connection with the sacrament.

The significance of these refinements will become clear as soon as we apply them to concrete instances. But first we must explain them more accurately.

With regard to the sacramental mystery, two factors evidently must be considered: first the mystery concealed in the sacrament; secondly the connection between this mystery as such and the sacrament, the visible thing. Only when both factors are present in a fully developed state can we speak of a sacramental mystery in the complete sense.

As concerns the first factor, there can be question only of a mystery in the strict theological sense, something truly supernatural, visible or perceptible neither to our senses nor to our reason. Thus it would occur to no one to call man or his body a sacrament or a sacramental mystery, merely because his soul is concealed in it; for the soul is something natural and, although not visible to the senses, is naturally knowable to the intellect.

With respect to the second factor, the connection of the supernatural mystery with the visible object, such connection may be either real or logical. The latter is the case when a visible thing houses some mystery within itself, and is the symbol and likeness of the mystery. The symbol or likeness enables me to make the mystery known to my understanding, or at an rate makes it possible for some other intelligence to acquaint me with the mystery. In this sense the Fathers sometimes speak of the sacrament of the Trinity in creatures. But this purely logical connection does not really cause the visible element to combine with the invisible element to form a whole. If the sacramental mystery is to have objective reality, there must be a real connection, as, for example, the connection between the divine person of Christ and His human nature, between the spiritualized body of Christ and the sacramental species, or between grace and the man endowed with grace. In the case of the logical connection the sacrament is indeed a sacrament, but a *sacramentum vacuum*, which does not really contain the mystery; in the case of the real connection it is a *sacramentum plenum*, that is, it is really filled with the mystery, it is full of mystery. Since in the latter case the mystery is actually present in the visible object, it is also actually present to him who sees the visible object, not indeed in the sense that he thereby perceives the mystery as it is in itself, but in the sense that when by faith he is apprised of the union of the two elements, he knows upon seeing the visible object that he actually has the mystery before him.

It pertains to the essence of the sacramental mystery that the mystery remain a mystery even in the sacrament. This would not be the case if the sacrament would literally manifest the mystery. Something must be, and remain, hidden in the sacrament, within its interior. This does not exclude the possibility that the sacrament may make known the inner nature and meaning of the mystery (as occurs in the Eucharist, wherein the species of bread and wine signify the nutritive and unifying power of Christ's body), or that the presence of the mystery in the sacrament may give evidence of itself by means of a few escaping rays (as, in the case of Christ's humanity, the hypostatic union shines forth through the miracles worked in virtue of it). It is only the essence of the supernatural mystery that may not become visible in the sacrament. This essence must ever remain the object of faith which, penetrating beneath the surface of the sacrament, lays hold of that which can be reached neither by the outer senses, nor by the intellect groping about in the realm of sensory perception.

Most of the mysteries of Christianity are sacramental mysteries in the sense that there is a real connection between the hidden element and the visible element. The Trinity is not one of these, at least directly in itself; it becomes such only indirectly in the God-man. But the first man, as he came forth from the hand of God, was a sacramental mystery, inasmuch as supernatural, invisible grace was joined to his visible nature. Still more the God-man was such; He is the great sacrament, the "evidently great *sacramentum* of godliness," as the Vulgate here significantly renders the Greek μυστήριον, "which was manifested in the flesh." [1] Here the supernatural in the most exalted sense is really and most closely united to the visible humanity, the flesh, as the humanity is called from its visible side, and in such a way that, although it is substantially

[1] Cf. I Tim. 3:16.

and personally present in the flesh, it remains hidden under the flesh. As the hypostatic union of Christ's flesh with the Logos is the mystery in the sacrament of the flesh, so this flesh itself is raised by the power of the divinity to a supernatural, spiritual mode of existence, to the mystery in the sacrament of the Eucharist, where it is linked with the visible appearances of bread so intimately that it completely replaces the substance that naturally goes with these appearances, and is actually made present through their agency. Thereupon also the Church, by virtue of its connection with the Incarnation and the Eucharist, becomes a great sacrament, a sacramental mystery. Although the Church is outwardly visible, and according to its visible side appears to be no more than a society of mere men, it harbors in its interior the mystery of an extraordinary union with Christ made man and dwelling within it, and with the Holy Spirit who fructifies and guides it.

In all these objects is verified the notion of sacramental mystery, as we have outlined it above. In all of them we have a visible, natural being, the natural contemplation of which suggests to us, at most, some faint idea of the mystery concealed in it. Faith alone assures us that such a mystery is really there, that a mystery really stands before us, present in the visible thing.

But what purpose is served, the question may be asked, by these subtle refinements and definitions of sacramental mystery?

It seems to us that such refinements and definitions would be sufficiently important and instructive even if they served only in the interest of science to develop and clarify as fully as possible the concept of Christian mystery. Their importance is increased by the fact that they make it clear that mysteries do not cease to be mysteries even when combined with visible things, and that the relation of mysteries to their opposite, the visible, duly appears only through their aid. They also bring to light the opposition and mutual relationship between faith and knowledge.

But apart from this subjective significance, the consideration of the sacramentality of many mysteries is of the greatest consequence for a deeper understanding of the entire system of the mysteries themselves.

2. To show that this is so, we have to answer the question: Why is it that in many parts of the Christian system a supernatural mystery, which is imperceptible to reason itself, is linked with natural

elements, even sensibly visible elements? Why are two such widely separated opposites joined together?

The answer to this question may be undertaken in two ways, according as we conceive the purpose of the union to be the entrance of natural and visible things into the supernatural and invisible world, or the appearance and representation of invisible and supernatural objects through the agency of visible things. Evidently the two courses must meet and affect each other. But if we wish to make our explanation more intelligible, we must consider them separately.

In the first place, why did God will that any visible object at all should be made the receptacle of a supernatural mystery? This question concerns man primarily, and with him the whole of visible nature, for it is in their favor that the mystery is given. Here the answer is simple. God willed to sanctify and transfigure not only created pure spirits, but also material nature which is visible to the senses, especially in man and with reference to man, by its union with the supernatural mystery placed in man. He wished to make not only spiritual, but also material nature His temple, and through the Holy Spirit to admit this temple to participation in a supernatural sanctity and glory. By substantially uniting the corporal with the spiritual in man, He brought spiritual and sensible nature together in the closest possible bond, in virtue of which corporal nature must have part in the supernatural elevation of the spiritual nature. But the glory with which material, corporal nature is to be invested was not meant to become immediately apparent. For the time being the supernatural is present in the natural only as a higher, heavenly consecration, and is not to reveal its resplendent beauty until later; the divine seed lies dormant within material nature, and its abounding energy will burst forth only at the end of time. In man particularly his visible body is sanctified along with his soul by the grace of the Holy Spirit abiding in him; that body possesses in this grace the seed of its future glorification, and so bears within itself a great mystery which at present we perceive only by faith.

The sacramental mystery acquires a still greater significance when the supernatural mystery not merely enters into the visible object, but makes its way to us in it and through it, and operates and communicates itself in it and through it as a vehicle or instrument. The former takes place, as we have seen, with man and visible nature, which merely receive the supernatural; the latter occurs in the God-man, who assumes His visible body to His divine person, and thereby raises it to be the bearer and vehicle of His divine power. Upon this truth rests the whole sacramental structure of Christianity. The essence of this structure consists not only in the fact that supernatural grace is given to the visible world as a hidden treasure, but that in its communication it is bound up with visible organs and instruments.

This commitment of the mystery to the visible, of the supernatural to the natural and particularly to the material, might at first sight seem to involve some debasement, and to be justifiable only on the basis of the natural imperfection of man on whom the supernatural is to be conferred, or of his degeneration which began with sin. This relation might be thought to be somewhat unnatural, and to rest upon purely medicinal grounds, as if man, a being sunk in sensuality, were in need of a sensible communication of the supernatural by reason of his very infirmity, and as if, installed in a new but salutary dependence on sensible nature, he were to be humiliated for his pride. Associated with this view is the notion that the sacramental character of Christianity is designed exclusively for fallen nature, so that such an order of things could not have found place in the original state; and that, while the sacramental character bears witness to the remarkable saving power of Christianity, it would by no means of itself, absolutely and by its very nature, pertain to a higher, more perfect economy of the universe, and of the supernatural in particular.

We are not at all inclined to deny that the supernatural institutions of Christianity have a medicinal function, an efficacy for the healing of human infirmity. We do not deny that the Son of God has come down to us in human nature, and still continues to dwell among us with His substance and power under a visible, sensible veil, in order to assist us in our weakness. Nor do we deny that our feeble powers are able to form a vivid notion of the supernatural, or even the spiritual, only under some sensible guise. Nevertheless we believe that something much deeper lies at the bottom of the whole sacramental order.

Our stand is based on the doctrine we have laid down about the mystery of the first man in his original state, and the mystery of the God-man. Already in Adam we observe a distinctive and remarkable interlacing of supernatural grace with the nature of man, even with his material side. The transmission of grace in that state was bound up with the transmission of nature. But since the generative faculty of human nature depends on the material component of that nature, and is exercised by a material act that is perceptible to the senses, grace also was bound up with the same act; grace was to come to Adam's descendants through the placing of this act, and hence in a sacramental manner, although in a fashion different from what is the case with the Christian sacraments.

The reason for this sacramental connection was evidently not to impress upon Adam's descendants, by means of a sensible act, an awareness of the grace imparted to them; at any rate this aspect is secondary. The reason must evidently be sought in the fact that God wished to treat grace as a good of the race as such, to link His supernatural fruitfulness with man's natural fruitfulness, to join both together in one harmonious whole, and thereby to give to the former a natural substratum and to the latter a supernatural consecration. Just as the material side of human nature was to have part in the supernatural transfiguration blossoming forth from grace, and grace was one day to manifest its splendor even in man's corporal nature, so, too, man's corporal nature was meant to become the vehicle for the grace in which the whole human family was to share. This is a truly imposing arrangement, from which we learn how wonderfully the divine wisdom intended to join the highest to the lowest, so that both would represent the fullest harmony of the universe in mysterious unity and mutual dependence, and so that what was high would display its mighty energy in what was low, and the low in turn would be raised from its native lowliness to share in the power of the high. Such was the sacramental character of the first man's original state, and such its sublime meaning.

The order established by the God-man must evince a sacramental character in a still higher sense, and for much weightier reasons.

That in the God-man a divine person should assume visible nature and take His place among men in human shape, has its motive not alone in the fact that man would thereby be enabled to know and love his God more easily under such visible form, but still more in the fact that this divine person wished to reveal Himself to the outer world in fullest measure, and to enter into the closest possible union with the whole human race. Further, it is only this entrance into visible and corporal human nature that enabled the Son of God to acquire a mystical body, which He did by uniting Himself with a race whose unity is essentially connected with its corporal nature, and by taking this whole race to Himself. As the corporal nature assumed by the Son of God is the necessary condition of His unity with the race, and this unity in turn is the foundation of the highest elevation of the race and hence of its participation in the supernatural, mysterious power of its head, so it was most fitting that the mysterious power of grace possessed by the Son of God should come to the race through the vehicle of His bodily humanity. Such relegation of the power of grace to a bodily vehicle is understandable. But we must go further and add: this connection, far from debasing grace or its recipient, was naturally adapted to honor and glorify both together incalculably more than they would have been honored and glorified without such a connection. For surely grace is most glorified when it is communicated in consequence of an inexpressibly intimate, personal relationship with God, whose very nature is poured out in it; and never is the recipient of grace more honored than when he is showered with divine favors not as a stranger, but as a member of the only-begotten Son of God.

The sublime union of God and His power of supernatural grace with visible, material nature is therefore brought about through the sacramental character of the God-man. For His flesh houses the fullness of the Godhead, and thus becomes a *caro vivificans*, a life-giving flesh, from which supernatural life flows to us. Naturally the flesh itself is marvelously transfigured, since it is the bearer of a supernatural power; and in Christ it is transfigured immeasurably more than it was in Adam. In Adam it was no more than the conductor of the power of grace, and there was no essential, substantial connection between the two. But the flesh of the God-man is, so to speak, a member of His divine person, and so becomes a real organ of the person in His supernatural acitivity.

If, then, Christianity is solidly sacramental in its foundation, and if it is precisely this sacramentality which brings out the full supernatural, mysterious grandeur of Christianity, the whole structure erected on that foundation must bear a sacramental stamp. If the

Son of God has come into contact with mankind in visible flesh and has committed His wonderful power to this flesh, His continuing presence here below and His substantial union with the whole of mankind, as well as His entire supernatural activity in our race, must be carried out in a sacramental manner. Otherwise the edifice would not correspond to its foundation, and the growing tree would deviate from the design and tendency contained in its root.

As the Son of God by His incarnation made His bodily unity with the race the basis of His supernatural unity with it, so likewise He had to crown this latter unity by bringing the first unity to its highest perfection. This He did by substituting Himself for bodily foods, which He changed into His flesh and blood. And as He conferred so remarkable a fruitfulness on His own flesh, so He had to extend this fruitfulness from His flesh to His mystical body, the Church, and to the material elements it uses. Thus the deifying, supernatural power of the God-man, which was to elevate and transfigure both man's spirit and his body, descended into the depths of corporal, material nature, in order to permeate and glorify the spirit by embracing it from both sides, from above and from below. Material nature, which ordinarily tends to draw the spirit itself down from its native eminence, was raised so high by the Incarnation that henceforward, endowed with divine energy, it was to cooperate in effecting the supernatural elevation of the spirit. So great was the blessing which the incarnation of the God-man shed over matter, that the flesh could become, and was made to become, the vehicle of the Holy Spirit. And the earth, to which man owes his bodily origin and his bodily nourishment, could become, and was made to become, his spiritual mother, while earthly elements were changed into spiritual, supernatural foods for him.

Such, if we are not mistaken, is the lofty idea we must have of the sacramental structure of Christianity, and of the nature and meaning of the sacramental mysteries themselves.

It will be observed that this sacramentality, or, in plain words, the real union of the supernatural with corporal nature, is itself a very great and very august mystery; it by no means explains away the mystery, or detracts from the supernatural significance of the mystery. This will become still clearer as we go on to consider in greater detail the sacraments of the Church in their stricter sense.

82. MYSTICAL NATURE OF THE SACRAMENTS OF THE CHURCH

By the sacraments of the Church in the narrower sense we under·stand those external signs by which the grace of Christ is conferred on us and is signified to us. This definition connotes the underlying truth that the sacraments involve a great mystery, and consequently that in their proper character as sacraments they are great mysteries.

If the sacraments were nothing but purely symbolic rites by which invisible things are represented, or if they were simply social acts and signs by which enrollment in the Church, admission to its functions, and the like, are effected, as in other human societies, they would in no way possess a mysterious character.

Nor would this be the case even if we considered the Church as a religious society founded by God, but prescinding from the supernatural elevation of its members to participation in the divine nature. Such a society might even be authorized to remit sins in the name of God by means of external, official acts, to reconcile its members with God, and to confer on them a documented right to assistance and aid on the part of God. But who would find anything mysterious in all this? Among men, too, offenses are forgiven, privileges distributed, and rights conferred by external acts. In such a view the sacraments would line up in the same way, for example, as the anointing of David as king, which, performed by divine order, imparted to him the royal dignity and at the same time brought with it the aid of God for the discharge of his duties. Even the application of the merits of Christ through the sacraments would not under these circumstances invest them with a mysterious character. Such an application would consist only in the official distribution of the rights and claims that Christ has merited for us. In this there would be nothing remarkable other than the fact that the merits of the God-man really are available for us. These merits, as we have pointed out, could not, on account of their superabundant riches, be restricted to a mere forgiveness of sins and a renewal of a natural ethico-religious life in man.

According to such a conception the sacraments would be more than mere signs for the vivid representation of an invisible thing; they would possess a true causality. But this would be only a moral causality, both in regard to its effect, which would be a mere moral relationship, and in regard to its mode of operation, which in the case of such an effect could be no other than purely moral. Nothing particularly extraordinary, nothing mysteriously great, will be apprehended in this.

The rationalist may take pleasure in thus brushing aside the supernatural. But according to Catholic conviction the supernatural must be firmly retained, at least to the extent that the effect to be achieved through the medium of the sacraments, sanctifying grace, cannot be a mere moral relation to God, but must be something altogether real, something mystically real. For it is a participation by man in the divine nature and the divine life. This effect cannot be attained through a simple approval of a man by God, but only through a real, supernatural intervention and operation of the Holy Spirit with all His divine and tremendous power.

However we may prefer to conceive the cooperation of the sacramental signs and their ministers in the production of grace in the soul, whether we would have the power of the Holy Spirit flow through them or would have it drawn down by them as pledges of Christ's merits, this much is certain: in the production of grace through the instrumentality of the sacraments an eminently real and miraculous divine activity of the Holy Spirit is in operation. Hence it is also certain that no purely moral power, but a hyperphysical power and efficacy of an extraordinary nature must in some manner or other be associated with the sacraments themselves, that is, the outward signs.

Accordingly we must undoubtedly think of the sacramental rites as occupying at least as high a plane as those outward actions, for example, words and touches, by which the saints were empowered by God to work external miracles in the sensible world, such as healing and raising from the dead. Whether the saints themselves and their outward actions cooperated in these miracles and how they did so; whether by their persons they merely merited the effect produced by God's grace, and by their outward actions they transferred their merits to the recipient of the miraculous effect, or whether the power of God passed to the recipient through them and their actions: this is a question about the way the miracle was worked through their agency. The reality of the miracle itself depends on the fact that the effect can be produced only by divine power; the actions of the saints are works of truly miraculous efficacy, but only in the sense that the production of the miracle, and therefore also the miraculous power, is in some way connected with them.

The miraculous power connected with the sacraments is still greater. What they produce is not a visible work in sensible nature, but an invisible work in the spirit of man, an effect absolutely and essentially supernatural, namely, participation in the divine nature and the divine life. In the case of miracles as ordinarily understood, supernatural power manifests itself in a visible effect. But here the effect is a profound and lofty mystery. Hence the sacrament itself, as concerns the mysterious power bound up with it, must be a sublime supernatural mystery.

Having already devoted sufficient discussion to the foundations of this connection, we can now with greater ease determine its nature more accurately.

It is acknowledged that the connection of the supernatural power of the Holy Spirit, the Spirit of Christ, with the organs of the Church has ties of close relationship with the Incarnation of the God-man and His union with the members of the race. By reason of His divine dignity, Christ, as head of the race, has truly merited all the gifts of grace for mankind. But His merits are applicable to individual men only on condition that they actually enter into possession of the right to grace which objectively has already been acquired for them. Christ wished to bring this about by means of external actions performed in His Church and in its name; to these actions He attached the communication of His merits. That is to say, as head of a mystical body which is likewise a visible body, He wished to summon men to fellowship in His honors and rights as members of this body. Therefore, to proceed in orderly fashion, He had to make the communication of His gifts dependent on the condition that men would become members of His mystical body by outward acts, or as members of it would enter into a special relationship with Him as their head. By virtue of such actions men were made worthy and were entitled to receive the divine power of grace in the keeping of the Holy Spirit who proceeds from their head. The merits of Christ descend to us through such actions, and draw the vitalizing grace of the Holy Spirit down upon us.

This is the so-called moral causality, or better, cooperation, of the sacraments in the communication of grace. In other words, the sacraments communicate grace to us in virtue of the moral value they possess by the fact that they are administered in the name of Christ and apply His merits. Even if the efficacy of the sacraments were restricted to the production of grace by this moral causality, the mystery would still be very great. That merit should be applied to us by means of sensible actions is not in itself so remarkable. But in the present case the greatness of the merit applied, and therefore the value of the action in which it is contained, is inexpressible, inconceivable. Indeed it is so great and sublime that the Holy Spirit Himself is thereby drawn down, and the highest good outside of God, the grace of divine sonship, is conferred on man.

Nevertheless, it seems, such causality does not bring out the efficacy of the sacraments to its full extent. Regarded as moral causes, the sacraments would hardly be real instruments of the grace-producing power of Christ and the Holy Spirit; they would rather be instruments employed by Christ to make us worthy of the grace to be received. We could not with any appropriateness say that the Holy Spirit works through the sacraments; strictly speaking, we should have to avow that the sacraments work upon the Holy Spirit to induce Him to exercise His sanctifying power. But the first of these two alternatives, that the Holy Spirit works through the sacraments, is too strongly emphasized in the language of Holy Scripture and the Fathers to permit of our overlooking it or explaining it in a moral sense. Moreover, the relation of the God-man to us, as outlined earlier, supplies a weighty argument for such causality, and at the same time seems to furnish a satisfactory explanation of the matter.

In His humanity the God-man has brought to the human race the fullness of His divinity; and along with His own person He has brought the Holy Spirit proceeding from Him. Not only by the merits of His humanity, but by the hypostatic union of His humanity with His divinity, He has brought the latter and the Holy Spirit down upon our earth. Thus the divine power comes to us in the humanity of Christ, and also through it, for it is the organ of the divine power. As this power reaches us through an organ closely connected with it, so it can and will spread over the whole race, and come to each individual, through other organs that are connected with that organ. The external actions of these organs, to which their efficacy is attached, are therefore not merely pledges assuring us of such efficacy, but are true vehicles of the power flowing into the members from Christ, the incarnate divine head. Hence their operation resembles that by which Christ permitted His miraculous power to go forth from Him through His outward actions, His words and touches. Such a connection is no doubt wonderful and inconceivable in the highest degree. But such it must be; it can and must be a mystery, because its foundation, the Incarnation, is the mystery of mysteries.

This manner of conferring grace through the sacraments is usually referred to as the physical causality of the sacraments. This does not mean that the outward sign contributes to the sacramental effect by its own nature. Rather it means that the outward sign is the true vehicle of a supernatural power that accompanies it or resides in it. Such causality is termed physical only in opposition to the moral causality exercised by merit. As it is in itself, it might better be called hyperphysical.

In the case of the Eucharist this cannot be contested, since the real union of Christ's humanity with ours must be of some real consequence. As far as possible we must hold fast to the same truth for the rest of the sacraments, seeing that they participate in the sacramental character of the Eucharist, and together with the Eucharist constitute a single great sacramental organism. It is clear that the sanctifying power of the Holy Spirit is present in the Eucharist quite otherwise than in the other sacraments. There it resides personally and substantially, in the life-giving flesh of the Word; in the other sacraments, which are merely actions, it cannot abide in this way, it can only be directed to the recipient by means of these actions while they are being performed. But it seems that we may not lightly deny this virtual, transitory union to them, without completely dissociating them from the Eucharist.[2]

However, let this be as it may. In any case we must cling to the truth that the Holy Spirit's supernatural power of grace, which goes forth from the God-man, is in some way connected with the sacraments of the Church. For by the reception of a sacrament the recipient enters into a special relationship with the God-man as his head, and by virtue of this relationship must also, as a member, share in the power of his head.

Such, in general, is the notion of the mystical nature of the Chris-

[2] See also sect. 68 above, and pp. 579 f. below.

tian sacraments, on which depend the inner structure of each sacrament, as well as the harmonious union and mutual relationship of
them all to one another, and also the mystical organization of the
Church itself. Let us go into the matter with somewhat greater
attention to detail.

83. The Inner Structure of the Individual Sacraments and Their Relation to One Another

The mysterious character just mentioned varies with the individual
sacraments. If we focus attention on their common effect, the supernatural grace which theologians call the *res sacramenti*, a mystery
hidden under the visible sign, we can discern no essential difference
among them. But the relations to the great sacrament of the God-
man in which the several sacraments place us and by which they
confer their common *res*, are essentially different in the various
sacraments. With reference to those relations, the common *res* takes
on a manifold significance and function.

First of all, leaving the Eucharist aside, we distinguish in the
remaining six sacraments two classes, those that consecrate and those
that heal. In the first class we enumerate baptism, confirmation,
holy orders, and matrimony; in the second class, penance and extreme unction.

1. We call sacraments of the first sort consecratory, because
they dedicate us to a supernatural destiny, and assign us a special,
permanent place in the mystical body of Christ.

By baptism we are received into the mystical body of Christ, and
thus are consecrated as members of Christ. Through this sacrament
we acquire for the first time a share in Christ's supernatural life. In
it we are born as children of God; at the same time, as members of
Christ, we are destined and obligated to glorify His heavenly Father
along with Him in a supernatural manner.

That we may become virile children of God and strong, energetic
members of Christ, confirmation is added as a sort of complement
to baptism, in order to attach us still more closely and firmly to
Christ, to confer on us a still higher consecration, and also to permit
supernatural grace to flow over us from Christ in richer abundance.
With this sacrament the supernatural consecration and rank of the
individual, simple members of Christ's body reach their perfection.

However, there must be some members who will represent the office and the functions of the head in the Church, and who with Christ and in His stead will be supernatural mediators between God and man. They must enter into a very special union with Christ, and receive a special consecration; and by this union and consecration they must share pre-eminently in supernatural grace. This is effected by holy orders, a sacrament which is a consecration par excellence, because it invests the recipient with the most sublime and holy function that is possible on earth.

Finally, those members of the body of Christ who unite with each other for the propagation of new members have a special supernatural place in the body of Christ. For, although Christ has reserved to Himself and His Church the rebirth of men as children of God, matrimony among Christians has essentially the end of procreating children exclusively for the body of Christ, to which husband and wife themselves belong. Christian parents accomplish this purpose by bringing into the world holy children,[3] that is, children marked for holiness. Hence the Christian marriage bond is necessarily more than an image of the mysterious union between Christ and the Church; it is also an organ of this union, and has to cooperate for the attainment of the same supernatural end, the propagation of God's children. Thus Christian marriage possesses a supernatural consecration by its very nature. The married couple are consecrated to God in a special way, and accordingly enter into a special union with Christ and His life of grace.

This consecration which the sacraments of the first category confer is, even apart from the grace which it brings, more than a moral relationship in the case of most of them; for it is bound up with a real, supernatural sign which the sacrament produces, and which really assimilates and unites us to Christ in supernatural fashion.[4] In the first three consecratory sacraments this sign is the mark or character of Christ, which is stamped on the soul as the seal of its special union with Christ. In matrimony alone a seal thus impressed on the soul would be out of keeping with the nature of the consecration. For on the one hand matrimony is not so much the consecration of one person as a consecrated union of two persons; and this

[3] Cf. I Cor. 7:14.
[4] This sign is the *sacramentum simul et res,* the "spiritual adornment" spoken of by the older Scholastics.

union, as we shall see later, receives its holiness from the holy character of the united persons. On the other hand matrimony receives its proper, characteristic seal in its consummation. For matrimony, according to the Apostle's teaching, is an image of its model, the union of Christ with the Church, in the oneness of the flesh; and this fact, too, accounts for the absolute indissolubility of its consecration, just as, in the case of the other consecratory sacraments, such indissolubility is bound up with the indelible character.

All of the consecratory sacraments confer supernatural, spiritual grace and oneness of life with God. But they do so in a manner that varies; for each of them places us in a specific relationship to Christ and His Church, and thus imparts to us a consecration that differs with the different sacraments. The divine grace associated with Christ and His Church is one; but it becomes our portion in different ways, according as in the organism of the body of Christ we are variously called to take part in the dignity or offices of the head, and consequently to share in the fullness of His grace to a greater or lesser extent. On the one hand the consecrations are differing titles to the grace to which they lay claim; on the other hand this grace varies with the different consecrations, so that with the aid of such grace we are enabled and obligated to measure up to the various ends imposed by the consecrations. On the basis of this double relationship to the consecration with which grace is connected, the grace corresponding to the several sacraments is called sacramental grace.

2. The consecration involved in the sacramental character or in the marriage bond properly constitutes the specific element in these sacraments. It is also the immediate and proximate effect of the sacraments, without which the sacrament could not exist at all or be *ratum*, valid; whereas it can exist, as far as its essence is concerned, even if at the time the sacrament is administered grace is not produced on account of some obstacle set up in the recipient. Accordingly the consecration occupies a middle position between the external sacrament and the *res sacramenti*. Hence, as theologians say, the consecration is *res simul et sacramentum: res* with respect to the external sacrament, by which it is signified and effected; *sacramentum* with respect to the grace to be produced, because this grace is dependent on the consecration, and is also to some extent signified by the real character impressed.

The distinction between *sacramentum, sacramentum simul et res*, and *sacramentum tantum* was originally applied by the medieval theologians to the Eucharist; later it was extended and made to apply analogously to the other sacraments. The distinction appears most clearly of all in the Eucharist, and springs spontaneously from the very nature of things. The outward sign of the Eucharist, the species of bread and wine, does not proximately and immediately contain and signify grace, but the body and blood of Christ, just as partaking of the sign signifies and is the partaking of the body of Christ and effects our union with it to form one body. It is only through the body of Christ and our union with it in one mystical body that its fullness of grace is communicated to us, and we share in the divine life coursing in it. In the Eucharist, therefore, the body of Christ is *sacramentum simul et res*. This fact enables us to perceive clearly the sacramental character of the Eucharist and the manner in which grace is imparted to us by this sacrament of sacraments. Since the other sacraments must produce grace in some similar way, a transfer of this distinction to them is well fitted to lead to a deeper understanding of them.

Many theologians have followed this procedure. However, attention was not always focused sharply enough on the profound and general import of the distinction, and thus a good deal of disagreement arose concerning the identity of the *sacramentum simul et res* in the other sacraments. As is clear from the foregoing, it consists in a special union with the God-man as head of His mystical body by which participation in the spirit, that is, in the divinity and the divine life of the God-man, is granted to us on the basis of a special supernatural title, and for a special supernatural end.

In the Eucharist grace is imparted to us by our real union with the substance of the body of Christ concealed under the external sacrament. Similarly grace is conferred in baptism by the membership in the body of Christ which the baptismal character entails; in confirmation by the consolidation of this membership which the sacrament effects, and which imposes on us the duty of manly strife at the side of Christ and for Christ; in holy orders by the elevation which its character imparts to us as organs of Christ's priestly functions; in matrimony by the creation of the sacred union of husband and wife with each other and with Christ for the purpose of extending His mystical body. And thus in these consecratory sacraments the *sacramentum simul et res* is the character or the sacred matrimonial bond, just as in the Eucharist it is the substance of Christ hidden under the external sacrament.

Accordingly the consecratory sacraments are truly supernatural, and hence mysterious in their power and effects, in a twofold way: first, because they produce and virtually contain supernatural grace, and with grace the principle of supernatural life and oneness of spirit with the Godhead; secondly, because they confer a supernatural consecration which elevates the recipient above his nature to an eminent position in the mystical body of Christ.

3. Somewhat different is the situation with those two sacraments which we have called medicinal. They do not raise the subject to a new supernatural rank and destiny in the body of Christ. Their immediate purpose is properly the expulsion of evil and of all that is connected with evil from the subject. But the way in which they accomplish this brings out their specifically supernatural character. They banish sin and its consequences precisely so far as sin is an obstacle to supernatural grace and is the very opposite of grace, and an evil which defiles not a mere man but a member of Christ, thus impeding that member in the exercise of his functions and the attainment of his goal. By their very nature they presuppose in the subject upon whom they work a supernatural place in the body of Christ, and hence work upon that subject from the standpoint of his organic union with the head. They heal Christ's member as such, either by re-establishing the living union with the head that had been destroyed, or by readjusting the existing union which had been impaired by venial sins, or by protecting the imperiled union, or lastly by assuring safe passage into eternity in the final decisive conflict.

The sacrament of penance has chiefly the first two of these effects, and the sacrament of extreme unction has the last two. In both of them we can determine their specific and supernatural character and their inner organization somewhat as we do in the consecratory sacraments, by means of a factor that is at once the *sacramentum* and the *res sacramenti*.

In the sacrament of penance this factor consists in the judicial remission of the unpaid debt in the sense of *debitum satisfaciendi*, or obligation to satisfy, which is an impediment to grace. Such remission implies the sinner's repentance. It also implies the application of the satisfaction of Christ the head, whereby the right to recovery of grace is conferred. It does not imply the granting of a new title to grace, but the annihilation of the opposing title and the resuscitation of the existing title, in virtue of which grace is communicated just as though a new title had been granted. The cancellation of the debt, as also the return of grace, is rooted in the character of the member of Christ, on the strength of which that member can do satisfaction himself and participate in the satisfaction of Christ, as well as share in Christ's merits and the power of His grace.

In the case of extreme unction it is more difficult to fix the *sacramentum simul et res*, the hub of the sacraments, for the reason that this sacrament has points of resemblance with the consecratory sacraments as well as with penance. It is a complement or supplement of the sacrament of penance, since its function is to remove the remnants of sin and its consequences, and, if need be, even grievous sins. It has a similar relationship to confirmation, since it is to prepare the recipient for the last and most momentous conflict of all, and equip him for gaining the all-important, decisive victory. If this last aspect is held to be predominant, as seems to us more correct, and if the effacement of the remains of sin is regarded as included in the preparation for the final conquest over sin and death, the *sacramentum simul et res* would be found in the consecration imparted with a view to this conquest. Such consecration would then, as is the case in baptism, imply purification from sin on the one hand, and on the other would involve grace along with the power necessary for victory.[5] The cancellation of the debt does not take place in the manner of a judicial process, as in the sacrament of penance, but in the form of a gratuitous cleansing, although it supposes sincere repentance, as in baptism, and also the firm purpose to make satisfaction and, where possible, to submit to the tribunal of penance. But the consecration mentioned above is not to be conceived as though Christ assigns to His member a new position, or a new, permanent function or office in His mystical body. It consists in this, that for the period of the crisis and peril Christ enters into a special relationship with His member in the position already occupied by the latter, so that he may hold his ground and triumph

---

[5] Accordingly extreme unction is predominantly a medicinal sacrament, for it consecrates the recipient only for victory over his own spiritual weakness and corporal illness.

over the obstacles standing in the way of the attainment of his goal. Hence extreme unction does not impress a sacramental character any more than matrimony and penance do; rather it has ties of relationship, although otherwise than matrimony and penance, with the character of baptism or confirmation.[6]

The medicinal sacraments, like the other sacraments, are essentially supernatural and mysterious, not only as regards their ultimate effect, sanctifying grace, but also in their inner structure and in the way they produce this effect. It is true that they forge no new organic bond with Christ, since they impress no character; nevertheless their entire efficacy is based on the character existing in the recipient or in the minister, and is therefore grounded upon and made available by the mystical organization of the body of Christ which the character implies, and is directed to the sanctification of the life that flourishes in that organism.

Although matrimony inaugurates a new holy state, it does not impress a new character, but rather derives its high supernatural import and the power of its grace from the character already present in the contracting parties. Hence this sacrament lines up with the medicinal sacraments as far as its inner structure is concerned. Further, since in matrimony the persons are not sanctified by their union, but the union is sanctified by the persons, the state which it intro-

---

[6] The *sacramentum simul et res sacramenti* in the case of the medicinal sacraments, somewhat as in the case of the consecratory sacraments, has so close and definite a relation to the *res tantum* (sanctifying grace) that even if, on account of some obstacle interposed by the recipient, grace is not produced, these sacraments can realize their proximate specific effect, and hence can be valid, even if they confer no grace. With regard to extreme unction this follows from the fact that the sacrament cannot be repeated during the same critical period of the illness; but surely we are not to suppose that a person who lacked the right disposition at the time of the reception is deprived of the sacramental grace if later on he rids himself of his defective disposition. As concerns penance, many excellent theologians are of the opinion that if a person who is burdened with a number of grave sins, remembers and hence confesses only some of them, but with a sorrow that cannot avail for the forgotten sins because its motive is the specific hatefulness only of those he recalls, the confessed sins are really remitted in virtue of the sacramental absolution, in the sense that God no longer looks upon them as titles of guilt which exclude the sinner from His grace. Of course, since the other sins are not included in the contrition, grace cannot be restored; and the remission itself cannot be complete, because it does not involve the recovery of God's friendship. Cf. Lacroix, *Theologia moralis*, lib. VI, no. 675.

duces is not a constitutive element in the mystical organism of the Church, but is only its offshoot.

4. To gain a deeper insight into the inner organization of the sacraments and the manifold forms in which it is manifested, we must (leaving the Eucharist out of account) distinguish two classes of sacraments: those which imprint a character, or the hierarchical sacraments, and the non-hierarchical sacraments. Hierarchical are those which, because of the character they imprint, build up the membership of Christ's mystical body and, by thus building up the body, draw the powerful graces of the head to the members concerned. These sacraments are baptism, confirmation, and orders. Non-hierarchical are those which, on the basis of the membership in the body of Christ effected by the character, transmit grace from the head by a special appointment to a definite function or office, or by removal of the impediments to grace. These sacraments are matrimony, extreme unction, and penance. The first three effect a real elevation of the recipient to a supernatural, organic unity with Christ, whereby unity of life with Him is conferred. The last three operate on the basis of this elevation and, with a view to the various relationships that may have been contracted, bring about the entrance of the recipient thus elevated into a special communication with the head. It is on the ground of the recipient's organic union with the head that grace is granted to him for the protection, preservation, or recovery of his high dignity.

If we are not mistaken, this line of thought gives us a deeper understanding of the real causality, the so-called physical causality, of the sacraments, of which we spoke above. This type of causality is usually attacked chiefly on the grounds that it is impossible to conceive how a sensible and quickly passing action, even though it be but an instrument, can produce in the soul a spiritual, and indeed an absolutely supernatural effect, which has only an indivisible instant in which to make its appearance.

When the effect of the sacraments simply as such is in question, the *res tantum*, or grace, is primarily meant. The sacramental cause corresponding to this effect is not the outward sign alone, the *sacramentum tantum*, but also the *sacramentum simul et res*, by which the external sacrament is made a *sacramentum ratum*, a sacrament validly administered. In the hierarchical sacraments the *sacramentum simul et res* is a truly real, internal sign, inhering in the soul of the recipient. Through the external sign which is perceptible to the senses these sacraments enter into relationship with the externally visible part of the source of all sacraments, the "great mystery [sacrament] of godliness" [7] in the God-man. Similarly, through the internal sign they are made parallel and are brought into contact with the internal, spiritual element of the God-man, the hypostatic union of the visible humanity with the Logos. From this union the humanity of Christ itself and all the sacramental rites draw their sanctifying and life-giving power.

The interior sacrament is, so to speak, the soul of the exterior sacrament. The latter is raised aloft into spiritual regions by the former so that it may be able to produce grace, and remains operative in the interior sacrament even after it has ceased to exist in itself. Further, just as the internal sacrament, which endures permanently, carries on the effect of the external sacrament with which it comes into existence, so in the case of those external sacraments which do not imprint a character, the internal sacrament can establish the point of contact which makes them capable of producing grace. The *sacramentum simul et res* pertaining to these latter sacraments is not a sacrament in the narrow sense, nor is it properly a *res;* it is no more than a moral relation, such as a state of freedom from sin, the marriage bond, or the resoluteness necessary for the last conflict. Consequently, if a real link between the external sacrament and grace is to be postulated in these sacraments, it must be situated in the character imprinted by the hierarchical sacraments.

On this supposition the activity by which the God-man produces grace is transmitted to the recipient directly and primarily by the character, and by the external sacrament only so far as it is connected with the character, with which and through which it operates as an organic unit. Of course the production of the character itself is not to be regarded as an effect of the already constituted sacrament; rather it is an effect which Christ, who cooperates with the sacrament and administers it, produces to round out and complete the external sacrament. Christ Himself effects the organic connection between the outward sign and the character.

It is clear that the structure of the various sacraments, and the organizing of them all into a unified system, are very closely connected with the inner structure and organism of the great mystery of

[7] Cf. I Tim. 3:16.

the Church. The sacramental nature of the Church as the mystical body of Christ is reflected in the sacraments; and the sacraments in turn form and sustain the organism of the Church, and make possible the circulation of its life-giving forces. The substantial sacrament of the Eucharist is the heart of the Church; but the sacramental functions are the arteries of the Church's life, and the organs by which the members of the body are formed and kept together in their manifold relations to the divine head.

It is no less clear that all the sacraments, like the Church itself, have an absolutely supernatural nature and mystical import. The Church itself can scarcely be regarded as the restored or healed body of the first Adam. It is the body of the new heavenly Adam put on by the Son of God Himself, a body which by its union with Him is raised infinitely high above its original condition, to say nothing of its purely natural condition. Likewise the sacraments of the Church, which in varying degrees elevate Adam's race and bring it into union with this body, as they also impart life within the framework of the same body, must be altogether supernatural and mysterious, and must unfold a supernatural activity which not only heals but elevates and glorifies nature.

It should not appear strange that in our general treatment of the sacraments we have laid such stress on their supernatural elevating causality rather than on their medicinal function, and have applied the term "medicinal" to two sacraments alone. This in no way con-tradicts the conventional presentation, in which all the sacraments are looked upon as healing agents for infirm humanity. The re-establishment of the supernatural order and the strengthening of the spirit against the tyranny of concupiscence counteract the condi-tion of ruin and confusion which has come over man as a result of original and personal sin. Hence all the sacraments, even the great *sacramentum pietatis* in which they are rooted, are an antidote against the poison of sin, which by its pestilential vapors has suf-focated supernatural life and corrupted natural life. Our illness is not a mere weakening of the higher life, but involves a true death of the soul which must be overcome by a formal regeneration. More-over, Christ wished not simply to restore what was lost, but to consolidate and crown in Himself the possession of the original gift, and therefore to build up an entirely new, higher order of things upon Himself as cornerstone. Therefore the sacraments can cure us only by enrolling us in this higher order and enabling us to draw a wholly new, heavenly life from it. They must heal by elevating and transfiguring. Only the sacraments that correct the destructive anomalies in the already constituted order correspond fully to the notion of a healing agent. This is so because, in the supernatural sphere, they perform the same function as medicine in the natural sphere, and operate in a similar way.

84. Mystical Nature and Significance of the Sacramental Character

The doctrine discussed above involves the consequence that the sacramental character is of exceedingly great and far-reaching importance in the sacramental organism of the Church. In referring to the character as sacramental, we should not restrict our concept of it to the fact that it is produced by some of the sacraments. We must realize that in the sacraments by which it is produced it is the center of their entire causality and significance, and that in the others it is the basis and point of departure of their whole activity. The character is the spiritual connection by which the external sacramental actions are drawn into the supernatural order. As *sacramentum simul et res* it is the soul of the external sacraments, and hence is a great mystery, no less than the *res* which it produces. This being so, we shall be richly repaid if we devote further study to the mystical nature and significance of the sacramental character.

1. The nature and significance of the character seem to us to come to this, that it is the signature which makes known that the members of the God-man's mystical body belong to their divine-human head by assimilating them to Him, and testifies to their organic union with Him. The character of the members must be a reflection and replica of the theandric character of this head. For, to become other Christs, the members must share in the character by which the head becomes Christ.[8] But the signature whereby Christ's humanity receives its divine dignity and consecration is nothing else than its hypostatic union with the Logos. Consequently the character of the members of Christ's mystical body must consist in a seal which establishes and exhibits their relationship to the Logos; their char-

[8] See above, sect. 51, no. 5.

acter must be analogous to the hypostatic union and grounded upon it.

We shall see that this idea is in accord with all that the Church and the sounder theologians teach concerning the character; indeed, it is this notion alone that can harmonize the various details of their doctrine. The haziness usually obscuring the concept of the character is to be referred chiefly to the fact that its relation to sanctifying grace and to the life of grace is not grasped with sufficient precision. On the other hand, the relation of the character to the mystery of grace must clearly bring out its mystical nature. Hence we wish to make this the starting point of our discussion of the subject.

The character and the grace of divine sonship have this in common, that they are both graces, that is, supernatural marks of God's favor, and that they both sanctify us. The grace of divine sonship is a mark of God's favor in the sense that the fatherly kindness of God is inseparably bound up with it, and is formally included in it, for the reason that it makes us supernatural likenesses of the divine nature; it is *gratia gratum faciens*, purely and simply. Further, it sanctifies us by formally endowing us with a holy disposition and a living union with God; [9] it is an unqualified *gratia sanctificans*. The character, on the contrary, renders us pleasing to God inasmuch as it brings out the fact that we belong to the Son of God, and sanctifies us in the sense that it confers on us a holy dignity, in virtue of which we are made worthy to share in the honor paid to the Son of God, and are commissioned to discharge high and sacred functions. In a word, it makes us pleasing to God and sanctifies us by the holiness of consecration. It is distinct from the grace present in us somewhat as the holiness which Christ's human nature formally possessed by pertaining to the Logos through the hypostatic union, was distinct from that holiness which formally consisted in the conformation of His human nature to the divine nature, and in the living union between the two.

We might say that grace is an ennobling and elevation of our nature and its activity by their glorification and transformation. But the character is an ennobling and elevation of the hypostasis, so far as it raises our hypostasis to a certain unity with Christ's hy-

[9] "Disposition" here signifies a metaphysical entity, a spiritual accident inhering in the soul as a new quasi-nature. [Tr.]

postasis, and empowers it to share in the consecration which the latter has through the divine dignity of the Logos. Although the character is not identical with *gratia gratum faciens* in the narrower sense, it cannot simply be reckoned among the *gratiae gratis datae*, because it is bestowed primarily not for the benefit of others but for the good of the possessor himself, and at the very least confers a higher consecration on him.

Despite this difference there is a close relationship and connection between the character and grace, a connection similar to that obtaining between grace in the humanity of Christ and the hypostatic union. In Christ the hypostatic union was the root from which the grace in His humanity sprang; it imparted an infinite dignity to the humanity, and guaranteed the enduring existence of this dignity. With us, too, grace springs from the character, not as though the character were the latent material that would yield grace after all obstacles have been removed,[10] but because it brings us into contact with Christ as the source of grace, as the heavenly vine whose branches we are through the character, and because it gives us a right actually to possess grace if we set up no impediment to it. The possession of grace, and grace itself, acquire a higher value because of their dependence on the character. This is true of the possession, because it is only through the character that we have grace as a good to which we are fully entitled, a good which is due to us as members of Christ. It is true of grace itself, because its pure gold is enhanced by the precious jewel for which it is a setting, and because the raiment of the adoptive child of God receives a far greater beauty from its connection with the seal of integration in the natural Son of God. But, as the character establishes and elevates grace in us by bringing us into organic union with the source of grace, it must likewise preserve grace in us and assure us of its possession for eternity. It gives us a right, as long as we are members of Christ and

[10] Oswalds' comparison [in *Die dogmatische Lehre von den heiligen Sakramenten der katholischen Kirche*] of the character with the latent principle of heat [as in the discarded caloric theory], and of grace with released heat, seems to us singularly unfortunate. For in the first place everyone who possesses grace (even without baptism) would also have to possess the character, just as whenever heat is released there must be some combustible matter which generates heat. Secondly, a principle of supernatural life, what is here called the "material of grace," would have to remain in the damned, even though it could never come to fruition; which is contrary to all theological conviction.

have not definitely forfeited our claim by our demerits, to participate in the life of Christ. It binds God's love so strongly to us that this love remains ever ready to give grace back to us even after we have trifled it away.

We note the following difference between our character and the character of Christ implied in the hypostatic union. Christ's character floods His soul with the fullness of grace, confers a simply infinite value upon this grace, and fixes it in His soul with an absolutely unshakable firmness. Our character produces in us only such measure of grace as corresponds to our capacity of reception, casts on this grace only a shadow of the infinite dignity of Him to whom our character joins us, and finally can find in the resistance of our will an impediment to the exercise of its influence. But it is clear that even with us the character is not destroyed when grace departs. The character persisting in us at the very least demands that we remain living members of Christ by grace; so that if we lose grace we tarnish the seal of our union with Christ, since we deprive it of the splendor that should normally encompass it.

2. With this observation we come to another point which is to be stressed in the character. At the same time we shall here discover new relationships to grace, and particularly to the destiny which the dignity and union with Christ sealed by the character confers and imposes upon us. That is, as members of the divine-human head we are *ipso facto* called to share in the activities to which He is called by His theandric character. This summons brings with it a fitness or authorization for participation in those activities, and an obligation to take part in them. The activity of the God-man is centered in His priesthood,[11] wherein the Logos transmits grace to creatures through His humanity, and the humanity, borne by the Logos, can and does convey to God the highest worship the creature can render.

According to the first of these relationships, the character we possess as members of Christ destines us, that is, empowers and obligates us, to a twofold participation in His sacerdotal activity. It qualifies us to accept, and obliges us to receive, the effects of the activity whereby the God-man dispenses grace in the sacraments; for the sacraments, with the exception of baptism, which imparts the character requisite to this purpose, can work their efficacy upon us only after we have been taken up into the organism of Christ's body,

[11] See above, pp. 411 f.

whose arteries are the sacraments. Secondly, the sacerdotal character in particular empowers and obliges its possessor to cooperate actively with the God-man as His organ in the office of dispensing grace. Passive participation in the distribution of grace is naturally of minor importance as compared with active participation; it is no real function, and the power to participate passively is no office in the ordinary sense. Nevertheless it requires a true authorization, as well as a special union with Christ and a configuration with Him; just as any member belonging to a body must in some way be conformed to the head and be joined to it if it is to have part in its life.

With regard to the worship that is to be offered to God, the designation or consecration which the character confers on us is obviously of far greater and more universal import. For all the characters empower and oblige us to participate, in greater or less degree, in Christ's acts of worship. Above all, the character conferred by the sacrament of holy orders so conforms the priest to Christ that he is enabled to re-enact, and by re-enacting to offer, the sacrifice of Christ, the *actio per excellentiam,* which involves the highest supernatural worship of God. But the baptismal character enables all others, if not to re-enact, at any rate to offer, this sacrifice to God as their own, as a sacrifice truly belonging to them on the strength of their membership in the body of Christ. Moreover, those who possess both characters are enabled and are called upon to offer themselves also to God as a living sacrifice, in the life of grace which their character brings with it. In this latter connection confirmation is added to baptism as its ordinary complement, and to holy orders as its ordinary substratum. Confirmation itself does not confer any new power for the performance of external acts or for participation in them; but it does corroborate the existing qualification and obligation for the carrying out of external and internal acts of worship. Hence every character anoints and consecrates us for active participation in the priesthood of Christ, that divine priesthood to which His humanity was ordained by the hypostatic union.

As Christ's divine-human character comprised, besides His priesthood, His prophetic and regal offices, we must add that in virtue of the sacramental character we, too, are called upon to share in His prophetic and regal offices, although neither the baptismal nor the sacerdotal character automatically involves the authorization to set ourselves up as spiritual teachers or rulers, particularly when there is question of juridical power that would bind others. The transmission of this purely social power, which does not directly set up a supernatural communion between God and man, cannot be attached to any special character; but it necessarily presupposes the baptismal character, and normally the sacerdotal character. Hence St. Thomas is quite right when he refers the character primarily to participation in Christ's priesthood. As the character is essentially a consecration, it is immediately ordained to the performance or reception of a *res sacra*, whereas the teaching or ruling power is restricted to the guidance of other persons, and therefore requires no special consecration on the part of him who is endowed with such power.[12]

Thus from every point of view the idea we expressed at the beginning is substantiated: that the character by which Christians are anointed and become Christians is analogous to the hypostatic union of the humanity with the Logos, which is what makes Christ what He is. Accordingly, when theologians declare that the sacramental character is a *signum configurativum cum Christo*, this is not to be understood of a similarity we have with the divine or the human nature in Christ—for this is founded on grace—but of a similarity, or better, both similarity and connection, with the stamping of the seal of the divine person upon the human nature.

3. It is true that from this point of view the character must be regarded as an extraordinarily great and inconceivable mystery. But in a body in which the head is characterized by so marvelous and inconceivable a signature, the shadow it casts upon the members of that body must likewise be something uncommonly exalted. This thought must put us on our guard against trimming down the notion of the character by restricting it to the limits of our feeble natural powers of comprehension, or in any way forming too superficial an idea of it.

a) The head receives His divine dignity and His divine priesthood, in a word, His true divine character, through so real a signature as the hypostatic union of the Logos with the humanity.

---

[12] Cf. *Summa*, IIIa, q.63, a.3. However, St. Thomas seems to us to have unduly narrowed the concept of the character, inasmuch as he regards it only as a signature attesting deputation, but does not look upon it as a seal of dignity.

Surely, then, we must receive the high dignity and the sacerdotal vocation falling to our portion as members of Christ, not by any purely external deputation or appointment, but through an interior, real impress of the signature of our head. The former is conceivable only if the head Himself were called to His higher dignity and His priesthood by a mere moral union with God, or by the simple will of God. A real distinguishing mark or seal is connected with our dignity and vocation. This connection has its ultimate basis not in the fact that the character is to make our dignity and vocation knowable to God or His angels, much less to ourselves, but in the fact that God wishes interiorly to engrave and more deeply to ground this dignity and vocation in us for His and our glorification. Thus also the grace which the character brings to us is not merely a favorable attitude toward us, but is divine life; and the Eucharistic Communion to which it entitles us is not merely a figurative, but a real and substantial, partaking of the body of Christ.

b) Secondly, we believe we must conclude that the character cannot be an arbitrary or artificial sign of the dignity and calling to which it bears witness, as is the case with external badges of human dignity. It must be a seal which by its very nature signifies the dignity to which it corresponds, a seal which really confers the dignity on the subject, and in fact raises the subject to this dignity. As long as the character is looked upon simply as a notification of appointment to certain functions, this interior relationship or union cannot be properly understood. But if it is regarded primarily as a sign of dignity, and especially as the real impress of the character by which our head possesses His divine dignity, the concept becomes much more adequate. Then the dignity and, in a secondary way, the qualification for the corresponding functions, are seen to be signified by the sealing, and also to be conferred and sustained by it, comprised in it. The sealing gives notice of our qualification for those functions only inasmuch as such qualification is imparted to us by our likeness to our divine-human head and our union with Him, both of which are contained in the impress stamped upon us.

c) Thirdly, there is no reason at all for supposing that the character is a modification of our consciousness, that is, a conviction impressed on us of our dignity and mission. Even if it were directly given for the purpose of awakening this consciousness in us, we should have to regard it, in line with the view of the Church, not as a subjective aptitude of the cognitive faculty for such consciousness, but as an objective mark by which the consciousness would be roused. But in reality the character has no immediate influence on our consciousness, for we cannot see it; we learn of its existence in the same way as we attain to a knowledge of our dignity, that is, by believing that it has been impressed upon our soul, and by the fact that in receiving the sacrament we have fulfilled the condition for its acceptance. Once this knowledge has been acquired, the reflection that our dignity and mission are so deeply and indelibly engraved in us, and shine with such luminous splendor in the eyes of God and His angels, must heighten the consciousness of our dignity and make our appreciation of it more vivid and constant.

d) In general, all those conceptions of the character which view it as an affection or quality of the faculties of the soul, whether of the intellect or of the will or both, seem to us defective. For the first and most essential element in the character is the dignity, the participation in the dignity of Christ, with which it clothes us; and this dignity directly elevates and transfigures the entire subject, the entire substance, just as in the order of grace most theologians assume, besides the transfiguration of the faculties, a transfiguration and elevation of the substance, to which they assign the dignity of divine sonship. Moreover, the character must be the point of departure and instrumental cause for the production of the whole of grace, hence not only of the virtues with which it endows the faculties, but likewise of the transfiguration which it accords to the essence of the soul. If a capacity for action is associated with the character, this capacity, so far as it is proper to the character and goes with it, consists not in an ability or disposition for the unfolding of higher vital activity in the inner faculties of the soul, but in the fact that it enables the subject to perform external actions as Christ's instrument or to receive the effect of such external activity. The character involves a capacity for the interior activity of the higher life only by reason of the grace which is bound up with it.

4. In short, we are not to think of the character as a vital faculty or a vital form that assimilates us to Christ. Rather we should say that the character is to the mystical body of Christ what the general configuration is to the members of the natural human body. This configuration is the form and structure by which the various members are fittingly accommodated to the structure of the head to which

they are to belong, and are therefore adapted, by virtue of their organic union with the head, to receive influence and life from it, as also to serve as organs for its activity. Similarity of structure is a condition for union with the head, and hence for conformity and agreement between the inner life and external activity. The organically formed and animated body gives us, on the whole, the most perfect image of the nature and significance of the mystical stamp impressed on the mystical body of Christ. A careful consideration of this figure will vividly recall to our minds all that we have thus far stated about the mystical nature of the sacramental character.

The mystery of the Church as the mystical body of Christ may be illustrated by the following analogies.

a) The members of the Church are in varying degrees conformed and joined to their head not as members of an external society, but as members of a living, organic body, by a real, inner configuration, and as such are to share intimately in the life of the head.

b) The inner organism, the hierarchical arrangement of the members in the mystical body of Christ, depends on this configuration, as is the case in a physical body.

c) In a physical body all the members are related by a common similarity and union with the head, even though such similarity and union may vary considerably. Likewise the sacramental character varies in form, according as it has to shape only the ordinary members which merely have part in the fellowship of the head, or the active members in which the head is to fight and struggle, or the special organs of the head that are to bring about and to sustain the union of the rest of the members with the head.

d) In a physical body the members are brought to conformity and unity of life with the head by the conformity of their structure and the resulting connection with the head. In the mystical body of Christ, similarly, we are raised to conformity with His divine nature and, if we have grace, to participation in His life, by the configuration and union with the divine-human head which are contained in the character.

e) In the human body one and the same soul fashions and shapes the members by its formative power, and at the same time apportions life to them. So also in the mystical body of Christ one and the same Holy Spirit stamps upon the members the likeness of their head and conveys the divine life of grace to them from the head. Although the impressing of Christ's character is properly the prototype of the impress stamped on the members, our character is called the seal of the Holy Spirit, for it is imprinted in us by Him. Grace, or charity, might more fittingly be called the seal of the Holy Spirit than the seal of Christ, because His own being, the fire of His life and love, is directly impressed therein. But there is such a close connection between these two impressions effected by the Holy Spirit that one is naturally designed to go with the other and to exist for the other; the two together constitute a single sealing and anointing. For normally the sealing contained in the character involves the sealing contained in grace, if no obstacle is present, and indeed that of the Holy Spirit Himself,[13] who comes to us with grace; the character receives its complement in grace. Conversely, it is only in the character that the grace of the Holy Spirit and the Holy Spirit Himself are closely and firmly implanted in the soul and impress their seal upon the soul.

f) Lastly, the formation of the members of the human body suffers impairment when life departs from them, and decomposition of the members results—a process that can occur only in organically constructed matter. In some such way, at least following the complete loss of the life of grace, the character, although it is not disintegrated, is robbed of its magnificent splendor, and there ensues in its possessor an unnatural disorder and disfigurement such as would be impossible without the character.[14]

Thus the mystery of the sacramental character is essentially bound up with the mystery of the Incarnation and its continuation in the mystery of the Church. Truly, it is the character which interiorly stamps and organizes the Church as the mystical body of Christ. It is the character which discloses to us the wonderful, supernatural sublimity of the sacramental order, and unites us with the great Sacrament of the God-man.

Further, the high consecration and eminent rank which the character imparts to us is, as was shown in section 83, the foundation for the supernatural significance of those sacraments that do not im-

---

[13] See above, sect. 30, no. 3.

[14] For an application of the dogmatic principles here laid down concerning the fellowship in life and activity enjoyed by Christians in the Church, see the encyclical of Pius XI, *Ubi arcano Dei* (December 23, 1922), on the cooperation of the laity with the apostolate of the hierarchy. [Tr.]

print a character. Particularly as regards matrimony, the fourth consecratory but non-hierarchical sacrament, the character is the source from which matrimony derives its whole supernatural consecration, as well as the bond connecting it with the mystical marriage of Christ and the Church, and showing that it is not merely the image, but the offshoot of that mystical marriage. In matrimony, further, the character clearly manifests the full range of its power and meaning, since it brings out the fact that those who possess it belong completely to Christ, body and soul, as His members.

We cannot follow up this line of thought without a more profound discussion of the sacramental nature of matrimony, a consideration of the utmost importance in our day. We are stressing this discussion for the added reason that in the course of it we wish to come back to ideas already mentioned.

CHAPTER XXI

Christian Matrimony

▪▪▪

85. The Mystery or Sacramentality of Christian Marriage

THE sacraments that imprint a character usher the subject into a new, supernatural state. In matrimony, too, the bridal couple enter into a new state, not in the sense that their persons receive a new consecration, but in the sense that henceforth a supernatural tie joins them together for the pursuit of a high and sacred objective. Entrance into the holy bond of matrimony brings with it sanctifying grace, just as the character does. Hence the matrimonial union itself must have a supernatural character; it must assign a definite, high position in the mystical body of Christ to the united pair, and a special vital force must flow to them from the head. The act by which the matrimonial union is contracted has a fruitfulness for grace. This fruitfulness is dependent on a supernatural, mystical, sacramental character which the marriage bond as such possesses.

Writers who treat of this point often fail in clarity. With regard to the sacramentality of matrimony, many theologians have paid no attention to the new, proper, mystical character that exalts sacramental marriage and that is the basis for its fruitfulness in the production of grace. Some have thought that marriage between Christians differs from marriage between unbaptized persons only by the fact that Christ, through a positive ordinance which does not touch the nature of the union, has attached special graces to sacramental marriage for the easier attainment of its end. In that case the supernatural holiness of matrimony would be only in the grace imparted at its contracting; it would not have its root in matrimony itself, and would be no more than an external embellishment that in certain circumstances could be lacking. The marriage union would have no supernatural character; and those who enter into it, the con-

tracting parties, would administer no sacramental rite. Consequently the contracting of marriage itself would not intrinsically
and essentially be a sacrament; only the supervening blessing which
the Church imparts in the name of Christ would be such.

If we wish to gain a clearer notion of this doctrine, we must go
back somewhat further.

1. Regarded from the purely natural standpoint, apart from all
positive divine ordination, matrimony is nothing but the fitting,
habitual union of man and woman for the propagation of the human
race.[1] The character and exigencies of this end are all that determine
the nature of the union. The sublimity of this end raises the marriage
contract above all other contracts. The demands of this end take
away from the contracting parties the power to lay down the conditions of their union according to their own arbitrary discretion.
Once they desire the end, they must enter into such relationship with
each other as is necessary for the realization of the end. The unity
and indissolubility of the bond are, as a rule, necessary for this purpose, but not indispensably and absolutely under all contingencies.
Therefore God has not in all cases insisted on these two conditions;
the absolute establishment of them rests upon the positive divine
law.

This positive divine law gives divine sanction to the conditions
of the marriage union. These conditions are usually demanded by
the end of matrimony, and are certainly required for its ideal perfection. So true is this, that from the time the divine positive law was
promulgated men can enter into no other matrimonial union than
the union thus sanctioned, and must guard its unity and indis-

---

[1] "Nature intends the race to continue: and this requires that children
shall be born and reared. This is the end for which the association of man
and woman is designed." It is the intention of nature that children, whose
condition of helplessness lasts for years, should enter into the inheritance
of their fathers, and should in turn do something for the progress of the
race. The responsibility for the rearing of the child rests upon the parents;
nature itself designates them for the office. (G. H. Joyce, S.J., *Christian
Marriage* [London and New York: Sheed and Ward, 1933], pp. 12 f.). After
the well-being of the child, in whom the race is to be continued, the well-
being of the husband and wife is designated by nature as a secondary end
of matrimony. "Each finds what is wanting to self supplied by the other"
(*ibid.*, p. 16). In connection with this chapter, a reading of *Casti connubii*,
the great encyclical on Christian marriage issued by Pius XI on December
31, 1930, will be found profitable. [Tr.]

solubility even if, by reason of peculiar circumstances, the end of matrimony should not require them.

The matrimonial union has a religious character even in view of its natural end. For there is question of bringing into the world new images of God, who are to honor and glorify God on earth from generation to generation. Therefore all the natural conditions necessary for the attainment of this end, and the union itself, have a religious basis, and the duties arising from the marriage state have, on account of this direct reference to God, a more sacred and holy character than all other natural or freely contracted obligations of men toward one another. When a man and a woman unite for the propagation of the human race, they not only assume obligations toward each other and their expected offspring, but they dedicate themselves to God for a holy service, the extension of His kingdom among rational creatures. And this dedication is all the more sublime inasmuch as the contracting parties enter into a closer union with God as the Creator of the souls of their children; God wills to extend His kingdom in them and with their aid. Hence the very end of marriage, even inasmuch as the matrimonial union rises from the consent of the contracting parties, reveals that the union itself, as well as the contract bringing it about, is a *res sacra* (in a wider sense, not in the specifically Christian sense). This alone, apart from all other considerations, is sufficient to show that the institution of matrimony is under all circumstances withdrawn from the competency of political and civil authority as such.[2]

It is because of the religious and sacred purpose of matrimony, and because of the fact that God Himself, as end and co-worker, is interested in the attainment of this purpose, that He has taken the marriage union under His own protection by positive law, as He has done with no other human relationship, and attaches a special sanction to it. The marriage union was intrinsically sanctified through this sanction; or better, the sanctity flowing from its end was completed and sealed by God's intervention.[3]

That is, for the realization of the purpose of matrimony, the procreation of children, God must directly intervene in order to

[2] I say, *as such;* for, if no properly religious or ecclesiastical authority had been established by God, we could presume that such authority is implicitly conferred by God on civil rulers, to the extent that it is absolutely necessary for the guidance of human society.

[3] Cf. Gen. 1:26-28, in conjunction with 2:18-25.

render the married couple fruitful. Hence He also willed to intervene directly in the union of man and wife which is directed to this
end, by not merely permitting them to dedicate themselves to this
sacred end and by accepting their dedication, but by positively con-
secrating them to this end by His own will, and thereby sealing
their union. Or let us put it thus: since it is only by acting as God's
instruments that the married couple can realize the end of matrimony through the exercise of their marital rights, God willed that
they should enter into the union not merely on their own authority,
but in His name.

This gave an essentially new turn to the meaning of the marriage
contract and of the marriage union itself. The good that was disposed of in the contract, the body as a principle of generation, was
reserved to God Himself as an instrument belonging to Him, as a
sacred thing, which the contracting parties could dispose of only
in the name of God. If they then proceeded to dispose of this good
in the name of God and surrendered it to each other, they could also
take possession of it only in God's name. In both respects they
could act only in virtue of the divine authority, and so henceforth
it was not so much they themselves who directly joined each other,
as God who joined them together through the intermediacy of
their consent. Consequent upon this special dependence on God in
which the married couple make the contract, the ensuing union is
necessarily withdrawn from their free disposal, even apart from
the actual exigencies of the end; God is an interested party whenever any question of the dissolution and extension of the bond arises.
His intervention unites the husband and wife more closely than they
could unite themselves; by making their union dependent on Himself, He has strengthened it and rendered it incapable of being shared
and dissolved. Of course, He is quite at liberty to permit it to be
shared and dissolved, if special reasons warrant. But under no circumstances can man by his own power, without divine authorization, dissolve or otherwise modify the union which he has contracted
in the name of God. "What God hath joined together, let no man put
asunder." [4] Obviously, no earthly power can exercise any jurisdiction at all over the substance of matrimony, any more than the
contracting parties can, since earthly authority has disposal only
of the rights of man, but never of the rights of God.

[4] Matt. 19:6.

As is evident, matrimony thus established and endowed with such a significance differs essentially from a marital union that would rest upon a contract entered into by a man and a woman on their own authority, on the basis of the Creator's intention as manifested in the difference of the sexes and according to legal norms easily derivable from the nature of things. But despite the fact that matrimony in this new form bears the impress of a positive institution which does not grow out of creation from below, but is introduced into creation from above by a special divine decree, this higher institution appears so natural that a fitting regulation of the union between man and woman can scarcely be envisaged without it. The thought can scarcely be entertained that God would refrain from fully vindicating the special right He possesses over the body of man as His instrument in the procreation of the human race, and would allow man to dispose of it as his own free personal property, even under the conditions which the nature of the end requires.

Also the dignity of man himself seems to demand that, as he must enter into a moral union with his marriage partner prior to physical union, so he should conclude a pact with God, and become united to his helpmate through God and in God. In any case, the ideal form of union between the sexes is found in matrimony thus instituted; right reason easily perceives that this is so, and hence without difficulty accepts it as actually intended and established by God. Indeed, this ideal form so readily commends itself to reason that it is generally taken as the form immediately and necessarily intended by the Creator's will. Such confusion is all the more understandable inasmuch as that ideal form was introduced by God from the beginning simultaneously with the creation of man, and practically everywhere throughout the human race, even where most of the other positive ordinations of God have been lost, has persisted as the only legal form. Yet we believe that at least in concept it must be distinguished from the other form immediately springing from the nature of things, and hence from the purely natural law, as a perfection and elevation thereof introduced by the positive will of God.

Thus, even prescinding from any supernatural rank and destiny of the contracting parties, we know that matrimony had from the beginning a sacred, religious character. This it had for two reasons: its relation to God as ultimate end, and particularly the actual intervention of God which comes into play when it is contracted. But this kind of sacredness does not pass beyond the bounds of natural sanctity. God comes in only as the first cause and as the natural end of man. Even though He intervenes positively, He does so only for the consolidation of the natural order with reference to a natural end.[5]

Because of this sacredness, a higher meaning, and in a certain sense something sacramental, can be discerned in the acts by which matrimony is contracted. There is incurred and signified something more than a simple contractual obligation, namely, a holy, religious union and binding force. This sacramentality is analogous to that which pertains to an oath, which in the ancient classical language was even called *sacramentum*. We note that a sworn promise does not simply set up an obligation in the person promising toward the person to whom the promise is made, but also makes him responsible to God, and in God to the recipient of the promise, so that a violation of the promise takes on a sacrilegious character. In like manner the married couple bind themselves in their contract not only to each other, but also to God, and are bound to each other by God. A further analogy with the sacraments is found in the fact that an objective consecration is imparted by God to the contracting parties to equip them for His service. With this consecration is intimately connected a divine blessing that directly guarantees the assistance of God to those who are joined in matrimony, inasmuch as the legitimacy of their union confers on them a legitimate claim to the divine concurrence which is necessary for the procreation of their children. But a genuinely sacramental character in the Christian sense is not discernible in all this, because the supernatural element is still missing.

2. The contract receives a properly sacramental character only when the members who enter into it are raised to a supernatural order, and unite for a supernatural end.

This was the situation in the beginning with our first parents in Paradise. They joined in marriage as children of God for the extension of God's supernatural kingdom. Their union was not merely religious, but supernaturally holy, as well in the members whom it

[5] Hence matrimony preserves its sacred character even after the collapse of the original state, and possesses it still among pagans, Jews, and all the unbaptized.

embraced as in the end to which it was ordained, and finally in the sanction of God, who intervened not to consolidate the natural order, but to found the supernatural order.

It is not at all farfetched to suppose that an increase of personal grace was connected with the entrance of our first parents into this mysterious union. This increase of grace would not come to them as a result of Christ's *opus operatum,* but *ex opere operantis,* somewhat as now an increase of grace attends one's entrance into a religious order. But in another respect a greater blessing was bound up with the marriage of Adam and Eve than with Christian marriage: as long as both remained in the state of grace, the Holy Spirit was so intimately present in them with His supernatural fruitfulness that without further ado the children begotten by them would come into existence not as mere children of men, but as children of God. When our first parents contracted their union with each other, they also entered into union with the Holy Spirit as the principle of supernatural grace, so that He cooperated with them not only with His creative power, but with His divine generative power. Thus the Holy Spirit, the source of supernatural blessing in the consummation of the union, became also the pledge and seal of the union in its very formation.

The fruit of Christian marriage does not come into being endowed with the grace of the Holy Spirit. Therefore it might appear that Christian marriage does not possess as high and supernatural a dignity as matrimony in Paradise. However, a more accurate consideration will show that the comparison favors Christian marriage.

Marriage between Christians is as much superior to marriage between the couple of Paradise as the Christian is superior to Adam in Paradise.

What is a Christian? In baptism he is received into the mystical body of the God-man through the character of Christ which is stamped upon him, and he belongs to it body and soul. When he contracts marriage with a baptized person, not merely two human beings, or even two persons simply endowed with grace, but two consecrated members of Christ's body enter into union for the purpose of dedicating themselves to the extension of this body. Whenever their union is rightly contracted, it can have no other intrinsic aim than to beget the children they look forward to for Christ, to whom the married couple themselves belong, just as on the other hand the children begotten by them in this union are themselves destined for Christ's body and for participation in its divine life. Accordingly, in the contracting of marriage itself the contracting parties can act only in the name of the divine head to whom they themselves belong, and for whom they function as His members. In particular, they can dispose of their bodies as generative principles only with the approval of Christ and according to the mind of Christ, for their bodies are no longer their own flesh, but the flesh of Christ.[6] They can unite with each other only on the basis of their oneness with Christ; the union of each with the divine head is carried over into the union which they contract with each other. The former union transfigures and consolidates the latter.[7]

Thus the matrimonial relationship between Christians is rendered supernaturally holy from every point of view: by reason of the supernatural character of the married couple themselves, by reason of the supernatural end, and by reason of the sublime intervention of God, to whom husband and wife are so closely linked. And this holiness is greater and more excellent than the holiness of marriage in the Garden of Eden, in the same measure that a member of Christ is superior to a man simply endowed with grace, or that the extension of the mystical body of the God-man is greater than the extension of the simple order of grace, or that the union of the Son of God with us in the Incarnation is above the simple indwelling of the Holy Spirit.

This characteristic excellence of Christian marriage is generally brought out by designating it as the "sacrament" of the union of Christ with the Church, with reference to the Apostle's words in the fifth chapter of the Epistle to the Ephesians. It cannot, in fact,

---

[6] This point seems to us of supreme importance, both theoretically and practically, for a deeper understanding of Christian marriage. From the latter standpoint, particularly, it shows that even with respect to the material object of the matrimonial contract all rights of earthly authority, and all unrestrained use of bodily functions by the husband and wife for the sheer gratification of the passions, are ruled out. We base our stand on the words of St. Paul in I Cor. 6:15–20: "Know you not that your bodies are the members of Christ? . . . Or know you not that your members are the temple of the Holy Ghost . . . and you are not your own?" The Apostle immediately draws the inference, and shows what an abominable crime it would be to rob Christ of the body belonging to Him by lascivious and illicit use, and to turn it over to a harlot.

[7] For what follows, see Eph. 5:21–33.

be more profoundly and beautifully expressed; but the entire wealth of meaning in the term must be comprehended.

"This is a great mystery" [or sacrament, according to the Vulgate and the Douay Version], says the Apostle; "I mean as applied to Christ and to the Church." He is speaking of the husband's obligation to love his wife as his own flesh and bone, as Christ has loved the Church as His flesh and bone. For this reason let a man leave even father and mother, from whose flesh and bone he issues, in order to cleave to his wife and become one flesh with her, as had been proclaimed to Adam in Paradise. It is at this point that St. Paul adds: "This is a great mystery," namely, this union and oneness of a man with his wife, "I mean as pointing to Christ and to the Church," which is the force of the Greek expression, εἰς Χριστὸν καὶ εἰς τὴν ἐκκλησίαν.

The sense in which marriage is said to be so great a mystery clearly depends on the meaning apprehended in its relationship to Christ and to the Church. This relationship can be understood either as symbolic or as real. According to the first interpretation, the Apostle would depict marriage in its natural character as a symbol of the supernatural union between Christ and the Church; in that case marriage itself would not be mysterious, but would only be a figure, itself empty of content, that would serve to call up before our minds a mystery extrinsic to it, that is, the union of Christ with the Church. Hence matrimony would be the sacrament of a mystery rather than a mystery, and a barren sacrament at that. Such, in fact, is marriage between non-Christians in our day; such was marriage everywhere before Christ, even among the chosen people who still looked upon it as a divine institution, although in this case it could not be regarded as a mere symbol, for it was set up by God as a prophetic type of the union between Christ and the Church, and was therefore brought into a closer relationship with this union. Even marriage in Paradise was no more than a perfect type of this mystery, although it possessed a mysterious character; for its mysterious character was not derived from any reference to Christ and His Church, at least not in the same way as in Christian marriage.

Christian marriage, on the contrary, has a real, essential, and intrinsic reference to the mystery of Christ's union with His Church. It is rooted in this mystery and is organically connected with it, and so partakes of its nature and mysterious character. Christian marriage is not simply a symbol of this mystery or a type that lies outside it, but an image of it growing out of the union of Christ with the Church, an image based upon this union and pervaded by it. For it not only symbolizes the mystery but really represents it. It represents the mystery because the mystery proves active and operative in it.

This is the way the Apostle intends it to be understood. He does not set out to illustrate the union between Christ and the Church from the nature of matrimony. He wishes to derive the nature and duties of Christian marriage from the union of Christ with the Church as the ideal and root of Christian marriage. To be sure, such derivation could be made to some extent even if there were no intrinsic connection between the two relationships, but only an analogy. But a procedure of this sort would take all the life out of the Apostle's forceful utterance; we should not at all be able to understand how at the end he could state so impressively: "This is a great mystery." If there is question of a mere comparison with a mystery, marriage itself could not be said to be a mystery, and particularly a great mystery, except by an extravagant hyperbole. It becomes a true mystery only if the great mystery of Christ vibrantly lives, operates, and manifests itself in it.

How does this take place? The Apostle teaches that baptism makes the Christian husband and wife members in the body of Christ, members of His flesh and bone. They have already been received into the mysterious union of Christ with His Church. As members of the bride of Christ they themselves are wedded to Christ; hence the mystery of the union between Christ and the Church is found in them also. They can rightfully unite with each other in matrimony only for the end which Christ pursues in His union with the Church, that is, the further extension of the mystical body of Christ. Since their attitude must be regulated by the spirit of Christ's union with the Church, they can act only in the name of Christ and the Church; for their bodies belong to Christ and His Church, and consequently the right of disposing of them pertains in the first instance not to the earthly bridal couple, but to the heavenly nuptials. Therefore their union presupposes the union of Christ with His Church, and joins with it to cooperate with it for a single supernatural purpose. They must cooperate precisely as members of the body of Christ in His Church, and hence as organs of the whole. Hence they must unite with each other as organs of Christ's body, as organs of the whole that was brought into being by the union of Christ with the Church. Thus their union, their alliance, becomes an organic member in the grand and richly varied alliance between Christ and His Church, a member encompassed, pervaded, and sustained by this mystical alliance, and participating in the lofty, supernatural, and sacred character of the whole. The member represents and reflects the whole.

The place of Christian marriage in the union between Christ and the Church is indicated most strikingly of all when depicted as a branching out or offshoot of that union. This emphasizes the fact that the married couple, for the very reason that their marriage is based upon the marriage of Christ with the Church, are wedded to Christ in their marriage to each other, and hence that they enlarge the union of Christ with the Church at one particular point for a determined end, reproduce it in a special form, and thus supply it with a new organ for the realization of that end. Accordingly their union with each other has its roots in the union of them both with Christ; it grows forth from that union and, like the branch on the tree, is at one and the same time an extension or continuation, a replica, and an organ of it.

This supernatural union of husband and wife as members and organs of Christ's body is therefore the heart of the great mystery of Christian marriage. But, since it signifies the still higher mystery of the marriage between Christ and the Church, it is likewise the sacrament of this mystery. And since it derives its own higher excellence from the latter mystery, of which it is the organ and image, we may further say that its mystical character lies in that sacramentality. However, the notion of sacrament must be taken in its full sense; the sacrament must be thought of not as a bare symbol of the mystery, but as interiorly permeated and transfigured by the mystery, or even as intertwined and, as it were, merged with it.

Thus understood, the sacramental relation of Christian marriage to the union of Christ with His Church stands revealed in the fullness of its extraordinary sublimity, thus excelling even marriage in Paradise. Christian marriage towers above marriage in Paradise because of the higher dignity of the concurring members, the higher purpose, and the closer relation to the marriage of the God-man with the Church, which it vividly represents. This higher rank is not impaired by the consideration that the children who are the fruit of Christian marriage do not forthwith, as in the marriage of Paradise, come into existence with divine life, in the resplendent beauty of grace. For, although marriage does not straightway transmit the life of grace to its offspring, it does confer grace as a member of the organism to which it belongs, in the sense that it brings forth children destined for rebirth by the flowering in them of the heavenly fruitfulness proper to the union of Christ with the Church; for that union lives on in Christian marriage. There is no doubt that in itself Christian marriage would be far more fitted to transmit grace than marriage as in Paradise. In the latter, grace had a very precarious connection with nature; in Christian marriage the fruit issuing from flesh belonging to the body of the God-man stands by its very nature in close relationship to the God-man and His grace. We may even say that this fruit issues from the marriage of the God-man with His Church, so far as the parents cooperate for the generation of their children as organs of the God-man in His name and for His name. If, notwithstanding, the children of Christian parents are not born in grace, the reason is that the God-man wishes to consecrate each of His members individually, that He does not wish to combine His supernatural fruitfulness in the Church with natural fertility, and that He desires to bring about the rebirth of the fruit of the flesh not in the flesh, but in the virginal womb of the Church.[8]

Although the sacramental efficacy of Christian marriage is not so manifest in the transmission of grace to the children born of this union, it is clearly revealed in the conferring of grace on the contracting parties. The inhabitants of Paradise, as has been stated, could acquire grace by contracting marriage as a work pleasing to God; but grace could not flow to them *ex opere operato*. But when a Christian man and woman contract marriage they enter into a closer union with the God-man as the bridegroom of the Church who abounds in grace. He Himself receives them and consecrates

---

[8] There is no certainly known substitute for the baptism of infant children. Cf. Denz., 712. This theological uncertainty does not contradict the doctrine of God's universal will to save, or the certain truth that God does not restrict His grace to the sacraments. But it does emphasize the heavy obligation resting on parents and guardians to arrange for the early baptism of children committed to their care. [Tr.]

them as active organs in His mystical body. Thus by reason of their new rank new grace and new life must flow into them from the source of the head. This is chiefly an increase of sanctifying grace, but it also involves a right to all the actual graces they need in their new state for the fulfillment of their sublime duties.

These graces come to the married couple not *ex opere operantis* but *ex opere operato*. For they acquire such graces by acting as organs and ministers of Christ and His Church in the contracting of marriage, and by contracting it they become organs of Christ and His Church. They gain these graces by attaching themselves, in their union with each other, to the union of Christ with the Church, since in their own alliance they reproduce and expand the union of Christ with His Church. For these reasons the marriage of Christ with the Church, upon which the entire communication of grace rests, must *ipso facto* manifest its power over grace in the matrimonial union between Christians as in its offshoot.[9]

Moreover, it follows from the nature of Christian marriage that the husband and wife must love each other not merely with natural love, but with supernatural love, as members of Christ and as representatives of His mystical nuptials with the Church. They must love and honor, educate and rear, their children not only as the fruit of their own bodies, but as the fruit of the mystical nuptials mentioned, that is, as children of God. They must take the place of Christ and the Church with regard to their children, as their teachers, guardians, and models. This is a lofty, supernatural vocation, which demands all the greater graces in proportion as they who are thus called are still in the grip of the weakness of the flesh, and in view of the fact that their children, who are burdened with the same infirmity, can be brought up to the full measure of Christ's maturity only at the expense of great effort. But all these graces really come to them from the marriage, so rich in graces, between Christ and the

[9] An essential difference between matrimony and the religious vows is discerned in the fact that in marriage the contracting parties act in the name of Christ and the Church, and are entrusted with a special office in the Church. By taking religious vows, to be sure, the member of the Church is more closely wedded to Christ, and so expresses more directly and perfectly the relation of the Church to Christ, than is the case in matrimony. Nevertheless the pronouncing of religious vows is not a sacramental act; it is an act of subjective, personal dedication, and merits grace only *ex opere operantis*. The objective form of the solemn vows of religion is no more than the effect of an act of ecclesiastical jurisdiction.

Church, that marriage to which they are dedicated as organs, and which is impressed, renewed, continued, and complemented in their own union.

The fruitfulness for the production of grace possessed by Christian marriage constitutes its sacramentality in the stricter sense. But this sacramentality is founded upon its inner, mystical nature, upon the sacramentality of the marriage union, so far as it is the figure and organ of the marriage between Christ and the Church, and must therefore be defined and clarified in terms of the latter.[10]

This is what we undertook to show in the beginning. Let us now draw the important consequences.

It is radically wrong to suppose that the grace of the sacrament of matrimony is produced by some blessing distinct from the contracting of the marriage union. This is no less false than to say that the grace connected with the sacrament of holy orders is brought about not by the act by which the priest is ordained, but by a special blessing. Marriage between Christians, provided it is otherwise legal, is essentially and under all circumstances a holy, mystical union, in which the bridal couple join and are joined in the name of Christ for the extension of His mystical body. They are therefore consecrated to a sacred office, not indeed by means of a new character, but on the basis of the baptismal character; consequently if any obstacles to grace have been set up, the grace of consecration is imparted once the obstacles are removed.

The priest's blessing could be the form of the sacrament, or the priest could be the minister, only if his positive cooperation were necessary for the valid contracting of marriage. This is not an absurd supposition. Since the bridal pair can enter into a true marriage only in the name of God, and since their union rests not upon a purely contractual obligation, but also upon the divine sanction that must have its part in the ceremony, it would evidently be pos-

---

[10] This truth enables us to perceive how we can demonstrate from Eph. 5:25–32 that matrimony is one of the seven sacraments. Although the text does not formally state that matrimony has the power to produce grace, the reasons why it possesses and must possess such power are there assigned as pertaining to its mysterious character. Thus the theological exegesis of the passage yields a proof, *ex visceribus causae*, that matrimony has the power to produce grace, a proof that should satisfy us even more than if a demonstration were forthcoming that the Apostle used the term *sacramentum* (μυστήριον) in our current sense.

sible, and in a certain respect perhaps even fitting, that this divine sanction should be audibly manifested by a representative of God, and that the validity of the marriage should be bound up with such manifestation. In this case the ratification (not the mere blessing) by the priest would constitute the complement of the contract, and hence also the form of the sacrament.

In actual fact, however, neither Christ nor the Church has made the validity of the marital union dependent on any act of sanction or blessing on the part of the priest. In all ages the Church has recognized that marriages contracted without the assistance of the priest are valid, and therefore sacramental, if nothing else stood in the way. In such marriages, therefore, the sacrament is administered simply by the bride and groom themselves when they make the contract. If, then, the bridal couple can do as much without the priest as they can by calling him in, and if there are not to be two essentially different forms for this sacrament, the ratification or blessing of the priest can never be the form, and the priest can never be the minister, of the sacrament.

Accordingly the bride and groom themselves, acting as members of Christ in His name and that of the Church, contract the sacramental marriage union by their expressed consent, and thereby acquire the grace attached to the union. The matrimonial contract itself is the outward sign, the *sacramentum tantum*, by which directly the marriage union, as the *sacramentum simul et res*, and last of all the *res tantum*, or grace, are signified and conferred.[11]

[11] Many are scandalized by the assertion that the ministers of the sacrament of matrimony are the contracting parties themselves, since in the case of the other sacraments the priest is at least the ordinary minister. In point of fact, we cannot state without qualification that the bride and groom are the ministers of this sacrament. For, since the first *res sacramenti*, the marriage union, is not conferred but only entered into by them, we cannot say that the bride and groom mutually convey to each other the grace attached to the union. On the other hand, since the contracting parties act essentially in the name of Christ and His Church, their act is essentially an act of sacred ministry, which engenders a *res sacra*, the marriage union, and consequently a consecration of the contracting parties and an objective sanctification, thereby involving grace. Just as the ministry of the bridal couple in the contracting of marriage has the special feature that it is exercised by the contracting or "drawing together" of a bond, so the fruitfulness for grace with which this ministry is endowed is marked by the characteristic that the contracting of the union brings with it the grace of state, and the bridal couple gain this grace, or draw it upon themselves, by contracting the union,

As the marriage union itself is sacred, so also the contracting of it is an essentially sacred act; whereas, on the supposition that it would figure merely as the matter of the sacrament, it could be profane, just as in baptism the water, and even the pouring of the water, can be profane.[12] The latter view separates the sacredness from the nature of matrimony, by holding that it comes in from outside. Those who favor this opinion believe that they raise the dignity of the sacrament by making it dependent on the cooperation of the priest, and that they bring marriage itself into closer relationship with the Church. Actually they divest it of its essential dignity, and sever its essential relationship with the Church. Matrimony preserves its essential dignity only if the contract itself is the sacrament; only thus do matrimony and the contract stand in close, physically necessary, and living relationship with the Church. As a truly sacramental act, the marriage contract is subject to the supervision, jurisdiction, and direction of the Church.[13] In order

---

and so they also "contract" the grace. Instead of calling the bride and groom ministers of the sacrament and of grace, we ought to use more general terms and say that they are executors of the sacrament, and agents—not transmitters —of the sacramental grace.

Melchior Cano, O.P., saw in the marriage contract the "matter," and in the blessing of the priest the "form" of the sacrament of matrimony. The words of the contracting parties, he thought, cannot be the "form" of the sacrament, for in themselves they constitute a merely "profane" action. As in the other sacraments, God imparts a sacramental stamp to the form through the agency of a special minister, in this case the priest. (*De locis theologicis,* lib. VIII, cap. 5). Against this view the well-known chapter "Tametsi" of the Council of Trent (Sess. XXIV, cap. 1; Denz., 990–2) teaches that so-called "clandestine" marriages, that is, marriages contracted by baptized persons through their mere free consent, without the assistance of the priest, are true and valid marriages, so long and so far as the Church does not declare them invalid, as, with the exception of a few extraordinary cases, it does in the present marriage legislation. Cf. *Codex Iuris Canonici,* can. 1094–1103. [Tr.]

[12] To be sure, as we brought out earlier, the act and the resulting union could possess a certain holiness of themselves and in themselves, but not the specifically Christian, sacramental holiness and efficacy imparted by Christ. In the supposition mentioned in the text, both the act and the union would be objects that are to be rendered holy.

[13] All those who wholly or partially withdrew the substance of matrimony, the establishment of diriment impediments, and the like, from the jurisdiction of the Church, maintained in support of their view that the marriage contract was not itself the sacrament, but at most the "proximate matter" of the sacrament, somewhat as the acts of the penitent are in the sacrament of penance, or the pouring of the water in baptism; or else that the marriage union was only the "remote matter," the object to be sanctified by the sacra-

that its dignity may be safeguarded, it must be administered in a sacred place and with the cooperation of the priesthood of the Church, so that its inner sanctity and relationship to Christ and the Church may be outwardly manifested. The assistance of the priesthood is required not to make the marriage holy, but because it is holy. Otherwise a marriage that for no valid reason is contracted without the blessing of the Church would involve only a sin of omission, whereas, as a matter of fact, it has a sacrilegious character.[14]

Certainly it is not without significance that the theory of the sanctification of marriage through the agency of the priest has been most strenuously advocated and proclaimed by that group which exerted every effort to eliminate from the realm of social life all that is supernatural in the Church. When as yet but few theologians had defended that theory, Gallicanism and Josephinism, as well as Jansenism, which was forging spiritual weapons for both and fought in alliance with both, were embraced by such people with surprising zeal. Since the battle had the semblance of a holy war, many well-meaning and learned theologians let themselves be won

---

ment. Against them many popes, especially Pope Pius IX, proclaimed in defense of the exclusive authority of the Church, that matrimony itself is the sacrament. And in fact, if the contract or the union were nothing but the matter of the sacrament, we could infer from the power which the Church has over the sacraments, only that it has the right to decide which contracts or unions it wishes to recognize as *materia sacramenti* and to sanctify by the sacrament. At any rate, it would be a difficult task, arguing from this standpoint, to defend effectively the exclusive right of the Church over matrimony. Of course, appeal could be made to the fact that matrimony is essentially a religious alliance which, as we ourselves stated above, must be exempt from the jurisdiction of the state, even prescinding entirely from Christianity: "What God hath joined together, let no man put asunder." But it is precisely this general religious character that in Christian matrimony becomes its specifically sacramental character; and if the latter is no longer recognized as essential, it boots nothing to appeal to the former.

[14] There can no longer be any doubt that marriage between Christians is sacramental by the very fact that it is valid. Again and again Pius IX solemnly proclaimed that the sacrament is not something accessory to matrimony, that the sacrament cannot be sundered from matrimony, and that the sacrament does not consist in the priest's blessing alone. And he designated it as the teaching of the Catholic Church that the sacrament pertains so necessarily to Christian marriage that no matrimonial union between Christians can be legitimate except in sacramental matrimony. See the *Syllabus*, prop. 66 and 73, and especially the Pope's letter of September 19, 1852, to the King of Sardinia. [Cf. Denz., 1766 and 1773; also 1640 and note 2: *Codex Iuris Canonici*, can. 1012.]

over, never suspecting that they were thereby placing most powerful weapons in the hands of the enemies of the Church.

Christian marriage is inextricably interwoven with the supernatural fabric of the Church; the greatest damage one can inflict on both is to tear them apart. When such a catastrophe occurs, matrimony completely loses its high mystical character, and the Church loses one of her fairest flowers, wherein her supernatural, all-pervading, transforming power was so splendidly revealed. Nowhere does the mystical life of the Church penetrate more deeply into natural relationships than in matrimony. In this sacrament the Church clasps to her heart the first of all human relationships, that upon which the existence and propagation of human nature depends, so as to make it wholly her own and transform it into herself. The bride of the Son, who as the head of the race has taken possession of the race, makes even the natural generative power of the race serve her purpose, and claims the legitimate use of that power exclusively for her own heavenly end. Nowhere has the truth more strikingly come to light that the whole of nature, down to its deepest roots, shares in the sublime consecration of the God-man, who has taken this nature to Himself. Nowhere does the truth more clearly appear that Christ has been made the cornerstone upon which God has based the preservation and growth of nature.

If, in the Apostle's teaching, Christian matrimony as the sacrament of Christ's union with the Church, and as its image and offshoot, is so great a mystery, then that union itself, and in it the Church, is a still greater mystery. It is a mystery that has its foundation in the wonderful works of the Incarnation and the Eucharist, and so alone can fully reveal their rich significance. In the following chapters we shall come to know this mystical side of the Church still better, as we turn our attention to the fruit and the ultimate goal of the supernatural activity of the Church.

PART SEVEN

The Mystery of Christian Justification

According to His mercy He saved us, by the laver of regeneration and renovation of the Holy Ghost, whom He hath poured forth upon us abundantly, through Jesus Christ our Savior; that, being justified by His grace, we may be heirs according to hope of life everlasting.

Titus 3:5–7

CHAPTER XXII

Nature of Christian Justification

▼▼▼

86. CHRISTIAN JUSTIFICATION AS RESTORATION OF ORIGINAL JUSTICE

THE effect and the goal of the Incarnation and of the whole economy of redemption, of the Church and its sacraments, is the justification of the redeemed human race here on earth, and ultimately the admission of men into the eternal glory and happiness promised to them.

The fruit corresponding to so marvelous and mysterious a sowing must itself be a great mystery. That this is so, we have already seen to some extent, when we were discussing the significance of the Incarnation and of the Church. We found this significance to consist chiefly in the fact that these two mysteries contain the germ of a supernatural union of men with God, and hence of a supernatural sanctification and glorification of them, to be effected by the Spirit and the power of God. We can infer the greatness of the fruit from the tremendous power of the seed, just as, conversely, we can gain a correct notion of the abounding wealth locked up in the seed only by observing the greatness of the fruit.

We shall first take up the question of Christian justification. By justification we mean all that relates to the acquisition or increase of Christian justice, and all that is instrumental in making man worthy of the attainment or increase of glory in the next world. It will become clear as we go on that the true essence of the mystery, the root of its mystical character, is better expressed by the term sanctification and rebirth from God than by the word justification. We must retain the latter, however, first because it is consecrated by ecclesiastical usage, and further because it directly connotes the special aspect of sanctification and regeneration we are here considering, that is, its relation to the removal of the state of sin. Besides, one of the chief concerns of our investigation is the discovery and clarification of the mystical element at the base of Christian justification.

The mysterious character of Christian justification must be revealed especially in its product, Christian justice. For, in accordance with the product is determined the mysterious character of the process by which it is brought about, and of the causes that work together for its production.[1]

1. If the phrase "to be justified" is taken to mean no more than the adopting of a right attitude conformable to God's law, along with the remission of the former injustice committed against God implied in such an attitude, it exhibits little or nothing that is mysterious. All of this is conceivable in the case of a man who stands in no supernatural relation to God, a man in the natural order who, after abandoning by sin the rightful station he should occupy with reference to God, subsequently returns, in response to the advances made to him by a forgiving God, to that station by the repentant recovery of the disposition which is pleasing to God. In this instance justification is but the correction of a disorder that breaks out in natural man, the restoration of man from his fall to his natural level. The justice thus effected is essentially something natural, even though it does not exclude a supernatural influence on God's side. There is no trace of any elevation of man above his nature. Hence what is the very heart of a supernatural mystery is lacking.

Rationalists may discern Christian justification in such a process, or reduce it to the latter. But a Catholic theologian cannot do so without explaining away the mystery of his faith in some utterly inane fashion. If he does not wish to shatter the whole mysterious organism of Christianity, he must conceive Christian justification as an essentially supernatural, mysterious work. In the relation of justification to the supernatural mysteries he must perceive the rigorous necessity, and hence also the possibility, of retaining and apprehending its supernatural, mysterious character.

In Christian justification he discerns particularly the restoration

[1] The reader will follow Scheeben better if he substitutes "holiness and justice" for simply "justice," "to be sanctified and justified" for "to be justified," and "sanctification and justification" for "justification." Later on Scheeben himself frequently expresses the association of the two ideas. [Tr.]

of that justice which Adam possessed prior to his sin, and which he lost by his sin. But this was a supernatural justice, infused into Adam's heart by the Holy Spirit. It was the justice of sanctity, an outpouring and reflection of the divine sanctity; it was a divine justice, and not merely a human or creatural justice. The last shred of this justice had been lost; but it was to be given back to us in Christian justification. Therefore justification must be a work no less great than was the infusion of the justice of Paradise. Like the latter, it must place man in a supernatural relation to God, put him in the right state for the attainment of his supernatural end, and equip him for the life he has to lead as an adoptive child of God, worthy of his heavenly Father. But this cannot be accomplished unless man is raised above his nature and placed in the state of divine sonship; in the Holy Spirit he must, in an ineffable manner, be reborn of God as His child, and thus be made to share, like the first man, in the divine nature. In a word, Christian justification as the restoration of original justice does not endow us with a mere natural, human justice, but recovers for us the supernatural justice of the children of God, along with all the sublime privileges which were either included in that state or resulted from it.

Thus the mystery of the original state leads us on to the mystery of the state of grace characteristic of Christianity.

But for that very reason Christian justification must be considered in terms of its opposition to the mystery of sin. However, the sin that Christian justification is meant to destroy cannot be regarded simply according to its natural side, as the derangement of the natural order. Sin must here be regarded according to the mysterious character it possesses in its opposition to the supernatural order of grace, particularly the grace of the original state. In this connection the state of sin is more than a disorder of the will. It is a complete estrangement and separation of man from God as his supernatural end, and is met with on God's part not by a simple displeasure—involving disfavor in the moral sense—but by a forcible ejection from the state of the children of God, a stripping away of the supernatural raiment of grace.

To join together again the severed strands of the supernatural bond with God, no mere change of the direction of man's will can suffice. If man is to be reunited to God as his Father, God Himself must raise him up again to His side, and through the Holy Spirit must pour forth into man's heart a filial love for Himself. If the sinner is to be freed from God's disfavor, it will not at all suffice for God to cover up the sinful deed with the cloak of forgetfulness, and simply to remit the guilt in response to the sinner's repentance. To forgive the sin fully, God must again confer on man that favor and grace which He had bestowed on him before he sinned. God must again draw man up to His bosom as His child, regenerate him to new divine life, and again clothe him with the garment of His children, the splendor of His own nature and glory. Only thus can justification completely and perfectly exterminate the sin as it exists concretely in its mysterious character. Therefore justification itself, which does away with so mysterious an evil, must be recognized as a supernatural mystery. Accordingly the mystery of sin, as also the mystery of original justice, looks to justification as a third mystery, which destroys the first and restores the second.

2. If we wish to form a truly adequate concept of Christian justification, which is essentially the justification of a sinner, we have to go still further into its relation to sin.

The sin which is to be uprooted by Christian justification is not actual sin as such; for actual sin, once committed, can never be undone, not even by the greatest miracle God is able to work in the order of grace. What is to be effaced is the aftereffect of actual sin, that is, habitual sin.

In habitual sin we distinguish the guilt from the disorder: the guilt which the sinner brought upon himself by offending God, and the disorder in which the sinful act takes permanent form. Both must be removed if the sinful state is to cease: the guilt by remission on God's part, the disorder by restoration of a right orientation toward God and union with God, which here consists in the habitual state of charity and the other virtues animated and sustained by charity.

Thus the justification of the sinner necessarily comprises two factors, one negative, the remission of the guilt, the other positive, the restoration of supernatural union with God. The result of the process is freedom from guilt and the possession of sanctifying grace. The first factor is, in a way, external to the justified person—it is the obliteration of the sin from the divine memory, in the sense that it is no longer imputed. The second is wholly internal to him, for it is the renovation, sanctification, and transfiguration of his being and his life. Or, if we regard the guilt as something clinging to the guilty person himself, it is no more than a purely moral relationship to God, the obligation of compensating for the offense offered to Him; hence its remission is nothing else than the canceling of this obligation. The infusion of supernatural justice, on the contrary, produces in the sinner something more than another moral relation to God. It produces a new, ontological quality, which inheres in his soul not only morally but physically.

The real mystery of justification might seem to be restricted to the second factor. And, indeed, its full greatness is primarily and directly revealed in this factor. For the renovation in question is a true miracle, greater even than the raising of a dead man to life; man is not merely healed of an abnormal disorder in his life, but recovers the seed of a new, divine life that had completely died in him. He is transformed in all his higher faculties, to the uttermost depths of his being. He is re-created to a new existence, in which he draws near to God, and God to him, in a way that defies description.

Compared with such a miracle, the remission of the guilt, considered in itself, appears to be rather easily conceivable, and to have little of the supernatural about it, especially as it can take place outside the supernatural order of things.

For all that, the remission of guilt in Christian justification takes on a quite distinctive, mysterious character: first, because the guilt to be effaced possesses such a mysterious character, inasmuch as it results from an infringement of the supernatural order; and secondly, because its remission also rests upon thoroughly supernatural grounds, namely, the infinite value of Christ's satisfactions, by which the debt is literally paid and canceled. But even apart from this, the remission of guilt in Christian justification may not in any way be separated from the interior renewal; it is inextricably intertwined with this renewal, necessarily forms a single whole with it, and therefore shares in its mysterious character.

For if the remission of the guilt is complete, it leads, in the supernatural order, to the wonderful interior renovation which is effected by grace and charity and, as we remarked above, terminates in it. For the remission is perfect only if everything that was lost through sin is restored.

On the other hand, the interior renovation brought about by grace and charity is the reason why the guilt is not only regarded in the external forum as though it had been remitted, but is truly eradicated from the soul of the sinner.

The first of these connections between the remission of guilt and interior renovation or transformation involves little difficulty, and is generally admitted. The second, on the contrary, is ordinarily heeded but slightly; but it is precisely this which brings us to the ultimate basis and the very essence of justification.

Under no circumstances is remission of the guilt following upon personal sin thinkable without a certain interior renewal and conversion of the sinner. For, as long as the sinner himself clings to his sinful will or does not retract his prior sinful will, God's all-seeing eye cannot look upon him as guiltless. The doctrine originally taught by Protestants about the non-imputability of the still-present sin was an utter absurdity, although it was given out as a mystery. But once we admit an interior renewal, at least by the adoption of a new and correct orientation of the will, the absurdity vanishes. A certain remission of the guilt is then possible, but not yet in the Catholic sense.

As long as the change of will is thought of as being actual and only morally habitual—and from the natural standpoint it cannot be otherwise—so that the inner renewal is restricted to the conversion thus conceived, remission of the guilt remains extrinsic to the sinner's renovation; and in itself it really is something extrinsic, because it is not formally included in the interior renovation. The turning of the sinner to God does not necessarily imply that God condones the guilt incurred. Baius perceived this, and therefore he could harbor the thought of teaching that charity could coexist in man with the state of mortal sin.[2] This proposition was condemned by the Church, chiefly for the reason that Baius, as far as we know, denied that the act of charity really involves the infused virtue of charity, that the latter involves the grace of adoption, and that sanctifying grace involves remission of the guilt.[3]

According to Catholic teaching, the interior renovation does indeed consist in a change of will, an alteration of its bent. But it also consists in a transformation and elevation of the will through

[2] Prop. 70 damnata: "Homo existens in peccato mortali sive in reatu aeternae damnationis potest habere veram caritatem: et caritas etiam perfecta potest consistere cum reatu aeternae damnationis." See also propositions 31 and 32 (Denz., 1070, 1031, 1032).

[3] Cf. propositions 15 and 42 (Denz., 1015 and 1042).

the infusion of the theological virtues, especially of the virtue of charity which, as the principle of a new supernatural life, transfers the will to an entirely new sphere. And this transformation of the will is essentially bound up with the inner elevation of our entire being by the grace of divine sonship and participation in the divine nature. Such a renewal of man necessarily and formally includes remission of the guilt, supplies a true basis and support for this remission, and invests it with a mysterious sublimity that it could never have outside of its connection with supernatural elevation.

That is to say, as long as we think of ourselves merely as God's creatures and bondsmen, we can be objects of the divine wrath and abhorrence on account of the guilt we have loaded upon ourselves, even though we are sorry for our sin. At least there is no intrinsic contradiction in the thought that we may repent of the sin and still be hated on account of it, especially in view of the fact that God is ever entitled to adequate satisfaction, which the creature himself can never render.

But if, instead of merely coming back to our offended Lord by our own activity, we pass from the condition of bondage to the bosom of God by a supernatural rebirth, that is, if we become God's children, we immediately cease to be objects of God's wrath and abhorrence. Among us men a son can be tragically at odds with his father and be an object of the latter's anger without ceasing to be a son. This is impossible with the sonship of God. The children of God participate as such in the divine holiness of their Father, in His very nature. Accordingly, as they cannot grievously offend their Father without *ipso facto* lapsing from their filial relationship to Him, so also by the very fact that they enter into such relationship they must be so pleasing to God that He can no longer look upon them as His enemies, as objects of His wrath. The light of grace, belonging as it does to the divine order, can no more endure the darkness of sin than it can continue to shine, once sin enters.

In the presence of this light, the shadows are dissipated, shadows of sins that have been committed, those shadows that remained behind in the guilt and caused the soul to appear disfigured and repugnant in God's sight.[4] Grace joins the creature so closely to

[4] *Catechismus Romanus*, par. II, c. 2, q. 38: "Grace is a divine quality inhering in the soul, and a sort of brilliant light which banishes all stain from our souls."

God that the soul, while it is in the state of grace, cannot be separated from God by any barrier of guilt. Grace, which bridges the infinite gap yawning between the creature and the divine nature, spans the still greater fissure caused by the upheaval of sin. By transforming man from a bondsman to a child of God, grace makes him also a friend of God, since God cannot but stand in a relation of friendship with His children as long as they remain His children. For this reason grace is called both *gratia sanctificans* (sanctifying grace) because it completely does away with all sinful disorder, and *gratia gratum faciens* (grace which renders one pleasing) because it makes the creature so pleasing in God's sight that God must deal with him as His friend and child.

Thus in Christian justification remission of sin is involved in the renovation and transformation brought about by grace. As grace itself is not just a favorable regard or benevolence manifested by God toward man, but a quality in man corresponding to such benevolence and favor, so the forgiveness of sin implied in that benevolence and favor is not a mere extrinsic relationship, but rests upon that intrinsic, real, supernatural quality we call sanctifying grace. God does not simply turn His eyes away from the guilt of sin; He no longer sees it, for the reason that He cannot allow it to remain in one who is so closely joined to Him by grace.

It might perhaps be contended that remission of guilt is not an effect of the infused grace, but a preliminary condition for it; that grace can enter into a man only so far as sin departs from him, and accordingly that the extirpation of sin must precede the coming of grace, thus being a special, independent effect produced by God, distinct from grace.

We willingly grant that grace can find place in man only so far as sin is banished from him. But it does not follow that the deletion of sin is not accomplished by grace. On the contrary, sin vanishes when grace pervades the soul, just as darkness flees before light. Grace itself drives sin forth, and makes room for itself in the soul by destroying all guilt, in the same way that the fire which seizes upon a green log devours the dampness barring its entrance by the very fact that it sets the wood ablaze.

This figure is taken from Holy Scripture itself. The prophet Malachias likens the justifying God-man to a refining fire: "and

He shall sit refining and cleansing the silver, and He shall purify the sons of Levi, and shall refine them as gold and as silver, and they shall offer sacrifices to the Lord in justice." [5] In the same manner, according to the words of the Baptist, the inner cleansing symbolized by baptism of water is effected by the Holy Spirit's baptism of fire. By the very fact that in grace the Holy Spirit envelops the soul with His divine fire, He expels the dross that clings to it, and burns away the chaff. With the infusion of His grace He enters the soul as a vitalizing breath, and as water that flows forth to give life. This breath scatters the encumbrance of guilt, and this water washes the soul clean of all the filth of sin. These figures also indicate that the sinful, disordered condition of the will, the root of guilt, is to be burned away by the fire of the Holy Spirit (that is, by the influence He exercises in prevenient actual grace rather than by the habitual grace which presupposes that the disordered condition has been corrected). Hence they also prove, against the Protestants, that the remission of guilt is not a mere covering up of sin that still persists in the will. More than this, they make it clear that the sinful will and act, which are things of the past, cannot even leave their shadows upon the soul, and hence that in every respect the sin is not just covered up, but is, as it were, burned away from the uttermost depths of the soul and annihilated. If, consequently, the Holy Spirit is exhibited as the principle of the forgiveness of sin, we are not to think merely of His influence upon the sinner's conversion, nor are we to regard Him simply as the representative of the divine mercy on account of which God remits our guilt. Rather we must look upon the infusion of His grace as the real, intrinsic cause that actually brings about the removal of the guilt of sin. [6]

This much, then, is certain: in Christian justification the remission of sin is accomplished by the infusion of supernatural grace, and that in so sublime, supernatural, and mysterious a fashion as to lie beyond the conjectural and apprehensive powers of reason. The remission of sin itself has the guise of a supernatural mystery by reason of the grace which effects it, just as, on the other hand, grace

[5] Mal. 3:2 f.
[6] "The efficient cause [of justification] is the merciful God who gratuitously washes and sanctifies, signing and anointing with the Holy Spirit of promise." Council of Trent, sess. VI, c.7 (Denz., 799).

manifests its mysterious greatness and the tremendous power of its divine holiness by necessarily and irresistibly expelling sin from the person who receives it.

3. Thus the remission of guilt, and the subsequent state of freedom from sin, cannot be fully understood unless we revert to the grace of divine sonship which is infused into the justified person, and perceive that the remission is rooted in this grace. Nor, on the other hand, can the mysterious character of our union with God, which is the positive side of justification and its effect, be fully appreciated apart from its relation to this same grace of divine sonship.

We have already pointed out that justice in our case must be supernatural; it must be a certain power and impetus infused into the faculties of the soul, enabling them to pursue and work for our supernatural end. The reason why this justice must be supernatural is that it is meant to be a justice not merely of human beings, but of God's children. It is conferred on man to the extent that he is elevated to God's sonship and for the reason that along with this grace of divine sonship he receives the gift of filial love for God and other powers needed for leading a divine life as it ought to be led by a child of God. Further, the justice in question is sustained and perfected by this same grace of sonship. The supernatural virtues make us pleasing to God because of the intrinsic excellence of the acts they enable us to perform, and also because of the fact that these acts are acts of an adoptive son of God, and give expression to his filial relationship to God. And so their power for meriting eternal glory rests not merely on the fact that they belong to the same supernatural order as heavenly glory itself, but especially on the fact that they are the acts of a person who, as a child of God, is entitled by his birth to receive that glory as his inheritance.

Accordingly, I cannot arrive at a true appreciation of the intrinsic excellence and value of the positive side of justification unless I realize that the grace of divine sonship is its root and prop. Owing to the grace of sonship, which is a participation in the divine nature and holiness, the justice rooted in that grace is clearly revealed to be a justice shot through with divine sanctity.

4. What do we conclude from all this? That both factors comprised in justification—the remission of sin and the assimilation to our supernatural end—are rooted in the grace of divine sonship and are based on that grace. At one and the same time the grace of son-

ship expels all guilt from us, and infuses into us a love for God which is the love of a child or a friend.

For this reason the Council of Trent, when propounding the true nature of justification, could confine itself to the statement that it is "a transference from the state in which man is born a son of the first Adam, to the state of grace and adoption of the sons of God." [7]

In these words the Council singles out the element that imparts to Christian justification its supernatural, mysterious character. We must cling to these words and make them our point of departure, if we would appreciate the full excellence of justification. If all theologians had done this, the notion of justification would have escaped the shallow and muddled treatment that has so often disfigured it.

Many inverted the proper procedure. Instead of starting with an adequate idea of God's adoptive sonship and then determining the concept of justice contained in this idea, they preferred to regard divine sonship as a relationship to God arising from human justice, which they looked upon as a right disposition connected with freedom from sin, and an inclination toward morally good conduct. Thereby they did away with the possibility of fixing upon anything supernatural in this justice, and could conceive of the divine sonship itself only in an extremely vague, if not altogether rationalist, fashion.

But if we follow the Council of Trent, and if with the Council we focus our attention on the fact that at bottom justification is a transition to the state of an adoptive child, to the state of the children of God, it emerges before our eyes with its greatness unimpaired. The grace of divine sonship is not formally identified with the justice to be realized in us, that is, freedom from sin and a bent toward morally good conduct; but it is the root of a particularly sublime justice, of a supernatural freedom from sin, which it excludes by intrinsic necessity, and a supernatural disposition and inclination toward good. In a word, it is the root of a supernatural, divine holiness, such as is right for the children of God by reason of their rebirth. The grace of sonship virtually comprises this supernatural justice, regarded as liberation from guilt and as union with God by charity. Accordingly the regeneration by which we enter into the sonship of God is the fundamental process in justification. It is

[7] Sess. VI, c.4 (Denz., 796).

precisely through this rebirth as children of God that we become free from sin and are again united with God in childlike love. The two factors which make up justice have their common basis and their inner unity in this rebirth, and at the same time derive their supernatural character from it.

According to the Council of Trent, therefore, the complete and exhaustive concept of the mystery of Christian justification may be expressed as follows: It is the transfer of man to the grace of divine sonship, along with the freedom from sin and living union with God implied in that grace and corresponding to it. In other words, it is a transition to the state of divine sonship and of the divine justice or sanctity corresponding to that state.

Distinctly present to the mind of the Council of Trent in its exposition of justification was the passage from St. Paul which we have placed at the head of this chapter: "According to His mercy He saved us, by the laver of regeneration and renovation of the Holy Ghost, whom He hath poured forth upon us abundantly, through Jesus Christ our Savior; that, being justified by His grace, we may be heirs according to hope of life everlasting." [8] The interior renovation by which we are saved and justified is here made parallel with regeneration from the Holy Spirit and in the Holy Spirit, who is poured forth upon us. It is this regeneration that makes us children of God and gives us a share in the Holy Spirit of God, that is, in His divine, holy existence and life. In regeneration we are sanctified primarily with regard to our assimilation to the holy divine nature, and secondarily with regard to the holy disposition of our will toward God, and to God's esteem of us as holy, in virtue of which He must exonerate us of our sinful guilt. In the rightly understood notion of the "renovation of the Holy Ghost," or sanctification by the Holy Spirit, the justification which the Apostle speaks of is associated with our rebirth as sons of God. And so it is the phrase "sanctification by the Holy Spirit," together with its underlying idea, that best describes Christian justification in terms of its mystical sublimity, and traces it back to its mystical root.

[8] Titus 3:5-7 (cf. sess. VI, c.7; Denz., 799).

87. High Point of Christian Justice. Its Difference from Original Justice

Thus described, the mysterious nature of Christian justification and of the state it engenders might appear to have reached the peak of its perfection. But in line with the doctrine we have previously set forth, concerning the significance of the Incarnation and its relations to grace, we must add, for a complete clarification of the specifically Christian character of justification, that we are justified not only by regeneration, but by our incorporation into the God-man as His members. Justification makes us living members of Christ's body, and justifying grace flows into us from this source. But as living members of Christ we have a higher dignity, a greater sanctity, and a more glorious power of pleasing God, than we should possess in virtue of grace alone, or than Adam possessed before his sin. When Christ begins to live in us by grace, His personal dignity and holiness are reflected upon us. Energized by this personal holiness of the God-man, grace must banish sin from us far more forcibly than it does of its own inherent power; it must make us much more pleasing to God, and must unite us more closely to Him, than it could of itself alone. And therefore our real union with the God-man must also invest the justice we receive through the grace of Christ with a greater power and a higher value.

Because God beholds His only-begotten Son linked to us in living union, He can no longer look upon our sin, any more than He can perceive His own Son separated from Him thereby. Further, because God's only-begotten Son Himself lives in us, His members, we are enabled to do more than render honor to the infinite Majesty of God in our feeble human way. We can do so perfectly, as far as this is possible at all, seeing that in union with Christ we offer to the divine Majesty a glory corresponding to His greatness. In union with Christ our justice becomes, in a certain sense, absolute justice.

This is the high point of the mystery of Christian justification. This is the point at which the organism established in mankind by the Incarnation reaches its summit here on earth.

Out of fear of drawing too close to the error of the Protestants and of undermining the truth that Christian justice is internal to the justified person, many theologians have held that this idea of extending the justice of the head to the members is a suggestion fraught with peril.

It would be dangerous, indeed, and instead of crowning would overthrow the very foundations of the mystery of justification, if it excluded justification by internal renewal and regeneration. It would still be dangerous even if it merely intimated that the inner regeneration by grace was not sufficient to make man truly just, that is, to expel sin from him and to equip him for leading a truly holy life. One who entertained either of these views would set himself in stark opposition to the Council of Trent.

In our explanation neither of these errors is maintained. Rather it is the very opposite that we propose. We vigorously insist that an inner renewal of man takes place, and that this suffices to render man truly just, and that in a supernatural manner. However, we add, if this inner justice is to be appreciated in its true worth as being more than merely that, if it is to be absolutely perfect, it must be regarded not simply as a replica of the personal justice of Christ, but as linked to that justice in real union, and hence as completed and crowned by it. Our internal justice is crowned and perfected by the personal justice of Christ our head in somewhat the way that the internal holiness and justice of Christ's humanity are crowned and perfected by the holiness and excellence of the divine person united with the humanity. We cannot envisage Christ's justice, the model of ours, as having any connection with us unless a living likeness of it is impressed upon our souls. Nor can we conceive this likeness and impress as disconnected from its exemplar. For the connection is based upon the relation of effect to cause, and also upon the organic unity of justified man with his infinitely just head.[9]

Through this same organic union with the God-man we necessarily enter into a closer union with the substantial, personal justice and holiness of Him who proceeds from the Son of God, the Holy Spirit who in a very special manner inhabits, pervades, and perfumes the grace He communicates to us.

Even apart from our union with the God-man, the Holy Spirit dwells substantially in the flame of holiness that is enkindled in us

[9] Cf. Suarez, *De Gratia*, lib. XII, c. 19, nos. 7 ff. Suarez infers from this doctrine that the merits of the justified Christian have a greater value. See also what we have stated on pp. 583–85 about the relation of the sacramental character to grace; it is the character that joins us to Christ as members.

at His fire. Like a seal, He stamps the image of His own sanctity upon our soul by His most intimate presence in us and His immediate contact with us. But this is a presence which the nature of supernatural sanctity in general necessarily brings to us.

Moreover, as we saw when treating of the mission of the Holy Spirit in grace,[10] grace renders us holy because it is an essentially holy quality in itself, and also because it makes us temples of the Holy Spirit, who takes up His abode in us along with grace. But as long as our union with the Holy Spirit is based on grace alone, it cannot properly add a new value to the sanctity already contained in grace, but can only disclose the full wealth of grace.

This new value is added only when grace is given us to make us living members in the body of Christ, hence when the Holy Spirit enters into the body of the human race along with the Son of God from whom He proceeds. From this moment on, the entire body possesses Him in His very person in a wholly new way, as the Spirit of the head. When this takes place, the holiness that He possesses in Himself belongs to us, over and above the holiness that He gives us as His effect; and that by a title which is not bestowed with grace as it is in itself. This new kind of holiness is added to the first as its complement, and invests it with an infinite value, an infinite dignity.

Thus in a certain sense it becomes true that we are just not alone by the justice of God which is produced in us by God, but also by the justice whereby God Himself is just. This can be boldly asserted without running counter to the Council of Trent. For the Council evidently intended no more than to repudiate the error of the Protestants, who rejected justice in the sense of a state intrinsic to man, and proposed as the essence of our justice merely a dead and, as it were, mechanical union with Christ and the Holy Spirit. We, on the contrary, require a living, efficacious union of the Holy Spirit with us, a union which communicates a holy quality to us. It is precisely this holy quality that we regard as the basis upon which the seal of supreme dignity and perfection is stamped on us, by the personal relation of the Holy Spirit to us.[11]

10 See section 28.

11 Our language is more temperate than that used by Thomassinus (*De Incarnatione*, lib. VI, c.7 ff.) and Lessius (*De perfectionibus moribusque divinis*, lib. XII, c.11), and we believe we have eliminated what is nonessential from the views of both. Petavius (*De Trinitate*, lib. VIII, c.7) argues brilliantly that a true hypostatic inhabitation began only at the time of the

Consequently the true character and sublimity of the mystery of Christian justification cannot be understood unless we realize that its term is more than just a supernatural justice, that of God's adopted children. We must associate with this a copossession of the personal justice and sanctity of Christ, the natural Son of God made man, and of the Spirit who proceeds from Him. Christian justice is what it is, not by a mere extrinsic denomination based on its origin from Christ and communication through Christ; it is such because it is the justice of a member of Christ. By an interior transformation the member receives an outpouring of sanctity from his head, and is at the same time overshadowed by the personal, divine holiness of his head and of the Holy Spirit belonging to Him.

Christian justification, thus conceived as the coming to life of the Incarnation in mankind, is seen to be so incomprehensibly great and extraordinary that the effect it produces leaves the supernatural justice of Adam far behind and places it quite in the shade, to say nothing of all natural justice, however noble it may be.

In Christian justification, to be sure, the whole of original justice, including its lower, material factors, is not given back to us. The full order and harmony of all the faculties of the soul are not restored. Inordinate concupiscence, particularly, is not completely suppressed and tamed. Thus there is lacking in us some of the order and harmony that pertained to Adam's justice; there is lacking the integrity of nature by which grace had originally been made so close an ally of nature, and had exercised such power in nature. But it would be folly to conclude from this that Adam was at bottom more just and more acceptable to God than we are, or that grace was more deeply rooted, and operated more energetically, in him than in us.

The true essence of supernatural justice undoubtedly consists in grace and charity, which render us pleasing to God and set us on the right path toward our supernatural end. The gifts of integrity have only a subordinate importance in comparison with this. Integrity did not invest sanctifying grace with a higher value, but rather received from grace its own higher significance. But union with

---

New Testament, when the Son of God brought the Holy Spirit down with Him at His incarnation. But Petavius seems not to have brought out with sufficient clarity how the Incarnation communicates to us the special hypostatic relation of the Holy Spirit.

our head, the God-man, and with His Spirit does impart a higher dignity and excellence to grace.

It cannot be denied that through the gift of integrity grace was originally enabled to strike deeper root in nature, was more tightly linked to nature, and was given more securely into the possession of nature, than would have been the case without integrity. But in spite of the lack of integrity, the taking up of our nature into the body of the God-man makes the alliance of grace with our nature still more intimate. Integrity was at bottom no more than a disposition for grace; it did not radically include grace within itself, but only prepared for its reception. Besides, this disposition was dependent for its very existence on the continuance of grace; it perished with grace, and therefore could not furnish a foothold for the recovery of grace. Quite other is the union of the Christian with the God-man, particularly when it is sealed with the sacramental character. This union does more than dispose us for the reception of grace; it confers upon us a strict right to grace, and virtually, radically postulates grace. In itself indissoluble, even in the presence of sin, it leads us back into grace the instant sin is removed, because of the indestructible power of the head to whom it unites us.

Accordingly all the advantages that Adam's gratuitous justice possessed in virtue of its association with integrity are not only compensated for in Christian justice owing to the fact that it is founded on the God-man, but they are superabundantly replaced. To manifest more strikingly the superior power and significance proper to Christian justice, God wished to leave it without that prop on the side of nature which Adam's grace possessed in the gift of integrity, and to demonstrate its might by its victory in open battle over the obstacles it encounters in nature. Through Christ grace is so deeply entrenched in nature that it requires no support in the latter; and it seizes upon nature so forcefully that in spite of resistance it is able to retain its grip. By enabling man to hold his course toward his supernatural end, and ultimately to arrive at his goal in the face of the disorder persisting in his nature, it places him in a position to put to the test the full supernatural hardiness of his justice, and out of the conflict with his inordinate appetites to emerge with greater glory for himself and to become more pleasing to God, than could have been the case without such conflict.

The power of God is made perfect in our infirmity: [12] such is the great law of Christian justice. The grace of Christ, which is held up by His own infinite power, can and must reveal itself in all its fullness by permitting the weakness of man arising from the lack of integrity to remain, and by then coming to grips with it and overcoming it. It is not through any defect in its intrinsic perfection that grace does not restore integrity to us. It could impart integrity to us, just as Adam received integrity by being constituted in grace. It could confer this gift on us in a still higher degree, even despite intervening sin; for the satisfaction of Christ has compensated for sin many times over. Indeed, the greater perfection of grace is shown by the very fact that it can dispense with integrity without in any way prejudicing itself. It actually does do without integrity in order to make the ensuing weakness of man serve its own purpose, and to unfold the full power of its strength in that weakness. For the sake of battle and merit, declares the Council of Trent, concupiscence has been allowed to remain in the baptized, in the members of Christ; hence not for any diminution, but for the glorification of their supernatural justice. And this is a greater glorification than would accrue to justice by the restoration of integrity.

Thus Christian justice, notwithstanding the lack of an external complement, is in many respects more sublime, more bountiful, and more mysterious than original justice. The man who is restored to grace in Christ is, for all the frailty of his nature, more intimately and wonderfully united to God than was Adam in the complete integrity of his nature. His state of justice is a greater supernatural mystery than Adam's state, and is all the more a mystery inasmuch as his state is not accompanied, as Adam's was, by a transfiguration of the whole nature, but is hidden under the infirmity, the misery, and the poverty of nature, like a pearl buried in mud, and is visible only to the eye of strong faith. Externally and in the lower faculties of his soul the justified Christian, unlike Adam, is still under the law of the sin, death, and corruption that came into existence with original sin. But the God-man, with His Holy Spirit, dwells in the profoundest depths of his soul, in the most hidden heart of his being; and amid the wreckage of sin builds Himself a temple that is the more sacred and precious the less it can be desecrated and damaged by the surrounding debris.

[12] Cf. II Cor. 12:9.

CHAPTER XXIII

The Process of Justification

‣‣‣

88. Justification as a Supernatural Process

IN this chapter we go back to the process by which Christian justification is brought about. This process, in its mysterious, supernatural character, must correspond to the product in which it issues. We can be rather brief in our treatment of this subject, since we have already become acquainted with most of the pertinent factors in preceding chapters.

Evidently Christian justification, or rather Christian justice as we have described it, cannot be a work of man. At best, man can retract and detest his sinful will by a naturally good act, and perhaps can perform some penance for his sin. But it is beyond his power to blot out his sin, or in any way to enter into a supernatural union with God.

Man cannot advance to the state of Christian justice even by the supernatural works he may perform with the aid of God's prevenient grace. Through the prevenient grace of God he does, indeed, receive the power to act supernaturally. But only God can so radically transform and renew his being and his faculties that he becomes a child of God and possesses in himself the principle of divine life, free from all grievous sin; only God who moves him to the acts preceding justification can work such a miracle. Man is utterly helpless in this matter, since the very power required for eliciting supernatural acts before or in justification is completely restored only by the full or partial bestowal of the supernatural principles comprised in the grace of divine sonship.[1]

Accordingly the conferring of the grace of sonship, as also of all the prerogatives associated with it, is exclusively the work of

[1] See *Natur und Gnade*, pp. 221 ff.

God. The grace is conferred through a mysterious activity of the Holy Spirit who, descending into the soul and dwelling therein with the fullness of His Godhead, inflames it with His divine fire and, by means of a stupendous regeneration, causes it to share in His own divine nature and sanctity. Thereby He excludes sin from the soul and, through the medium of the supernatural virtues of faith, hope, and charity, He brings the soul into harmony with its supernatural end.

Therefore the Council of Trent declares: "The efficient cause of justification is the merciful God who gratuitously [hence without any merit on our part] washes and sanctifies, signing and anointing with the Holy Spirit of promise, who is the pledge of our inheritance"; that is, the inheritance of us, the children of God.[2]

But as we saw in a previous connection, the sacred humanity of Christ is the organ whereby the Holy Spirit enters into the whole mystical body of Christ, and dwells in it with His supernatural power and activity. The sacraments in their turn are the secondary organs whereby Christ's humanity, or rather the divine power emanating from it, is ordinarily directed toward us, and comes into contact with us. Consequently we must regard the sacred humanity of Christ and the sacraments of the Church as the channels through which the sanctifying power of the Holy Spirit reaches us in justification. Hence justification in its substance is accomplished not by an unfolding from within, but by an extraordinary influence and infusion from above and from without.

It is true, further, that man cannot draw Christian justice into himself from above, in the sense of acquiring a real right to its infusion by his activity. As the source from which this justice flows must be supernatural, so the act by which it is acquired and with which it is bought must have a supernatural value, a value so great as to be truly the equivalent of the goods to be purchased. But man is absolutely incapable of putting forth such an act, even with all the graces that precede justification, to say nothing of his purely natural powers. None of his efforts can be regarded as equivalent either to the infinite debt he has contracted with God, or to the infinite good he is invited to possess in grace. Nor is any other creature, though already constituted in grace, able to render such satisfaction or acquire such merit for him. Only the God-man could

[2] Sess. VI, c.7; Denz., 799.

fully discharge the debt by His passion, only He could merit the grace of the children of God for us by His obedience; for the value of His passion and obedience is infinite.

Hence He, and He alone, is also the moral cause of justification, that is, the cause by which God is moved to impart justifying grace to us. And since He ordinarily makes us partakers of His merits through the sacraments, these too, in a subordinate way, are moral causes of our justification, as pledges of His merits.

Thus with respect to the efficient and moral causes, which are the really decisive principles, the process of justification is seen to operate from without, or rather from above, as descending from God and Christ, to renew man in his interior and to apply to him in a supernatural manner the effect of God's power and Christ's merit. If justification is truly a supernatural work, it cannot be brought about except by supernatural causes that stand outside and above man, and that operate in a supernatural way.

The person to be justified is not coproductive, but passive and receptive, in respect to this causality.

Consequently, in the case of those who labor under no personal iniquity, and in general in those who are as yet incapable of personal activity, the entire process of justification is reduced to communication and influence from without. This is the case with infants in baptism. Here the process has simply the character of an ineffable, supernatural generation, to the exclusion of all cooperation between the person generated and his begetter.

With adults the case is different. With them too, according to the Council of Trent, justification takes place by a reception (not by a production, or cooperation in the production) of grace and the accompanying gifts. But the reception must be voluntary; it must be such that man freely approaches and receives the justification held out to him by God. Hence the grace which comes down from above is met by an ascent from below; the descent of the supernatural into nature is matched by an effort of the latter to raise itself. In this case also the activity of God, regarded in its power and efficacy as the communication of supernatural existence and life, remains a true generation. But it is such only so far as the production of the higher existence and life in the soul is accomplished by a formal marriage of God with the soul.

In this figure both the physical and the ethical character, and thereby the entire mystery of the process of justification, find expression. With regard to the physical factor, the metaphor stresses the moral interchange that takes place between God and man in justification. In this mutual exchange it emphasizes the physical concurrence and the real union of God with the soul in the fructification that issues in the soul's supernatural existence and life. Thus it marks the whole process as something indescribably lofty, wonderful, and mysterious. The idea of regeneration points out that in justification man not only returns to the purity of his natural existence, but rises to a supernatural existence and life. In like manner the idea of marriage intimates that justification consists not only in a simple reconciliation and abolition of enmity, but in the inception of a supernatural friendship, indeed in an elevation of the soul to the rank of spouse of God, an elevation whereby God clasps the soul to Himself and pours forth His own Spirit into it.[3]

The actual union of God with the soul, wherein the soul receives from God the seed of the Holy Spirit out of which the soul arises to the life of His children, is undoubtedly supernatural and mysterious. So also must be the meeting wherein God holds out His hand to the soul to lift it up to so intimate and lofty a union; and the soul, grasping the proferred hand, strains upward toward this union, prepares itself for it, and rids itself of all obstacles to it. Not with its natural freedom can the soul go to meet the heavenly bridegroom, prepare a welcome for Him, and receive Him into itself. No; that the soul may mount so high, its freedom must be elevated and sustained by the power of the same Holy Spirit who wills to descend into the soul. Only when illuminated by His light, only when simultaneously driven and drawn by His might, can the soul turn to Him, approach Him, and attain to actual union with Him. As the Holy Spirit at His entrance seals and crowns His union with the soul, so by His influence upon the soul He has the initiative for the first

[3] This conception of interior justification is faithful to scriptural usage. In the Old Testament, cf. Osee 2:19; Isa. 54:4–6 and 62:4 f.; Ezech. 16:7–14. In the New Testament, Christ calls Himself the bridegroom: Matt. 9:15; Mark 2:19 f.; Luke 5:34. John the Baptist applies the same name to Christ in John 3:29. The bride is both the Church as a whole and all the individual members: Matt. 22:2–14; Rom. 7:4; I Cor. 6:15–20; II Cor. 11:2. This sacred marriage begins in time, is subject to all the vicissitudes of time, and will achieve its perfection only at the end of time in the new City of God: Apoc. 19:7–9; 21:2; 22:17. For the whole idea, the best text of all is Eph. 5:22–32. [Tr.]

beginnings of that union. Only between these two poles, the inception and the consummation of the union, does the activity pertaining to the soul in justification come into play. It is rooted in the one, and strives toward the other; it concurs with the one, and paves the way for the other, and thus cooperates supernaturally for the consummation of the soul's mysterious espousals with God.

Let me make my point clear. The soul cooperates in the marriage, but not in the generation; that is, the soul does not cooperate as efficient cause for the production of grace, as though grace proceeded from the soul too; for grace comes to the soul from God alone. But by complying with God's prevenient actual grace, the soul does cooperate to the end that God may find a welcome in it, and an opportunity for the exercise of His generative power. The soul cooperates formally in the contracting of the bond which is sealed in the infusion of grace. Its whole activity is but a disposition for the reception of the grace designed for it by God, or is this very reception. Herein is found the supernatural significance and mysterious character of the soul's activity.

89. Nature and Value of the Subjective Dispositions Which Have Part in Justification

In another place [4] we have attempted a fuller explanation of the internal organization of these dispositions, and of their relation to the actual attainment of justification. However, we were then primarily concerned with the relation of nature to grace in a general way, without taking account of the communication of grace as affected by sin and the Incarnation.

Since the present question has to do with the communication of grace to the sinner through the mediation of the God-man, we may not omit these factors from our consideration. Hence we shall have to assign a threefold supernatural function to the dispositions that work together in justification: first, a reaction against sin; secondly, a firm attachment to the mediator of our reconciliation and reunion with God; thirdly, a movement toward reception of justifying grace. For remarriage between God and the soul that has fled His arms will be possible only so far as the sinner seeks to undo his

[4] *Natur und Gnade*, pp. 241 ff.; cf. *The Glories of Divine Grace*, Bk. V.

wrong, appropriates to himself Christ's satisfaction to fill out his own shortcomings, and sincerely desires union with God, which he claims and hopes for through the merits of his mediator.

In its reaction against sin and its accession to the satisfactions and merits of Christ, the soul moves in the supernatural sphere no less than in its striving for grace. The soul must react against sin as a supernatural evil, that is, as a violation of the supernatural order established in the world by God, and as an obstacle to grace. And if attachment to its head, the God-man, is to raise it to the level of that head and is to be a genuine, living union with Him, such attachment must be effected by God's mysterious action. For, as the Savior says, "No man can come to Me except the Father, who hath sent Me, draw him." [5] Thus from every point of view the activity which, under God's supernatural influence, disposes the soul for justification and leads to it, has a mystical character.

This truth does not stand forth so clearly if the function attributed to the disposition is conceived in a purely negative manner, as a *remotio obicis*, or removal of an impediment. For the simple removal of obstacles to a union, or in general to any effect, does not of itself take on the character of that to which it gives place. In our case, however, even the *remotio obicis* has a supernatural character, because it is essentially connected with the ascent of the soul toward grace. The soul must remove the obstacle to grace, that is, the sin that has been committed, not simply by giving up its sinful will, but by reacting against the sin incurred and by striving to annul its effects in respect to grace. But how can this be done unless the soul resolutely turns to the law of grace, detests the sin as a violation of that law, and endeavors to make amends for the sin precisely as such a violation?

This consideration implies that the *remotio obicis* is not the only factor in the disposition required for justification. Such a disposition must also have a positive function: besides making room for grace, it leads to the reception of grace. Herein is directly revealed the supernatural character which the disposition gets as a movement toward a supernatural objective.

But how does this disposition put the soul on the path to grace? First, the soul experiences a sincere longing for grace, and desires to

[5] John 6:44.

receive it from God. God Himself engenders this yearning in the soul by His prevenient grace. That very fact confers on the soul a claim for the realization of its desire, and consequently disposes for the reception of grace, just as any well-ordered desire is a disposition for its realization. If this longing is the fruit of an elevation of the soul, whereby the soul is already beginning to embrace God with the love of a friend and bride, it is so effective that the marriage with the soul is immediately brought to pass by God, and in that same instant God and the repentant soul meet in a holy kiss. If the soul does not soar quite so high, and seeks grace and the friendship of God from motives that do not proceed from pure charity, God does not come at once; He lets the soul wait, just as the soul keeps Him waiting, and He offers His grace only in the actual reception of His sacraments.

The longing with which the soul goes to meet God's justifying action puts it in vitalizing contact with God's activity. The activity of the soul and the activity of God are joined not negatively, but positively. The connection becomes still closer if the soul, with a lively faith in God's power and promises, confidently expects that God will bestow the longed-for grace. As the soul strains toward grace by its longing, so it draws grace down to itself by its confidence, not as though it strictly merited grace, but because God has vouched for the fulfillment of this expectation without any merit on man's part. The soul does not merit grace, but obtains it by entreaty. The positive worthiness of the soul to receive grace can be designated as merit only in the sense that any positive worthiness to receive a gift, even such as does not rest on an equivalent service, can be termed merit. This sort of merit does not deny, but affirms, the gratuitous character of grace, especially in view of the fact that it is inspired by God Himself, and is effective only so far as God cannot gainsay Himself.

As the yearning leads to confidence, so confidence supposes the yearning. And as the yearning is flawless and operates flawlessly only when it springs from pure love of God, so the confidence can without further delay bring on the desired union with God only when man, out of pure love for God, does his part in entering into the divine espousals and, pinning all his hopes to his love, trusts that God will no longer hold back. Love such as this takes all uneasiness out of the confidence, because it is already a prelude to close intimacy with God. Without such love, the fear of still being unreconciled with God can be removed only by the sacrament of penance.

Alongside the yearning for marriage with God and confidence as to its realization, a third factor must be considered. This is the readiness and determination of the soul to live in conformity with the grace to be received, to put it to good use, and to remain faithful to it; in other words, the surrender of the soul to the heavenly bridegroom and complete submissiveness to Him. This attitude is necessarily connected with a sincere longing for grace. Confidence would turn into presumption if man were not prepared on his side to correspond to the awaited grace. But not even this readiness has the character of a service to be rewarded by grace. It is no more than a resolve to render service in the future, when in the state of grace, in the actual marriage with God.

But, once the nuptials are celebrated, the soul's readiness has more than the negative function pertaining to the willingness to have sin removed, or even to the detestation and repentance of sin. By his readiness to cherish and preserve grace, the sinner is prepared positively for its reception; here precisely is the point at which the upward movement of the soul and the power of God's grace come into closest contact, permeate each other, and are linked together. By its longing, the soul advances toward grace; by its longing, it brings grace down; but by the surrender of itself to grace, it receives grace. When the soul obediently submits to the desired and awaited yoke of grace, God lowers the yoke upon it. In thus obediently submitting to the divine bridegroom, the soul becomes His bride in all truth, and receives from Him the seed of life which it is ready to nurture in itself.

This takes place particularly when the surrender of the soul to God is motivated by pure love of Him, hence when the soul on its side falls in fully with God's designs and is perfectly subjected to Him. For when this happens God cannot delay in giving Himself to the soul with His grace. But if the surrender to God and submissiveness to Him proceed from other motives, if the soul submits only to God's inflexible right and law, and is prepared to live up to the law of grace only in this guarded fashion, it does not enter into immediate contact with God but approaches Him from afar. Hence it cannot expect that God on His side will come running on the instant.

In such circumstances the soul can achieve union with God only by the actual reception of the sacrament.

Thus, in addition to reaction against sin by repentance, there are three ways in which the soul that is to be justified or wedded to God can and should advance toward the divine bridegroom and union with Him in grace, and so do its part to usher in this union: by desire, confidence, and surrender. In all three ways the soul, with its will elevated by prevenient grace, sets out upon a supernatural flight. This flight appears in its full mystic sublimity and import especially when it is accompanied and upborne by a love for God which is that of a bride for her spouse. The creature as such can love God only with the love of a stranger or a handmaid. But when the creature loves God with the love of a bride or a son, its act is supremely supernatural, and its love is closely linked and related to the supernatural love which God has for the creature, and by which He unites Himself to the creature in grace.

Therefore this pure, supernatural love is called by theologians the soul or "form" of the dispositions leading to the divine espousals, or of the moral, subjective elevation of the person to be justified, whereby his physical and objective elevation to the state of grace is initiated. But we are not to suppose that without such love there could occur in the soul no supernatural upsurge that would preserve for the process of justification its physico-ethical character, and hence the idea of the marriage with God which exhibits that character. For even though the soul aspires to union with the divine bridegroom from motives other than pure love for Him, it can mount high enough for God in His unparalleled mercy to meet the soul halfway, and along with grace to infuse, at least in the habit of charity, the love that is still lacking though desired. But in this case the contact and linking together of the activity of God and man is obviously not so direct, or so nicely adjusted, or so vibrant with life. There is lacking the soul, the "form" of the subjective elevation, the flame leaping up from the depths of the soul, in which the soul is to meet and merge with the flame of the Holy Spirit that darts down upon it.

To uphold even in this case the full significance of the ethical factor (preparation for justification) and its immediate contact with the physical factor (justification itself), Von Schäzler takes the following view. He assumes that whoever approaches the sacrament with attrition, but has failed to rise to an act of perfect charity, is elevated to that height by the sacrament itself. He concludes that the person does not receive grace from God until he passes over into the habit of charity by an act of charity, thus meeting the infusion of grace on God's part with filial love on his own part.[6]

As long as this view allows that the penitent cannot be obligated to bring more than an *attritio non formata* (attrition that falls short of perfect love) to his reception of the sacrament, no theological objection need be raised. But the difficulties that experience urges against the existence of such an act of love in the reception of the sacrament might be rather hard to solve, even though it should be claimed that the act does not have to be explicitly formulated. At any rate, justification brought about in such a way would be more worthy and perfect; and it is also possible to contend that, if the sinner does not do all in his power to prepare himself for justification, the justification lacks some of the beauty and nobility that should attend it.

In a passage already referred to several times,[7] the entire process wherein the soul readies itself for union with its divine bridegroom and draws near Him in humble yearning and confidence and sincere submissiveness, was compared to the part played by the Mother of God in her espousals to the Holy Spirit, of whom she was to conceive the only-begotten Son of God. As the Son of God was conceived in the womb of the Virgin by assuming human nature to His person, so He is to be reborn in the soul by communicating a supernatural likeness of Himself. To avoid needless repetition, we must refer our readers to this passage.

However, we wish to stress one point in this comparison which sheds a most revealing light on the inner nature of the process of justification. Mary did not conceive the Son of God in her womb as efficient cause; by her activity which was upborne by the prevenient grace of the Holy Spirit, by her humility, her longing, and her love she merely made herself ready for fructification by the Holy Spirit. In like manner our soul cannot generate habitual justice in itself by the activity in which it engages under the prevenient, excitating

[6] Konstantin von Schäzler, *Die Lehre von der Wirksamkeit der Sakramente ex opere operato* (Munich, 1860), especially sect. 24 ff., where the relation and cooperation of the objective and subjective factors in justification are worked out with great detail and erudition.

[7] *Natur und Gnade*, pp. 248 ff.

grace of God and the stirring breath of the Holy Spirit. This habitual justice is the supernatural virtue of charity and the grace of divine sonship, in a word, the likeness of the divine nature and holiness. The interior renovation of the justified man is the fruit of divine activity not mediately but immediately, just as immediately as the communication of the first prevenient grace. It is and ever remains the direct work of God, a most amazing work, almost as amazing as the conception of the Son of God in Mary's womb.

90. CHRISTIAN JUSTIFICATION AS A MYSTERY OF FAITH

In Scripture and the teaching of the Church, Christian justification and the resulting justice are closely associated with Christian faith. The Apostle calls justice simply a "justice of the faith." [8] Since the Reformation, this relation of justification to faith has often been made the object of profound and thorough discussion in controversy with Protestants, and many beautiful and magnificent things have been said and written about it. The relation is of special interest for us; it is our strongest proof of the mysterious character of Christian justification and, if rightly explained, will contribute notably to an understanding of the mystery.

A truth that can be known, pursued, and attained only by supernatural faith, a truth that is so inseparably linked and interwoven with faith, must be a specific object of faith, and must be a mystery of faith in the strictest sense. Conversely, the far-reaching influence which faith, according to the teaching of the Church, exercises in justification, can be set forth and grasped only if justification is understood in the manner described above, as an absolutely supernatural work.

The following observations will fully elucidate both these assertions.

First of all, it is clear that the justification to be effected in us can be brought home to our consciousness solely through faith. With our reason we perceive only those works of God that fall within the province of sensible or spiritual experience. If justification consisted merely in a moral change of heart, accompanied by remission of sin on the part of God, it might actually, at least on its positive side, be perceived by us in its consummation and in the causes that

[8] Rom. 4:11.

cooperate for its production. Faith would then be necessary at most to assure us of the remission of sin. But justification achieves its essential perfection in an inexplicable, deeply interior renewal and transformation, a regeneration of the soul out of God's inaccessible light, and so is as completely hidden from our eyes as this light itself. The *gloria Dei*,[9] the glory streaming forth from God which really makes us pleasing in His sight, the glory which was lost to us by sin and is restored to us by the grace of divine sonship, is properly its specific object, and is a true mystery of faith. Only in faith can we perceive what Christian justification consists in, and under what conditions it is realized in us. Only in faith do we have experience of the gracious decree whereby God wills to communicate Himself to us in so astounding a way because of Christ's merits.[10]

But faith is not limited to bringing justification to our notice. Since faith alone is capable of doing this, and since justification is accomplished not by a simple regeneration, but by a conscious marriage with God, faith must be a main factor in the process itself. Faith is the root and mainspring of all the activity whereby man aspires to justification; it is the bond linking God's justifying activity to man's dispositive activity.[11] It impels man toward God as the source of justice, and draws the justifying power of grace from God down upon man. Consequently we may say that in both its converging factors, the activity of God and the activity of man, the

[9] Rom. 3:23.
[10] We do not, of course, mean to suggest that faith gives us assurance of the actual arrival of the state of justification. In fact, we have indicated the contrary, namely, that we cannot attain to complete certitude in this matter, inasmuch as experience is not able to make us evidently conscious that the necessary supernatural quality actually informs our preparatory acts.
[11] Above, on p. 638, we singled out the surrender of self to God as the factor that establishes contact between the divine and the human activity. But there we were viewing the matter from another angle: we had in mind the junction which takes place in the meeting and interpenetration of two intersecting motions; and the surrender to God is the apex of the movement and activity by which man advances toward God. On the other hand, the confidence engendered by faith is of such great moment not so much because it conducts man to God, but rather because it draws God's activity down to man. Reaction against sin, desire for grace, and surrender to God signalize the inadequate effort which man contributes to the process of justification; whereas the confidence emanating from faith is significant because it coincides with the calling forth of God's activity.

whole process is sustained by faith, and receives from faith its identifying signature.

Let us consider the question somewhat more fully.

It is faith, and faith alone, from which proceeds all the activity that man directs toward the acquirement of justification. This is in accord with the Apostle's words: "Without faith it is impossible to please God"; and "he that cometh to God must believe that He is, and is a rewarder to them that seek Him." [12] The whole activity in question, if it is to have any positive meaning, must be aimed at the supernatural goal which it points out to us. But how could we direct our activity to the goal if we did not know where the goal is, and were not even acquainted with the roads that lead to it? And how could we obtain this knowledge except through faith? In particular, how could we abhor sin as the rupture of our friendship with God, long for grace, and subject ourselves to its laws, unless faith lighted up our course before us and spurred us on? Accordingly faith is the first step we take, led by God's hand, to surmount our nature and set out upon the road of salvation. Faith is also the mainspring of every other movement by which we draw near to God in a supernatural way. The supernaturalness that must characterize our activity in preparing for justification is equally dependent on elevating grace and on faith; our actions derive their higher worth and meaning from both grace and faith.

Indeed, our entire activity is at bottom nothing but an attachment to God by faith, a longing, a surrender, and a subjection foreshadowed, expressed, and inaugurated in the act of faith. This attachment to God does not stop with knowledge, but advances to action; when it reaches this stage it is called a living faith. The designation is the more striking since it intimates that the importance of our activity in the matter of justification consists not so much in a meritorious act performed by us, as rather in a movement, fired by faith, leading toward the reception of unmerited grace.

This is one way faith concurs in justification, and is the way that was chiefly denied by the Reformers, but upheld against them by the Catholics. The Reformers countered by putting more stress on another kind of cooperation proper to faith, and often enough, perhaps, this has not received sufficient attention from Catholic the-

[12] Heb. 11:6.

ologians. We mean the function of faith as an organ by which the grace of justification itself is grasped and drawn down. Against the exclusive insistence on this aspect of faith, as also against the preposterous conception which the Reformers had of its mode of operation, Catholic theologians have ever entered a victorious protest. But they have often neglected, by failing to exploit their advantage, to fell their adversaries with their own weapons.[13]

When the Apostle speaks of justification by faith, he is no doubt following up the thought that we neither produce justification in ourselves nor merit it, but are to expect it from God's grace and mercy through the merits of Christ. This expectation is at bottom nothing but the faith in God's promises that is buoyed up by unshakable confidence. In holding this, the Protestants are right. But the admissibility and necessity of other movements for the reception of the awaited grace, factors likewise proceeding from faith, are not thereby excluded. Rather, they are essentially included and presupposed, if the nature of the awaited grace at all admits of such dispositions or postulates them. The latter is in fact the case, as is evident if the awaited grace is conceived, in accord with Catholic teaching, as a worthy object of believing expectation, and if the real reason for the necessity of such expectation is apprehended.

Why and to what extent does the Apostle demand, in the process of justification, the confident expectation that grace will be granted by the goodness and mercy of God as promised to us? Can the reason be that we are not to be interiorly justified, but are only to be clothed with the justice of Christ? But such a justification is no justification. Even if it were, it is not in any case a proof of the miraculous efficacy of God's sanctifying power, but rather a sign of His powerlessness in the face of sin. Yet the Apostle insists that justifying faith is a wonder-working faith,[14] a faith in God "who quickeneth the dead, and calleth those things that are not as those that are," [15] a faith such as Abraham had when he believed that the

---

[13] Thus spoke Scheeben in the full vigor of his youth. When, as an older man, he was preparing the second edition of the present work, he usually deleted or tempered such expressions. Apparently he missed the forceful term, *niederschlagen*, here employed. [Tr.]

[14] *Wunderglaube*: Scheeben seemingly means a faith that is miraculously realized in man, a faith that is absolutely unwavering in its expectation that all the divine promises will be carried out to the letter. [Tr.]

[15] Rom. 4:17.

barren Sara would become fertile,[16] and that Isaac would be raised from the dead; [17] that very faith by which we believe in the resurrection of Christ to a new, glorified life.[18]

A marvel such as this, so triumphant and supernatural a proof of the divine love and power, is found only in the Catholic doctrine of justification, a justification through regeneration by the Holy Spirit, through the communication of the divine nature and the divine life, through the wonderful renewal and sanctification of the entire essence of the soul. Only justification in the Catholic sense can be the object of the superb, believing confidence which the Apostle requires for justification, and to which he ascribes its attainment. He demands this believing trust in God because he knows that we cannot call down so great a wonder by our own works and merits, and attributes justification to this faith, because he is aware that faith alone summons God's marvels down from heaven.

Miraculous effects of other kinds are likewise credited to faith. Faith in the power and goodness of the God-man was, as a rule, the chief condition for His miraculous deeds, and the main factor that evoked the unfolding of His miraculous power. Naturally, if a person can point to no merits or, even when equipped with such, calls for an extraordinary manifestation of God's power, he can base his action only on faith in God's love and omnipotence, only on an appeal to His promises and an acknowledgment of His infinite might. By faith man, as it were, clasps God to himself, draws the divine power down, and applies it to himself. So faith is, in fact, the organ by which man comes into contact with the source of grace and drinks from it.

The importance of faith in this connection is so great that the faithful of the Old Testament could, by belief in the coming Redeemer, anticipate the efficacy of His merits. After the redemption, special external organs of God's supernatural activity in the sphere of grace were instituted by Christ, organs designed by Christ to transmit the marvelous effects of grace to the subject contacted by them. But if the subject is capable of a personal cooperation in the matter of his salvation, and wishes to share in the efficacy of those organs, he must approach them with faith and transfer their power

[16] Rom. 4:18 f.
[17] Rom. 4:17; cf. Heb. 11:17–19.
[18] Rom. 4:24.

to himself by faith. And when the activity which proceeds from faith, and by which man disposes himself for grace, has reached such a pitch that, as far as his part is concerned, he again enters into friendship with God, then faith straightway anticipates the power of the sacrament, and draws grace down into the soul before the actual reception of the sacrament.

Obviously this wonder-working faith does not exclude active belief on man's part, but rather implies it. This faith excludes only such activity on man's part as would confer on him a strict claim to the miraculous effect, or would wholly or partially produce the effect which in its totality can proceed only from the divine omnipotence. If God wishes the greatness of His gifts to be held in honor and if He wishes to accomplish His wonders with power and also with wisdom and love, He can and must require on the part of the subject an activity whereby the subject, aroused and accompanied by the light of faith, prepares himself for the reception of so great a boon, draws close to God led by God's own hand, and opens his heart to God's supernatural influence.

Inasmuch as faith prepares man for the reception of the precious gift of justification and induces God to bestow it, the two factors that enable faith to cooperate in the process and expedite it, imply and complement each other. They are both so indispensable that one requires the other, and both together are borne up by the supernatural character of justifying grace. Here again is exemplified the amazing precision of Catholic dogma, and at the same time the need of utmost accuracy in analyzing the supernatural character of its content.

91. THE MYSTERY OF SECOND JUSTIFICATION

Justification is accomplished. The mysterious rebirth of the soul in a burst of light from the heavenly Father, and its ineffably intimate espousals with the Holy Spirit, have taken place. Has the mystery of justification at length run its course?

Grace is a living force that must unfold and develop. It must bring forth fruits and, in its own turn, by these fruits must grow. The proper unfolding of the supernatural principle of life placed by God in the soul must be as supernatural and mysterious as this principle itself. In this unfolding, the mystery of justification reaches ever farther, striving toward its final perfection.

That the flowering of infused, supernatural justice in works of justice, or the practice of the supernatural virtues, is in itself thoroughly supernatural in character, is obvious. Both the activity of the soul in its intimate union with the Holy Spirit who fructifies it, and the products of this activity, that is, supernatural vital acts, are so wonderful and sublime that, with regard to this property, they are withheld from the perception even of that soul to which they pertain.[19] Rightly the Apostle refers to the life of true Christians as a hidden life: "Your life is hid with Christ in God." [20] As this life streams forth from the bosom of God and is nourished and grows with divine light, it lies open in all its glory to the eyes of God alone. Only a supernatural illumination through the Word of God or through a higher light can give us information about it. Evidently, no communication through the word of faith is able to assist us in obtaining a vivid notion of it. And the inner experience and illumination vouchsafed to us here below to a greater or lesser extent can serve only to afford us an anticipatory glance into the depths of the mystery and to fill us with greater awe at its boundless sublimity.

This vital activity of the justified man is the inception and preparation of the wonderful life which the adoptive children of God are to lead in the bosom of their Father, in the beatific vision of God; it is an anticipation of the divine life which is to flower in them when they share fully in the divine nature. Its high mystical character is best expressed by saying that it is the same kind of activity as that of the blessed in heaven. This is why its value is so great that it enables us in a true sense to merit the vision; and so this meritorious value, too, is a great mystery.

Notwithstanding the remarkable power and high value of the acts performed by the children of God, we may not conclude that the grace of justification can be thereby increased in the way that in the domain of nature the natural faculties are perfected and strengthened by exercise. Such a notion, exaggerating as it does the efficacy of the actions in which the life of grace unfolds, would debase the mysterious and lofty character of grace itself. Since

---

[19] For a fuller discussion of the nature of this vital activity and the specifically supernatural acts proceeding from the infused virtues, see *Natur und Gnade*, pp. 167 ff.

[20] Col. 3:3.

grace is a participation in the divine nature, as Christian justice is a participation in the divine sanctity, it can no more proceed from man in its growth and increase that it can in its first beginnings. Before as well as after, grace and justice at all the stages of their development must be directly infused by God through the influx of new light and new vital energy. Our activity in the state of grace serves only to merit the communication of a new measure of grace, and hence to unlock, as it were, the wellsprings of grace and divert its stream to ourselves.

Should the increase of the life of grace in us appear less mysterious and sublime on this account? Nothing could be farther from the truth. Is not God's immediate action in the augmentation of grace, the continued rebirth of man from God's bosom, the summit of mystery? Is not the traffic between man and God, the interchange between the fruits of grace on the part of man and the distribution of grace on the part of God, something that wholly transcends our earthly experience? Is this not a continuation and constant renewal of man's mystic marriage with God inaugurated by justification, with the sole difference that then the soul drew near to her heavenly bridegroom only with longing desire, whereas now, by the fruits already born to God, she truly merits the increase of His favor and a richer fructification through His grace?

Second justification, *iustificatio secunda*, as theologians term the increase of justice,[21] is no less remarkable than first justification, if it but be conceived according to the analogy of the latter. The difference between the two speaks in favor of the former. That is why we insisted that the mystery of justification does not come to a close with entrance into the state of justice, but continually grows. In fact, it grows with the increase of intimacy in the soul's marriage with God and the interchange that flourishes between them.

But this mystery does not attain its ultimate perfection until the spouse of God, after bearing rich fruits of love and fidelity to her bridegroom, is led home by Him to His Father, and is adorned with the crown of His glory. The mystery of justification looks to the mystery of glorification as its natural goal and consummation.

---

[21] The restoration of lost justice is also occasionally called *iustificatio secunda*. We are not including a consideration of second justification in this sense, since it is essentially no more than a reproductoin of first justification, and is not an augmentation of the latter.

PART EIGHT

The Mystery of Glorification and the Last Things

Eye hath not seen, nor ear heard, neither hath it entered into the heart of man, what things God hath prepared for them that love Him.

1 Cor. 2:9

CHAPTER XXIV

Glorification and the Beatific Vision

▀▀

92. SUPERNATURAL GLORIFICATION IN GENERAL AS THE CONSUMMATION OF THE MYSTERY OF FAITH

THE justification and sanctification of man is the proximate, present fruit of the supernatural, mysterious organism instituted by the Incarnation, or better, the blossom whose fruit will mature when time gives way to eternity: the supernatural glorification and beatitude of man and of all creation.

That this last end, in which the mystery of the Incarnation and grace culminates, this supreme consummation of all things, which projects beyond time into eternity and reaches above all that is earthly into heaven, is a mystery, a great and majestic mystery, can scarcely be called into question.

In general, everything that still lies hidden in the womb of the future has an air of mystery for us. But especially, and quite apart from the economy of the supernatural, we regard as a mystery all that concerns our lot beyond the grave. How matters will stand with us on the other side, even in the natural course of things, how our life will go on and how we shall rest at the end of the turmoil of our temporal existence, we can conceive only with supreme effort. Hence the haziness, the obscurity, and the uncertainty which plague the mind that is left to its own resources in this sphere; difficulties which at times appear so great as to engender the conviction that everything regarding the afterworld is absolutely hidden from reason, and is the object of faith alone.

However, if we should entertain the idea that the mystery of faith consists only in the fact that man's destiny in the future world is beyond the reach of present experience, and that only the darkness of the grave veils it from our sight, we would completely mistake its true nature. To the extent that man's state beyond the grave is his natural end and pertains to his natural destiny, it cannot be entirely impervious to reason. For the mind that has been rightly formed and cultivated, it must be discoverable with sufficient certainty and in rather clear outline. That the soul is immortal, that it will continue its spiritual life on the other side of death, and will enjoy a happy, peaceful repose in the knowledge and love of God, or, in case it departs this world in God's enmity, will eternally suffer for its sin, at odds with God and itself: these are not real mysteries at all. These are simple philosophical truths which, to be sure, can in many ways be obscured by intellectual bias, but which pertain properly to the sphere of sound reason. If Christianity conveyed to us about the next life no higher truths than these, it would undoubtedly help to correct many errors into which reason falls. But it would in no sense throw open a new domain that is altogether beyond the reach of reason.

In reality it does both, and the latter more than the former. Salvation (*salus animarum*), the final perfection and happiness of souls which revelation bids us hope for, is heralded by the Prince of the Apostles as the consummation of Christian faith (*finis fidei*),[1] not the goal of reason. This is a consummation which faith alone can make known to us, to which faith alone can lead us. It is an end pictured to us and brought home to us exclusively by faith, "the substance of things to be hoped for, the evidence of things that appear not," [2] that is, of things that are not accessible to our natural perception either in themselves or in their causes. "Eye hath not seen," says the Apostle, "nor ear heard, neither hath it entered into the heart of man [even by way of conjecture], what things God hath prepared for them that love Him." [3] This truth is taught us by "the wisdom of God in a mystery, a wisdom which is hidden, . . . which none of the princes [the great and the wise] of this world knew." [4] The wisdom of the creature cannot, by studying his nature and speculating on his natural destiny, discover the goal to which he is to tend according to God's decree. The Spirit of God alone, who "searcheth all things, yea, the deep things of God,"

[1] Cf. I Pet. 1:9: "Reportantes finem fidei vestrae, salutem animarum."
[2] Heb. 11:1.
[3] Cf. I Cor. 2:9.
[4] Cf. I Cor. 2:7 ff.

and fathoms the abyss of divine power and love, only He, according to the Apostle, can reveal to us what God has allotted to us from out the depths of His being, and what He still intends to give.[5]

Does not all this express in the clearest terms that in the perfection and beatitude of the creature we have before us a mystery in the fullest and highest sense of the word? So distinctly is this fact enunciated that even the nature of the mystery is indicated. We have here a mystery because the perfection and beatitude of the creature, as held out to us by faith, consist not in the development and maturing of a seed contained in the creature's nature, or in the unleashing of an energy buried in the creature's depths, but in the outpouring of the divine nature upon the creature, in the disclosing of the depths of the divinity.

If the perfection and beatitude of the creature are no more than a growth and maturing of its nature, the mystery in the proper sense ceases. It is preserved and its greatness appears only if there is question of an elevation of the creature above its natural sphere, of a transfiguration of the creature by participation in the divine nature.

We believe we cannot give a better, deeper, and at the same time more adequate account of the essence of the mystery than by presenting it under the aspect of transfiguration. Hence we shall endeavor to clarify the mystery along these lines.

In a certain sense we might say that the creature is transfigured when the energy and fire latent in its nature are loosed and made known to the outer world, when its inherent beauty is displayed, and its own light is intensified and brought to full brilliance. In this sense even the natural condition of the separated soul that is freed from its repressive confinement in the body and that manifests its full spiritual power, would be a state of transfiguration, just as during our present life every refinement and enhancement of its spiritual mode of life can be regarded as a kind of transfiguration. But transfiguration of this sort will not give us our supernatural mystery; nor is it a glorification in the proper sense of the word.

True glorification takes place when an object is transformed and sublimated not by the intensification of its native splendor, but by the accession of a splendor from without. Thus when we say that a seed achieves glorification in the splendor of the plant that grows forth from it, we are using figurative language. So, too, the

[5] Cf. I Cor. 2:10–12.

notion of glorification is verified in the perfection and beatitude of a spiritual creature only to the extent that the creature is suffused from without by a radiance emanating from the divine nature, which is purest spiritual and celestial fire. By the fire of this sun the creature is not only developed and perfected as the seed is brought to maturity in the plant, but it is metamorphosed into the likeness of the divine nature, and so is made to reflect and radiate the divine splendor and light of the divinity.

The Apostle expresses this thought with great precision in a classical passage. "But we all," he says, "beholding the glory of the Lord with open face, are transformed into the same image from glory to glory, as by the Spirit of the Lord." [6] It is true that St. Paul is not here treating explicitly of glorification in the next life; he is speaking primarily of that transformation which the Spirit of God effects in us here on earth, of the renewal of the inward man, as he calls it in the following chapter.[7] However, this renewal culminates in the perfection of the next life. In both cases there is a real transformation of man, a recasting by which he is changed from his own form (*a propria forma*) into the form, the image, and the glory of God. In both cases a true rebirth from God is brought to pass, a clothing of the creature with the splendor of the divine nature. In both cases a transformation into a radiant likeness of the divinity is effected by the fire of the Holy Spirit into which we are plunged: and it is this that we look upon as the very essence of glorification. In both cases this transfiguration is a deification of man by his participation in the nature of the Godhead.[8]

Ordinarily we refer to the deification and rebirth of man during this life as sanctification rather than transfiguration. We do not call it transfiguration because here the divine fire poured forth upon us gives only a hint of its brightness in a few faint rays, displaying for the most part the warmth of its love. A further reason is that, for the present, the divine splendor of God's children lies dormant in them as in a bud or seed, to burst forth into full magnificence only on the other side of the grave. But the luster of this faint glow, the loveliness of this bud, is an earnest of the immensity of that glory

[6] See II Cor. 3:18.

[7] "The inward man is renewed day by day" (II Cor. 4:16).

[8] For positive proof of all this, see sect. 57 above, and Casinius, *Quid est homo*, c.6.

which God will shower upon us in the future life. The splendor of grace, the *lumen gratiae*, which imparts so breath-taking a beauty and attractiveness to our souls in the eyes of God and makes them temples of the Holy Spirit, is the dawn of the light of glory, the *lumen gloriae*, wherein God will so suffuse us with His own glory that, like a crystal globe illuminated by the sun, we shall reflect it in ourselves.

Such a transfiguration, such a charging of the creature with divine glory, is obviously a most wonderful and supernatural work, a mystery that is beyond the reach of the intellect, and that remains inconceivable and unfathomable even after it has been revealed. It is a mystery that passes all comprehension: the mystery of a new creation, which we can grasp only by believing in God's word, and adhere to only by trusting in God's inexhaustible power and love.

This mystery manifests itself first and foremost in the spiritual creature, and hence also in the spiritual part of man. For only the spirit, which by its very nature bears a certain resemblance to God in the simplicity and vitality of its being, can be made, by the approach of God and the might of His Spirit, to share in the divine nature and be filled with God's glory and beatitude. Material nature, and so also the bodily side of man, has no capacity for deification. It is too remote from God, and has too little in common with Him, to enter into so intimate a union with Him. But who would on that account deny that the same transforming power of the Godhead which changes the spirit into a living likeness of itself, can also, and actually will, lay hold of material nature and impart to it a glory and perfection which immeasurably transcend its natural mode of being, its natural condition? If God has promised to create a new heaven and a new earth, we may not restrict this newness to the greater abundance of natural forces that the new nature will possess, and to their better organization. On the analogy of the transfiguration of the spirit, we shall have to say that material nature too, like spiritual nature, will be raised above its native condition by God's miraculous power. This material nature will be clothed and permeated with a new splendor, which cannot be explained by the enhancement and combination of natural properties and forces, any more than the supernatural life of the spirit can.

This is certain in the case of man's corporal nature, which ac-

656 THE MYSTERIES OF CHRISTIANITY

cording to the Apostle will be spiritualized,[9] and by this spiritualization will be freed from its natural frailty, and will be charged with supernatural splendor and power. This spiritualization is for corporal nature what deification is for spiritual nature. Although not so great a perfection as the latter, it is equally miraculous, because in both instances only the supernatural, elevating power of God's Spirit can be the efficient cause. The same Spirit of God divinizes the soul, and, as a sort of redundance and reflection of such divinization, effects the spiritualization of the body, just as He had done in a preparatory and rudimentary fashion in the case of the first man. As with the first man, here too, and to an even greater degree, He must bring the body of God's children, who have entered their Father's house, into harmony with the deified soul, and make it conformable to that soul. With man, at all events, He must work upon material nature the way He does upon spiritual nature, and consequently must transmute the body with a dazzling fire and splendor that could never be produced by any natural force whatever, whether spiritual or corporal. The chief reason for this is that the glorification of the body, no less than that of the soul, is regulated and demanded by the mystery of the Incarnation, which achieves its full perfection in the glorification of the entire creature.

In general, the Incarnation and the supernatural organism established by it must be taken as the point of departure and the pattern determining our notion of supernatural glorification. The explanation and the norm of the glory that is to be revealed in the creature are not found in the creature's natural destiny, but in the inconceivably high dignity and consecration which the creature has received from its union with the God-man, and through Him with God.[10] The creature's glory must be the same, if not in degree at

---

[9] "It is sown a natural body, it shall arise a spiritual body" (I Cor. 15:44). We shall see later that the notion of spiritualization probably does not completely explain the transfiguration of the body; in any case it is the main factor in the latter.

[10] This point could well receive particular attention in our efforts to extend a knowledge of Christianity. Many of our contemporaries who openly profess that they are not Christians believe in a continued happy existence of the soul with God, without suspecting that this is a specifically Christian truth. The Christian origin of this belief should be insisted on; likewise its dependence on the doctrine, the death, and especially the resurrection of Christ. There are still many non-Christians who cling to remnants of Christian revelation. [Tr.]

any rate in kind, as that which pertained to Christ's humanity in virtue of the hypostatic union. "Such as is the earthly [Adam]," says the Apostle, "such also are the earthly [children]; and such as is the heavenly, such also are they that are heavenly. Therefore as we have borne the image of the earthly, let us bear also the image of the heavenly." [11] Because of His heavenly, divine origin from the bosom of God, Christ, even in His humanity, had to be clothed with a heavenly, that is, divine, glory deriving from the Godhead.

A like heavenly, absolutely supernatural glory is to be the lot also of all those who in Christ and through Him have been taken up to God's bosom. The glory to which Christ's humanity was destined by virtue of the hypostatic union could not be natural; by the same token the glory of His members cannot be natural. Their glory must transcend all that is natural, in the same measure that the dignity and consecration which they have as Christ's members transcend all nature; and indeed, as we have mentioned, in body as well as in soul. For their bodies, too, have been taken into Christ's mystical body and, like His own body, are consecrated and sanctified by His person.

If we view the matter from this standpoint, we shall not be surprised that the transfiguration of man surpasses all natural comprehension, as it transcends all nature. If anywhere, the statement of the Apostle must hold good here, that God "is able to do all things more abundantly than we desire or understand, according to the power that worketh in us." [12] This is why St. Paul so often speaks of the inexhaustible riches of the glory that awaits us in the next life, and is lost in admiration at his contemplation of it.

But it is St. Maximus Martyr who gives expression to the full greatness of the mystery: "The transfiguration or deification of the creature surpasses all that is natural and finite. It is an immediate and infinite action of God, and tends to an infinite effect; it is almighty and all-powerful. In those who are the objects of this action there arises an inexpressible, and more than inexpressible, joy and rapture, for which in the whole of nature we can find neither explanation nor conception, neither representation nor description." [13]

[11] Cf. I Cor. 15:48 f.
[12] Eph. 3:20.
[13] *Cent. oecom.*, IV, c.19. The passage will be found in my edition of Casinius, *Quid est homo*, pp. 275 f. (*PG*, XC, 1312; cf. *ibid.*, 609).

However, to gain a clearer notion of the scope of this mystery, we must consider in detail the nature and effects of the state called into being by the transforming activity which God exercises in the creature, and especially in man.

93. The Glorification of the Spirit in the Beatific Vision: the Mystery of Eternal Life

Glorification or deification so fills the spirit with divine light that the spirit is rendered capable of a knowledge that in itself belongs to God alone: the immediate intuition of the divine essence. In this intuition is revealed the depth and sublimity of the light of glory (*lumen gloriae*); in it is wrought the most magnificent and incomprehensible of all the miracles of God's supernatural activity in the creature, a miracle by which the creature is raised to full participation in the divine life and to a share in the enjoyment of the divine happiness; a marvel so excelling nature and reason, that next to the Incarnation there is no greater. This pre-eminently is the mystery the Apostle had in mind when he proclaimed that no eye has seen it, no ear has heard it, and that it has entered into the heart of no man.

But such would not be the case if its reality, or even its sheer possibility, could be known by natural reason. For then it would fall within the natural orbit of the reason, and reason would not need to rise by faith above its native lowliness to lay hold of it.

Only a complete misunderstanding of the absolutely supernatural character of the last end actually appointed for us can give occasion to such an assumption. For the fact of the beatific vision, or our actual destination to it, could be known by reason only if it were an end physically necessary for the created spirit, an end to which God had to destine the spirit, in order to give its nature the perfection required of it. But on that hypothesis the entire Catholic doctrine of grace would go by the board; the beatific vision would not become our inheritance through a gratuitous adoption into the sonship of God, but we would have a true title to it by nature. As long as our destination to the beatific vision is a pure grace of God, we can come to know that it is a fact, and can hold fast to it with certitude, solely by belief in the revelation wherein God makes known His gracious will to give Himself to us. Thus far, all Catholic theologians must be at one.

But they do not all agree that knowledge of the possibility of the beatific vision surpasses the powers of reason. Many think that the essential idea of the mystery and the necessity of faith are sufficiently guarded if the actual existence of the beatific vision is held to be concealed from the eye of pure reason. Perhaps so; but at any rate the sublimity of the mystery and the dignity of faith are impaired if the content of faith can be so easily penetrated and grasped by reason. Even many natural things, possessed of no great excellence, can remain hidden from us as far as their actual existence is concerned, without on that account being numbered among the mysteries of faith. Indeed, most natural objects are such that we cannot apprehend their inherent possibility with a priori knowledge, but only from the fact of their actual existence. How grievously, then, would the beatific vision be debased and divested of its depth and greatness if the concession were to be made that reason, prescinding from the revealed fact of the mystery, could of itself arrive at a knowledge and a notion of its possibility!

No, the beatific vision is an unparalleled wonder, a supernatural marvel of the highest kind; and no one who recognizes it as such would dream of wishing to conceive its possibility a priori.

Let us reflect for a moment on the conditions which theologians require for the realization of the mystery, and which from the very nature of the case must be required. The immediate intuition of God in His very essence is in itself natural and proper only to the three persons who possess the divine nature. If the creature is to be elevated to such power, he also must be made to share in the divine nature by a communication of divine light, in which alone the divine essence can be rendered visible. "Those who possess God in the beatific vision," says the Roman Catechism, "although they retain their own proper substance, are clothed with an extraordinary and almost divine form, so that they seem to be gods rather than men." [14]

This is not all. That the divine essence may be really comprehended and beheld as it is in itself, it must be so closely joined to the intellect, and must penetrate so deeply into it, as to become present to it not by means of an impressed species, but by itself. It must be-

[14] P. I, c. 13, q. 6: "Qui illo fruuntur, quamvis propriam substantiam retineant, admirabilem tamen quandam et prope divinam formam induunt, ut dii potius quam homines videantur."

come no less present than the impressions emanating from a material object, as required for sensory knowledge, are present to the eye of sense. Under these conditions, theologians teach, the intuition of God is possible for the created spirit; and, we should like to add, it is these conditions alone that make the possibility of the intuition of God conceivable.

But who would maintain that even the possibility of these conditions is a priori conceivable for our natural reason? Who can fail to perceive that the fulfillment of them is a marvel beyond all marvels? What could enable reason to understand how God can fill with His own light the finite, limited creature, that stands so far beneath Him, and unite the creature so intimately with Himself, as though the creature were itself of divine nature; how the creature can be made like to God in that faculty of cognition which is the most conspicuous and characteristic excellence of His divine nature, as well as in that most intimate possession and fruition of His essence, which is due to God Himself only because of the absolute identity of the knower and the known? [15] If this is not an incomprehensible wonder, then such does not exist at all; then none of God's extraordinary activities in the order of grace, which here reaches its peak, can be characterized as wonderful or absolutely supernatural.[16]

Only a superficial regard, which does not at all penetrate to the heart of the matter, can be cast over the abyss of divine power and love here opened up, and then proceed to draw the notion of the intuition of God within the radius of rational ideas, and treat this notion according to the norm of the latter. Even those theologians, at least the sounder ones, who hold that the possibility of the beatific vision is naturally knowable, do not for a moment contend that its inner nature is conceivable; they base their view on an indirect, external, and hence more negative procedure, which depends on certain presumptions.

[15] This ineffable deification, or assimilation to God in His specifically divine property, is what the Beloved Disciple has in mind when he says: "We shall be like to Him, because we shall see Him as He is" (I John 3:2). In the same passage St. John proposes for our contemplation the beautiful and tender love that God has for us as our Father.

[16] On the nature and conditions of the beatific vision, see the incomparably clear and profound exposition of St. Thomas, *Contra Gent.*, III, 52 ff. The Roman Catechism (P. I, c.13, q.6 ff.) here closely parallels the Angelic Doctor.

They maintain, in the first place, that the possibility of the beatific vision cannot be denied, even from the standpoint of natural reason. In this they are quite right; but only because natural reason must confess that God can do more than we can grasp and conceive; and further, because reason can no more demonstrate the impossibility than the possibility of the beatific vision. Reason demonstrates that the beatific vision is not naturally possible, even though the powers of nature should be enhanced to the limit of their capacity. Hence reason also shows that this possibility, if there is such, must rest on a supernatural foundation, which reason itself cannot investigate. Hence the intrinsic possibility remains ever uncomprehended and undemonstrable.

But, they continue: the spiritual creature has a natural desire for the intuition of God; and this natural longing cannot be aimed at something impossible. Let this desire be set forth in the strongest terms: in any case it is no more than a presumption for the possibility of the intuition of God; it does not make the beatific vision conceivable in itself. But even this presumption is not demonstrative. For, first of all, the desire is not of such a nature that it necessarily requires satisfaction, or postulates the real existence of its object, thus presupposing the possibility of the object: this is against Catholic doctrine. If such a desire is assumed, it can be nothing else than the general wish of nature to be united with God as perfectly and intimately as possible. This longing exists; but can we infer from it what kind of perfection, what kind of union with God, is possible for the creature? On the contrary, must we not rather infer from the fact that a certain perfection or union with God is possible, that it really falls under that general and indefinite desire of nature? Nothing is more agreeable to the natural bent and wishes of the rational creature than perfect knowledge and intuition of its Creator. But nothing more transcends the creature's natural powers and destiny, and therefore nothing more surpasses all natural concepts, than this very intuition, by which the creature is raised above itself and carried up to the inaccessible light of the Godhead, into the bosom of the Father, to the side of the only-begotten Son, there to possess the same glory as His, and to enjoy the same happiness.

Accordingly, if we choose to admit a natural longing for the beatific vision—but only in the sense mentioned—we must add that the object of the desire is an absolutely supernatural mystery, which natural reason, left to itself, is unable to conjecture. Otherwise the Apostle could not say that what God has prepared for those who love Him has entered into the heart of no man, and that only the Spirit of God, who plumbs the depths of the Godhead, could have enlightened us concerning this great gift.[17]

The mysterious character of the immediate vision of God is brought out still more clearly by the following consideration.

The vision of God, the possession it entails, and the fruition of God based on it, constitute in a very true sense the inheritance of the children of God. This happiness is the same as that which God Himself enjoys, which belongs to Him alone by nature, and which on that account can become the joint possession only of those whom God has made partakers of His own dignity and nature, and whom He has transferred from the state of bondage to His family. The happiness of heaven is a good which we can acquire only as heirs of God and coheirs of Christ. For only as heirs and children of God can we have a right to possess and enjoy God as He possesses and enjoys Himself; and only as coheirs and members and brothers of God's only-begotten Son can we lay claim to behold His Father as He beholds Him, face to face. So greatly does this good excel all the claims and expectations of nature, that God's own Spirit has to enter into us in order to convey the promise of it to us, and to give us, in the possession of Himself, the pledge and guaranty of this promise. Therefore even the possession of this pledge accords us a blissful peace of so exalted a kind that, as the Apostle observes, it surpasses all (natural) understanding, and makes our hearts exult with rapture such as nature can never know.

However, since the possession and enjoyment of God, which His children acquire as the inheritance due to their high rank, are inconceivable without a great elevation and transfiguration of their life, and since the beatific vision, in which the possession and enjoyment of God are concentrated, is itself an act of divine life, the entrance of the children of God into their inheritance must be a new rebirth from the bosom of God, inasmuch as it is a new participation in the divine life. Through this rebirth a divine vital energy pours into the creature. It enlarges his powers of comprehension in such a way that he can apprehend the divine essence which enters into the innermost depths of his spirit. In the knowledge and love of

[17] Cf. I Cor. 2:9–12.

it he can unfold a most sublime life, a life that is wonderfully rooted in God and has its nourishment in God: a truly divine life, whereby the creature lives in God, and God lives in the creature.

Even natural life, whether spiritual or sensitive, has the guise of a profound mystery as far as our reason is concerned. Much more, then, and in much higher a sense, this divine, supernatural life of the creature in God and of God in the creature must be regarded as an unfathomable, ineffable mystery.

The term usually occurring in Sacred Scripture and ecclesiastical language to characterize this life—eternal life, *vita aeterna*—could, superficially considered, appear to have simply the force of bringing out its mysterious transcendence. If, in enunciating the predicate "eternal," we think only of the imperishableness, the immortality of life, evidently no supernatural mystery is implied. The created spirit is by nature immortal; even its natural life is imperishable, and in that sense eternal. The eternity of the spirit and its life is so evident that our natural reason has to admit it; it is so intelligible that the opposite is quite unintelligible.

But the term cannot be understood in so jejune and common a sense. Thus restricted, it obviously fails to reflect the lofty and solemn idea Christ had in mind when He used it to proclaim a blessing of such superlative magnificence; nor does it convey the sense the Church intends in placing the word at the conclusion of its Creed. Moreover, the Savior expressly describes eternal life as a life that is to flow into us in consequence of our union with Him as the natural Son of God and with His eternal Father; as a life that in Him and from Him is transmitted by the Father to all those who by faith or in the Eucharist receive Christ's own vitality into their hearts. Hence it must be a supernatural life, infused into the creature from above, and emanating from the Godhead. If it is called eternal life in this connection, its eternity must lie in the fact that it imparts to us a share in the absolutely eternal life of God.

The eternal life promised us by Christ is eternal not only because it is in some way or other immortal and imperishable, but because it is an outpouring of the absolutely eternal life of the Godhead, a life absolutely without beginning or end, as well as without change. This life is no longer rooted in a vital principle which, though indestructible, hovers on the brink of nothingness, but it is directly rooted in the eternal, primal source of life that never had a beginning. Thus its duration is endowed with an infinitely more tenacious stability than any natural life. Therefore it is incomparably more indestructible and immortal than natural life. Not only is it immortal, but, like the divine life, it is also unalterable and immutable in its immensely richer simplicity.

The natural life of the created spirit, though imperishable, is subject to the flight of time. It cannot unfold all its power in a single act, but must advance by a continuous succession of distinct acts. But the life which the spirit lives in God resembles the divine life; everything concerning this life is centered in God and around God; all that the spirit knows and loves, it knows and loves in God and through God. In its natural life, while gravitating toward God in various ways, the spirit incessantly rotates around God, so to speak, like a planet around the sun. But in its supernatural life it comes to rest, with unalterable peace, in God Himself, embracing in a single act of knowledge and love of God all the stages of development that in natural life are dispersed over a lengthy and diversified course. The spirit that lives in God and with God rises superior to the laws of the earthly flight of time (*tempus* in the narrower sense), and also is above the flight of time that measures the duration of the spiritual creature (*aevum*), and shares in the prerogative of changeless repose which is unattainable by the natural creature and is proper to God alone. Since the life of the glorified spirit is wholly divine and flows from God in whom it has its source, it is eternal in the manner of God's life, and so its eternity is at once the consequence and a distinctive mark of its divine character. To emphasize the perfection of this life, and its relation to the life of the divinity, the Son of God could well content Himself with designating it as eternal life.[18]

But there is another reason why the Son of God insisted on the term eternal life to signalize the life that is to be supernaturally conveyed to us through His mediation. In the beautiful Eucharistic discourse reported in the sixth chapter of St. John, He does not speak exclusively of the life of our soul, but refers explicitly to that life which He wishes to confer upon our entire nature, soul and body. Indeed, He goes so far as to place a special emphasis on the life of the body, by promising us that it will rise again after temporal death.

[18] On the subject of eternal life, see St. Thomas, *Contra Gent.*, III, c.61, which deals with the question of participation in the eternal life of God through the beatific vision.

The body is mortal by nature, and dies; the eternal duration of its life is a supernatural miracle so striking that it compels our attention. And therefore the Savior could with good reason stress the excellence of the life which flows from Him into our entire being by saying that it is eternal, particularly as, on the whole, unfading freshness and complete immunity to dissolution and decay constitute the highest perfection of life.

With this observation we come to the second of the chief elements in the glorification of our nature: the transfiguration of the body and of bodily life.

CHAPTER XXV

Transfiguration of the Body

~~~~~~

94. The Resurrection and Transfiguration of the Body as Correlative Factors of a Single Mystery

IN the teaching of faith about the perfection of our nature on its bodily side, two phases are distinguishable: first, the simple restoration of the union between soul and body, plus the assurance that this union will never again be dissolved; secondly, the transfiguration of the body and of bodily life, or its spiritualization along the lines of the divinization of the spirit and its life. This glorification, as has been shown, and as will become clearer as we go on, is undoubtedly a supernatural mystery. But the question might be raised whether likewise the restoration of the body that is to be glorified and its eternal preservation in life is a true mystery considered in itself alone.

This question is much in order, seeing that the restoration of the body and of its life, its resurrection from the dead, does not necessarily entail the glorification of the restored life, as we know from the case of those whom Christ raised from the dead here on earth. Again, God could conceivably preserve such a life from a second death by a special providence, without rendering it immune to dissolution by an internal transformation and spiritualization.

Undoubtedly the simple restoration of the body and its life after death, particularly after the total decomposition and dissolution of the body, is essentially a supernatural work, so far as it cannot be brought about without an immediate, extraordinary manifestation of power on the part of God. In the same way the unbroken, uninterrupted maintenance of the life so restored could not take place without God's extraordinary concurrence. But such restoration and preservation would, on the present hypothesis, affect the body and

666

its life only so far as, under other circumstances, both could be restored naturally and could be preserved in a natural way, at least for some time. Fundamentally, therefore, only the mode of operation is supernatural; the product of the causality is natural, for this product is the body and its life in their natural condition.

If we were compelled to regard this restoration or preservation of natural life as an effect that would necessarily fall within the province of man's natural destiny, it would not, despite its miraculous character, extend beyond the range of natural reason. It would be a mystery only in the sense that any of the miracles God works in the visible world are mysteries for us. And, as a matter of fact, we have the possibility of the chief effect, resuscitation from the dead, visibly before our eyes in many examples. But the supposition is untenable. It cannot be maintained that God must of necessity preserve everlastingly or restore human nature in its totality, particularly according to its lower side. Since bodily life is subject to corruption by its very nature, and actually succumbs to the forces of dissolution, and since it can be eternally preserved or restored only by a miracle, the presumption is that it has no claim to immortality and resuscitation. Even for the perfection and happiness of the soul the everlasting duration of its union with the body is not essentially requisite. The soul can be happy without the body by the enjoyment of spiritual goods, as in fact the souls of the departed are during the interval of separation from their bodies. Indeed, a union of the soul with the body, without a supernatural transfiguration of the latter, would be more of a hindrance than a requisite for the soul's full enjoyment of its higher beatitude and the full unfolding of its spiritual life. Rightly, to be sure, we say that death has come into the world through sin, and that death is an anomaly that ought to vanish once the sin to which it is linked has been remitted. But we also know that according to Catholic doctrine the immortality of the first man was a supernatural, free grace of God, to which nature had no claim. Since, according to Catholic teaching, nature had no title to immunity from death, much less has it a title to a miraculous restoration after death.

All the rational arguments advanced to persuade us of a future resurrection from the dead are nothing but reasons for the congruity of such resurrection, not for its necessity; reasons, therefore, which can make resurrection from the dead credible, perhaps even probable, but which can engender no certain conviction. It is fitting that for His glory God should give eternal existence to human nature, the microcosm, the meeting point of all creation, that He should extend the immortality of the soul to the body, and that He should eternally reward man in his body, since man has labored for the honor of God in his body and by means of his body. But these reasons are not sufficiently cogent to postulate and motivate so tremendous a miracle as would here be called for. They lose all their force by the circumstance already mentioned, namely, that the body, if not transposed to a condition of supernatural transfiguration, would hinder the full development of spiritual life, and hence would block the higher happiness of man, as well as the greater glory of God in His creation. Accordingly, from a purely natural, philosophical standpoint, the presumption must be against resurrection rather than for it.

The really decisive grounds for the resurrection of the dead and the everlasting life of the body belong to a higher region, to a supernatural order of things. They are of a mysterious nature, and therefore impart a truly mysterious character to the structure which they support.

Let us see how Holy Scripture accounts for the resurrection of the dead. We shall look in vain in the sacred writings for any indication that the resurrection is founded on a natural right of our nature. The only possible way of arriving at such a conclusion would be to resort to a number of passages in which Scripture bases the resurrection upon Christ's merits, whereby He destroyed sin. But this recourse would be valid only if Christ had annihilated sin as a mere violation of the natural order, whereas the truth is that He overcame sin as the ruin of the supernatural order. The God-man reconquered for us the right to bodily immortality, a right that had been granted us in the beginning, only because His death was powerful enough utterly to vanquish sin as the despoiler of supernatural goods.

On the other hand, the immortality of our body and its resurrection are accounted for in a number of classical texts on the grounds of our supernatural union with the God-man as the channel of a higher vitality which flows into us from the divinity.

In the sixth chapter of the Gospel according to St. John, the Savior derives our title and our hope for bodily immortality from our supernatural union with Him by faith in His divinity, and by partaking of His life-giving flesh. This union is so intimate that we are in Him as He is in the Father. Therefore we are to have our life through Him and from Him as He has His life through the Father and from the Father. He depicts the resurrection from the dead as a superhuman, scarcely imaginable wonder, which can be looked for only if a bread from heaven, replete with divine power, is given to earthly, mortal man. For the Apostle, too, the strongest argument for our resurrection is that Christ, the God-man, our head, has risen from the dead by the power of His divinity.[1] According to the Apostle, we shall share in Christ's resurrection principally for the reason that the divine, life-giving Spirit of Christ and His eternal Father abides in us, the living members of Christ: "If the Spirit of Him that raised up Jesus from the dead dwell in you, He that raised up Jesus Christ from the dead shall quicken also your mortal bodies, because of His Spirit that dwelleth in you."[2]

The Fathers likewise, such as Irenaeus[3] in the earliest times, explain our resurrection on the grounds of our supernatural union with the God-man. And since the best way of bringing about this union is to partake of His life-giving flesh, they, following the example of the Savior, point to the Eucharist as the primary source and chief title of our immortality and the resurrection of our body. Especially striking is the statement of St. Cyril of Alexandria: "No otherwise can that which is corruptible by its very nature [therefore not only by sin] be made alive [that is, be raised to incorruptible life and be preserved therein], than by being bodily joined to the body of Him who by His nature is life itself [and hence eternal life], that is, to the body of the only-begotten."[4] In saying this, however, St. Cyril does not contend, any more than the Savior Himself does, that our union with Christ must be unconditionally sacramental. Obviously he means merely to affirm that, to be able to claim and eventually obtain bodily immortality, we must be supernaturally united to the God-man as members of His mystical body, either perfectly through the Eucharist, or imperfectly by faith and baptism.

Such are the glorious, supernatural reasons upon which Sacred

---

[1] Eph. 2:5 f.; Col. 2:12 f.
[2] Rom. 8:11.
[3] Especially *Adv. Haer.*, lib. V, in many passages.
[4] *Comm. in Ioan.*, lib. X, c.2; *PG*, LXXIV, 341.

Scripture and the Fathers base our title and our hope of bodily immortality, and specifically of resurrection. These reasons are strong enough to justify our expectation of the great miracle that is here called for, whereas natural arguments can scarcely give us the faintest inkling that it will some day be realized.

If we look closely, we see that the grounds alleged, as laid before us by Sacred Scripture and the Fathers, do not merely transcend nature, but are deduced from the supernatural order at its very peak. They pertain not to the simple order of grace, but to the plane that is proper to the organism constructed on the hypostatic union. They are all reduced to the truth that we are members in the mystical body of the only-begotten Son of God.

Undoubtedly grace, by which man is elevated to the eminent rank of an adopted child of God, would be sufficient of itself, at least infinitely more so than the natural dignity and destiny of man, to account for the great miracle that is to be wrought in the human body. The sonship of God is a miracle and a source of miracles which at times, as, for example, in the immediate vision of God, are even greater than the grace of divine sonship itself. It summons man to a new, divine life in his soul. Why should it not merit for him also the restoration and continuance of his corporal life, even though this would involve a great miracle?

Nevertheless Sacred Scripture assigns our relation to Christ, our head, as the chief ground of our resurrection to immortal life. And this fact has a deep meaning in its own right. For one thing, our incorporation in Christ is the reason for grace itself, and hence also for the privileges that flow to us from Christ. Again, in the last analysis grace implies no more than sanctification and elevation of the spirit, and exercises its proper vital energy in the spirit. It does not embrace man's entire being, including his lower nature. Hence there is no contradiction in the thought that the soul might be cut off, and remain eternally cut off, from the body in the enjoyment of the happiness destined for it by grace, as in fact the souls of the blessed, although separated from their bodies for an indefinitely long time, enjoy their beatitude in perfect contentment. But through the Incarnation man's entire being was taken up into the person of the Logos, and is elevated, supported, permeated, and sanctified by His divine person. In the absolutely eternal person of the Son of God the body He assumed necessarily receives a call and a claim to everlasting existence. The same call and claim are received by the bodies of all the living members that have been mediately incorporated in the God-man's own body. The fact that the eternal God has entered into perishable flesh and has taken that flesh up with Him to the bosom of the eternal God, is the final and supreme reason for its everlasting duration and its triumphant victory over death. It is this fact which imprints the stamp of eternity upon the flesh.

Therefore we conclude: our hope for the resurrection and immortality of our body is based not on nature, but on the supernatural mysteries of grace and the Incarnation, or briefly, the mystery of our mystical oneness with the God-man.

This consideration does away with the difficulty that made the restoration of union with the body seem incompatible with the state of the spirit's complete perfection and happiness. For it not merely requires that the soul should re-enter into union with the body, but at the same time stipulates that this should be a glorified union, that the body itself should be clothed with a supernatural glory corresponding to the glory and happiness of the soul. And thus the body, far from being a heavy burden on the soul, serves rather for the full manifestation and completion of the soul's glory and happiness.

Without such a transfiguration, we said above, a resuscitation and everlasting preservation of bodily life is unthinkable. We must say now that the resuscitation may not be separated from the transfiguration: only the body that is destined for glorification at its reanimation has a destiny for resurrection at all. There is no resurrection unto eternal life without glorification. Although resurrection as such is a supernatural mystery, in reality it fuses with transfiguration into a single mystery. The supernatural reasons which require the resurrection of the body for a life that is nevermore to be dissolved, also require the glorification of that body and its life; both are required *per modum unius*, that is, the one in relation to the other.

This is a double relationship. Our living oneness with the God-man demands the resurrection of our body only so far as the body may be and must be glorified. The reason for this glorification is not merely that the body may not hinder, but that it may enhance and manifest the glory of the soul. On the other hand, the everlasting duration of the newly awakened life is fully assured, established, and effected only by the glorification of the body. Glorification of the body, as a spiritualization of its life, suppresses all that could expose it to death anew after its resurrection, namely, its natural frailty and corruptibility. Glorification guarantees that the body henceforth will never again die, that it is really raised beyond death's reach and is truly immortal. Without such glorification the body would remain intrinsically mortal, and would be guarded against the actual approach of death only by God's special protection. Without transfiguration, the endless duration of the body's life would ever be precarious, hazardous, not grounded in any quality of its own, and hence would not be the full property of the risen body, as it must be if it is to appear as the end result of the closed order which begins with grace.

What follows from this? It follows that the entire mystery of man's perfection in his corporal nature, including his resurrection and the everlasting existence of his body, is concentrated in the mystery of his glorification. This is why at the outset we pointed simply to this glorification as the proper object and fruit of man's supernatural perfection. The glorification that comes to the body by virtue of its incorporation in Christ, its destiny for participation in the glorification of the soul, ensures its everlasting life, just as the deification of the soul accords to the soul an eternal, divine life. And it ensures this so perfectly that the body becomes as truly immortal through a supernatural quality, as the soul is immortal by nature. Indeed, it seems that we must go so far as to say that through this supernatural quality everlasting life is imparted to the body in a still higher sense than pertains to the created spirit by nature. For the glorified body shares in the eternity of God, although indirectly through the soul. Along with the soul, it is raised beyond that variability and fluctuation of time to which the created spirit is subject despite its immortal nature. The body, too, is transported to a state of immutability and unalterable repose, such as God alone naturally possesses and can claim as His own.

But to understand this better, we must devote further study to the nature and effects of the transfiguration of the body.

This problem no doubt involves considerable difficulties, the more so since theologians have as yet devoted comparatively little attention to its solution. The difficulties are rooted in the very object under consideration, which is so sublime and mysterious that attempts to understand it must encounter many setbacks. These very difficulties are not the least proof of its supernatural eminence.

Nevertheless, in accord with the data before us, besides some other items we have listed elsewhere, we will try to give as clear an idea as possible of the glorification of the body and its effects.

95. Detailed Description of the Transfiguration of the Body

In general the glorification of the body may be said to consist in the conquest of its materiality, that is, in the exclusion of the imperfections which flow from its materiality. The materiality of the body is, as it were, the rust which the transfiguring fire of the Holy Spirit, who dwells in the body through the soul, is to consume, in order to confer on the body a purity, or refinement, which transcends its nature and which of itself pertains only to the immaterial spirit. Accordingly such glorification appears primarily as a refining of the body by divine power, as well as a spiritualization, that is, an assimilation to the condition of the immaterial spirit.[5]

The materiality of the body gives rise to certain defects that distinguish the body from the spirit, encumber the spirit in its natural union with the body, and drag the spirit down to the material condition of the body. The chief of the defects of the body are its crassness, its corruptibility, and its inertness. To offset these imperfections, the glorification of the body brings about the three qualities of subtility, incorruptibility or impassibility, and agility.

That these three qualities are communicated to the body in virtue of its glorification, is generally admitted. Not so general is the explanation of them, particularly in the case of the first quality, which is the one that penetrates most deeply into the stronghold of corporal nature.

This subtility is patently the opposite of the body's crassness. The crassness or grossness of the body is the most immediate and natural consequence of its materiality; just as the subtility or refinement of the spirit is the result of the simplicity which is involved in its im-

[5] On what follows, cf. St. Thomas, *Suppl. in IIIam*, q.82 ff.; Suarez, *In IIIam.*, tom. II, disp. 48.

materiality. If this crassness is removed, the body undergoes a profound modification, and is conformed to the spirit; it is spiritualized. By crassness, it should be noted, we mean no more than the property by which bodies occupy space, that is, exclude other bodies from the same place, and are themselves excluded by other bodies. If this quality were wholly eradicated, the glorified body would lose the power of occupying space and of excluding other bodies therefrom. Evidently this is not the case, else the glorified body of Christ could not have been touched by the disciples. Touching supposes spatial resistance in its object. Such an extinction of crassness is neither conceivable nor necessary. It is not conceivable, for then the body would lose an essential power, and would no longer be a spiritualized body, but would simply cease to be a body. Nor is it necessary, because the power of resistance and of occupying space is a proper perfection of the body, and the withdrawal of it would not confer any greater happiness on the soul. But this happiness is the decisive factor determining whether the body is to take its place at all in the system of divine works. If this quality were to cease, the continued existence of the body as such would no longer have any meaning.

What is really an imperfection to be suppressed, what really makes the body defective and limited with regard to its extension, and constitutes what we properly call the crassness of the body in a disparaging sense, is its dependence on space, the fact that it is naturally excluded by other bodies from the space they occupy, and hence that it is not sufficiently imponderous and subtle to be able to exist in the same place with them, as can a spirit which does not exist spatially at all. If, alongside its power to resist other bodies, the body should be endowed with the prerogative of not being impeded by the resistance of other bodies but of penetrating them despite their resistance, then in addition to its natural perfection it acquires a mode of existence proper to the spirit, and takes part in the refinement of the spirit without losing its own character. In this sense the Fathers speak of the subtility of Christ's glorified body, in virtue of which He passed unimpeded through closed doors, but immediately afterward allowed Himself to be touched. A number of the Fathers expressly describe this quality as a consequence of His transfigured, glorious state.[6]

St. Thomas is of the opinion that the subtility implied in glorifica-

[6] Cf. Suarez, op cit., sect. 5.

tion cannot be understood in this way.[7] He bases his view on two reasons: first, because the body's independence of space would be so extraordinarily supernatural that compenetration with another body could not be the result of a quality supernaturally imparted to it, but could be accomplished only by an extraordinary exercise of divine omnipotence in each case; secondly, because such a permanent quality would be pointless, since the distinction of bodies according to spatial position pertains to the manifold beauty of heaven. St. Thomas, therefore, thinks that by subtility is to be understood no more than a certain spiritualization of the body in a larger sense, which he designates as the subjection of the body to the soul.

If this were so, we should have to forgo holding that subtility is a special *dos* of the same order as the other *dotes;* it would be the sum total, or the basis and result of the others. We shall come back to this idea later. But it is a fact that the notion of subtility, as the term is here employed to signify one of the four [8] properties of the glorified body, is derived from the above-mentioned phenomena observed in the glorified body of Christ, and so we believe that it must be retained in the sense we have explained. The arguments advanced by St. Thomas are deeply thought out, but perhaps they are not altogether conclusive. For if the divine omnipotence can bring it about that one body penetrates others, and therefore that it is temporarily able to surmount the resistance of other bodies, we should think that God can, of course by a standing miracle of His omnipotence, communicate this privilege to the body as a permanent property to be used at will. And it certainly would not be pointless. Even though a permanent penetration of bodies would do away with the visible order of the heavens, it pertains to the perfection of the body that the soul can at any moment transport it to any spot it desires. For the unrestricted use of such a privilege, the power to penetrate any body lying in its path, and to pass right through it, would appear, if not necessary, at any rate very much to the point.

The other two qualities by which the body, owing to its materiality, is distinguished from the spirit to its disadvantage, are corruptibility and inertness.

[7] St. Thomas, *op. cit.,* q.83, a.2.
[8] Apparently Scheeben is here looking upon impassibility as a separate quality; later on in this section he does not distinguish it from incorruptibility. [Tr.]

By corruptibility is meant the capacity for suffering which is proper to the body as such, and by which it can be altered, disintegrated, decomposed. By inertness is understood the unwieldiness, the ponderousness whereby the body is prevented from responding to every impulse put forth by the soul, and from serving the soul as an instrument for whatever activity it chooses. That these two imperfections are absorbed by the glorification of the body is unquestioned; incorruptibility or impassibility and agility are alleged precisely in this sense among the endowments of the glorified body. By its glorification the body receives a supernatural incorruptibility and impassibility such as the spirit has by nature; and at the same time it receives a mobility that enables it without difficulty to accompany the spirit anywhere, just as if it were a spirit itself.

Thus we can understand tolerably well what glorification accomplishes as a refinement and spiritualization of the body, and how it makes the body conformable to the soul by overcoming its materiality.

But we must penetrate still more deeply into the foundation and significance of this spiritualization. Man's body is glorified and spiritualized not as an independent being, but as a body informed and animated by the spiritual soul. By its spiritualization it is made conformable not to some spirit extraneous to itself, but to the spirit inhabiting it. And since, as a human body, it exists only by the spirit that animates it and for the good of that spirit, its conformity to the spirit must have its proper basis and full significance in the spirit. The conformity must be brought about on the grounds and for the purpose of its subjection to the spiritual soul.

St. Thomas gave expression to a remarkably profound thought when he stated that the glorification of the body (in the three qualities thus far mentioned) is at bottom nothing but a full subjection of the body to the soul.[9] For the materiality of man's body is sur-

---

[9] *Op. cit.*, a. 1: "Therefore others say that the complete perfection whereby human bodies are said to be subtile proceeds from the dominion which the glorified soul, as the form of the body, exercises over the body. On this account the glorified body is said to be spiritual, in the sense that it is entirely subject to the spirit. The first subjection, whereby the body is subject to the soul, gives the body a share in the specific being of the soul, inasmuch as it is subject to the soul as matter to form; and secondly, the body is subject to the soul with regard to the other operations of the soul, so far as the soul is a principle of movement. Accordingly, the first reason for the body's spirituality is subtility, and secondarily agility and the other properties of

mounted by the fact that the spirit inhabiting it perfectly pervades and dominates it with supernatural power.

The spirit, as vital principle, also rules the body in a natural manner, in the functions of natural life and in movement. But this dominion is not unlimited. It has its limits in the very materiality of the body; and these limitations are such that not only is the spirit's absolute control of the body obstructed, but the spirit itself is restricted in the exercise of its own liberty. Not only is the spirit unable to free the body from its dependence on space, to suppress its passibility, and to employ it as an instrument for any activity it wills; the spirit itself for its part is to some extent pinned down under the oppressive materiality of the body fettered to it. The spirit cannot exist with its substance in any place where its body cannot exist; the spirit, while united to the body, is involved in the latter's passibility; and lastly, the spirit itself is in many ways hampered in its inner activity by the cumbersomeness of the body. "The corruptible body is a weight on the soul."

The soul's dominion over the body can be made complete only by the power of God's Spirit. Raised to a higher degree of spirituality in its own being, and, as it were, immersed in divine fire, the glorified soul can lay hold of the body, permeate it, and dominate it in an incomparably more effective way than it could by its natural power. Therefore it can absorb whatever corporeal properties could be alien to it or oppose it or obstruct it. This complete impregnation of the body by the spiritual soul is, in the concrete, the cause of the spiritualization of man's body. This point has to be grasped before the spiritualization of the body can be made fully clear.

If the body is controlled by the soul in so dominant a manner that the limits of the body's materiality are broken through, the first consequence of this is the subtility, the sublimation of the body, in virtue of which, if our explanation given above is to remain, the body can exist wherever the soul itself is able to exist. St. Thomas, who does not admit this explanation, supplies another,[10] which we

the glorified body. And therefore, as the theologians explain, the Apostle in treating of spirituality touches on the gift of subtility; and Gregory says in the fourteenth book of his *Moralia* that the glorified body is called subtile because it is an effect of spiritual power. With this in mind, it is easy to solve the objections, which have to do with the subtility that is brought about by rarefaction."

[10] *Ibid.*

can adopt along with our own in order to complete it and impart further depth to it. The very domination by the soul involves a certain refining of the body, a removal of the crass, dense character by which its materiality blocks it off from a thorough impregnation by the spirit. Crassness is a hindrance that prevents a body from penetrating and from being penetrated, just as tenuousness (for example, the rarefaction of the air) imparts a capability for penetrating and for being penetrated. The surmounting of the obstacle and the conferring of penetrability is in our case the effect of the soul itself, which by divine power impregnates the body. The immediate result of this operation is naturally that subtility which enables the body to be impregnated by the soul; a secondary result is the other aspect of subtility relative to space, whereby the body can exist with the dominant soul wherever the soul itself is able to exist.

We see from this that St. Thomas, in denying the subtility of the glorified body in the latter sense, intends to set aside only a secondary factor; but he has a deep grasp of the proper character of subtility itself, and of the basic nature of the body's spiritualization.

The other two properties of the glorified body, that is, incorruptibility and agility, are more easily and conclusively inferred from the soul's absolute dominion over the body. If the body is so completely under the sway of the soul that its materiality is wholly repressed and neutralized, and is, so to speak, absorbed in the spirit, it can no longer be assailed, injured, or destroyed by any of those causes that formerly had power over it on account of its materiality. Especially it cannot be affected in such a way that the soul would be involved in its suffering. Rather, the body must be completely dependent on the soul. Far from placing any obstacle in the path of the soul's activity, it must permit itself to be moved and controlled in every respect according to the soul's good pleasure.

Thus the three factors mentioned as contributing to the glorification of the human body are essentially related to the supernatural, absolute dominion of the soul over the body. They are effects of the supernatural power with which the soul is endowed by the Spirit of God. But just as they are effects of the soul's dominion over the body, so at the same time they are conditions under which alone this dominion can exist and be maintained in its perfection. In other words, the soul's enjoyment of full dominion over the body is the result, and hence also the end, of the qualities imparted to the body by the soul's absolute sway over it. For the soul, acting in the power of the Holy Spirit, effects the spiritualization of the body not for the sake of the body, but that the soul itself may be liberated from all the limits and ties of materiality, and may be able to use the body without hindrance as a flexible instrument for its own good.

This is why we stated above that the subjection of the body to the soul is at once the cause and the purpose of the body's spiritualization. This may seem to be contradictory, but actually it is not. The subjection is the cause of the spiritualization of the body so far as the body is permeated and dominated by the soul, and is its end so far as the absolute dominion is rendered possible by the spiritualization.

It is evident, and no further demonstration is required, that so perfect a subjection of the body to the soul, a subjection which the admirable conformation of the former to the latter partly procures and partly supposes, is not only most extraordinary, but rises above all claims of human nature. Hence it is at least as much a mystery as the gifts of integrity were in the first man. For those gifts were merely the prelude to this glorification which completely transforms nature. In a certain way integrity achieved what this glorification achieves, but only because it also rested on a sort of glorification effected by the Holy Spirit. However, it was not a glorification that radically sublimated the body and its life, or made impossible the revival of its natural shortcomings, and hence its complete dissolution. The natural defects were merely covered up and suspended, but were not eliminated by an interior transformation. Such transformation takes place only in heavenly glorification; and therefore Adam's immortality was only a *posse non mori* (a power of avoiding death), not a *non posse mori* (impossibility of dying). Hence the mystery of glorification transcends the mystery of integrity as greatly as the *non posse mori* excels the *posse non mori*.

Integrity, as we stated earlier, was meant to rectify and purify nature so that nature, as a burnished and unspotted mirror, might receive the light of God's grace. In the same way the rectification and purification of nature by glorification must make nature an unsullied mirror for the reception of the light of glory, in which God grants the soul to behold Him face to face. And as integrity was intended to emancipate the soul that had been called to the sublime liberty of the children of God from the bonds of the flesh, and to make it the body's master, so in actually entering into the full possession of the liberty of the children of God the soul must be perfectly freed from the ties of the flesh and must be given absolute dominion over it.

What we observed previously regarding the relation of integrity to the grace of divine sonship, has a parallel in the relation of the body's glorification to the glorification of the soul. This relation brings out the full mysterious character of glorification and manifests its full significance.

But if the glorification of the body exists simply for the glorification of the soul, we must discover in it something more than we have proposed up to the present. Those of its effects that we have thus far specified are at bottom only a refinement and purification of the body and its life, but they do not constitute a positive glorification. They conform the body to the spirit, but not to the glorified, deified spirit. They enable the body to share in the natural spirituality of the soul, but not in its supernatural glorification. They are only preliminary conditions for participation in the divine glorification of the soul; but as such they are also directed to that end. Precisely because the body is entirely conformed to the spirit, is completely impregnated and dominated by it, and is, so to speak, fused with it, it can and should be enveloped by the glorifying fire of the divinity, and reflect the divine glory of the soul. When earthly fire frees gold from its dross, it communicates itself to the gold and sets it aglow. Likewise when the Spirit of God refines the body with His heavenly fire, He must prepare the way for raising it to a state of glowing brilliance, whereby He confers on it a new, supernatural power and glory, so that the words of the Apostle may be fulfilled: "It is sown in dishonor, it shall rise in glory; it is sown in weakness, it shall rise in power." [11]

The purity and refinement which the body receives in its spiritualization impart to it a great beauty and glory; and the complete subjection of the body to the soul confers on bodily life an incomparably greater power and energy than it had from nature. But this beauty, although received in a supernatural manner, is nothing but the natural beauty of the soul radiating through the body; and the power coursing triumphantly through the body is the natural vitality of the soul. Again, a higher beauty and an enhanced life

[11] See I Cor. 15:43.

redound in the body from the light of glory in the soul, whereby the soul sees the face of God. We would expect the tremendous rapture and ecstasy of the soul that enjoys the vision of God to transfigure the bodily countenance and pervade the entire natural life with glowing happiness, much more than in the case of natural joy. But this direct redundance of the effects of the light of glory is not an overflow of this light itself; since the light is purely spiritual it cannot of itself confer a higher splendor on the body and make it literally radiant. Indeed, if the soul were not furnished with a supernatural power for regulating the life of the body, the limitless energy of the light of glory might end by completely paralyzing the lower activity of the soul, instead of elevating it. These two sources do not yield that effect which we usually, and not without reason, associate with the glorification of the body, namely, that it is really bathed and permeated with its own supernatural radiance, which imparts to it a greater beauty and a greater power. Although we cannot attain to any clear understanding of this point, the notion itself seems to be well founded, as we indicated previously when treating of glorification in general.

If the transfiguration of the body is to be proportionate to the glorification of the soul, God must confer on the body a corporeal radiance suitable to its nature, just as He confers spiritual illumination on the soul. This corporeal radiance must excel the nature of the body and all natural light as much as the light of glory in the soul is above its nature and all natural spiritual illumination. And like the light of glory, it must glorify both the substance and the life of the body, imparting a higher beauty to the former, a higher energy and strength to the latter. It must do all this in so exquisite a way that the beauty, although in the body, is not itself visible to the bodily eye, and the energy enables the body to concur in vital acts in which, as far as its nature goes, it could not concur.[12]

Despite their intrinsic difference, these two lights are so closely related that one can be regarded as a consequence of the other; the two can even be regarded as one. The *lumen corporis*, although not

[12] It seems to us that this idea of the glorification of the body best corresponds to the expressions used by Scripture, as well as to the analogy of faith. However, as we are well aware, very many theologians believe that the light of bodily glorification is natural in substance, that is, that it results from a combination of the energies which produce natural light, or from an intensification of natural vital energies.

ignited at the *lumen animae*, and though certainly not identical with it, is naturally connected with it, on account of the union of the body with the soul. It should even make the body, as far as is consistent with its nature, conformable to the glorified soul, and should cause it to reflect the soul's glory. Besides, both are effects of the same divine fire of the Holy Spirit, who extends the influence He exerts on the soul over to the body, and glorifies the body only with reference to the soul. In this sense the glory of the body can be understood as a redundance of the glory of the soul, and both together as an outpouring of divine power and glory flooding the entire man.

96. The Glorification of Material Nature

Not only the human body, but the whole of material nature, is moving toward a state of glorification, in which it is to realize its final purpose and attain its eternal repose.

We have to view this transformation according to the analogy of the glorification of the human body, with which it is closely connected. For as the body is the domicile of the soul, material nature is the domicile of the whole man. The human body is derived from material nature and does not abandon its organic connection with matter even when united to the spirit. By a natural conformity, therefore, the glorification of the human body must be communicated to the nature which encompasses it and is bound up with it, so that this nature may become a worthy dwelling place for glorified man, and in its totality have a share in the glory shed over man, its highest pinnacle.

If the glorification of material nature in general must be represented after the analogy of the glorification of the human body, it is manifestly an absolutely supernatural mystery. For this transfiguration will result in a glory that infinitely surpasses all the powers and exigencies of nature, and hence can be neither known nor conceived by the natural intellect.

True, the Apostle says that creation which was subjected to frustration against its will sighs for the revelation of the glory of God's sons, in order to be delivered from the tyranny of corruption.[13] But from this we may not infer that such glorification is the

---

[13] Rom. 8:20–22.

natural end of creation. For the glory whose revelation creation awaits is the supernatural glory of the children of God, a glory to which man himself is called only in consequence of his gratuitous adoption by God. Therefore it is only in virtue of its connection with the children of God that nature can expect this glory, which falls to its portion as a reflection and overflow and revelation of the glory of God's children. If nature sighs and yearns for this glory, if according to St. Paul its present sufferings are, so to speak, the birth pangs of the glory that is to come, it sighs and yearns not of itself, but through the same divine Spirit who, as the Apostle so beautifully says directly afterward, pleads in our hearts with unutterable groanings, and is the seed and pledge of their future glory. This glorification is for material nature as much a complete transformation and rebirth to a higher existence and life, a new heavenly creation, as is the sanctification and transfiguration of the soul by grace.

The deepest and strongest motive for the glorification of the human body was found in the Incarnation of the Son of God; the same is true here. The most valid claim that material creation has for a glorious transfiguration is the fact that it is organically united to the body assumed by the God-man, and that through the hypostatic union it has become the consecrated temple of the Son of God, and so must reflect the divine glory that has come to it. By descending into material nature, the Son of God has raised it high above its own native condition, and through His Spirit must renew and glorify it in a manner becoming its high estate. In the Son of God creation is drawn up with Him to the highest heavens, to the bosom of the Godhead, and so must lay aside its earthly nature and put on a heavenly nature; it must become heavenly in the highest and noblest sense of the word.

This new heavenly condition, which comes into exsitence not by evolution but by a miraculous transformation, is so full of mystery that we can scarcely form even a rough notion of it, to say nothing of a clear idea. Pursuing the analogy of the transfiguration of the human body, we must stop at saying that it consists, on the one hand, of a suppression and repression of materiality, particularly of the corruptibility, inconstancy, and perishableness resulting therefrom, and on the other hand, of a communication of supernatural beauty and energy.

This much, it appears, must be said; it may not be of much help for a clearer description, but at least contributes to a deeper understanding of the mystery. The natural splendor of the universe as we know it here on earth depends chiefly on the sun situated at its center: from the sun energy and light flow forth to the celestial bodies dependent on it. In the same way there is a sun in the glorified world, from which its supernatural splendor is derived. For spiritual beings, this sun is the infinitely luminous substance of God, who assembles all the blessed spirits in Himself and around Himself, to pervade, glorify, enliven, and saturate them with divine light in unchangeable repose. But for the material world the sun is the body of the Son of God, from which alone its supernatural, spiritualizing, and deifying splendor can proceed and in fact does proceed. Around Christ's body, as around its center, the glorified world must arrange itself. That body must be for it what the natural sun is for the terrestrial world, and what God is for the glorified spirit world. Thus in glorification the entire natural world is lifted from its former base and set upon a new foundation and provided with a new organism which is inherently immutable. Thus it becomes a new heaven and a new earth, the glorious City of God, which has no need of earthly sun or moon: "for the glory of God hath enlightened it, and the Lamb is the lamp thereof"; [14] and into it the waters of life flow, not from any earthly source, but from the throne of God and of the Lamb.

97. Negative Transfiguration, or the Mystery of the Fire of Hell

Opposed to the mystery of justification and grace is the mystery of sin. So, likewise, opposed to the shining mystery of heavenly glorification, whereby God crowns the work of His grace and rewards the justice of man, there must open up an abyss of darkness and nothingness into which the justice of God thrusts those who have abused the grace offered them, and have turned its blessing into a curse.

Our very reason informs us that God will be a just judge, who will reward the good and punish the wicked. And reason teaches us this not through a difficult and involved process of deduction, but

[14] Apoc. 21:23.

through the clear, decisive voice of conscience. Further, that this requital, whether of good or of evil, will be everlasting and never-ending, may be easily learned by natural reason, even if not with the same clarity. Once the immortality of the soul is admitted, it follows as a matter of course that God will never cease to reward the good. But it also follows that He will never cease to punish the wicked. Otherwise we should have to assume that no definite term has been set for the time of probation, and suppose a periodic return of such an opportunity. Without denying the absolute possibility of this hypothesis, there is little probability of its realization; at any rate reason can assume the contrary just as well, without running into any greater difficulties. Briefly, the eternity of the retribution at least can pertain to the final consummation of the natural order, and is therefore not to be classified as belonging to an order of things that is completely hidden from the intellect.

With our reason alone, of course, we cannot determine very many details about the mode of eternal retribution, whether for the good or for the bad. But as long as there is question only of retribution for the fulfillment or non-fulfillment of the natural law, we have to assume that the retribution itself is contained within the boundaries of nature, and hence that the reward of the good would consist in the more or less perfect attainment of their natural end, and the punishment of the wicked in the loss of that end, together with an interior derangement and laceration of soul corresponding to the gravity of their guilt. A truly miraculous, supernatural intervention on the part of God, to raise the good above their nature and to degrade the wicked beneath their nature, appears inadmissible in our supposition, and lies entirely beyond the calculations of natural reason, since it is outside the province of the natural order.

But if we regard the justice and the sin of man in the supernatural order, there must be a correspondingly supernatural and mysterious mode of retribution. In the case of remuneration this is clear: it consists in the miraculous glorification of man in body and soul by the divine fire of the Holy Spirit. And since sin, in its opposition to supernatural grace and justice, is a supernatural evil by which the creature rebels against the infinitely tender kindness of the Holy Spirit, God's reaction against it must take on a quite different character from what it does in the natural order. The infinitely powerful might of God must, with the same supernatural force with which it draws the just to itself in order to glorify and beatify them, repel the sinner from itself in order to degrade him beneath his nature, and to overthrow and crush him to the same degree that it had planned to raise him above his nature and to overwhelm and fill him with the fullness of divine existence and life.

We would be wide of the mark if we were minded to restrict the punishment due to sin, considered as a violation of the supernatural order, to the *poena damni*, or privation of the beatific vision. For, in violating the supernatural order, sin, besides destroying charity and grace, by which we are called to the beatific vision, is a positive offense and dishonoring of God in His fatherly rights. This is much more grievous than an offense against God as supreme Lord, and therefore draws down upon the sinner a positive chastisement. In support of the opposite view it might be alleged that the older theologians were accustomed to say that the *poena damni* corresponds to the *aversio a Deo*, while the *poena sensus* or *afflictiva* corresponds to the *conversio ad creaturam*,[15] and that sin in the supernatural order differs from sin committed in the natural order only in the *aversio a Deo*. But by *aversio a Deo* these theologians understood primarily the abandonment, the refusal of the love that was due; and to this refusal corresponds in fact the *poena damni*, just as the possession of the beloved good corresponds to love. In the inordinate *conversio ad creaturam*, on the other hand, they saw a positive contempt of the supreme Good to which the sinner preferred a finite good, and hence a real dishonoring of God. To this dishonor corresponds vengeance on the part of God's outraged honor, the *poena afflictiva* which crushes pride. On account of this equation with the dishonor done to God, the *inordinata conversio ad creaturam* has a meaning in the supernatural order essentially different from the meaning it has in the natural order, and therefore entails not only a rejection from the bosom of God, but also a *poena afflictiva* of a special kind.

Accordingly the state of punishment visited on the sinner is not merely the negation, but the reverse, of divine glorification, and in its way is as supernatural and mysterious as the latter. It, too, is a sort of supernatural transfiguration of nature, accomplished by the fiery power of the divinity, not in the positive sense that the sinner's nature is transformed into a sun shining with the light of glory and

[15] Thus, for example, St. Thomas, *Contra Gent.*, III, c. 145.

radiant with happiness, but in a negative sense, so far as nature, without being actually annihilated, is so utterly degraded, so completely stifled and laid waste, that it incessantly perceives and feels itself hovering on the brink of annihilation. The appalling frightfulness of this state consists in the fact that the creature not only tortures itself by the inner conflict of its malice and its unsatisfied appetites, but is plunged into a vastly deeper sea of misery and unhappiness by a supernatural force which lays hold of it and imprisons it, so that it succumbs to the weight of a supernatural, overpowering action from without. It is devastated by an external agent even more than it devastates itself.

Still, it is evident that in the supernatural order the corrosion of the damned by the poison of their own malice is as horrible as the malice itself. Even if the *poena damni*, regarded as the loss of a supernatural good not irresistibly desired by the creature and not freely craved by the damned, did not constitute such a great torment, it certainly does so since it involves, besides the loss of fellowship in love with God and the blessed, a hate and fury against God and the blessed proportionate to the supernatural fellowship in love. This hate, combined with the consciousness of utter powerlessness to make itself felt, interiorly racks the damned in such a way that it tortures them still more terribly than the effects of God's wrath against them. Thus understood, the *poena damni* is the most excruciating punishment of the damned, and is thoroughly supernatural in character.[16]

It lies in the nature of things that the punishment of the sinner in the supernatural order can scarcely be described otherwise than as the effect of a devouring fire, if only for the reason that, as has been stated, it is the reverse of the supernatural glorification and beatitude of transfiguration. This designation is the more apt in view of the fact that even in the natural world we are unable to conceive a more violent mode of destruction or a more frightful torment than that which is caused by the consuming force of material fire. But it is clear that fire in the supernatural order, whether its function is positive or negative transfiguration, cannot be regarded simply as material or natural fire. There is question chiefly of a devastation or glorification, respectively, of the spirit, and of so mighty a devastation or glorification that the spirit is completely enveloped and

[16] See above, sect. 40 f.

transformed by the fire that lays hold of it. Material, sensible fire has no natural effect at all upon the spirit as such; nor does the spiritual fire of love or malice that naturally flares up in the spirit itself possess any transforming power.

In the last analysis this fire can be nothing else than the spiritual and supernatural fiery might of the divinity which stands outside and above the spirit, either to elevate and glorify it by drawing the spirit to itself, or to debase and destroy it by repelling and subjugating it. Divine power alone is able to glorify the spirit by raising it to a higher existence, and to reduce it to the brink of annihilation, that is, so to crush it that naturally it would have to expire, and yet does not expire, so that it may feel the unalloyed misery of its predicament. This is the sense in which Scripture asserts that God is a consuming fire.[17] If, then, we wish to gain a deeper idea of the extent of the punishments of hell, we must place these thoughts in the foreground: as the just are permeated by the tender fire of the divine love which envelops them, the wicked are debased and devoured by the weight and the fire of divine wrath, a wrath exactly proportionate in greatness and might to the love which, offered to the creature and scorned by him, has been changed into hatred.

But might it not appear that in equating this fire with God's wrath and spiritual might we are interpreting the fire of hell in a purely figurative and symbolic sense? This may at first sight seem to be the case. In reality this course leads to an understanding of the meaning and possibility of hell-fire in a material sense.

If we should refer the spiritual fire, which rakes and consumes the damned, exclusively or principally to their inner laceration and malice, it would obviously have no connection at all, or the very slightest connection, with an external, material agent. Actually, however, we apprehend this fire in the terrible might of the divine wrath, which stands outside and above the spirit, and which intends to smother and destroy the spirit; and we contend that it is quite understandable that the divine wrath should employ a material agent as the instrument of its activity. Although matter in itself has no power over the spirit as such, in the hand of God, as the instrument of His might, it can acquire such power supernaturally. Indeed, since matter in itself possesses no power over the spirit, it is eminently fitted and qualified for this activity of God's. For the debasement

[17] Deut. 4:23 f.: "Beware lest thou ever forget the covenant of the Lord thy God . . . because the Lord thy God is a consuming fire, a jealous God."

and overthrow of the spirit which is in question here—a lowering beneath its nature—will best be effected if the spirit, deprived of its natural liberty and impassibility, is chained to matter by the power of God and subjected to its action and its tyranny.

The force which the material agent possesses for the devastation and overthrow of the spirit is not its natural energy, but the power of God, who most completely and strikingly attains His end, and celebrates the most brilliant triumph over His enemies by employing so deficient an instrument. Without the concurrence of the consuming power of the Godhead, the material agent could not be thought of in this connection as operative at all. On the other hand, without the material instrument the power of God would not celebrate so glorious a triumph over His enemies. The two factors require and complement each other.

Hence the notion of a material agent, far from being excluded by the emphasis placed on the spiritual fire of the divinity, is accounted for, clarified, and rendered intelligible only on this hypothesis. But, it will be objected, is not this material agent, which operates not by its own power but by the power of God, likewise fire only in a figurative and symbolic sense? Evidently the material agent need not be perfectly identical in substance with our natural, earthly fire. The idea is perhaps not untenable that other material substances may in the hand of God accomplish the same effect as our natural fire.[18] For the latter cannot act upon the pure spirit merely by its natural properties, which require a chemical process for their operation. Nor can the pure spirit really burn, in any proper sense of the word. Nor can it formally experience the sensation of burning, which is essentially an animal experience. There is no doubt that our material agent, though furnished with a supernatural devastating power, can be termed fire only in an analogous sense. Its supernatural energy makes it essentially different from our natural fire.

For all that, it is not a purely symbolic fire. It would be symbolic fire only if the agent thus designated were in a quite different order, that is, in the domain of the spirit. I speak symbolically when I discourse about the consuming power of love, or of anger. But here

[18] Some conclude from this, and not without reason, that the devils, who at present are not yet confined to a definite place, suffer the pain of fire from their contact with any material substance, hence also from the air in which they may be moving about.

everything is on the same level. We have a material agent that exercises a destructive and devouring activity upon another substance, but does so in a higher sense and in a much more terrifying manner than natural fire is able to do. Precisely the aspect under which fire is here regarded, and the function which Sacred Scripture intends principally to express and illustrate under the notion of natural fire, that is, its power to destroy and to cause that pain which is produced in a sentient being at the climax of its conflict with material nature,[19] is present in the agent which we call supernatural fire, and in a far greater and higher degree than in natural, chemical fire. Just as I call God a spirit not in a symbolic but in a proper sense,[20] and indeed, in a more proper sense than my own soul, although I derive the idea of spirit from my soul and apply it analogously to God, so that material agent can be called fire in the proper sense, and even in a more proper, or rather, in a higher sense, than the material fire to which I chiefly attach the term fire; for what I mean by that name is verified in the former more perfectly and in a higher degree than in the latter.

In any case, when interpreting Scripture and the teaching of tradition about hell-fire, its similarity and analogy to natural fire must be defended as long and as strictly as possible. Simply because no adequate similarity between them as regards their nature and causality presents itself to our imagination, we may not consider ourselves justified in arbitrarily bringing out the dissimilarity, and in making a mere symbol out of the analogy, so as by the fire of Gehenna to understand, for instance, the heat of ungratified passions. The repeated and straightforward expressions of Scripture, as interpreted by the Fathers and theologians, stress at least these two points: the fire signifies a devouring action upon the damned

[19] My esteemed teacher, C. H. Vosen (*Das Christentum und die Einsprüche seiner Gegner*, 2nd ed., p. 429), has brought out this point well. I believe I must differ with him only in this one detail, that I do not account for the conflict with material nature simply in terms of the interior repugnance which the condemned spirit experiences toward external objects, but primarily by the influence these objects exert upon the spirit as instruments in God's avenging hand.

[20] We are here using the term "proper sense" not as opposed to analogous sense (for the notion of spirit, as applied to God, is surely analogous), but, as intimated in the text, in opposition to symbolic sense, according to which Holy Scripture refers to Christ as the lion of Juda [Apoc. 5:5], a rock [I Cor. 10:4], and the like.

from without, and this action is associated with a material agent. No legitimate interpretation of Scripture can ignore these two points. We could relinquish them only if their impossibility or incongruity were evidently demonstrated. But up to the present no theologian has pointed out any impossibility. The Fathers and theologians admit no more than that they are incomprehensible. However, in conceding this and even frankly emphasizing it, and thereby explaining the fire of hell as a miracle of God's omnipotence which must be retained despite its inconceivability,[21] they give us to understand that they believe irrevocably in the existence of both elements, and that they regard as quite untenable any symbolic interpretation of the fire as the burning smart of unsatisfied passions, which would do away with the miracle. Nor are there any other theological reasons to prevent us from admitting such a miracle, and actually finding it in the words of Scripture. Rather, the analogy of faith leads us to expect a miracle of God's punitive justice here. Even if the words of Scripture and the teaching of the Fathers were not so telling, if they merely allowed of such an interpretation, we should have to be on the watch for some such miracle.

We need not be surprised that the rationalist, who looks at everything from a natural standpoint, regards the whole doctrine as impossible and incomprehensible, and that sometimes even Catholic theologians who view the matter somewhat from the same standpoint, excessively water down the idea. As has been stated, the action of fire upon the spirit as such is naturally impossible. It is possible only supernaturally, in virtue of a terrible reaction on the part of God against the sinner, and its searing assault is explicable only in view of the peculiar character which sin has in the supernatural order as the rebellion of man against supernatural grace. The notion of this frightful ravaging of the spirit by material fire is based fundamentally on the idea of the divine, spiritual fire with which God intended to suffuse the soul in grace. The notion must stand or fall with this idea. The attenuation of the latter involves the attenuation of the former; and if we do not have recourse to the latter, we shall have great difficulty in conceiving and defending the former.

It is this punishment of fire that characterizes the state of the

[21] Thus St. Augustine, *De civ. Dei*, lib. XXI (*PL*, XLI, 724; *CSEL*, XL, 2, 536), insists that the devils suffer from material fire "in an unimaginable, yet real manner."

damned as the reverse of a mysterious order, and so it is itself a true mystery, the terrifying nature of which surpasses the perception and concepts of natural reason as much as the magnificent splendor of glorification does. It is a mystery of torment, suffering, and terror, which the purely natural reason can no more conjecture and conceive than it can fathom the mystery of the malice of sin and contempt of grace, from which it sprang.

This same mysterious character of infernal punishment also entails corporal chastisement for man in particular, and determines its nature.

The very circumstance that man has to endure eternal punishment in his body is at least *de facto* connected with the supernatural order of grace. The miraculous resuscitation of the body and its permanent conservation for eternal punishment is inseparably related to the resurrection and conservation of the body for the reception of everlasting reward. If the latter did not occur, the former would not occur either. But if the latter takes place, the former must take place also, if the manner and intensity of the punishment are to correspond to the reward. Since the glorious resurrection of the body can have its motivation only in the supernatural order of grace, the resuscitation of the body for punishment must be the specific consequence of the violation of that order.

As concerns the punishment itself, it must clearly be conceived, on the one hand, after the analogy of the punishment of the spirit, and on the other hand, as a state which is inversely proportionate to the glorification of the bodies of the blessed; it must be a punishment that qualitatively and quantitatively is so great and terrible that it immeasurably surpasses all the forebodings and concepts of natural reason.

It must be the result of a supernatural force which penetrates and devours the body without destroying it, and through the body dreadfully racks and tortures the soul fettered to it. I say: it must be the result of a supernatural force; otherwise the punishment of the body would be proportionate neither to the punishment of the soul nor to the glory of the transfigured body; and moreover, natural forces consume only if they destroy. As in the glorification of man God exalts and beatifies soul and body by the same divine power, so in the case of punishment He must degrade and inflict pain on soul and body by this same power, but in reverse order. For

God effects the glorification of the body by causing it to be dominated and spiritualized by the soul. But the debasement of the body is a means He uses for the greater abasement of the soul. The body is to drag the soul along with it in its catastrophic ruin. The soul is rightly punished by being deprived of its dominion over the body and by being subjected to the body's mastery, just as the fairest reward of the soul consists in its absolute dominion over the body.

In consequence of the glorification and spiritualization of the body, a divinely enkindled light, perceptible to the senses, suffuses the body with exquisite, superterrestrial beauty and splendor. In like manner, with the degradation of the body is associated a bodily malady, caused by divine power and hence supernatural, but not on that account less sensible, whereby the body is laid waste and tortured. Operating like a natural fire, this formidable affliction brings the body to the verge of annihilation, and makes the soul entrapped in the body experience the very torment, but in a far more terrible degree, that it would experience from natural fire at the height of its disintegrating violence.

The material agent by which God reduces the body to this condition of intolerable heat and causes in the soul the searing pain it experiences as the vital principle of the body, is obviously fire in a much more proper, true, and real sense than that which racks and tortures the soul directly. But it differs from natural fire in this respect, that its flame is not the result of a natural, chemical process, but is sustained by divine power, and therefore does not dissolve the body which it envelops, but preserves it forever in the condition of burning agony. It remains ever a supernatural fire in its origin, in its mode of operation, and in the incomparable intensity of the torment it inflicts.

From this it follows that the fire of hell acts upon the body, and upon the soul as vital principle of the body, otherwise than upon the soul not yet reclothed with the body, or upon pure spirits. In the first case it can cause a real sensation of burning; in the latter, as remarked above, it can naturally neither burn the soul in any proper sense nor produce in it the sensation which our soul experiences when the body is exposed to fire. By the divine power it can produce in the spirit only an analogous, but none the less terrible, and even a greater, havoc and suffering. Therefore the Savior could use the same term to designate the fire which is prepared for man when resurrected to his damnation, and that prepared for the devil and his angels; because in both cases it is the same agent which is employed by the might of the divine wrath to produce different effects according to the varying susceptibilities of the subject.

It might appear as if the positive punishment of man, since it affects both body and soul, were greater than that of the pure spirits, whose sin is essentially more malicious and more deserving of punishment than the sins of men. But we must remember that the human soul is by its very nature more capable of suffering, and in particular is more susceptible to the influence of material causes, than the pure spirit. Therefore its suffering does not involve so great a degradation and abasement beneath its nature as when the angels are subjected to a material agent. Further, the degree of God's reaction against the sinner is to be measured according to the enormity of the malice, and a greater intensity of this reaction can abundantly compensate for the special form which it takes in the case of man.[22]

[22] In general, on the fire of hell, see the learned and comprehensive treatise of Suarez, De angelis, c.12 ff., where practically all the pertinent literature has been taken into consideration; St. Thomas, De spirit. creaturis, q.2, art. ult.; Lessius, De perf. div., lib. XIII, c.30.

PART NINE

The Mystery of Predestination

> Blessed be the God and Father of our
> Lord Jesus Christ, who . . . chose us in
> Him before the foundation of the world
> . . . [and] hath predestinated us unto the
> adoption of children through Jesus Christ
> unto Himself, according to the purpose of
> His will.
>
> Eph. 1:3–5

CHAPTER XXVI

Nature of Predestination

▀▀▀

98. General Notion of Predestination and Its Mysterious Character

THE glorification of man and of all creation is the goal of the great, mysterious order of things which has unrolled before our eyes, and the crown of all the supernatural works of God, which achieve their full consummation therein.

It might appear that our gallery of mysteries comes to an end with this glorification. And in fact we find that there are no further supernatural works of God which may not be reduced to those we have already passed in review. But beyond and above the works of God, we have still to consider the decree and plan from which those works go forth; for they come into being and run their course according to the pattern and under the influence of that plan.

Both in itself and in its influence upon the unfolding order of the universe, this decree or plan must be an absolutely supernatural mystery, impervious to natural reason. It is the great mystery of predestination.

Predestination: a portentous, awesome word in theology, the cross of the brooding intellect, the terror of the apprehensive conscience. At first glance it appears to be a somber mystery, and seems to be the more so, the less its true supernatural and hidden character is understood. But as soon as it is moved back to the proper distance and is inspected from the right point of view, it stands before us, for all the obscurity of its secret nature, as a luminous and splendid truth. Although its ramifications are lost in dim and, to some extent, alarming regions, its shining core emits most cheering and comforting rays.

Let us endeavor to outline the mystery from this standpoint.

697

In the most general sense predestination is a decree of God, an inner decision of the divine wisdom and will, whereby God resolves and determines what He Himself will bring to pass. In the Apostle's words, it is the counsel of the divine will whereby God works all things,[1] or, according to St. Augustine, whereby He disposes within Himself what He intends to accomplish.[2]

In this general sense divine predestination has a bearing on all the works of God. Everything that He does and effects is predestined by Him through an eternal decree before it is carried out in time.

However, in the Sacred Writings God's predestination is not stressed in a uniform way for all His works. Scripture, it is true, reduces all visible works to God's decree, as, for example, when it states: "Whatsoever the Lord pleased He hath done, in heaven, in earth."[3] But it lays special emphasis on predestination only when it speaks of decrees that are not manifest in visible creation, but come to our knowledge through a divine communication of a very intimate sort, and in which we do not infer the decree from the work, but know the work from God's preconceived plan. This is the case particularly with regard to those supernatural works of God that do not automatically come to our knowledge even at their realization. Such are the hypostatic union of the Son of God with a human nature, the inner workings of the economy of redemption, and the elevation of created nature to participation in the divine nature by grace and glory. In speaking of such works, the Apostle is careful to emphasize the eternal, gratuitous decree locked up in God's bosom, from which these works proceed; and he represents that decree as the pre-eminent object of revelation and faith. Thus, for example, he says: "To me, the least of all the saints, is given this grace . . . to enlighten all men that they may see what is the dispensation of the mystery which hath been hidden from eternity in God, who created all things; that the manifold wisdom of God may be made known to the principalities and powers in heavenly places through the Church, according to the eternal purpose which He made, in

[1] "Who worketh all things according to the counsel of His will" (Eph. 1:11).

[2] "In sua quae falli mutarique non potest praescientia, opera sua futura disponere, id omnino nec aliud quidquam est praedestinare" (*De dono perseverantiae*, c.17, no. 41; *PL*, XLV, 1019).

[3] Cf. Ps. 134:6.

Christ Jesus our Lord." [4] The entire supernatural order is here exhibited as the unfolding of a mystery hidden in God; but this mystery is nothing else than the infinitely resourceful plan that is based upon the God-man, a plan of the divine wisdom and love that will be communicated to creatures with an astounding generosity they could never have imagined.

Hence when we speak of the mystery of predestination, we understand this term to mean, in the sense of Holy Scripture, the plan and decree of God's supernatural works; and, owing to the supernatural and obscure character of the object, we also take predestination itself to be a mystery.

According to the definition thus far discussed, predestination is equivalent to plan or counsel in general, and therefore refers simply to the objects or products of the divine activity. Usually, however, the word is employed in a more graphic sense, with a special turn. "To destine" does not mean simply, as a rule, to decree an action, or to order a task to be performed; we associate it with the subject, the person, to whom and for whom something is to happen: *praedestinare alicui aliquid*, to destine something for someone. Thus the Apostle speaks of the supernatural wisdom which God has foreordained before the beginning of time for our glorification; [5] and the Savior talks about the kingdom which was prepared for the just from the foundation of the world. The object of predestination is here a gift that God is to bestow on the creature.

If such gifts are supernatural, that is, if they surpass the nature and the natural claims of man, the foreordaining of them is evidently a mystery; and since all the gifts of the higher order of grace are supernatural in this way, the predestination of them also falls within the order of mystery. Concerning this there is no further difficulty.

But the most proper meaning of predestination, as well as the essence of the mystery, stands out only if we regard it as the destiny, the designation of a being for the attainment of a preordained end. It is in this most characteristic sense that we have to understand predestination here. For it is in this sense that it is the soul of the divine government of the world, and the principle that regulates the working out of the order of things as God intends.

[4] Eph. 3:8–11.
[5] Cf. I Cor. 2:7.

This destiny can be conceived in two ways: that God appoints an end for man, and then allows him to pursue, achieve, or earn it by his own activity; or that God Himself not only predetermines what is to be the goal of man's endeavor, but also leads him toward that goal, and effectively influences his progress toward it. These two ways of designating or predestinating do not exclude each other; they can very well imply each other, as the self-activity of man is joined to an impulse coming from God, and God's inciting activity stimulates and calls forth man's self-activity. Manifestly the second kind of designation better fulfills the notion of predestination. For here it is properly seen to be the cause of the movement of man to his end, the *ratio transmissionis creaturae rationalis in finem*, in the pithy formula proposed by St. Thomas.[6]

As a principle of movement, therefore, as *ratio transmissionis*, God really operates in all the actions of His creature, including those of its natural development. Rational creatures, too, who are endowed with liberty and consequently with self-movement and self-determination, cannot freely tend even toward their natural end unless they are moved by God at least to good in general through the powers and impulses received from Him. In no sphere is there or can there be an absolute self-movement of the creature toward good. However, the moral freedom of the creature is not at all destroyed by its dependence on the divine impulse; rather, it draws therefrom its entire motive force and energy.

Some theologians of the modern era have sought to discover the mystery of predestination in this general dependence of man's self-activity on the divine movement and foreordination. If this were the case predestination would not be a specifically Christian mystery; it would be a simple rational truth, even though more or less obscure in its inner nature; it would belong to the same category as creation, on which its necessity and nature rest.

Christian predestination, the real mystery of predestination, is something quite different. It completely surpasses nature, and is the reason of a movement which is wholly distinct from that which is common to all natural movements.

Although nature can pursue and attain its natural end only in consequence of divine destination and activity, God has placed the seed of its growth in nature itself; as long as it unfolds in its own

[6] *Summa*, Ia, q. 23, a. 1.

sphere, the entire movement can be regarded as proceeding from nature. It does not need to be elevated and sustained by any new interior force. The source of the development is contained in nature itself; and in order that motion may flow forth from it, it requires at most only such further assistance as will initiate activity and prepare the way for it.

In Christian predestination, on the contrary, man is destined by God for an end which lies beyond the range of natural powers, which nature of itself can neither attain nor merit, and to which of itself it stands in no vital relationship. The divine love manifested in ordaining man to this end is truly lavish and gracious. No less imposing is the divine power that comes into play in communicating to nature an activity it could never attain by itself. That man may receive the power to strive after that supernatural end, he must mount above his nature. He must let himself be elevated, raised by God. He must, as it were, let himself be borne toward his end upon the wings of God's grace. Here the full force of the *transmissio in finem* is revealed; for man progresses toward his goal not by any power lying in his own nature, but is raised up and carried by a higher power that speeds him toward it.

Hence Christian predestination is essentially supernatural, as well in the decree of God's free, gratuitous love in which it is anchored, as in the goal at which it aims and the activity which it generates. At the same time the notion of predestination is perfectly verified in the supernatural character of the divine foreordination and activity. The supernaturality of predestination involves and determines its mysterious character. The mystery of predestination lies in God's sublime decree, unfathomable by any human wisdom, by which He appoints men to their supernatural end and guides them toward it.

It is the decree of the divine will, whereby God "hath predestinated us unto the adoption of children through Jesus Christ," [7] "to be made conformable to the image of His Son." [8] This decree manifests itself step by step in the call to grace, justification, and the eventual glorification of man.

Looked at from this point of view, predestination is the cause of our salvation, and therefore is of the utmost importance in theology;

[7] Eph. 1:5.
[8] Rom. 8:30.

it is also the object of lively controversy. We have now to study it more closely.

99. Universal or Virtual Predestination, and Particular or Effective Predestination

Predestination is fundamentally identical with God's supernatural salvific will, by which He directs the movement of His creatures toward their supernatural end.

The divine will to save, according to the unanimous teaching of all Catholic theologians, is twofold: on the one hand it is universal, and refers to all men, even those who, as a matter of fact, fail to achieve salvation; on the other hand, it is particular, and refers to those who actually reach their foreordained end.

Ordinarily, when God's will to save is designated as predestination, it is only this latter sense, to the exclusion of the former, that is understood. Hence predestination is taken to mean the divine decree whereby men are effectively brought to their end. Accordingly the mystery is placed at that point which marks off the particular, effective salvific will from the universal salvific will. We are of the opinion that the universal salvific will, too, can and must be called predestination, and that the center of gravity of the mystery is found therein, for the reason that it is the root and kernel of the particular salvific will. If this turns out to be the case, the light shining in the heart of the mystery will illuminate us with rays of uncommon brilliance.

In point of fact, if God's universal will to save is serious and efficacious, God had from eternity the design to call all men to a supernatural end, and also, as far as lies in Him, to guide them toward it. In pursuance of this intention, God begins to draw man to Himself by His prevenient grace, to incline man to his supernatural end, and to spur him on to the attainment of it, with the purpose of leading him to it effectively, provided man does not refuse his consent and cooperation to grace. What else does this mean but that God has predestined man to a supernatural end, and continues to predestine him? Sacred Scripture, it is true, refers predestination primarily to the actual, effective leading of man to salvation or the sonship of God. St. Paul, in the first chapter of his Epistle to the Ephesians, in his own name and in the name of his readers praises

God for choosing and predestining them. No one would maintain that the Apostle here had in mind only God's particular salvific will, of which no one can know whether it will issue in complete fulfillment as far as he is concerned, or is going to be realized only with regard to the "holy and unspotted" who have the grace of adoption.

Particular, effective predestination, by which God actually assists man to procure his end, is only an offshoot, a flowering of this universal predestination, is virtually contained in it, and issues from it.

As the tendency and inclination to good, which precedes the deliberate advertence of the will, passes over to actual movement when the free will accedes to it, so the divine will to move really moves when the will of man accedes to it under the influence of grace, and makes God's design his own. As the carrying out of the impulse to which God inspires the creature presupposes the consent and cooperation of the creature's free will, so on the part of God the will to carry through the impulse supposes foreknowledge of this cooperation and is consequent upon it, and is therefore essentially a *praedestinatio consequens*, consequent predestination. But, as should be carefully noted, it is consequent not upon any works performed by the creature or his meritorious movement toward the supernatural—with regard to these it remains antecedent, as their efficient cause—but only in reference to the creature's cooperation, which likewise precedes the work and the effective movement.

Universal predestination and particular predestination are at bottom only one. They are distinct only as different stages. The second is based on the first, and for its execution requires the intervention of God's foreknowledge.[9]

[9] "Antecedent will is the name applied by theologians to God's conditional will, or the will whereby God wills inasmuch as He Himself is concerned. The other, that is, consequent will, is called absolute. The distinction between the two has nothing to do with any difference in affection or in the manner of willing in God, but has reference to the connotation of the terms and our manner of understanding. When God is said to will the salvation of all as far as lies in Him and antecedently, the ordering of all men to salvation is connoted, with regard both to the nature that has been given to them and to the grace that has been offered them. For God has given to all a nature whereby they can know Him, seek Him when they know Him, find Him when they seek Him, and cleave to Him when they find Him, and thus obtain salvation. Likewise, He offered grace when He sent and offered His Son, whose merit suffices for the salvation of all. He also gave and made known laws and commands relating to salvation. Further, He Himself is at

Surely the power by which God conducts and moves man to his end is present in His universal salvific will; the particular salvific will implies only the effective use of this power by the will of man under the influence of grace. Hence it appears to us to be a thoroughly distorted view to ascribe a special power to particular predestination as opposed to universal predestination, and in this sense to call it *praedestinatio efficax*, efficacious predestination. As distinct from universal predestination, it should rather be termed effective (in Latin, *efficiens*, or *effectiva*, or *effectrix*). For if God's universal will to save is in earnest, it must be efficacious, since it makes the striving after salvation abundantly possible for the creature.[10]

---

hand to all who seek Him, and is close to all who call upon Him. Therefore to will man's salvation antecedently means to place him on the road to salvation, and to assist him in his desire to arrive at the goal. Hence antecedently to will to save does not connote salvation [as actually conferred], but rather the fact that man is fully equipped to attain salvation. But consequently or absolutely to will to save is the same as to give salvation to him whom God foresees will achieve salvation through His help and grace, and connotes the actual obtaining of salvation." (St. Bonaventure, *In I Sent.*, dist. 46, a.1, q.1). For St. Augustine, effective predestination involves God's foreknowledge. St. Augustine perceives in predestination not simply foreknowledge, but foreknowledge of a divine effect; and so he invariably adds to the divine operation the prevision of the effect that is to be produced. He often speaks in this vein in his works *De praedestinatione sanctorum* and *De dono perseverantiae*. Thus in the latter (no. 41; PL, XLV, 1018) he says: "In giving His gifts to anyone, God undoubtedly foresaw to whom He was going to give them, and prepared them in the light of His prevision. . . . For to dispose His future works in the light of His foreknowledge, which is not subject to error or change, this and nothing else is meant by predestination." St. Augustine always used the term *praedestinare* of God's effective will to save. The relation of the latter to the universal salvific will and to prevision is given by St. Augustine's faithful disciple Prosper, in the *Responsiones ad cap. obiectionum Gallorum* (no. 8; PL, LI, 172): "He who says that God does not will all men to be saved, but only a certain number of the predestined, speaks more harshly than he ought concerning the depth of God's inscrutable grace; for God wishes all men to be saved and to come to the knowledge of the truth, and He fulfills the design of His will in those whom, having foreknown, He predestined . . . so that they who are saved, are saved because God willed them to be saved; and they who are lost, are lost because they merited to perish." Elsewhere (*Responsiones ad cap. obiectionum Vincentianarum*, c.12; PL, LI, 184) Prosper says of the reprobate: "By their own will they departed, by their own will they fell. And because their fall was foreknown, they were not predestined. But they would have been predestined if they had returned and remained in holiness and truth."

[10] The Latin *efficax* can, to be sure, signify the force which is actually operative, as well as the force which suffices and equips for action. Primarily, how-

But if this is so, if particular predestination is essentially one with universal predestination and draws its power therefrom, evidently the mystery of predestination must be found not in particular predestination alone, but also, or rather primarily and principally, in universal predestination.

The mystery is nothing else than the supernatural character of predestination in general, as is clear from the fact that it incites man and fits him for a progress beyond his nature and, if he cooperates, effectively achieves this purpose. The supernatural element of the process involved in predestination does not consist in the passage from the impulse to the actual motion, but in the elevation of man by a supernatural impulse, so far as the motion toward a supernatural end is thereby made possible for him and, as soon as he accedes to the impulse, is actually carried through. Of course, the transition from impulse to motion in man's cooperation must also take place in a supernatural way, but only for the reason that man, in order to cooperate in a supernatural movement, must be stimulated and sustained by a proportionate impulse.

If the mystery of predestination is looked at from this point of view, as rooted in the supernatural nature of God's universal will to save, it is seen to be a mystery as elevating as it is sublime. It appears to us to be such particularly in those properties usually regarded as the most prominent, but also as the most obscure aspects of its mystical character.

We mean the gratuitousness and the infallibility of predestination. As long as we restrict these properties to particular, effective predestination, we shall be entangled in the most perplexing problems, and shall be hard put to it to defend the sincerity of God's universal will to save. But in our view of the matter, this sincerity is triumphantly vindicated, and the two properties of predestination, as the necessary consequences of its supernaturalness, accord us the

---

ever, it signifies capacity for action, hence sufficient force, *vis sufficiens;* and so *efficax* should not be used as the opposite of *sufficiens.* For this reason most theologians make a distinction between *efficacia virtutis* and *efficacia connexionis* (i.e., *virtutis cum effectu reapse prodeunte*). But why is not the latter designated by the word which indicates its relationship to the former, and simply called *efficientia?* If *gratia effectrix,* to be really *effectrix,* still needs a special *efficacia virtutis,* which man does not have by the mere fact that he has *gratia sufficiens,* it is not apparent how the latter can be regarded as truly sufficient.

strongest motive for humble gratitude mingled with wholesome fear and the most comforting hope.

Both properties, gratuitousness and infallibility, taken together constitute what is generally known as the absolute or unconditional character of predestination. Because it is supernatural, predestination is evidently not subject to any condition on the side of nature, since God is neither moved nor can in any way be moved by nature for the predestination of nature; nor can obstacles present in nature hinder Him from carrying out the decrees of predestination. The gratuitousness of predestination makes it unconditional in the first sense, and the infallibility of predestination makes it unconditional in the second sense.

100. The Gratuitousness of Predestination

According to the teaching of the Church and of Sacred Scripture, predestination is, in the fullest sense of the word, gratuitous or unmerited on our part, and is in general independent of all that is purely human or outside of God. In other words, it is independent of everything that is not connected with God's predestination. This gratuitousness is based on the supernaturalness of our end, and is therefore a true mystery. This end absolutely transcends our nature. Nature has no claim at all to it; it becomes ours only through the supernatural merit of the God-man. This is true especially in view of the fact that by sin nature lost the relation to the supernatural end which originally it had received in Adam. Consequently nature cannot make a step toward that end by its own activity, and cannot merit it by its own works, even if these are quite pure and perfect in their kind. Nature cannot even summon forth the slightest efficacious or fruitful striving for it. Hence the plan or purpose by which God destines nature to the supernatural end and wills to lead it to that end, proceeds solely and entirely from His sheer goodness and the superabundant grace He bestows on us in Christ and for the sake of Christ; but this plan of God's is quite unmotivated and unconditioned from our side. No merits, great or small, either of nature or of nature's works, precede it; the plan itself precedes all meritorious works or cooperation. In both respects, therefore, the *propositum salvandi* is a *voluntas antecedens, quam nihil antecedit et quae antecedit omnia nostra merita*, an absolutely antecedent will, which no merit precedes, and which precedes all our merits.

This absolutely antecedent will of God, which is independent of us, ought not to frighten us. Rather it ought to call forth our thanks to God, who wills to confer on us a good so sublime that we cannot merit it by our own efforts. Further, it ought to call forth our confident hope that we will attain salvation, since we are all efficaciously drawn and spurred on to it. All our meritorious works, including our very cooperation with grace, depend on prevenient grace, which is given to us without any merit on our part. But God gives this first grace to all men (or at least holds out the prospect of it to them), and thereby gives them the power and the impetus to consent to it, to cooperate with it, and so to draw ever closer to their goal.

Since particular predestination is nothing but universal predestination regarded from the standpoint of its actual realization in the human will, it likewise can be said to be absolutely gratuitous and unmerited, that is, as concerns all good works and merits that lie outside it and precede it. Strictly speaking, it is not induced or merited even by the merits springing from grace. We do, of course, merit glory by the works of grace; and so we can, in a certain sense, say that we prevail upon God to confer glory on us, or that we merit the *propositum dandi gloriam*, so far as glory is a special work of God, a special stage in the order of salvation, in which one element can and does depend on another. But we merit heavenly glory only by the fact that God destines us to it as our end, and incites us to it by His grace; and predestination in the narrower sense is not exactly God's decree to give us glory, but the will by which He conducts us to it: the *consilium quo nos transmittit in finem gloriae*. Neither by natural nor by supernatural merits can we earn the actual impetus which God gives us to arrive at the goal. But the utilization of the movement itself which God gives us is dependent on the condition that we accept it, that we consent to the impulse received from God, and that we allow ourselves to be moved and carried along; in a word, that we cooperate with and through God's prevenient grace.

Accordingly, particular predestination in no way takes our merit into consideration, but only our cooperation. With our cooperation it brings forth meritorious works in us, and leads us to our end through them. It is the cause of our merits, and so is not subsequent but antecedent to our foreseen merits. But it is such only with respect to the prevision of our cooperation (*praescientia cooperationis nostrae*), and hence is not independent of our supernatural liberty and its activity as procured by universal predestination and prevenient grace. And it differs from universal predestination only in this respect, that the latter abstracts even from the prevision of our actual cooperation. Therefore it would be best to say that it is neither *ex praevisis meritis* nor *post praevisa merita*, nor simply *ante praevisa merita* or independent of them, but *per merita praevisa in cooperatione liberi arbitrii a gratia moti et informati, qua cum ipsa gratia praeveniente cooperatur;* that is, through merits foreseen in the cooperation of the free will as moved and informed by grace, whereby the free will cooperates with the prevenient grace itself.

Thus presented, the true significance of the gratuitous nature of predestination is perceived, and the mystery, owing to its supernatural character, stands forth as a true mystery; as the object of our grateful wonderment and not as an object of terror; as the source of our supernatural liberty and not as an obstacle to it; as the best and most exalted motive of our supernatural hope, and not as a cause of anxious alarm.

101. The Infallibility of Predestination

The second supernatural property of predestination is its infallibility. This is undoubtedly more than the mere inerrancy and immutable certainty of the divine foreknowledge, whereby God perceives that the elect will arrive at their goal; for in the same way God also knows that the reprobate will fail to attain their end. It is the infallibility and immutable certainty of the decree by which God conducts the elect to their goal.

We must discern its true meaning in the fact that it is the basis and motive of that supernatural and unshakable hope whereby all men during this life must expect, through God's love and power, that they can and ought to achieve their supernatural end. Therefore its efficacy must be found in universal predestination, of which particular predestination is the mere manifestation and expression. It is based not so much upon the divine knowledge as upon the divine faithfulness and the divine power whereon our hope relies.

In Christ and on account of Christ, God has extended to us the fatherly love He bore toward Christ as His Son and has made us the coheirs of Christ. Through this love God has destined us for a supernatural end. Therefore He owes it to His love that, as long as we are still wayfarers on this earth (*in statu viae ad finem*), He remain true to Himself, and lead us through all the intervening steps to our sublime goal. But this is so only if we do not refuse cooperation to His grace or, in the words of St. Augustine, if we do not scorn His mercy in His gifts. God wishes to recognize us as His children. He has loved us all in His Son, and has predestined us to be made conformable to the image of His Son. Therefore He must call us all to faith and justice by His prevenient grace. If we heed this call, He must justify us; and if we guard the justice we have received up to the very end, He must glorify us.[11]

Thus in virtue of His universal supernatural love, God on His part must infallibly and unfalteringly lead us toward our goal. That is, He must on His part infallibly do everything that is necessary and sufficient for the attainment of our end; but the actual attainment of that end depends on our cooperation, which is inherently wavering and uncertain. Hence, so far as our hope is anchored in God, as alone it can and must be, it is unfailing. It is this hope, which all men must have, that the Apostle intends to commend and substantiate in the passage just cited from the Epistle to the Romans. Consequently his words must refer not to particular predestination as such, but, at least virtually, to universal predestination; for the latter alone is the basis of our universal hope.

The infallibility of particular predestination consists in the fact that God infallibly foresees the result of the efficacy of universal predestination, which in itself is unfailing. The infallibility that corresponds to God's love and faithfulness is not necessarily rooted in a special preference of God for the effectively predestined; rather it flows *ipso facto* from His universal salvific will under the prevision of human cooperation. Hence it is present principally and primarily in the antecedent will to save, and only as a result of this fact in particular predestination which, as consequent will, in the sense explained above, proceeds from the antecedent will, and objectively manifests the efficacy of the latter in man's cooperation.

In the same passage of the Epistle to the Romans, the Apostle

[11] Rom. 8:29 f.

further bases our supernatural and unshakable hope on God's irresistible power. "If God be for us, who is against us?" This is the
second reason for the supernatural infallibility of predestination.
Since God has foreordained us to an end infinitely surpassing all
created effort, He also places at our disposal His own infinite power
that sets aside every obstacle, so that through God who is with us,
and for the sake of God who has loved us so unstintingly, we may
overcome in all things.[12] In prevenient grace the divine love turns
over to us its own omnipotence which nothing can withstand, so
that no creature in heaven or on earth, no power, neither death nor
life, neither height nor depth, can separate us from the love of
Christ, or can stay us on the road to our goal, as long as we allow
grace to have its way in us.[13]

Even our natural frailty, even the evil disposition of our will
which precedes grace, is paralyzed by grace as far as its operation
is concerned, so that it cannot detain us on the road along which God
wishes to lead us, if only we do not barricade ourselves against grace.
And grace possesses this unfailing, invincible, and all-conquering
power and efficacy even if it does not actually bring about the complete transformation of the will. For it places in the will so strong
an impulse toward good that the previous disposition can no longer
hinder the conversion of the will, and endures only to the extent
that the will withdraws from the influence of grace. But when the
will is converted, the conversion or actual turning toward good is
an effect of that supernatural power of grace which the will receives
and permits to work in itself. In short, the antecedent will of God
so powerfully moves us toward our end through prevenient grace,
which is given to everyone, that all the barriers set up in its path,
whether they come from outside or from our nature or even from
the will itself, are virtually overcome and eliminated, and are no
longer insuperable obstacles, if we really wish to consent to grace.

In this sense, then, we can speak of an intrinsic infallibility of
universal predestination, arising from its supernatural character. As
a result, the infallibility of particular predestination does not consist simply in God's foreknowledge of the free activity of our will,
but rather in His foreknowledge of an effect that proceeds from His
unfailing, supernatural divine love and power. It is, therefore, like

[12] Rom. 8:37.
[13] Cf. Rom. 8:35-39.

the gratuitousness of predestination, a true, supernatural mystery, which is based on the supernatural character of our end, and is as comforting as it is sublime.

It is also quite clear that this infallibility of predestination does not destroy man's freedom, but is the foundation of his highest freedom. What St. Augustine says of grace applies equally to predestination: *non aufert, sed statuit libertatem*. That is, inasmuch as effective predestination involves God's prevision of man's free cooperation, it presupposes the exercise of liberty. And inasmuch as universal predestination (as *efficax*) spurs man on to the pursuit of his end, and hence to cooperation with grace, it empowers him to exercise his liberty, or better, elevates natural liberty to the supernatural plane, and raises it so high above its natural weakness and all arresting obstacles, that failure to cooperate can in no way be ascribed to a deficiency in freedom, but only to a misuse of it. With regard to this strengthening of the will against obstacles, predestination operates through grace primarily upon fallen man, in order to make an invincible, unshakable steadfastness in good possible for his will, and to capacitate him for a perseverance which the mere absence of obstacles did not impart to the first man.

CHAPTER XXVII

The True Mystery of Predestination

■■■

102. THE CATHOLIC DOCTRINE OF PREDESTINATION AS OPPOSED
TO RATIONALIST AND ULTRAMYSTIC VIEWS

OUR exposition of the nature of predestination according to
Catholic teaching will receive new light if we examine closely
the one-sided counterproposals, or rather mutilations of the mystery,
which have appeared in the course of time.

The true mystery of predestination stands in the middle between
two extremes, which either completely abandon one or other of its
two organically connected elements, or at any rate put such excessive
emphasis on one that the other is neglected. Either the self-activity
of man is too much stressed, to the exclusion of God's guidance of
man's preliminary steps and continued progress, or the divine guidance is represented as driving and hurrying man along in such a
way that his own movement and advance are obscured. The former
is the rationalist and naturalist doctrine, the latter is the ultramystic
and ultra-supernaturalist view, which however, when carried to its
logical conclusion, degenerates to a rationalist mechanism.

Let us begin with the naturalist or rationalist teaching.

The orthodox doctrine maintains that God's free love moves Him
to rouse us and urge us toward our end by His prevenient grace.
The naturalist theory, on the contrary, excludes all movement
emanating from God and passing over to us, hence the *transmissio
in finem*, and with it predestination itself as its principle. It contends
that man by his own free will gives himself the first impulse, the first
thrust toward his end. Hence it teaches that of himself man moves
himself, and thereby moves God to lend him aid and support for
carrying out the purpose he has formed, and eventually to allot him
an eternal reward.

In the first view God moves Himself (gratuitously) and us (with love and power that in themselves are infallible); and, provided that we permit ourselves to be moved, He perceives in our movement an effect of His predestination. In the second view man moves both himself and God, and God sees in this movement only an effect produced by man; God Himself can exercise no excitating influence on this effect; all God can do is to help it along by assisting man to surmount incidental obstacles, and crown it with His reward.

In the first case predestination precedes the prevision of merits, for it is their cause. In the second case predestination comes after the prevision of merits, for these depend chiefly on man; it presupposes the activity and movement of man, and so is no longer a real predestination by which man is conducted to his end; it is no *praedestinatio movens in finem*, but is only a predestination of the reward which man is to receive for his labors.

This naturalist teaching was most strongly marked in the Pelagians. They looked upon human liberty not as the active indifference which pertains to the will even under the influence of grace and, generally speaking, under any divine impulse that anticipates the will's decision in favor of good, but as an unconditional independence of God and of all divine impulse, whereby the will could of its own power determine itself to good no less than to evil. When man turns to evil, he acts without God and is the principal agent and cause; the same is true, according to Pelagius, when he decides in favor of good. As man can give himself the first impulse toward evil, so he can give himself the first impulse toward good; and as God does not impel and predestine us to evil, but by His prevision merely foresees evil as an effect in which He has no part, so He can foresee good as a human effect which is quite independent of Him. If God wishes to take part in any way, He must await the decision of the human will, whereupon He can abet it with supporting grace, and thus assist man to carry out his purpose, his *propositum*. Grace does not work upon the will itself in such a way as to set it in motion. Grace is but an instrument subject to the will and placed at its disposal, so that the will, in the face of all impediments, can successfully carry out the motion it has itself initiated. In this conception man really predestines himself, since he does not, as Augustine says, line up his *propositum bonum* with the divine plan and permit it to issue therefrom, but gives direction to the divine plan by his own.

Such a doctrine, taken as it stands, contradicts not only supernatural, mysterious predestination to eternal life, but even that predestination which is proper to the natural order. For even in the natural order the will does not move itself to natural good by the same way as it does to evil, but inclines to the former in virtue of an impulse to good placed in it by God. This is why the arguments which St. Augustine advances against the Pelagians are not always taken from the order of grace, as, for example, when he says that for every good action of the will it is necessary that the good appeal to the will, that the will feel itself drawn to good, and that there be in the will a motive force impelling it to good. Indeed, at times he is little concerned whether the prevenient impulse of the will's decision in favor of good is in nature itself, that is, in the sphere of nature, or whether it is absolutely above nature, in supernatural grace, since the Pelagians on principle exclude not only the supernatural impulse, but in general every impulse affecting the will from without.

If this Pelagian doctrine contradicts the natural order, much more pronounced is its opposition to the supernatural order of salvation, in which man can do nothing of himself, even though aided by all the energy and propelling force at nature's command. Whatever man is capable of doing in this order, he can achieve only so far as he is borne up by the prevenient, unmerited, supernatural grace of God. Man acts in the supernatural order only to the extent that God by His supernatural influence makes it possible for him to act, and consequently acts in him. Man's entire activity or movement emanates originally and chiefly from the decree and invitation of God, and is carried out only by the will of man as stirred by God. In whatever man does, God perceives not an effect of man's decision which is independent of Him, but an effect of His own plan, which precedes and evokes the decision of man that is necessary for the execution of the action. To carry out His purpose, God needs no disposition of the human will as a presupposition for His call, since His call is powerful enough to evoke the necessary cooperation of the will; nor can a preceding contrary disposition in the will be the absolutely decisive reason why God's decree regarding man should come to nought. Such is the supernaturalist doctrine which St. Augustine proposes against the Pelagians.

In consequence of erroneous views about the true import of this doctrine, inferences have been drawn from it which contradict the character of predestination as presented by us, especially with regard to the relation of particular to universal predestination. Attempts have been made to set up St. Augustine as the champion of an ultra-mystical theory of predestination, whereas in point of fact he really intended to advocate no more than the simple, truly mystical and supernatural character of predestination in opposition to the rationalist conception of the Pelagians.[1]

[1] According to some interpreters, St. Augustine makes no allowance for the conditioning of effective predestination by God's foreknowledge of man's free cooperation, but holds that this cooperation is determined by an efficacy proper to predestination, so that it unfailingly results from God's decree, and consequently does not determine the decree in any way, even to make it effective; the cooperation, rather, is determined by the decree. This is inferred from certain expressions, for example, that God moves man to action, that He even causes man's willing, that His will to save cannot be frustrated by man's will, that God does not have to wait for the consent of man's will, and others of like nature. However, St. Augustine declares explicitly and repeatedly that he defends no other predestination than that which is consonant with the necessity and gratuitousness of prevenient grace. (See *De dono perseverantiae*, nos. 41, 42, 54; thus he says in no. 42 [*PL*, XLV, 1019]: "Let them [Augustine's Semipelagian adversaries] realize that this doctrine of predestination overturns only that pernicious error which holds that grace is given in accord with our merits.") Hence he maintains that predestination is independent of the activity of man's free will prior to grace, and therefore that the activity of free will for eternal salvation is dependent on grace and gratuitous predestination, in virtue of which grace is given. Consequently he demands only that grace exercise such determining influence on natural freedom as is consistent with the nature of prevenient grace. But this implies no more than that free will can go into action only when stimulated by the impulse received, that the action, if it takes place, must be referred not only to the will which moves itself but also to the impulse of the grace which incites it, hence that the necessary cooperation of the will with grace is instigated and made possible by grace itself, and finally that God, who is able to rouse the will in a great variety of ways and in a most compelling manner, can evoke such cooperation even though the will was stubbornly pursuing an opposite course prior to the reception of grace. This and nothing else is what St. Augustine sets out to vindicate against the Pelagians.

Therefore, when he says that God effects man's very act of willing, he is arguing against the Pelagians, who contended that man alone elicits his act of willing with the natural power which, to be sure, he has received from God, and that God does no more than carry it through to its consummation. Augustine merely declares that God by His grace gives man the power and the impetus to will in a salutary fashion, and consequently that this willing, as the act of a will which has been elevated and stimulated by God's grace,

That many of the expressions employed by St. Augustine have a predeterminist complexion is not to be wondered at, if we reflect that he had to make every possible effort to batter down all the props, even to the very last, from under the Pelagians. He had to insist that no use of free will independently of grace could in any way affect predestination, but that rather every use of freedom that would have an influence on eternal salvation had to be utterly dependent on predestination. Therefore it was quite natural that in his polemical office he should slight God's universal, conditional salvific will and emphasize the particular, absolute salvific will, and that as a rule he should pay no heed to the relationship between the two, especially the transition from one to the other. For if he had more forcibly stressed the connecting link between them, that is, God's prevision of human cooperation, the Semipelagians would

---

is also a work of God. He does not conclude from this that God effectively brings about this act of willing only so far as man is moved by Him to cooperate.

Further, when he states that God does not await man's willing, he is taking his stand against the position that God cannot induce man to act, but must wait until man has set himself in motion prior to grace and independently of grace. He does not deny that God, after inciting man to good, awaits man's cooperation in order that grace may bear fruit.

This is not contradicted by Augustine's repeated insistence that God's will to save cannot be frustrated by man's will. By this he means frustration in the sense advocated by the Pelagians, who held that God could not take the initiative with a man who blocked God's grace with a perverted will, and consequently that the malice of man had greater power than the mercy of God. Accordingly he maintained only that God, by the inner force of grace, is able to paralyze every resistance set up in the way of His grace. It does not follow that grace and predestination cannot be frustrated in any way at all; it follows merely that they are not thwarted by an insurmountable obstacle, that they are thwarted only so far as God permits, and only so far as God does not, from the treasury of His omnipotence, overwhelm the will with graces which He knows would bring about man's cooperation.

Hence there is no basis for ascribing to particular predestination in the doctrine of St. Augustine a special efficacy in virtue of which its infallibility is not conditioned by the prevision of man's cooperation with reference to the fact of such cooperation. According to St. Augustine, particular predestination excels universal predestination only in the *efficientia*, the actual revealing of the efficacy found in the latter. In attributing efficacy to the former, he is merely regarding it from the standpoint of its oneness with the latter, as the concrete manifestation of the latter, but not as opposed thereto. But he does set it up in opposition to the Pelagian view of God's salvific will, which has no power to move men, but lets itself be called forth and determined by their autonomous, natural activity.

inevitably have distorted this to suit their own purposes, and in the given circumstances St. Augustine himself would scarcely have found the right terms to expound, in a completely unequivocal way, the true significance of that factor.

The ultramystical conception, which is diametrically opposed to the view combatted by St. Augustine, is in general characterized by its attachment to the idea that the influence of God's action upon the will is a predetermination, which the movement of the will resulting from its impetus cannot recognize at all, or only with the greatest difficulty, as a self-movement, as a product of the will's free self-determination.[2]

We call it ultramystical, because it stresses the mystical element of predestination beyond all limits. However, by going too far, it ends up by debasing this mystical element, and so reduces the living mystery to a more or less dead mechanism. For if I emphasize God's motive influence upon the will so excessively that the latter is simply put in motion without moving itself, I deprive that influence of its noblest property, namely, that it places man in a position to determine himself, not only upon the natural plane, but also upon the supernatural plane, to which he is raised by God's grace.

Where the free self-movement and self-determination of man under God's moving influence are expressly excluded, hence where predeterminism is advocated in its unmitigated crudity, we have before us an open denial of the Christian mystery of predestination. This error, no less injurious to God's power and transcendence than the opposite error of naturalism, deeply degrades man in the very faculty wherein God proposes to raise him to the highest level.

Even if the mystery is not entirely destroyed, its true character is distorted, and its distinctive greatness is obscured. At least this is the case if God's moving influence upon the will is so conceived that the cooperation of the will or its self-determination must spring from the force of the existing impulse with an inner infallibility, if not with absolute necessity. If anyone can distinguish between this infallibility and necessity, let him approve of this view. We are unable to do so, particularly if infallibility is to be understood strictly; for from a given cause the only effect that follows with absolute infallibility is an effect which cannot fail to result, and

[2] Proponents of this system are, among others, Calvin, Baius, Jansenius, and Karl Barth. [Tr.]

which therefore is so determined in its cause that it cannot be absent as long as the cause is in operation.

God's motive influence is unintelligible without some interior modification of the will by grace. It is not enough for grace merely to refrain from interfering with the act of the will, or to do no more than equip the will for action. Grace must incline the will to action, and that not simply from without, by proposing to it enticing objects which attract it, but from within, by impelling it, as the Thomists assert against Molina, although in point of fact the latter does not deny any of this. But there is not the slightest ground for inferring that the direction thus given to the will without the will's cooperation infallibly involves its self-determination. All that follows is that such self-determination, if it takes place, ensues only on the basis of and in virtue of the disposition caused by God.

The effort made by Thomistic and Augustinian theologians to secure the clearest possible recognition of man's utter dependence on God in his moral acts, and particularly in his supernatural acts, was in itself most laudable. However, as St. Bonaventure remarks, piety is more inclined to attribute too much to grace than to the natural freedom of the will. At all events, the dignity of grace is best safeguarded in the view that we advocate. For in the work of salvation we attribute absolutely nothing to natural freedom, not even cooperation with grace; such cooperation does not take place either outside of or alongside of or even under grace. The power and the incentive to cooperate with grace are conferred on the natural will by grace alone. Cooperation is an act of the supernatural freedom imparted by grace; hence in the matter of salvation man is completely dependent on the grace of God. But if this dependence is to redound to man's glory, and if it is to be truly glorious also for God Himself and His grace, it must raise man so high that he will move himself as freely, and will have as much control over himself in the supernatural order, as in the natural order. Only thus does grace prove to be a force that ennobles natural freedom but does not destroy it. Only thus is the power of God's influence upon man revealed in its full splendor; for God does not rest content with elevating man to a supernatural life, but renders this life truly man's own, by making the exercise of it dependent on man's own self-determination. Is man less dependent on God simply because God in His power makes a great achievement partly dependent on man?

Consequently we believe we are justified in maintaining that the advocates of *gratia praedeterminans* and of *gratia victrix* have disfigured what is most sublime in God's predestination and most glorious for Him, and what is in itself the heart of the mystery. We have still further reasons for this stand.

The defenders of *gratia praedeterminans* hold that the physically predeterminative force of grace is a property pertaining essentially to every effective influence of God upon the rational creature, and hence also to that divine influence whereby the rational creature is moved to naturally good acts. This very contention reveals that such efficacy is not a specific prerogative of the supernatural movement by which God conducts the creature to eternal life, and consequently that it cannot constitute a specifically Christian mystery. If this theory were true, the excellence of Christian predestination would lie only in the object toward which it moves man, and in the elevation of the faculty of the will as the principle of supernatural acts. But even this elevation of the will to a higher sphere is undermined if the will does not really determine itself in this sphere, and hence does not become the true lord of its higher domain. On the other hand, if even in the natural order no movement is regarded as occurring through predetermination, but every movement is the result of the active liberty and energy bestowed on us, the supernatural movement appears doubly remarkable. It does so for two reasons: first, because it leads us toward a supernatural end; secondly, because God so completely entrusts the principle of this movement to our keeping that in our ascent from earth to heaven we are not only borne aloft, but we ourselves fly upon the wings with which we have been equipped.

But the doctrine of *gratia victrix* as proposed by the Augustinians obscures the great mystery of Christian predestination much more than the Thomistic conception of the will's activity does. The central point of the Thomistic theory is the movement produced in the interior of the created will by God and the enhancement of its natural energy by a supernatural energy in the movement toward the supernatural end, in brief, the real, physical, or hyperphysical influence of God. In the Augustinian system this central point is relegated to the background, to make room for a moral influence, an influence brought about by the stimulation or delight of the will. Even though the stimulation should be irresistibly attractive, the movement of the will by God is no more extraordinary than the movement of the will by sensible concupiscence, against which grace is supposed to strengthen the will. The necessity of the *delectatio coelestis* is demanded in this system not by the absolute supernatural character of the act in question, but by the moral weakness of our will. The higher attractiveness of this *delectatio* implies neither a motion of the will emanating from its interior, where only the Creator can affect it, nor an elevation of the faculty of the will to a higher sphere, which would inform and animate it supernaturally so as to make it capable of supernatural activity. Therefore, if we postulate these latter factors and explain them by saying that God's physical influence is also a moral influence which simultaneously confers physical and moral energy upon the will and thereby establishes its full freedom for action, we shall grasp the idea of the movement of the will by God far more profoundly and vividly without any *gratia victrix* than do the theologians in question with their *gratia victrix*.

On the other hand, in acknowledging the connection between prevenient grace and the actual movement of the will simply as a connection founded on fact, and in subjecting it to God's providence only so far as God foresaw it through His *scientia media*, the Molinists and Congruists do not in any way impair the mystery of Christian predestination, provided they retain what is substantially true in the doctrine of the Thomists and Augustinians. This for the most part they have done, particularly their leaders, Molina and Suarez.

However, it seems to us that the brilliant theologian, Gregory of Valencia, following in the footsteps of St. Thomas, has most profoundly and clearly brought into prominence the real mystical and supernatural character of predestination and of the movement of man by God.[3] According to Gregory, man's progress toward his ultimate supernatural goal takes place as follows.

[3] See Gregory of Valencia, tom. II, disp. 8, q.3, punct. 4; q.5, punct. 4, sect. 8; Dominic Soto, *De natura et gratia*, II, c.18; other Thomists, e.g., Cajetan, Medina, *In Iam IIae*, q.113, a.6 and 8; Vasquez, *In Iam IIae*, disp. 211. With regard to the substance of the doctrine, almost all of the older theologians are in accord with those named. However, most of them do not acknowledge that the act whereby man's first supernatural turning to God

In order to evoke in man a self-active, supernatural movement of the will, God must transport man to a higher sphere of life, must form, animate, and fructify his natural faculty by a supernatural complement, and must ennoble and transform it, as the body is formed and animated by the infusion of the soul. This elevation, formation, and actuation of the natural faculty is the cardinal point of the entire supernatural movement of man by God. It is a movement in the most proper sense of the word, because it is a transference from potency to act, not to *actus secundus* but to *actus primus*, by which the potency is formed and receives the power and inclination to perform supernatural acts. It is brought about by God alone as efficient cause, in the same way that nature was called into being by God alone. Therefore it produces in us a new, higher nature whereby we are endowed in our interior with a capacity for and an inclination toward supernatural good, just as we are endowed by nature itself with regard to natural good. Accordingly, as God, the Creator of nature, is the principle of everything that man does on the basis of and in conformity with his natural tendency to natural good, and moves man by his nature even where in virtue of his nature man moves himself, so in a higher way, by elevating and transforming nature, God is the moving principle of everything that man does in his own right through his higher vital principle. This movement is, therefore, the starting point for all the other movements which, as activities of man, proceed from it. It is a real movement, physical as opposed to moral, hyperphysical as opposed to natural, an impress which God stamps upon the faculties of the soul that they may pass over to active movement, and thereby attain an end which they could not attain by themselves.[4] This movement brings it about that supernatural activity is man's very own, since it places the principle of activity deep within his faculties. Hence the activity is not something merely produced from outside, but springs forth and issues from a principle of life within the soul. As there is no influence exercised by God on man which is more powerful and thoroughgoing than the movement whereby man's very

---

is effected requires the intermediacy of an infused habit. On this question see my *Natur und Gnade,* beginning of chap. 4. Space does not permit us to discuss all the angles of the theory proposed and to preclude every possible misunderstanding.

[4] Cf. St. Thomas, *Summa,* Ia, q.9, a.1: "What is moved, acquires something by its motion, and attains to what it had not possessed before."

nature is transformed and elevated, so there is none which more solidly establishes and more satisfactorily explains the independence and self-activity of the person moved. This movement gives us our supernatural freedom, which enables us to cooperate as actively in supernatural acts as we do by means of our natural freedom in natural acts.

However, as intimated above, this movement of man by God is but the most fundamental factor and the cardinal point in the process by which man's salutary striving for his supernatural end is made possible. To carry out this movement in man, God must induce man to accept it; and after God has accomplished this, He must rouse man to activate himself and avail himself of the principles of life conferred on him. In the first phase God initiates the movement mentioned; in the second phase He makes it fruitful. He accomplishes both by means of actual grace, which is not, like habitual grace, the end and radical principle of a movement, but is rather in itself a movement, and by that very fact is capable of eliciting and calling forth a further movement. In itself the actual, excitating, and soliciting grace has no mystical, supernatural character in its influence on the will. But whenever, as here, its function is to move the will to accept a supernatural force or to actuate such a force already within the will, whenever it is to draw the will up to a higher region or induce it to move forward within that region, it must participate in the supernatural character of this force.

Our conception of the movement of the will in the direction of supernatural activity would be very superficial if we sought to regard such supernatural activity as a product of the purely natural will under the influence of actual grace. Actual grace becomes a truly moving force only in connection with or accession to habitual grace, from which the movement, that is, the vital activity of the soul, has to originate. It brings about supernatural activity in the will only when it entails the imprinting of the divine vital principle in the soul, or finds it there already. The two kinds of divine influence, the exciting influence of actual grace and the informing influence of habitual grace, complement and suppose each other. Both together constitute the complete *gratia motrix* on which man's salutary effort and activity depend. But the actual result of this *gratia motrix* depends on the free decision of the will which it is to move, and that in two ways, according as man is already animated by habitual grace or not.

In the second case (prior to justification), man's decision coincides with the reception of habitual grace, by which he is to obtain his supernatural freedom. This decision is like the opening of his eyes for the reception of the light that enables him to see: by making the decision, man makes his elevation and formation by God possible. In the first case (subsequent to justification), on the contrary, man makes his decision under the influence of actual grace by using his supernatural freedom to release the force lying dormant in habitual grace. In the second case the decision of the will entails a simple surrender to God, who draws the will to Himself in order to elevate; in the first case, it involves an application and unfolding of the supernatural motion conferred on the will by God. In the second case, not only the simple result, but the entrance of the complete *gratia motrix* depends on the decision of the will, since the *forma impressa* makes its appearance only if the will accepts it; but in the first case the complete *gratia motrix*, that is, both the formal principle and the excitation, is present prior to the decision of the will, although the will can remain unresponsive to its inducement.

But as regards its outcome, this dependence of the divine motion on the voluntary decision of the person who is to be moved does not interrupt the continuity or impair the supernaturalness of the divine impulse. In neither of the instances discussed above is the decision of the will a foreign element forcing its way unbidden into the supernatural process. Such would be the case only if the will had to give its assent quite apart from God's supernatural influence, or if God issued to the will only an external invitation to accede to the impulse emanating from Him. No, if the will determines itself, it makes its decision in response to the internal attraction and urging of God's prevenient grace; for grace stirs the will interiorly. Therefore the decision itself is supernatural in character, as is the grace in virtue of which it ensues. The decision of the will is, as it were, beset on two sides: by actual grace, which per se affects the soul and operates therein only morally, and by habitual grace, which informs the soul physically. Thus the decision is evoked by the former and fructified by the latter, and so the will puts forth a vital act that is both free and supernatural.

Such is the truly mystical theory of the supernatural *transmissio hominis in vitam aeternam*, a theory most illuminating in its mystical greatness and splendor. St. Thomas points to predestination as its principle and foundation. In the theory thus presented, grace does not obscure liberty, and liberty does not obscure grace; rather, grace is the basis of a mystical freedom, and this freedom reveals the full mystical power and significance of grace. The two factors are organically knit together; one pervades the other. The natural will with its natural freedom is not opposed to grace but, influenced and informed by grace, is raised up and endowed with supernatural energy and freedom, and thus becomes an intrinsic part of the supernatural process.

103. PREDESTINATION AS ELECTION AND SELECTION

Before dealing with the somber, forbidding aspect of predestination, we wish briefly to consider it under another form, the luminous form in which Holy Scripture lays it before us.

Sacred Scripture and, in the spirit of Scripture, the Fathers and theologians, refer to predestination as election. That is to say, the decree by which God proposes to conduct us to our supernatural end is a free, gratuitous choice whereby He singles out and wills to admit certain souls to the possession of Himself as His children, His spouses. The sublimity of the dignity, and the greatness of the riches of His grace and glory, mark this choice as an act of His supernatural providence. The soul has nothing in its nature or its natural, free activity that could ever make it worthy of being chosen by God; but at the same time it has nothing that could unconditionally deter God from choosing it. The goodness of God and the merits of Christ constitute the sole motive governing His choice; but this motive is infinitely efficacious. The actual elevation of the soul to the august state intended for it by God can take place either by simple regeneration, as in the case of infants, or by formal espousals, as in the case of adults, who must advance to meet their heavenly bridegroom at the reception of sanctifying grace, through the disposition which precedes it, and at the reception of glory, by perseverance in grace to the end. All human souls are chosen, and consequently called, by God's universal salvific will to be His children and spouses. But only those who actually receive baptism, or who respond to

God's choice of them up to the very end with a counterchoice of their own, effectively and absolutely constitute the elect, and are separated out from the multitude of those who are merely chosen in the sense that God has created all men for eternal bliss.

It is clear that this election is as unmerited and infallible, and in the same form, as predestination, with which it is at bottom identical. God does not choose us because we have chosen Him; but through His choice, through the call whereby He invites and draws us, He makes it possible for us to choose Him. The election (*electio*), like predestination, issues from the unmerited, but absolutely reliable and powerful love (*dilectio*) by which God has called us to supernatural union with Himself. This love, although wholly unmerited on our part, gives us confident assurance that we will attain our end, just as if the election depended on the natural bent of our will over which we alone have control. But this love becomes actually selective, and inextricably ties the bond between God and man, only so far as God foresees man's counterchoice and response which He evokes. It is not in our power, of course, to effect our choice and call; but it does depend on us to follow the call and thereby, in the words of the Apostle, to make our election and our call really effective and certain.

Up to this point we find in the election, as also in predestination, nothing but cheerful light, nothing but comforting truths that instill in us the most confident assurance concerning the attainment of the supreme Good. We have every reason to make our own the sentiments expressed by the Apostle at the beginning of the Epistle to the Ephesians, and to praise and glorify God for the mystery of His predestination and election.

But the same Apostle cries out to us in the Epistle to the Philippians: "With fear and trembling work out your salvation. For it is God who worketh in you both to will and to accomplish, according to His good will." [5] Since we can work out our salvation only in dependence on the divine influence whereby God calls and moves us, we must submit to His influence with fear and trembling, lest by rebelling against it we take upon ourselves a heavier burden than if we had to work out our salvation by our own efforts. For then we would wantonly fling away our happiness, and would thrust aside the hand of God stretched out to save us, and would frustrate the

[5] Phil. 2:12 f.

tender exertions He puts forth in our behalf out of sheer goodness and love (*pro bona voluntate*). Further, since our endeavor is conditioned by God's influence, and since this influence depends exclusively on God's unconstrained good pleasure which we can of ourselves in no wise merit, we have grounds to fear that God will withdraw His saving hand once we have defied Him, that He will no longer help us with His prevenient grace, at least not with the same abundance of grace He had previously intended for us, and that He will forsake us, since we have forsaken Him. Thus we would wander ever farther from our vocation and destiny. In this fear, the Apostle admonishes us, we must guard against ever resisting a grace. With trembling we must eagerly receive all of God's inspirations, and allow ourselves to be used and guided by Him as willing instruments in His hands.

However, this formidable aspect of predestination and election is no more than a shadow which we ourselves cast, and so we have it entirely in our own power to dissipate it. We can readily perceive that neither God's mercy nor man's free will is here jeopardized in any way. Still, the curse laid upon man by divine justice springs from this very mercy which man, abusing his freedom, so basely scorns and contemns.

Dark clouds gather when we reflect that God in His omnipotence could undoubtedly show mercy even to those who, as a matter of fact, resist His grace, and that those who actually follow His call would quite likely have trifled grace away like the others, if their graces and the circumstances in which they were placed had been different. Here a special predilection of God for the latter and a certain rejection with regard to the former seem to emerge, and indeed in such wise as to precede the actual use or abuse of human freedom, since it depends precisely on that predilection or rejection whether God places man in those circumstances in which He knows that man will cooperate with His grace or not.

If the fact that God, although He could do so, does not save all men from abusing their free will and the grace they have received, is represented as an effect of God's rejection of these men, the procedure must surely appear to be unjustified and terrifying. Actually, however, it is nothing but an indication that God in His prevenient love does not will the salvation of those men to such a degree or with such resoluteness that He intends to see to it that they will definitively and unfailingly attain to salvation no matter what the cost. There is, to be sure, no reason in men themselves why God should secure some rather than others against the final abuse of their free will. But neither is there any reason why God must shield all men against such abuse, once He has made it possible for all to make a good use of their freedom. No doubt, those who are placed under a system of providence wherein they can cooperate with grace and, as is foreseen, will cooperate, must thank God not only for grace itself, but also for the effective congruity of grace, and they must regard the latter as a special benefit. But the others cannot on that account complain against God, who had bestowed on them His prevenient grace which they had not merited, and was prepared to save them if they had been willing to cooperate with that grace.

The matter shapes up somewhat differently in the case of infants, who receive or do not receive baptism before their death, according to the incidence of external circumstances, without any reference to the use of their free will. Those who are lost without any personal fault of their own can have no complaints concerning the gratuitous providence which effectively extends grace to others, because they neither had any right to such grace, nor are held personally responsible for the non-possession of grace, and hence do not suffer the loss of their natural goods and rights. Consequently, if the saving mercy of God never reaches them effectively, God is not to be blamed any more than in the case of those adults who had indeed experienced His mercy, but did not continue to avail themselves of it up to the very end.

The varying efficacy of the divine salvific will in the distribution of internal and external graces, on which man's cooperation and hence the attainment of his end depend, is appropriately termed the selection of graces, which is to be carefully distinguished from the effective election of persons, as we shall see immediately.

That there can be and really is such a selection of graces, a dispensing of graces in greater or lesser measure dependent on God's free will, is beyond question. We may not conceive of God's universal will to save as though it were uniform for all, or the product of equal love for all, without any regard to the way man actually corresponds to grace, as the Pelagians contended. As God does not always desist immediately because of man's refusal to cooperate, and often seeks to draw him by new means, so too, prior to His prevision of man's cooperation and independently of it, He distributes to the one greater graces, to another lesser, to one such graces as He foresees will be effective, to another graces the fruitlessness of which is not unknown to Him, and appoints for one the end of the course while he is in the state of grace with or without his co-operation, for another when he is lacking in grace through his own fault (or without his fault, in the case of unbaptized children). This selection of graces does not in any way contradict God's universal will to save, but rather gives it the specific form in which it applies to particular men. It would contradict God's salvific will only if God, in selecting graces, were to pass over some men entirely, and were to confer on them no grace at all whereby they could attain salvation. Indeed, since the universal will to save is itself pure grace, it is in the nature of things that God, to manifest Himself as the Lord of His gifts, should not make it avail equally for all men.

On God's liberty in selecting graces, and on the variety of graces within the framework of the universal salvific will, depends in great part whether the universal will to save is to take the form of the particular will, and whether the virtual and conditional is to pass over into the effective and definitive, or will turn into reprobation. But we may not associate with this selection of graces the effective, definitive, particular salvific will itself, or the definitive election of persons, as if God had from the beginning formed the absolute, unconditional resolve to admit some to glory and others not, and hence to give to some graces that would effectively lead thereto, but to refuse such graces to others. Otherwise there would be no difference between the antecedent and consequent will with reference to the actual attainment of salvation. Further, as regards those who are not to attain salvation, it would be impossible to perceive how God could have a serious will effectively to admit them likewise to salvation, in the event that they would cooperate with His grace. For such a will presupposes that God has not, for His part, fixed the number of the predestined independently of His prevision of men's cooperation; otherwise He Himself would have to see to it that none of those whom He had not predestined should find their way into that number by cooperating with grace. Although God can elect some to the effective attainment of salvation by a will that is unconditional from the very beginning, He cannot from the outset proceed to exclude any. There must be certain limits to the selection of graces, for God does not endeavor to bring about the salvation of all men with equal energy, with equal solicitude, with equal forebearance; nevertheless He has the serious design to assist everyone effectively provided he cooperates, and consequently to predestine all effectively.

In the light of the principles governing the standpoint taken by us, no contradiction is discoverable either in predestination or in the selection of graces that have a part in carrying it out. There is nothing to contradict either the justice and mercy of God, or the rights and reasonable claims of man; and the hidden judgments of God's providence cannot be regarded as gloomy, unsolvable enigmas merely because the principles which warrant their leniency or severity have not been divulged by reason and revelation. God's works are so unfathomable for us because His decrees and their bearing on individual cases, regarding definite men or persons, as also the way God combines mercy with justice in particular details and in the whole plan, can be appraised and discerned by us only with extreme difficulty, and as a rule only after the appearance of the effect. In this connection man cannot and may not intrude upon God's exalted ways; he may neither make demands on God nor criticize His arrangements. With full acknowledgment that all the ways of the Lord are mercy and truth, man must reverently adore the decrees of infinite wisdom, love, and holiness, and must be on his guard lest by his arrogant prying he call justice down upon himself rather than mercy.

These are the somber regions and, because of their uncertainty and the severity of the divine justice, they are to some extent ominous regions in which, as we stated at the beginning, the ramifications of the mystery of predestination lose themselves. But above these regions is diffused the reassuring light of dawn, as we can see if we let our eye dwell on the points of light and the comforting features that characterize the mystery as a whole: that is, if, we hold fast to the truth that God in His unutterable and wonderful love has destined and chosen all men for eternal, supernatural union with Himself, and that repudiation and exclusion from this union commence only when man scorns the great love of his Creator and predestines himself to perdition. In the salutary fear of changing this astounding love by our own fault into a hatred no less awesome, we should lower our gaze with grateful wonderment into the abyss of the divine goodness which is the beginning of the unsearchable ways of the Lord, whereas His incomprehensible judgments lie along those paths where we ourselves constrain our God to walk. Most of all, let us reverently contemplate, in the depths of the wisdom and of the knowledge of God, that decree which God has revealed to us with the greatest definiteness and certainty, that decree by which God has loved all men in His own only-begotten Son and has showered them with all heavenly benediction, that decree by which He decided, out of the profoundest depths of His Godhead, to build up all men upon His Son as the cornerstone, and through the power of the Holy Spirit to make them temples of His glory, provided they do not prove unwieldy stones and deserve by their own fault to be rejected by the Architect.

Christ is the center, the foundation, the ideal, and the end of the whole supernatural world order and of the decree by which it is governed and brought to realization. From Him this decree derives its sublimity, its effectiveness, and its universality. All men are predestined in the predestination of Christ; for, in assuming His own body, Christ has taken the whole race as His body. When Christ arrived on our earth the race was a *massa damnationis;* but in Him it has become a *massa benedictionis*, upon which God's love is lavished more insistently, more abundantly, and more graciously than upon the original man. Man had been held back from the attainment of his supernatural end not only by his natural unworthiness, but by sin and the disorder of his nature. But God raises him through Christ above all his weakness and unworthiness, and leads him to glorious triumph in victorious battle over sin, hell, and the flesh. The infallibility of predestination, even of the universal predestination which we spoke of above, the infallibility which is based on God's universal love and the corresponding unfolding of His power, has its deepest motivation and its highest significance in Christ.

PART TEN

The Science of the Mysteries of Christianity or Theology

> We speak wisdom among the perfect; yet
> not the wisdom of this world. . . . But
> we speak the wisdom of God in a mystery,
> a wisdom which is hidden, which God
> ordained before the world unto our glory.
>
> I Cor. 2:6 f.

CHAPTER XXVIII

Theology as Science

▲▲▲

104. THE MYSTERIES AS THE PROPER SCIENTIFIC DOMAIN OF THEOLOGY

WE have completed our survey of the mysteries of Christianity. We have seen that the central truths of Christianity are and always remain real mysteries for man's natural reason, that is, truths that reason of itself can neither perceive as actually existing nor understand in their nature, except through analogous concepts that remain ever obscure and inadequate. But we believe we have shown that, if we go back to the basic reason why these truths transcend our intellectual powers, namely, their supernatural character, and place them in order according to this point of view, they will mutually set off and illuminate one another, and combine to form a marvelous system in which the divine majesty of Christianity will be reflected in all its greatness. Thus we have gathered rich material and have undergone a number of experiences that enable us to judge to what extent a scientific knowledge of the Christian mysteries is possible, and how it is to be organized so as to impart to us a more thorough understanding of the nature, the method, and the position of the science of the Christian mysteries, or of the scientific character of theology.

The question whether and to what extent theology is a true science in its own right, a science quite distinct from philosophy, is of prime importance in our day, as we remarked in the Introduction. On the basis of the data that have been established, we will try to make a contribution to the solution of this problem.

By science we understand objectively a system of correlated truths which can and should be known in their interconnection; or, subjectively, the system of cognitions by which the objective system is known in terms of the interrelationship of its parts. This provisional definition does not perhaps contain everything—certainly not explicitly—that may be considered when we speak of science. But it suffices for the purpose of opening up our discussion. We will bring forward the remaining elements more suitably at the proper time.

Frequently no more than a formal, subjective difference is admitted between philosophy and theology, with exclusive reference to the *principium quo* of knowledge. Thus it is said that theology as such is based upon positive faith, upon surrender to the authority of another who possesses knowledge, that is, God, whereas philosophy rests upon evidence personally controlled by the one who knows or, as many prefer, upon credence in one's own intellect.

But if no objective difference corresponds to this subjective distinction as its basis, theology can scarcely be called a proper, truly autonomous science. Who would reasonably speak of two independent sciences, if one person knew a series of mathematical truths from principles evident to him, while another person, to whom the same series was known, merely accepted these principles on faith? In both cases we would have the same science of mathematics, and even the same branch of it. The only difference is that the first mathematician would have a perfect mastery of his science, while the other would have a very imperfect acquaintance with it.

The case is no different with theology. If a person were to know on the basis of faith only the truths which he could know in philosophy on the basis of rational principles and natural experience, theology would evidently be no more than a grasp of what is objectively a rational science, or of objects proper to philosophy. It would be a knowledge that is less perfect because of the defect of evidence, even though it might well be more perfect because of higher certitude. Theology would have a different mode of cognition, but not a different objective sphere. Indeed, it would move exclusively in the sphere of philosophy; it would simply be philosophy in another form.

Theology is an independent science in its own right only if it has its own province in which philosophy is not able to follow by its native power; if it possesses its own objects of cognition, which lie outside the reach of rational principles; if, consequently, its proper mode of cognition, faith, is required by the very nature of its object, or conversely, if its proper mode of cognition enables it to pass beyond the frontiers of pure reason and to illuminate a higher domain.

But does theology really possess a higher province of its own? That it can, nobody will be able to deny even from the philosophical point of view, unless in foolhardy presumption he hopes to measure the compass of truths that God can reveal, and therefore the range of infinite, divine knowledge, according to the norm of created, finite knowledge. That it actually does, is clear from all we have said about the supernatural mysteries of Christianity. These mysteries would not be true mysteries unless they lay outside the radius of human reason, and in general of every created reason. But if they are to be mysteries, we cannot acquire knowledge of them through any light of our own, but only by receiving light from Him before whom no mystery can stand.

There are two kinds of truths, whether considered objectively as they exist in themselves, or subjectively in our knowledge of them. There are two essentially disparate kinds of truths, because there are two essentially different modes of being and of manifestation, which must be subjectively known in different ways precisely because they are objectively different.

In the creature we have to consider primarily the nature of things, chiefly that of the rational creature, its powers, its constitutive elements, its destiny to the end it is to reach, its essential relations to other natures and especially to the absolute, divine nature. And in this divine nature we have to consider its relation to created nature, in which it is mirrored as in an image, but is not really manifested in its innermost being. Whatever belongs per se to created nature, and whatever of the uncreated nature is manifested in it, we call natural truth, and all of this can be the object of the creature's natural knowledge. All of this constitutes a clearly defined system of knowable truths, an object of science. The cognitive light which is proper to this order and illuminates it is the organ of nature, the intellect; and the corresponding actual knowledge, the cultivation and actuation of the intellect, is rational science or philosophy. This is not to imply that the created intellect, especially in man, can perfectly and without exception know all natural things. We prescind from the question, how far reason can advance within this sphere. We content ourselves with the observation that it cannot progress beyond it.

If there is yet another realm of being above the one just mentioned, if beyond the natural there exists something that is truly supernatural in substance, something that, while it is based on the natural, does not grow out of the natural; and particularly if there is a closely knit order of supernatural things, then there is a sphere of reality and truth which can in no way be known by the organ of nature, reason as left to itself. This is a sphere which extends as much beyond nature's cognitive faculty and principles of cognition as it projects beyond nature itself; in a word, which is suprarational to the degree and for the reason that it is supernatural. This domain of truth is essentially distinct from that which reason and philosophy can rule. Consequently it forms the object of a special science. Not only is it in actual fact known by faith, on God's authority; it cannot be known in any other way; and so it constitutes a proper object of knowledge that is specific to faith.

The opposition between the two spheres will appear in clearer light if we adopt a somewhat more concrete mode of procedure. Only too often the difference between the two provinces is admitted without a definite, concrete conception of their contents, and without any thought being given to their dimensions and boundaries. Particularly in the case of supernatural truths, their mutual interdependence is not sufficiently taken into account, although their domain can in no other way be rounded off into a well-ordered whole.

If there were only a few isolated supernatural truths, they would undoubtedly project beyond the sphere of philosophy, but more as an incidental appendage to philosophy than as a complete and self-contained body of truths. At all events, they would scarcely be looked upon as the object of a proper science. A domain requires a certain extension; a scientific domain implies a circle drawn round a central truth according to definite laws. However, supernatural truths are certainly something more than mere isolated units intended to serve for the completion or embellishment of the natural order of things. To be sure, they do not create any new substances as substrata for a new order; rather, the substances in the natural and supernatural orders are the same, namely, God and creature. But supernatural truths call into being other and higher relationships and connections between these substances than the nature of the creature requires and engenders of itself. On the one hand they raise the creature to a plane infinitely above its nature and bring it infinitely closer to God than it was by nature; and on the other hand they make available a truth about God that was not available to created nature as such, namely, His being as it is in itself in the Trinity of divine persons. The high point of this order, and its end, is the perfect union of the rational creature with God by participation in His own glory, and the intuition of Him face to face in the Blessed Trinity. All the other supernatural truths are hierarchically organized in subordination to this end, and embrace specifically all that has been ordained for the appointing, the pursuit, and the attainment of this end. Consequently, if we regard the natural order as the ordering of nature to the end which essentially corresponds to it, and the supernatural order as the ordering of the creature to a supernatural end, the two orders will be sharply differentiated by their proper ends. The end is the principle and the norm of whatever is drawn to it, at any rate in the measure that things are drawn to it.

Perhaps we can give a clearer and more profound exposition of the matter as follows. The domain of natural things is formed by a circle of truths which links together created natures as such. It embraces only such things as concern created nature itself, its development, and its essential relations. Objectively, of course, God also is the center of nature and the natural order, inasmuch as created nature proceeds from Him by an act of His will, and is drawn back to Him as its final end. But God is to be considered here not immediately and in Himself, but only in His relations to the creature, and moreover the eye which contemplates the entire order is in the creature. Natural things form, so to speak, an eccentric circle with two centers, created nature on the one hand and God on the other, in the first of which is located the eye that surveys the whole order.

The supernatural truths, on the contrary, are grouped directly not around the created nature, but around the divine nature. They are not concerned with any development of the divine nature, which on account of its infinite wealth is not, like created nature, capable of and in need of development. They have to do only with the communication, manifestation, and glorification of the divine nature that proceed from God's infinite riches. God communicates Himself also in the production and perfecting of created nature, but not in His own proper nature, which infinitely transcends all creation. The supernatural communication we are speaking of is exclusively of the latter kind. It takes place according to a series of three descending steps: first, by the substantial and total communication of the divine essence in the Trinity; secondly, by hypostatic union in the Incarnation of the Son; and thirdly, by participation in grace and glory on the part of men. This communication of divine nature proceeds from God in a higher manner than does created nature, and hence returns to Him in a higher manner than is the case with created nature; that is, it returns to God as its end by union with Him and glorification of Him. Created nature here ceases to be a real center of the supernatural order. It is to be considered only so far as, clad with the divine nature, it is received into the circle of the life proper to the divine nature. Consequently, to survey this order our eye must, as it were, be located in the divine center of the circle, since we can perceive it only by belief in God's revelation, and so we must contemplate it with an eye that is indeed ours, but must look through God's eyes. Hence the sphere of the supernatural order is a simple circle with one center.

If we wish to give a brief description of both spheres, we may put it thus: the natural, rational sphere is an eccentric circle with two related centers, that of created nature and that of the divine nature, a circle whose radius vector consists in the relationship in which the various truths stand toward the regulation and development of created nature and its subordination to the divine nature; whereas the supernatural order is a simple circle with one center, that of the divine nature, a circle whose radius vector consists in the relationship in which the various truths stand to the supernatural communication and manifestation of the divine nature.

In the interest of greater clarity, let us proceed to put this description of the respective spheres to the test by applying it to the supernatural truths of which there is chiefly question. We can do this the more easily inasmuch as we have but to glance back over the results of our previous studies.

To the supernatural sphere belong: the Trinity, as the supernatural, internal, essential, and total communication of the divine nature, and as the principle, ideal, and end of every supernatural communication of itself to the creature; man's original justice, as the state of the first, original elevation of man to participation in the divine nature, and as the aggregate epitomizing all the privileges given to him in consequence of this elevation; sin in general, and original sin in particular, as the negation and destruction of the supernatural union with God conferred by participation in the divine nature; the Incarnation, as the highest and most intimate supernatural communication of God outside Himself, and as the second principle, end, and ideal of the supernatural union of mankind with God, to be re-established by the redemption; the Eucharist, as the means of closest union of men with the God-man, their head, and through Him with God; the Church, as the mystical body so closely joined to the head, and as the mysterious organ of the God-man; the sacraments, as the instruments of the supernatural activity of God, Christ, and the Church; Christian justification and the entire process which initiates and consummates it, as the restoration of the supernatural participation in the divine nature lost by sin; the glorification of man in soul and body, as the climax of his participation in the divine nature; and finally predestination, as the decree existing in God, whereby God wills to communicate His own nature to creatures in a supernatural way, and effectively achieves its communication.

Accordingly theology, as opposed to philosophy, is an independent science in its own right because, in addition to its own theological principle of cognition, it has its own specifically theological sphere. Its principle of cognition is called theological because it is based upon the Word, the Logos of God, and has its motive and formal object in Him; its sphere and the truths comprised in it, its material object, are theological because God Himself is directly and immediately considered therein as the center of the supernatural order, and as the principle and term of the communication of His nature. In a word, it is theology because what it says comes from God, and because it speaks about God. Philosophy, on the contrary, speaks from the viewpoint of created nature, that is, in virtue of its natural light; it also speaks primarily and directly about created nature, and only secondarily of God, as the principle without which nature cannot exist, and the end outside of which nature cannot come to rest.[1]

[1] Cf. St. Thomas, *In Boeth. de Trin.*, q.20; *Summa*, Ia, q.1, a.1 ff.; *In 1 Sent.*, prol. In his brief against Frohschammer, Pius IX gives the gist of our thought in the following words: "To dogmas of this kind [those proper to faith alone] pertain primarily and unmistakably all that concerns man's

This way of looking at the matter may appear to confine the province of theology within excessively narrow limits. For, surely, its principle of cognition is not restricted to the supernatural order, but extends to the natural order, both potentially and actually. Divine faith is no more limited to a definite sphere than is God's knowledge upon which it rests. As faith is able to pass beyond the bounds of reason, it can very well diffuse itself over the sphere of reason and dominate it. And, as a matter of fact, God has revealed and proposed for our belief a number of truths that do not in themselves belong to the supernatural order, such as creation, the spirituality and immortality of the human soul. As a general rule, theologians include in the sphere of theology all that falls within the purview of its principle of cognition.

But from this there follows immediately only one conclusion, that in a certain respect the sphere of theology objectively overlaps the sphere of philosophy. It does not follow that the supernatural order of things cannot be regarded as the specific object of theology. For, even if the supernatural order is regarded as only a part of the province of theology, still it is the nobler and higher part, and is that very part in which theology excels philosophy. Nor is this all; the natural truths in which theology is on common ground with philosophy are of minor importance and are contemplated under a different light, but they are also studied from a different angle and in a way demanded by the higher light of faith and by the bearing of these secondary truths on the primary truths.

Since faith or, as the case may be, theology, has to deal with the supernatural order of things, it can and must extend to the natural order, without of course relinquishing its own proper object. Natural things form in great part the substructure of the supernatural order which, as its very name connotes, is built up on the natural order. Therefore, if God wills to reveal the supernatural to us, or if we, following the lead of His revelation, hope to gain an adequate grasp of it, both revelation and our understanding which depends on faith must take advantage of the enlightenment afforded by that substratum. This truth should be evident in view of the fact that

---

supernatural elevation and his supernatural dealings with God, and all that is known to be revealed for this purpose. And assuredly, since such dogmas are above nature, they cannot be reached by natural reason and natural principles" [Denz., 1671].

natural things themselves are taken up into the supernatural order, and the latter, in the last analysis, is nothing but an elevation of created nature on the one hand, and a manifestation and communication of the divine nature on the other. Thus, for instance, the mystery of the Trinity can neither be revealed nor be grasped without a further elucidation of God's nature; nor can we form an idea of the compass and meaning of the supernatural elevation of human nature, as effected by grace and glory, or by the hypostatic union, unless we take into account human nature itself and its natural condition.

This statement of the reasons requiring the inclusion of natural truths within the orbit of theology indicates also the aspect and relation under which those truths here apply. They are not considered for their own sake, as in philosophy, so far as they form a proper, independent object of cognition, but so far as a knowledge of them is requisite for the understanding of another, higher object. They do not constitute the proper end which theology aims at, but simply provide the material which is worked into the structure of the supernatural truths of theology, or the foundation upon which that structure is erected.

Hence it is possible that certain truths, such as creation from nothing, may be of major concern to both philosophy and theology; but they will be so in different ways. Thus creation is a cardinal point in philosophy, in the sense that without it the existence of finite beings cannot be explained, and their relation to their first cause cannot be rightly and satisfactorily determined. But in theology it constitutes the basic condition without which we are unable to conceive the assumption so necessary to the supernatural order, the infinite distance between the divine nature which elevates and the human nature which is to be elevated, and the absolute dependence of the latter on the former.[2]

[2] The following passage from St. Thomas (*Contra Gentiles*, II, 4) contains some profound observations on the different points of view from which theology and philosophy look at the same objects. The heading of the chapter is: "That the Philosopher and the Theologian View Creatures from Different Standpoints." The text continues:

"It is clear from the foregoing that the teaching of the Christian faith considers creatures inasmuch as a certain likeness of God is reflected in them, and inasmuch as error with respect to them leads to error about God. And so creatures are regarded from different angles by the teaching of faith and by human philosophy. Human philosophy considers them as they are in themselves. Hence we find that the different divisions of philosophy corre-

Another objection may be lodged against our description of the orbits proper to philosophy and to theology: it seems that we completely fence off the province of the supernatural from the contemplation of natural reason, as though the latter had no right to enter the supernatural domain; whereas, in point of fact, the supernatural must have the same relationship to nature's principle of

---

spond to the various classes of things. But Christian faith does not consider creatures as they are in themselves; for instance, it regards fire not inasmuch as it is fire, but inasmuch as it represents the majesty of God, and is in some way directed to God Himself. For, as is said in Ecclus. 42:16 f., 'Full of the glory of the Lord is His work. Hath not the Lord made the saints to declare all His wonderful works?'

"Therefore the philosopher and the believer in revelation are concerned with different aspects of creatures. The philosopher considers such points as pertain to them by nature, for example, that fire tends upward. The believer considers only those matters about creatures that belong to them in their relations to God, such as that they are created by God, that they are subject to God, and the like.

"Hence the teaching of faith cannot be accused of imperfection if it overlooks many properties of things, such as the configuration of the heavens, and the laws of motion. In the same way the physicist is not concerned with the same properties of a line as the geometrician, but only with those that pertain to it as the term of a natural body.

"Such points, however, as are studied by philosopher and believer alike, are treated according to different principles. The philosopher draws his conclusions from the immediate causes of things. But the believer argues from the first cause, and shows, for instance, that a truth has been divinely revealed, or that a certain line of conduct makes for the glory of God, or that God's power is infinite. Hence the speculations of the believer should be called highest wisdom, as dealing with the highest cause, according to Deut. 4:6: 'This is your wisdom and understanding in the sight of nations.' And therefore human philosophy serves this higher wisdom. In token of this, divine wisdom sometimes argues from the principles of human philosophy, just as, among philosophers, first philosophy uses the resources of all the sciences to establish its own position.

"Further, the two sciences do not follow the same order. For in the science of philosophy, which regards creatures in themselves, and proceeds from them to a knowledge of God, the first consideration is about creatures, and the last about God. But in the science of faith, which studies creatures only in their relationship to God, the consideration of God precedes, and that of creatures comes afterward. And this is the more perfect procedure, and is more like God's knowledge; for He discerns other beings by knowing Himself.

"Wherefore we shall follow this latter order; having discoursed in the first book about God as He is in Himself, we have now to treat of the beings that have their origin from Him."

cognition, reason, that it has to nature itself, with which it is wedded. This much, in any case, is incontestable: no matter how the relationship between the natural and the supernatural is conceived, as long as the latter remains truly supernatural, reason, relying on its own resources, can no more rule the supernatural sphere than nature can encompass it or cause it to issue forth from nature itself. Reason may well strive, with the aid of analogous concepts, to understand the supernatural objects that have been proposed to it, and to suggest explanations of their real or ideal truth with some degree of plausibility; but mere plausibility will not enable us to master truth or to rule its domain. Therefore, as long as philosophy is taken to mean the science of pure reason, the supernatural cannot be referred to its sphere. How reason is related to the supernatural order, and what value reason's own insight into that order may have for the scientific formulation of theology, we shall see later.

Only those supernatural events that appear visibly or perceptibly, the so-called miracles, pertain to the realm of philosophy; not indeed of abstract philosophy, which is concerned only with the inner, necessary relationships of things, but of applied philosophy, which aims at understanding every fact it encounters. To distinguish this sort of object from the strictly supernatural, which lifts the creature above the whole domain of nature, it could be called, in conformity with its ontological character, preternatural; although this classification could include many other objects which, because they escape our notice, do not strike our attention in such a way as to arouse wonderment. At all events, they should not be confused with what is strictly supernatural. As a rule, they are but the echo, the outward reflection, the visible garb of the strictly supernatural, as in the case of Adam the gift of integrity with respect to his sanctity, or in the case of Christ His miraculous works with respect to the hypostatic union, or in the case of the saints their miraculous deeds, their mystical states, and their influence on others, with respect to their exalted union with God. But from these visible phenomena, as we have shown in the case of the original state and the Incarnation, the heart of the mystery from which they burst forth can only be vaguely surmised; reason cannot penetrate the shell and reach the kernel as it is in itself. Miracles by themselves do no more than indicate with some probability that a supernatural order exists. They bring us to certitude and introduce us to the supernatural order only by the fact that they are, so to speak, the divine seal by which its heralds are proved to be accredited.

If we sum up the various points that have been made, the difference and the relationship between the spheres of theology and philosophy may be stated as follows.

The two spheres are related to each other as higher to lower, the building to its foundation, the temple to the forecourt, and heaven to earth. This relationship obtains whether the sphere of theology is regarded as the higher precisely because it is distinct from its substructure, or whether the lower is thought of as included in the higher, the foundation in the house, the forecourt in the temple, and the earth as encompassed by heaven. Reason, like the Gentiles in Old Testament days, remains standing in the outer court of God's temple, while faith, like the chosen people of God, enters into the interior of the temple. The highest privilege of reason is its ability to press on within the limits of the outer court up to the threshold of the inner court. This is the same as saying that reason can do the following: first, it can contemplate and pass judgment on the supernatural phenomena surrounding the supernatural sphere, and the fact of revelation as the portal which invites entrance into it; secondly, if the curtain veiling the interior is drawn aside by revelation, it can from afar off venture a timid, uncertain glance at the glories of the sanctuary, without, however, approaching any closer; for this is possible for faith alone.

105. Scientific Knowledge of Theological Truths

If theology has a proper sphere of cognition objectively and essentially distinct from that of philosophy, the question arises whether and how we can gain a scientific knowledge of the subject matter belonging to this sphere, hence whether theology can have a scientific value for us subjectively. We shall see that the scientific knowledge possible here is radically different from philosophical knowledge, but that, if we have a correct appreciation of this difference and of the general conditions of scientific knowledge, it amply satisfies the requirements of such knowledge.

Scientific knowledge of a truth requires, first of all, that we be able to justify the certitude with which we affirm its objective reality. In philosophy we do this when we trace the assumed truths back to the fundamental principles of natural cognition, and so let the natural light of reason be our guaranty for the objective truth of the assumption. In theology we cannot thus infer its specific objects from evident rational principles or facts. We can learn of their existence from God alone, and hence God's veracity and infallibility must be our guaranty. God gives assurance of a particular truth by the very fact that He has revealed it. But, since this assurance is not immediately evident to us, we must further determine whether God has really vouched for the truth accepted by us. The demonstration of this devolves upon philosophy; the procedure to be followed is essentially philosophical. Accordingly, if this were the only condition required for a scientific knowledge of the object of theology, the scientific element in theological knowledge would pertain entirely to philosophy: the scientific knowledge in question would not be specifically theological. But that is not the only consideration, as we shall proceed to show.

The opinion has been expressed that, if certain knowledge of theological truths can receive only indirect authentication from philosophy, and if the principles from which it proceeds can be accepted on faith alone, no properly scientific knowledge at all is possible for theology itself, because scientific knowledge must proceed from evident principles. Or, as those who advance this opinion declare, if we cling to this notion of scientific knowledge, and insist on applying it to the sphere of theology, we make a rash attempt to wrest certitude about the objects of theology from evident principles and facts of reason alongside and outside the certitude of faith, and end up by representing this latter certitude as a scientific knowledge of revealed truths.

If a scientific knowledge of the truths of faith had to be purchased at this price, we should do better to forgo it entirely and rest content with simple belief. In fact, this sort of scientific cognition is incompatible with the supernatural sublimity of the object of faith. It is suitable only to things of nature; and we must prefer simply to accept the supernatural on faith, particularly so far as it benefits us personally, rather than know the natural ever so perfectly. Scientific cognition of this kind is, indeed, applicable to a certain portion of the teachings of faith, to that portion which does not constitute the specific province of theology; but it is common to both theology and philosophy. In a word, it is applicable to the order of nature, which is the substructure of the supernatural order. The possibility of such science is not prejudicial to the sublimity of faith. Rather, the fact that reason corroborates the verdict of faith wherever it is able to follow faith, gives us a new assurance that faith requires no further confirmation from reason in those areas where reason cannot follow.

But is it true that the idea of scientific cognition requires a resolution into evident principles? The account that scientific knowledge has to render in order to justify the acceptance of a truth does not demand any more than that I trace the conclusion back to a certain, incontestable principle. It is the certainty of the principle, not the evidence as such, which justifies the acceptance of a conclusion. Evidence enters the question only to the extent that it reveals the certainty of the principle in the absence of other motives. The certainty of the principles which I, believing in God's infallible word with a faith elevated by grace, possess regarding the fundamental truths made known by divine revelation, is as great as, indeed even greater than, the certitude of the evident truths of reason vouched for only by my own intellect, not by the divine intellect. Consequently these principles enable me to render at least as strict an accounting of the certitude of the conclusions derived therefrom as I could render with the aid of evident principles apprehended by reason.

Of course, the criterion of revelation and faith always presupposes the criterion of natural evidence. Therefore it might appear that the accounting which the former enables us to give of a truth is, in the last instance, resolved into the latter, as though faith were only a derived, subordinate criterion, and hence could not take its place alongside and above the criterion of evidence as the basis of a new, higher scientific cognition. This would, indeed, be the case if the certitude of faith grew out of the certitude engendered by the evidence of the fact of revelation and of God's veracity, and if, consequently, it derived its entire force from such certitude. But this rational certitude is no more than a simple preliminary condition that renders the motive of faith accessible to us. After we are aware of the existence of the divine authority, the will sustained by grace raises the understanding to the heights of that authority, to find repose therein, to rely upon it, and to draw from it a certitude which the understanding could never attain by its own intuition or investigation.[3] And thus, although setting out from rational evidence, we gain through the will and grace a new, firmer, and higher vantage ground from which we can render a more satisfactory account of the certitude of those truths which lie within its orbit, than we could from our original starting point.

Therefore, although scientific knowledge of theological truths, as concerns their certitude, can proceed from faith alone and can be founded on faith alone, it is and ever remains a true scientific knowledge, despite its difference from what we call scientific knowledge in philosophy.

There are two ways in which a truth that falls within the orbit of theology can be scientifically established on the grounds of faith and revelation. First, if the truth is explicitly revealed *in individuo*, we can bring forward and discuss the testimonies that have led to the conviction that it is revealed. If the Church, acting as judge, has pronounced on the matter, we are not absolutely bound to scrutinize the evidence on which the definition is based. But even then, science can and should give an account of the reasons underlying the definition, not so much with the intention of corroborating it, as rather to trace it back to its principles and to refute its adversaries. When, however, such a definition is not forthcoming, examination of the evidence is the only way to establish the truth in question on the grounds of faith, unless it can be demonstrated from its connection with another truth that has certainly been revealed. This type of demonstration is called positive, not exactly because it reduces the truth in question to a positive revelation, but rather because it simply shows that this truth is immediately and implicitly contained in the deposit of that revelation and hence, without further formality, is to be held firmly with the assent of faith. It is at bottom nothing but the ascertaining of a supernatural fact as such. It does not so much proceed from faith as issue in faith; it proceeds from faith only inasmuch as, in virtue of a general acceptance of whatever is contained in the fonts of revelation, it comprises the individual truths of this deposit, and so makes them the subject of the act of faith. This sort of procedure is essentially historical; it is a special kind of history. Since it is not rooted wholly in faith itself, but rather leads to faith, it is not completely theological. Notwithstanding, it is usually called

[3] Cf. *Natur und Gnade*, pp. 179 ff.

theological, to differentiate it from the method of philosophy. It is thus designated, however, from the viewpoint of its term, not from the viewpoint of its principle, since the endeavor of philosophy is to demonstrate a thing not as credible but as evident. It is known as theological because it justifies belief in a definite truth, not because by belief in one truth it establishes the certitude of another truth. As was remarked above, it does not effectively lead to belief in a definite truth except on the supposition of a general belief in the whole deposit of truth contained in the fonts of revelation. When this is the case, the result of the procedure is apprehended and embraced with supernatural certitude.

Theological demonstration in a narrower sense proceeds from definite truths already accepted on faith, with a view to deducing other truths from them with certitude. Here faith is properly the root from which knowledge issues in the theological sphere. The truths immediately apprehended by faith are the principles, or fundamental truths. From these and upon them I build up a structure of truths sustained and supported by them, the reasons which enable me to render an account of everything else that I accept or hope to receive in the domain ruled by faith, and arrive at certitude therein. The first method mentioned above has the function in theological science that the critique of the principles of knowledge has in philosophy. This critique has the purpose of subsequently enabling the structure of philosophical science to be erected with certain knowledge upon the principles that have been established. In the same way the science of theology cannot rest content with establishing the principles to be believed. It is only after they have been established that the proper structure of theology can be erected on the foundations that have been laid.

Since faith merely makes new principles available to us, but does not confer any new power of reasoning on us, the utilization of those principles devolves upon our natural reason, which must apply them according to the ordinary rules of inference. It is reason that draws other truths from the revealed truths, and vindicates them. The form of its procedure is the same as the method employed in philosophy. But the basis on which it rests, and the principles from which it proceeds, are different, more secure, and of a superior order. As in philosophy, the intellect works with its own reasoning power. But this power is here elevated and sustained by a higher power, the power of faith, which it serves and by which it is fructified and ennobled. Therefore the product of its activity is far more excellent than the product of philosophical speculation; through faith it rules a higher domain than it possessed of itself and, other things being equal, it rules this domain with greater sureness than its own powers equip it for ruling its own domain.

Of course, the certitude attained by inference from the principles of faith is not as great as that of the principles themselves, and it decreases the farther we get from the principles in deducing our conclusions, or in proportion as the evidence of the demonstration grows dimmer. But as long as the connection between conclusion and principle is equally evident, the theological inference always engenders a higher certitude than the corresponding philosophical inference.

By reasoning from truths that I believe in, I can infer others that are not in themselves revealed and I can obtain certitude concerning them. Moreover, I am able to deduce such truths as I already believe in and hold without the intermediacy of any reasoning process, from still other, likewise believed truths, and so can render a double and triple account of them. Such deduction is not per se required that I may adhere with certitude to those truths in a reasonable manner. There is no need for deduction of this sort, just as, absolutely speaking, there is no need of a proof from tradition or Scripture when the Church proposes some article for belief. Nor, of course, may we prefer the certitude obtained by means of inference to the certitude of faith. Even on the philosophical level, truths known only by deduction from others cannot surpass in certitude the principles on which knowledge of them rests. Much less can this be the case in theology, where the principles are immediately vouched for by God, whereas the inferences depend on the correctness of the reasoning process, which in itself is open to error.

Our certitude throughout the theological sphere would be most perfect of all if God had also revealed explicitly all those truths that now we can know only by deduction. And so we must be heartily grateful to Him for having expressly revealed and proposed for our belief, besides the principles that are indispensable, also many of the conclusions derived from them. Nevertheless, even in the case of truths assented to with divine faith, science must endeavor to infer truth, and so confirm truth with truth. For it must be a matter of concern to science that every truth be substantiated as perfectly as possible, and in every possible way. This is accomplished in theology if each proposition of faith is seen to be formally revealed in itself, and also virtually in others.

It must further be of concern to science to comprehend the aggregate of revealed truths in their logical connection, in order to know them as a whole in which one part postulates the others, and all parts together are sustained by the whole. To this end it must seek to reduce the truths of faith to the fewest possible simple truths, which virtually contain all the others. Not all the truths belonging to the province of theology can be reduced to a single principle, any more than in other sciences; one reason for this is that theology comprises many truths that are in every respect contingent. But the unity of its cognitive principle can be achieved in a high degree throughout the several departments of its province, as we attempted to show in some detail when treating of the Trinity.

The establishment of a logical connection between the truths of faith is of greatest consequence when the principle from which I deduce another truth comprises the intrinsic reason underlying the reality of this truth, as, for example, when I infer the distinction between the divine persons from the productivity of the First Person. In this case not only the certitude, but an understanding of the conclusion is intrinsically involved in the reasoning process, and so certitude attains its final perfection. The demonstration is a *demonstratio propter quid* (a priori), as opposed to a *demonstratio quia* (a posteriori); it is scientific demonstration par excellence. However, full use of this kind of demonstration can be made in theology only when the basic reasons are directly revealed. In many cases the basic ontological principle must be demonstrated analytically (a posteriori); and then, of course, certitude regarding it rests on certitude regarding its effects, and insight into its connection with these effects can only assist our understanding of them, but cannot directly establish our certitude concerning them.

106. THE UNDERSTANDING OR *INTELLECTUS* OF THE OBJECTS OF FAITH

Investigation into the certainty of the truths to be believed, or rather, into the judgment to be pronounced on their actual existence, and establishment of that certainty on logical grounds, constitute only one factor in the scientific knowledge of any class of objects. Hand in hand with this must go a second factor, which pertains to every kind of knowledge, but especially to scientific knowledge, namely, the apprehension or conception of the object as really known, whereby an account is rendered not of the judgment concerning its existence, but of the content of the object, or of the objective reality itself. We call this conception scientific when it represents the object definitely and distinctly, and in such a way that we can conceive the possibility and the principle of its actual existence. Furthermore, when there is question of a system of truths, we must also be able to perceive the relation in which the various truths stand to one another, and owing to which they imply and postulate one another, and hence reflect in us subjectively the objective systematic order in its cohesion and unity.

As distinguished from the judgment about the existence of the object, this apprehension is known as the *intellectus* or understanding of its content, that is, the insight whereby we penetrate into its very essence, and in particular explore the conditions on which its real existence is based. In its narrower sense, this understanding is restricted to an apprehension of the inner core or essence of the thing, and penetrates only to that conception of its intrinsic possibility which is contained in such apprehension. But so far as we advance beyond this and endeavor to account for its existence, and seek and find the reason why the thing is or has to be, the apprehension is an act of the *ratio*, especially if the relation of the individual truths to a higher whole is taken into consideration. However, since *intellectus* and *ratio* (understanding and reason) are but a single faculty of the soul, the entire apprehension of the content and principles of a truth that is accepted or to be accepted as established, can be called *intellectus*, or understanding.

The understanding of the object which is to be accepted as existing must in a certain respect precede the judgment pronounced on its actual existence, since I can assert nothing as existing unless I have some knowledge of what it is. An understanding of the possibility, and of the cause which turns the possible into the actual, is by no means necessary for this. As a rule, such understanding follows knowledge of the existence of the object, and requires a closer, more searching investigation. But in any case this understanding, if it precedes the judgment about actual existence, will greatly facilitate belief in it, and will later strengthen and confirm belief, as, on the contrary, lack of such understanding would impede and prejudice belief. Indeed, full awareness of the impossibility of a thing, and of the lack of any cause to bring it into being, would make belief in its existence utterly impossible.

Let us see to what extent in the realm of faith an understanding of its objects is possible, and in what sense the claim of theology to be a science alongside philosophy and distinct from it can be made good.

1. The understanding of truths accepted on faith is of a quite different order from the understanding of things known through mediate or immediate perception. In the domain of reason we acquire a notion of objects in the same way that we achieve certitude of their existence, that is, by the fact that these objects immediately or mediately confront us, and so at one and the same time assure us of their existence and impress their image upon us. We gain a concept of the objects from the objects themselves. Under the guidance of this concept and according as we retire to a greater or lesser distance from the object immediately conceived, we can with greater or lesser clarity and facility investigate the possibility of the objects, the principles of their existence, and their connection with other objects similarly conceived.

When supernatural truths are proposed to us by revelation, they remain invisible to us; they do not send their rays into the eye of our minds. Consequently they can no more project an image of their content toward us than we can become certain of their existence otherwise than through faith. Hence we do not have the same understanding of them as we have of the objects of philosophy; we have no such comprehension as would suppose their visibility or cause them to become visible. Our understanding of them must be achieved by means of natural concepts acquired by way of philosophical speculation; revelation itself clothes them with the forms and habiliments of these concepts.

In what, then, does the task of scientifically apprehending the objects of faith chiefly consist? Does it consist in this, that reason forces these objects into the conceptual forms it has found on the natural plane? The supernatural towers above the natural, and cannot be enclosed in the forms of the latter. If the supernatural and hence suprarational character of the objects of faith is to be safe-guarded, the concepts proper to reason must themselves be elevated, sublimated, and transformed according to the norm of the revealed proposition. A simple clarification, purification, and rectification, such as philosophy undertakes when dealing with the confused, inexact, and distorted notions of everyday experience, is not sufficient; such a process is necessary even for a correct scientific conception of natural things. Nor may the concepts be applied in the full, concrete value they have in the case of natural things; they may be transferred to the supernatural sphere only according to their highest aspects, those wherein natural things resemble supernatural things. We can designate this operation no better than by calling it a trans-figuration, which takes place through the agency of revelation and faith, somewhat in the way that sensible representations are raised to the spiritual plane by the spiritual light of the intellect.

This is the procedure we have applied and carried through in a practical way in the mysteries of the Trinity, the Incarnation, and the Eucharist. With the rest of the mysteries we have merely touched upon it.

Evidently this method of forming concepts is essentially different from philosophical abstraction; for it cannot be accomplished by reason alone, but only with the cooperation of a higher light, that of divine revelation, which supplies both the proposition and the norm governing the process.

It is just as evident that the *intellectus*, or understanding, of super-natural truths thus effected cannot be as clear and lucid as under-standing on the philosophical level. However, owing to the sublimity of the object into which it affords us a glimpse, and despite its lesser clarity, such understanding is by far the more valuable; and the philosophical concepts themselves, by serving as the substratum of the transfiguration, are of higher scientific import than if they were formed in their own sphere in a manner conformable to their own proper object.

In spite of the obscurity clinging to them, the concepts thus trans-figured give us a sufficiently exact and definite notion of supernatural objects. Therefore they enable us to understand, at least to some extent, the subject matter of the proposition we accept on faith, and to reflect on it.

For this reason they can serve as the basis for a further understanding of the objects of faith, by demonstrating the remaining factors required for their conceivability.

2. A feature pertaining to the understanding of an object is that we understand not only what it is, but also how and why it can be and really is. For an adequate conception of an object it is not enough that we have some idea of it; we must also be able to apprehend and conceive it as capable of realization and as realized.

The first condition for the existence of a thing is its intrinsic possibility, the absence of contradiction in the object. Insight into this results immediately, at least negatively, from the fact that we have a true, adequate, even if not exhaustive, idea of the object, that in general we conceive it to be what it really is. For if I conceive of an object, which in itself involves no contradiction, in such a way that I inevitably must unearth an evident contradiction in my conception, the conception cannot but be false. Only a positive insight into the manner in which the constituent notes of an object agree and fit well together, admits of degrees, according as the conception of the object is more or less clear and adequate. This is present to some extent in every correct apprehension of the notes; but in the case of purely analogous concepts it is so slight that it can scarcely be taken into account.

Accordingly, if analogous concepts correctly represent the objects of faith, they must make us aware that we perceive no evident contradiction in the latter. But since their correctness depends on their transfiguration and their sharply defined analogous value, we cannot exclude all contradiction until we have established this analogous value with complete accuracy. Conversely, in proportion as we neglect analogy and endeavor to compress supernatural objects within the dimensions of natural concepts, the notes must become incompatible, and hence the object must be inconceivable. Thus supernatural objects cannot be positively conceived as possible if the concept depends exclusively on analogy. Hence they are much less capable of being positively conceived than the objects of philosophy. But since even in these latter objects positive possibility plays no great role in science, at least in its deeper regions, on account of the obscurity attending even direct concepts, no one can attribute any peculiar disadvantage to theological science on the score that it does not get very far in this regard. However, the inconceivability of which there is question here, results from that very sublimity of the objects of theological science which constitutes its greatest dignity, and which necessarily entails some sort of inconceivability. The possibility of these objects is simply taken for granted by faith in their actuality, just as on the philosophical level possibility is presumed when it is manifested in actualization, as, for example, with regard to the union of the soul with the body.

3. The second condition for the possibility of a thing's existence is that there be a cause that has power to actualize it; this is extrinsic possibility. If I am already convinced of the existence of a thing, it is evident to me that such a cause exists. But thereupon I further desire to know what this cause is, and how it is able to produce the effect. As a rule, it is easy to find out what can and must be the cause of a given effect, since the effect itself bears witness to its cause. But the very fact that we ordinarily come to a knowledge of the cause in terms of its effect makes it much more difficult for us to learn of the properties that enable the cause to produce the effect, in such a way that we can detect the production itself.

In theology, too, the cause of the supernatural objects is soon discovered; it can be no other than the supreme cause, God. It is also easy to perceive that those objects, in order to be brought into being by God, require infinite power and wisdom. But how those effects are contained in God's infinite power and wisdom, and how they can be brought to light, we are much less able to perceive with our reason than we are to understand the production of created natures. We can perceive only that God in His infinite power and wisdom is able to accomplish infinitely more than we can ask and understand. Yet faith makes known to us a most stupendous activity that takes place within God Himself, in the Trinitarian productions, which enable us in some degree to understand positively how, in addition to producing other natures outside Himself, God can communicate His own nature to them in a supernatural manner.

But to discover what in God is the principle of all His supernatural works *ad extra*, the intellect may not rest content with the concept of God gained through its own efforts. It must take as its basis the higher, more comprehensive concept made accessible by revelation. Situated upon this vantage point, the intellect sees not only how God virtually comprises in Himself all His supernatural effects, but also how He is their ideal, their exemplary cause, and consequently has them in Himself as the real exemplar of them. The Trinitarian unity and the Trinitarian relations, as we showed earlier, are the prototype from which God Himself derives the idea of His supernatural relations *ad extra* and of His union with the creature in the Incarnation and grace. And thus we too, through our knowledge of this ideal, can come in some way to know how supernatural works are contained in God and proceed from Him.

Moreover, the clear apprehension of the way the efficient cause is able to produce the effect, and actually produces it, is of subordinate importance in all sciences, since forces are known only from their effects and are valued in terms of these effects. Even the forces studied in the natural sciences remain veiled in a mysterious obscurity. The scientific reduction of effects to their causes is nothing but the ascertainment of the laws which govern the production of the effects, and in accordance with which one effect involves another. From this truth we conclude further that the force which can produce one effect is able to produce another, related effect. A similar procedure may be adopted in studying the supernatural effects produced by God. To some extent God's sublime visible works could be adduced in proof of His mysterious power. But, since these works lie in a wholly disparate sphere, strictly scientific procedure requires that the possibility of a supernatural effect be illustrated by the possibility of another that is just as marvelous or even more so, as when the Fathers prove the possibility of the mysteries of grace and the Eucharist from the Incarnation.

4. The understanding demands an insight into the possibility of the object to be accepted on faith. After this demand has in some measure been satisfied, the understanding inquires more insistently than ever into the "why" of the real existence, that is, into the purpose to be attained by giving existence to the object, or the motive which explains the actualization of a definite idea. In a certain respect this question still concerns the possibility of the effect, since the power of the cause does not suffice for the effect unless the cause has an end which it pursues in producing the effect, and which determines it to this effect. But the question also touches on the necessity of the effect, since the end really intended, so far as it is a decisive factor in the emergence of the effect, necessarily involves the effect. To be sure, there are also means which are not absolutely necessary for the attainment of an appointed goal. But in that case they are

THEOLOGY AS SCIENCE 757

chosen by an intelligent cause only to the extent that the cause
intends to realize the objective in an especially perfect way, and
for this perfection the means chosen is absolutely demanded.

In its insight into the relationship of means to end, and into the
meaning and necessity of the various mysteries, theology is in a
most fortunate position, and can exercise a most fruitful and encouraging activity. However, none but genuinely relevant claims
should be made for this insight. The pretensions of the intellect
would be quite unwarranted and rash if it were to claim that the
free works of God were absolutely necessary, or if it were to presume
to discover within its own native domain the ends which motivate
these works, especially if they are supernatural. There can be no
more than a relative necessity for God's free works, that is, they
can be necessary only in relation to an end actually intended by
God. The purpose of such things as belong to a supernatural order
cannot be found outside that order, although evidently the concomitant realization of subordinate aims for the good of the natural
order is not excluded. Assuredly it is reason that has to gain an insight into the aims of God's supernatural works, and thereby an
understanding of their significance. But reason acquires this understanding not by reading the book of nature, but by reading the book
of divine revelation, in which God has laid open His mysterious
works themselves, together with their meaning and design. Far from
doing away with faith, such understanding, no matter how clear
and comprehensive it may be, can take possession of its object only
in conjunction with faith or revelation.

How we should regard this aspect of the understanding of the
objects of faith, we have tried to show in a practical way in the
mysteries of the Incarnation and the Eucharist. In general we may
say that an understanding of such objects can be achieved and
realized in two ways. We can start with the work in question, and
by analyzing its nature infer the destiny that can and ought to be
fitting for it. Or if, as is frequently the case, God Himself has expressly revealed certain definite aims, we begin with the purpose
and from it deduce the existence and nature of the works necessary
for its attainment. In both cases the understanding evidently remains
within the theological sphere.

It is clear that the effort to gain an insight into the purposes of
God's works cannot rest content with their proximate ends, but

must press on to the ultimate end beyond which there is no other. Thus, for instance, in accounting for the mystery of the original state, it is not sufficient to list the lordly prerogatives it conferred on man; we must advance further to the beatitude which man was called to attain, and to the supernatural glorification of God which he was to render thereby. Moreover, we must look upon the various mysteries as members of a great whole, in which the purpose of any one mystery is determined not only by its individual character, but also by its bearing on the whole. We must observe how the members of this whole are designed for one another in God's plan, how they are built up on one another, how all the mysterious works of God are connected with the mystery of the Godhead as their principle, and how they are strung together for the communication of God to the creature and for His own glorification. In a word, we must gain an insight into the wonderful plan of the supernatural order, and so endeavor to appreciate the significance of the individual mystery in terms of its relationship with the whole, and the whole in its harmonious unity as resulting from the proportion and correlation of the several parts.

By means of this insight, we then proceed in our conception to acquire a grasp of the objective system of the truths of faith. If the organic system of the objects to be known constitutes an objective science, evidently subjective science consists primarily in an apprehension and intellectual reflection upon the objective system. And if such apprehension is to a very high degree possible in the domain of faith, despite the fact that we are aware of the existence of the system only by faith as distinct from evident knowledge and understand its constituent parts only by means of analogous concepts, theology can be a science with as full right as philosophy or any other natural science.

5. Theologians and philosophers of a former age defined subjective science as *notitia rerum ex causis*, the knowledge of things in terms of their causes. This definition briefly sums up all that we have said about scientific activity in the field of theology.

By *notitia* is here meant not the certitude of the judgment regarding the existence of a thing—for even in the natural sciences this is derived not from causes but from effects—but the general apprehension of the object in the light of all the factors on which its nature and existence depend. First of all, we have the formal cause, the inner determination of the object's essence, on which also its intrinsic conceivability and possibility depend; in theology we attain to this by the employment of analogous concepts. Secondly, we have the efficient cause, on which the thing's capacity for external actualization depends; this we find, as also the exemplary cause, in God, regarded from the viewpoint of His supernatural power and perfection, although we do not have an adequate grasp of God's power and its relation to the objects. Lastly, we have the final cause, which we recognize in the various subordinate supernatural ends, and in the last instance in the greatest supernatural glorification of God.

The mystery in God, the Trinity, has no proper cause. It is, rather, the ultimate foundation of all the other mysteries as their root, ideal, and last end. But, although it has no proper cause, it possesses within itself a reason for itself. Thus in God's supernatural interior fruitfulness science discerns the root, in the interior communication and glorification of God the end, and in the relations and unity of the persons the form, which characterize the mystery. But it takes its place in the system of the remaining mysteries as their principle, for science must attend to the relation of cause to effect no less than to the relation of effect to cause.

The only question that could still be asked is whether material causality is not also to be assigned a function in theology. If by material cause we understand, in a loose sense, not a constituent of the object itself, but the substratum in which a particular object is placed, we can say fittingly that the material cause which forms the substructure of strictly theological, supernatural objects is none other than the natural order of things, upon which and over which the supernatural is erected. The study of this order as it is in itself is primarily the task not of theology but of philosophy. Theology has only to pay heed to the relation in which the natural stands to the supernatural, and in particular should endeavor to foster the conviction that the supernatural does not contradict the natural, but joins itself thereto in a most felicitous manner so as to crown and perfect it.

For instance, theology has to show that the Trinity of persons in God does not conflict with the unity and infinity of the divine nature, but rather exhibits that nature in all the glorious light of its infinity. It has to show that the supernatural endowment of the first man does not run counter to the concept of human nature, but transfigures it by harmonizing all its nobler elements, suppresses only natural defects, and the like. Further, since the supernatural can be nothing but an elevation and transfiguration of nature, theology must be mindful of nature in its unfolding of the supernatural, and must adjust the various phases of the supernatural to nature. Thus, for example, the working of habitual and actual grace in the soul must be accommodated to the several faculties of the soul, as well as to the relation of these faculties to one another and to their specific properties, in such a way that it does not contradict their nature, but ennobles and perfects it.[4]

The conception and appreciation which theology has of the relation of the natural to the supernatural suppose the most accurate knowledge obtainable of the former. Since this is in itself a purely philosophical knowledge, philosophy must prepare the ground for the theological edifice and lay the foundation for it. But philosophy cannot define this relationship itself. For the perception of this relationship a knowledge of the other term is also necessary, and such knowledge can be gained only from God's revelation. If philosophy could arrive at this knowledge by itself, the supernatural would have to be virtually contained in the natural, and would have to have the natural for its principle, not merely for its substructure. The plot of ground on which a building stands does not acquaint me with its relations to the building, or with the building itself, even though the contour of the building is conditioned by the shape and size of the lot.

In this matter of determining the relation of the supernatural to the natural, theological knowledge comes into its closest contact with philosophical knowledge, but without merging with it. Here, as everywhere, theology is essentially marked off from philosophy by the fact that its object and the standpoint from which it has to proceed are furnished by revelation, and are not the proper stock in trade of the intellect itself. True, it is the natural understanding, the natural reason, with which we must work in our endeavor to know the truths of revelation, and with which we achieve some insight. But this is made possible only by the fact that under the

---

[4] This plan is carried out by St. Thomas on an imposing scale in Part II of the *Summa*, where his ordinary procedure is to take a sound presentation of nature, its powers, and its life as the foundation whereon he may subsequently erect the edifice of the supernatural order.

guidance of revelation the intellect rises above its own sphere, grasps the higher objects, contemplates them from all angles, and analyzes them in the light of the transfiguration of its own concepts. In the process of understanding the supernatural, reason must constantly regard revelation as the source and norm of its conception of the object, just as in the judgment about the existence of this object it must look to revelation as the principle of its certitude, whereas in both respects philosophy is restricted to the natural light of reason.

CHAPTER XXIX

Faith and Reason

••

107. The Organic Unity of Understanding and Faith in Theological Knowledge

THE closing paragraph of the preceding chapter makes it clear that the *intellectus rerum creditarum*, the understanding of things accepted on faith, not only does not exclude belief in these objects, but necessarily supposes it. Full, scientific knowledge of the supernatural order of things is possible only in conjunction with faith. In addition to well-founded certitude about a truth, full scientific knowledge requires an apprehension of its ontological grounds. Similarly, a simple apprehension of objects without a certain judgment about their objective truth does not verify the notion of scientific knowledge. The conception of supernatural objects does not in itself include a positive guaranty of the truth of the objects conceived even in the ideal order, to say nothing of the real order. It does not do so in the real order: with the exception of the Trinity, supernatural objects are essentially contingent; hence any conviction I may have that they are conceivable does not entail their real existence. Likewise in the ideal order, with regard to the objective possibility of their realization: since I do not fully comprehend them with my analogous concepts, and can do no more than ascertain that I myself find no contradiction in them, I am not in a position to judge positively that they are objectively possible.

With all my inspection of supernatural objects, I cannot form a positive judgment as to their objective possibility and actual existence except by belief in divine revelation, which simultaneously proposes them for my conception and vouches for their objective truth. Hence, even though I may arrive at a concept as connected with another and as evidently proposed therein, I cannot judge of the objective truth of the former except through the faith whereby I assent to the objective truth of the latter; for I can never deduce one supernatural truth except from another that is likewise supernatural. And although in virtue of my understanding of revealed objects I may perceive the dependence of an object on its ontological grounds, I can acquire a sure knowledge of its objective truth only so far as I am apprised of the existence and the character of these grounds by faith.

Consequently I can mentally reconstruct the objective system of supernatural truths with conviction of its objective verity, only to the extent that I hold fast in faith to the cardinal point around which it revolves, and the principles from which it develops. Often such a principle is directly expressed in the revealed truth; and then without further ado I can evolve the system from it. At times, however, the fundamental idea underlying one or more explicitly revealed truths can be ascertained only by an analysis of them. The former is the case, for example, in the Trinity. But in the Incarnation we were obliged, at least in part, to pursue a different route in order to discover the end it is meant to achieve.

In the Trinity we found our principle in the inner productivity and fruitfulness of the divine nature. All the other mysteries are contingent works of God. The principle leading to our knowledge of them is located in the purposes they are to realize; by realizing these purposes they become linked with the mystery of the Trinity as their ultimate end.

These principles supposed, all the truths issuing from them in theology may be explained with the strictest scientific precision, and may be deduced with the most rigorous scientific consistency. But the roots themselves, the first principles, cannot be inferred by the application of a strictly scientific process. Any explanation of their tenor must rest content with analogy, and their certainty can be guaranteed only by faith.

Nevertheless, if these principles are rightly grasped, our very apprehension of them renders them in some measure probable and acceptable to the intellect, at times even to the degree that we may come to look upon them as self-evident, and take their objective truth for granted.

We must give a somewhat more detailed explanation of this point. If it is put clearly, it closes off the source of most of the misunder-

standings that arise with regard to the essential character of theological science.

If I rightly understand and weigh the import of a theological
principle—for instance, that there are inner productions in God's
knowledge and love, that God has destined man for the immediate
vision of Himself, or that in the redemption He wills simultaneously
to reveal His infinite mercy and justice—then with my unaided
reason I can straightway become aware that I perceive no evident
contradiction in these objects. I perceive no such contradiction
among the objects themselves or with what reason by itself knows
to be well established concerning the nature of God and man. Consequently I become aware that reason has no grounds for vetoing
the acceptance of such principles. Reason does not pronounce upon
the ideal truth of the principles. But, on the supposition of their objective conceivability, reason can perceive that, if they are brought
to realization, God would be revealed both *ad intra* and *ad extra* in
all the magnificent splendor of His infinity, and man would be
elevated to an unimaginable height of dignity and blessedness. Hence
reason sees that the lofty idea it has acquired of God by its own
powers would be strikingly substantiated, and that the most extravagant cravings of human nature would be superabundantly
satisfied. Reason must admit to itself that the infinity of God can
and must embrace a host of perfections that are not reflected in the
mirror of creation. And as soon as it has the slightest clue to go
on, its very nature impels it continually to think as highly as
possible of God in regard to His own being and to His activity in
the outer world, and to expect for itself the best that it could receive
from the infinite goodness of God.

Accordingly reason does not shrink from such truths; it even
feels itself drawn to them and feels an inclination to presume their
reality. Though but dimly grasped, the coherence of these truths
with objects known and valued by reason, and therefore with reason
itself, engenders a certain kinship between them and reason. On
this kinship depends the attractive force whereby they charm our
reason and sway it in their favor. This disposing of reason in favor
of a truth rests not so much upon the intelligibility of the truth as
upon the goodness and beauty of its content. It has an analogy with
the *pius credulitatis affectus*, the pious disposition to believe, which
is the starting point of positive, supernatural faith. Indeed, it is the

natural stock on which the grace leading to theological faith is grafted, to elevate and sublimate it. Hence it is in itself a certain natural faith, a certain surrender of the will to the supernatural object. It inclines reason to accept the latter, although it can impart no definite certitude. Although it cannot of itself banish doubt, it sets up a bias in favor of the truth, and so makes impossible an absolute indifference on the part of reason toward that truth. However, this indifference is not completely eliminated except by positive belief in divine revelation, which undeniably vouches for the objective truth that had previously been presumed. Thus, too, the presumptive disposition itself acquires true vitality and efficacy only through supernatural grace, which exhibits the supernatural objects to us in a favorable light and causes our will to experience the power of attraction they exert. But even grace conduces to certitude only by inclining us to a willing surrender to divine revelation.

If we are not mistaken, this account gives us the best explanation of the psychological possibility and the true import of the utterances and the method of many great theologians who, while emphatically professing the absolute necessity of positive faith for a sure knowledge of the mysteries, often proceed as though they wished to raise such knowledge to certitude independently of faith. We may not ascribe either an overoptimistic esteem for man's intellectual powers or an obvious logical inconsistency to such learned and holy men as Anselm, Bonaventure, and Richard of St. Victor. Their mode of procedure may be partly explained on the ground that the power of faith as "the substance of things to be hoped for, the evidence of things that appear not," [1] brought the mysteries so close to them. Or perhaps the power of faith unconsciously raised their spiritual vision so high that they thought they beheld the invisible, and supposed they could illuminate others with the abundance of their own light. They did not always clearly differentiate between the natural standpoint of the intellect and the level to which revelation raises the intellect. Yet, as we saw earlier, [2] St. Bonaventure and Richard sometimes make the proper distinctions. But we must not forget that the ideal disposition that we spoke of above was a prominent feature of their intellectual life, even apart from theological faith. Hence they thought that whatever was presented in

[1] Heb. 11:1.
[2] See p. 39.

the form of supreme goodness and perfection would be acceptable even to one who was as yet an unbeliever, in the genuine conviction that a person who once looked at the mysteries of faith from this angle would readily embrace external revelation, and so would in some measure have anticipated belief in it.

They speak of *rationes necessariae* with which, independently of Scripture, they desired to demonstrate revealed dogmas. But this is to be understood in the sense that they wished to establish the various teachings of faith with necessary, inescapable logic from causes and principles which, taken strictly, cannot be known with certitude except by belief in positive revelation, but which would not be denied by anyone of good will who has not closed his mind to the majesty of God and the sublimity of man's destiny. This is true particularly where there is question of justifying or explaining the data of revelation which depend on those causes and principles. Thus, for instance, St. Bonaventure could assume that no one would refuse to grant that the infinite divine goodness is essentially communicable in an infinite way, a principle from which he draws out the entire doctrine of the Trinity. Thus also St. Anselm did not think that anyone would care to dispute that there is a real production of a Word and a sigh in the divine knowledge and love, just as there is in human knowledge and love, on the analogy of which we conceive the divine. Nor did he think anyone would deny that man is destined for the intuitive vision of God, or that in the redemption God wished to assert His justice and His mercy alike in a perfect manner. Therefore with full confidence he could go on to deduce the details of the dogmas of the Trinity, original justice, and the Incarnation. With both doctors this procedure is all the easier to understand inasmuch as the genius of St. Bonaventure veered toward idealization rather than analysis, and St. Anselm, who was the first to break ground in the matter of treating dogma scientifically, was not yet in a position to devise a method that would be well defined and sound from every point of view.

St. Thomas is more cautious. He found speculative theology in a higher and more complex stage of development and systematization and was able, in the full flight of his genius, to analyze everything supremely well. In countless passages he declares that the starting points of the mystical portion of theology can be rendered intelligible only by comparisons and analogies, and can in some measure be made plausible and acceptable only by their agreement with truths already mastered by reason. Often he goes so far as to draw attention to the dangers and drawbacks that may arise from the claim to have demonstrated these fundamental truths on rational grounds. This appears clearest of all in the Trinity, as we saw previously.

With regard to man's supernatural destiny, on the other hand, his procedure often resembles that of St. Anselm. He infers the existence of this destiny from man's natural cravings to behold the Cause of all things, a craving that cannot remain ungratified. And in the *Summa contra Gentiles* he even seems to place this destiny and all that follows from it in the category of natural truths. Indeed, it is not until the fourth book (he had treated of this subject in the third), after he has finished dealing with truths attainable by reason itself, that he takes up the roll of true mysteries. How this particular procedure is to be understood, we have tried to explain in another place.[3] It is enough to remark here that St. Thomas consistently bases the necessity and importance of supernatural faith on the fact that the intellect can be made ready for the attainment of the supernatural goal of the beatific vision and can be conducted to it only by faith. The intellect, by force of its very nature, aspires to a perfect knowledge of the ultimate reality, but it keeps this reality definitely in view only by supernatural faith. This view is the condition of that efficacious, dynamic striving which issues in attainment of the objective.[4]

[3] See pp. 659–62.

[4] Cf. *Summa*, IIa IIae, q.4, a.1 ff.; *De veritate*, q.14, a.11; and especially *In III Sent.*, d.23, q.1, a.4, quaestiunc. 3 in corp: "All things that act in pursuance of an end must have a tendency toward that end, and a certain inception of it; otherwise they would not be acting for an end. However, the end to which the divine generosity has foreordained or predestined man, namely, the fruition of God Himself, completely surpasses the powers of created nature; for 'eye hath not seen, nor ear heard, neither hath it entered into the heart of man, what things God hath prepared for them that love Him' (I Cor. 2:9). Man's natural equipment does not confer on him a sufficient inclination to such an end, and so something must be added to man to give him an inclination to that end, just as his natural powers impart to him an inclination to an end that is connatural to him. These superadded gifts are called theological virtues, for three reasons. First, as concerns their object: for, since the end to which we are ordained is God Himself, the required tendency consists in actions whose object is God Himself. Secondly, with regard to their cause for, as that end is appointed unto us by God, and

Accordingly, whoever wishes to refrain from undermining knowledge of supernatural truths by depriving it of the first condition of scientific knowledge, the unshakable certainty of its principles, must of set purpose take belief in the principles as his foundation. Whatever understanding is possible in this sphere does not do away with faith or engender a knowledge independent of faith. On the contrary, the entire function of such understanding is discharged by the fact that it leans upon faith or leads to faith. And so by the science of faith is to be understood either the purely rational demonstration of the fact of revelation, which disposes to faith, or the scientific understanding of the objects revealed. This latter understanding conduces to faith or strengthens readiness to embrace it, but does not impart full conviction of the truth of the object apprehended except in faith and by faith.

With respect to the objects of faith, therefore, such understanding of them as is possible should never be called a real knowing as distinct from faith, as if it constituted a proper, complete knowledge that would take its place at the side of faith. To be real knowledge, it must be as intimately associated with faith as faith is with it, if not more so. The profound observation, *Fides quaerit intellectum*, is adequately appreciated only in conjunction with another, *Intellectus quaerit fidem*. Both, faith and understanding, complement and postulate each other for the organic unity of a knowledge imparted by God concerning truths revealed by Him. By faith I accept the word of God; with my understanding I apprehend it. Only if I have both together do I make my own the knowledge which God has uttered in the Word, and thus become a true knower myself.

Without carefully qualifying our statement, we cannot say that through the activity of the intellect faith passes over into knowledge as a further stage of cognition, and that this is brought about not by self-surrender but by self-development. For ordinarily we give the name faith to that stage of supernatural knowledge in which we understand the truths we believe only so far as some grasp of

---

not by our nature, God alone produces in us an inclination toward the end; and so they are called theological virtues, in the sense that they are caused in us exclusively by God. Thirdly, from the point of view of natural knowledge: for the tendency to this end cannot be known by natural reason, but only by revelation; and so they are called theological, inasmuch as they are made known to us by information that comes from God. Consequently philosophers have no knowledge of them."

them is indispensable for holding a definite object as true. In this sort of understanding the object is known only in vague outline; it is not known with clarity and precision in its various facets, its inner organism, its principles, and its connection with other objects. At this stage faith is naturally the predominant element, and understanding has scarcely any importance as compared with our acceptance of the truth. If, however, understanding is cultivated along the lines just indicated, the cognitive process inaugurated by faith enters upon another and higher stage, in which it is called knowledge. But one who thus knows and one who simply believes are not distinct as two individuals, the first being aware of a definite thing by ocular evidence, the second by receiving information about it from another person. Rather they are as two individuals, both of whom perceive a thing with their own eyes, hence through the same medium; but one stands in front of the object scarcely adverting to it, while the other scrutinizes it from all sides in a scientific spirit, examines the interrelation of the parts and studies their functions, and generally seeks to account both for the whole and for the details. Something of the sort would ensue, for instance, if the same plant were placed before an uneducated man and before a botanist. Or perhaps we should do better to say: they are in the position of two men who together listen to a report of a momentous event that is recounted in great detail. Both have to rely on the word of the narrator; but one of them catches only a few outstanding facts, while the other comprehends the logical coherence of the development and learns so much that he is able to appreciate both the motivation and the significance of each fact.

Moreover, the reasoned probability of theological principles which, as we said above, results from a deeper understanding of them, can be strengthened in yet another way. This other way is by detecting in the unfolding of the principles the wonderful coherence and harmony whereby all the truths of the supernatural order are related to one another and to the truths of the natural order. It seems that false principles cannot be at the basis of a system of truths in which not the slightest contradiction can be found, in which each detail is perfectly adapted to the whole, in which every fresh examination uncovers new unifying threads, a system which in the course of the centuries discloses an increasing fruitfulness, which exhibits itself not merely in one but in a thousand different departments

as the consummation of natural truth, and with ever deeper perception reveals new points of contact with the latter.[5] This indirect
proof can easily rise to certitude with a person who carefully surveys the whole vast sweep of the system. Yet it can never, by any
process of demonstration, afford an insight into the principles themselves. It merely engenders the conviction that the principles of such
a system, which man cannot reach by his own efforts, must be revealed by God, and therefore must be accepted by faith in the word
of God.

108. The Supernatural Stimulus in Our Understanding of the Truths of Faith

Up to this point we have said nothing of the influence of supernatural grace on the *intellectus fidei;* and the same is true, at least
in part, of our treatment of faith itself. We have regarded this understanding as a purely intellectual operation which, to be sure, is connected with the external revelation that has been accepted or is to
be accepted on faith, but supposes no other light in the thinking
subject than the light of reason itself.

If the reasoned conviction of the fact of revelation and of credibility, or the *intellectus credibilitatis,* is to lead to supernatural, theological faith, it must be elevated, transfigured, and stimulated by a
supernatural light, the *lumen fidei.* In like manner, if the understanding of the truths of faith (the *intellectus rerum credendarum*)
is to be at all vivid, and hence in junction with faith is to result in a
truly vital grasp of the truths believed, there must be found in the
believing subject something more than simple faith or the grace
formally required for faith itself. There must be found a supernatural disposition that is more or less closely connected with faith and
the grace of faith. It is this disposition which effects a certain spiritual
kinship and harmony between the believer and the supernatural objects.

The logical operations by which an understanding of the supernatural is achieved with the aid of rational concepts, in themselves
suppose no more than an external proposal of the objects and a
sufficient cultivation and docility of the intellect on the part of the

---

[5] Newman uses this argument to good advantage in his *Essay on the Development of Christian Doctrine,* pp. 93, 437 ff. [Tr.]

subject, without being absolutely dependent on a supernatural, inner light or on the moral disposition of the subject. Even in the sphere of the higher natural truths lying within the radius of reason, man often requires an auxiliary illumination from God, and must bring with him a good moral disposition of will, so that the light of his reason may not slumber ineffectually or be smothered as soon as it starts to rise. If this is so, then in the case of supernatural truths the natural receptiveness of the intellect for all truth will hardly suffice for a vivid and dynamic conception of them. A supernatural light will be needed to display the objects to their best advantage, and to elevate reason to their level. In the soul there will have to grow forth a life that will enable the objects to strike root in the soul itself.

This is the sense in which the Apostle says: "The sensual man perceiveth not these things that are of the Spirit of God; for it is foolishness to him, and he cannot understand, because it is spiritually examined. But the spiritual man judgeth all things." [6] By sensual man (that is, natural or animal man), is here meant the man who with his entire nature is opposed to the Spirit of God, whereas the spiritual man is the man who is not only raised above the animal man, but is animated and pervaded by the Spirit of God. Unless man is in some way or other moved, enlightened, and animated by the Spirit of God, he cannot actively grasp "the doctrine of the Spirit" [7] concerning the deep things of God, and the gifts that are drawn out of these depths.[8] Without the Spirit's illumination, supernatural objects must ever appear strange to us, and our relations with them must lack vitality. But this illumination makes them shine in our eyes with a favorable light, and brings them close to us. Even if it does not actually enable us to behold them, at any rate it places them before us so plainly and clearly that we could almost be persuaded we saw them.

By this illumination of the Holy Spirit, as has been indicated above, we understand first a more or less perfect, immediate enlightenment of our reason about the matter to be believed, an enlightenment normally connected with the grace of faith, or even conveyed by this grace. Secondly we understand by this illumination the radiation, through faith itself, of the love and life of the

[6] See I Cor. 2:14 f.
[7] Ibid., 2:13.
[8] Ibid., 2:10–12.

Holy Spirit. Therein our faith becomes a living faith, informed by sanctifying grace, and its objects come into close contact with the soul by a real manifestation of themselves.

In the first of these illuminations the Holy Spirit opens up "the ear of our heart," moving it to a willing, resolute surrender to the word of revelation, and at the same time "enlightens the eyes of our heart," that we may know, or correctly and vividly conceive, the objects of revelation, which the Apostle refers to as our supernatural calling, the riches of the glory of the divine inheritance, and in general as the exceeding greatness of the divine power over us.[9] It is chiefly this illumination that brings about the transfiguration of our natural concepts, so necessary for an apprehension of supernatural truths. Strictly speaking, such transfiguration and transformation can be undertaken by the unaided reason, acting in conformity with external revelation. But if no corresponding inner light illuminates our understanding, the concepts lose their vitality and precision in the very process of being recast, owing to the introduction of analogy. They are not of the same order as the objects, which they represent under forms that always remain unsuited to them.

The illumination we are speaking of can precede faith, and then it makes for a firmer and more cheerful acceptance of faith. Or, in the case of one who already believes, it can make its influence felt with increasing power later, whether in response to man's loyal cooperation or in pursuance of God's free choice of graces. In general, however, the dispensing of divine grace is mainly dependent on man's humble consciousness of his own powerlessness; and this is particularly true of this grace. The more man trusts in the power of his own reason, and boldly sets out with nothing but its murky lantern to explore the ocean of the divine mysteries, the more dimly will the supernatural light illuminate his way, and the more obscure and confused will his conception be.

In this connection, the word of the divine Savior holds: "Unless you become as little children, you shall not enter into the kingdom of heaven." [10] As we must become little in our persons if we wish to be reborn of God, so we must enroll in God's school as infants, and must allow ourselves to be led into the depths of His mysteries clasping His hand, and guided by His light. Indeed, whoever re-

[9] Cf. Eph. 1:17–19.
[10] Matt. 18:3.

fuses to become little in this way will not even reach what he is actually capable of reaching with his natural faculties. God's curse will rest upon his undertaking, and under its weight his enterprise will inevitably founder. But where a childlike spirit prevails unspoiled, neither great intellectual culture nor a skilled human teacher is needed for a vivid conception of the most august truths; for the Holy Spirit's anointing teaches us concerning all things.[11] Grace often manifests its enlightening power preferably to those very people who are truly small in respect to their intellectual equipment, so that they not infrequently apprehend the mysteries of God more surely and clearly than the most learned philosophers, and the supernatural is as easily grasped by them as the natural. Indeed, their perception and clarity in the domain of the mysteries seem greater at times than their powers of comprehension in worldly and natural affairs.

Sometimes children, in whom we can scarcely instill the most ordinary notions of earthly matters, vividly conceive and, as it were, imbibe the most sublime truths that are placed before them. How can we explain this fact if not by the grace of the Holy Spirit who by His illumination stirs up a holy hunger in their hearts, and enables them receive such truths as easily as the eye drinks in pictures of material objects? Of course, this supernatural light does not in itself engender any abstractly formulated and organically integrated conception of the mysteries, as true science demands. Ideas of this sort can be acquired only by study and a methodical cultivation of the intellect. But such study receives its higher efficacy and consecration, its blessing and its life, from that illumination.

We might add that the eye of the heart must be cleansed of pride, as well as of every other defilement, in order to have the power of acquiring a lively understanding of God's mysteries. An egotistical spirit, and especially sensual cravings which rule the heart, not only make the heart unworthy of God's enlightening grace, but paralyze grace and snuff out the very light that normally illuminates the intellect. Even in the natural sphere such vices darken the mind respecting quite evident truths, whenever they emerge beyond the circle in which concupiscence moves, or go so far as to oppose these truths in open hostility. How much more must the supernatural light presuppose a circumcised heart and a pure, consecrated eye, if it is to

[11] Cf. I John 2:27.

prove effectual! As only the pure of heart can see God, so they alone can here below grasp the mysteries with a clarity and vividness akin to vision, because they alone hold up a pure, untarnished mirror to the light of the Holy Spirit's grace.

Humility and purity of heart, as considered here, are obviously not independent of grace. On the contrary, they are produced by the Holy Spirit and by faith which is already operative. To that extent they have a certain analogy with the second kind of influence listed above, whereby the Holy Spirit graphically brings the truth of our faith home to us. But in themselves these two virtues do not positively raise us above nature, in such a way as to bring us closer to revealed truths than we were by nature. In themselves they merely remove the obstacles to our approach, and make us responsive to the double radiation of the light and the life-giving warmth of the Holy Spirit.

The second kind of radiation emanating from the Holy Spirit comes to this: by its light it causes the truths of faith to illuminate us from without, and by its warmth and energizing power it places us in a real, living communication with them. It makes these truths, so to speak, live in us, and us in them, and brings them to our consciousness in all their vibrant reality. The consequence of this influence is that we are enabled to grasp their content more readily, and can, in a way, confirm their existence by our own inner spiritual experience.

The supernatural life growing out of faith under the action of the Holy Spirit, the life whereby faith becomes objectively a living faith in its real and moral implications, further causes faith to become a living faith. What effects this is the illumination it confers by bringing the invisible objects of faith close to us. This takes place in a variety of ways.

First, if faith is animated by the love which the Holy Spirit infuses, this love sets up in us a relationship of intimate union with the objects of faith, for all of them reveal to us in many forms the infinite lovableness of God. By love that knows no distance, the lover is placed in the object loved, to embrace and permeate it. The mind is carried along in this flight of the heart. Its power of vision becomes keener and stronger in proportion as the heart craves to possess the object loved. And the attraction which the object of faith exercises upon the heart, as also the joy and rapture which every ray of its beauty arouses, is taken by the intellect as a proof of the splendor and reality of the object.

Secondly, the love infused by the Holy Spirit works in the soul itself a transformation whereby the soul is assimilated to the objects loved and becomes a mirror of them. Moreover, it is assimilated to the exalted goodness and love of God, the very foundation and root of all the mysteries. Indeed the mysteries are but revelations and fruits of the one truth that God is in all reality a *bonum summe communicativum*, a supremely communicable Good. To one who has clearly grasped this truth, even the greatest and most sublime mysteries will appear understandable and comprehensible. But only he who discerns in himself the power and the nature of divine love, on whom the Holy Spirit has lavished His own love, who has been, as it were, transformed by this love into God and Christ, and who, in the words of the Apostle, has in him the mind that was in Christ Jesus, will vividly perceive the full force of this truth. Such a one will understand how the infinite divine goodness could impel the Father to communicate His entire nature to the Son and the Holy Spirit, to send His Son into the outer world, and to surrender Him up to the most ignominious and agonizing death.

Lastly, in consequence of the inspiration of the Holy Spirit there grows out of faith the entire higher life in which we endeavor to regulate our conduct in conformity with the truths of faith and stamp their laws upon our souls. This higher life must be regarded as a sort of real revelation of those truths and a practical confirmation of their existence. As a result of believing in those truths, we can almost feel in ourselves a certain power, along with the spiritual peace and consolation conferred on us by our living in accord with them. This power enables us to experience their wonderful efficacy for satisfying the deeper needs and the nobler cravings of our nature. It reveals to us in our Christian life the truth of Christianity, and draws its mysteries down from their transcendental remoteness to the closest and most intimate proximity to us.

Thus in these three ways the faith which lives in love places us in vital relationship with the truths that are but dimly grasped by faith alone. It also imparts to us such a vivid conception of them that we can almost believe we are seeing them.

But no matter how keen such perception may become, it will never do away with faith itself or make faith superfluous, since at all points it supposes faith as its principle. Without the anchor of faith our heart is always in danger of leading us astray. If we insisted on heeding the thrust, the emotions, and the feelings of the heart alone, all our certitude about supernatural truths would evaporate into empty subjectivism. The voice of the heart may be listened to only in conjunction with faith and the objective criteria of external revelation. The heart may serve as proof and corroboration, but never as a substitute for revelation and faith.

The same holds with even greater urgency as regards the inner light which is joined to the grace of faith. This light may assist us to apprehend the truths of faith correctly; but it does not enable us actually to see them. Besides, it is psychologically impossible for us readily to ascertain with sureness that the light by which we think we behold a thing is really a true light, unless it pertains to the intellect as such. If, prescinding from the objective and external revelation to which it corresponds, we wish to follow that light alone, we are no more secure from visionary fanaticism than we are from emotional excess.

Hence we conclude: both the supernatural light shining in the grace of faith, and the union with the objects of faith that flows from faith, whereby we penetrate into the objects, and they become, as it were, a part of ourselves, both serve, and are even necessary, to acquaint us with the mysteries, and to turn the lifeless and artificial conception of them—the only conception possible for unaided reason—into a living, graphic understanding; but they can never bring about an intuition in the proper sense.

That light is merely a faint glimmer in the night of our intellect, the dawn of the light of vision. It leads us securely only when we cling in faith to our divine Guide, who tells us what He has Himself beheld. That union does indeed establish a contact with the objects, and according to circumstances stirs us powerfully and fills us with anticipatory joy. However, in the darkness of our night, nothing but faith, in which we receive these objects from the hand of God, makes a firm and sure grasp of them possible for us.

Faith will be replaced only by the light of glory, in which alone we no longer need to cling to God's word, because God will flood us with the light in which He sees; it is from the fullness of this light that He speaks. He will take us to His bosom, the source and center of all the mysteries, and will place us in an immediate and real communication with them all.

However, since the light of grace and the life of grace are an anticipation of the light of glory and of life in the bosom of God, we can perhaps say that the natural understanding and supernatural faith are formed and vitalized by grace into a perfect, living knowledge. Hence we can also say that an anticipation of the future vision is germinally contained in faith, obscure though it may be of itself. But faith derives the principle of this vitality not from reason, but from the very divine source whence it itself arises. Faith brings it down from the infinite light of the divinity, in order to imbue the intellect with supernatural illumination, just as faith itself formally enriches reason with the certitude of supernatural principles. This principle of vitality comes down with faith, because it consists in two of the seven gifts of the Holy Spirit. All these gifts, in a higher or lower degree, accompany at least the faith that is animated by grace in the just, and are designed to guide the theological virtues to their full perfection. The two gifts we are speaking of are understanding (*intellectus*) and wisdom (*sapientia*): understanding, so far as it sharpens our sight in a supernatural way, enabling it to penetrate into the truths believed and to grasp them clearly and accurately; wisdom, so far as, in consequence of the affective unity contained in love and of our kinship with the objects of faith, it confers on us a certain spiritual discrimination and relish whereby our judgment about these objects is made easily and naturally.[12]

[12] On the gift of understanding, see St. Thomas, *In III Sent.*, d.35, q.2, a.2, quaestunc. 1 ff.; *Summa*, IIa IIae, q.8. The Angelic Doctor discusses the gift of wisdom in *In III Sent.*, d.35, q.35, a.1; a better treatment is found in the *Summa*, IIa IIae, q.45, a.2: "Wisdom implies a certain rectitude of judgment that is in accord with the divine reason. Rectitude of judgment can be regarded in two ways: first, with reference to perfect use of reason, secondly, from the point of view of a certain connaturality with the object about which judgment is to be pronounced. Thus, in matters pertaining to chastity, he who has mastered the science of moral theology judges rightly, once he has investigated the question; but another person, who has the habit of chastity, judges rightly about the same matter because this virtue is, so to speak, connatural to him. Therefore, with regard to divine matters as investigated by reason, the ability to judge aright pertains to the wisdom which is an intellectual virtue. But the ability to pass correct judgment about such matters by a sort of connaturality with them belongs to wisdom as a gift of the Holy Spirit. Thus Dionysius says, in chapter 2 of *De divinis nominibus*:

This supernatural acumen and this supernatural relish, standing at the head of the list among the gifts of the Holy Spirit, instill into unlearned souls that are, however, pure, unsophisticated, and God-loving, that instinctive clarity and assurance in the most august questions of theology, which frequently scholars can but marvel at in amazement. Yet these same gifts also guide the scholar most rapidly and securely in the use of his reason on the supernatural plane. At the same time they imbue his thoughts and words with that heavenly ointment which, by the light it gives and the perfume it emits, so powerfully quickens the eye and lovingly stirs the heart of the disciples and readers of the saintly doctors of the Church.

109. General Relation Between Reason and Faith in the Genesis of Philosophical and Theological Knowledge

In accordance with this doctrine, we may readily determine the general relation between the factors that work together for the production of theological knowledge, that is, reason and faith. In dealing with this subject, we must touch upon the lively controversies enkindled in recent times by the revival of the adage, "philosophy is the handmaid of theology."

The metaphorical cast of this proposition has given rise to a number of misunderstandings, which only an accurate interpretation of its meaning can correct. We are of the opinion that in many respects this metaphor illustrates the true relation between philosophy and theology, but that it must be supplemented by another metaphor which brings out that relation more profoundly and adequately, and

---

'Hierotheus is perfect in divine things, because he not only learns, but experiences them.' This connatural sympathy with divine things is the result of charity, which unites us to God, according to I Cor. 6:17: 'He who is joined to the Lord is one spirit.' Therefore the wisdom which is a gift has its cause in the will, for its cause is charity; but its essence resides in the intellect, whose act is to judge correctly, as was stated above." The gift of knowledge belongs here, too; but its position is inferior to that of understanding or wisdom.

On the relation of these gifts to faith, St. Thomas teaches (*Summa*, IIa IIae, q.4, a.8 ad 3): "The perfection of the gifts of understanding and knowledge exceeds the perfection of that knowledge which is proper to faith, from the point of view of greater clarity, but not as regards firmer assent. For the whole certitude of understanding and knowledge, considered as gifts, arises from the knowledge that belongs to faith, just as the certitude of conclusions arises from the certitude of principles."

has the further advantage that it tones down the harsh and objectionable features of the first figure. In putting forth our view, we will at the same time proceed further and illustrate the relation with two analogies. These, drawn as they are from the very essence of Christianity, propose not a natural symbol, but the supernatural ideal according to which that relationship is objectively constituted.

First of all, we should note that philosophy and theology are not being compared here according to the nature and range of their respective objects. Nor are they compared subjectively as the sums of the correct elements of knowledge acquired by drawing out their respective principles of cognition. For under these two aspects they have only a static, not a dynamic, relation to each other, whereas the latter is expressed in the formula quoted above. There is question rather of the relation between the two principles of cognition, natural reason and supernatural faith, and also of the relation between the respective activities whereby theology and philosophy are built up into subjectively complete sciences. With this presupposed, it is easy to determine the sense in which philosophy is the handmaid of theology, or, more exactly, the sense in which reason is the handmaid of faith.

1. In the first place, natural reason is, in dignity and power, a lower cognitive principle than faith. It ranks below faith in a very important respect, namely, in the range and inerrancy of its illumination. Faith reaches as far as the communication of the divine knowledge and, in supernatural reliance thereon, shares in its infallibility. In a word, it represents the divine reason as opposed to human reason. This opposition between reason and faith does not formally imply the idea of the positive subordination of reason to faith. But, as soon as a real relationship is set up between them, reason is dependent on faith and proceeds from faith.

This occurs when man is called to faith, or actually receives the gift of faith. In this case reason has to work for the good of faith as for a higher principle, and in dependence on faith as on a higher principle. To this extent reason has to serve faith, or be its "handmaid."

Reason has to work for faith in two ways: first, to prepare a place in the soul for faith itself; secondly, once faith has taken possession, to bring about an understanding and development of its contents. Thus reason serves theological knowledge as a higher science by helping to impart it in its principle and in its subsequent development. In the first connection reason is a *praeambula* (forerunner), in the second a *pedisequa* (attendant) of faith.

As *praeambula*, reason goes before faith, exploring the natural order of things upon which is erected the supernatural order to be known by faith and from which must be acquired the notions that, when illuminated by analogy, are to be applied to the conception of the supernatural order. Again, reason precedes in order to convince the soul of the existence and credibility of supernatural revelation, and hence of the licitness and obligation of belief in it. In virtue of man's vocation to faith, reason may no longer work exclusively for itself when investigating natural things in its effort to win control over the domain of natural truths. It is called upon to build a throne for faith and to utilize its natural knowledge as a pattern for the higher knowledge to be gained through faith. Further, owing to this same vocation, reason is under orders not to ignore the facts by which revelation comes to its attention, but must ponder them carefully so as thereby to open the door of the soul to faith. Reason cannot, of course, inaugurate faith; for faith is ushered in and set upon its throne by the free will elevated by grace.

From this point on, reason is called upon to work for faith as *pedisequa*, so that faith can develop the rich resources of its own subject matter. Reason must strive more to promote the development of faith than its own good, since the object of faith is immeasurably nobler and more worthy than its own proper object, and comprises everything that reason longed for by nature, but could not reach by its own efforts. Therefore reason must place its natural concepts at the disposal of faith, and must endeavor to elucidate the objects of faith according to the norm of revelation by determining to what extent such concepts can be analogously applied to them. In the same way reason must devote its natural associative and discursive powers to the task of discovering the interconnection between the truths of faith and the motivation of the one by the other. It must also strive to bring out all the implications of each of the truths by unfolding the full wealth of the consequences potentially contained in them.

Thus reason is to serve faith by laboring in its behalf. Of course its assignment to this higher office does not deprive it of the right of working for itself. Far from losing this right, it can serve faith efficiently only by fully developing its own talent. Still less does it lose the physical power of exercising its own activity as before, and particularly of ruling its own domain. On the contrary, its higher destiny gives it the new power, in conjunction with faith, of rising above its own natural sphere. It is not degraded but ennobled by its assignment to the service of the higher science, just as the private citizen is ennobled when he enters the service of the state.

In exerting itself in behalf of faith, reason is dependent on faith in all its efforts, since every cause is dependent on the end to which its activity is to be directed; and also because it is influenced and ruled by faith in the exercise of its functions. This latter dependence flows from the former. For he who is under orders to labor for a definite end must so regulate his procedure as really to attain the objective; and of course he may not imperil it. Thus the maidservant who has agreed to place her services at the disposal of a master must first of all abstain from everything that would be contrary to his interest; secondly, the maidservant must do what will conduce to his advantage, as he desires, and not according to her own whims.

Moreover, so far as reason is to be active on behalf of faith, it may not pronounce any judgment, even in its own sphere, that would prejudice faith or would subvert faith, in the psychological impossibility of two simultaneously contradictory judgments. Further, when laboring in the specific domain of faith, reason must take faith as the basis and norm of its whole activity, since only thus can it really be of effective service for the cultivation of faith. For unless it had faith to sustain it, it could draw no certain conclusions; and unless it conformed to the norm of the revealed proposition, it would not be able to determine how far its concepts were analogously applicable, and consequently could not form correct ideas of supernatural things. Therefore it must take faith as the principle of its argumentation, and the proposition given by faith as the model for the recasting of its concepts. Accordingly there are two ways in which reason must exert itself in dependence on faith.

However, this sort of dependence of reason on faith does not destroy its natural liberty and autonomy, but rather imparts to it a higher freedom, and even raises it to a higher plane, although it can remain there only by clinging to faith. A higher sphere of activity is thereby opened up to it, which faith alone can authorize it to undertake. This does not mean that its natural range of action is curtailed, or that henceforth it can rule over its own domain only with the permission of faith. Within its own sphere it is prevented only from abusing its power, since for the future it is restrained from setting up errors against faith, and consequently from accepting falsehood for truth. The true liberty and autonomy of reason, its freedom to search for clear, untarnished truth in the light of its own principles, is but assured by the joint reign of faith over its province. This liberty is doubly assured if reason, in addition to being on its guard against pronouncing judgment prejudicial to the infallible authority of faith, endeavors to make the data of faith the goal of its own investigations, and thus lightens the task of discovering truth by itself.

Briefly, the dominion of faith over reason involves only the joint rule of faith over the natural sphere; and this joint regency is limited to the function of a protectorate set up for the maintenance and furtherance of reason's own natural freedom and sovereignty. On the other hand, the dominion of faith elevates reason to joint regency in the supernatural domain of faith, over which reason of itself had no dominion at all, and in any case can acquire no more than the dominion proper to a vassal.

Nowhere do we find more perfectly verified the profound truth of the wise adage, "to serve God is to reign." For the rule of faith is at bottom nothing but the rule of the divine reason, which takes possession of our souls in faith. If human reason submits to the demands of the divine reason or reverently follows its lead, divine reason assures human reason of its rightful dominion over natural truth, and admits it to a dominion, though only a dominion proper to a vassal, over a higher kingdom of truth. The full force of the Savior's statement applies here: "If you continue in My word . . . you shall know the truth, and the truth shall make you free." [13] Divine truth, which we take secure possession of in faith, can and will keep our reason free from the domination of any error that contradicts it, will aid it in its investigations to pursue an undeviating course toward truth, and will never permit it to be misled by a will-o'-the-wisp. And as the Son of God has made us free in the highest sense by endowing us with the liberty of the children of God, so our reason will be supremely free when, elevated above its natural limits, it not only overthrows error, but like the eagle, borne on

[13] John 8:31 f.

the wings of faith, it can soar up to the heights of the most secret truth.

We may regard the relation involved in reason's service from the standpoint of the activity it exerts on behalf of faith, or from the standpoint of its dependence on faith in that activity. Then this relation is not that of a slavish subjection and subordination in which reason would no longer retain any rights or power for itself, nor is it the relation of a tyrant, to whom God might say, as Pharao said to Joseph: "Without thy commandment no man shall move hand or foot in all the land of Egypt." [14] It is not even the relation of an ordinary subject to his master, but the relation of a subject privileged and ennobled by special service to his prince. Assuredly it is not a slavish relation, for it can rise effectively and endure only so far as reason recognizes it voluntarily, and the will of man enters into it freely. [15]

2. Because of this element of freedom, the relation is conveyed far more profoundly, clearly, and adequately, and at the same time

[14] Gen. 41:44.

[15] Our doctrine might, perhaps, appear to involve the consequence that faith is the servant of reason, no less than reason is the servant of faith; for faith can exist and operate only in a certain dependence on reason, and in any case is in a position to render notable services to reason. But this view is excluded by our definition of the relationship servitude entails, as given above. Not every kind of dependence is the basis for a relationship of subordination. The higher can be dependent on the lower, and require its services; indeed the lower, by its very nature, is often a prerequisite for the higher. In this sense a king is dependent on his subjects, for he cannot defend and rule his kingdom all by himself; thus also a housewife may be dependent on her maid for the management of her establishment. In the same way theological knowledge, so far as it is possible for us during this life, is dependent on the activity of the intellect and on philosophical knowledge. There could be no question of faith without such activity, nor could the knowledge which rests on faith be cultivated without philosophical reasoning. But it does not follow, nor would such a conclusion occur to any thoughtful person, that theology is the servant of philosophy on that account. For theology remains the higher science; whatever it requires from philosophy it simply takes, as having a rightful claim to it. Nor is the higher in any way subordinate to the lower simply because it works for the good of the lower, or performs some service for the lower. Everything that is higher can be useful to the lower, since it possesses greater wealth and power. God Himself, the All-highest, serves His creatures by procuring many goods for them; but He is not on that account subordinate to them. Accordingly, although faith brings advantages to philosophy, and to that extent serves reason, it does not in any sense occupy a menial position with respect to philosophy.

more nobly, if we describe it as the relation of a bride to her bride-groom. The preservation, enhancement, and elevation of reason's natural liberty by its union with faith, which is not explicitly brought out in the relation of the handmaid to her lord, is as fully stressed in our comparison as is reason's subordination and sub-missiveness to faith. For the wife must acknowledge the husband as her head and lord, particularly when she is originally of lower rank than the husband, and is called to union with him only because he is pleased to invite her to share his higher estate. This view of the matter also corresponds to the general relation between nature and grace (or God as the dispenser of grace), as we have suggested on several occasions, and is but a special application of this doctrine to the relations existing between the light of nature, reason, and the light of grace which operates through faith. Lastly, it gives a more accurate idea of the inner union and fusion, the intimate, real co-operation of reason and faith in the genesis of their common product, theological knowledge. This is not the case with the other metaphor, drawn as it is from a purely moral union between two persons.

Although pertaining to different spheres, the two illuminations are compatible, and are of the same species, since both issue from the same source, the depths of the divine wisdom. Hence they can come together again in close union. And they ought to be joined, to complement and sustain each other, especially for the production of theological knowledge of the divine mysteries, of which reason is by nature receptive, and in which it satisfies its deepest cravings and highest desires. Reason by itself cannot generate this knowledge. It requires the fructifying seed of faith, which must furnish reason with principles and a standard for formulating its thought, and by the light of its accompanying grace must empower reason to co-operate effectively in the generation of theological knowledge. In a word, faith must convey to reason the subject matter and law of the higher knowledge, and provide the stimulus for pursuing it. But without reason, faith is no less unable to unfold and develop its content. That is why faith must deposit this content in the womb of reason, and cause it to be nurtured and formed there. Reason is doubtless receptive as regards faith; but it conceives in order to clothe and develop the object it has conceived. Hence in the gen-eration of theological knowledge reason and faith unite to constitute a single principle; they operate in each other and through each other. With regard to this function, therefore, reason appears in all truth as the bride of faith. Reason is raised from its natural lowliness to a mysterious union with the divine light of faith. Since this union cannot take place unless reason freely acknowledges the superior dignity and the rights of faith, and willingly admits the entrance of faith into its womb, both the character of the union and the form it assumes must be envisaged as a marriage.

It is clear that by entering into this union with faith as bridegroom, reason must be subordinate to faith and must be submissive to it. This subjection of the bride to the bridegroom is the necessary consequence of the union, the natural correlative of the bridegroom's descent to the bride and of the bride's elevation to union with the bridegroom. Reason must be submissive to faith especially in their common activity in the theological sphere, by dedicating its entire effort to the service of faith, and by receiving from faith the law of its behavior. Even in its own proper actions and omissions, reason may not proceed as if it stood alone. It may utter no opinion that opposes the law of its bridegroom, and as a true bride must endeavor even in its own affairs to follow the path pointed out by faith's superior wisdom. Reason may no longer regard itself as isolated, because it is no longer isolated. Much less may it look upon the curtailment of the liberty it possesses in the abstract as a misfortune, for the enjoyment of true liberty is not thereby impeded, but is safeguarded and enhanced.

3. Like the nuptials of nature with grace, the yoking of reason with faith in the theological sphere has its fairest and most sublime ideal in the espousals of the noblest of purely human beings, the Virgin of virgins, with the Holy Spirit, whereby she became the mother of Him who is personal Wisdom incarnate.

Mary, bride of the Holy Spirit, conceived of Him the personal Word of eternal Wisdom. Under the action of the Holy Spirit she gave her own flesh to that Word, and in her womb fashioned the flesh that had been animated by the Holy Spirit, thereupon to present Him to the world embodied in visible form. In like manner reason, wedded in faith to the same Holy Spirit by His grace, conceives, in the light of faith shed by Him, the divine truth contained in the word of God. Reason offers to that truth the matter required for its intellectual formulation, and clothes it, so to speak, with the forms of its own natural ideas. Thereby reason makes that truth intelligible and apt for embodiment in human phraseology. For reason cannot reflect divine truth in its divine vastness and splendor. This can occur only in the light of glory, where reason contributes nothing but a potency for the reception of this light and for its own transfiguration. Mary had to clothe the personal Wisdom of the Son of God in the unpretentious raiment of the "form of a servant," [16] so that later this "form of a servant" might become the "form of God," not of course by annihilation but by transfiguration. So likewise here below reason has to invest divine truth with the garments of its own lowliness, only to behold the veil drop later, and without the intermediacy of earthly forms to gaze on the Divine in the full purity of its natural brilliance.

As the summons to become the Mother of the God-man involved the highest dignity for Mary, and raised her from a humble maid to be the Queen of all creation, thus also there is no greater distinction for reason than its vocation to cooperation with faith in the generation of theological knowledge, whereby it is elevated beyond its native lowliness to the highest nobility. Mary rose to the dignity of Mother of God by the humble obedience of a handmaid of the Lord. With this obedience she assented to the invitation of her divine bridegroom, and even in her high estate preserved the humility fitting for the Lord's handmaid. So too, reason can receive faith only by the humble acknowledgment of the rights of revelation and an obedient assent to God's call. Even in its intimate union with faith, it must remain conscious of its subjection to faith. With the humility of a maidservant, reason may not contradict faith, but, mistrustful of self, must gladly submit to the infallible guidance of faith. In both cases, however, the bride's dignity ensures that the obedience will be a free and liberating, noble obedience, which is not under the constraint of harsh subjection to a master. On the contrary, this obedience proceeds from a tender devotedness that fittingly corresponds to the gracious kindness of the lord.

Therefore he who is repelled by the axiom, "philosophy is the handmaid of theology," should turn his thoughts to the handmaid of the Lord and the merit of her humility; he should think of her

[16] Phil. 2:7.

who is the pinnacle of human eminence and dignity in her attitude toward the divine. For by her humble submissiveness and by her sublime union she prefigures the perfect relationship of all that is human with the divine.

4. In line with our discussion up to this point, the God-man Himself would have to be considered not so much a type of the relation between reason and faith as a type of their joint product, theological knowledge. We will come back to this idea. Nevertheless, from the viewpoint of the two principles of activity, the divine and the human nature which enter into the composition of the God-man, I can also look upon Him as a figure of the relation between the two principles, faith and reason.

One of the chief features of marriage, the free union between the parties, cannot of course be found here, since the human nature of Christ has never had independent existence apart from the Logos. Besides, at first sight the autonomy of Christ's human nature almost seems to have vanished in the person of the Logos. This indeed is the case so far as hypostatic autonomy is meant. But neither do reason and faith possess hypostatic autonomy; for in our present supposition both pertain to one and the same subject. Hence their difference and their relation can be illustrated by this very comparison, according to a point of view that is completely lacking in the other analogies.

a) The two natures in Christ, despite their hypostatic union, exist alongside each other unmingled, as the higher and the lower; for both together constitute the whole Christ. This, too, is the way reason and faith exist unmixed alongside each other in the believer, as the principles of the two highest sciences, philosophy and theology. These two taken together invest the knowing subject with proprietorship over the highest domain of knowledge.

b) Owing to its integrity, the human nature in Christ preserves its own proper energy and mode of operation, its own activity that proceeds from the human nature itself and exists in its own right. Thus likewise reason keeps its own activity, even after it has been joined to faith in the same subject. Hence it has the power and the right to know, in virtue of its own principles, the truths that lie within its radius, that is, to cultivate pure philosophy.

c) However, as Christ's human nature, owing to its union with the Logos, cannot and may not exercise its own activity as if it had separate existence, but must conform to the divine nature and will, so reason in a believing Christian cannot and may not philosophize independently of every other consideration, but must cherish harmony with faith in its philosophical speculations.

d) On the other hand, in those activities which the human nature of Christ cannot carry through by its own power, it must not only be conformed to the divine nature, but must let itself be used by the latter as an instrument of its activity, so that the two natures may work in and through each other in theandric action. In like manner, whenever there is question of cultivating knowledge that is not purely philosophical but is theological, reason must develop its activity in and through faith.

Would anyone contend that, in consequence of this close and necessary harmony and union between the operations of Christ's two natures, the natural freedom of the human nature is not elevated and transfigured, but curtailed? Or would anyone say that the activity of the human nature ceases to be truly human when it performs what is proper to it by its own power, although in accord with the divine nature? Why, then, should the natural freedom of man's reason be lost, when all it has to do is to seek and embrace truth in harmony with faith, and in common with faith to engender a knowledge of supernatural truths? Why should it cease to operate in a purely philosophical and a truly philosophical manner when, in developing and drawing out the principles placed in it by God, it strives to enter into accord and remain in accord with the wisdom of God that faith has revealed to it with the greatest certitude? And even if activity of this sort were no longer to be called purely philosophical, should reason on that account completely isolate itself from faith, to which it is joined in so close a union?

Thus the various natural figures and analogies, which a deep contemplation of the nature of Christianity yields, complement one another, and furnish us with a good illustration of the relations between reason and faith. In this relationship the sharp distinction between the two factors is preserved in unity, and necessary independence is maintained in subordination. Indeed, the union of both is based upon their very difference, and the subordination of the lower to the higher is shown to be the supreme elevation of the former.

110. Theology as Wisdom both Human and Divine

It remains for us but to cast a glance at theology itself, as the subjective science of faith already acquired or yet to be attained, in its relation to the sciences of pure reason, and to compare it with them from the standpoint of scientific excellence. In view of the foregoing discussion we can be quite brief. Let us begin by seeing to what degree theology verifies the conditions on which the absolute and relative perfection of a science depends.

These conditons are partly objective, partly subjective.

If we consider a science as objective, its perfection consists in the greatest possible universality, uniformity, and sublimity of its subject matter. For the perfection of any system is proportionate to the multitude and value of the items that make it up, and the order by which they are brought together in unity. Hence the unity of a science need not be sought exclusively in the unity of the cognitive principle from which all its truths may be deduced as conclusions. This sort of unity pertains to the subjective perfection of a science. Moreover, it is not attainable by us men in any physical science (such as physics, zoology, or psychology), and least of all in philosophy, if philosophy is not to lose itself in abstract formulas and degenerate into barren speculation. The essential objective conditions are admirably realized in the subject matter of theology. For theology embraces all things in heaven and on earth, the natural as well as the supernatural, although the former only with respect to the latter, and hence the most sublime objects. Primarily it contemplates the supreme and most simple unity, the divine nature, and secondarily all other beings, so far as they are taken up into a union with God so intimate that, according to the profound expression used by the Apostle, God is all in all.[17] Its proper subject matter is first and foremost the supernatural unity of the divine persons among themselves in the interior of the divine nature, and the union of all creatures with God and one another in a unity which, though reason could never suspect it, is an imitation of the divine ideal. Objectively, therefore, by reason of its subject matter, theology is the most universal, unified, and sublime science that can be conceived.

The subjective perfection of a science is nothing but the perfe⸗

---

[17] Cf. I Cor. 15:28.

tion of the knowledge with which we comprehend the system as it is actually constituted. This perfection depends on three factors: (1) the logical connection between the various truths and their reduction to the fewest possible principles; (2) the certainty or evidence of these principles themselves; (3) the coincidence of the cognitive principles with the real principles or real foundations of the system. If these three conditions are verified, knowledge reaches its greatest simplicity, certitude, and profundity.

1. It would be unreasonable to require that all the truths known in any science should be reduced to a single principle. Yet it does unquestionably pertain to the greater perfection of its simplicity that the entire network of truths should be reducible as conclusions to the fewest possible premises, so that a formal unity in the mind of the knower may be established. This is actually the case in theology, no less than in philosophy. If we examine the *Summa theologica* of St. Thomas, we find that in almost every section dealing with supernatural truths he places at the beginning a single article of faith, from which, as from a premise, he proceeds with mathematical rigor to infer all the truths connected with the topic in question. Thus at the head of his Trinitarian doctrine he places the single proposition taken from revelation, that there are real processions in God. From this proposition he derives, in a methodical and perfectly concatenated series, the entire profusion of those wonderful truths that revelation and theology have made accessible concerning this subject. In the *Prima Secundae* he starts with the supernatural destiny of man as his principle and leads up to the beatific vision as his end. He adopts this procedure in order scientifically to deduce all the conclusions bearing on man's supernatural progress toward God. On man's supernatural destiny he bases his whole theory of the meritorious virtues, the supernatural law, and grace.

2. Only in one detail does theology seem, at first sight, to rank below other sciences: the principles, the fundamental truths from which it proceeds, are not known by intrinsic evidence, but are accepted on faith. We spoke of this matter above. That the principles of theology are not evidentially known, but must be believed, is accounted for by their supernatural eminence, not by any uncertainty or unreliability on their part. Because of their eminence, they can be known clearly and evidently by God alone with the light natural to Him, and by us only through the light of glory. But even

in our present state we are more certain of them than we are of the principles of philosophy. Since, as regards the mastery of a science, there is as much question of the certainty as of the evidence of the principles, we can say that the higher certitude in theology amply compensates for any deficiency in intrinsic evidence.

3. The value of a science depends on a perception of the objective grounds on which its several truths are ultimately based, even more than it depends on the evidence of the principles or the connection of the conclusions with them. In philosophy this perfection is unattainable; our intellect mounts to a knowledge of a cause only from its effects, with the aim of returning with greater clarity from the cause to the effects. Transcendental philosophy alone makes the claim of being independent of effects in its investigation of causes. It would wish to transcend effects and penetrate into the cause immediately, so as to have an intuition of the effects in the light of the cause. But what is impossible for philosophy is, by the grace of God, possible for theology. Theology is the true transcendental science, and is able to employ the synthetic method in the highest perfection possible for us.

God alone, per se, knows immediately the ultimate foundation of all things, His own essence, and perceives how all things proceed therefrom by His free will. Through the light of glory He shares His knowledge with the blessed, admits them to immediate intuition of His essence, and in it enables them to perceive all the other objects of theology, and even those of philosophy. In faith we do not, of course, attain to intuitive knowledge; but our knowledge is based on God's vision, and so we anticipate the vision proper to the blessed. By faith we have an immediate knowledge of God Himself, the supreme Cause, of His omnipotence, and of the divine decree and plan according to which He is pleased to act in the outer world. And thus we are empowered to survey the whole vast range of theological truths from their heart and center, as is possible in no other science (except, perhaps, abstract mathematics), and also the domain of natural beings, to the extent that these, as explained above, are illuminated by supernatural revelation.

However, as at present we behold neither the divine essence, nor the power, the goodness, and the plan of God in the clearness of vision, but only in the dim light of faith, our understanding of the way God acts and communicates Himself is far from being a perfect knowledge. Nevertheless God has revealed to us the connection of the natural and supernatural orders with their causes, particularly their final and exemplary causes. From these supreme ends and exemplars which He pursues in His plan we can infer, if not all details, at any rate the chief elements of the supernatural order. God's ultimate aims and ideals, as is the case with everything that has to do with the planning and execution of His activity, are derived from Himself, from His own essence. From this essence, as made known to us by revelation, we can understand in turn how and why God has ordained the designs of His wisdom as He has, and not otherwise. Thus by faith we struggle through to the *rationes aeternae* of all temporal things; and these reasons comprise, in addition to the source, the motive and the norm of the wonderful structure of the universe.

Accordingly faith, which at first sight seems to negate science, actually establishes us in the possession of the most excellent of all sciences. When in faith we follow the theologians in their eagle flight under the guidance of the Evangelists, we share in God's own knowledge, and transcend all creation, so as finally to attain to the summit of all being. From there we command a view of all things in their utmost harmony and unity.[18]

From all this it follows that theology is more than simply one science out of many; it is the most excellent and precious of them all. Among the various sciences (*scientiae*) it is the one which as the wisdom (*sapientia*) par excellence, divine wisdom, towers majestically over all human sciences.

The qualities characterizing theology as a perfect science are identical with the qualities usually associated with wisdom. Its primary concern is not with created things, but with divine things, with God; it deals with created things only to the extent that they are related to God, proceed from Him, are united to Him, and serve for His glorification. Indeed, as regards God Himself, theology fastens its gaze chiefly on the interior mysteries of His bosom and His heart, and outside of God follows up mainly the extension of the Trinitarian productions and the assumption of creatures into the Trinitarian unity. It perceives and judges all things in the light

[18] The finest example of a theological treatise that gives methodical explanations throughout in the light of the attributes and plans of the first principle of all being, is the *Breviloquium* of St. Bonaventure.

of the most basic and certain principles, from the viewpoint of their deepest, most hidden causes and their highest ends. It contemplates the temporal only in the light of the eternal reasons (*rationes aeternae*), according to the eternal designs of God and the destiny of the temporal for reception into the divine eternity. To the dweller in time theology reveals his own ultimate and supreme destiny as well as the road that leads thereto, and hence instructs him to regulate his life and conduct in the wisest manner. It shows him the supreme Good in the possession of which he is to enjoy a superhuman happiness, and grants him even here below a faint foretaste of its heavenly sweetness. Consequently theology is, like no other science, a *scientia sapida*, a science full of delights.

At bottom theology is all this because it flows from the source of all wisdom, the divine wisdom, more directly and in purer and fuller flood than all the other sciences. Unlike these sciences, which do not rise above the level of human wisdom, it deserves to be called divine wisdom. As product of the natural reason, in whose womb it is conceived, formed, and brought to birth, it does not disown its earthly conception and generation, and so remains at the same time a truly human science: just as the Son of God is true man, because born of woman. But as Mary's Son, who was not conceived of earthly seed but came down into her womb from heaven, is a God-man, and therefore infinitely excels not only all the rest of the sons of men but His very mother herself, so, too, theology, generated as it is of divine light in the womb of reason, is not a purely human, but a divine-human wisdom and science. Like a heavenly queen, theology surpasses all merely rational sciences, and takes all of them, together with the very intellect from which it is sprung, into its service.

Between theology, considered as divine wisdom poured out upon man and, so to speak, taking human form in him, and the incarnate, personal Wisdom of God in Christ, a surprisingly close analogy and kinship is discernible.

The Incarnation of the personal Wisdom of God is, first of all, the source through which divine wisdom is communicated to us, according to the Apostle's phrase: "Christ Jesus, who of God is made unto us wisdom." [19] By taking our flesh, the personal Wisdom of God has flooded it with "all the treasures of wisdom and knowl-

[19] See I Cor. 1:30.

edge," [20] thence to pour those treasures out upon all flesh. By His human speech and by the inner illumination which enables us to believe in His authority, He unlocks for us the fullness of His knowledge. Through faith we receive the incarnate, personal Wisdom of God into ourselves, so that He dwells in our hearts. By His presence in our souls He becomes, as it were, the sun which, diffusing its light and at the same time stimulating and sustaining our own personal activity, generates our divine-human wisdom as a reflection of Himself. Living on in this reflection, the divine Wisdom is reborn in our hearts, embodies us in Himself, and thus in a mysterious, ineffable way becomes our Wisdom, too.

The incarnate, personal Wisdom of God continues, so to speak, His Incarnation in the communication and generation of our own divine wisdom. Hence He is manifestly the ideal of our divine wisdom in regard to its origin and nature. For, as in the Incarnation the personal Wisdom of God was sent into human nature to be hypostatically united to it, so God sends Him, the sharer of His throne, down from His heaven into holy souls,[21] to enlighten them with grace and faith, and fill them with His own brilliance. And, as the personal Wisdom assumed human flesh and blood in Mary's womb and transfigured them with His divine power, so in the depths of our souls He assumes flesh and blood from our human thoughts and concepts, by suffusing and sublimating them with His higher light, by bringing Himself to conception in them, and thus making His riches our own.

For all that, He remains invisible here below under the form He thus assumes, as He did in the flesh that was united to the Godhead, but prior to the Resurrection was not perfectly illuminated with the splendor of divinity. And although even here below we can savor the sweetness of the Spirit of divine Wisdom, this is only a slight foretaste, which no more stills the aching desire of our heart for an unobstructed sight of Him than the beatific vision enjoyed by Christ's humanity excluded the capacity to suffer. The weakness attending our earthly nature continues to cling to our theological wisdom, as the infirmity of the flesh clung to the earthly Christ. Our wisdom can become wholly divine only when the weakness of nature, besides being fructified and imbued with divine light, is com-

[20] Col. 2:3.
[21] See the Book of Wisdom, chap. 9.

pletely absorbed in it. Not until then can the sweet and lovable Spirit of divine Wisdom fill us with the fragrance of His undiminished sweetness and lovableness, and satiate us with the torrent of His bliss; just as the incarnate Wisdom did not send the Spirit to us until after the resurrection and glorification of His body.

Finally, the incarnate Wisdom of God is the supreme end and object of theology, and the focus of its continually evolving wisdom. For the God-man is the most concrete and the greatest objective revelation of God, and the junction point, if not the root, of the whole system of Christian truths. Theology bases itself on His visible manifestation, but with the aim of pressing on to His invisible glory and that of His Father; and from the divine eminence He occupies it descends again, to trace out the shaping and perfecting of His mystical body. On the one hand, God "hath shined in our hearts, to give the light of the knowledge of the glory of God, in the face of Christ Jesus," [22] in the visible, human form of the invisible image of the Father. On the other hand, we find the sum and substance of the whole of theological wisdom in the wisdom of "the mystery of Christ" and of the "unsearchable riches" contained in Him, in the outpouring of which "the manifold wisdom of God" is made known.[23]

Of course the objective center, the root, and the summit of the entire supernatural order is the Triune God, or the bosom of the eternal Father, from which Christ Himself came forth, and to which He returns with His mystical body. But as long as we have not yet entered with Christ into the very bosom of the eternal Father, and must be content to behold the invisible in the visible, He Himself in His earthly form is the way upon which we must travel in our ascent to that summit. Our theological wisdom, which is at once human and divine, must attach itself to Him primarily in His humanity, in order to scale the heights to His divinity, to His unity with the Father.

Thus from every point of view our theological wisdom is bound up with the incarnate, personal Wisdom of God, is conformed to Him, and receives from Him its characteristic divine-human signature. Subjectively as well as objectively it is specifically Christian; for it is the science of the great mystery of Christ, and is the result

[22] See II Cor. 4:6.
[23] Eph. 3:4, 8, 10.

of divine anointing and illumination. Owing to the unpretentious form in which it appears, and the enigmatical obscurity in which its objects are revealed, it is scorned by the world, in the same way that the Son of God was despised when in the form of a slave He went down to death upon a cross. Like the cross of Christ, theology appears to haughty human wisdom as foolishness and weakness. But "the foolishness of God is wiser than men; and the weakness of God is stronger than men." [24] Therefore in facing the wisdom of this world we may, with the Apostle, in holy pride "speak the wisdom of God in a mystery, a wisdom which is hidden, which God ordained before the world unto our glory." [25] In the grace of God we may consider ourselves blessed by reason of "all riches of fullness of understanding, unto the knowledge of the mystery of God the Father and of Christ Jesus, in whom are hid all the treasures of wisdom and knowledge," and in whom we, too, shall be filled to repletion.[26]

The enlightened Christian need envy no one but the blessed in heaven on account of the lucidity, the depth, and the fullness of their knowledge. But the same faith as that in which we anticipate their vision holds out to us the sure promise that its imperfections and obscurity will vanish if, following its directions, we strive devotedly and perseveringly to reach its divine object. Faith is the prophet within our very spirit, presaging the full unveiling of the mysteries of God, the morning star of the day of eternity, the bread of our childhood in the kingdom of God, which rears us to the maturity of the wisdom of Christ.

May the love of the Holy Spirit, which can never fall away, the love which forms the bond between time and eternity, between heaven and earth, between yearning anticipation and blissful vision, the love that surpasses understanding and even now plunges us into the depths of the heart of God, raise us up with its heavenly power to the bosom of "the Father of lights," that together with His Son we may behold Him face to face, and may "be like to Him, because we shall see Him as He is," and as we ourselves "are known by God." [27]

---

[24] See I Cor. 1:25.
[25] Ibid., 2:7.
[26] Col. 2:2, 3, 10.
[27] Jas. 1:17; I John 3:2; Gal. 4:9.

Index

Abasement: of Christ, 426; impossible in God, 423 ff.

Absolute, the, 73, 128

Abu-Qurra, 391 and note

Activity, supernatural, 647

Activity of Christ: excellence of, 411; infinite value of, 456; ordained to man's salvation, 428; sacramental character of, 566; *see also* Causality of Christ's activity

Activity of God
in the beatific vision, 658
in creatures, 150 f.
in deification of man, 654, 656 f.
in glorification of man, 680 ff.
in justification, 631-35, 637, 641
known by faith, 755
in predestination, 700, 709, 722
in resurrection of the body, 666

Actual grace: relation to habitual grace, 722 f.; *see also* Grace; Prevenient grace

Actual sin: destructive power of, 249, 257; distinction between habitual sin and, 251 f.; habitual sin as effect of, 616; illustration of, 263; punishment of, 277

Adam (*see also* First man)
Christ as the new, 376, 402, 456
compared with Christ, 323-30, 364, 386 f.
Cyril of Alexandria on the new, 380
derivation of Eve from, 182, 374
elevation to supernatural order, 209, 314
function in conferring of grace, 386
generative activity of, 458
immortality of, 667, 669
inheritance of original justice from, 231-36
integrity of, 329, 387
limited power of, 330
mortality of, 329
mystery of, 314
natural head of the race, 233, 365, 386

Adam (*continued*)
original state of, 212
purpose in elevating, 357
sin of, 265, 280, 283 f.
transmission of grace from, 564
type of Christ, 184 f., 235 f.
union with God, 315
unity of the race in, 232, 367

Adduction theory in transubstantiation, 497

Adoptive sonship, grace of
basis in human nature for, 383
conferred in justification, 631
conferred through the sacraments, 570
conformity to God in, 169
Cyril of Alexandria on, 383
destroyed by sin, 326, 619
elevation of man by, 619
the Eucharist and, 489, 493 f.
exemplar of, 142 f.
fellowship with God and Christ in, 492
foundations of, 143 f.
function of the Holy Ghost in, 169 f.
illustration of, 384
through the Incarnation, 382 ff.
through membership in Christ, 383
merited by Christ, 449
motivation of, 142
mystery of, 383 f.
nature of, 141, 583, 619
presupposition of, 142
purchased by Christ's blood, 452 ff.
as purpose of the Incarnation, 380 ff.
relation of sanctity to, 623 f.
through sanctifying grace, 145 f., 168, 382
synonyms of, 211
vocation to, 325

Adults, justification of, 633 ff.

Agility of glorified body, 673, 676, 678

Albert the Great, St., 104 note

Alexander of Hales: on the Holy Ghost, 109; on object of supernatural love, 128 note; on original justice, 226 and note

797

Alger of Liége: on Christ's Eucharistic existence, 476 note; on fellowship with Christ, 487 note; on reception of the Eucharist, 524 note

Ambrose, St.: on Holy Ghost, 110 note; on names of Third Person, 97; on union with Holy Ghost, 160 note

Amor beatificus, 448

Amor sacerdos, 445 and note

Analogous concepts: in apprehension of mysteries, 11 and note; inadequate for representing the Trinity, 47, 118; in names of the Holy Ghost, 114; in representing objects of faith, 754, 759; *see also* Analogy

Analogue of Holy Ghost's procession, 95 note, 181-89

Analogy
    between Christ and theology, 793 ff.
    between divine and created hypostasis, 83
    between divine and human generation, 89 ff.
    between divine and human personality, 80 ff.
    between divine knowledge and love, and human knowledge and love, 59 ff.
    in hypostatic union, 320 ff.
    illustrative of the sacramental character, 590
    of relation between faith and reason, 784-88
    in theological knowledge, 754, 759

Anchor of faith, 776

Angel in Canon of the Mass, 507 and note

Angels
    announcement of Christ's birth by, 421
    Christ's sacrifice and the, 444
    commerce between men and, 267
    effect of the Incarnation on, 403
    existence of, 238
    the fallen, 264 f., 267
    fellowship of man with, 238
    grace of the, 238
    natural knowledge of, 43
    permitted to fall, 429
    punishment of the wicked, 694
    relation of original justice to, 237
    relation to Christ, 402 f.
    sin of the, 263 ff.
    union with Christ, 401

Anointed, the, 331 f., 398, 432

Anointing of Christ, 331 f., 381, 443: John Damascene on, 333 note; Peter Chrysologus on, 381 and note

Anselm, St.
    Cur Deus homo of, 428
    demonstration of the Trinity, 25 and note
    on divine personality, 81 note
    Monologium of, 56
    on original sin, 305
    theological procedure of, 765 ff.

Appearance of Christ, external, 336

Appropriation: of divine activity in the missions, 176 ff.; of divine attributes, 133 ff., 145 f., 151

Appropriations: in Scripture, 135; Thomas Aquinas on, 134 note

Aquinas; *see* Thomas Aquinas, St.

Architect, the divine, 730

Arrha (pledge), 158 and note, 159

Ascension, sacrificial significance of Christ's, 436 f.

Assumption of human nature, 317, 358, 366

Athanasius, St.
    on Christ's body, 518
    on Christ's union with the race, 367 note
    on the Father as "source" of the Trinity, 74 note
    on the grace of Christ, 390 note
    on the Holy Ghost, 111 note
    on the mediation of Christ, 408
    on the purpose of the Incarnation, 379 and note
    on the Spirit of the Son, 393 note
    on union with Christ, 390 note

Atonement: as end of Christ's sacrifice, 452; liberty of God in demanding, 345, the motive of God in exacting, 426

Attachment to God by faith, 643

Attributes of God, 27 ff.: manifestation of, 415

Attributes of the God-man, 322-33

Attrition, 640

Augustine, St.
    on animation of the mystical body, 394
    on the cause of original sin, 285 f. and note
    on Christ as the first fruits, 441 and note
    on Christ's sacrifice, 438 note
    on Christ's union with the race, 367 note
    on the Church as spouse of Christ, 373 and note
    definition of predestination, 698 and note

Augustine (*continued*)
on the dissolution of integrity, 277 and note
on divine personality, 81 note
on freedom of will in predestination, 711
on holocausts, 439 note
on Holy Communion, 525
on the Holy Ghost, 64 f., 164 note
on mystical union between head and body, 371 note
on names of the Holy Ghost, 110 and note
on names of the Third Person, 97 and note, 99 note
opposition to Pelagians, 714 f. and note
on original justice, 214 f., 228
on original sin, 301 f. and note
on predestination, 703 note, 713 f., 715 and note
on the procession of the Holy Ghost, 106
on the purpose of the Incarnation, 378 and note, 382 and note
on sacrificial fire, 436 note
on salvation without the Incarnation, 344 note
on study of the Trinity, 148
Trinitarian view of, 74 note
on the Trinity, 56
Authority: of the Church, 549; teaching, 550; withdrawal of matrimony from civil, 595 f. and note, 608 note
Authority, divine: in theological knowledge, 745 f.
Aversio a Deo, 256, 279, 686

Baius, Michael: on compatibility of charity and sin, 618 and note; condemnation of, 286 and note
Ballerini, Antonio, 464 note
Baptism
function of, 572, 586, 602
of infants, 604 note
initiation into the Church by, 542
justification by, 633
and the mystical body, 375
relation to Christian marriage, 602
relation to confirmation, 586
sacramental character in, 586
sacramentum et res in, 575 f.
union with Christ through, 374 f.
Basil, St.: on deification of man, 316 note; on the Father as "source" of the Trinity, 74 note; on original justice, 227 and note

Beatific vision, the
anticipated in faith, 791, 796
conditions for, 659 f.
controversy on, 659-62
credibility of, 417
deification of man in, 659 f.
desire of, 661
destiny to, 417 f., 658
elevation of life in, 662 f.
foretaste of, 129
happiness of, 658, 662, 681
as inheritance of children of God, 662
knowledge in, 658, 662, 664
known by revelation, 658 f.
love of God in, 662, 664
meriting of, 647
miracle of, 658, 660
mysteries unveiled in, 796
mystery of, 653, 658-62
nature of, 159, 652 f., 658
possession of God in, 526, 658, 662
preparation for, 647
privation of, 686
supernaturalness of, 658, 661 f.
Thomas Aquinas on, 767, 790
transcendence of, 661 f.
transfiguration of life in, 662
Beatific vision of Christ, 325 ff.: necessity of, 448; reconciliation of merit with, 448-52
Beatitude: of God, 125; inauguration of, 129; nature of, 653 (*see also* Beatific vision); transfiguration of man in, 653
Being, infinite, 27
Belief, obligation of, 551, 780
Bernard, St.: on Christ's sacrifice, 436 note; on the Holy Ghost, 65 and note, 110, 171 note; on infusion of the Holy Ghost, 160 note; on purpose of the Incarnation, 420 note
Blessed Virgin Mary, the
compared with priesthood of the Church, 546
conception of Christ by, 640, 785
dignity of, 786
as ideal of theology, 785 ff.
Immaculate Conception of, 444, 464 f.
mother of God, 786
mother of the God-man, 464
the new Eve, 465
obedience of, 786
Blood of Christ, the
bond between God and world, 446
Clement of Alexandria on, 524 note
infinite power of, 444, 453

Blood of Christ (*continued*)
  presence in the Eucharist, 469
  price of our redemption, 452
  procession of the Holy Ghost symbolized by, 445 f. and note
  shedding of, 445
  symbolized by wine, 528
Body of Christ, the
  Athanasius on, 518
  center of the glorified world, 684
  corporal extension of, 516
  existence in the Eucharist, 470, 473-76
  the glorified, 426
  immortality after the Resurrection, 519
  indivisibility in the Eucharist, 473
  instrument of divine activity, 477, 512
  presence in the Eucharist, 469
  qualities of, 519
  seed of immortality, 504
  subtility of, 674
  unaugmented by transubstantiation, 498 f.
  union of the faithful in, 484; *see also* Mystical Body of Christ
  union of the mystical body with the real, 547
Body, glorification of (*see also* Body, transfiguration of)
  communicated to material nature, 682
  compared with divinization of the soul, 666
  demanded by the Incarnation, 656
  meaning of, 673
  taught by faith, 666
  Thomas Aquinas on, 676 and note
Body, the glorified
  agility of, 673, 676, 678
  beauty of, 680 f.
  conformed to the glorified soul, 682
  eternal life of, 664
  immortality of, 671 f., 679
  impassibility of, 673
  incorruptibility of, 673, 676, 678
  power of, 680 f.
  qualities of, 673-81
  refinement of, 673, 676, 680
  relation of the soul to, 677 f.
  spiritualization of, 656, 673, 676 ff.
  subtility of, 673 ff., 677
  supernatural radiance of, 681
Body, the human: crassness of, 673 f., 677; inertness of, 673, 676; natural defects of, 673; natural mortality of, 665, 667
Body, resurrection of the
  basis of, 668-71

Body, resurrection of (*continued*)
  brought about by God, 666
  Cyril of Alexandria on, 669 and note
  distinct from glorification, 666 f.
  founded on the Incarnation, 671
  Irenaeus on, 669 and note
  John Chrysostom on, 389 and note
  miracle of, 669 f.
  mysterious character of, 666, 668
  notion of, 666
  rational arguments for, 667 f.
  relation of grace to, 670
  relation of transfiguration to, 671
  scriptural account of, 668 f.
  as share in Christ's resurrection, 669
  supernaturalness of, 666-71
  taught by faith, 666
Body, transfiguration of
  beatitude completed by, 671
  distinct from resurrection, 666 f.
  general notion of, 673
  influence of the soul on, 677 f.
  materiality overcome in, 673
  mysterious character of, 666
  proper to heavenly glorification, 679
  purpose of, 679 f.
  relation of resurrection to, 671
Boethius on divine personality, 81 note
Bonaventure, St.
  on appropriations, 134 note
  demonstration of Trinity by, 34 note, 39 and notes
  on God's goodness, 128 note
  Greek Trinitarian tradition followed by, 74 note
  on original justice, 226 and note
  on original sin, 292 and note
  on possessing God, 158 note
  on predestination, 703 note
  on the procession of the Holy Ghost, 109
  on the second Trinitarian procession, 64, 76 note
  theological procedure of, 765 f.
Bond, matrimonial: indissolubility of, 594, 596; unity of, 594, 596
Bread: from heaven, 516; representative of the faithful, 500
Bread, accidents of: function in the Eucharist, 473 f.; preserved in the Eucharist, 474
Bread, substance of: relation of accidents to, 474; replaced by Christ's body in the Eucharist, 473 f., 497, 500
Bread and wine: appearances in the Eucharist, 469

Bride of Christ: the Church as, 541; human nature as, 373

Caesarius of Arles, St.: on sacrifice of the mystical body, 511 note; on transubstantiation and interior conversion, 504 note
Calor Verbi, 499 and note
Cano, Melchior: on marriage, 607 note
Caritas creata, 161
Casinius, Antonius: *Quid est homo*, 209 note, 301 note, 316 note
Casti connubii by Pius XI, 594 note
Catechismus Romanus; see Roman Catechism
Categories, Christian mysteries and Aristotelian, 478
Causality of Christ's activity: explanation of physical, 457-60; instrumental, 457, 461-64, 788; moral, 452-56, 463; objections against physical, 460 ff.; physical, 456 f., 462 f.
Causality of the sacraments; *see* Sacraments, causality of
Cause: difference between principle and, 121; nature of instrumental, 460
Certitude: in philosophy, 745; in theology, 745, 749
Character, sacerdotal, 585 f.
Character, sacramental
  absent from some sacraments, 578
  analogies of, 590 f.
  analogy between hypostatic union and, 582 f., 587
  in baptism, 586
  basis for recovery of grace, 629
  in confirmation, 586
  connection of matrimony with, 578, 592, 600
  defective notions of, 588 f.
  difference between hypostatic union and, 585
  disfigured through sin, 591
  effects of, 583 ff.
  function in production of grace, 580, 584 f., 588 f.
  in holy orders, 586
  importance of, 582
  impressed by the Holy Ghost, 591
  knowledge of, 589
  mystery of, 582 f., 587
  nature of, 573, 582, 587-91
  necessary for reception of sacraments, 585
  obligations involved in, 585 f.

Character, sacramental (*continued*)
  participation in Christ's activity through, 585
  permanence of, 585, 591, 629
  production of, 580
  related to Christ's priesthood, 585 f.
  related to Christ's prophetic and regal offices, 586 f.
  relation to the Incarnation, 591
  relation of sanctifying grace to, 583-86
  as sign of dignity, 588
  significance of, 582-92
  as *signum configurativum cum Christo*, 587, 589
  Thomas Aquinas on, 587 and note
  union with Christ through, 583 ff., 629
Character, theandric, 582, 585
Charity: infused virtue of, 619, 641; nature of divine, 248; *see also* Love
Christ (*see also* God-man; Son of God)
  achievement of, 454
  activity of, 411, 428, 456
  Adam compared with, 323-30, 364, 386 f.
  anointing of, 331 ff., 377, 443
  Athanasius on grace of, 390 note
  attributes of, 322-33
  blood of; *see* Blood of Christ
  born anew in the Church, 547
  bridegroom of the Church, 543, 546, 604
  center of creation, 430
  center of the supernatural order, 730
  the Christian as another, 377 and note
  constitution of, 317-22, 333
  cross of; *see* Cross of Christ
  death of, 518
  dignity of, 324, 337, 444
  divinity of, 337, 400, 454
  divinity denied by Jews, 516 f.
  dominion over suffering and death, 329 f.
  erroneous views about, 314, 319 f.
  existence of, 336
  external appearance of, 336
  first fruits of the race, 440 ff.
  free will of, 448-52
  God's love for man in, 709
  grace merited by, 453, 569
  grace of, 331, 456 f.
  head of the race, 354, 387 f., 403; *see also* Headship of Christ
  humanity of; *see* Human nature of Christ
  identical with God-man, 333

Christ (*continued*)
incorporation in; *see* Incorporation in Christ
kingship of, 412, 428
living and acting in His members, 371, 397
mediation of; *see* Mediation of Christ
merits of; *see* Merits of Christ
miracles of, 336 f.
mystery of, 3, 332
the new Adam, 376, 402, 456
one person in, 318
operative in the Church, 544
predestination in, 730
present in the Eucharist, 469-78; *see also* Eucharistic existence of Christ
priesthood of, 412 f., 432; *see also* Priesthood of Christ
prophetic office of, 412
reborn in the faithful, 547
recovery of integrity from, 387
re-establishment of all things in, 403
relation of angels to, 402 f.
relation of human race to, 501
representative of the race, 437
resurrection of; *see* Resurrection of Christ
riches of, 333
sacrifice of; *see* Sacrifice of Christ
sacrificial victim, 436; *see also* Sacrifice of Christ; Sacrificial victim
sanctity of, 168
self-renunciation of, 328, 443, 450
source of grace, 387 and note, 390-95, 456
sufferings of; *see* Sufferings of Christ
task of, 454
theandric character of, 582, 585
transfiguration of, 326 ff., 331, 337
two natures in, 317, 406, 478
type of theological knowledge, 787 f.
ultimate end of creation, 429
union of Christians in one, 333, 376
unity of, 318
victim in Eucharistic sacrifice, 505 f.
Christian: as another Christ, 377 and note; description of a, 599
Christian Marriage by G. H. Joyce, 594 note
Christianity (*see also* Mysteries, Christian)
adversaries of, 3
attempts to modify, 3 f.
charm of mysteries in, 5 f.
mysteries essential to, 4
mysterious character of, 3

Christianity (*continued*)
need of revelation to, 16
rejection of, 3
relation of mysteries to, 3, 15
relation of original state to, 615
revelation of, 4
sacramental structure of, 563, 565
scientific understanding of, 18
teaching about next life in, 652
Christians: marriage between, 595, 605 f., 609 and note; power experienced by, 775; reason for name of, 381
Chrysologus; *see* Peter Chrysologus, St.
Chrysostom; *see* John Chrysostom, St.
Church, the
activity of priesthood in, 546-50
analogies illustrating, 590 f.
authority of, 549 f.
as body of the God-man, 541 ff.
as bride of Christ, 541, 546, 610
care of children in, 548
Christ born anew in, 547
competency in matters of faith, 551, 557
connection between matrimony and, 610
cultural contributions of, 557 note
different from other societies, 540 f.
divine institution of, 539, 543, 553
doctrinal definitions issued by, 747
equated with the mystical body, 543, 552, 581
Eucharist the heart of, 542, 552, 581
exercise of government in, 552
fellowship with Christ in, 542
fertility of, 549
formation of, 553
function of sacraments in, 581
functions of, 541 f., 550-57
functions of members of, 555 and note
general notion of, 539-42, 545
glory of, 557
goal of, 549, 613
guided by the Holy Ghost, 551 f.
hierarchy of, 552
Holy Ghost the soul of, 545
importance of, 542
inadequate notion of, 567
incomprehensibility of, 540
infallibility of, 549, 557
initiation into, 542
inner nature of, 540 ff.
integration of members in, 543
invisible aspect of, 540
maternal organization of, 546-50, 555
membership in, 542 ff.

Church (*continued*)
as mother, 546-50, 557
mystery of, 539-42, 548, 557 f.
organization of, 545-49, 555
organs of Christ in, 545, 556
origin of, 539
powers of, 550-57
representatives of Christ in, 545
revelation requisite for knowing, 540 f.
sacramental nature of, 581
sacraments of; *see* Sacraments
sacrifice offered by, 507, 510, 548
as society, 539 f., 553
steps in entering, 543
supernaturalness of, 540 ff., 553, 558
teaching office of, 549 f.
temple of the Holy Ghost, 544
unity of, 552 ff.
visibility of, 539
Circumincession of the divine persons, 150, 178
City of God, 684
Clandestine marriage, 607 note
Clement of Alexandria: on the blood of the Lord, 524 note; on the Word, 529 note
Coal, glowing: figure of Christ, 459 and note, 463, 514 and note
Cognition: certitude of natural, 745; reason and faith as principles of, 779
Cologne, Council of (1860), 11 note, 26 note, 36 note
Command imposed on Christ, 450
Communicatio idiomatum between Christ and His members, 371 and note
Communication of divine goodness, 357
Communication of divine nature
to Christ's mystical body, 363
to creatures, 141, 143, 206 f.
within the Godhead, 46, 74, 141
in the Incarnation, 358, 421
per modum naturae, 93 f.
twofold aspect of, 398
Communion, Holy
Alger of Liége on, 524 note
Augustine on, 525
Cyril of Jerusalem on, 488 and note
divine life conferred by, 523 ff.
effects of, 523-27
fellowship with Christ in, 487 and note, 493, 528
John Chrysostom on, 485 and note, 528 note
John Damascene on, 488 and note, 492 note

Communion (*continued*)
natural refection compared with, 483, 493
possession of God pledged in, 526 f.
possession of the God-man in, 526
preparation for, 523
purpose of, 500
reason for name of, 492
reception of the Logos in, 524
relation of the Consecration to, 486
Robert Grosseteste on, 492 note
significance of, 523-27
two functions of, 523
union with Christ in, 462 f.
Compensation for sin, 313
Comprehensor, 448 f.
Concepts, transfiguration of natural, 772; *see also* Analogous concepts
Concupiscence
Christ's freedom from, 329 f.
as factor in original sin, 291 ff.
force of, 307
freedom from, 216
not removed in justification, 630
origin of, 216, 275 f., 278
Condition of fallen man, 303
Confidence in God, 129: as disposition for justification, 637, 640, 644 f.
Confirmation (sacrament): function of, 572; relation of baptism to, 586; relation to extreme unction, 577; sacramental character in, 586; *sacramentum et res* in, 575 f.
Congruism, 720
Conscience, law of, 247
Consecration (Mass): relation of Holy Communion to, 486; as sacrificial action, 507
Consequences of sin: in the natural order, 249; in the supernatural order, 249; *see also* Sin
Conservation, 205
Constitution of Christ, 317-22, 333
"Construction" of the Trinity, 35, 50, 55 note
Conversio ad creaturam, 686
Conversion: of bread into Christ's body, 497; difference of transubstantiation from natural, 498; transubstantiation as supernatural, 498
Corpus Christi, office of, 379 note
Correspondence with grace, 638, 707 f., 724
Corruptibility of human body: as natural defect, 673; nature of, 676; overcome

Corruptibility of human body (*cont.*)
  by quality of incorruptibility, 673, 676
Corruption: deliverance from, 682; through sin, 349
Council in Trullo (692), 488
Councils
  Cologne (1860), 11 note, 26 note, 36 note
  Florence (1441), 81 note
  Lateran IV (1215), 26 note
  Toledo XI (675), 64, 133 note
  Trent; see Trent, Council of
  Trullan (692), 488
  Vatican (1869), 11 note, 553
Crassness of human body: as natural defect, 673; nature of, 674; overcome by quality of subtility, 674 f., 677 f.
Creation
  as cause of nature, 204
  definition of, 87
  exclusion of instrumental causality in, 461
  exemplar of, 141
  motive of, 141
  not a mystery, 204
  purpose of, 130, 429, 725
  subjected to frustration, 682
  supernatural end of, 682 f.
  unknown to pagan philosophy, 204
Creator, 141
Creatures: end of, 421, 423; free will of, 451
Creed: appropriations in the, 134; purpose of the Incarnation in the, 421
Cross of Christ, the: fruits of, 436; relation of the Mass to, 509; restoration of the world and, 427; sacrifice on, 519 f.
Culpability of original sin, 283-88, 295
Cultus of the Holy Ghost, 166
Cur Deus homo by St. Anselm, 428
Cyprian on virginity, 188 and note
Cyril of Alexandria, St.
  on adoptive sonship, 385
  on Christ as first fruits, 440
  on Christ as source of grace, 387 note, 391
  on Christ as the new Adam, 380
  on Christ represented by glowing coal, 459 note
  on Christ's sacrifice, 438 note
  commentary on St. John, 530-34
  on Eucharistic teaching of Nestorius, 480 note
  on the Incarnation, 352 and note

Cyril of Alexandria (*continued*)
  on the lily as figure of Christ, 463 note
  on mediation of Christ, 408 note
  on motivation of the Incarnation, 353, 531
  on names of the Holy Ghost, 113 and note
  against Nestorius, 351
  opponent of Eastern rationalism, 530
  on procession of the Holy Ghost, 111 note
  on purpose of the Incarnation, 380 f. and notes
  on relations between the Trinity, Incarnation, and Eucharist, 489, 530-35
  on resurrection of the body, 669 and note
  on sharing in the divine nature, 392 note
  on significance of the Incarnation, 533
  on "Spirit" as applied to Third Person, 98 note
  on the Spirit of the Son, 393 note
  on union with God through Christ, 407 and note, 532 ff.
Cyril of Jerusalem, St., 488 and note

Damascene; see John Damascene, St.
Damned, punishment of the, 686-94
David, anointing of, 567
Dead, resurrection of the; see Body, resurrection of
Death: of Christ, 518; freedom from, 216; nobility of, 455; sin as cause of, 667
Debitum incurrendi peccatum originale, 465 note
Defilement of sin, 256 ff., 279
Deformity in original sin, 279, 284-88
Deicide, 270
Deification: of Christ's human nature, 323; of the first man, 315
Deification of man
  Basil on, 316 note
  in the beatific vision, 659 f.
  through the Eucharist, 487 f.
  Gregory of Nyssa on, 316 note
  incorruption as factor in, 390
  Maximus Martyr on, 657 note
  meaning of, 316, 378, 654
  in original justice, 211
  as purpose of Incarnation, 337 ff., 488
  by transfiguration, 654; see also Transfiguration of man
  transubstantiation as model of, 502 f.

Delectatio coelestis, 720
Demonstratio: propter quid, 750; *quia,* 750
Demonstration: in theology, 747-50; of the Trinity, 50-54
Dependence on God, 204
Depravity of mankind, 309
Destiny: natural, 652; supernatural, 417 f., 658, 699 ff.
Devil, the
  captivity under, 307 and note
  conquest of, 310 f.
  dominion of, 307 f.
  efforts to destroy mankind, 267
  influence in the world, 271, 294
  punishment of, 694
  slavery of, 307 and note
Diabolical sin, 264
Dieringer, F. X., 114, 420 note
Dispositions for justification, 635-40
Distinction
  among the divine persons, 52, 54, 115
  between *efficacia virtutis* and *efficacia connexionis,* 704 note
  between essence and person in God, 48, 51, 120 and note
  between mystery and sacrament, 558 f.
  between power of orders and power of jurisdiction, 550
  between *sacramentum, sacramentum et res,* and *sacramentum tantum,* 575
Distribution of graces, 727 f.
Divine attributes, 27 ff., 134: manifestation of, 415
Divine cognition, expression of, 62
Divine generation, notion of, 87 f.
Divine intellect, activity of the, 56
Divine justice in predestination, 729
Divine knowledge, expression of, 57-63
Divine law, regulation of marriage by positive, 594, 597
Divine life: communicated in the beatific vision, 658 f., 662, 664; communication of Christ's, 501; infused into the members of the Church, 544 f.
Divine love
  disinterestedness of, 422
  in election to beatitude, 725
  in the Eucharist, 479, 503
  expression of, 57-64
  for men, 410, 709
  poured forth in the Eucharist, 487
  in predestination, 729 f.
  revealed in the Incarnation, 419
  selective, 725

Divine mercy: exhibited in the Incarnation, 419; in predestination, 729
Divine missions; *see* Missions, divine
Divine nature, the
  activities of, 56
  communicated in the hypostatic union, 738
  communicated in three ways, 738
  communicated to creatures, 141-43, 358, 737
  communicated within the Godhead, 46, 74, 141
  different ways of possessing, 88
  inconceivability of, 47
  knowability of, 26, 45 f., 735
  life of, 56
  participation in; *see* Participation in the divine nature
  unicity of, 73
Divine person, notion of, 80 ff.
Divine persons, the
  absoluteness of, 81 f.
  circumincession of, 150, 178
  designated by relative terms, 83
  distinction among, 52, 79, 133
  entrance into creatures, 154 ff., 159, 175
  external works common to, 133, 135, 151
  holiness of, 111
  hypostatic possession of, 166
  hypostatic presence of, 160 ff.
  identity in essence of, 68, 115, 150
  independence of, 82, 121, 149
  infinity of, 150
  inseparability of, 149, 178
  love among, 128
  omnipresence of, 150, 157
  presence of, 158 f.
  relationship among, 51
  relativity of, 51, 81, 115
Divine productions (*see also* Productions in God)
  hypostatic and personal, 79
  immanence of, 66
  personal character of, 73
  products of, 62, 65-69, 73-80
  prolongation in the God-man, 313
  revealed in the God-man, 313
  substantiality of, 66 ff.
Divine sonship, 168 f.; *see also* Adoptive sonship, grace of
Divine will, activity of, 56
Divine wisdom; *see* Wisdom, divine
Divinity: of Christ, 337, 400, 454; replenishment of human souls with, 525

Divinization; *see* Deification

Döllinger, J. von, 495 note

Dogma: of the Eucharist, 470; Pius IX on nature of, 739 note; precision of Catholic, 646; of the Trinity, 26, 50, 63

Dominion of the devil, 307 f.

Donum, Holy Ghost as, 107, 156, 530

Donum Dei, 161

Dove as symbol of the Holy Spirit, 150, 154 and note, 446 note

Duns Scotus: on attempt to demonstrate the Trinity, 29 note; on original justice, 226 and note; on procession of the Holy Ghost, 108 and note

Earth, the new, 655, 684

Education, powers of the Church in, 550-57

Effects attributed to the Holy Ghost: creation in general, 190 ff.; gifts to rational creatures, 192 ff.; in guiding creatures to God, 195 ff.

Elect, the, 708: who constitute, 725

Election, divine
cause of, 725
effective, 725
formidable aspect of, 726
gratuitousness of, 725
identical with predestination, 724
infallibility of, 725

Elevation of human nature: effects of, 376; in hypostatic union, 317 f., 322; as purpose of the Incarnation, 377, 419; in sanctifying grace, 317 f., 619

Elevation of man
basis of, 399
in the beatific vision, 662
through Christ, 730
described by Leo the Great, 378 note
through the Incarnation, 395, 398 ff., 419
to participation in the divine nature, 205 f.
relationship of restoration to, 399 f., 318 f.

Elevation of material nature, 402

Elevation, supernatural: basis in the race for, 354; for infants and for adults, 724; nature of, 205; *see also* Adoptive sonship, grace of; Sanctifying grace

End; *see* Last end

Entreaty, grace obtained by, 637

Epiphanius on the Holy Ghost, 97

Essence, intuition of divine, 658 f.; *see also* Beatific vision

Eternal life
of the glorified body, 664
imperishableness of, 663 f.
meaning of, 663
miracle of, 665
mystery of, 663 ff.
participation in God's eternity in, 663 f.
root of, 663
Thomas Aquinas on, 664 note

Eternal productions; *see* Divine productions

Eucharist, the (*see also* Eucharistic existence of Christ)
agency in divine missions, 528
defective views of efficacy of, 502
discourse of the Savior on, 516 f.
dogma of, 470
faith required in, 470
fellowship with Holy Spirit in, 488
function in mission of the Holy Spirit, 528
heart of the Church, 542, 552, 581
heavenly food, 503 f., 513
incomprehensibility of, 470
Lutheran doctrine on, 476
meaning of the name, 530
means of union with Christ, 374, 482, 528
mystery of, 469-78, 561
natural food compared with, 483 ff., 493, 514
Paschasius Radbertus on, 486 note
perfection of Christ's mediation in, 491
pledge of immortal life, 525
position among Christian mysteries, 479, 481, 494 ff.
prolongation of the Incarnation, 485 f., 493, 522
purpose of, 479-82, 486, 493
reception of; *see* Communion, Holy
relation of the Incarnation to, 477 f., 485-89, 494 ff.
relation of the Trinity to, 477 f., 489-96, 528
sacramentum et res in, 575
as sacrifice, 494 ff.; *see also* Eucharistic sacrifice
significance of; *see* Significance of the Eucharist
spiritual life nourished by, 513 f.
teaching of faith about, 469
union with Christ in, 482, 493, 669

Eucharistic existence of Christ
  Alger of Liége on, 476 note
  concealment of glory in, 472
  divine character of, 473 f., 476
  divine-spiritual, 512-21
  glory of, 473, 514, 519
  material manner of, 473
  Peter de Blois on, 476 note
  power of, 515
  purpose of, 512
  relation of the hypostatic union to, 476
  the Resurrection compared with, 514 f.
  sacramental mode of, 522
  significance of, 512-22
  spiritual character of, 473, 475, 512-21
  supernatural character of, 472-76
  threefold mode of, 471, 512
Eucharistic sacrifice, the (see also Mass; Sacrifice of Christ)
  characteristics of, 508 ff.
  Döllinger on, 495 note
  form of, 506, 510
  function of the Consecration in, 507 f.
  function of the Holy Ghost in, 509
  in heaven, 519
  as holocaust, 506, 510, 520
  oblation in, 508; see also Sacrificial gift
  relation of the Cross to, 509
  sacrificial action in, 506-10
  significance of transubstantiation in, 505-11
  theory of, 507-10
  true sacrificial character of, 505
  unbloody manner of, 506
  union with Christ in, 501, 505, 518
  victim in, 505; see also Sacrificial victim
Eucharistic species, presence of Christ under the, 469
Eunomians, the, 85
Eutychian notion of Christ, 320
Eve: derived from Adam, 182, 374; Mary as the new, 465; reason for name of, 185; sin of, 265 f.; supernatural production of, 183
Evidence: function in theological knowledge, 746 f.; in scientific knowledge, 746
Existence, possibility of, 754 f.
Existence of Christ: indemonstrable on rational grounds, 338 f.; necessity of revelation to show, 336
Ex opere operantis, grace conferred, 599, 605 and note

Ex opere operato, grace conferred, 599, 604 f.
Extension of hypostatic union, 366, 369, 373
Extension of mystical body, 602
Extreme unction: connection with other sacraments, 577; the function of, 576; the medicinal character of, 577 and note; sacramentum et res in, 578 note

Faith
  activity of God known by, 755
  activity of the Holy Spirit in, 771-75
  anchor of, 776
  animated by love, 774 f.
  attachment to God by, 643
  as basis of theological science, 747 f.
  beatific vision anticipated in, 791, 796
  in Christ, 337
  competence of the Church in matters of, 551, 557
  consummation of, 652
  criterion of, 746
  demanded by Christ, 516
  dependence of reason on, 779, 782, 785
  development of, 780 f.
  as disposition for justification, 637, 642
  elevation of reason by, 748 f., 761, 780
  fostered by the Incarnation, 417
  function in justification, 644
  function in knowledge of God, 57
  function in theology, 734, 744, 748
  gifts of the Holy Ghost and, 777 f.
  grace of, 770 f., 776
  higher stage of, 769
  humility in, 774
  illumination required in, 771 f.
  inauguration of, 780
  infallibility of, 779, 782
  initiation into the Church through, 542
  justification by, 644
  knowledge of God through, 791
  knowledge of the plans of God through, 792
  and knowledge of the Trinity, 54, 122
  light of, 770, 776
  light of glory anticipated in, 777
  living, 772, 774-77
  man's cooperation in, 772
  miracles credited to, 644 f.
  as mode of cognition in theology, 734
  motive of, 746
  necessary for understanding the supernatural, 762 f.
  obligation of, 551, 780

Faith (*continued*)
ordinary meaning of supernatural, 768 f.
in Protestant theology, 643 f.
purity of heart in, 774
reason and, 15 ff., 778-88
reason as *pedisequa* of, 780
reason as *praeambula* of, 780
reason in service of, 780 ff.
relation to justification, 641-46
relation to the mystical body, 375
replaced by the light of glory, 776
representative of divine reason, 779
science of, 768, 789
scriptural definition of, 652 and note
service of reason to, 780 ff.
service to reason, 782 f. and note
source of, 777
supernatural stimulus in, 770-78
theology as science of, 789
Thomas Aquinas on, 767 and note
ultimate perfection of man taught by, 666
and understanding, 768, 770
union of reason and, 784-88
vocation to, 779
wonder-working, 644 ff.
Faith, objects of
conditions for understanding, 770-74
efficient cause of, 759
exemplary cause of, 759
final cause of, 759
formal cause of, 759
function of reason in understanding. 757, 760
illumination of, 771-74
natural concepts in understanding, 752 f.
objective truth of, 762 f.
represented by analogous concepts, 754, 759
subjective science of, 758
sublimity of, 753
supernatural character of, 753
suprarational character of, 753
system of, 758
understanding of, 752-61, 768
union with, 774, 776
Fall, the: God's reason for permitting. 429; relation to the Incarnation, 422
Fallen man: condition of, 303; effect of predestination on, 711; restoration of, 419, 423; *see also* Original sin
Father as name of First Person in God, 84
Fatherhood of God extended to man, 358, 383 f., 493

Fathers of the Church
on Christ as source of grace, 391
on Christ's body, 518
on deification through the Eucharist, 488 ff.
on the Eucharist as extension of the Incarnation, 485 ff.
on Eucharistic union with Christ, 483 f.
on the purpose of the Incarnation, 378-82, 419 f.
on relation between the Logos and human nature, 373 and note
on resurrection of the body, 669
on the sacrifice of the Church, 511 and note
Fault: distinct from guilt, 251 and note; in original sin, 284 f.
Fellowship with Christ: Alger of Liége on, 487 note; in the Church, 542; effected by Holy Communion, 487 and note, 493, 542; through the sacraments, 569
Fellowship with God, 172, 395: in Holy Communion, 527
Fellowship in grace, basis in mankind for, 235
Fellowship in the mystical body, 539, 542
Ferrandus the Deacon, 438 note
Filiation, divine; *see* Adoptive sonship, grace of
Finis fidei, 652 and note
First man: deification of, 315; immortality of, 667, 669; sacramental mystery of, 560; twofold mystery in, 219; *see also* Adam
First person in God: characteristic of, 51; name of the, 84; present in the Word, 67; principle of the other two persons, 121, 134; principle of the Word, 74 f., 79
Florence, Council of (1441), 81 note
Foreknowledge of God: intervention in predestination, 703 and note; regarding man's cooperation with grace, 727 f.; relation of predestination to, 708 f.
Formal element: of original justice, 223; of original sin, 288 ff., 305
Formation (production), 89
Francis de Sales, St.: *The Love of God*, 99 note, 527 note; on the product of divine love, 58
Franzelin, J. B.: on Eucharistic presence, 472 note; on transubstantiation, 499 note

Free will: mystery of Christ's, 448; nature of Christ's, 448 f., 452; see also Will, human

Friendship with God, 127

Frohschammer, J., 20 and note, 739 note

Fulgentius, St.: on Christ's union with the race, 367 note; on the name of the Holy Spirit, 98 and note; on union in charity, 172 note

Garden of Eden, marriage in, 598, 600, 604

Garnier, J.: De haeresi Nestorii, 480 note

Generation: conditions requisite for, 87; different from other kinds of production, 87; different from spiration, 88-95; intellectual, 90 f.; notion of, 87 ff.

Generation of the Son of God, 85-95, 423: as basis of adoptive sonship, 142, 493 f.; Thomas Aquinas on, 91 note

Gift: as applied to the Holy Ghost, 107, 109, 156; God's supreme, 109; notion of, 107

Gift of integrity; see Integrity

Gifts of the Holy Ghost, 777

Glories of Divine Grace by Scheeben, 527 note, 635 note

Glorification: crown of God's supernatural works, 697; of material nature, 682 ff.; mystery of, 666-73, 683 f.; relation to integrity, 328; seed of, 562; see also Body, glorification of; Transfiguration of man

Glorification of God
through Christ, 354, 363, 430 f.
through Christ's sacrifice, 432
as end of the Incarnation, 396 f., 421, 425 f.
through the Eucharistic sacrifice, 495
finite, 358
by the incarnate Son, 397 f., 419, 425 ff.
through the Incarnation, 342, 354, 396 f.
infinite, 358, 396
means for promoting, 397
by the mystical body, 396 ff., 427, 495
as purpose of God's external works, 357
by sacrifice, 431
unnecessary to God, 342

Glorified body; see Body, glorified; Body, transfiguration of

Glory: of Christ's human nature, 323, 657; meriting of heavenly, 707

Glory of God: as purpose of Trinitarian revelation, 130; as supreme end of the Incarnation, 419, 425 ff.

Glory, light of
dawn of, 655
effect on glorified body, 681
faith as anticipation of, 777
faith replaced by, 776
God's knowledge communicated in, 791
mystery of, 658

God
activity of; see Activity of God
attributes of, 27 ff., 415
Bonaventure on goodness of, 128 note
Christ as the revelation of, 795
center of Christian mysteries, 775
center of the natural order, 737
dependence of creatures on, 204
difference between creatures and, 206 f.
as exemplary cause, 755, 759
external activity of, 135; see also Activity of God
glorification of; see Glorification of God
idea in the Old Testament, 30
invisibility of, 27
justice of, 684
knowability of, 26 ff., 125
knowledge and love in, 57
love for man, 309 and note, 325, 377
man's knowledge of, 791
natural concept of, 45, 125, 128
perfection of knowledge in, 791
personality in, 73
principle of all being, 26, 141
principle of grace, 457, 461
productivity in, 37, 73
purpose in external works, 357
reaction against sinners, 685
relations in, 52 f., 81, 115
simplicity of, 47, 51, 87
sovereignty of, 451
summit of supernatural order, 795
supernatural knowledge of, 737
three persons in, 26, 51; see also Divine persons; Trinity
true idea of, 31
vitality of, 30 f., 56

God-man, the (see also Christ; Son of God)
Adam as type of, 184 f., 235 f.
adoration of, 358

God-man (*continued*)
anointing of, 331 ff.
attributes of, 322-33
as complement to Adam, 354 f., 376, 387 f.
constitution of, 317-22, 333, 406
difficulty of describing, 315
dignity of, 324, 337, 426
fellowship of grace in, 235
first-born of all creatures, 364, 401
founder of the Church, 540
function in rescuing man, 400
head of material nature, 401
head of the angels, 401 ff.
head of the Church, 401
head of the human race, 364 ff., 376; *see also* Headship of Christ
identical with Christ, 333
inseparability from God, 325
invisibility of, 336
mediatorship of, 405-14; *see also* Mediation of Christ
mystery of, 313, 319
power of, 566
principle of fellowship with God, 396
relationship to human race, 366-71, 406
relationship with the Trinity, 359-64
reparation wrought by, 376
sacramental character of, 565
sacramental mystery of, 560
as substitute for Adam, 354 f., 376, 386 f.
as supernatural head, 235, 376
as supreme revelation of God, 795
task of, 447
triumph of, 400, 426
two natures in, 317, 406, 478
unity of, 318
visibility of, 336, 540
Grace (*see also* Adoptive sonship; Sanctifying grace)
accompanying religious vows, 605 note
and adoptive sonship, 146, 623 f.
caused by God alone, 457, 461
of Christ, 331, 456 f.
communicated through Christ, 456 f.
congruity of, 727
correspondence with, 638, 707 f., 724
Cyril of Alexandria on Christ as source of, 387 note, 391
disposal of treasures of, 551
distribution of, 727 f.
of divine sonship; *see* Adoptive sonship, grace of
enlightening power of, 770-73, 776 f.
of faith, 770, 776

Grace (*continued*)
first, 707
fruits of, 646
function in revelation, 765
habitual; *see* Sanctifying grace
incompatible with sin, 326, 619 f., 623
increase of, 646 ff.
life of, 777
merited by Christ, 453, 569
obtained by entreaty, 637
opposition of sin to, 248, 685
in patristic terminology, 315
perseverance in, 711, 724
prevenient; *see* Prevenient grace
relation of bodily resurrection to, 670
relationship of the Incarnation to, 398
in the sacrament of matrimony, 593, 604-7
sanctification through, 670
sanctifying; *see* Sanctifying grace
sin as impediment to, 326, 619, 636
sin remitted by infusion of, 620
source in Christ, 387 and note, 390-95, 456
transmission from Adam, 564
the Trinity as source of, 141
union with God by, 159, 317, 619 f.
Graces, selection of: God's liberty in, 728; God's salvific will and, 728; limits of, 729; meaning of, 727; relation to predestination, 729
Gratia capitis, 456, 458
Gratia gratum faciens, 583, 620
Gratia motrix, 722 f.
Gratia praedeterminans, 719
Gratia victrix, 719 f.
Gratiae gratis datae, 155
Grave, darkness of, 651 f.
Gregory the Great, St.: on the Incarnation, 373 note
Gregory of Nazianzus, St.: on anointing of Christ, 333 note; on Christ as source of grace, 391 and note; on the Father as "source" of the Trinity, 74 note; against the Macedonian heresy, 181 f. and note
Gregory of Nyssa, St.: on Christ as source of grace, 391 and note; on deification of man, 316 note; on elevation of the race, 377; on the Father as "source" of the Trinity, 74 note; on transubstantiation, 498 and note
Gregory of Valencia on predestination, 720-24
Günther, Anton, 16 note, 125

Günther's school on the Incarnation, 338
Guilt: distinct from fault, 251 and note; of habitual sin, 253, 616; inherited, 303; in original sin, 286 ff., 353; state of, 250
Guitmund on the Eucharist, 515 note

Habitual grace; see Sanctifying grace
Habitual sin
analysis of, 253 f., 616
definition of, 252
deformity of, 253, 257, 616
distinct from actual sin, 251 f.
guilt of, 253, 616
remission of, 616
survival of sinful act as, 250, 256, 616
Handbuch der katholischen Dogmatik by Scheeben, 57 note, 333 note, 550 note
Happiness: the body not essential to heavenly, 667; in heaven, 658, 662, 681; participation in the divine, 658, 662
Headship of Christ, the
over all creation, 401 ff.
over the Church, 401
in communication of divine life, 389-96
in elevation of the race, 398 ff.
influence of, 456
meaning of, 364 f.
mystery of, 366, 376
perfection of, 456
representative of the members, 438, 494
significance of, 501
Heaven: Christ's spiritual sacrifice in, 519; happiness of, 658, 662, 681; the new, 655, 684
Hell: conquest of, 310; punishments of, 686-94
Hell-fire: action of, 689 f., 693; errors about, 691; nature of, 687-93; reality of, 688-91, 693; supernatural character of, 688 ff., 693
Hereditary sin; see Original sin
Heresies on the Incarnation, 320, 346 f.
Hermes, George, 16 note
Hierarchy of the Church, 552
Hilary of Poitiers, St.: on Christ's union with the Church, 486 and note; on Christ's union with the race, 367 note; on the purpose of the Incarnation, 378; on relation between Trinity and Eucharist, 490 ff.; on union

Hilary of Poitiers (*continued*)
with God through Christ, 407 and note
Holiness: disposition for, 221, 230; nature of original, 210; relation of integrity to original, 220 f.; see also Justice and holiness; Original justice; Sanctity
Holocaust: Augustine on, 439 note; Christ's sacrifice as, 436, 442, 519; the Eucharistic sacrifice as, 506, 510, 520; living, 435; of the whole Christ, 439
Holy Communion; see Communion, Holy
Holy Ghost (*see also* Spiration; Third Person in God)
activity in faith, 771-75
activity in the Church, 545
activity in the sacraments, 568-71
Ambrose on, 110 note, 160 note
analogy for procession of, 185
appropriations of, 190-97
ascription of hypostatic union to, 332 note, 360 note
Athanasius on, 111 note
Augustine on, 64 f., 110 and note, 164 note
Bernard on, 65 and note, 110, 171 note
bond of peace, 172
cause of original justice, 231 ff.
cause of supernatural glorification, 680, 682, 685
the Church as temple of, 544
as Comforter, 111, 177
communication of, 172
in communication of divine life, 393 ff.
compared to stream of living water, 104 and notes
cultus of, 166
Cyril of Alexandria on names of, 113 and note
defects in analogue of, 182, 187
devotion to, 447 note
distinct from divine love, 65
as *donum*, 107, 156, 530
as *donum hypostaticum*, 161 ff.
effects attributed to, 190-97
Eucharistic sacrifice effected by, 509
Fulgentius on name of, 98 and note
gifts of, 777
guest of our soul, 167 ff.
guidance of the Church by, 551 f.
hypostatic mission of, 385 f.
indwelling of; see Indwelling of the Holy Ghost

Holy Ghost (*continued*)
    inspiration of, 775
    Methodius on, 185 and note
    mission of, 156 and note; see also Mission of the Holy Ghost
    name of, 186
    not generated, 94
    object of supernatural love, 174
    as Paraclete, 111, 162 f., 177
    person of love, 77
    personality of, 75 ff., 101
    pledge of divine love, 164, 174, 385
    possession of, 165, 170, 385 f.
    production of, 76, 102 f., 111
    as real product, 65
    seal of unity, 170 ff.
    sigh of love, 66, 77, 88
    soul of the Church, 545
    spiration of, 76, 102 f., 111
    Spirit of divine life, 393
    Spirit of the mystical body, 394
    symbols of, 103 f.
    unguent of Christ, 332 and note
    the world as temple of, 237, 402
Holy of holies, 436
Holy orders; see Orders, holy
Hope: fostered by the Incarnation, 417; Maximus Martyr on, 417 note; of salvation, 707, 710
Hoppe, L.: on the Eucharistic sacrifice, 510 note; on the prayer "Supplices te rogamus," 507 note
Human body as member of Christ, 370; see also Body, human
Human nature
    assumed by Christ, 317, 322, 358
    elevated by grace, 317 f.
    elevated by hypostatic union, 317 f., 378 note
    enriched by hypostatic union, 321
    epitome of all creatures, 358, 362 f., 401
    reasons for assumption of, 362 f.
    transmission of, 364
Human nature of Christ (see also Hypostatic union)
    activity of, 330 f., 570; see also Activity of Christ
    assimilated to God, 331
    beatific vision of, 325 ff.
    channel of grace, 458 f.
    communication of grace from, 331
    continuity of the race with, 462 f.
    deification of, 323 ff.
    dignity of, 377, 584

Human nature of Christ (*continued*)
    divine control of, 326, 788
    as first fruits of the race, 368
    fruitfulness of, 566
    glory of, 323, 657
    grace of, 331, 458, 565
    holiness of, 324 ff., 377
    immune from concupiscence, 329 f.
    impeccability of, 326 f.
    as instrument of divinity, 330 f., 477, 565
    instrumentality in production of grace, 457-60
    integrity of, 327-30
    merit of, 331; see also Merits of Christ
    model of glorified man, 656 f.
    mortality of, 329
    natural condition of, 424
    organ of the Logos, 458, 462, 565
    participation in divine nature, 322 ff., 458
    passibility of, 328 f.
    power of, 330 f., 565
    reality of, 324
    sinlessness of, 326 f.
    spiritual contact with, 462 f.
    supernatural condition of, 323 f.
    supernatural life of, 389
    threefold mystery in, 331
    transfiguration of, 323 ff., 331, 565
    union with God, 326, 458
    value of activity of, 330
Human race
    Adam as head of, 233, 365, 386
    assumed by Christ, 370 and note, 565, 730
    as body of Christ, 367 ff., 390, 565
    changed into divine race, 396
    dignity through Christ, 388, 565
    natural ancestry of, 365
    participation in Christ's sufferings and actions, 370 and notes
    priesthood of, 398
    relation to Christ, 501
    represented by Christ, 438
    share in Christ's sacrifice, 438
    solidarity of, 363, 366, 376
    specific unity of, 363
    union with Christ, 366-75, 464, 565
    unity of, 364 f., 368, 376
Humanity of Christ; see Human nature of Christ
Hypostasis: analogy between divine and created, 83; definition of, 70; impor-

Hypostasis (*continued*)
tance in definition of person, 69;
kinds of, 71; original meaning of, 70;
see also Person

Hypostatic union, the (*see also* Incarnation)
absence of contradiction in, 321
ascribed to the Holy Ghost, 332 note, 360 note
between bread and Christ's body excluded, 500
consequences in Christ's Eucharistic existence, 476
in the created order, 318
different from sanctifying grace, 316 f.
effect on creatures, 407
effects in the mystical body, 377
effects on Christ's human nature, 317 f., 406, 513 ff.
exemplary cause of supernatural elevation, 502
extension of, 366, 373, 377
gratia capitis and, 458
impossibility of fused natures in, 318, 322
indicative of infinite perfection, 321
mystery of, 316, 318, 561
nature of, 317-22, 406
purely personal, 319 f.
relation of the Mass to, 509
relation to the Trinity, 321
revelation of, 319 f.
supernatural character of, 318 ff.
supreme among unions, 325
unicity of purely personal, 319

Image of God: man as, 317, 434; substantial; *see also* Word of God
Immaculate Conception, 444, 464 f.
Immolation, association with Christ's, 496
Immortality
Christ's body as seed of, 504
of eternal life, 663 f.
of the first man, 667
hope of bodily, 668, 671
preternatural gift of, 390, 668
restored right of bodily, 668
of the soul, 652, 663
Impanation, 505
Impassibility of glorified body, 673: nature of, 676
Impeccability of Christ, 326 f.
Impediment to grace: removal of, 636; sin as, 636

Incarnation (*see also* Hypostatic union)
acknowledgment of mystery in, 313
analogous concept of, 316
as basis of adoptive sonship, 383
bodily resurrection based on, 671
connection of theology with, 795
connection with original sin, 353 ff.
Cyril of Alexandria on, 352 and note, 380 f. and notes
effected by the Trinity, 133 and notes, 151
effects of, 420 f., 423, 613
goal of, 613; *see also* Purpose of the Incarnation
in God's providence, 355
Gregory the Great on, 373 note
illustrations of, 316, 543
impossibility of philosophical demonstration of, 338
inadequate view of purpose of, 418
intelligibility of, 335
knowability of, 335 ff.
lack of natural motivation for, 339
mission of the Son in, 151, 154, 180
misunderstanding of, 313
moderate rationalism on, 338
motivation of, 353-56, 404; *see also* Significance of the Incarnation
motivation undiscoverable by reason, 338-50
mysterious decree of, 345, 354
mystery of, 322, 353, 404
nature of, 314
necessity of faith to appreciate, 356
objective ends of, 414 f.
pattern of glorified nature, 656
position in God's plan, 428 ff.
possible without the Fall, 422 f.
prolongation in the Eucharist, 485 f., 493, 522
purpose of, 172, 354 f., 377-89; *see also* Significance of the Incarnation
rationalist distortion of, 351
rationalist rejection of, 341, 346
redemption possible without, 343-47
relation of the Eucharist to, 477 f., 485-89, 494 ff.
relation of the Fall to, 422
relations to the angels, 363
relationship to grace, 398, 422
relationship to the Trinity, 398
remission of sin through, 420
renewed in the Mass, 510
restricted to the Son, 360 f.

Incarnation (*continued*)
  significance of; *see* Significance of the
    Incarnation
  the Son's activity in, 134
  subjective ends of, 415 and note
  subordinate end of, 421
  supernatural character of, 423
  supernatural motivation of, 348, 350,
    353-56
  supposition for necessity of, 355
  supreme motive of, 419, 425 ff.
  unmotivated by man's fall, 349 f.
  unmotivated by man's need of recon-
    ciliation, 347 f.
  unmotivated by need of satisfaction,
    344-47
  from viewpoint of man, 421 f.
Incommunicability as characteristic of
  hypostasis, 70
Incomprehensibility: of Christian mysteries, 11, 19; of the Trinity, 47, 118,
  121
Incorporation in Christ, 366-71
  claim to resurrection contained in,
    670 ff.
  effect of, 486, 493 f.
  effected by Holy Communion, 523,
    528
  essential characteristic of, 376
  in the Eucharist, 483 ff., 493 f.
  through the Incarnation, 383
  through justification, 625
  in transubstantiation, 500 f.
Incorruptibility of glorified body, 673:
  nature of, 676, 678
Incorruption of transfigured body, 390
Independence of the divine persons, 82,
  121, 149
Indissolubility: of consecratory sacraments, 574; of the marriage bond,
  594, 596
Indwelling of the divine persons, 160
Indwelling of God: in Christ, 336; in
  man, 317
Indwelling of the Holy Ghost
  in the Church, 545
  distinct from sanctifying grace, 168
  effects of, 163, 627
  as formal cause of holiness, 167
  through grace, 165
  hypostatic, 160-64, 166-71, 385 f.
  through justification, 627
  in man's body, 673
  in the mystical body, 488
  as prolongation of His eternal proces-
    sion, 386

Ineffabilis Deus (papal bull), 355 note,
  465 note
Inertness of the human body: as natural
  defect, 673; nature of, 676; overcome
  by quality of agility, 673, 676
Infallibility: of the Church, 549, 557; er-
  roneous notion of, 554; of faith, 779,
  782; of predestination, 705 f., 708-11,
  730; of the supreme pontiff, 554-57
Infants: baptism of, 604 note; justification of, 633; the lot of unbaptized,
  727
Infinite Being, 27
Infinity of the divine persons, 150
Inhabitation of the Holy Ghost; *see* Indwelling of the Holy Ghost
Inheritance of the children of God, 662
Inseparability of the divine persons, 149,
  178
Inspiration of the Holy Ghost, 775
Instrumentum coniunctum, 330, 456
Integrity (preternatural gift)
  of Adam, 329
  Augustine on dissolution of, 277 and
    note
  of Christ's humanity, 327-30, 787
  difference between sanctity and, 217
  as disposition for grace, 230, 296, 629
  dissolution of, 276 f.
  erroneous views on, 217, 219
  function of, 220, 230, 275
  nature of, 216-20, 273, 296
  not restored in Christian justification,
    628 ff.
  prelude to glorification, 679
  purpose of, 221, 275, 679
  relation of holiness to, 220 f.
  relation of sanctifying grace to, 628 f.,
    680
  relation to glorification, 328, 679
  relation to transfiguration, 387, 679
  supernatural character of, 217 f., 277
  transmitted privation of, 296
Intellectus, 751
Intellectus credibilitatis, 770
Intellectus fidei, 770
Interchange of properties between Christ
  and members, 371 and note
Intuition of divine essence, 658 f.; *see also*
  Beatific vision
Irenaeus, St.: on mediation of Christ, 409
  and notes; on the purpose of the Incarnation, 380 and notes; on resurrection of the body, 669 and note; on
  union with Christ, 392
Isidore of Pelusium, 420 note

Jesus: meaning of name, 333; mystery in, 333; *see also* Christ; God-man

Jews, the: rejection of Christ by, 516 f.; sacredness of marriage among, 598 note

John the Baptist, St., 621

John Chrysostom, St.
on Christ as first fruits, 442 note
on Christ's union with the race, 370
on Holy Communion, 485 and note, 528 note
on meaning of procession, 104
on redemption and regeneration, 420 note
on resurrection in Christ, 389 and note

John Damascene, St.: on anointing of Christ, 333 note; on effects of Holy Communion, 488 and note; on Holy Communion, 492 note; on salvation through Christ, 401 note; on transubstantiation, 498 note

Joyce, G. H.: *Christian Marriage*, 594 note

Jurisdiction: definition of, 551; in matrimony, 596, 608 and note; power of, 550 f.

Justice: as freedom from sin, 623; notion of original, 211; *see also* Holiness; Original justice; Sanctity

Justice, Christian
acquisition of, 613, 623 f., 632
compared with Adam's justice, 628 ff.
difference between original justice and, 628 ff.
as extension of Christ's justice, 625-30
increase of, 613
internal, 625-28
law of, 630
modeled on Christ's justice, 626
nature of, 626 f., 641
product of justification, 614
rooted in the God-man, 629
sanctity of, 622
superior to Adam's justice, 628, 630

Justice and holiness
conferred on Adam, 209
faulty notion of, 210
meaning of, 210 f.
reasons for defective views on, 213
relation between, 623 f.
scriptural account of, 214
supernatural character of, 211
various views of, 212 ff.

Justification
activity of God in, 631-35, 637, 641
of adults, 633 ff.

Justification (*continued*)
through anticipation of Christ's merits, 645
attachment to Christ in, 635 f.
attrition in, 640
by baptism, 633
through Christ, 632
Christian justice as product of, 614
confidence as disposition in, 637, 640, 644 f.
consciousness of, 641 f. and note
cooperation in process of, 633 ff., 645
defective notions of, 623, 644
dispositions for, 635-40
in ecclesiastical language, 613
effected by the Incarnation, 613
efficient cause of, 632
elevation of will in, 618
essence of, 613, 623, 628
ethical factor in, 639
by faith, 644
faith as disposition for, 637, 642
final perfection of, 646
function of faith in, 644 ff.
fundamental process in, 623
goal of, 648
greatness of, 617, 623, 628
high point of, 625-30
incorporation in Christ through, 625
increase of grace in, 646 ff.
of infants, 633
instrumentality of sacraments in, 632 f.
integrity not restored in, 628 ff.
by internal renewal, 626 ff., 633, 654
love for God in, 638 ff.
man's part in, 631, 633 ff.
as marriage of the soul with God, 633 ff., 637 ff., 648
meaning of, 613 f. and note, 616, 623 f.
moral cause of, 633
movement toward grace in, 635-40
mystery of, 613-24, 641-46
mystery of second, 648
nature of, 623 f., 627, 632
negative aspect of, 616-21
opposition to sin, 615 f., 619 f., 623
physical factor in, 639
positive effect of, 616, 622 ff.
practice of virtue in, 647
preparation for, 638 ff., 646, 724
process of, 616, 623, 631-35
rationalist notion of, 614
reaction against sin in, 635 f., 639
relation of faith to, 641-46
relation of regeneration to, 613, 623 f., 632 ff.

Justification (*continued*)
  relation of sanctification to, 613, 623 f.
  remission of guilt in, 616-22
  removal of sin in, 614-22, 631
  restoration of original justice in, 614
  restoration of union with God in, 616-
    24, 632
  result of, 616
  rooted in grace of adoptive sonship,
    622
  in sacrament of penance, 638 f.
  Schäzler on, 639 f. and note
  second, 646 ff.
  supernaturalness of, 614-24, 631, 641
  surrender of soul in, 638, 643
  Trent on, 623 and note, 627, 632 and
    note
  two factors in, 616, 624
  union with God in, 634 f.

Kenosis, 424
Kiss: as applied to the Holy Ghost, 160,
  171; as attestation of love, 65 and
  note, 100
Kleutgen, Joseph: on the Trinity, 57 and
  note
Knowledge
  autonomy of reason in philosophical,
    780 ff., 788
  in the beatific vision, 658, 662, 664
  Christ as type of theological, 787 f.
  conditions of scientific, 744 f., 768
  difference between divine and human,
    67, 77 f.
  difference between philosophical and
    theological, 744
  evidence in scientific, 746
  evident principles in scientific, 745
  external expression of divine, 59, 66, 78
  external expression of human, 58, 66,
    78
  generation of theological, 784-88
  of God: through faith, 791; *in Verbo*,
    163
  of God's works, 201
  internal expression of divine, 60 f., 66,
    78
  internal expression of human, 59 ff.
  limitations of human, 8 f., 201, 761
  notion of scientific, 744, 762
  of objects of faith, 763
  perfection of God's, 791
  requirements of scientific, 744 f.
  theological: two factors in, 778; union
    of faith and reason in, 784-88; union

Knowledge (*continued*)
  of faith and understanding in, 762,
    768 f.
Kuhn, Joseph, 30 note, 119 note, 122 note
Kulturkampf, 557 note

Lamb of God, 436
La Puente, Luis de, 162 note
Last end, the
  attainment of, 709
  failure to attain, 708
  hope of attaining, 707
  known by faith alone, 652
  mystery of, 651, 657
  relation of meritorious works to, 707
  supernaturalness of, 658 f., 661 f., 706
Lateran, Fourth Council of (1215), 26
  note
Latreutic sacrifice; *see* Sacrifice, latreutic
La vierge Marie et le plan divin by A.
  Nicolas, 465 note
Law of conscience, 247
Learned ignorance, 8
Legislative power, 550
Leo the Great, St.
  on Christ's sacrifice, 438
  on Christ's union with the race, 367
    note
  on Eucharistic union with Christ,
    486 f. and note
  on exaltation of human nature, 378
    note
  on purpose of the Incarnation, 379 and
    note, 382 and note
  on restoration of man, 419 f. and note
Life
  culmination of supernatural, 504
  definition of, 32
  divine; *see* Divine life
  eternal; *see* Eternal life
  the Eucharist as nourishment of spir-
    itual, 513 f.
  glory of the next, 657
  of God, 30 ff., 56
  nature of Christian, 647
  obscurity of future, 651
  sustenance of supernatural, 484, 493
Light of glory; *see* Glory, light of
Liturgies: effect of the Eucharist in the
  ancient, 488; the Eucharistic sacrifice in the ancient, 509
Liturgy: of the Apostolic Constitutions,
  488 and note; of St. Basil, 488 and
  note; of St. Chrysostom, 488 and
  note

Logos, the, 62, 151, 331: incarnation of, 353; relation of Christ's humanity to, 331, 373, 524; union with the divine, 524; union of man's whole being with, 670; see also God-man; Second Person in God; Son of God; Word of God

Love
in Christian marriage, 605
difference between divine and human, 67, 77 f.
divine; see Divine love
external expression of divine, 59, 66, 79
external expression of human, 59, 66
faith animated by, 774 f.
internal expression of divine, 62 ff., 66 ff., 79
internal expression of human, 59, 61, 78
process of divine, 62
production of human, 61 and note
tendency of affectual, 99

Love for God: in the beatific vision, 662, 664; effected by grace of divine sonship, 622; fostered by the Incarnation, 417; in justification, 638 ff.; motives of, 128 f., 417

Love of God by St. Francis de Sales, 99 note, 527 note

Lucifer, 269

Lugo, John de: on Eucharistic presence, 472 note

Lully, Raymond, 25

Lumen animae, 682

Lumen corporis, 681

Lumen fidei, 770

Lumen gloriae, 655, 658

Lumen gratiae, 655

Luther, Martin: denial of Eucharistic sacrifice, 505

Lutheran doctrine of the Eucharist, 476

Malebranche on the Incarnation, 342

Malice of mortal sin, 250, 255

Man
activity of the justified, 647
beneficiary of the Incarnation, 419-22, 427 f.
center of God's plan, 357
deification of; see Deification of man
dwelling place for glorified, 682
elevation of; see Elevation of man
as focal point of creation, 238
as image of God, 317, 434
mortality of, 216, 665
rebirth of, 654
supernatural excellence of, 237

Man (continued)
transfiguration of; see Transfiguration of man
united with woman in matrimony, 372

Mankind: God's love of, 309 and note; depravity of, 309; unity of, 182; see also Human race

Manuale (anonymous) on intuition of God, 418 note

Marriage (see also Matrimony)
as analogy between faith and reason, 784 f.
clandestine, 607 note
as figure of Christ's union with the Church, 235 f., 543 f.; see also Marriage, Christian
of God with the soul, 633 ff., 637 ff., 648
Melchior Cano on, 607 note
between members of Christ, 599 f., 605 f.
mystical, 543

Marriage, Christian
assistance of the priest in, 609
blessing imparted by the priest in, 606, 609 and note
characteristic excellence of, 600
compared with marriage in Paradise, 599 ff., 604
connection between the Church and, 610
doctrine of St. Paul on, 601-3, 610
education of children in, 605
end of, 573, 599, 610
figure of Christ's union with the Church, 235 f., 543 f., 601 ff.
form of, 606 f. and note
fruit of, 599, 604
grace at contracting, 593, 604-7
the "great mystery" of, 601-3, 610
love between husband and wife in, 605
minister of, 606 f. and note
organ of Christ's union with the Church, 573, 602 f., 605
sacramentality of, 606 and note, 608 f. and note
sacredness of, 606 ff.
supernatural fruitfulness of, 236, 604 ff.
supernaturalness of, 600, 603, 610
transmission of grace in, 604
validity of, 607 ff. and notes
vocation of husband and wife in, 605

Marriage bond, indissolubility and unity of, 594, 596

Martyrs, 439

Mary; see Blessed Virgin Mary

Mass: angel in Canon of, 507 and note;
relation to the hypostatic union, 509;
relation to the Resurrection, 509; re-
newal of the Incarnation in, 510;
sacrificial action in, 507; see also
Eucharistic sacrifice; Sacrifice of
Christ
Massa benedictionis, 730
Massa dammationis, 730
Material element of original justice,
223
Material element of original sin, 291, 305
Material nature
    elevation of, 402, 562, 683
    glorification of, 682 ff.
    incapable of deification, 655
    presence of the supernatural in, 562
    spiritualization of the body's, 656, 673,
        676 ff.
    transfiguration of, 655
    union of the supernatural with, 566
Materiality overcome in glorification,
673
Matrimonial union; see Union, matri-
monial
Matrimony (see also Marriage)
    consummation of, 574
    contracted on God's authority, 596
    definition of natural, 594 and note
    end of, 594 f.
    as illustration of the mystical body,
        372 ff.
    intervention of God in, 595 f.
    jurisdiction of, 596, 608 and note
    as natural institution, 597
    original form of, 597
    in Paradise, 598 f., 601, 604
    sacramentality of pre-Christian, 598
    state of, 593
Matrimony (sacrament)
    conferring of grace in, 593, 604-7
    connection of sacramental character
        with, 578, 592, 606
    the contract as sacrament in, 608
    function of, 573
    husband and wife as ministers of, 607
        and note
    inadequate view of, 593, 608 note, 609
    matter and form of, 607 note, 608 and
        note
    Pius IX on, 608 note, 609 note
    production of grace in, 593, 604-7
    relation of baptism to, 602
    res sacramenti in, 607 and note
    sacramentum et res in, 575, 607
    sacramentum tantum in, 607

Mattes, W., 14 note
Maximus Martyr, St.: on deification of
    man, 657 note; on hope, 417 note; on
    purpose of the Incarnation, 379 and
    note
Maximus of Turin, St., 389 note
Mediation of Christ, 405-14
    active, 410-13
    Athanasius on, 408
    based on divine procession, 411
    on behalf of creatures, 411
    character of atonement in, 414
    communication of grace through, 635
    culmination in the Eucharist, 491
    culmination of, 413
    Cyril of Alexandria on, 408 note
    effect of, 414
    functions of, 413
    Irenaeus on, 409 and notes
    moral, 413
    mystery of, 414
    notion of, 405, 414
    Paschasius Radbertus on, 491 f. and
        note
    Paulinus of Nola on, 409 note
    in reconciliation, 405
    relationship of His priesthood to, 412
    sacrificial, 443
    substantial, 405-10, 413
    Tertullian on, 409 f. and note
    two ways of conceiving, 409
Melchisedech, Christ a priest according
    to order of, 443, 518
Members of Christ
    communication of divine life to, 389-
        96, 625
    divine filiation of the, 493
    elevation of, 378, 565
    holiness of, 378, 565, 625
    through the Incarnation, 383
    through justification, 625
    living, 625
    marriage between, 599 f., 605 f.
    participation in the Eucharistic sacri-
        fice by, 494 ff., 548
    priesthood of the, 398
    union with Christ in sacrifice, 501, 505,
        510
    union with the Holy Ghost, 385 f.
Mercy, divine: exhibited in the Incarna-
    tion, 419; in predestination, 729
Merit: cause of supernatural, 708; condi-
    tions of, 448, 451; heavenly glory as
    object of, 707; limitations of crea-
    ture's, 449; restrictions of Adam's,
    234

Merits of Christ
  all supernatural gifts through the, 388
  applied through the sacraments, 567, 569
  distinctive feature of, 235, 449
  free will and the, 447-52
  infinite, 455, 567
  justification by anticipation of, 645
  possession of God through the, 331
  possible without suffering, 454
  union with God purchased by the, 413
Metaphysics, supernatural, 478
Methodius, St.: on the Holy Ghost, 185 and note
Microcosm, the, 237, 362, 401
Miracle: of the beatific vision, 658, 660; of the hypostatic union, 407
Miracles
  causality of the saints in, 568
  of Christ, 336 f.
  credited to faith, 644
  interest of philosophy in, 743
  relation of the supernatural to, 743
  worked by men, 336
  wrought by divine power, 568
Mission of the Holy Ghost: function of the Eucharist in, 528; hypostatic, 385 f.; relation to the Son's mission, 529; see also Missions, divine
Mission of the Son of God: crowned in the Eucharist, 528; in the mystical body, 363, 396; relation to the mission of the Holy Ghost, 529; see also Missions, divine
Missions, divine
  activity of God in, 151 f.
  activity of the Holy Ghost in, 176 f.
  agency of the Eucharist in, 528
  appropriations of activity in, 176 ff.
  carrying out of the, 152, 176 ff.
  connection with the processions, 149
  different from human missions, 149
  effect of the, 150, 157
  hypostatic, 157, 160, 385 f.
  images of, 157
  by impression of the persons sent, 155 ff.
  without local motion, 150
  notion of, 150 ff., 155, 175 f.
  as prolongations of eternal processions, 157
  purpose of, 177 ff.
  real, 154
  restricted to the Son and the Holy Ghost, 149
  in sanctifying grace, 147, 154 ff., 165

Missions (continued)
  symbolic, 153
  Thomas Aquinas on, 148 note
  Trinity and Triunity manifested by, 179
  union of kinds of, 173 ff.
  visible, 153
Möhler, Adam: on effects of the Eucharist, 501 and note
Molina, Luis de: on predestination, 718, 720
Molinism, 720
Monologium by St. Anselm, 56
Morbida qualitas, 301
Mortal sin: malice of, 250, 255; nature of, 250; peculiar to the supernatural order, 250
Mortality of Christ, 329
Mortality of man: natural, 665, 667; origin of, 216
Motivation of the Incarnation, 353-56; see also Significance of the Incarnation
Motive of sin: in Adam and Eve, 265 f.; in Lucifer, 269
Mysteries: abundance of natural, 9; Christianity replete with, 3; obscurity of, 5
Mysteries, Christian
  conditions for understanding, 19, 735
  defective views of, 13 ff.
  God the center of, 775
  importance of, 13
  incomprehensibility of, 11, 19, 733
  position of the Eucharist in, 479, 481, 494 ff.
  as the proper domain of theology, 735-44
  purpose in isolating, 17
  rejected by rationalism, 20, 351
  relation of natural truths to, 15 f.
  relationship between, 477 ff., 527 ff., 758
  revelation of, 304
  sublimity of, 17
  supernatural organism of, 481, 758
  supernaturalness of, 17
  suprarationality of, 17
  system of, 14, 18, 733
  the Trinity as foundation of, 759
  unveiled in the beatific vision, 796
Mystery: in creation, 201-9; excluded from God's knowledge, 8; general notion of, 7 ff., 10, 651; religion inseparable from, 6; sacrament as synonymous with, 558

Mystery, Christian: essential elements of, 11; notion of, 10 f., 12 and note, 561

Mystery, sacramental, 558-66
essence of, 560
in general, 558
importance of, 561
mysteries of Christianity as, 560
in the original state, 564
significance of the, 561-66
theological mystery in, 559
two factors in, 559
visible element of, 559

Mystery in man, views on the, 203

Mystery of the beatific vision, 653, 658-62

Mystery of Christ, the, 3, 332 f.: incomprehensibility of, 335; indemonstrability of, 335 f.

Mystery of eternal life, 663 ff.

Mystery of glorification, 666-73, 683 f.

Mystery of iniquity, 245, 272 f., 307

Mystery of justification, 613-24, 641-46

Mystery of mysteries, 25

Mystery of original sin, 203 f., 353; see also Original sin

Mystery of predestination, 697-701, 712, 725; see also Predestination

Mystery of the Church, 539-42, 548; see also Church

Mystery of the Eucharist, 469-78, 561; see also Eucharist

Mystery of the Incarnation, 322, 353, 404; see also Incarnation

Mystery of the original state, 203; see also Original justice

Mystery of the Trinity; see Trinity

Mystical body contrasted with real body, 369

Mystical body of Christ, the
animated by the Holy Ghost, 394
Augustine on animation of, 394
building up of, 546 ff.
the Church as, 543, 552, 581
communication of divine life in, 392
destiny of, 439
divine nature communicated to, 363
extended through matrimony, 602
glory of, 657
growth of, 548
matrimony as illustration of, 372 n.
meaning of, 369
narrower sense of, 375
office of priests in, 546-50
presupposition of, 375
relation of baptism and faith to, 375
in relation to the whole race, 375, 390

Mystical body of Christ (continued)
represented in Christ's sacrifice, 439
rights of, 390, 394
supreme function of, 431

Naclantus on divine filiation, 384 note

Natur und Gnade by Scheeben, 128 note, 209 note, 631 note

Natural ancestry of the race, 365

Natural concept of God, 45, 125, 128

Natural order; see Order, natural

Natural union, 319 f.

Natural works of God, 202

Nature: corruption of, 303; as substratum of the supernatural order, 740, 746

Nature, divine; see Divine nature

Nature, human; see Human nature

Nestorianism: denial of the Real Presence in, 480 and note; the Incarnation in, 347; notion of Christ in, 320

Nestorius: denial of original sin by, 351; idea of the first man, 351; obscure doctrine on the Eucharist, 480 note; opposed by Cyril of Alexandria, 351; rejection of the God-man by, 351

Nicolas, A.: La vierge Marie et le plan divin, 465 note

Nirschl, J., 250 note

Objective revelation of the Trinity, 137 ff.

Ointment, divine, 332 f.

Old Law, symbolic sacrifices of the, 520

Old Testament, the
description of the future Redeemer in, 331 note
faith in the Redeemer in, 645
idea of God in, 30, 128
revelation through prophets in, 340
on union of Israel with Christ, 370 and note
union with Christ in, 375

Omnipresence of the divine persons, 150, 157

Oneness with Christ; see Union with Christ

Order, the natural: description of, 737 f.; elevation of, 741; God the center of, 737; as substructure of the supernatural order, 740, 746

Order, the supernatural
description of, 737 f.
enumeration of truths of, 738 f.
God as center of, 795
highest end of, 737, 795

Order, the supernatural (*continued*)
insight into, 758
nature as substructure of, 740, 746
necessity of faith for understanding, 762 f.
opposition of sin to, 247
re-establishment of, 353
Orders, holy: excellence of, 586; function of, 573; sacramental character in, 586; *sacramentum et res* in, 575 f.
Orders, power of, 550
Origin of sin, 261-67: theological opinion on the, 268-72
Original justice
Alexander of Hales on, 226 and note
Augustine on, 214, 228
Basil on, 227 and note
Bonaventure on, 226 and note
complex nature of, 222
conditions for preservation of, 282 f.
distinction between grace and integrity in, 225, 230
Duns Scotus on, 226 and note
effected by the Holy Ghost, 228
formal element of, 223
function of integrity in, 224
as gift to nature, 229 ff.
gratuitousness of, 235
hereditary character of, 231
material element of, 223
the material universe and, 237
mystery of, 223 f., 232 ff.
propagated by natural generation, 233
reason for name, 229 f.
relation of angels to, 237
restricted sense of, 225 f.
supernaturalness of, 229, 615
Thomas Aquinas on, 226 and note
transmission of, 230-34, 282, 296
union of holiness and integrity in, 222-28
universality of, 230-36, 282
when conferred, 225
Original sin
Ambrose on, 305
analysis of, 274-80, 282-88
attempts at rational demonstration of, 309
Augustine on, 285 f. and note, 301 f. and note
Bonaventure on, 292 and note
condition for knowing, 303 f.
connection with the Incarnation, 353 ff.
consequences of, 301, 306

Original sin (*continued*)
contrasted with state of pure nature, 301 f.
culpability of, 283-88, 295
culpable cause of, 284 f.
defective view of, 291 ff.
definition of, 284
deformity of, 279, 284-88
different from personal sin, 306
distinction between fault and deformity in, 285
and divine justice, 304
and divine mercy, 304 f.
elements composing, 273
formal element of, 288 ff., 305
guilt in, 286 ff.
hereditary character of, 284
imputability of, 283
inherence of, 285
knowability of, 281, 303
material element of, 291, 305
metaphorical expressions for, 300 ff.
as *morbida qualitas*, 301
mysterious character of, 204, 273, 305
mystery of the, 203 f.
nature of, 204, 290
nature of deformity in, 288-94
as opposed to integrity, 274
as opposed to sanctity, 275
poison of, 300
possibility of, 281 f.
punishment of, 308
rational speculation about, 307
rationalist distortion of, 351
in relation to Adam's sin, 284
in relation to original justice, 282 ff., 294
scholastic doctrine on, 302 and note
somber character of, 304
stain of, 300
three mysteries presupposed in, 303
transmission of, 282, 295-99
voluntariness of, 283, 286 f., 295
as wound, 300
Original state: mystery of the, 203, 305; relation of Christianity to the, 615; sacramental character of the, 564
Oswald on the sacramental character, 584 note

Paganism, sacredness of marriage in, 598 note
Pantheism, 125
Papacy: position in the Church, 553, 555; *see also* Pope

Paraclete, the, 111, 162 f., 177; *see also* Holy Ghost

Paradise: command given in, 265; justice in, 615; marriage in, 598, 600 f., 604; transfer of man to, 215

Participation in the divine nature
in the beatific vision, 658, 662, 664
through Christ as head, 390
by Christ's human nature, 322 ff., 738
Cyril of Alexandria on, 392 note
elevation of man to, 205 f.
through the Eucharist, 479, 488, 495
through grace, 619, 622, 738
likeness to the God-man through, 316, 382
the mystery of, 139, 207, 378
Peter Chrysologus on, 317 and note
transfiguration of man by, 653
union with God in, 408

Pascal, Blaise, 203 and note

Paschasius Radbertus: on Christ as mediator, 491 f. and note; on the purpose of the Eucharist, 486 note

Passibility of Christ, 328 f.

Passion of Christ: connection of sin with, 428; sacrificial character of, 437; satisfaction and merit in, 454, 632

Pastoral office, 551 f.

Pastoral power, the
distinct from power of orders, 551
functions of, 552-56
infallibility of, 554
subject of, 555
transmission of, 552
unity of, 552 ff.

Patristics, relation of Scholasticism to, 302 note

Paulinus of Nola on Christ's mediation, 409 note

Pelagianism: on God's will to save, 727; opposed by St. Augustine, 714 f. and note; predestination according to, 713 ff.; rationalist character of, 480

Pelagius: on predestination, 713; rejection of original sin by, 351

Penance (sacrament)
function of, 576
judicial process in, 577
justification in, 638 f.
relation to extreme unction, 577
remission of sin in, 576
sacramentum et res in, 578 note

Perdition, self-predestination to, 729

Perfection attainable without the Incarnation, 340 f.

Per modum naturae, communication of divine nature, 93 f.

Peristerium, 530

Perseverance in grace, 711, 724

Person (*see also* Hypostasis)
definition of, 71, 80
dignity of Christ's, 425
distinct from nature and essence, 71
distinction between hypostasis and, 71
in German theology, 69
importance in theology, 69
notion of divine, 80 ff.
rights of a, 72

Personal inhabitation of the Holy Ghost, 160-64, 166-71, 385 f.

Personality
analogy between divine and human, 80 ff.
Anselm on divine, 81 note
Augustine on divine, 81 note
Boethius on divine, 81 note
conditions requisite for, 71
essence of, 72
as perfection of spirit, 69
retained in reception of grace, 316

Persons in God, 26, 51; *see also* Divine persons; Trinity

Perspective in theology, 19 f.

Petavius on distinction between divine generation and procession, 94 note

Peter (apostle), faith of, 517

Peter de Blois on Christ's Eucharistic existence, 476 note

Peter Chrysologus, St.: on anointing of Christ, 381 and note; on participation in the divine nature, 317 and note; on the purpose of the Incarnation, 379 and note

"Philosopher's cross," the, 302

Philosophical significance of the Trinity, 124 ff.

Philosophy
applied, 743
certitude in, 745
distinct from theology, 733 f., 744, 760
handmaid of theology, 778, 786
limitations of, 761, 791
nature of, 124, 735, 739
relation of theology to, 744 f., 760, 778-88
revelation not necessary for, 125 f.
study of miracles in, 743

Pius IX: on matrimony, 608 note, 609 note; on the nature of dogma, 739 note

Pius XI: *Casti connubii* (encyclical), 594 note
Pius credulitatis affectus, 764
Pledge of divine love as name of the Holy Ghost, 67, 112
Poena afflictiva, 686
Poena damni, 686 f.
Poena sensus, 686
Pontificale Romanum on the Eucharistic sacrifice, 510 note
Pope, the: dependence of priests and faithful on, 552; dignity of, 556; infallibility of, 554 f.; plenitude of power in, 552-57
Possession of the divine persons, 158, 166
Possibility, intrinsic, 754
Power
  experienced by Christians, 775
  of jurisdiction, 550
  legislative, 550
  of orders, 550
  pastoral, 551-56
  sacerdotal, 551
  of the supreme pontiff, 552-56
  teaching, 550
Praedestinatio efficax, 704 and note
Praevisa merita, 708
Predestination
  activity of God in, 700, 709, 722
  antecedent, 703 and note
  Augustine on, 703 note, 713, 715 and note
  Augustinian theologians on, 718 ff.
  Bonaventure on, 703 note
  as cause of salvation, 701
  in Christ, 730
  consequent, 703 and note
  cooperation of free will with, 703, 708 f., 725
  defective theories of, 712-20
  defined by St. Augustine, 698 and note
  divine providence in, 724
  effect on fallen man, 711
  effective, 702 ff., 709 f.
  as election, 724
  freedom of man's will in, 700, 708 ff.
  fundamentally identical with God's salvific will, 702
  general notion of, 698
  God's foreknowledge in, 703 and note, 708 f.
  God's love in, 729 f.
  God's mercy and justice in, 729
  gratuitousness of, 706 ff., 724

Predestination (*continued*)
  Gregory of Valencia on, 720-24
  infallibility of, 705 f., 708-11, 730
  Molina on, 718, 720
  mysterious character of, 697-701, 708, 730
  nature of, 698 ff., 712
  object of, 699
  particular, 702, 705, 709
  predeterminist theories of, 717
  process of, 701, 705, 709
  proper meaning of, 699, 707
  properties of, 705
  Prosper of Aquitaine on, 703 note
  rationalist view of, 712 ff.
  relation of particular to universal, 702, 705, 707 f.
  scriptural sense of, 698, 702
  self-activity of man in, 700, 703, 725
  significance of, 708, 725, 730
  somber aspects of, 697, 725, 728
  supernaturalness of, 700 f., 705 f.
  theological importance of, 701
  Thomas Aquinas on, 700 and note, 724
  Thomistic theory of, 718 ff.
  ultramystic view of, 717-20
  unconditional, 706
  universal, 702, 704 f., 730
  unmerited, 706
  virtual, 703
Predestined, number of the, 728
Predeterminism in predestination, 717
Preparation for justification, 638 ff., 646, 724
Prevenient grace: dependence of merit on, 707; elevation of will by, 639; supernatural activity through, 631, 640; vocation to faith and justice by, 709
Prevision; *see* Foreknowledge of God
Priest: activity of Christ through the, 545, 556; blessing imparted in marriage by the, 606, 609 and note; definition of, 437; function in the Church, 546-50, 555; relationship to Christ and to the Holy Ghost, 556
Priesthood: activity in the Church, 546-50; of the race, 398
Priesthood of Christ, the
  activity of Christ centered in, 411, 585
  eternal, 444
  exercised on behalf of creatures, 412
  according to the order of Melchisedech, 443, 518
  perfection of, 436

Priesthood of Christ (*continued*)
relation of mediation to, 412
relation of sacramental character to, 585

Priesthood of the Church, the
Blessed Virgin compared with, 546
dignity of, 548, 556
educational authority of, 551
fruitfulness of, 549, 556
motherhood compared with, 547, 556
mystery of, 548

Prince of darkness, 310

Principle: of all being, 26, 141; difference between cause and, 121

Privation of justice, 251

Process of justification, 616, 623, 631-35

Procession: meaning of, 96, 103-5; Albert the Great on, 104 note

Procession of the Holy Ghost
Alexander of Hales on, 109
Augustine on, 106
as basis of adoptive sonship, 143 ff.
Bonaventure on, 109
Cyril of Alexandria on, 111 note
Duns Scotus on, 108 and note
Ruiz de Montoya on, 108 note
Thomas Aquinas on, 108

Procession of the Son continued in the Incarnation, 359

Processions: in God, 53, 68, 149; prolongation of divine, 147, 155; see also Divine productions

Production: of the Second Person, 79, 87-95; in theory of transubstantiation, 498; of the Third Person, 79, 88

Production in God, 53, 56-65 (see also Divine productions)
existence of, 56
the first, 74 f., 85
generation as the first, 85
meaning of, 74
the second, 75 f., 85
spiration as the second, 76, 102, 111

Productivity in God, 37, 73

Products of divine productions, 62, 65-69, 73-80

Prolongation: of divine processions, 147, 155, 423; of Trinitarian relations, 136 f., 445, 494; of the Trinity in the Incarnation, 359-62, 396

Propagation of original justice, 230-34

Propensity to sin, 251, 259, 279 ff.

Properties of the glorified body, 673-81

Proprietorship restricted to persons, 72

Prosper of Aquitaine on predestination, 703 note

Protestantism: justification in teaching of, 627; non-imputability of sin taught in, 618; see also Reformation

Providence, divine: hidden judgments of, 729; the Incarnation and, 355; plans of, 404; in predestination, 724; in redemption of man, 454

Prudentius: *Apotheosis*, 390 note

Pseudo-Dionysius on Holy Communion, 492 note

Punishment
everlasting, 685
gravity of eternal, 687, 691, 693
nature of eternal, 686-94
of original sin, 308
of personal sin, 255, 287, 684-94
supernatural aspect of eternal, 687

Purpose of the Incarnation, 172, 354 f., 377-89 (see also Significance of the Incarnation)
Athanasius on, 379 and note
Augustine on, 378 and note, 382 and note
Bernard on, 420 note
Hilary of Poitiers on, 378
Irenaeus on, 380 and notes
Leo the Great on, 379 and note, 382 and note
Maximus Martyr on, 379 and note
Peter Chrysologus on, 379 and note
Thomas Aquinas on, 417, 422

Qualitas morbida, 301

Qualities: of Christ's body, 519; of wisdom, 792

Qualities of the glorified body: connection with the soul's happiness, 674; explanation of, 673; number of, 673, 675 and note; reason for, 679; supernaturalness of, 678

Quid est homo by Casinius, 209 note, 301 note, 316 note

Race; see Human race

Ratio, 751

Rationalism
attitude toward theology, 20
defective view of sacraments in, 567 f.
notion of justification in, 614
predestination according to, 712 ff.
rejection of Christian mysteries by, 351
rejection of hell-fire by, 691
rejection of the Incarnation by, 341, 346

Rationalism, moderate: efforts to conceive the Incarnation, 338
Rationes aeternae, 792
Raymond Lully, 25
Raymond of Sabunde, 37 and note
Real Presence, the: of Christ in the Eucharist, 470 f.; connection of Eucharistic sacrifice with, 495; undivided in many hosts, 512
Reason
autonomy of, 780 ff., 788
dominion of faith over, 779, 782, 785
elevated by faith, 748 f., 761, 780
and faith, 15 ff., 778-88
faith as representative of divine, 779
function in theology, 744, 747 f., 780-88
limited in knowing God, 57
as *pedisequa* of faith, 780
as *praeambula* of faith, 780
in service of faith, 780 ff.
service of faith to, 782 f. and note
union of faith with, 784-88
Reasoning, two methods of, 335
Reatus culpae, 251 and note, 255
Reatus poenae, 251 and note, 256
Reconciliation with God: without the Incarnation, 347 f.; possibility of, 347; after repeated sins, 347
Rectitude of nature, 216 ff.; *see also* Integrity
Redeemer: described in the Old Testament, 331 note; function of the, 333, 353; *see also* Christ; God-man
Redemption, the
effect of, 613
effected by the God-man, 376, 454
as end of Christ's sacrifice, 452
free will and, 447
goal of, 613
inadequate views of, 502
without the Incarnation, 343-47, 423
methods of, 346, 354
modern theories of, 452
notion of, 353
Re-establishment of the supernatural order, 353
Reformation, the: defective views of redemption in, 502; on the function of faith in justification, 643 f.; theory of man's depravity in, 502; *see also* Protestantism
Regeneration: effects of, 624; as fundamental process in justification, 623; relation between justification and, 613, 623 f., 632 ff

Relations in God, 52 f., 81, 115; *see also* Divine persons; Divine productions; Trinity
Relationship: of creatures to God, 141; among the divine persons, 51, 81, 115
Religion inseparable from mystery, 6
Remission of sin: effected by Christ's sacrifice, 452; through the Incarnation, 420; interior renewal in, 616-22, 624; repentance required for, 636, 639; in the sacrament of penance, 576
Renovation, interior, 618 f.
Repentance: required for remission of sin, 636, 639; in the sacrament of penance, 576
Reprobation, 726, 728 f.
Reproduction: of Christ's body in transubstantiation, 498 ff.; of Trinitarian relations, 136 f., 141 f.; *see also* Prolongation
Res sacramenti: in Christian matrimony, 607; notion of, 572, 578 note, 579
Restoration: through Christ, 209, 352, 354 f.; of nature, 343, 352; relationship to elevation of man, 399 f.
Resurrection of Christ: effected by the Holy Ghost, 518; Eucharistic state compared with, 514 f.; man's resurrection modeled on the, 669; relation of Mass to the, 509; sacrificial significance of the, 436, 443
Resurrection of the body; *see* Body, resurrection of
Retribution: as effect of sin, 251; eternal, 685
Revelation
attitude toward, 7, 16
in the beatific vision, 129
belief in divine, 765, 780
criterion of, 746
demonstration of fact of, 745, 747, 768
divine works and, 11
of God's plan, 792
of individual truths, 747
mysteries a category of, 13, 18
necessary for knowing beatific vision, 658, 661
reason and, 15 ff., 780; *see also* Faith
of supernatural truths, 740
of the Trinity, 28
Reward, everlasting, 685
Richard of St. Victor
contributions to Trinitarian doctrine by, 56
demonstration of the Trinity by, 25 and note, 38 and note, 40

Richard of St. Victor (*continued*)
  Greek Trinitarian tradition followed
    by, 74 note
  on necessity of faith for knowledge of
    Trinity, 50
  theological procedure of, 765 f.
  on the Third Person, 76 note
Rites, function of sacramental, 568
Robert Grosseteste (of Lincoln) on
    Holy Communion, 492 note
Roman Catechism, the: on the beatific
    vision, 659 and note; on original jus-
    tice, 211, 223, 228; on sanctifying
    grace, 619 note
Rosmini, condemnation of transubstan-
    tiation theory of, 499 and note
Ruiz de Montoya: on the divine mis-
    sions, 148 note; on the procession of
    the Holy Ghost, 108 note; on the
    Trinity, 51, 57 note
Rupert of Deutz on Christ's sacrifice,
    521 note

Sacrament
  definition of, 567
  inadequate notion of, 567
  mystery as synonymous with, 558
  original meaning of, 558
  relation of interior to exterior, 580
  wider sense of, 559
Sacramental character; *see* Character,
    sacramental
Sacramental mystery; *see* Mystery, sac-
    ramental
Sacramental order, basis of, 563
Sacraments, the
  activity of the Holy Ghost in, 568-71
  causality in producing grace, 568; *see
    also* Sacraments, causality of
  common effect of, 572
  connection of the Eucharist with
    other, 571
  connection with structure of the
    Church, 580
  consecratory, 572-76
  contact with Christ in, 464
  difference among, 572
  effect of, 568 f.
  effect of hierarchical, 579
  effect of non-hierarchical, 579
  efficacy of, 570
  efficacy of medicinal, 578
  hierarchical, 579
  immediate purpose of medicinal, 576
  indissolubility of consecratory, 574

Sacraments (*continued*)
  instrumentality of, 568; *see also* Sacra-
    ments, causality of
  justification through, 632 f.
  medicinal, 572, 576 ff., 581
  merits of Christ applied through, 567,
    569
  miraculous power of, 569
  mysterious character of, 567, 569
  non-hierarchical, 579
  ordinary means of grace, 464
  production of grace by various, 575
  proximate effect of consecratory, 574
  rationalist view of, 567 f.
  relationship among, 572-82
  specific element of consecratory, 574
  structure of medicinal, 578
  supernaturalness of, 581
  system of, 580
  two classes of, 572, 579
Sacraments, causality of
  exemplified in the Eucharist, 571
  hyperphysical, 571
  moral, 569
  mystery of, 571
  objection against physical, 579
  physical, 571, 579 f.
Sacramentum, 558
Sacramentum et res: in Christian matri-
    mony, 607; function of, 573 f., 579;
    in medicinal sacraments, 578 note;
    nature of, 579 f., 582; in various sac-
    raments, 575 ff., 578 note
Sacramentum plenum, 560
Sacramentum ratum, 579
Sacramentum tantum, 575, 579: in Chris-
    tian matrimony, 607
Sacramentum vacuum, 559
Sacred Heart, 447 note
Sacrifice
  alteration of gift in, 433
  distinction between offerer and gift in,
    433
  distinctive features of, 433 ff.
  general notion of, 432
  glorification of God by, 431
  material, 435
  minimum requirements of, 433
  nature of oblation in, 433
  realized ideal of, 435 f.
  significance of oblation in, 433
  specific meaning of, 432
  in the spirit world, 432 f.
  suffering in propitiatory, 426
  supposition of interior, 435
  surrender of self in, 432-35

Sacrifice (*continued*)
  symbolic, 431, 434
  theory of, 508
  of the whole Christ, 494 ff.
Sacrifice of Christ (*see also* Eucharistic
    sacrifice; Mass)
  Augustine on, 428 note
  Bernard on, 436 note
  connection between satisfaction and
    merit in, 454
  continued in His members, 494
  continued in the mystical body, 439,
    494
  as culmination of His life, 437
  Cyril of Alexandria on, 438 note
  effects of the, 441 f.
  efficacy of the, 443
  essence of the, 432
  Eucharistic, 494 ff.; *see also* Eucharistic
    sacrifice
  form of the, 432
  as holocaust, 436, 442 f.
  ideal of all sacrifice, 432
  ideal of the community's sacrifice, 439
  impetratory character of, 432, 443
  infinite value of, 435, 442 ff.
  latreutic character of, 432, 442 f., 452
  Leo the Great on, 438
  mediatorial character of, 443
  merit of, 447
  meritorious value of, 453 ff.
  nature of, 432, 435
  offered by the Church, 507, 510
  offered for the universe, 438, 444
  participation in the Eucharistic, 495
  propitiatory character of, 432, 442
  propitiatory value of, 452 ff.
  re-enaction of, 494 ff.
  representative of divine love, 444 ff.
  rooted in the Trinity, 446
  Rupert of Deutz on, 521 note
  significance for the universe, 444 ff.
  significance of transubstantiation in,
    505-11
  significance of the Resurrection and
    Ascension in, 436 f., 443
  social character of, 437
  as thankoffering, 443
  union of offerer and victim in, 435 f.
Sacrifice, latreutic: characteristic of
    Christ's sacrifice, 431 f.; definition
    of, 434 note; end of, 432; perfection
    of, 431, 433, 435
Sacrificial gift (*see also* Sacrificial vic-
    tim)
  distinct from offerer, 433

Sacrificial gift (*continued*)
  effect of transubstantiation on man's,
    506
  offered through consecration, 507
  presented by the community, 437
  representative character of the, 437
  significance of donation of the,
    433 f.
  value of the, 508
Sacrificial ideal realized, 433
Sacrificial oblation, significance of,
    434 f.
Sacrificial victim, the (*see also* Sacri-
    ficial gift)
  alteration required in, 433
  Christ as the eternal, 519
  destruction of, 433, 505
  ennobling of, 434 f.
  in Eucharistic sacrifice, 505 f.
  God's possession of, 426, 519
  significance in annhilating, 434
Saints: causality in working miracles,
    568; motive in suffering, 426
Salvation
  God's choice of all men for, 724
  hope of, 707, 710
  without the Incarnation, 344
  notion of, 652
  predestination as cause of, 701
  worked out with fear and trembling,
    725 f.
Salvific will of God
  absolute, 703 note
  antecedent, 703 and note, 706, 728
  conditional, 703 note, 728
  consequent, 703 and note, 709, 728
  effective, 702, 704, 728
  particular, 702 f., 728
  predestination fundamentally identical
    with, 702
  twofold, 702
  universal, 702, 704 f., 724
Sanctification: through the Holy Ghost,
    113; relation between justification
    and, 613, 623 f.; transfiguration and,
    654
Sanctifying grace (*see also* Adoptive
    sonship; Grace)
  incompatibility of sin with, 326, 619,
    623
  lost through sin, 326, 619
  nature of, 568 f., 620, 648
  relation of actual grace to, 722 f.
  relation of integrity to, 628 f.
  Scotist theory of, 212
  as source of integrity, 221

Sanctity (*see also* Holiness; Justice; Justice and holiness)
causes of human, 167
of Christ, 168
formal cause of, 167
meaning of, 112
opposition of sin to, 245, 251, 619 f.
perfected through glory, 326
possible without integrity, 297
as state of the soul, 167
Satisfaction: application of Christ's, 577; through Christ, 330, 617, 632; impossible by sinner's efforts, 346, 453, 619; offered in Christ's sacrifice, 442 f., 453; sin remissible without, 344, 354
Schäzler, K. von: on justification, 639 f. and note
Schlünkes, F., 292 and note
Scholasticism: distinction between *amor notionalis* and *amor essentialis* in, 63 note; notion of original justice in, 223; original sin in, 302 and note; relation of Patristics to, 302 note
Science
apprehension of object of, 751
meaning of, 733
natural, 735
objective, 733, 758
objective perfection of, 789
subjective, 733, 758
subjective perfection of, 789 f.
sublimity of theological, 789, 792 f.
transcendental, 791
understanding of object of, 751
unity of theological, 789
universality of theological, 789
Scientia media, 720
Scientia sapida, 793
Scotists: sanctifying grace according to, 212; on the spiration of the Holy Ghost, 107
Scotus, Duns: on original justice, 226 and note; on possessing the Holy Ghost, 108 and note; on Richard of St. Victor's Trinitarian demonstration, 29 note
Scripture, Sacred: appropriations in, 135; on Christ's union with the race, 370 f.
Second justification, 646 ff.
Second Person in God: names of the, 84, 98; as personal Word of God, 77; production of the, 87-95; procession from the Father, 84; *see also* Logos; Son of God; Word of God

Selection of graces, 727 ff.
Self-consciousness as mark of personality, 72
Self-determination in predestination, 717
Self-renunciation of Christ, 328, 443, 450
Self-surrender in justification, 638, 643
Sigh of love, the Holy Ghost as, 66, 77, 88
Significance of the Eucharist
in Christ's sacramental existence, 512-22
in continuation of Christ's sacrifice, 494-97
as extension of the Incarnation, 486-89, 494
in general, 479-82
in incorporation in Christ, 483 ff.
in reception of Holy Communion, 523-27
Significance of the Incarnation
in Christ's mediatory office, 405-14
in communicating divine life, 389-96
in communicating divine nobility, 376-89
Cyril of Alexandria on, 380 f. and notes, 533
in glorification of God, 396 f., 421, 425 f.
in prolongation of Trinitarian processions, 360 ff., 396, 416
in redemption of man, 419-22, 613
subjective, 415-18
survey of, 398 ff., 403, 416
for the whole universe, 401 ff.
Significance of predestination, 708, 725, 730
Significance of transubstantiation: for Eucharistic sacrifice, 505-11; for incorporation in Christ, 500 f.; for interior renewal, 501; for man's transformation, 502 ff.
Significance of the Trinity: philosophical, 124 ff.; in prolongation of Trinitarian relations, 136 f.; in reproduction of Trinitarian relations, 136 f.; theological, 127 ff., 180
Simplicity of God, 47, 51, 87
Sin
of Adam and Eve, 265 f.
actual; *see* Actual sin
as affront to God, 344, 686
of the angel, 263 ff.
as annihilation of likeness to God, 258
as aversion from God, 256, 262, 274
committed by child of God, 345
compensation for, 313, 427

Sin (continued)
  conquest of, 428, 668
  consequences of, 249-59; see also Punishment
  as conversio ad creaturam, 256, 274, 279
  defilement of, 256 ff., 279
  definition of, 244 f.
  diabolical, 264
  difference between personal and original, 306
  difference in men and in angels, 266
  effect in rebellious angels, 265
  effects in the sinner, 246-51, 255, 266
  God's purpose in permitting, 309
  gravity in the supernatural order, 346
  habitual; see Habitual sin
  as hatred of God, 264
  as impediment to grace, 636
  incompatibility of grace with, 326, 619 f., 623
  incomprehensibility of, 255
  knowability of, 244
  mortal, 250, 255
  motive of the first, 265 f.
  mysterious character of, 245 ff., 616
  as a mystery of evil, 243 ff.
  in the natural order, 245 f.
  nature of, 243, 248, 686
  origin of, 261-67
  original; see Original sin
  possibility of, 259 ff.
  presuppositions of, 261 f.
  as privation of supernatural justice, 251
  propensity to, 251, 259, 279 ff.
  punishment of, 255 f., 287, 686-94
  as rebellion against Christ, 268-72
  relation to the Incarnation, 421
  remission through infusion of grace, 620
  remitted in sacrament of penance, 576
  removed in justification, 614-22
  as stain on the soul, 256 ff., 279
  state of, 615; see also Habitual sin
  in the supernatural order, 246 ff., 636, 685
  theological, 244, 256
  venial, 257
Sin, hereditary; see Original sin
Sin, original; see Original sin
Sinlessness of Christ, 326 f.
Sinners, punishment of, 684-94
Society, the Church as a, 539 f.
Socinianism, 347
Solidarity of human race, 363, 366, 376

Son of God, the (see also Second Person in God; Word of God)
  fellowship with, 179
  generation of, 85-95, 423
  God's love of man in, 709
  head of the Church, 539
  mission crowned in the Eucharist, 528
  mission in the Incarnation, 153, 359, 363
  model of God's adopted sons, 383 f.
  as object of our happiness, 175
  reborn in creatures, 179
  threefold manifestation of, 478
Son of man; see Christ; God-man; Son of God
Son as name of the Second Person, 84
Sonship, adoptive; see Adoptive sonship
Soul, the
  acts of, 77
  as analogon of Christ's Eucharistic existence, 474
  as cause of body's accidents, 475
  dominion of body by, 677-80
  effect of sin on, 252 f.
  as form of the body, 320, 676 f.
  immortality of, 652, 663
  infusion of, 458
  marriage of God with, 633 ff., 637 ff., 648
  powers of the glorified, 677 f.
  surrender in justification, 638
  worthiness to receive justification, 637
Speculation, theological, 749
Spiration of the Holy Ghost, 76, 102 f., 111
Spirit: meanings of, 96-102; as name of the Third Person, 97 f.; original sense of, 97
Spirit, Holy; see Holy Ghost; Third Person in God
Spiritualization of the glorified body: cause of, 677; effected by the Holy Ghost, 656, 680; foundation of, 676 f.; nature of, 656, 673
Spiritus Christi, 385
Spiritus vivificans, 549
Stain of original sin, 300
Status exaltationis, 424 note
Status exinanitionis, 424 note
Status viae, 326, 709
Suarez, Francis: on the divine missions, 148 note; on justification, 626 note; on punishments of hell, 694 note; on salvation without the Incarnation, 344 note; on the Trinity, 51 note, 57 note

Subsistence, 70, 72

Substance: distinction between hypostasis and, 70; oneness of the divine, 150; relationship between accident and, 478

Subtility of the glorified body, 673 ff., 677

Suffering, motive of the saints in, 426

Sufferings of Christ: justification of, 428; in His mystical body, 370 and note; motives of, 425 f.; relation of sin to, 427

Summa contra Gentiles by St. Thomas Aquinas, 767

Summa theologica by St. Thomas Aquinas, 790

Supernatural, the: distinct from the natural, 202; understanding of, 770

Supernatural elevation; *see* Adoptive sonship; Elevation of man

Supernatural elevation of creatures, 205 ff.

Supernatural fellowship with God, 206; *see also* Participation in the divine nature

Supernatural metaphysics, 478

Supernatural order; *see* Order, supernatural

Supernatural union with God, 220; *see also* Union with God

Supernatural works of God, 202, 755

Suppositum; *see* Hypostasis

Suprarationality of mysteries, 17

Syllabus of Pius IX, 609 note

System of Christian truths, 14, 18, 763

Tertullian on Christ's mediatorship, 409 f. and note

Theandric character, 582, 585

Theodore Abucara, 391 and note

Theodore of Mopsuestia, rejection of original sin by, 351

Theodoret: on Eucharistic union with Christ, 483 note; on the Incarnation and the Eucharist, 480 note

Theological significance of the Trinity, 127 ff., 180

Theological virtues, 619: Thomas Aquinas on, 767 note

Theology
apprehension of ultimate causes in, 759, 792
cause of objects of, 755
certitude in, 745, 749, 790
Christ as ideal of, 793 ff.
as Christian wisdom, 795

Theology (*continued*)
cognitive principle of, 734, 739, 750
conditions for independence of, 723
connection of the Incarnation with, 793 ff.
consistency of principles of, 764
deduction in, 749, 763
defective views on the nature of, 740, 742
demonstration in, 747-50
distinct from philosophy, 733 f., 744, 760
as divine wisdom, 792 ff.
evidence of principles of, 790
function of faith in, 734, 744, 748
function of reason in, 744, 747 f., 780-88
God's wisdom as source of, 793
historical procedure in, 747
infallibility of principles of, 745
logical coherence of, 790
material causality studied in, 759
nature of, 739, 748
as participation in God's knowledge, 792
perspective in, 19 f.
philosophy as handmaid of, 778, 786
place of natural truths in, 740 f.
pre-eminent among sciences, 792
principles accepted on faith, 763 f., 768, 790
progress of, 86
proper object of, 734-44, 792, 795
rationalist attitude toward, 20
relation of evidence to, 746 f.
relation of natural to supernatural truths in, 759 f.
relation of philosophy to, 744 f., 760, 778-88
as science of faith, 789
scientific excellence of, 789, 792 f.
scientific knowledge of, 744-50
scientific value of, 744
as a special science, 17 f., 733 f., 739
specific domain of, 734-44
subject matter of, 789
sublimity of, 789, 792 f.
supreme end of, 795
Thomas Aquinas on nature of, 739 note
union of faith and understanding in, 762, 768 f.
unity of, 789
unity of cognitive principle in, 750
universality of, 789
use of analogous concepts in, 754, 759

Third Person in God (*see also* Holy Ghost)
  Ambrose on names of the, 97
  Augustine on names of the, 97 and note, 99 note
  communication of the divine nature to, 75
  created analogue of, 95 note, 181-89
  essential holiness of, 112
  lack of name parallel to Son, 95
  names of, 84, 96 ff., 110 ff.
  personality of, 76
  procession of, 79; *see also* Procession of the Holy Ghost
  product of divine love, 77 ff.
  Richard of St. Victor on, 76 note
  as seal of unity, 97
  spiration of, 76, 102 f., 111
Thomas Aquinas, St.
  on appropriations, 134 note
  on the appropriations of the Holy Ghost, 190-97
  avoidance of rationalism in Trinitarian doctrine, 34
  on the beatific vision, 767, 790
  on the causality exercised by Christ, 456
  on the difference between theology and philosophy, 741 note
  on the divine missions, 148 note
  on eternal life, 664 note
  on friendship with God, 128 note
  on the generation of the Son, 91 note
  on the gifts of the Holy Ghost, 777 note
  on glorification of the body, 676 note
  on the indemonstrability of the Trinity, 26 and note, 41 and note
  on man's supernatural destiny, 790
  on motivation of the Incarnation, 417, 422
  on the nature of theology, 739 note
  on original justice, 226 and note
  on possessing God, 158 note
  on predestination, 700 and note, 724
  procedure in Trinitarian doctrine, 54 ff., 68, 790
  on the procession of the Holy Ghost, 108
  on relation of the natural to the supernatural, 760 note
  on sacramental character, 587 and note
  on salvation without the Incarnation, 344 note
  on subtility of the glorified body, 674 f. and note, 677 f.

Thomas Aquinas (*continued*)
  Summa contra Gentiles, 767
  Summa theologica, 790
  on supernatural faith, 767 and note
  theological procedure of, 766 f., 790
  on the theological virtues, 767 note
Toledo, Eleventh Council of (675), 64, 133 note
Transcendency of the Incarnation, 342
Transfiguration: of natural concepts, 772; negative, 686-93; relation of integrity to, 387, 679
Transfiguration of Christ, 323 ff., 331, 337
Transfiguration of man (*see also* Body, transfiguration of)
  in the beatific vision, 662
  effected by the Holy Ghost, 654, 656
  mystery of, 655, 657
  nature of, 653 f.
  by participation in divine nature, 653
  patterned on the Incarnation, 656
  relation of sanctification to, 654
  supernaturalness of, 653, 655
Transformation: of the faithful into Christ, 501-4, 544, 775; inadequate to explain transubstantiation, 498 f.; of will, 618
Transmission of original justice, 230-34, 282, 296
Transmission of original sin: erroneous theory of, 299; explanation of, 298; as juridicial inheritance, 299; nature of, 295 ff.
Transubstantiation, 497-511
  adduction theory of, 497
  Caesarius of Arles on, 504 note
  deification of man modeled on, 502 f.
  Franzelin on, 499 note
  Gregory of Nyssa on, 498 and note
  inadequacy of adduction in, 497
  inadequacy of transformation in, 498 f.
  incorporation in Christ effected by, 500 f.
  John Damascene on, 498 note
  meaning of, 497 ff.
  minimum requirements of, 497
  natural conversion different from, 498
  production of Christ's body in, 498
  relation of interior renewal to, 502, 506
  reproduction of Christ's body in, 498 ff.
  sacrificial action constituted by, 506-10
  significance of, 500-511
  union with sacrificial Victim by, 506

Trent, Council of
  on Christ as source of grace, 457 and
    note
  on concupiscence, 630
  on efficient cause of justification, 632
    and note
  on matrimony, 607 note
  on the nature of justification, 623 and
    note, 624, 627
  on original justice, 227
Trinitarian productions, continuation of,
  129, 359-62, 494
Trinitarian relations, extension of, 136 f.,
  142, 445
Trinity, the (see also Divine persons; Divine productions)
  absence of contradiction in, 119 ff.
  attempts to demonstrate: by Gün-
    ther's school, 26; by Raymond
    Lully, 25; by Richard of St. Victor,
    25, 29 note, 38 and note; by St.
    Anselm, 25, 34 and note; by St.
    Bonaventure, 34 note, 39 and note
  Augustine on, 56, 74 note, 148
  certitude of productions in, 56
  "construction" of, 35, 50, 118
  criticism of attempts to demonstrate,
    29-43
  distinction between persons and es-
    sence in, 120 note
  dogma of, 26, 50, 63
  essence of, 26, 141
  foundation of all Christian mysteries,
    759
  function of faith in knowledge of, 54
  God's purpose in revealing, 127, 130,
    142; see also Significance of the
    Trinity
  inconceivability of, 47 f., 118, 121 f.
  indemonstrability of, 26-29, 42, 125
  mysterious character of, 25, 48
  necessity of, 313
  necessity of productions and proces-
    sions in, 54
  as object of theology, 131, 759
  objective revelation of, 136 ff.
  philosophical significance of, 124 ff.
  procedure in explaining, 53 ff.
  prolongation through the Incarnation,
    359-62, 396
  ramifications in the order of grace,
    147 f.
  reflection of, 131 f., 139
  relation of created world with, 147
  relation of the Eucharist to, 477 ff.,
    489-96, 528

Trinity (continued)
  relation to other dogmas, 131 ff., 528
  relations of the God-man with, 359-64
  relationship of the Incarnation to, 398
  revelation of, 28
  root of the dogma of, 118
  Ruiz de Montoya on, 51, 57
  significance of; see Significance of the
    Trinity
  supernaturalness of, 43 ff.
  teaching of the Church on, 26
  theological demonstration of, 50-54
  theological significance of, 127 ff., 180
  Thomas Aquinas on, 74 note, 790
  transcendental character of, 125, 127
  unity in, 114 ff., 179
Triunity in the Trinity, 114 ff., 179
Trullan Council (692), 488
Truth: knowledge of created, 735;
    knowledge of supernatural, 736;
    principle of supernatural, 736;
    sphere of supernatural, 736; two dif-
    ferent kinds of, 735
Truths, natural: domain of, 737; place in
    theology, 740 f.; relation of super-
    natural truths to, 736, 743 f., 759 f.
Truths, supernatural
  ascertaining of, 747, 750
  competency of reason in, 742 ff.
  enumeration of, 738 f.
  harmony among, 750, 769
  hierarchy of, 737
  indirect proof of, 769 f.
  interdependence of, 736
  knowledge of God conveyed by, 737
  objective system of, 763
  as objects of a special science, 736
  relation of natural truths to, 736,
    743 f., 759 f.
  revelation of, 740
  understood by children, 773
Truths, system of, 751, 763, 769
Truths, theological
  connection between, 750, 769
  faith as basis of, 747 f.
  inconceivability of, 754 f.
  reduced to few principles, 750
  scientific knowledge of, 744-50
  scientific value of, 764
  understanding of, 752-61, 768

Unbelief, 271
Understanding: gift of, 777; of revealed
    truths, 752-61, 768
Unguent of the Holy Ghost, 332 and
    note

Union: between body and soul, 320, 434, 676; natural, 319 f.; in one Christ, 333, 366-75; *see also* Incorporation in Christ; Mystical body of Christ

Union with Christ
Athanasius on, 390 note
effects of, 513
energy imparted by, 513
in the Eucharist, 482, 493, 528
in the Eucharistic sacrifice, 501, 505, 518 f.
in glorifying God, 397, 495
in Holy Communion, 500, 543, 566
Irenaeus on, 392
Leo the Great on, 486 f. and note
living and organic, 375, 397, 625
marriage as analogy of, 483 f., 493
in the Old Law, 375 and note
physical, 483
prior to baptism, 375
purpose of, 378
through the sacramental character, 583 ff.
satisfaction through, 376

Union of Christ with the Church: Christian marriage as organ of, 573, 602, 605; Christian marriage rooted in, 601 f.; Christian marriage as the sacrament of, 600; marriage as figure of, 235, 543, 601 ff.

Union with God
through Christ, 406 f., 411 f.
Cyril of Alexandria on, 407 and note, 532 ff.
in divine missions, 154, 159
in eternity, 179
in the Eucharist, 479 f., 489, 493
by grace, 159, 317, 619 f.
Hilary of Poitiers on, 407 and note
in justification, 634 f.
natural, 348
in love and fruition, 130
potency in nature for, 320
purchased by Christ's merits, 413
purpose of, 408
restored by Christ, 313
two kinds of supernatural, 220

Union with the Holy Ghost, 626 f.; *see also* Indwelling of the Holy Ghost

Union, hypostatic; *see* Hypostatic union

Union, matrimonial: nature of, 372; sacred character of natural, 595, 597 f. and note; sanctification of, 578; supernatural character of, 593; *see also* Marriage; Matrimony

Unity
of Christ, 318
of the Church, 552 ff.
of the human race, 363-66, 368, 376
of the marriage bond, 594, 596
three kinds of real, 534
in the Trinity, 114 ff., 133, 179

Universality of the original justice, 230-36

Valencia, Gregory of: on predestination, 720-24

Vasquez, Gabriel: on Eucharistic union with Christ, 483 note

Vatican Council: on mysteries, 11 note; on the papacy, 553

Venial sin, 257

Verbum, 34; *see also* Logos; Word of God

Viator, 448 f.

Victim; *see* Sacrificial victim

Virgin of virgins, 785: as image of the Holy Ghost, 188; *see also* Blessed Virgin Mary

Virginal life, excellence of, 188

Virtue of charity, 619, 641

Virtues, supernatural: acts performed through, 622; practice of, 647

Virtues, theological, 619

Vision, beatific; *see* Beatific vision

Vita aeterna, 663

Vitality of God, 30 f., 56 f.

Vocation: in Christian marriage, 605; to faith, 779; to glorification of God, 396 f.; of man, 141, 396 f., 709

Voluntariness of original sin, 283, 286 f., 295

Vosen, C. H., 690 note

Vows, religious, 605 note

Wayfarers, state of, 709

Will: activity of the divine, 56; salvific; *see* Salvific will of God

Will, human
conversion of, 710
cooperation with grace, 638, 707 f., 718
curtailment of, 308
freedom of Christ's, 447-52
freedom in predestination, 700, 708 ff., 724
holiness of Christ's, 330
transformed by infused virtues, 618 f.
undestroyed by original sin, 308

Wisdom: gift of, 777; sum and substance of theological, 795; theology as Christian, 795

Wisdom, divine
common to three divine persons, 77
communicated to men, 794
incarnate and personal, 786, 793 ff.
in predestination, 729
in redemption of man, 423
source of theology, 793
the Spirit of, 794 f.
as supreme end of theology, 795
theology as, 792 ff.

Woman, union with man in matrimony, 372

Word of God, the (see also Logos)
Clement of Alexandria on, 529 note
distinct from divine knowledge, 65
divine knowledge expressed in, 66

Word of God (continued)
equal to the Father, 75, 358
expression of the Father's majesty, 358
external utterance of, 361
generation of, 87-91
origin from the Father, 75, 79
personality of, 75
production of, 74 ff., 87
as real product, 65

Works: meritorious, 707; supernatural, 397, 697 f.

Works of Christ: merit of the, 448 f., 452; value of, 448

Works of God: knowledge of the, 201 f., 641; the natural, 202; purpose of external, 357, 421; the supernatural, 202, 755

Worship: through Christ, 413; expressed in sacrifice, 435